PRENTICE HALL

MIDDLE GRADES

MATH
TOOLS FOR SUCCESS

Solution Key
Course 3

PRENTICE HALL
Simon & Schuster Education Group
A VIACOM COMPANY

ISBN: 0-13-427782-1

Printed in the United States of America.

 2 3 4 5 6 7 8 9   01 00 99 98 97

Table of Contents

Chapter 1 Drawing Conclusions from Data

1-1 Organizing and Displaying Data

Pages 5–8

Think and Discuss pp. 5–6

1. rock music

2. urban contemporary and country music

3. **a.** Bar graph; compares amounts of money spent on rock music.

   b. Line graph; compares changes of amounts spent over time.

4. stacked bar graph

5. sliding bar graph

Work Together pp. 6–7

Check students' work.

6. Sales increased from 1988 to 1992.

7. 1991

8.

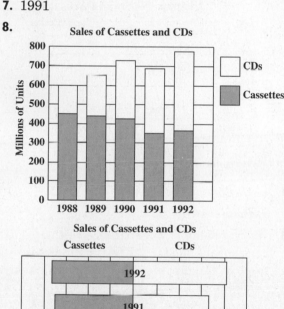

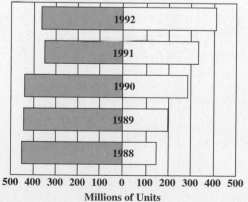

9.

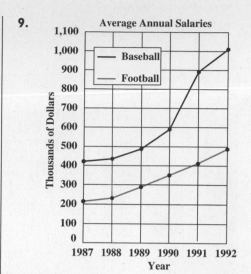

Mixed Review p. 7

1. circle

2. multiple line

3. Accept any reasonable estimate. Sample: 69,000

4. Sample: 6

5. 1,890 mi

On Your Own p. 8

10.

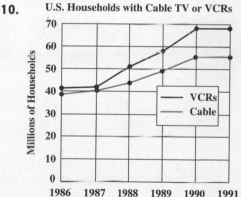

11.

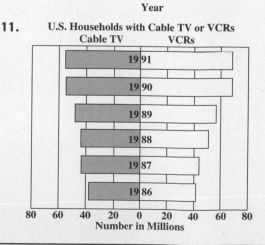

12.

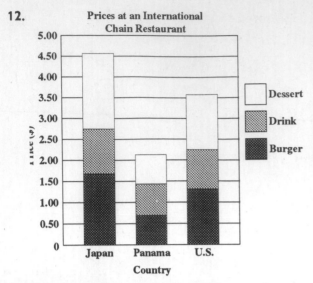

Prices at an International Chain Restaurant

13. Sample answer: In a double bar graph, it is easier to compare the number of boys to the number of girls. In a stacked bar graph, it is easier to see the total number of students.

14. 24.8 million T

15. about 4 times greater

16. Answers may vary. Sample: An advantage of giving percents is that you can compare parts to the whole. A disadvantage is that the exact amounts of each part are not given.

1-2 Reading Graphs Critically

Pages 9–11

Think and Discuss pp. 9–10

1. Sample answer: The different scales make the data look different.

2. the second graph

3. the first graph

4. 52 million passengers used Dallas-Fort Worth Airport and 65 million used Chicago O'Hare. 65 million is not twice as many as 52 million.

5. the O'Hare Airport manager

6. a. Sample: include the values between 0 and 45 million

  b. Sample: The data from the other airports would be graphed as bars that are shorter than the one used for Los Angeles.

Work Together p. 10

Answers may vary. Sample answers:

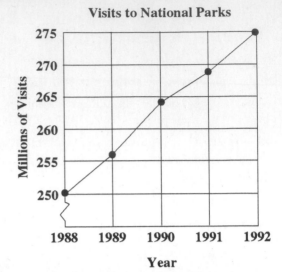

Visits to National Parks

Visits to National Parks

On Your Own p. 11

7. a. *National Geographic*

  b. *Reader's Digest*

8. Writing sample: The distance on the horizontal scale for the first 8 million is the same as the distance for each 2 million more.

9.

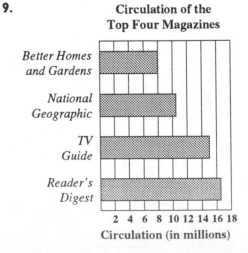

Circulation of the Top Four Magazines

10.

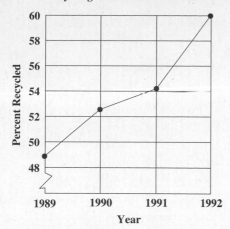

Recycling of Soft Drink Containers

11.

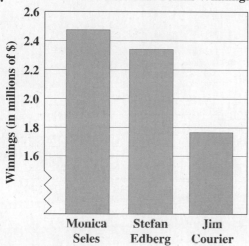

1991 Professional Tennis Winnings

12. Answers may vary.

Mixed Review p. 11

1. 1462

2. 284

3. bar graph

4.

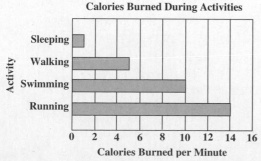

Calories Burned During Activities

5. 72 beats/min $\times$ 60 min/h $\times$ 24 h/d $\times$ 7 d/wk = 725,760 beats/wk

1-3 Displaying Frequency

Pages 12–15

Think and Discuss pp. 12–13

1. a. ‖‖‖ ‖‖ ; 8

   b. Sample: r, ‖‖‖ ‖‖ ; 8

   c. r and t

Try These p. 14

2. 9–11

3. 17

4.

Numbers of Books	Tally	Frequency
0–2	‖	2
3–5	‖	1
6–8	‖‖‖	5
9–11	‖‖‖ ‖	6
12–14	‖‖	3

5. a. 9

   b.

Numbers of Medals	Tally	Frequency
1	‖‖‖	4
2	‖	2
3	‖	2
4	‖	1
5	‖	1
6	‖	1
7		0
8		0
9	‖	2
10	‖	1

   c.
```
X
X
X  X  X                X
X  X  X  X  X  X     X  X
_____
1  2  3  4  5  6  7  8  9  10
```

6. a. $5.50

b. Answers may vary. Sample:

Cost of Binder	Tally	Frequency
$2.00 – $2.99	III	3
$3.00 – $3.99	III	3
$4.00 – $4.99	I	1
$5.00 – $5.99		0
$6.00 – $6.99		0
$7.00 – $7.99	II	2

c.

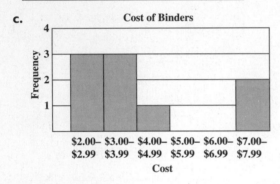

Cost of Binders

9. a. 25

b.

Interval	Tally	Frequency
55–59	III	3
60–64	III	3
65–69	II	2
70–74	II	2
75–79	IIII	4
80–84	II	2

c.

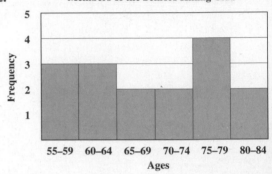

Members of the Seniors Hiking Club

10. a. Answers may vary. Sample table given.

Interval	Tally	Frequency
240–289	II	2
290–339	II	2
340–389	IIII	4
390–439	IIII	4
440–489	I	1
490–539	I	1
540–589	I	1

b. Sample:

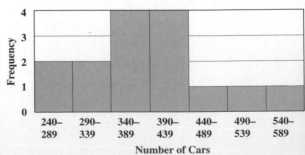

Cars in Industrialized Countries

On Your Own pp. 14–15

7. a.

Hours	Tally	Frequency
0	II	2
1	ҬI+ II	7
2	ҬI+ II	7
3	IIII	4
4	II	2

b.

```
      x    x
      x    x
      x    x
      x    x    x
      x    x    x
  x   x    x    x    x
  x   x    x    x    x
 _____
  0   1    2    3    4
```

8. Critical Thinking: The intervals overlap.

11. Writing: Sample answer: A histogram with small intervals will have more bars of shorter height. One with larger intervals will have fewer bars that are taller.

12. Research. Check students' work.

Checkpoint p. 15

1.

Weekly Leisure Time

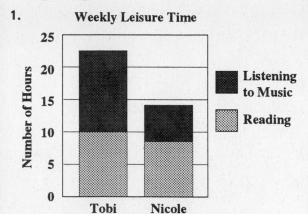

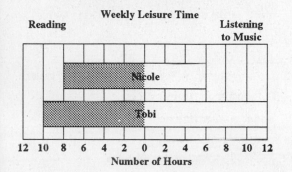

2. Sample: The scale on a graph can be altered to make the data misleading. For example, starting the scale at a number other than zero and using small units can exaggerate the results.

3. Sample:

Grades	Tally	Frequency
0–68	I	1
69–76	III	3
77–84	IIII	4
85–92	IIII	4
93–100	IIII	5

4. Sample:

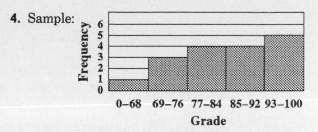

Mixed Review p. 15

1. 29

2. 92

3.

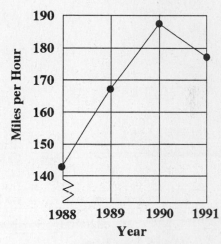

4.

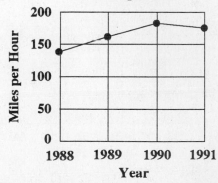

5. 98

1-4 Analyzing Measurements of Data
Pages 16–19

Think and Discuss pp. 16–18

1. mode

2. mean

3. median; $5.00

4. **a.** mean: $5(4.25) + 3(5.00) + 5.25 + 4(6.00) = 65.5$;
   $5 + 3 + 1 + 4 = 13$; $\$65.50 \div 13 = \$5.04$
   median: $5.00
   mode: $4.25

   b. The mean changes, but the median and mode stay the same.

Mixed Review p. 18

1. $35 - 29 = 6$

2.

Number	Tally	Frequency
29	I	1
30	II	2
31	I	1
32	I	1
33	III	3
34	II	2
35	II	2

3.

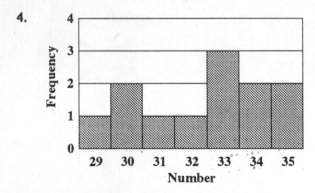

4.

4.

5. $2 \times 3 \times 2 = 12$

Work Together p. 18

Answers may vary. See students' work.

Try These p. 18

5. $\dfrac{1 + 1 + 2 + 2 + 3}{9} = 1; 1; 0$

6. $\dfrac{70 + 80 + 84 + 90 + 92 + 100}{6} = 86; 87;$ no mode

7. $\dfrac{\$11.70}{8} = \$1.4625 \approx \$1.46; \$1.35; \$1.25$ and $1.75

8. median; data may vary widely, causing outliers.

9. mode; data are not numerical.

10. mean or median; data will be close.

11. median; use mean if there are no outliers.

12. $\dfrac{2(4) + 3(5) + 6 + 4(7)}{2 + 3 + 1 + 4} = 5.7; (5 + 6)/2 = 5.5; 7$

On Your Own p. 19

13. $\dfrac{7 + 2(8) + 4(9) + 2(10)}{1 + 2 + 4 + 2} = 8.\overline{7}; 9; 9$

14. $\dfrac{2 + 1 + 3 + 2 + 3 + 4 + 6 + 5 + 4 + 1 + 2}{12} = 2.75;$

$\dfrac{3 + 2}{2} = 2.5; 2$ (occurs 3 times)

15. $\dfrac{690.4}{7} \approx 98.629; 98.7; 98.7$ (occurs twice)

16. $\dfrac{1(1) + 5(3) + 3(4) + 1(5)}{1 + 5 + 3 + 1} = 3.3;$

3; 3 (occurs 5 times)

17. mode; non-numerical data

18. median; outliers

19. mean or median; no outliers

20. Answers may vary. Check students' work. Sample: You would use the mode to describe results of a survey that asks students about their favorite kind of fruit (non-numerical data). You would use the mean for the average temperature during the month of September, because the temperature is likely to be fairly constant. You would use the median to describe the number of books people read over summer vacation, because some people might read a lot of books and others might read almost no books.

21. **a.** $87 \times 6 = 522$ and $522 - (89 + 92 + 78 + 83 + 83) = 97$

   b. 78 83 83 x 89 92
   $\dfrac{83 + x}{2} = 85$
   $x = 87$

22. 427; 427.5; 431

Problem Solving Practice

Page 20

1. 9 1-by-1 squares, 4 2-by-2 squares, 1 3-by-3 square.

    $9 + 4 + 1 = 14$ squares in all.

2. Let x, $x + 1$ and $x + 3$ be the integers. Thus $x + x + 1 + x + 3 = 193$.

    $3x + 4 = 193$

    $3x = 189$

    $x = 63$

    Thus the three integers are 63, 64, and 66.

3. Notice: $4 = 3 + 1$

    $6 = 4 + 2$

    $\vdots$

    $18 = 13 + 5$

    Thus, $24 = 18 + 6$. Answer is 24.

4. 1 through 100: 10 3's in ones' place

    10 3's in tens' place

    101 through 200: 10 3's in ones' place

    10 3's in tens' place

    201 through 300: 10 3's in ones' place

    10 3's in tens' place

    1 3 in hundreds' place

    301 through 343: 5 3's in ones' place

    10 3's in tens' place

    43 3's in hundreds' place

    $20 + 20 + 21 + 5 + 10 + 43 = 119$ 3's

5. $4 \cdot 7 \cdot 28{,}000 = 784{,}000$ lb per week

    $\frac{784{,}000}{2{,}000} = 392$ T per week

6. 12-package box: $12 \times 300 = 3{,}600$ sheets for $72.00. So $72.00 \div 3{,}600 = \$.02$ per sheet.

    6-package box: $6 \times 200 = 1{,}200$ sheets for $30.00. So $30.00 \div 1{,}200 = \$.025$ per sheet.

    Thus the 12-package box is the better buy.

7. $3 \cdot 105 - (112 + 96) = 315 - 208 = 107$ is score on third game.

8. $T + Y = 160$

    $Y + U = 180$

    $U + P = 200$

    So $T + Y - (Y + U) = 160 - 180 = -20$

    Thus $T - U = -20$

    Then $(T - U) + (U + P) = -20 + 200 = 180$ lb

    So $T + P = 180$

9. 20 through 29: 20, 24, 26, 28; 4 numbers

    40 through 49: 40, 42, 46, 48; 4 numbers

    60 through 69; 4 numbers

    80 through 89; 4 numbers

    Total: 16 numbers

1-5 Conducting a Survey

Pages 21–23

Think and Discuss pp. 21–22

1. **a.** 46,800

    b. No; sample was heavily Midwestern.

    c. The % decreases as students get older.

    d. Not necessarily. The trend may be different for other areas of the country.

2. closed-option

3. The question assumes you like eggs.

4. The question makes Car A seem more desirable.

Mixed Review p. 22

1. $100 - 63 = 37$

2. $1320 \div 16 = 82.5$

3. $\frac{(83 + 78)}{2} = 80.5$

4. 73 (occurs 4 times)

5. $35 + 85 + 45 = 165$ min $= 2$ h 45 min

    $9{:}00 - 2{:}45 = 6{:}15$

Work Together p. 22

5–7. See students' work.

On Your Own pp. 22–23

8. The question assumes that you have a brother and that he is your friend.

9. The question makes kittens sound more desirable.

10. **a.** 263,000 consumers 14 and older; 263,000

    b. no

    c. closed-option

11. No; many students entering the building may know nothing about your bus stops.

12. No; people who attend museums may have similar tastes.

13. Writing. Sample: Are you a caring, concerned citizen who recycles cans, or do you pollute the environment by throwing cans away? Do you recycle cans?

14. Sample: 80% of all dentists responding to our survey liked Dazzle Toothpaste.

Decision Making pp. 22–23

1–6. Answers will vary.

1-6 Scatter Plots

Pages 24–27

Think and Discuss pp. 24–26

1. $x = 178$ cm, $y = 180$ cm

2. Samples: The point (119, 116); the lowest point.

3. Sample: the taller a person is, the wider his/her arm span is.

4. A

5. Sample: No, different people may draw lines with slightly different slopes.

6. Temperature decreases as latitude increases.

7. Scatter plot

8. (58, 39)

9. No; not all the points fall on the line.

10. a. Sample: No. The points are widely scattered.

   b. Sample: No. The points do not approximate a line.

11. Height vs. arm span: positive
Temperature vs. latitude: negative
Active volcanoes vs. elevation: none

Mixed Review p. 26

1. Sample: What is your favorite food?

2. Sample: Do you prefer junk food or health food?

3.
```
X
X          X
X          X
X          X          X
X    X     X          X
_____
5    6     7     8     9
```

4. $77 \div 12 = 6.41\overline{6}$; $\dfrac{6 + 7}{2} = 6.5$; 5 (occurs 5 times)

5. Let x be what Kim earned. So Al earned $x + \$5.50$.

Thus $x + (x + 5.50) = 22.50$

$2x + 5.50 = 22.50$

$2x = 17.00$

$x = \$8.50$

Kim earned $8.50 and Al earned $14.00.

Work Together p. 26

Sample:

Hours Slept	Minutes of Homework
8	15
9	45
7.5	30
10	90
6	0

Hours of Sleep vs Minutes of Homework

12. positive

13. negative

14. none

15. negative

16.

	A	B	C	D	E	F	G
1	Year	Farms	Acres				
2	1910	6,366	139				
3	1920	6,454	149				
4	1930	6,295	157				
5	1940	6,102	175				
6	1950	5,388	216				
7	1960	3,962	297				
8	1970	2,954	373				
9	1980	2,440	426				
10	1990	2,143	461				
11							
12							
13							
14							
15							
16							
17							

Number of Farms vs. Number of Acres

17.

	A	B	C	D	E	F
1	Player	Jordan	Pippen	Paxson	Grant	Cartwright
2	Ave. Points per Game	35.8	20.8	10.3	9.2	6.3
3	Most Points in 1 Game	46	26	16	18	10

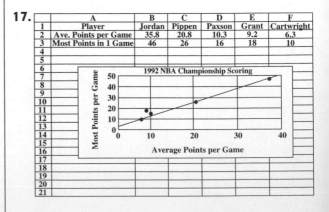

1992 NBA Championship Scoring

18. Sample: An example of a set of data with positive correlation would be height and length of foot. In general, as height increases so does the length of the foot. As you drive a car, the farther you drive on a tank of gas, the less gas there is in the tank. This is an example of negative correlation. There should be no correlation between the number of pets a person owns and the number of books he or she reads in a year.

19. Critical Thinking: not necessarily

Checkpoint p. 27

1. $6.\overline{7}$; 7; 7

2. 48.5; 47; no mode

3. mode; non-numerical data

4. median; data contain outliers.

5. Sample: Do you use an alarm clock to wake you?

6.

Distance	% of ID'd
100	2
93	4
82	6
68	8
60	10
48	12

Eye Chart Symbols Identified at Different Distances

1-7 Stem-and-Leaf Plots

Pages 28–30

Think and Discuss pp. 28–29

1. 7; 20

2. Two data items are 15.

3. 15; 9 and 15

4. Sample: The stem-and-leaf plot lists each number.

Try These pp. 29–30

5. 20, 21, 22

6. 0, 0, 0, 7

7. 21.3; 20.0

8.

2	0 0 2 7
3	5 8 9
4	0
5	1
6	
7	2

2|0 means 20

9.

	Set A		Set B
	9	16	3
	9 8 6 5	17	5 8
	6 4 3 0	18	0 0 2 6 7
		19	1

means 169 ←—9 | 16 | 3 —→ means 163

A: median, 179; no mode;
B: median, 180; mode, 180

On Your Own p. 30

10.

0	2 6 9
1	3 3 7 8 9
2	4 6 7 7
3	0 2 5

2|7 means 27

19; 13 and 27

11.

3	2 7
4	3 5
5	0 0 2 8
6	3 7 9 9

3|2 means 3.2

5.1; 5.0 and 6.9

12.

87	3 5
88	1 3
89	9
90	0 8
91	5 7
92	0 0 1

87 | 3 means 873

904; 920

13. Sample: Yes; including a stem of 5 with no leaves presents a better picture of the distribution of the data.

14. $40 - 27 = 13$ mi/gal

15. 33 mi/gal

16. 18 mi/gal

17.

Females		Males
8 3 3	20	
6 5 3 2	21	
0	22	8 8
9	23	2
	24	3 3 6 7
	25	1 9

means 22.0 ← 0 | 22 | 8 → means 22.8

18.

Girls		Boys
9 8 8	5	9 9
3 3 2 1 1 0 0	6	0 1 2 3 3 4 5 5

means 58 ← 8 | 5 | 9 → means 59

Mixed Review p. 30

1. $100 - 55 = 45$

2.

Interval	Tally	Frequency
51–60	||	2
61–70	ⅢⅠ	6
71–80	|||	3
81–90	||	2
91–100	|||	3

3.

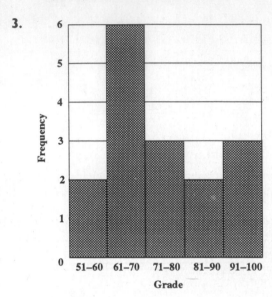

4. negative

5. $3(\$6.95) + \$5.75 = \$26.60$;
$\$30 - \$26.60 = \$3.40$

Practice

Page 31

1.

Physical Education Class Choices

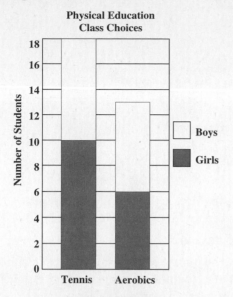

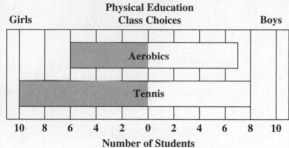

2. $51 \div 14 = 3.64$; 4; 4; $7 - 1 = 6$

3. $256 \div 4 = 64$; $(67 + 56) \div 2 = 61.5$; no mode; $85 - 48 = 37$

4. $\$34.25 \div 5 = \$6.85$; $\$6.50$; $\$6.50$; $\$8.00 - 5.75 = \$2.25$

5. 92; 92; 92; 0

6. $61.5 \div 7 = 8.8$; 8.8; 8.8 and 8.9; $9.2 - 8.2 = 1$

7. $36.6 \div 6 = 6.1$; $(5.7 + 6.2) \div 2 = 5.95$; no mode; $8.9 - 3.1 = 5.8$

8.

Number	Tally	Frequency
0	II	2
1	III	3
2	II	2
3	III	3
4	II	2
5	I	1

```
                x           x
    x     x     x     x     x
    x     x     x     x     x     x
    0     1     2     3     4     5
```

9.

Number	Tally	Frequency
15	I	1
16	III	3
17	II	2
18	I	1
19	I	1
20	I	1

```
          x
          x     x
    x     x     x     x     x     x
    15    16    17    18    19    20
```

10. Sample:

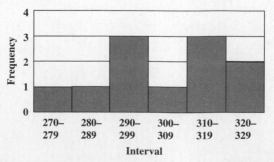

11. Sample:

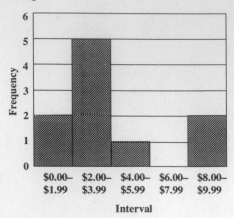

12. mode; non-numerical data

13. median if there are outliers, or mean if there are none

14. mean, but use median if there are outliers.

15.

19	0 8
20	7
21	0 0 5 6 7 9
22	2 5 9

19|8 means 198

16.

59	1 5
60	4 6
61	5 8 8 8
62	0 2 4

59|1 means 59.1

17.

	Set A		Set B	
		0	2 5	
	5 2	1	7 9	
5 3 3 2		2	1 2 5 5	
	4 3	3		

means 12 ◄—2 | 1 | 7—► means 17

18.

	Set A		Set B	
		4	0 2	
	3 1	5	1 2 8	
9 5 4		6	3 7	
	1	7		
	7	8		

means 5.1 ◄—1 | 5 | 1—► means 5.1

1-8 Box-and-Whisker Plots
Pages 32–35

Think and Discuss pp. 32–33

1. The median is the middle value in the data, not the middle value of the box.

2. The data are widely distributed.

3. No; the quartiles would remain the same because the new numbers would still be the greatest data items.

4. Find the mean of the two middle values of the lower half.

5. median, range

Mixed Review p. 33

1.

3	1 2 3 8
4	5 5 5
5	0 0 2

3|1 means 31

2. $52 - 31 = 21$

3. 45

4. 45

5. $x + (x + 1) + (x + 2) + (x + 3) + (x + 4) = 50$

$5x + 10 = 50$

$5x = 40$

$x = 8$

The five numbers are 8, 9, 10, 11, 12.

Work Together p. 34

Answers will vary. Sample:

Hand Spans in Centimeters

□ Girls
▨ Boys

Try These p. 34

6. 85

7. 70

8. 90

9. 100

10. 50

11. $100 - 50 = 50$

12.

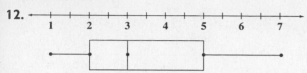

13.

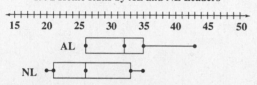

1992 Home Runs by AL and NL Leaders

On Your Own pp. 34–35

14.

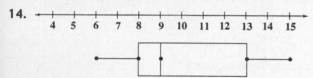

15.

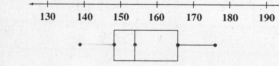

Average Miles per Hour of Daytona 500 Winners

16.

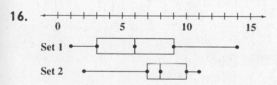

Sample: The median is 6 for Set 1 and 8 for Set 2. The data in Set 2 are more tightly clustered around the median than the data in Set 1. The range of the data is 13 for Set 1 and 9 for Set 2. Although the median for Set 2 is greater than the median for Set 1, Set 1 has a greater distribution of data values.

17.

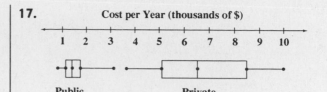

Sample: The median is $1,414 for public colleges and $6,658 for private colleges. The data for public colleges cluster tightly around the median, indicating that the data are relatively close in value. The wide range of data for private colleges, and the long box used in the plot, indicate the wide variation in the cost of private colleges. The longer whiskers used in the plot for private colleges indicate the existence of distant outliers in both directions from the median.

18. No; data sets of various sizes may have the same ranges and quartile values.

19. Yes: if all values between them are also the same.

20.

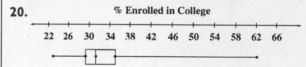

21. A

22.

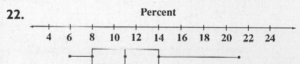

1-9 Choosing an Appropriate Graph

Pages 36–38

Think and Discuss pp. 36–37

1. The sum of the percents is not 100, since the data items do not represent "parts" of the same "whole."

2. data showing parts of a whole

3. Yes; a bar graph displays a comparison of amounts.

4. No; a line graph is used to indicate change over time.

5. No; a scatter plot is used to show a relationship between two sets of data.

6. No; a stacked bar graph is used to compare categories of data.

Mixed Review p. 37

1. $110 - 80 = 30$

2. $1,040 \div 11 = 94.54$

3. 90

4. 88

5.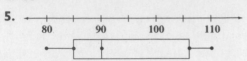

6. $\$34 + \$8.50 = \$42.50$; $\$42.50 \div \$9 = 4.72$
   Thus 4 tapes can be bought.

Try These p. 37

7. line graph; shows change over time

8. bar graph; compares quantities

9. scatter plot; shows a relationship between two sets of data.

On Your Own p. 38

10. line graph

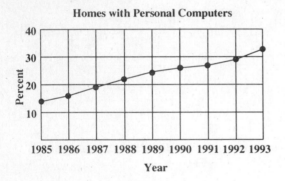

11. scatter plot

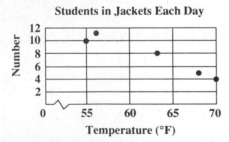

12. bar graph

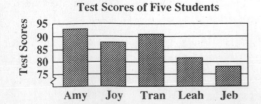

13. box-and-whisker plot

14. C

15. Sample: Your family budget can be displayed on a circle graph or in a bar graph. The circle graph will show the different budget items as parts of the whole family income. The bar graph will compare amounts spent on each budget item.

16. Sample:

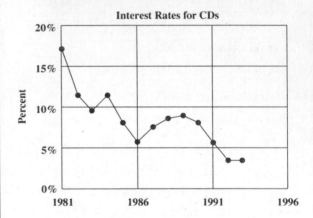

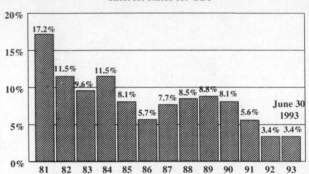

Checkpoint p. 38

1.

Set A		Set B
7 6 5 0	11	2 8 9
9 9 5 0	12	7 8 9
5 5 2	13	0 8
	14	1 3 5

means 132 ←—2│13│0—→ means 130

2.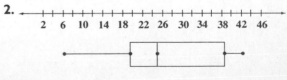

3. D

1-10 Too Much or Too Little Information

Pages 39–41

1. A survey asked students how many hours they spend per week listening to music.

2. the mode and the median

3. **a.** none

   b. The box-and-whisker plot shows the median.

4. Answers may vary. Sample: the number of students surveyed

5. Answers may vary. Sample: The 28 data items could have been listed.

Try These p. 40

6. not possible; need to know how much time Maria spent at bakery

7. Let x be the number of homers McGriff hit. Then Gonzales hit $x + 8$ homers.

   Thus $x + (x + 8) = 78$

   $2x + 8 = 78$

   $2x = 70$

   $x = 35$ homers for McGriff

8. not possible; need to know regular price of rolls

On Your Own pp. 40–41

9. The numbers of chairs in the rows are 8, $8 + 3, 8 + 6, \ldots, 8 + 11(3)$. Thus their total is $12(8) + 3(1 + 2 + \cdots + 11) = 96 + 3(66) = 96 + 198 = 294$.

10. Let x be number of quarters. Then $x + 3$ is the number of dimes.

    Thus $\$.25x + \$.10(x + 3) = \$3.45$

    $0.25x + 0.10x + 0.30 = 3.45$

    $0.35x + 0.30 = 3.45$

    $0.35x = 3.15$

    $x = 9$

    So there are 9 quarters and 12 dimes.

11. Let x be first number.

    Thus $x + (x + 1) + (x + 2) + (x + 3) + (x + 4) = 415$

    $5x + 10 = 415$

    $5x = 405$

    $x = 81$

    The numbers are 81, 82, 83, 84, and 85.

12. Let w be width.

    Thus $2w + 2(w + 12) = 100$

    $4w + 24 = 100$

    $4w = 76$

    $w = 19$ is width

    $w + 12 = 31$ is length

13. First 4 games: $4(75) = 300$ min

    Winners play next 2 games: $2(75) = 150$ min

    Winners play next 1 game: 75 min

    Total time: 525 min = 8 h 45 min

    Express 4 P.M. as 16:00 and subtract 8:45 from 16:00 to get 7:15 A.M. starting time.

14. $470 \div 5 = 94$ km/h

    $805 \div 94 = 8.56$ h

    Thus she will arrive within 9 h

15. 49

16. Let the smaller number be x. Then the larger is $15 - x$.

    Thus $3x - 2(15 - x) = 5$

    $3x - 30 + 2x = 5$

    $5x - 30 = 5$

    $5x = 35$

    $x = 7$

    $15 - x = 8$

    The numbers are 7 and 8.

17. $4 \cdot 3 \cdot 5 = 60$

18. 1 number in 1st row

    2 numbers in 2nd row

    3 numbers in 3rd row, etc.

    Thus in n rows we have the numbers 1 through $(1 + 2 + \cdots + n)$.

    This means that in 8 rows we have the numbers 1 through $(1 + 2 + \cdots + 8)$; that is, 1 through 36. Finally, we can see that in 14 rows we have the numbers 1 through $(1 + 2 + \cdots + 14)$; that is, we have the numbers 1 through 105. So, 100 is in the 14th row.

19. $21 change:

One $20 plus one $1

Two $10 plus one $1

Four $5 plus one $1

One $10, two $5, one $1

One $10, one $5, six $1

Three $5, six $1

Total of six different ways.

Mixed Review p. 41

1. A

2. C

3. B

4. Sample: Name your favorite movie from the following: *Aladdin*, *Beauty and the Beast*, *Snow White*, or *Sleeping Beauty*.

5. 6:00 P.M.

Wrap Up

Pages 42–43

1.

School Chorus Members

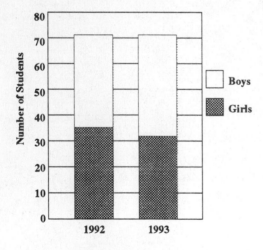

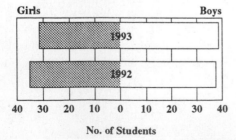

2.

School Chorus Members

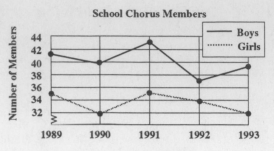

3.

Age	Tally	Frequency
51–60	﹉﹉ l	6
61–70	﹉﹉	5
71–80	﹉﹉ l	6
81–90	l	1

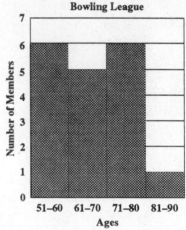

4. $1210 \div 18 = 67.\overline{2}$; $(68 + 65) \div 2 = 66.5$; 78

5. Writing sample: What is your favorite citrus fruit? Is your favorite type of fruit a citrus fruit?

6.

```
6 | 3 5 7
7 | 2 5 8 8 9 9 9
8 | 5 5 9
9 | 0 9

9 | 0 means 90
```

7. Juice Prices (in cents)

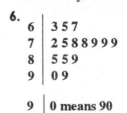

8. B

9. not enough info; need to know how much time for breakfast

Getting Ready for Chapter 2 p. 43

1. $\pi r^2 = 3.14 \times 3^2 = 3.14 \times 9 = 28.26$ in.^{2}
2. $\pi r^2 = 3.14(4.2)^2 = 55.389$ cm^2
3. $\pi r^2 = 3.14(0.45)^2 = 0.63585$ m^2
4. $\pi r^2 = (\frac{22}{7})(\frac{3}{4})^2 = \frac{22}{7} \cdot \frac{9}{16} = \frac{99}{56}$ in.^{2}

Assessment

Page 46

1. 1990; $250 = 2(125)$
2. bar graph; compares quantities

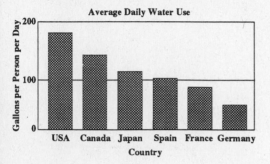

Average Daily Water Use

3.

Subscribers (in millions)	Tally	Frequency
55					3
56				2
57			1
58				2
59				2

```
        x
x       x               x       x
x       x       x       x       x
55     56      57      58      59
```

4.

	Career Earnings of Top Golfers (in millions of dollars)	
Male		**Female**
	1	9
	2	5 5 8
	3	2 3 4 5
8 7	4	2
9 7 4 3 1 1	5	
	6	
1	7	

means 4.7 ⟵ 7 | 4 | 2 ⟶ means 4.2

5. $27.3 \div 9 \approx 3$; 3.2; 2.5 (millions of dollars)
6. Sample: Of math, English, and history, which is your favorite subject?
7. $6(90) - 444 = 540 - 444 = 96$
8. The median, mode, and range mean that 4 data items must be 19, 23, 26, 26. The 5th data item is 21, since the mean is 23, and $5(23) - (19 + 23 + 26 + 26) = 21$.
9. C
10. Negative correlation

Cumulative Review

Page 47

1. C; $(7 + 8) \div 2 = 7.5$
2. A; non-numerical data
3. B; $12 + 5 = 17$
   $17 + 6 = 23$
   $23 + 7 = 30$
4. A; $18{:}39 - 11{:}36 = 7{:}03$
5. D; $35.7 \div 7 = 5.1$
6. B; $\frac{12}{1} = \frac{x}{30}$
   So $x = 30 \cdot 12$
   $x = 360$ students
7. B
8. D
9. D
10. D; Use Guess and Test.

Chapter 2 Patterns in Geometry

2-1 Angles of Circles
Pages 51–53

Work Together p. 51

Central Angle	Inscribed Angle
1. $m\angle AOB = 120°$	$m\angle ACB = 60°$

2. Check students' work.
Sample:
Diagram 1

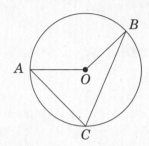

Diagram 2

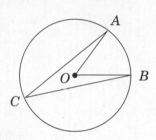

Central Angle	Inscribed Angle
Diagram 1: $m\angle AOB = 140°$	$m\angle ACB = 70°$
Diagram 2: $m\angle AOB = 40°$	$m\angle ACB = 20°$

3. The measure of the central angle is twice the measure of the inscribed angle.

Think and Discuss pp. 51–52

4. The sum of the measures of the non-overlapping central angles of a circle is 360°.

5.

Number of congruent angles	Sum of the measures of the central angles	Measure of each central angle
3	360°	360° ÷ 3 = 120°
4	360°	360° ÷ 4 = 90°
5	360°	360° ÷ 5 = 72°
6	360°	360° ÷ 6 = 60°

6. half of a circle

7. The endpoints of any semicircle are also the endpoints of a different semicircle.

8. Samples: $\widehat{XZ}, \widehat{YZ}, \widehat{YW}, \widehat{WZ}$

9. $m\angle RPT = 2m\angle RST = 2(52°) = 104°$

10. $m\angle RPT = 2m\angle RST$
$98° = 2m\angle RST$
$98° \div 2 = m\angle RST$
$49° = m\angle RST$

On Your Own pp. 52–53

11. A

12. $\overline{AB}, \overline{AH}, \overline{AD}, \overline{AF}$

13. Sample: (one of the following)
$\overline{DH}$ or $\overline{BF}$

14. Sample: (three of the following)
$\overline{CE}, \overline{BF}, \overline{EG},$ or $\overline{HD}$

15. Sample: (one of the following)
$\angle BAD, \angle BAH, \angle HAF,$ or $\angle FAD$

16. $\angle CEG$

17. $m\angle 1 = \frac{1}{2}(134°) = 67°$

18. $m\angle 2 = 2(50°) = 100°$

19. $m\angle 3 = 2(42°) = 84°$
$m\angle 4 = \frac{1}{2}m\angle 3 = \frac{1}{2}(84°) = 42°$

20. a. Accept reasonable estimates.
  b. $m\angle ABC = 120°$
  $m\angle DEF = 72°$
  $m\angle HIJ = 90°$
  c. $\angle HIJ$ is a right angle since $m\angle HIJ = 90°$.
  d. $\frac{90°}{360°} = \frac{1}{4}$ so $\widehat{HJ}$ is $\frac{1}{4}$ the circumference of circle I.

21. Check students' drawings.
Sample:

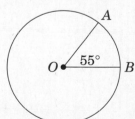

22. Check students' drawings.

Sample:

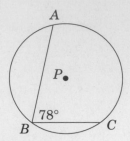

23. a. $m\angle ROT = 360° \div 2$, or $180°$, since $\overset{\frown}{RST}$ is a semicircle.

b. $m\angle RST = \frac{1}{2} m\angle ROT = \frac{1}{2}(180°) = 90°$

24. $93°$; $66 + 27 = 93$

25. No; the angles do not have the same intercepted arcs since B and C are different points.

26. Sometimes; a chord is a diameter only when it passes through the center.

27. Never; the endpoints of a chord lie on the circle. Only one endpoint of a radius lies on the circle.

28. Sometimes; the inscribed angle and central angle may not have the same intercepted arc.

29. always

30. Answers will vary.

Sample: The cable company would try to make the most efficient use of cable by routing along the shortest routes.

Mixed Review p. 53

1.

Data	Tally	Frequency
22	II	2
23	II	2
24	I	1
25	III	3
26	II	2
27	II	2

2.

```
                    x
       x    x       x    x    x
       x    x    x    x    x    x
      ────────────────────────────
      22   23   24   25   26   27
               Number
```

3. Double bar graph; Six different bars will show the data for the categories and adjacent male and female bars will illustrate the average data for each category.

4. $\frac{3}{16} \cdot 11 = \frac{3}{16} \cdot \frac{11}{1} = \frac{33}{16}$ or $2\frac{1}{16}$

5. $\frac{18}{5} \cdot 6 = \frac{18}{5} \cdot \frac{6}{1} = \frac{108}{5}$ or $21\frac{3}{5}$

6. $6 \cdot 5 \cdot 4 \cdot 3 \cdot 2 \cdot 1 = 720$

2-2 Measuring Circles

Pages 54–57

Think and Discuss pp. 54–55

1. because $d = 2r$

2. a. Circumference is the distance around the circle and area is the amount of space inside the circle.

b. No; circumference is measured in linear units and area is measured in square units.

3. a. Use $C = \pi d$, 3.14 for π and 8 for d.

$3.14 \boxed{\times} 8 \boxed{=}$ **25.12**

The circumference is 25.12 cm.

Use $A = \pi r^2$, 3.14 for π and 4 for r.

$3.14 \boxed{\times} 4 \boxed{x^2} \boxed{=}$ **50.24**

The area is 50.24 cm².

b. Answers may vary.

Sample: The value for π is rounded.

Work Together pp. 55–56

4. The radius of circle O is the length of $\overline{OD}$, 3 cm.

$r = 3$, $C = 2\pi r$

$2 \boxed{\times} \boxed{\pi} \boxed{\times} 3 \boxed{=}$ **18.849556**

The circumference is about 18.8 cm.

5. $\overset{\frown}{DE}$ is $\frac{1}{4}$ the circumference of circle O. Since $\angle DOE$ is a right angle and $\frac{90}{360} = \frac{1}{4}$, $DE = \frac{1}{4} C$.

Using the results of Exercise 4,

18.849556 $\boxed{\div}$ 4 $\boxed{=}$ **4.712389**.

The length of $\overset{\frown}{DE}$ is about 4.7 cm.

6. $A = \pi r^2$

$\boxed{\pi}$ $\boxed{\times}$ 3 $\boxed{x^2}$ $\boxed{=}$ **28.274334**

The area is about 28.3 cm^2.

7. The area of the shaded wedge is $\frac{1}{4}$ the area of the circle.

28.274334 $\boxed{\div}$ 4 $\boxed{=}$ **7.0685835**

The area of the shaded wedge is about 7.1 cm^2.

8. $\frac{60}{360} = \frac{1}{6}$

  a. Use $C = 2\pi r$, $r = 6$, and $\overset{\frown}{FG} = \frac{1}{6}C$.

    2 $\boxed{\times}$ $\boxed{\pi}$ $\boxed{\times}$ 6 $\boxed{\div}$ 6 $\boxed{=}$ **6.2831853**

    The length of the intercepted arc, $\overset{\frown}{FG}$, is 6.3 cm.

  b. Use $A = \pi r^2$, $r = 6$ and the area of wedge $= \frac{1}{6}A$.

    $\boxed{\pi}$ $\boxed{\times}$ 6 $\boxed{x^2}$ $\boxed{\div}$ 6 $\boxed{=}$ **18.849556**

    The area of the wedge formed by $\angle FPG$ and the circle is 18.8 cm^2.

9. $\frac{120}{360} = \frac{1}{3}$

  a. Use $C = 2\pi r$, $r = 10$ and $\overset{\frown}{JK} = \frac{1}{3}C$.

    2 $\boxed{\times}$ $\boxed{\pi}$ $\boxed{\times}$ 10 $\boxed{\div}$ 3 $\boxed{=}$ **20.943951**

    The length of the intercepted arc, $\overset{\frown}{JK}$, is 20.9 in.

  b. Use $A = \pi r^2$, $r = 10$ and the area of wedge $= \frac{1}{3}A$.

    $\boxed{\pi}$ $\boxed{\times}$ 10 $\boxed{x^2}$ $\boxed{\div}$ 3 $\boxed{=}$ **104.71976**

    The area of the wedge formed by $\angle JQK$ and the circle is 104.7 in.^{2}.

Try These p. 56

10. Use $C = 2\pi r$ and $r = 5$.

2 $\boxed{\times}$ $\boxed{\pi}$ $\boxed{\times}$ 5 $\boxed{=}$ **31.415927**

The circumference is about 31.4 cm.

11. Use $A = \pi r^2$ and $r = \frac{d}{2} = \frac{12}{2} = 6$.

$\boxed{\pi}$ $\boxed{\times}$ 6 $\boxed{x^2}$ $\boxed{=}$ **113.09734**

The area is about 113 m^2.

12. Use $C = \pi d$ and $d = 7$.

$\boxed{\pi}$ $\boxed{\times}$ 7 $\boxed{=}$ **21.991149**

The circumference is about 22 in.
Use $A = \pi r^2$ and $r = \frac{d}{2} = \frac{7}{2} = 3.5$ in.

$\boxed{\pi}$ $\boxed{\times}$ 3.5 $\boxed{x^2}$ $\boxed{=}$ **38.48451**

The area is about 38.5 in.^{2}.

13. Use $d = \frac{C}{\pi}$ and $C = 12.6$ m.

12.6 $\boxed{\div}$ $\boxed{\pi}$ $\boxed{=}$ **4.0107046**

The diameter is about 4 m.
$r = \frac{d}{2} = 2$ m

The radius is about 2 m.

On Your Own pp. 56–57

14. Use $C = \pi d$ and $d = 5$.

$\boxed{\pi}$ $\boxed{\times}$ 5 $\boxed{=}$ **15.707963**

The circumference is about 15.7 m.
Use $A = \pi r^2$ and $r = \frac{d}{2} = \frac{5}{2} = 2.5$ m.

$\boxed{\pi}$ $\boxed{\times}$ 2.5 $\boxed{x^2}$ $\boxed{=}$ **19.634954**

The area is about 19.6 m^2.

15. Use $C = 2\pi r$ and $r = 4.5$ cm.

2 $\boxed{\times}$ $\boxed{\pi}$ $\boxed{\times}$ 4.5 $\boxed{=}$ **28.274334**

The circumference is about 28.3 cm.
Use $A = \pi r^2$ and $r = 4.5$ cm.

$\boxed{\pi}$ $\boxed{\times}$ 4.5 $\boxed{x^2}$ $\boxed{=}$ **63.617251**

The area is about 63.6 cm^2.

16. Use $\pi = \frac{22}{7}$ and $d = 14$ in.

$C = \pi d = \frac{22}{7}(14) = 44$

The circumference is 44 in.
Use $r = \frac{d}{2} = 7$.

$A = \pi r^2 = \frac{22}{7}(7)^2 = 154$

The area is 154 in.^{2}.

17. Use $\pi = 3.14$ and $d = 2$ cm.

$C = \pi d = (3.14)(2) = 6.28$

The circumference is 6.3 cm.
Use $r = \frac{d}{2} = 1$ cm.

$A = \pi r^2 = 3.14(1)^2 = 3.14$

The area is 3.14 cm^2.

18. Use $\pi = 3.14$ and $r = 10$.

$C = 2\pi r = 2(3.14)(10) = 62.8$

The circumference is 62.8 in.

$A = \pi r^2 = 3.14(10)^2 = 314$

The area is 314 in.^{2}.

19. Use $d = \frac{C}{\pi}$ and $C = 132$.

$132 \boxed{\div} \boxed{\pi} \boxed{=} \mathbf{42.016905}$

$42.016905 \boxed{\div} 2 \boxed{=} \mathbf{21.008452}$

The diameter is about 42 cm and the radius is about 21 cm.

20. Use $r = \frac{d}{2} = \frac{1}{2}(\frac{C}{\pi}) = (\frac{C}{2\pi})$ and $C = 226$ in.

$226 \boxed{\div} 2 \boxed{\div} \boxed{\pi} \boxed{=} \mathbf{35.969017}$

Divide inches by 12 to get feet.

$35.969017 \boxed{\div} 12 \boxed{=} \mathbf{2.9974181}$

Divide feet by 3 to get yards.

$2.9974181 \boxed{\div} 3 \boxed{=} \mathbf{0.9991394}$

The radius is about 36 in., 3 ft, or 1 yd.

21. $r = 3$ and $\frac{45}{360} = \frac{1}{8}$

a. $\overset{\frown}{ED} = \frac{1}{8}C$ and $C = 2\pi r$

$2 \boxed{\times} \boxed{\pi} \boxed{\times} 3 \boxed{\div} 8 \boxed{=} \mathbf{2.3561945}$

The length of $\overset{\frown}{ED}$ is 2.4 cm.

b. Area of shaded wedge $= \frac{1}{8}A$ and $A = \pi r^2$.

$\boxed{\pi} \boxed{\times} 3 \boxed{x^2} \boxed{\div} 8 \boxed{=} \mathbf{3.5342917}$

The area of the shaded wedge is 3.5 cm^2.

22. $\overset{\frown}{QS} = 18.8$ and $\frac{120}{360} = \frac{1}{3}$

a. Use $r = \frac{d}{2}$, $d = \frac{C}{\pi}$ and $\overset{\frown}{QS} = \frac{1}{3}C$, so $C = 3(\overset{\frown}{QS})$.

$$\overset{d}{\overbrace{3 \boxed{\times} 18.8 \boxed{\div} \boxed{\pi}}} \boxed{\div} 2 \boxed{=} \mathbf{8.9763388}$$

r

The radius of circle P is about 9 cm.

b. Answers may vary.

Sample: Multiply 18.8 by 3 to find the circumference. Divide C by π to find the diameter. Divide d by 2 to find the radius.

23. $C = 2\pi r \approx 2(3.14)(10) \approx 62.8$

The circumference of a circle of radius 10 is about 63.

A. $P = 4(10) = 40$

B. $P = 4(20) = 80$

C. $P = 10 + 20 + 10 + 20 = 60$, $P \approx C$

D. $P = 5 + 12 + 5 + 12 = 34$

24. Accept reasonable estimates.

About 120; $C = 122.67\pi$

$C = 385$

$\frac{C}{3} =$ about 120 or 130

25. Use $A = \pi r^2$.

radius of outer circle $= 2 + 3 = 5$

radius of inner circle $= 2$

area of outer circle $= \pi(5)^2 = 25\pi$

area of inner circle $= \pi(2)^2 = 4\pi$

a. area of the outer ring

$=$ area of the outer circle

$-$ area of the inner circle

$= 25\pi - 4\pi = 21\pi$

$21 \boxed{\times} \boxed{\pi} \boxed{=} \mathbf{65.973446}$

b. Subtract the area of the inner circle from the area of the outer circle.

The area of the outer ring is about 66.0 cm^2.

26. Use $A = \pi r^2$.

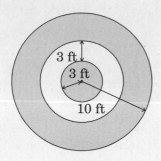

Combined area of the two gardens

= area of inner garden
    + area of outer ring garden

= $\pi(3)^2 + [\pi(10)^2 - \pi(3 + 3)^2]$

      ↑   ↑

   area of   area of
   outer   middle
   circle   circle

= $9\pi + [100\pi - 36\pi]$

= $9\pi + 64\pi$

= 73π

$73\ \boxed{\times}\ \boxed{\pi}\ \boxed{=}\ $ **229.33626**

The combined area of the two gardens is about 229.3 ft^2.

Mixed Review p. 57

1.

U.S. Population

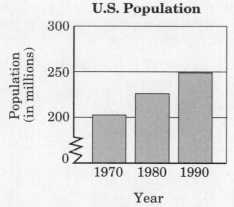

Year

2.

U.S. Population

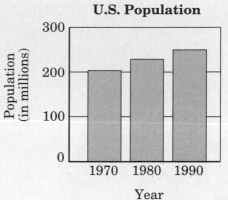

Year

3.

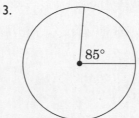

4.

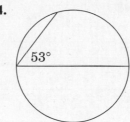

5. There are 60 min × 24 h per day, or 1,440 min in each day. 20,000 minutes would be $\frac{20,000}{1,440}$ or about 13.9 days. Thus 20,000 minutes would have passed from the first day of October during October 14.

2-3 Look for a Pattern

Pages 58–60

1. a. Area

   b. Answers may vary.

      Sample: The area of the larger (4π ft^2) is 4 times greater than the area of the smaller (π ft^2).

2.

Diameter	2 ft	3 ft	4ft
Radius	$2 \div 2$ = 1 ft	$3 \div 2$ = 1.5 ft	$4 \div 2$ = 2 ft
Square of the Radius	1 ft^2	2.25 ft^2	4 ft^2
Cost	$36 (1×36)	$81 (2.25×36)	$144 (4×36)

3. cost $\approx$ 36 $\times$ square of radius

4.

5 ft	6 ft	7 ft	8 ft
2.5 ft	3 ft	3.5 ft	4 ft
6.25 ft^2	9 ft^2	12.25 ft^2	16 ft^2
$225	$324	$441	$576

The largest size available for $500 is 7 ft in diameter.

5. yes

Try These p. 59

6. Make a table that shows the number, pattern, and triangular number.

Number	1	2	3	4
Pattern	1	1+2	1+2+3	1+2+3+4
Add to Pattern	$\frac{1(2)}{2}$	$\frac{2(3)}{2}$	$\frac{3(4)}{2}$	$\frac{4(5)}{2}$
Triangular Number	1	3	6	10

...	10	...	45
	1+2+$\cdots$+10		1+2+$\cdots$+ 45
	$\frac{10(11)}{2}$		$\frac{45(46)}{2}$
	55		1035

To determine the nth triangular number, you add $1 + 2 + 3 + \cdots + n$, or find $\frac{n(n + 1)}{2}$.

7. Make a table.

Money in box at night	$2	$3	$4	$5	$6
Pattern	2(2.50)	3(2.50)	4(2.50)	5(2.50)	6(2.50)
Money in box the next morning	$5	$7.50	$10	$12.50	$15

There would be $15 in the box in the morning if Keith put $6 in the night before.

On Your Own pp. 59–60

8. Pick a number: n

add 7 to it: $n + 7$

multiply the sum by 3: $3(n + 7)$

subtract 6: $3(n + 7) - 6$

end up with 45: $3(n + 7) - 6 = 45$

Solve: $3(n + 7) - 6 = 45$

Make a table to solve the equation.

n	$3(n + 7) - 6$	? = 45
1	$3(8) - 6 = 18$	$\neq 45$
5	$3(12) - 6 = 30$	$\neq 45$
10	$3(17) - 6 = 45$	$= 45 \checkmark$

The equation could also be solved.

$3(n + 7) - 6 = 45$

$3n + 21 - 6 = 45$ Multiply $n + 7$ by 3.

$3n + 15 = 45$ Combine like terms.

$3n + 15 - 15 = 45 - 15$ Subtract 15 from each side.

$3n = 30$

$\frac{3n}{3} = \frac{30}{3}$ Divide each side by 3.

$n = 10$

9. Make a table.

Day	1	2	3	4
Pay	$0.15	$0.30	$0.60	$1.20

Day	5	6	7	8	9
Pay	$2.40	$4.80	$9.60*	$19.20	$38.40†

* more than $5 a day: 7 days

† more than $20 a day: 9 days

10. 12 houses: 146, 156, 160, 162, 164, 166, 168, 176, 186, 196, 206, 216

11.

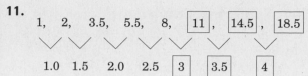

$$1, \quad 2, \quad 3.5, \quad 5.5, \quad 8, \quad \boxed{11}, \quad \boxed{14.5}, \quad \boxed{18.5}$$

$$1.0 \quad 1.5 \quad 2.0 \quad 2.5 \quad \boxed{3} \quad \boxed{3.5} \quad \boxed{4}$$

12.

No. of free throws	by 4 P.M.	next game	following game	total
Kris	n	5	3	$n + 5 + 3$ $= n + 8$
Velvet	$2n$	2	0	$2n + 2 + 0$ $= 2n + 2$

The total number of free throws Kris made is the same as the total number of free throws Velvet made. Make a table to determine when the total number of free throws Kris made is the same as the total number of free throws Velvet made, i.e., when $n + 8 = 2n + 2$.

n	$n + 8$	$2n + 2$
1	9	4
2	10	6
3	11	8
4	12	10
5	13	12
6	14	14

$n = 6, 2n = 2(6) = 12$

Kris made 6 free throws by 4 P.M. Velvet made 12 free throws by 4 P.M.

13. Look for a pattern.

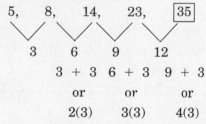

$$5, \quad 8, \quad 14, \quad 23, \quad \boxed{35}$$

$$3 \quad \quad 6 \quad \quad 9 \quad \quad 12$$

$$3 + 3 \quad 6 + 3 \quad 9 + 3$$
$$\text{or} \quad \quad \text{or} \quad \quad \text{or}$$
$$2(3) \quad \quad 3(3) \quad \quad 4(3)$$

Juan will buy 35 cards the next week.

14.

Circle	1	2	3	$\cdots$	6
No. of points on circle	3	4	5	$\cdots$	$6 + 2$ $= 8$

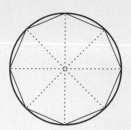

15. Make a table to find on what day Walter and Jackie both ride the bus to go shopping:

Bus days for Walter	6	12	18	24
Bus days for Jackie	8	16	24	32

Walter and Jackie will both ride the bus on the 24th day.

16. Look for a pattern.

No. of people	1	2	3	4	5	6	7	8	9
Cost ($)	8	16	23	29	34	38	41	43	44
Difference	8	7	6	5	4	3	2	1	

a. A buffet breakfast for 7 costs $41. If each person bought breakfast individually, the cost would be $7 \times \$8$, or $56.
The group saves $\$56 - \$41$, or $15.

b.

No. of people	Cost for the person	Cost for the restaurant at $5 per person
1	8	5
2	16	10
$\vdots$	$\vdots$	$\vdots$
6	38	30
7	41	35
8	43	40
9	44	45

The restaurant begins to lose money when serving 9 people. Thus, the restaurant can serve 8 people or fewer without losing money.

17. Answers will vary.

Mixed Review p. 60

1. Arrange the numbers in order from least to greatest.

   −10.3, −4.6, −4.1, 5.6, 6.4, 7.5

   Find the middle number, the average of −4.1 and 5.6.

   4.1 $\boxed{+/-}$ $\boxed{+}$ 5.6 $\boxed{=}$ $\boxed{÷}$ 2 $\boxed{=}$ **0.75**

   The median is 0.75.

2. mean: $= \dfrac{-10.3 + 5.6 - 4.1 + 7.5 + 6.4 - 4.6}{6}$

   10.3 $\boxed{+/-}$ $\boxed{+}$ 5.6 $\boxed{-}$ 4.1 $\boxed{+}$ 7.5 $\boxed{+}$ 6.4 $\boxed{-}$

   4.6 $\boxed{=}$ $\boxed{÷}$ 6 $\boxed{=}$ **0.0833333**

   The mean is $0.08\overline{3}$.

3. Use $C = 2\pi r$ and $r = 8$.

   2 $\boxed{×}$ $\boxed{\pi}$ $\boxed{×}$ 8 $\boxed{=}$ **50.265482**

   The circumference is about 50.3 cm.

4. Use $C = \pi d$ and $d = 7$.

   $\boxed{\pi}$ $\boxed{×}$ 7 $\boxed{=}$ **21.991149**

   The circumference is about 22.0 in.

5.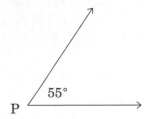

6.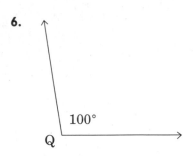

7. Make a table to find Yoshi's age when her mother is twice as old.

Yoshi's age	8	...	13	...	18	...	20	21	22
Mother's age	30	...	35	...	40	...	42	43	44

   Yoshi is 22 when her mother is twice as old.

2-4 Exploring Congruent Triangles

Pages 61–64

Work Together p. 61

yes

Check students' work. Samples given.

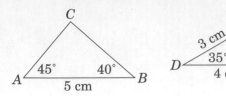

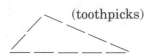

(toothpicks)

Think and Discuss pp. 61–63

1. Answers will vary.

   Samples: stop signs, pennies, bricks in a walkway

2. **a.**

Vertex	R	S	T
Corresponds to vertex	L	K	J

   b. $RSTW \cong LKJN$

   c. $\angle R \cong \angle L$, $\angle S \cong \angle K$, $\angle T \cong \angle J$, $\angle W \cong \angle N$, $\overline{RS} \cong \overline{LK}$, $\overline{ST} \cong \overline{KJ}$, $\overline{TW} \cong \overline{JN}$, $\overline{WR} \cong \overline{NL}$

3. **a.** SAS

   b. SSS

   c. ASA, since the vertical angles are congruent.

4. **a.** Vertical angles are $\cong$.

   b. ASA, since $\angle ABC \cong \angle EDC$, $\overline{BC} \cong \overline{DC}$, and $\angle BCA \cong \angle DCE$.

   c. Corresponding parts of $\cong \triangle$s are $\cong$.

   d. $AB = ED = 82$, or 82 yd

On Your Own pp. 63–64

5. $\angle B \cong \angle H$, $\overline{AB} \cong \overline{KH}$, $\overline{CB} \cong \overline{GH}$
   $\triangle ABC \cong \triangle KHG$ by SAS

6. $\overline{MO} \cong \overline{ST}$, $\overline{MN} \cong \overline{SR}$, $\overline{NO} \cong \overline{RT}$
   $\triangle MON \cong \triangle STR$ by SSS

7. no

8. $\angle T \cong \angle K$, $\overline{TR} \cong \overline{KJ}$, $\angle R \cong \angle J$
   $\triangle RTS \cong \triangle JKL$ by ASA

9. $\angle B \cong \angle E, \overline{BC} \cong \overline{EC}, \angle BCA \cong \angle ECD$
$\triangle ABC \cong \triangle DEC$ by ASA

10. $\overline{EH} \cong \overline{GF}, \angle EHF \cong \angle GFH, \overline{FH} \cong \overline{HF}$
$\triangle EFH \cong \triangle GHF$ by SAS

11. Answers may vary. Sample given. The triangles that form the supports of the swing set are congruent. Mass-produced items need to have parts that are exactly the same dimensions each time they are produced, so that parts are interchangeable for repair and always meet design and safety specifications.

12. C: **A.** SAS, **B.** SSS, and **D.** ASA

13. a. $\angle ABD \cong \angle CBD$
b. $\overline{AD} \cong \overline{CD}$

14. a. $\overline{RS} \cong \overline{MP}, \angle R \cong \angle M, \overline{RT} \cong \overline{MN}$
$\triangle RST \cong \triangle MPN$ by SAS
b. $PN = ST = 8$ in., $m\angle N = m\angle T = 59°$, $m\angle P = m\angle S = 72°$

Checkpoint p. 64

1. $\angle NPT$

2. $\angle RQT, \angle RQP, \angle PQS, \angle PQT, \angle SQR, \angle SQT$

3. $\overline{NT}$

4. Samples: $\widehat{PST}; \widehat{RNS}$

5. Use $A = \pi r^2$, $r = PQ = 6.5$
$\boxed{\pi} \boxed{\times} 6.5 \boxed{x^2} \boxed{=}$ **132.73229**
The area is about 132.7 cm^2.
Use $C = 2\pi r$.
$2 \boxed{\times} \boxed{\pi} \boxed{\times} 6.5 \boxed{=}$ **40.840704**
The circumference is about 40.8 cm.

6. Make a table.

Day	1	2	3	...	6
Blocks jogged	3	$3+1(4)$ $=7$	$3+2(4)$ $=11$	...	$3+5(4)$ $=23$

Andrea jogged 23 blocks on the sixth day.

7. B; A, C, and D each have 4 prongs, B has only 3 prongs.

Mixed Review p. 64

1.
```
3 | 6 9
4 | 5 7
5 | 2 5 7
6 | 3 3 3 4 5
```
3|6 means 36

2. 36, 39, 45, 47, 52, 55, 57, $\overset{mode}{\overline{63, 63, 63}}$, 64, 65,
median: $\frac{55+57}{2} = 56$
The median is 56, and the mode is 63.

3. 4

4. triangle

5.

Generation	Jorge
1	2 parents
2	2(2), 2^2 or 4 grandparents
3	2(2)(2), 2^3 or 8 great-grandparents
4	2(2)(2)(2), 2^4 or 16 great-great-grandparents
⋮	⋮
8	2(2)(2)(2)(2)(2)(2), 2^8 or $\boxed{256}$ ancestors in the 8th generation back.

2-5 Quadrilaterals and Triangles
Pages 65–67

Think and Discuss pp. 65–66

1. trapezoid: b
parallelogram: a, c, d, e
rectangle: a, c
rhombus: a, e
square: a

2. a. square
b. trapezoid
c. rectangle
d. parallelogram
e. rhombus

3. A quadrilateral with exactly 2 pairs of congruent sides; kite

4. a. $\triangle ABC \cong \triangle CDA$
b. $\overline{AB} \cong \overline{CD}$
c. $\overline{BC} \cong \overline{DA}$
d. $\angle B \cong \angle D$

5. **a.** They are ≅.

   b. It is true for rectangles, rhombuses, and squares, because they are all parallelograms. It is not true for trapezoids, because they have only one pair of parallel sides.

6. The nonparallel sides are ≅.

7. An equilateral triangle is a type of isosceles triangle because it has at least two ≅ sides.

8. Answers may vary. Check students' drawings. Sample:

   a.

   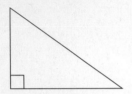

   b.

   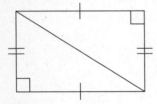

Work Together p. 66

rectangle: 2 congruent right triangles

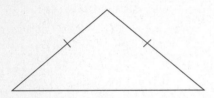

square: 2 congruent right isosceles triangles

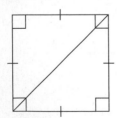

rhombus: **a.** 2 congruent obtuse isosceles triangles

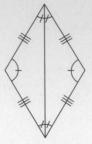

b. 2 congruent acute isoseles triangles

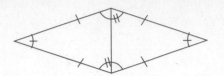

parallelogram: 2 congruent triangles

On Your Own p. 67

9. parallelogram; $\overline{AB} \cong \overline{CD}$; $\overline{AD} \cong \overline{CB}$; $\angle A \cong \angle C$; $\angle B \cong \angle D$

10. rectangle; $\overline{XW} \cong \overline{VU}$; $\overline{UX} \cong \overline{VW}$; $\angle X \cong \angle W \cong \angle V \cong \angle U$

11. rhombus; $\overline{EF} \cong \overline{FG} \cong \overline{GH} \cong \overline{HE}$; $\angle E \cong \angle G$; $\angle F \cong \angle H$

12. square; $\overline{JK} \cong \overline{KL} \cong \overline{LN} \cong \overline{NJ}$; $\angle J \cong \angle K \cong \angle L \cong \angle N$

13–18. Answers will vary. Check students' drawings.

Samples:

13.

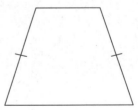

14.

15.

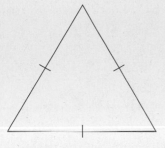

16.

17.

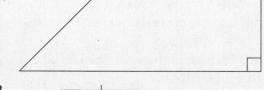

18.

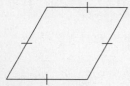

19. all

20. $\triangle BAD, \triangle BCD, \triangle JKL, \triangle JNL$

21. $\triangle WTU, \triangle WVU, \triangle DAB, \triangle DCB$

22. $\triangle JKL, \triangle JNL$

23. $\triangle WTU, \triangle WVU, \triangle PRS, \triangle TSP$

24. $\triangle PRS, \triangle STP$

25. $TUVW, ABCD$

26. C; rhombus

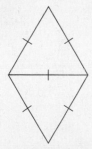

27. Answers may vary. Sample: All squares are both rhombuses and rectangles. Some rhombuses and rectangles are squares.

Mixed Review p. 67

1.

1	9
2	2 6 9
3	7

1 | 9 means 19

2. 19, 22, 26, 29, 37

      ↑

   median

The median is 26.

There is no mode.

3. False; $\angle L \cong \angle R$ and $\angle N \cong \angle T$.

4. True

5. False; a triangle has no diagonals.

6. Let $n, n + 1,$ and $n + 2$ represent the whole numbers.

$$n + n + 1 + n + 2 = 702$$
$$3n + 3 = 702$$
$$3n = 699$$
$$\frac{3n}{3} = \frac{699}{3}$$
$$n = 233$$
$$n + 1 = 234$$
$$n + 2 = 235$$

The numbers are 233, 234, and 235.

2-6 Angles of Polygons

Pages 68–71

Work Together p. 68

1.

Polygon	Number of Sides	Number of Triangles Formed	Sum of Angle Measure
Triangle	3	1	180°
Quadrilateral	4	2	360°
Pentagon	5	3	540°
Hexagon	6	4	720°

2. The sum increases by 180°; each additional side creates one more triangle.

3. The number of triangles formed is 2 less than the number of sides.

Think and Discuss pp. 68–69

4. a. 5; 2 less than 7 (number of sides of a heptagon)

  b. $5(180°) = 900°$

5. a. $100 - 2 = 98$

   b. $98(180°) = 17,640°$

6. number of triangles formed $\times$ 180°

     $(10 - 2) \times 180°$

        $\uparrow$

     number of
sides of a
decagon

     $8(180°) = 1440°$

7. a. $180° \div 3 = 60°$

   b. equilateral

8. a. $360° \div 4 = 90°$

   b. square

Try These p. 70

9. $48° + 65° = 113°$

The sum of the measures of the angles of a triangle is 180°.

The measure of the third angle is

    $180° - 113° = 67°$.

10. $14 - 2 = 12$

11. $(9 - 2) \times 180°$

    $7(180°) = 1,260°$

12. The sum of the measure of the angles of a pentagon is

    $(5 - 2) \times 180°$

    $3(180°) = 540°$.

The measure of each angle of a regular pentagon is $540° \div 5 = 108°$.

On Your Own pp. 70–71

13. hexagon; 6 sides

14. nonagon; 9 sides

15. octagon; 8 sides

16. heptagon

17. decagon

18. $79° + 23° = 102°$

    $m\angle B = 180° - 102°$

    $m\angle B = 78°$

The triangle is acute.

19. $45° + 90° = 135°$

    $m\angle J = 180° - 135°$

    $m\angle J = 45°$

The triangle is right.

20. $68° + 15° = 83°$

    $m\angle S = 180° - 83°$

    $m\angle S = 97°$

The triangle is obtuse.

21. a. $(8 - 2) \times 180°$

      $6(180°) = 1080°$

   b. $1080° \div 8 = 135°$

22. The sum of the measures of the angles of a decagon is:

    $(10 - 2) \times 180°$

    $8(180°) = 1,440°$

The measure of each angle of a regular decagon is:

    $1,440° \div 10 = 144°$

23. right; the sum of the two non-right angles of a right triangle is 90°.

24. In a nonregular polygon, the angles are not all necessarily $\cong$.

25. $145° + 115° + 152° + 87° + 150° = 649°$

The sum of the measures of the angles of a hexagon is:

    $(6 - 2)(180°) = 4(180°) = 720°$

The measure of the sixth angle is:

    $720 - 649° = 71°$

26. Check students' drawings.

The sum of the measures of the angles of a pentagon is 540°. The sums should be the same. If there is a difference, it may be due to difficulty in measuring accurately.

27. B; $180°(n - 2)$

28. hexagon

    $(6 - 2) \times 180° \div 6 = \frac{4(180°)}{6} = 120°$

29. pentagon

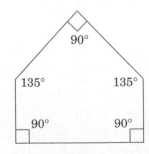

30. Answers may vary. Sample: Saba's method; it is more direct.

31. a.

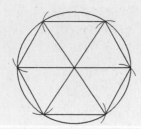

b. See figure; 6 equilateral triangles. The measure of each angle of each triangle is 60°.

c. regular hexagon; there are six ≅ sides and six 120° angles.

Mixed Review p. 71

1. 7, 9, 9, 33, 36, 41, 52, 55

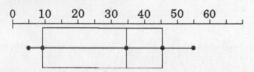

    Q1   Median   Q3

Median = $\frac{33 + 36}{2}$ = $\frac{69}{2}$ = 34.5

quartile 1 = $\frac{9 + 9}{2}$ = 9

quartile 3 = $\frac{41 + 52}{2}$ = 46.5

lower extreme: 7

upper extreme: 55

```
 0   10  20  30  40  50  60
```

2. 40, 55, 65, 74, 77, 79, 90, 98

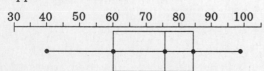

    Q1   Median   Q3

Median = $\frac{74 + 77}{2}$ = 75.5

quartile 1 = $\frac{55 + 65}{2}$ = 60

quartile 3 = $\frac{79 + 90}{2}$ = 84.5

lower extreme: 40

upper extreme: 98

```
30  40  50  60  70  80  90  100
```

3. True

4. False; A parallelogram is sometimes a rectangle.

5. Two corn muffins and a glass of milk cost $1.80. One corn muffin and a glass of milk cost $1.25.

    1.8 − 1.25 = 0.55

One corn muffin costs $.55.

    0.55 + m = 1.25

    0.55 + m − 0.55 = 1.25 − 0.55

    m = 0.7

A glass of milk costs $.70.

2-7 Polygons and Tessellations
Pages 72–75

Work Together p. 72

1.

Regular Polygon	Measure of Each Angle	Number of Polygons Sharing Each Vertex	Tessellation
triangle	60°	6	yes
square	90°	4	yes
pentagon	108°	–	no
hexagon	120°	3	yes
octagon	135°	–	no
decagon	144°	–	no

2. Answers may vary.
Sample: If the measure of each angle is a factor of 360°, the polygon can be used to form a tessellation.

Think and Discuss pp. 72–73

3. Answers may vary. Sample given. The design along $\overline{BC}$ is the image of the design along $\overline{BA}$ rotated 270° about B.

4. Answers may vary. Sample given. The design along $\overline{DC}$ is the image of the design along $\overline{AD}$ rotated 180° about D.

5. 1 and 12, 2 and 11, 3 and 6, 4 and 5, 7 and 10, 8 and 9

On Your Own p. 73

6. Check students' drawings. Samples given.

a.

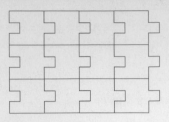

b.

7.

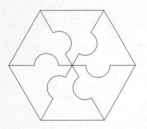

8.

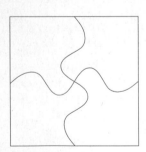

9.

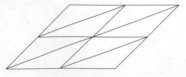

10.

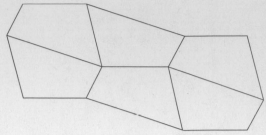

11.

12.

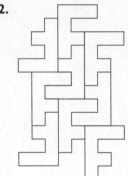

13.

14. Check students' drawings.

15. Answers will vary. Sample:

The measure of each angle is 108°. Since 108 is not a factor of 360, the figure will not tessellate.

16. C

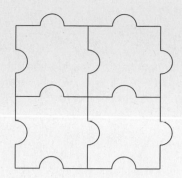

17. Check students' drawings.

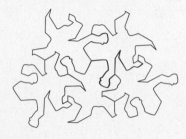

Mixed Review p. 75

1. $\frac{45}{360} = \frac{1}{8}$

$PQ = \frac{1}{8}C, C = 2\pi r,$ and $r = 6.$

$2 \;\boxed{\times}\; \boxed{\pi} \;\boxed{\times}\; 6 \;\boxed{\div}\; 8 \;\boxed{=}\; \mathbf{4.712389}$

The length of the intercepted arc, $\overset{\frown}{PQ}$, is about 4.7 cm.

2. $(n - 2) \times 180° = 900°$

$n - 2 = \frac{900}{180}$

$n - 2 = 5$

$n - 2 + 2 = 5 + 2$

$n = 7$

The polygon is a heptagon.

3. $(n - 2) \times 180° = 1080°$

$n - 2 = \frac{1080}{180}$

$n - 2 = 6$

$n - 2 + 2 = 6 + 2$

$n = 8$

The measure of each angle is $1{,}080° \div 8 = 135°.$

4. Make a table.

Number of coins	1	2	...	10	...	14	15
quarters	\$.25	\$.50	...	\$2.50	...	\$3.50	\$3.75
dimes	\$.10	\$.20	...	\$1.00	...	\$1.40	\$1.50
nickels	\$.05	\$.10	...	\$.50	...	\$.70	\$.75
total	\$.40	\$.80	...	\$4.00	...	\$5.60	\$6.00

Toni has 15 of each coin.

2-8 Constructing Perpendicular Lines
Pages 76–78

Work Together p. 76

Answers may vary.

1. Fold X onto Y.

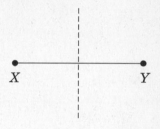

2. Fold $\overline{XY}$ onto itself with P on the fold line.

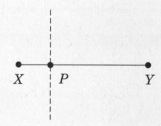

3. Fold $\overline{XY}$ onto itself with Q on the fold line.

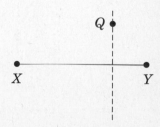

Think and Discuss p. 76–77

4–5. Check students' drawings.

The drawings should resemble the text drawings.

6. a. $\overline{LM} \cong \overline{LN}, \overline{MO} \cong \overline{NO}, \overline{LO} \cong \overline{LO}$; SSS

   b. Corresponding parts of $\cong$ triangles are $\cong$.

   c. $\overline{LM} \cong \overline{LN}, \angle MLP \cong \angle NLP$, $\overline{LP} \cong \overline{LP}$; SAS

   d. Corresponding parts of $\cong$ triangles are $\cong$.

   e. $m\angle MPL = 90°, m\angle NPL = 90°$

   They are $\cong$ and supplementary.

7. a. midpoint

   b. perpendicular bisector

8.

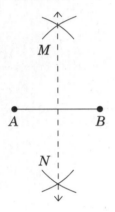

   • Draw $\overline{AB}$.

   • Open the compass to more than half the length of $\overline{AB}$. Put the top of the compass first at A and then at B, and draw arcs above and below $\overline{AB}$. Label the points where the arcs intersect M and N.

   • Draw $\overleftrightarrow{MN}$.

   • The perpendicular bisector of $\overline{AB}$ is $\overleftrightarrow{MN}$.

On Your Own p. 78

9. Diagrams may vary. Check students' drawings.

The drawings should resemble the steps of Exercise 5.

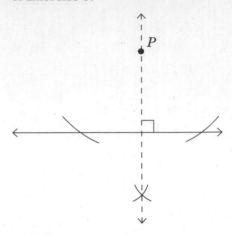

10. Check students' drawings.

The drawing should resemble the steps of Exercise 4.

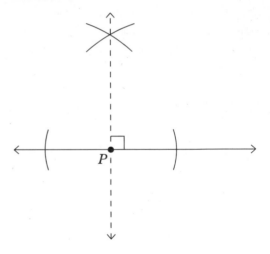

11. Check students' drawings.

The drawing should resemble the steps of Exercise 8.

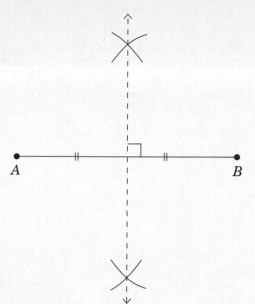

12. B

13. Diagrams may vary. Check students' drawings.

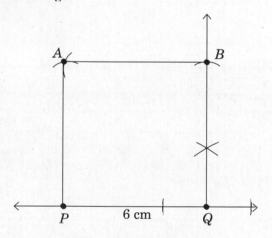

- Draw $\overline{PQ}$. (Extend both ends.)
- Construct a perpendicular line at Q.
- Measure a length equal to PQ on the perpendicular line at Q. Label the end B.
- Draw $\overline{QB}$.
- Measure a length equal to PQ from B and from P. Label the point of intersection A.
- Draw $\overline{PA}$ and $\overline{AB}$.

14. Diagrams may vary. Check students' drawings.

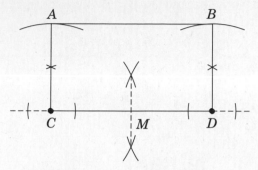

- Draw $\overline{CD}$. (Extend both ends.)
- Determine the midpoint of $\overline{CD}$ by constructing the perpendicular bisector of $\overline{CD}$. Label the midpoint M.
- Construct perpendicular lines at C and D.
- Measure length equal to $\frac{1}{2}CD$ or $\frac{1}{2}CM$ on the perpendicular lines at both C and D. Label the ends A and B.
- Draw $\overline{AB}$.

15. a. Check students' drawings.

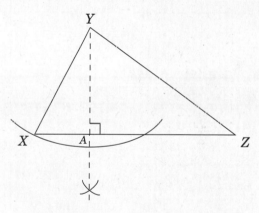

- Construct a perpendicular line from Y to $\overline{XZ}$. (See Exercise 5.)
- $\overline{YA}$ is the altitude of $\triangle XYZ$ from Y.

b. Sample: The area of $\triangle XYZ$ is $\frac{1}{2}$ times the length of the base (XZ) × the length of the height or altitude (YA) to this base. In $\triangle XYZ$, the area, $A = \frac{1}{2}(XZ)(YA)$.

16. a. $\overline{UW} \cong \overline{VW}$, $\overline{UR} \cong \overline{VR}$, $\overline{WR} \cong \overline{WR}$; SSS

b. Corresponding parts of $\cong$ triangles are $\cong$.

c. $\angle URW$ and $\angle VRW$ are right angles.

Mixed Review p. 78

1. $90° - 32° = 58°$

2. Check students' drawings.

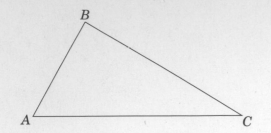

3. Answers may vary. Sample given. A *tessellation* is a design formed by a repeating geometric figure that completely covers a plane leaving no gaps.

4. Answers will vary. Samples: triangles, squares

5. The distance traveled by the tip of the minute hand in one hour:

$$2\pi(8) = 16\pi \text{ in.}$$

in 24 hours:

$$24(16\pi) = 384\pi \text{ in.}$$
$$\approx 1,206 \text{ in.}$$
$$\approx 100.5 \text{ ft}$$

2-9 Parallel Lines

Pages 79–82

Work Together p. 79

1. Answers may vary.

2. Answers may vary.

3. Sample: ∠2 and ∠3; ∠1 and ∠4; ∠6 and ∠7; ∠5 and ∠8; ∠1 and ∠5; ∠4 and ∠8; ∠2 and ∠6; ∠3 and ∠7

4. Samples: ∠1 and ∠2; ∠3 and ∠4; ∠5 and ∠6; ∠7 and ∠8; ∠1 and ∠3; ∠2 and ∠4; ∠5 and ∠7; ∠6 and ∠8

5. a. Check students' work.

b. Sample: When 2 parallel lines are cut by a non-perpendicular transversal, 4 acute angles and 4 obtuse angles are formed. All of the acute angles are ≅ and all of the obtuse angles are ≅. In addition, each acute angle is supplementary to any one of the obtuse angles. If the transversal is perpendicular to the parallel lines, then all of the angles formed are right angles and ≅.

Think and Discuss pp. 80–81

6. ∠4 and ∠8

7. The corresponding angles are on the same side of the transversal and in corresponding positions on each parallel line. The alternating interior angles are on alternating sides of the transversal and on the interior of the two parallel lines.

8. Answers will vary. Samples: ∠2 and ∠4, ∠7 and ∠8, ∠5 and ∠6, etc.

9. ∠1 and ∠3, ∠2 and ∠4, ∠5 and ∠7, ∠6 and ∠8

10. ∠2 and ∠7, ∠3 and ∠6

11. ∠1 and ∠5, ∠5 and ∠6, ∠6 and ∠2, ∠2 and ∠1, ∠3 and ∠7, ∠7 and ∠8, ∠8 and ∠4, ∠4 and ∠3

12. ∠1 and ∠6, ∠2 and ∠5, ∠3 and ∠8, ∠4 and ∠7

13. If two parallel lines are cut by a transversal, then corresponding angles are congruent, alternate interior angles are congruent, and vertical angles are congruent.

14. a. 55°

b. Answers may vary.

$m\angle 1 = 180° - m\angle 3$
$\qquad = 180° - 55°$ ∠1 and ∠3 are
$\qquad = 125°$ supplementary angles.

$m\angle 2 = m\angle 3 = 55°$ Vertical angles are ≅.

$m\angle 4 = 180° - m\angle 3$
$\qquad = 125°$ ∠3 and ∠4 are supplementary angles.

c. 125°; $m\angle 5 = m\angle 1$ Corresponding angles are ≅.

d. $m\angle 6 = m\angle 3 = 55°$
$m\angle 7 = m\angle 3 = 55°$
$m\angle 8 = m\angle 4 = 125°$

Try These p. 81

15. $m\angle 2 = m\angle 1 = 70°$

16.

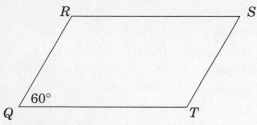

$m\angle Q = 60°$
$m\angle R = 180° - 60° = 120°$
$m\angle S = m\angle Q = 60°$
$m\angle T = m\angle R = 120°$

17. Answers may vary. Sample given. The angle made by the transversal and the first parallel line must be a right angle, since the lines are perpendicular. Since corresponding angles of parallel lines are congruent, the transversal and the second parallel line would intersect at right angles. Thus the transversal is perpendicular to both parallel lines.

On Your Own pp. 81–82

18. ∠6, ∠7: adjacent and supplementary

19. ∠6, ∠8: vertical and congruent

20. ∠2, ∠4: alternating interior and congruent

21. ∠3, ∠5: corresponding and congruent

22. ∠1, ∠7: none and neither

23. ∠1, ∠5: none and congruent

24.

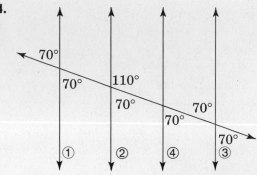

1. Vertical ∠s ≅.
2. Supplementary ∠s.
3. Vertical ∠s ≅.
1, 2, 3, 4. Corresponding ∠s ≅.
If a pair of corresponding ∠s are ≅, then the lines are parallel.

25. on either side of the existing sewage line above the lake or below the lake, each parallel to the existing sewage line

26. a. $m\angle 2 = m\angle 1 = 50°$

b. $m\angle 3 = 180° - m\angle 1 = 180° - 50° = 130°$

c. $m\angle 4 = 90°$

d. $m\angle 5 = 180° - 50° - 90° = 40°$

27. a. ∠EBC and ∠ABC are supplementary.
$m\angle EBC = 180° - 140° = 40°$
$140° + 40° + 85° = 265°$
The sum of the measures of the angles of a quadrilateral is 360°.
$m\angle C = 360° - 265° = 95°$

b. trapezoid; only one pair of sides is parallel.

28. a. all

b. rectangles, squares

c. rhombuses, squares

29. Answers will vary.

Mixed Review p. 82

1. Use $C = \pi d$ and $d = 5$ cm.

| π | × | 5 | = | **15.707963** |

The circumference is about 15.7 cm.

2. Use $r = \frac{C}{2\pi}$ and $C = 44$ in.

$$44 \boxed{\div} 2 \boxed{\div} \boxed{\pi} \boxed{=} \textbf{7.0028175}$$

The radius is about 7 in.

3–4. Check students' drawings. Answers will vary. Samples given.

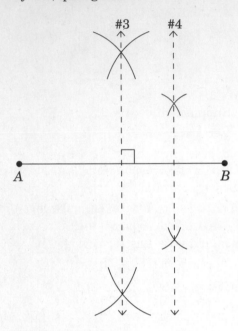

5. 5:42 A.M. to 7:42 P.M. is 14 h.

7:42 P.M. to 8:17 P.M. is 35 min.

The length of the day is 14 h 35 min.

Problem Solving Practice

Page 83

1. (1, 2), (1, 3), (1, 4), (1, 5), (1, 6)   5 ways

(2, 3), (2, 4), (2, 5), (2, 6)   4 ways

(3, 4), (3, 5), (3, 6)   3 ways

(4, 5), (4, 6)   2 ways

(5, 6)   <u>1 way</u>

15 committees

2.

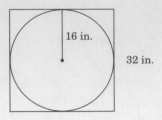

32 in.

$A = \pi r^2$

$$\boxed{\pi} \boxed{\times} 16 \boxed{x^2} = \textbf{804.24772}$$

The area is about 804.2 in.^{2}.

Instead of using the π key, the approximate value 3.14 can be used for π.

$3.14 \times 16^2 = 803.84$

The area is about 803.84 in.^{2}.

3. Let D represent the number of quarters David has.

Daniel has three times as many quarters as David.

   $3D$

Matthew has three more quarters than David.

   $D + 3$

Make a table.

David D	Daniel $3D$	Matthew $D + 3$	Total quarters	Value ($)
1	3	4	8	2.00
2	6	5	13	3.25
3	9	6	18	4.50
4	12	7	23	5.75
5	15	8	28	7.00
6	18	9	33	8.25
7	21	10	38	9.50

David has 7 quarters.

Daniel has 21 quarters.

Matthew has 10 quarters.

4. Work backward. The clown had 5 balloons at the end of 1 hour. During the second 30 minutes she gave away half of the balloons she had left plus 5.

At the end of the first half-hour she had

$(5 + 5) \times 2 = 20$ balloons.

During the first 30 minutes, she gave away half of the balloons she had plus 5. She must have started with

$(20 + 5) \times 2 = 50$ balloons.

The total number of balloons the clown started with was 50.

5. Twice the sum of the length and the width is 20. The sum of the length and width is 10.

Make a table to determine the possible integer values for the length and the width.

Possible		Sum
Length	Width	
9 cm	1 cm	10 cm
8 cm	2 cm	10 cm
7 cm	3 cm	10 cm
6 cm	4 cm	10 cm
5 cm	5 cm	10 cm

6. Find a pattern.

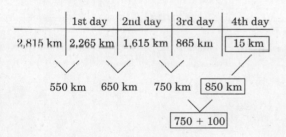

$865 \text{ km} - 850 \text{ km} = 15 \text{ km}$

No; they would be 15 km from home.

7. The total number of postcards and letters is 15.

Let L represent the number of letters.

$15 - L$ represents the number of postcards.

Each postcard costs \$.19

so $15 - L$ postcards will cost $0.19(15 - L)$.

Each letter costs \$.29

so L letters will cost $0.29L$.

Make a table.

Letters L	Postcards $15 - L$	Cost of letters $0.29L$ (\$)	Cost of $(15 - L)$ postcards $0.19(15 - L)$ (\$)	Total cost (\$)
1	14	$0.29(1) = 0.29$	$0.19(14) = 2.66$	2.95
2	13	$0.29(2) = 0.58$	$0.19(13) = 2.47$	3.05
3	12	$0.29(3) = 0.87$	$0.19(12) = 2.28$	3.15
4	11	$0.29(4) = 1.16$	$0.19(11) = 2.09$	3.25
5	10	$0.29(5) = 1.45$	$0.19(10) = 1.90$	3.35
6	9	$0.29(6) = 1.74$	$0.19(9) = 1.71$	3.45

Colleen mailed 9 postcards and 6 letters.

2-10 Constructing Parallel Lines

Pages 84–85

Think and Discuss p. 84

1. Answers will vary. Samples:

top and bottom edges of chalkboard, opposite sides of a door frame

2. Check students' drawings.

3. Corresponding angles are congruent, so the lines are parallel.

Work Together p. 85

4. Diagrams may vary.

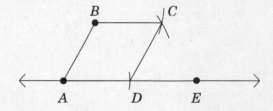

5. Diagrams may vary.

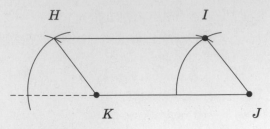

On Your Own p. 85

6.

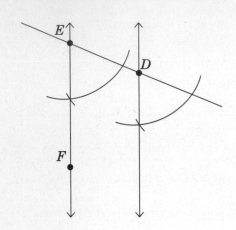

7.

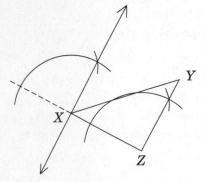

8.

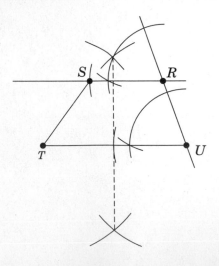

9.

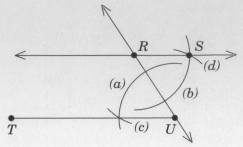

Steps

1. Draw $\overleftrightarrow{RU}$.
2. Draw arc (a) with compass point at U and arc (b) with compass point at R using the same setting.
3. Measure the distance between the points where arc (a) intersects $\overline{TU}$ and $\overleftrightarrow{RU}$ (arc (c)).
4. Mark the width on arc (b) by placing the compass point at the point where arc (b) intersects $\overleftrightarrow{RU}$ (arc (d)).
5. Draw $\overleftrightarrow{RS}$.

10.

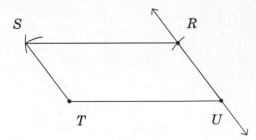

Mixed Review p. 85

1. hexagon
2. 10
3. $\angle 1$ and $\angle 5$, $\angle 2$ and $\angle 6$, $\angle 3$ and $\angle 7$, $\angle 4$ and $\angle 8$
4. $\angle 3$ and $\angle 6$, $\angle 4$ and $\angle 5$

5.

1st digit 3 possibilities (3, 4, 5)	2nd digit 3 possibilities (3, 4, 5)	3rd digit 3 possibilities (3, 4, 5)
333	433	533
334	434	534
335	435	535
343	443	543
344	444	544
345	445	545
353	453	553
354	454	554
355	455	555

total possibilities $= 3(9) = 27$

2-11 Square Roots

Pages 86–88

Work Together p. 86

4×4

5×5, 3 left over

6×6, 2 left over

Think and Discuss pp. 86–87

1. 5, since $5^2 - 25$

2. $49 = 7^2$

3.

Counting number	1	2	3	4	5
Square of number	1	4	9	16	25

Counting number	6	7	8	9	10
Square of number	36	49	64	81	100

4. $36 < 38 < 49$

$\sqrt{36} = 6$ and $\sqrt{49} = 7$

so $6 < \sqrt{38} < 7$

5. 28 $\boxed{\sqrt{\ }}$ **5.2915026**

$\sqrt{28} \approx 5.3$

6. -9 and 9, since $(-9)^2 = 81$ and $9^2 = 81$

Try These p. 87

7. -10 and 10, since $(-10)^2 = 100$ and $10^2 = 100$

8. -8 and 8, since $(-8)^2 = 64$ and $8^2 = 64$

9. -20 and 20, since $(-20)^2 = 400$ and $20^2 = 400$

10. $49 < 56 < 64$

$\sqrt{49} = 7$ and $\sqrt{64} = 8$

so $7 < \sqrt{56} < 8$

11. $81 < 94 < 100$

$\sqrt{81} = 9$ and $\sqrt{100} = 10$

so $9 < \sqrt{94} < 10$

12. $121 < 125 < 144$

$\sqrt{121} = 11$ and $\sqrt{144} = 12$

so $11 < \sqrt{125} < 12$

13. 56 $\boxed{\sqrt{\ }}$ **7.4833148**

$\sqrt{56} \approx 7.5$

14. 94 $\boxed{\sqrt{\ }}$ **9.6953597**

$\sqrt{94} \approx 9.7$

15. 125 $\boxed{\sqrt{\ }}$ **11.18034**

$\sqrt{125} \approx 11.2$

On Your Own pp. 87–88

16–24. $A = s^2$, where A represents the area and s represents the length of the side of the square. You can find s by finding the principal square root of A.

16. $s = \sqrt{36}$ in. $= 6$ in.

17. $s = \sqrt{100}$ yd $= 10$ yd

18. $s = \sqrt{144}$ ft $= 12$ ft

19. $s = \sqrt{121}$ cm $- 11$ cm

20. $s = \sqrt{0.01}$ km $= 0.1$ km

21. $s = \sqrt{0.64}$ m $= 0.8$ m

22. $s = \sqrt{2.25}$ in. $= 1.5$ in.

23. $s = \sqrt{\frac{9}{16}}$ in. $= \frac{3}{4}$ in.

24. $s = \sqrt{\frac{49}{100}}$ ft $= \frac{7}{10}$ ft

25–27. To find the area, find the square of s.

25. $A = (7.5 \text{ m})^2 = 56.25 \text{ m}^2$

26. $A = (\frac{1}{4} \text{ in.})^2 = \frac{1}{16}$ in.^{2}

27. $A = (\frac{2}{3} \text{ yd})^2 = \frac{4}{9}$ yd^2

28. $49 < 54 < 64$

$\sqrt{49} = 7$ and $\sqrt{64} = 8$

so $7 < \sqrt{54} < 8$

29. $144 < 148 < 169$

$\sqrt{144} = 12$ and $\sqrt{169} = 13$

so $12 < \sqrt{148} < 13$

30. $225 < 250 < 256$

$\sqrt{225} = 15$ and $\sqrt{256} = 16$

so $15 < \sqrt{250} < 16$

31. 13, since $13^2 = 169$

32. $53 \boxed{\sqrt{}}$ **7.2801099**

$\sqrt{53} \approx 7.3$

33. $89 \boxed{\sqrt{}}$ **9.4339811**

$\sqrt{89} \approx 9.4$

34. $0.27 \boxed{\sqrt{}}$ **0.5196152**

$\sqrt{0.27} \approx 0.5$

35. $2704 \boxed{\sqrt{}}$ **52**

$\sqrt{2704} = 52$

36. $3481 \boxed{\sqrt{}}$ **59**

$\sqrt{3481} = 59$

37. $289 \boxed{\sqrt{}}$ **17**

$-\sqrt{289} = -17$

38. $191 \boxed{\sqrt{}}$ **13.820275**

$-\sqrt{191} \approx -13.8$

39. $r^2 = \frac{A}{\pi}$ and $A = 804 \text{ m}^2$

$r^2 = \frac{804}{\pi}$

$r = \sqrt{\frac{804}{\pi}}$

$804 \boxed{\div} \boxed{\pi} \boxed{=} \boxed{\sqrt{}}$ **15.997536**

The radius of the circle is about 16 m.

40. The area of the larger square is 49 in.^{2} so the length of the side is 7 in., since $(7 \text{ in.})^2 = 49 \text{ in.}^2$.

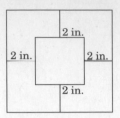

The length of the smallest square is 7 in. $-$ 2 in. $-$ 2 in. $=$ 3 in.

The area of the smallest square is (3 in.)^2, or 9 in.^{2}.

41. There is no number that when squared is a negative number.

Checkpoint p. 88

1. $\angle 1$ and $\angle 5$, $\angle 2$ and $\angle 6$

$\angle 3$ and $\angle 7$, $\angle 4$ and $\angle 8$

2. $\angle 3$ and $\angle 6$, $\angle 4$ and $\angle 5$

3. $\angle 1$ and $\angle 2$, $\angle 2$ and $\angle 4$

$\angle 3$ and $\angle 1$, $\angle 3$ and $\angle 4$

$\angle 5$ and $\angle 6$, $\angle 6$ and $\angle 8$

$\angle 8$ and $\angle 7$, $\angle 7$ and $\angle 5$

4. $\angle 1$ and $\angle 4$, $\angle 2$ and $\angle 3$

$\angle 5$ and $\angle 8$, $\angle 6$ and $\angle 7$

5. Answers may vary.

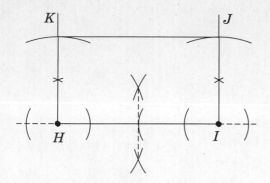

6. 4, since $4^2 = 16$

7. 70, since $70^2 = 4{,}900$

8. 0.5, since $(0.5)^2 = 0.25$

9. -16, since $(-16)^2 = 256$

10. $\dfrac{(5-2)180}{5} = \dfrac{3(180)}{5}$

$3 \boxed{\times} 180 \boxed{\div} 5 \boxed{=} \mathbf{108}$

The measure of each angle of a regular pentagon is 108°.

Mixed Review p. 88

1. Use $C = 2\pi r, A = \pi r^2, r = 15$ in., and $\pi = 3.14$.

$2 \boxed{\times} 3.14 \boxed{\times} 15 \boxed{=} \mathbf{94.2}$

$C = 94.2$ in.

$3.14 \boxed{\times} 15 \boxed{x^2} \boxed{=} \mathbf{706.5}$

$A = 706.5$ in.^{2}

2. Use $C = \pi d, A = \pi r^2, d = 11$ cm,

$r = \dfrac{11}{2}$ cm $= 5.5$ cm, and $\pi = 3.14$.

$3.14 \boxed{\times} 11 \boxed{=} \mathbf{34.54}$

$C \approx 34.5$ cm

$3.14 \boxed{\times} 5.5 \boxed{x^2} \boxed{=} \mathbf{94.985}$

$A \approx 95.0$ cm^2

3. Diagrams may vary.

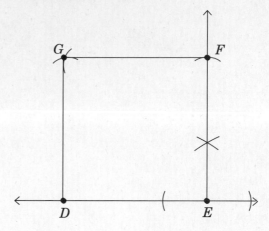

4. $8^2 = 64$

5. $5^2 = 25$

6. Make a table.

Blue (gallons)	Red (gallons)	Violet* (gallons)
3	2	5
6	4	10
9	6	15

* 3 parts blue plus 2 parts red yields violet. A proportion could also be solved.

$$\frac{3 \text{ parts blue}}{5 \text{ parts violet}} = \frac{x \text{ parts blue}}{15 \text{ parts violet}}$$

$$\frac{3}{5} = \frac{x}{15}$$

$$5x = 3 \cdot 15$$

$$x = \frac{3 \cdot 15}{5}$$

$$x = 9$$

The painter needs 9 gal of blue paint to make 15 gal of violet paint.

2-12 The Pythagorean Theorem

Pages 89–92

Work Together p. 89

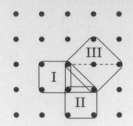

1. I: 1 unit^2

   II: 1 unit^2

   III: 2 unit^2

2. Answers will vary.

   Sample: area I + area II = area III

3.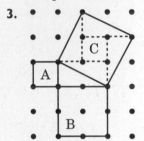

   A: 1 unit^2

   B: 4 unit^2

   C: 5 unit^2

4. Answers will vary.

   Sample: area A + area B = area C

   $$1 + 4 = 5$$

Think and Discuss pp. 89–90

5. **a.** $\overline{RT}$

   b. $\overline{RS}$ and $\overline{ST}$

   c. $(RT)^2 = (RS)^2 + (ST)^2$

   $(RT)^2 = 12^2 + 5^2$

   $\quad\quad\ = 144 + 25 = 169$

   $RT = \sqrt{169} = 13$ in.

6. **a.** hypotenuse

   b. 26 m, since it is the longest side.

Try These pp. 90–91

7. hypotenuse: $\overline{EF}$

   legs: $\overline{DE}$ and $\overline{DF}$

8. hypotenuse: $\overline{PR}$

   legs: $\overline{QR}$ and $\overline{QP}$

9. $a^2 + b^2 = c^2$

   $3^2 + 4^2 \overset{?}{=} 5^2$ Substitute 5 for c,

   $9 + 16 \overset{?}{=} 25$ the length of the
   longest side.

   $\quad\quad 25 = 25$

   Yes. The triangle is a right triangle.

10. $a^2 + b^2 = c^2$

    $8^2 + 9^2 \overset{?}{=} 10^2$ Substitute 10 for c,

    $64 + 81 \overset{?}{=} 100$ the length of the
    longest side.

    $\quad\quad 145 \neq 100$

    No. The triangle is not a right triangle.

11. $c^2 = a^2 + b^2$

    $c^2 = (7)^2 + (4)^2$ $a = 7$ m, $b = 4$ m

    $c = \sqrt{7^2 + 4^2}$

    $7\ \boxed{x^2}\ \boxed{+}\ 4\ \boxed{x^2}\ \boxed{=}\ \boxed{\sqrt{}}$ **8.0622577**

    hypotenuse ≈ 8.1 m

12. $a^2 + b^2 = c^2$

    $3^2 + b^2 = 8^2$ $a = 3$ ft, $c = 8$ ft

    $b^2 = 8^2 - 3^2$

    $b = \sqrt{8^2 - 3^2}$

    $8\ \boxed{x^2}\ \boxed{-}\ 3\ \boxed{x^2}\ \boxed{=}\ \boxed{\sqrt{}}$ **7.4161985**

    leg ≈ 7.4 ft

On Your Own pp. 91–92

13. $RT^2 = RS^2 + ST^2$

    $RT^2 = 8^2 + 15^2$ $RS = 8$ cm, $ST = 15$ cm

    $RT = \sqrt{8^2 + 15^2}$

    $8\ \boxed{x^2}\ \boxed{+}\ 15\ \boxed{x^2}\ \boxed{=}\ \boxed{\sqrt{}}$ **17**

    $RT = 17$ cm

14. $AB^2 + BC^2 = AC^2$

    $AB^2 + 12^2 = 20^2$ $BC = 12$ in., $AC = 20$ in.

    $AB^2 = 20^2 - 12^2$

    $AB = \sqrt{20^2 - 12^2}$

    $20\ \boxed{x^2}\ \boxed{-}\ 12\ \boxed{x^2}\ \boxed{=}\ \boxed{\sqrt{}}$ **16**

    $AB = 16$ in.

15. $DE^2 + EF^2 = DF^2$

$DE^2 + 6.1^2 = 8.1^2$ $EF = 6.1$ m

$DF = 8.1$ m

$DE^2 = 8.1^2 - 6.1^2$

$DE = \sqrt{8.1^2 - 6.2^2}$

8.1 $\boxed{x^2}$ $\boxed{-}$ 6.1 $\boxed{x^2}$ $\boxed{=}$ $\boxed{\sqrt{}}$ **5.329165**

$DE \approx 5.3$ m

16. $GI^2 = GH^2 + HI^2$

$GI^2 = 5^2 + 5^2$ $GH = 5$ cm, $HI = 5$ cm

$GI = \sqrt{5^2 + 5^2}$

5 $\boxed{x^2}$ $\boxed{+}$ 5 $\boxed{x^2}$ $\boxed{=}$ $\boxed{\sqrt{}}$ **7.0710678**

$GI \approx 7.1$ cm

17. $a^2 + b^2 = c^2$

$16^2 + 63^2 \stackrel{?}{=} 65^2$ Substitute 65 for c,

$256 + 3969 \stackrel{?}{=} 4225$ the length of the longest side.

$4225 = 4225$

Yes. The triangle is a right triangle.

18. $a^2 + b^2 = c^2$

$15^2 + 35^2 \stackrel{?}{=} 40^2$ Substitute 40 for c,

$225 + 1225 \stackrel{?}{=} 1600$ the length of the longest side.

$1450 \neq 1600$

No. The triangle is not a right triangle.

19. $a^2 + b^2 = c^2$

$7^2 + 9^2 \stackrel{?}{=} 12^2$ Substitute 12 for c,

$49 + 81 \stackrel{?}{=} 144$ the length of the longest side.

$130 \neq 144$

No. The triangle is not a right triangle.

20. $a^2 + b^2 = c^2$

$2.0^2 + 2.1^2 \stackrel{?}{=} 2.9^2$ Substitute 2.9 for c,

$4.0 + 4.41 \stackrel{?}{=} 8.41$ the length of the longest side.

$8.41 = 8.41$

Yes. The triangle is a right triangle.

21. $a^2 + b^2 = c^2$

$2.8^2 + 4.5^2 \stackrel{?}{=} 5.3^2$ Substitute 5.3 for c,

$7.84 + 20.25 \stackrel{?}{=} 28.09$ the length of the longest side.

$28.09 = 28.09$

Yes. The triangle is a right triangle.

22. $a^2 + b^2 = c^2$

$5^2 + \left(\sqrt{56}^2\right) \stackrel{?}{=} 9^2$ Substitute 9 for c,

$25 + 56 \stackrel{?}{=} 81$ the length of the longest side.

$81 = 81$

Yes. The triangle is a right triangle.

23. $c^2 = a^2 + b^2$

$c^2 = 17^2 + 17^2$ $a = 17$ cm, $b = 17$ cm

$c = \sqrt{17^2 + 17^2}$

17 $\boxed{x^2}$ $\boxed{+}$ 17 $\boxed{x^2}$ $\boxed{=}$ $\boxed{\sqrt{}}$ **24.041631**

The length of a diagonal is about 24.0 cm.

24. Answers may vary. Sample given. To find the distance across a room, measure the lengths of two adjacent walls of the room to create a right triangle with the walls as legs and the distance across the room as the hypotenuse.

25. Figure 1: $a = 2.5$ cm, $b = 1.7$ cm,

$c = 3.0$ cm

Figure 2: $a = 2.1$ cm, $b = 1.8$ cm,

$c = 2.2$ cm

Figure 3: $a = 2.1$ cm, $b = 1.8$ cm,

$c = 3.2$ cm

a. Figure 2: acute triangle

$a^2 + b^2 = 2.1^2 + 1.8^2$ $c^2 = 2.2^2$

$= 4.41 + 3.24$ $= 4.84$

$7.65 > 4.84$

b. Figure 3: obtuse triangle

$a^2 + b^2 = 2.1^2 + 1.8^2$ $c^2 = 3.2^2$

$= 4.41 + 3.24$ $= 10.24$

$7.65 < 10.24$

26.

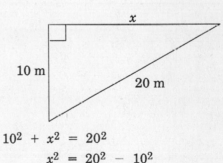

$10^2 + x^2 = 20^2$

$x^2 = 20^2 - 10^2$

$x^2 = 400 - 100$

$x^2 = 300$

$x = \sqrt{300}$

$x \approx 17.3$

The buoy on the surface is located about 17.3 m from the place where the diver started.

27.

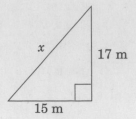

$$x^2 = 15^2 + 17^2$$
$$x = \sqrt{15^2 + 17^2}$$

15 $\boxed{x^2}$ $\boxed{+}$ 17 $\boxed{x^2}$ $\boxed{=}$ $\boxed{\sqrt{}}$ **22.671568**

The pond is about 22.7 m from the base camp.

28.

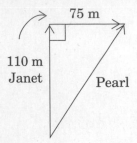

Janet: 110 m + 75 m = 185 m

Pearl: $\sqrt{110^2 + 75^2}$ m

110 $\boxed{x^2}$ $\boxed{+}$ 75 $\boxed{x^2}$ $\boxed{=}$ $\boxed{\sqrt{}}$ **133.13527**

≈ 133 m

Janet walked farther by 185 m − 133 m, or 52 m.

29.

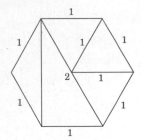

Divide the upper (right-hand) half of the hexagon into three equilateral triangles. Since each side of the equilateral triangles has length 1, the hypotenuse of the inscribed right triangle has length 2.

$$x^2 + 1^2 = 2^2$$
$$x^2 + 1 - 1 = 4 - 1$$
$$x^2 = 3$$
$$x = \sqrt{3} \approx 1.7$$

Answer: D; about 1.7 units

30. Answers may vary. Samples given.

Pythagorean triple	$a^2 + b^2 = c^2$
3 • 4 • 5 etc.	$3^2 + 4^2 = 5^2$ etc.
3, 4, 5	$3^2 + 4^2 = 5^2$ $9 + 16 = 25$ $25 = 25$
5, 12, 13	$5^2 + 12^2 = 13^2$ $25 + 144 = 169$ $169 = 169$
7, 24, 25	$7^2 + 24^2 = 25^2$ $49 + 576 = 625$ $625 = 625$
8, 15, 17	$8^2 + 15^2 = 17^2$ $64 + 225 = 289$ $289 = 289$
9, 40, 41	$9^2 + 40^2 = 41^2$ $81 + 1600 = 1681$ $1681 = 1681$
16, 63, 65	$16^2 + 63^2 = 65^2$ $256 + 3969 = 4225$ $4225 = 4225$

31. Answers may vary.

Mixed Review p. 92

1. mode

2. median

3. 9, since $9^2 = 81$

4. 11, since $11^2 = 121$

5. Sandy earns $40 per 8 hours or $5 per hour.

In $\boxed{1.5}$ hours Sandy will earn

1.5($5) or $7.50.

Practice

Page 93

1. $\overline{ER}, \overline{ED}, \overline{EA}$

2. Samples: $\angle RDA, \angle ADK, \angle RDK$

3. $\overline{RD}, \overline{DK}, \overline{AD}$

4. Samples: $\angle REA, \angle RED$

5. $m\angle ADR = \frac{1}{2}m\angle AER$

$m\angle ADR = \frac{1}{2}(80°)$

$m\angle ADR = 40°$

6. $m\angle AER = 2\,m\angle ADR$
   $m\angle AER = 2(45°)$
   $m\angle AER = 90°$

7. Use $A = \pi r^2$, $r = \frac{1.5\text{ m}}{2} = 0.75$ m, and
   $\pi \approx 3.14$.

   $3.14\ \boxed{\times}\ 0.75\ \boxed{x^2}\ \boxed{=}\ \textbf{1.76625}$

   The area is 1.77 m².
   Use $C = \pi d$, $d = 1.5$ m, and $\pi \approx 3.14$.

   $3.14\ \boxed{\times}\ 1.5\ \boxed{=}\ \textbf{4.71}$

   The circumference is 4.71 m.

8. Use $r = \frac{C}{2\pi}$, $A = \pi r^2$, and $C = 314$ ft.

   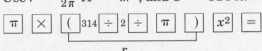

   7846.0204

   The area of circle E is about 7850 ft².

9. area of shaded region $= \frac{3}{4}$ area of circle or
   0.75 area of circle
   Use area $= \pi r^2$ and $r = 5$ cm.

   $0.75\ \boxed{\times}\ \boxed{\pi}\ \boxed{\times}\ 5\ \boxed{x^2}\ \boxed{=}\ \textbf{58.904862}$

   The area of the shaded region of circle A is
   about 58.9 cm².

10. $AC = 5$ cm, $AB = 5$ cm
    $BC^2 = AC^2 + AB^2$
    $BC^2 = 5^2 + 5^2$
    $BC = \sqrt{5^2 + 5^2}$

    $5\ \boxed{x^2}\ \boxed{+}\ 5\ \boxed{x^2}\ \boxed{=}\ \boxed{\sqrt{\ }}\ \textbf{7.0710678}$

    $BC \approx 7.1$ cm

11. $m\angle B = m\angle L$ since $\triangle HLQ \cong \triangle DBF$
    $m\angle L = 60° = m\angle B$

12. $m\angle F = m\angle Q$
    $m\angle Q = 180° - (60° + 70°)$
    $m\angle Q = 180° - 130°$
    $m\angle Q = 50° = m\angle F$

13. $DF = HQ$
    $HQ = 11.3 = DF$

14–16. Check students' drawings.

14. False

15. False; a trapezoid can have at most two right
    angles. Any quadrilateral with three right
    angles must have a fourth right angle,
    making opposite sides parallel. A trapezoid
    has exactly one pair of parallel sides.

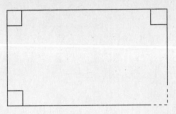

16. True

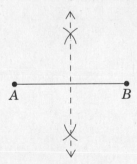

17. $m\angle 1 + 50° = 180°$
    $m\angle 1 = 180° - 50°$
    $m\angle 1 = 130°$

18. pentagon:
    sum of the measures of the angles is
    $(5 - 2)180° = 540°$
    $120° + 115° + 90° + 125° = 450°$
    $m\angle 2 = 540° - 450°$
    $m\angle 2 = 90°$

19. $m\angle 3 = 140°$
    $m\angle 3 + m\angle 4 = 180°$
    $140° + m\angle 4 = 180°$
    $m\angle 4 = 180° - 140°$
    $m\angle 4 = 40°$

20. Answers may vary. Check students' work.

21. $a^2 + b^2 \overset{?}{=} c^2$
    $15^2 + 20^2 \overset{?}{=} 25^2$
    $225 + 400 \overset{?}{=} 625$
    $625 = 625$

    Yes. The triangle is a right triangle.

Wrap Up

Pages 94–95

1. $m\angle AYP = \frac{1}{2}m\angle AOP$

   $m\angle AYP = \frac{1}{2}(60°)$

   $m\angle AYP = 30°$

2. Use $C = 2\pi r$ and $r = AO = 6$ cm.

   $2 \;\boxed{\times}\; \boxed{\pi}\; \boxed{\times}\; 6 \;\boxed{=}\; \textbf{37.699112}$

   The circumference is about 37.7 cm.

   Use $A = \pi r^2$ and $r = 6$ cm.

   $\boxed{\pi}\; \boxed{\times}\; 6 \;\boxed{x^2}\; \boxed{=}\; \textbf{113.09734}$

   The area is about 113.1 cm².

3. $m\angle AOP = 2\,m\angle AYP = 2(30°) = 60°$

   $r = OP = 3.5$ in.; $d = 2r = 7.0$ in.

   $\frac{60}{360} = \frac{1}{6}$

   length of $\widehat{AP} = \frac{1}{6}C$ and $C = \pi d$

   $\boxed{\pi}\; \boxed{\times}\; 7 \;\boxed{\div}\; 6 \;\boxed{=}\; \textbf{3.6651914}$

   The length of $\widehat{AP}$ is about 3.7 in.

   Answer $\boxed{B}$ is correct.

4. $\overline{CR} \cong \overline{CQ}$, $\angle R \cong \angle Q$,

   $\angle PCQ \cong \angle TCR$ (Vertical angles are $\cong$.)

   Yes; $\triangle PQC \cong \triangle TRC$ because of ASA.

5. $m\angle R + m\angle T + m\angle PCQ = 180°$

   $48° + 42° + m\angle PCQ = 180°$

   $90° + m\angle PCQ = 180°$

   $m\angle PCQ = 180° - 90°$

   $m\angle PCQ = 90°$

6. It is a parallelogram, and it has 4 right $\angle$s.

7. octagon: 8 sides

   sum of the measures of the angles

   $= (8 - 2)180°$

   $= 6(180°)$

   $= 1080°$

8. hexagon: 6 sides

   measure of each angle of a regular hexagon

   $= \frac{(6-2)180°}{6}$

   $= \frac{4(180°)}{6}$

   $= 120°$

9. $\angle 1$ and $\angle 3$, $\angle 2$ and $\angle 4$, $\angle 5$ and $\angle 7$, $\angle 6$ and $\angle 8$

10. $\angle 8$, $\angle 6$, $\angle 1$

11. $m\angle 6 + m\angle 7 = 180°$

    $75° + m\angle 7 = 180°$

    $m\angle 7 = 180° - 75°$

    $m\angle 7 = 105°$

12.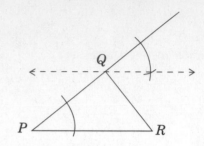

13. 9, since $9^2 = 81$

14. 0.8, since $(0.8)^2 = 0.64$

15. -11, since $-(11)^2 = -121$

16. 15, since $15^2 = 225$

17.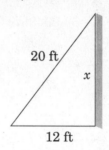

    $(12)^2 + x^2 = (20)^2$

    $x^2 = 20^2 - 12^2$

    $x^2 = 400 - 144$

    $x^2 = 256$

    $x = 16$

    The ladder is 16 ft up the side of the house.

18.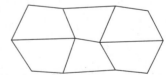

19.

time	1 min	2 min	3 min	4 min	5 min	6 min
amount	25¢	34¢	43¢	52¢	61¢	70¢
difference		9¢	9¢	9¢	9¢	9¢

6 min: $25¢ + (6 - 1)9¢$
$$= 25¢ + 5(9¢)$$
$$= 25¢ + 45¢$$
$$= 70¢$$

Getting Ready for Chapter 3 p. 95

1. $8b = 8(5) = 40$

2. $a + c = 3 + 10 = 13$

3. $4 \cdot b - 2 \cdot a = 4 \cdot 5 - 2 \cdot 3$
$$= 20 - 6$$
$$= 14$$

4. $\dfrac{6b}{ac} = \dfrac{6(5)}{3(10)}$
$$= \dfrac{30}{30} = 1$$

5. $a(b + c) = 3(5 + 10)$
$$= 3(15) = 45$$

6. $a \cdot b + c = 3 \cdot 5 + 10$
$$= 15 + 10 = 25$$

Assessment

Page 98

1.

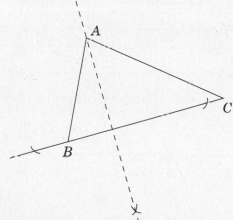

2. B; $LM^2 + MC^2 = LC^2$, so $\triangle LMC$ is a right triangle.
$LM \neq MC \neq LC$, so $\triangle LMC$ is scalene.
The triangle is a right scalene triangle.

3. $r = 5.8$ cm
$\dfrac{60}{360} = \dfrac{1}{6}$ since $m\angle EKA = 60°$

a. area $= \pi r^2$
area $= \pi(5.8)^2$
area ≈ 105.7 cm^2

b. $C = 2\pi r$
$C = 2\pi(5.8)$
$C \approx 36.4$ cm

c. $\widehat{AE} = \dfrac{1}{6}C$
$\widehat{AE} \approx 6.1$ cm

d. area of shaded region $= \dfrac{1}{6}$ area of circle
$\approx \dfrac{1}{6}(105.7$ cm$^2)$
≈ 17.6 cm^2

e. $m\angle EDA = \dfrac{1}{2}m\angle EKA$
$m\angle EDA = \dfrac{1}{2}(60°)$
$m\angle EDA = 30°$

4. A rectangle and a parallelogram are alike in that both pairs of opposite sides are parallel and $\cong$. They are different in that in a rectangle the measure of each angle is 90°, while in a parallelogram the measure of each angle may or may not be 90°.

5. first 4 lines for $28; each line thereafter at $6.50 per line
10 lines: 4 for $28   = $28   or $28
6 at $6.50 per line = 6($6.50) or $39
total $67
The cost of a 10-line ad is $67.

6. a. true

b. false; The sum of the measures of the angles of a triangle is 180°. If one angle is obtuse, the measure of the obtuse angle is greater than 90°. Thus, the sum of the remaining two angles is less than 90°. It is impossible to have a right angle less than 90°.

c. true

7. decagon: 10 sides
sum of the measures of the angles is
$(10 - 2)108° = 8(180°)$
$$= 1440°$$

8. $a^2 + b^2 \overset{?}{=} c^2$

$ 2^2 + 4^2 \overset{?}{=} 5^2$

$ 4 + 16 \overset{?}{=} 25$

$ 20 \neq 25$

The triangle is not a right triangle.

9. a. 13, since $13^2 = 169$

b. 1.1, since $1.1^2 = 1.21$

c. -20, since $-(20)^2 = -400$

10. $d^2 = 10^2 + 10^2$

$ d^2 = 100 + 100$

$ d^2 = 200$

$ d = \sqrt{200}$

$ d \approx 14.14$ cm

11. a. no

b. yes; $\triangle PRQ \cong \triangle SRT$ by SAS, since $\overline{PR} \cong \overline{SR}$, $\overline{QP} \cong \overline{TR}$, and $\angle PRQ \cong \angle SRT$.

12. a. alternate interior

b. none of the above

c. corresponding

d. adjacent

Cumulative Review

Page 99

1. B; A is $\cong$ by ASA.

B does not have to be $\cong$.

C is $\cong$ by ASA.

D is $\cong$ by ASA.

2. B

3. C; $\overline{(M)}$ T W Th F

M $\overline{(T)}$ W Th F

M T $\overline{(W)}$ Th F

M T W $\overline{(Th)}$ F

M T W Th F

$\overline{(M)}$ T W Th F

every 6th week

4. A; $11^2 = 121$ and $12^2 = 144$

$ 121 < 135 < 144$

$ 11 < \sqrt{135} < 12$

5. D; $\angle 2$ and $\angle 4$

6. C

7. A; area $= 36\pi$ in.^{2}

area $= \pi r^2$; $\pi r^2 = 36\pi$

$r^2 = 36$

$r = 6$ in.

$C = 2\pi r$

$C = 2\pi(6)$

$C = 12\pi$ in.

8. B; 1 day \$1.35

$\boxed{\text{2 days \$2.70}}$ 3 days \$4.05

She can buy a full lunch 2 days a week.

9. D; $\frac{(n-2)180°}{n} = 140°$

Guess and test can be used.

Try different values of n.

$n = 7$: $\frac{(7-2)180°}{7} \neq 140°$

$n = 8$: $\frac{(8-2)180°}{8} \neq 140°$

$\boxed{n = 9: \frac{(9-2)180°}{9} = 140°}$

The number of sides is 9.

10. C; average $= \frac{36 + 40 + 85 + 63}{4}$

$36 \boxed{+} 40 \boxed{+} 85 \boxed{+} 63 \boxed{=} \boxed{\div} 4 \boxed{=}$ **56.**

The average (mean) number of cars is 56.

Chapter 3 Integers and Variable Expressions

3-1 Graphing Integers on the Number Line

Pages 103–105

Think and Discuss pp. 103–104

1. **a.** to the right of zero
   b. to the left of zero
   c. The line extends indefinitely in both directions.

2. **a.**

   b. 8, −8 and 12, −12

3. 5

4. Sample:

   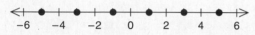

5.
   ```
   |<---- 2 units ---->|<---- 2 units ---->|
   ├---------|---------|---------|---------┤
   -2                  0                    2
   ```

6. The absolute value of 12
   |12| = 12

7. No; the distance from zero to a number is always positive or zero.

8. −3, −2, −1, 0, 1, 2, 3;
   |−3| = 3 < 4, |−2| = 2 < 4,
   |−1| = 1 < 4, |0| = 0 < 4, |1| = 1 < 4,
   |2| = 2 < 4, |3| = 3 < 4

9. Chlorine; it is the furthest to the right on the number line.

10. Chlorine, −30°F;
    Oxygen, −297°F;
    Nitrogen, −320°F;
    Hydrogen, −423°F;
    Helium, −452°F

On Your Own pp. 104–105

11. −129

12. −571

13. 2,000,000

14. Yes; Kansas reached −40°C.

15. Alaska

16. D; A contains $\frac{1}{2}$, B contains −3.2, and C contains 2.5 and −2.5.

17. U; −48

18. V; −2

19. T; 12

20. W; −35

21. X; −19

22. S; −23

23. |−14| = |14| since 14 = 14

24. 3 > −4

25. |−3| < |−6| since 3 < 6

26. 6 > 0

27. |−25| > |−1| since 25 > 1

28. 0 < |−5| since 0 < 5

29. |75| < |−210| since 75 < 210

30. |1| > 0 since 1 > 0

31. 28 > −35

32. −13 > −16

33. Sample: The whole numbers are a subset of the integers.

Mixed Review p. 104

1. Mean = $\dfrac{4 + 5 + 9 + 2 + 2 + 3}{6}$

   $\boxed{4}\boxed{+}\boxed{5}\boxed{+}\boxed{9}\boxed{+}\boxed{2}\boxed{+}\boxed{2}\boxed{+}\boxed{3}\boxed{=}$

   $\boxed{÷}\boxed{6}\boxed{=}$ **4.1666667**

   Mean = $4.1\overline{6}$

2. Mean = $\dfrac{98 + 95 + 91 + 98 + 95 + 95}{6}$

   $\boxed{98}\boxed{+}\boxed{95}\boxed{+}\boxed{91}\boxed{+}\boxed{98}\boxed{+}\boxed{95}\boxed{+}\boxed{95}\boxed{=}$

   $\boxed{÷}\boxed{6}\boxed{=}$ **95.333333**

   Mean = $95.\overline{3}$

3. $c^2 = a^2 + b^2$
   $c^2 = 7^2 + 24^2$ $a = 7, b = 24$
   $c^2 = 49 + 576$
   $c^2 = 625$
   $c = 25$

4. $c^2 = a^2 + b^2$

$c^2 = 9^2 + 12^2 \qquad a = 9, b = 12$

$c^2 = 81 + 144$

$c^2 = 225$

$c = 15$

5. 24(47)

1,128 books

3-2 Writing Variable Expressions
Pages 106–108

Think and Discuss pp. 106–107

1. $6.5h$

2. a. $2n$

  b. $0.75x$

3. a. $2n = 2 \cdot 5 = 10$; $n = 5$

    Five hot dogs cost $10.

  b. $0.75x = 0.75 \cdot 8 = 6$; $x = 6$

    Eight cartons of juice cost $6.

4. Answers may vary.

  Samples:

Variable expression	Another word phrase
$n + (-3)$	the sum of n and -3
$k \div 8$	a number divided by 8
$y - 6$	a number decreased by 6
$15 - b$	b less than 15

5. a. $27 + y$

  b. $x - 13$

  c. $\dfrac{n}{-10}$

  d. $17m$

6. a. Multiplication and addition

  b. Sample: 1.5 more than twice a number

Try These p. 107

7–10. Answers may vary. Samples given.

7. $m - 6$; m = mother's height

8. $3b$; b = no. of calories in a slice of bread

9. $j + 3$; j = Jill's age

10. $12e$; e = Eric's age in years

11. $2m$

12. $-12 + x$

13. $-4y$

14. $\dfrac{3}{w}$

15. $a + 18$

16. $n - 17$

Mixed Review p. 107

1. 14, 14, 31, 33, 50

  ⎣⎦

  mode: 14

2. 8, 17, 17, 19, 34

  ⎣⎦

  mode: 17

3. $-7 < 7$

4. $|-32| = 32$ since $32 = 32$

5. $342 + 1{,}257$

  total attendance: 1,599

6. 12 min + 15 min = 27 min

  Cara needs to leave her house 27 min before school starts or 27 min before 8:00.

  7:33

On Your Own p. 108

17. $n - 6$

18. $|x| + 7$

19. $9|x|$

20. $12x + 4$ for $x = \frac{1}{2}$

  $12\left(\frac{1}{2}\right) + 4 = 6 + 4$

            $= 10$

21. $17 - n$ for $n = 12.5$

  $17 - 12.5 = 4.5$

22. $(30 \div z) + 19$ for $z = 6$

  $(30 \div 6) + 19 = 5 + 19$

                $= 24$

23. $52y - 16$ for $y = 1\frac{1}{2} = \frac{3}{2}$

  $52\left(\frac{3}{2}\right) - 16 = 78 - 16$

                $= 62$

24. **b**; $35x$

25. **e**; $35(7)$

26. **d**; $n + 35$

27. **c**; $m - 35$

28. **a**; $35 - 7$

29–32. Answers may vary. Samples given:

29. $n \div 3$; a prize amount divided into 3 equal parts

30. $3 + a$; Katerina won 3 events more than last year.

31. $-(-x)$; the opposite of the opposite of a number

32. $7w - 5$; five fewer than seven times the number of hours worked

33. a. $241n$

b. Answers may vary. Sample: $263n$; total number of cars owned by n thousand inhabitants of Spain.

34. C; n fewer eggs than 6

$6 - n$

3-3 Adding Integers

Pages 109–112

Work Together p. 109

1. a.

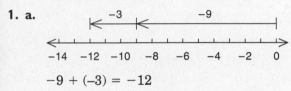

$-9 + (-3) = -12$

b.

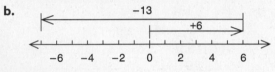

$6 + (-13) = -7$

c.

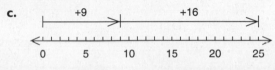

$9 + 16 = 25$

d.

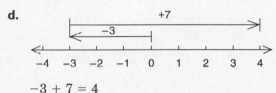

$-3 + 7 = 4$

e.

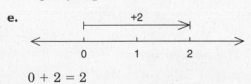

$0 + 2 = 2$

f.

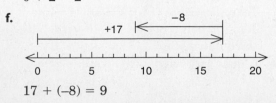

$17 + (-8) = 9$

2. Answers may vary. Sample:

Same sign: add absolute values and keep same sign.

Different signs: subtract the absolute values and use the sign of the addend with the greater absolute value.

Think and Discuss pp. 109–111

3. a. $|-9| = 9, |-3| = 3$

b. negative

4. a. $|17| = 17, |-8| = 8$

b. $17 - 8 = 9$

c. positive

5. -6; $6 + (-6) = 0$

Mixed Review p. 110

1. 4 since $4^2 = 16$

2. 7 since $7^2 = 49$

3. $b + 7$

4. $f - 6$

5. -9

6. $-(-2) = 2$

7. 7 since $3(7) = 21$ or $21 \div 3 = 7$

Try These pp. 111–112

6. a.

holes	1	2	3	4
strokes	$3 + (+2)$	$4 + (-1)$	$5 + (-2)$	$4 + (+3)$
	5	3	3	7

b. $+2 + (-1) + (-2) + (+3) = +2$

2 above par

c. To "be at par" means the sum of the number of strokes above or below par is zero. The total for the first 4 holes is $+2$. So the number of strokes above or below par for hole five is -2 since $+2 + (-2) = 0$. Since par is 4, the player must take $4 + (-2)$ or 2 strokes at hole 5 for her total score.

7. $13 + (-12)$

$|13| - |12| = 13 - 12$ ← Subtract absolute values.

$= 1$

$|13| > |-12|$ ← Use the sign of the integer with the greater absolute value.

$13 + (-12) = 1$

8. $12 + (-4)$

$\quad |12| - |-4| = 12 - 4$

$\qquad\qquad = 8$

$\qquad |12| > |-4|$

$\quad 12 + (-4) = 8$

9. $-4 + 6 + 4$

$\quad -4 + 6 + 4 = (-4 + 4) + 6$

$\qquad\qquad\quad = 0 + 6$

$\qquad\qquad\quad = 6$

10. $-45 + (-67)$

$\quad |-45| + |-67| = 112 \quad \leftarrow$ Add the absolute values.

$\quad -45 + (-67) = -112 \quad \leftarrow$ Both addends have the same sign; use the sign for the sum.

11. $-13 + (-4)$

$\quad |-13| + |-4| = 17$

$\quad -13 + (-4) = -17$

12. $14 + (-62)$

$\quad |-62| - |14| = 62 - 14$

$\qquad\qquad = 48$

$\qquad |-62| > |14|$

$\quad 14 + (-62) = -48$

13. $-2 + 3$

14. $1{,}800 + (-750)$

15. $-53 + 28$

On Your Own p. 112

16. $9 + (-3)$

$\quad |9| - |-3| = 9 - 3$

$\qquad\qquad = 6$

$\qquad |9| > |-3|$

$\quad 9 + (-3) = 6$

17. $-9 + 3$

$\quad |-9| - |3| = 9 - 3$

$\qquad\qquad = 6$

$\qquad |-9| > |3|$

$\quad -9 + 3 = -6$

18. $-9 + (-3)$

$\quad |-9| + |-3| = 9 + 3$

$\qquad\qquad = 12$

$\quad -9 + (-3) = -12$

19. $9 + 3 = 12$

20. $-8 + 0 = -8$

21. $-8 + 8 = 0$

22. $-11 + (-9)$

$\quad |-11| + |-9| = 11 + 9$

$\qquad\qquad = 20$

$\quad -11 + (-9) = -20$

23. $11 + (-9)$

$\quad |11| - |-9| = 11 - 9$

$\qquad\qquad = 2$

$\qquad |11| > |-9|$

$\quad 11 + (-9) = 2$

24. $-23 + 15$

$\quad |-23| - |15| = 23 - 15$

$\qquad\qquad = 8$

$\qquad |-23| > |15|$

$\quad -23 + 15 = -8$

25. $-17 + 18$

$\quad |18| - |-17| = 18 - 17$

$\qquad\qquad = 1$

$\qquad |18| > |-17|$

$\quad -17 + 18 = 1$

26. $|-13| + (-13)$

$\quad |-13| - |-13| = 13 - 13$

$\qquad\qquad = 0$

$\quad |-13| + (-13) = 0$

27. $-37 + 33 + (-32) + 29 + 18$

$\quad = -4 + (-32) + 29 + 18$

$\quad = -36 + 29 + 18$

$\quad = -7 + 18$

$\quad = 11$

a. yes; The total is positive.

b. 11 points

c. Answers may vary. Sample: Group the negative values and the positive values. Then estimate to determine total value.

$\quad -37 + (-32) \approx -40 + (-30)$

$\qquad\qquad\quad = -70$

$\quad 33 + 29 + 18 \approx 30 + 30 + 20$

$\qquad\qquad\quad = 80$

$\quad |80| > |-70|$

The total is positive.

28. Team A: $+ 30 + (-40) + (-15) = -25$

Team B: $+ 4 + (-40) + (-9) = -45$

Team B had a net loss of 45 yards after its third down.

29. $|-45| + |10| = 45 + 10$

$\qquad\qquad = 55$

55 yards

30. Check students' work.

3-4 Subtracting Integers
Pages 113–115

Work Together p. 113

1. a. $9 \boxed{-} 10 \boxed{=} -1$
$9 - 10 - -1$

b. $27 \boxed{+/-} \boxed{-} 8 \boxed{+/-} \boxed{=} -19$
$-27 - (-8) = -19$

c. $15 \boxed{-} 6 \boxed{+/-} \boxed{=} 21$
$15 - (-6) = 21$

d. $35 \boxed{+/-} \boxed{-} 12 = -47$
$-35 - 12 = -47$

e. $7 \boxed{+/-} \boxed{-} 18 \boxed{+/-} \boxed{=} 11$
$-7 - (-18) = 11$

f. $10 \boxed{-} 12 \boxed{=} -2$
$10 - 12 = -2$

g. $22 \boxed{-} 4 \boxed{+/-} \boxed{=} 26$
$22 - (-4) = 26$

h. $15 \boxed{-} 10 \boxed{+/-} \boxed{=} 25$
$15 - (-10) = 25$

i. $15 \boxed{+/-} \boxed{-} 10 \boxed{=} -25$
$-15 - 10 = -25$

2. a. $9 \boxed{+} 10 \boxed{+/-} \boxed{=} -1$
$9 + (-10) = -1$

b. $27 \boxed{+/-} \boxed{+} 8 \boxed{=} -19$
$-27 + 8 = -19$

c. $15 \boxed{+} 6 \boxed{=} 21$
$15 + 6 = 21$

d. $35 \boxed{+/-} \boxed{+} 12 \boxed{+/-} \boxed{=} -47$
$-35 + (-12) = -47$

e. $7 \boxed{+/-} \boxed{+} 18 \boxed{=} 11$
$-7 + 18 = 11$

f. $10 \boxed{+} 12 \boxed{+/-} \boxed{=} -2$
$10 + (-12) = -2$

g. $22 \boxed{+} 4 \boxed{=} 26$
$22 + 4 = 26$

h. $15 \boxed{+} 10 \boxed{=} 25$
$15 + 10 = 25$

i. $15 \boxed{+/-} \boxed{+} 10 \boxed{+/-} \boxed{=} -25$
$-15 + (-10) = -25$

3. Corresponding expressions are equivalent.

4. Answers may vary. Sample:
They are opposite.
To subtract an integer, add its opposite.

Think and Discuss pp. 113–114

5. Sample: a $12 debt

6. $-12 - (-15) = -12 + 15$
$\qquad = 3$
The treasury contains $3.

7. $-7 + 4 = -3$
You still owe him $3.

8. $-7 + (-4) = -7 - 4$
$\qquad = -11$
You would owe him $11.

Mixed Review p. 114

1. false; Parallel lines *do not* intersect.

2. true

3. $-5 + 2 = -3$

4. $-7 + (-3) = -7 - 3$
$\qquad = -10$

5. $927 \boxed{\times} 63 \boxed{=} \mathbf{58401}$
$927 \times 63 = 58{,}401$

6. $23868 \boxed{\div} 52 \boxed{=} \mathbf{459}$
$23{,}868 \div 52 = 459$

7. $12 \boxed{\times} .07 \boxed{=} \mathbf{.84}$
$12 \times \$.07 = \$.84$

On Your Own pp. 114–115

9. $9 - (-1) = 9 + 1$
$\qquad = 10$

10. $5 - 8 = 5 + (-8)$
$\qquad = -3$

11. $6 - 9 = 6 + (-9)$
$\qquad = -3$

12. $-16 - (-2) = -16 + 2$
$\qquad = -14$

13. $27 - 52 = 27 + (-52)$
$\qquad = -25$

14. $19 - (-12) = 19 + 12$
$= 31$

15. $-10 - (-8) = -10 + 8$
$= -2$

16. $11 - (-25) = 11 + 25$
$= 36$

17. $|-12| - 17 = 12 + (-17)$
$= -5$

18. $-28 - 28 = -28 + (-28)$
$= -56$

19. $-28 - (-28) = -28 + 28$
$= 0$

20. $|-17| - |-12| = 17 + (-12)$
$= 17 - 12$
$= 5$

21. $-36 - |29| = -36 + (-29)$
$= -65$

22. $10 - (-14) = 10 + 14$
$= 24$

23. 27, 20, 13, $\boxed{6}$, $\boxed{-1}$, $\boxed{-8}$, $\boxed{-15}$

$-7 \quad -7 \quad -7 \quad -7 \quad -7 \quad -7$

24. 8, 5, 2, -1, $\boxed{-4}$, $\boxed{-7}$, $\boxed{-10}$, $\boxed{-13}$

$-3 \quad -3 \quad -3 \quad -3 \quad -3 \quad -3 \quad -3$

25. 14, 7, 0, -7, $\boxed{-14}$, $\boxed{-21}$, $\boxed{-28}$, $\boxed{-35}$

$-7 \; -7 \; -7 \quad -7 \quad -7 \quad -7 \quad -7$

26. 3, 5, 2, 4, 1, 3, 0, $\boxed{2}$, $\boxed{-1}$, $\boxed{1}$, $\boxed{-2}$

$+2 \; -3 \; +2 \; -3 \; +2 \; -3 \; +2 \quad -3 \quad +2 \quad -3$

27. opposite

28. positive

29. Answers may vary. Sample:
They are equivalent;
$8 + 6 = 8 - (-6)$

30. $x + y$
$4 + (-7) = -3$ $\quad$ $x = 4, y = -7$

31. $10 - z$
$10 - (-3) = 10 + 3$ $\quad$ $z = -3$
$= 13$

32. $y - z$
$-7 - (-3) = -7 + 3$ $\quad$ $y = -7, z = -3$
$= -4$

33. $x + y - z$
$4 + (-7) - (-3) = 4 - 7 + 3$ $\quad$ $x = 4, y = -7,$
$= 4 + 3 - 7$ $\quad$ $z = -3$
$= 7 - 7$
$= 0$

34. $y - 20 + x$
$-7 - 20 + 4 = -27 + 4$ $\quad$ $x = 4, y = -7$
$= -23$

35. $35 - z + x$
$35 - (-3) + 4 = 35 + 3 + 4$ $\quad$ $x = 4, z = -3$
$= 42$

36. $|y| - |z|$
$|-7| - |-3| = 7 - 3$ $\quad$ $y = -7, z = -3$
$= 4$

37. $z + |y|$
$-3 + |-7| = -3 + 7$ $\quad$ $y = -7, z = -3$
$= 4$

38. $y - (-z)$
$-7 - (-(-3)) = -7 - 3$ $\quad$ $y = -7, z = -3$
$= -10$

39. decreases

40.

0 m	28°C
1500 m	20°C

$20°C - 28°C = -8°C$

41. Sample:
Each 1,500 m increase in altitude represents an 8°C decrease in temperature. A height of 10,000 m from 9,000 m is an increase of 1,000 m or $\frac{2}{3}$ of a 1,500 m increase and represents $\frac{2}{3}$ of an 8°C decrease in temperature.

$\frac{2}{3}(-8°) \approx -5°$

The approximate temperature at a height of 10,000 m is $-20°C + (-5°C) = -25°C$.

42. Sample: 34,284 feet; $29,028 + 5,256 = 34,284$

43. Answers may vary.

Sample: U.S. Customary:

12 in. = 1 ft, 3 ft = 1 yd, 1 mi = 5,280 ft

Problem Solving Practice

Page 116

1.

	sports car	a van	pick-up truck	a convertible
Al	☐ ④	× ③	× ④	× ④
Barbara	× ①	× ③	☐ ⑥	× ①
Carla	× ②	× ③	× ⑤	☐ ⑤
Dan	× ③	☐ ③	× ③	× ③

× indicates not a possibility.

☐ indicates answer.

① Barbara's friends own the convertible and the sports car. Barbara does not.

Put an × in sports car and convertible slots for Barbara.

② Carla does not own a sports car.

Put an × in sports car slot for Carla.

③ Dan's name rhymes with van.

Put ☐ in van slot for Dan. Put ×'s in other slots for Dan and for van.

④ Put ☐ in sports car slot for Al since it is the only remaining slot for sports car.

Put ×'s in remaining slots for Al.

⑤ Put ☐ in convertible slot for Carla since it is the only remaining slot for convertible.

Put an × in the remaining slot for Carla.

⑥ Put ☐ in pick-up truck slot for Barbara since it is the only remaining slot for pick-up truck.

Answers: Al: sports car; Barbara: pick-up truck; Carla: convertible; Dan: van.

2. Work backward using:

Friday, 600 crates and 40 fewer crates each day before.

Friday, 600 crates;

Thursday, 560 crates; (600 − 40)

Wednesday, 520 crates; (560 − 40)

Tuesday, 480 crates; (520 − 40)

Monday, 440 crates; (480 − 40)

3. not enough information given; need to know how many students are in the class

4. at 8:00 A.M.: 460 empty spaces

at 11:00 A.M.: 460 − 324: 136 empty spaces

Then every 15 minutes an average of 6 cars left and 14 cars came or a total of 14 − 6 or 8 spaces filled.

Every hour contains four 15-minute periods for a total of 32 spaces filled.

at 12 noon: 136 − 32 or 104 empty spaces

at 1 P.M.: 104 − 32 or 72 empty spaces

at 2 P.M.: 72 − 32 or 40 empty spaces

at 3 P.M.: 40 − 32 or 8 empty spaces

at 3:15 P.M.: 8 − 8 or 0 empty spaces

The garage was filled by 3:15 P.M.

5. Find a pattern:

week		1		2		3	
stickers	10		12		16		22	
difference		2		4		6		8

4		5		6		7		8
30		40		52		66		82
	10		12		14		16	

Jake's little sister will have 82 stickers at the end of the eighth week.

6. 3 years = 36 months

52,193 mi − 45,000 mi = 7,193 mi

(over 45,000 mi)

The total cost is $900 down + $198 a month for 36 months + 7,193 mi at $.12 per mile:

900 + 198(36) + .12(7,193):

900 $\boxed{+}$ 198 $\boxed{\times}$ 36 $\boxed{+}$ .12 $\boxed{\times}$ 7193 $\boxed{=}$

8891.16

Mr. Juaney paid $8,891.16.

3-5 Multiplying and Dividing Integers

Pages 117–120

Think and Discuss pp. 117–118

1. It is negative.

2. a. Answers may vary.

Sample: When one factor is negative, the product is negative. When both factors are negative, the product is positive.

b. It is positive.

c. $(30)(-3) = 90$

d. Sample: $-10 \cdot (-10) = 100$

3. positive; The product of two negatives is positive.

4. a. $9 \cdot 12 = 108$:

$108 \div 12 = 9$,

$108 \div 9 = 12$

b. $-30 \cdot 5 = -150$:

$-150 \div 5 = -30$,

$-150 \div (-30) = 5$

c. $25 \cdot (-10) = -250$:

$-250 \div (-10) = 25$,

$-250 \div 25 = -10$

d. $-13 \cdot (-4) = 52$:

$52 \div (-4) = -13$

$52 \div (-13) = -4$

5. a. positive

b. negative

c. negative

Try These pp. 118–119

6. $18 \cdot (-3) = -54$:

$-54 \div 18 = -3$,

$-54 \div (-3) = 18$

7. $-12 \cdot 4 = -48$:

$-48 \div 4 = -12$,

$-48 \div (-12) = 4$

8. $-6(-9) = 54$ ← same sign

9. $(-5 \cdot 6) \div (-5) = -30 \div (-5)$ ← same sign

$= 6$

10. $48 \div (-8) = -6$ ← different signs

11. $-5 \cdot (-4 - 2) = -5 \cdot (-6)$ ← work inside parentheses

$= 30$

12. $48 \div (-19 + 11) = 48 \div (-8)$

$= -6$

13. $-3 \cdot 2 \cdot (-4) + (-6) = -6 \cdot (-4) + (-6)$

$= 24 + (-6)$

$= 18$

14. $-32 + (-8) \cdot 4 = -32 + (-32)$

$= -64$

On Your Own pp. 119–120

15. $3 \cdot (-4) = -12$:

$-12 \div 3 = -4$,

$-12 \div (-4) = 3$

16. $-7 \cdot (-2) = 14$:

$14 \div (-2) = -7$,

$14 \div (-7) = -2$

17. $-5 \cdot 8 = -40$

18. $-12 \cdot (-2) = 24$

19. $-56 \div (-7) = 8$

20. 210 $\boxed{+/-}$ $\boxed{\div}$ 15 $\boxed{=}$ **−14**

$-210 \div 15 = -14$

21. 4 $\boxed{+/-}$ $\boxed{\times}$ 6 $\boxed{+/-}$ $\boxed{\times}$ 7 $\boxed{\times}$ 2 $\boxed{=}$ **336**

$-4 \cdot (-6) \cdot 7 \cdot 2 = 24 \cdot 7 \cdot 2$ ← multiply from left to right

$= 168 \cdot 2$

$= 336$

22. 3 $\boxed{+}$ 3 $\boxed{\times}$ 4 $\boxed{+/-}$ $\boxed{=}$ **−9**

$3 + 3 \cdot (-4) = 3 + (-12)$ ← multiply

$= -9$ ← add

23. 84 $\boxed{+/-}$ $\boxed{\div}$ $\boxed{(}$ 3 $\boxed{+/-}$ $\boxed{\times}$ 4 $\boxed{)}$ $\boxed{=}$ **7**

$-84 \div (-3 \cdot 4) = -84 \div (-12)$ ← multiply within parentheses first

$= 7$ ← divide

24. Answers may vary.
Sample: Count the number of negative factors. If the number of negative factors is even, the product is positive. If there is an odd number of negative factors, the product is negative.

25. product: 4   ← The signs are the same since the product is positive.

sum: −5   ← The sign is negative since the sum is negative.

Possible combinations for a product of 4 are: −1, −4 and −2, −2.
Only −1 and −4 have a sum of −5.
Answer: −1, −4

26. product: −6   ← signs different
sum: −5   ← largest absolute value is negative

Possible product combinations: −1, 6; −2, 3; −6, 1; −3, 2.
Only 1 and −6 have a sum of −5.
Answer: −6, 1

27. product: −4   ← different signs
sum: 0   ← absolute values are the same

Possible product combinations: −1, 4; −2, 2; −4, 1.
Only −2 and 2 have a sum of zero.
Answer: −2, 2

28. 14 $\boxed{+/-}$ $\boxed{\times}$ 327 $\boxed{+/-}$ $\boxed{=}$ **4578**
−14 • (−327) = 4,578

29. 448 $\boxed{+/-}$ $\boxed{\div}$ 14 $\boxed{=}$ **−32**
−448 ÷ 14 = −32

30. 1134 $\boxed{\div}$ 54 $\boxed{+/-}$ $\boxed{=}$ **−21**
1,134 ÷ (−54) = −21

31. 23 $\boxed{\times}$ 212 $\boxed{+/-}$ $\boxed{\times}$ 43 $\boxed{=}$ **−209668**
23 • (−212) • 43 = −209,668

32. 712 $\boxed{-}$ 83 $\boxed{\times}$ 2 $\boxed{+/-}$ $\boxed{=}$ **878**
712 − [83 • (−2)] = 878

33. 786 $\boxed{+/-}$ $\boxed{\times}$ $\boxed{(}$ 567 $\boxed{+/-}$ $\boxed{-}$
489 $\boxed{+/-}$ $\boxed{)}$ $\boxed{=}$ **61308**
−786 • [−567 − (−489)] = 61,308

34. B; −8 • 6 = −48
     ↑ ↑
borrow from 6 friends
$8

35. a. −40,230
b. −40,230 ÷ 3 = −13,410 ← 3 ft = 1 yd
−13,410 yards

36. −95; 95 ft below

37. −20; descent of 20 ft/min

38. Yes; Sample: the diver can make it to −95 ft in 5 min, since (−20) • 5 = −100.

Mixed Review p. 119

1. yes; The measure of each angle of a regular hexagon is (6 − 2) • 180° ÷ 6 or 120°. 120° + 120° + 120° = 360° so a regular hexagon can form a tessellation.

2. no

3. $19 - x - y$
$19 - 2 - 4 = 19 - 6$ ← $x = 2, y = 4$
$= 13$

4. $y - 10 - (-x)$
$4 - 10 - (-2) = 4 - 10 + 2$ ← $x = 2, y = 4$
$= 6 - 10$
$= -4$

5. $199 + 1 - 60 = 200 - 60$
$= 140$

6. $17 - 10 \div 2 = 17 - 5$
$= 12$

7. 7 h for 365 nights in a year:
$7(365) = 2,555$ h

Checkpoint p. 120

1. $|76| = 76$ since $76 = 76$

2. $-19 < |-23|$ since $-19 < 23$

3. $|-2| > 1$ since $2 > 1$

4. $-3n$

5. $\frac{m}{12}$

6. $-7 + (-12) = -19$

7. $-15 + 8 = -7$

8. $-32 - (-11) = -32 + 11$
$= -21$

9. $-a + (-b)$

$$-19 + (-(-3)) = -19 + 3 \leftarrow a = 19, b = -3$$
$$= -16$$

10. $-2a - 13$

$$-2(19) - 13 = -38 - 13 \quad \leftarrow a = 19$$
$$= -51$$

11. $-15b + (-1)$

$$-15(-3) + (-1) = 45 + (-1) \quad \leftarrow b = -3$$
$$= 44$$

3-6 Mental Math
Pages 121–123

Think and Discuss pp. 121–122

1. yes; $0 + a = a + 0$ by the commutative property and $a + 0 = a$ by the identity property.

2. $(-6) + 46 + 17 + (-11) =$
$46 + 17 + (-11) + (-6)$
Commutative property used to reorder the numbers
$$= 46 + 17 + [(-11) + (-6)]$$
Associative property used to group the negative numbers
$$= 46 + 17 + (-17)$$
$$= 46 + 0$$
Identity property used to add zero to 46
$$= 46$$

3. Yes; because of the commutative and distributive properties

Work Together p. 122

Answers may vary.
Sample:
$$50 - 3(14.95) = 50 - 3(15 - 0.05)$$
$$= 50 - 45 + 0.15$$
$$= 5.15$$

$5.15 change

Try These p. 123

4. Sample: You can group numbers that can be combined easily.

5–12. Answers may vary. Samples given.

5. $-3 + 14 + (-7) + 6$
$$= -3 + (-7) + 14 + 6 \quad \text{Comm. Property}$$
$$= (-3 + (-7)) + (14 + 6) \quad \text{Assoc. Property}$$
$$= -10 + 20$$
$$= 10$$

6. $4 \cdot 356 \cdot 25 = 4 \cdot 25 \cdot 356 \quad \text{Comm. Property}$
$$= (4 \cdot 25) \cdot 356 \quad \text{Assoc. Property}$$
$$= 100 \cdot 356$$
$$= 35,600$$

7. $(32 + 87) + 13 = 32 + (87 + 13) \, \text{Assoc. Property}$
$$= 32 + 100$$
$$= 132$$

8. $2(13 + 50) = 2 \cdot 13 + 2 \cdot 50 \quad \text{Dist. Property}$
$$= 26 + 100$$
$$= 126$$

On Your Own p. 123

9. $4 + (-3) + 6 + (-7)$
$$= 4 + 6 + (-3) + (-7) \quad \text{Comm. Property}$$
$$= (4 + 6) + (-3 + (-7)) \quad \text{Assoc. Property}$$
$$= 10 + (-10)$$
$$= 0 \qquad\qquad\qquad \text{Additive Inverse}$$

10. $-2 \cdot 34 \cdot (-5) = -2 \cdot (-5) \cdot 34 \, \text{Comm. Property}$
$$= (-2 \cdot (-5)) \cdot 34 \qquad \text{Assoc. Property}$$
$$= 10 \cdot 34$$
$$= 340$$

11. $-2(5 \cdot 46) = (-2 \cdot 5)46 \qquad \text{Assoc. Property}$
$$= (-10)(46)$$
$$= -460$$

12. $-5 + 2 + 18 + -45$
$$= -5 + (-45) + 2 + 18 \quad \text{Comm. Property}$$
$$= (-5 + (-45)) + (2 + 18) \, \text{Assoc. Property}$$
$$= -50 + 20$$
$$= -30$$

13. $25(-198) = 25(-200 + 2)$
$$= -5,000 + 50$$
$$= -4,950$$

14. $1.8(-5) = -5(1.8)$
$$= -5(1 + 0.8)$$
$$= -5 - 4$$
$$= -9$$

15. $4 \cdot \$1.99 = 4(\$2 - \$.01)$
$= \$8 - \$.04$
$= \$7.96$

16. $103 \cdot \$22 = \$22(103)$
$= \$22(100 + 3)$
$= \$2,200 + \$66$
$= \$2,266$

17. false; $7 \cdot 6 + 4 \neq 7 \cdot 4 + 6$ Order of operations.
Multiply before adding
$42 + 4 \neq 28 + 6$
$42 + 4 \neq 28 + 6$
$46 \neq 34$

18. false; $-6(9 - 2) \neq 6(11)$
$-6(7) \neq 6(11)$
$-42 \neq 66$

19. false; $13 \cdot 9 \neq 10 \cdot 9 + 3 \cdot 3$ Distributive property
is not correctly setup:
$117 \neq 90 + 9$ $13 \cdot 9 = (10 + 3) \cdot 9$
$= 10 \cdot 9 + 3 \cdot 9$

20. false; $10 + (-12) \neq 12 + (-10)$
$-2 \neq 2$ Using the commutative
property of addition:
$10 + (-12) = -12 + 10$,
not $12 + (-10)$

21. a. Total changes in temperature from
Monday to the end of Thursday:
$+11 + (-14) + 9 + (-6)$
$= [+11 + 9] + [(-14) + (-6)]$
$= 20 + (-20)$
$= 0$
The temperature on Thursday will be the
same as on Sunday, 32°F.

b. Sample: commutative and associative
properties

22. Answers may vary. Samples:
Percentage of gold is measured in karats;
distance at sea is measured in leagues; a
ream of paper is 500 sheets.

Mixed Review p. 123

1. Use $C = 2\pi r$ and $r = 9$ in.

$2 \boxed{\times} \boxed{\pi} \boxed{\times} 9 \boxed{=}$ **56.548668**

$C \approx 56.5$ in.

2. Use $C = 2\pi r$ and $r = 4$ cm.

$2 \boxed{\times} \boxed{\pi} \boxed{\times} 4 \boxed{=}$ **25.132741**

$C \approx 25.1$ cm

3. $8 \cdot (-4) \cdot (-10) = [8 \cdot (-4)] \cdot (-10)$
$= (-32) \cdot (-10)$
$= 320$

4. $-(-30) \div 6 = 30 \div 6$
$= 5$

5. Make a table for the first 10 days until the
nickel and the penny are saved on the same
day.

Day	1	2	3	4	5	6	7	8	9	10
Nickel (one every 5 days)					5¢					5¢
Total Value of Nickels					5¢				10¢	
Penny (one every 2 days)		1¢		1¢		1¢		1¢		1¢
Total Value of Pennies		1¢		2¢		3¢		4¢		5¢

Every 10 days Bart saves 15¢.
At the end of 30 days, Bart will save $3(15¢)$
or 45¢.

3-7 Guess and Test
Pages 124–126

1. a. 89

b. Centaurian: 4;
Tripodian: 3

c. 319

d. Sample: There are 3- and 4-legged
scientists and you have to find how
many of each there are.

2. a. $89 - 45$ or 44 Tripodians

b. $4 \cdot 45 = 180$

c. $3 \cdot 44 = 132$

d. $180 + 132 = 312$
no; $312 \neq 319$

3. More; because Centaurians have more legs
than Tripodians and this guess didn't have
enough legs.

4. Answers may vary. Sample given.
Try 52 Centaurians.

a. $89 - 52$ or 37 Tripodians

b. $52 + 37 = 89$

c. $52 \cdot 4 + 37 \cdot 3 = 208 + 111$
$= 319$

d. yes; a total of 319 legs

5. Answers may vary. Sample:
Seeing that the first guess was 7 legs too few, add 7 to the original guess.

Try These pp. 125–126

6. Try: 900 m for the first day.
The second day Jesse swam
900 m + 250 m = 1,150 m
total: 900 m + 1,150 m = 2,050 m
900 m and 1,150 m satisfy the conditions of the problem.

7. Conditions: 40 birds and cats
110 animal feet
each bird has 2 feet
each cat has 4 feet

a. Try: 25 birds
40 − 25 or 15 cats
$25 \cdot 2 + 15 \cdot 4 = 50 + 60$
$= 110$ legs
25 birds and 15 cats satisfy the conditions of the problem.

b. Answers may vary. Sample: Guess how many birds and cats there are. There should be a combined total of 40 birds and cats. Multiply 2 times the no. of birds and 4 times the no. of cats. Find the sum. If the sum does not equal 110 animal feet, then your guess is incorrect.

On Your Own p. 126

8. sum: −9
difference: 5
Guess and Test can be used.
Try: two negative integers −7 and −2
sum: −7 + (−2) = −9
difference: −2 − (−7) = 5
−7 and −2 satisfy the conditions of the problem.

9. Conditions:
total miles for three days: 1,000 mi
No. of miles in second day = no. of miles in first and third days combined
Rosa drove one half the total number of miles on the second day, $\frac{1}{2}$ (1,000) or 500 miles.

10. a. No; 40 − 3 = 37, pairs of twins cannot total an odd number of people.

b. There can be 6 combinations of twins and triplets since there can only be 2, 4, 6, 8, 10, or 12 sets of triplets.

11. Guess and Test can be used.
Try: 32 pairs of tennis sneakers
2(32) or 64 pairs of basketball sneakers
32 + 64 = 96 total

32 pairs of tennis sneakers and 64 pairs of basketball sneakers satisfy the conditions of the problem.

12. Use Guess and Test.
Try: Izumi at 120 y
White at 120 − 4 or 116 y
120 + 116 = 236 y total
116 y and 120 y satisfy the conditions of the problem.

13. 2(2)(2)(2)(2)(2) = 64
64 players

Mixed Review p. 126

1–2. Answers may vary. Samples given.

1. adjacent sides of window frame

2. top and bottom of window frame

3. 12 + (−1) + 8 + (−9)
   = (12 + 8) + [(−1) + (−9)]
   = 20 + (−10)
   = 10

4. $20 \cdot 6 \cdot 5 = (20 \cdot 5) \cdot 6$
   $= 100 \cdot 6$
   $= 600$

5. William is 16 years old.
William's father is three times as old as William: 3(16) or 48 years old.
William's brother is $\frac{1}{2}$ his father's age:
$\frac{1}{2}$(48) or 24 years old.

3-8 Exponents and Multiplication
Pages 127–130

Think and Discuss pp. 127–129

1. $V = s^3$, $s = 5$ cm
$V = (5 \text{ cm}) \cdot (5 \text{ cm}) \cdot (5 \text{ cm})$
$V = 125 \text{ cm}^3$

2. Answers may vary. Sample:

$(-4)^4 = (-4)(-4)(-4)(-4);$

$-4^4 = -(4)(4)(4)(4)$

They are opposite.

3. $(-2)^3 = (-2)(-2)(-2) = -8$

$-2^3 = -(2)(2)(2) = -8$

4. 5 $\boxed{y^x}$ 4 $\boxed{=}$ $\boxed{+/-}$ **−625**

$-5^4 = -625$

5. **a.** 12 $\boxed{y^x}$ 0 $\boxed{=}$ **1**

$12^0 = 1$

15 $\boxed{+/-}$ $\boxed{y^x}$ 0 $\boxed{=}$ **1**

$(-15)^0 = 1$

(Some calculators will give an error reading when a negative value is raised to a zero power.)

3 $\boxed{y^x}$ 0 $\boxed{=}$ **1**

b. Any nonzero number raised to the 0 power is 1.

6. $2^3 = 8$

7. $16 = 2 \cdot 2 \cdot 2 \cdot 2 = 2^4$

$16 = 4 \cdot 4 = 4^2$

$a = 4, b = 2$

8. **a.** $5x^3$

$5(2^3) = 5(2)(2)(2) = 5(8) = 40$

b. $(5x)^3$

$(5 \cdot 2)^3 = 10^3 = 10(10)(10) = 1{,}000$

9. **a.** $6 \cdot a \cdot a \cdot a \cdot a = 6a^4$

b. $6a \cdot 6a \cdot 6a \cdot 6a = (6a)^4$

10. **a.** The exponent of the product is the sum of the exponents of the factors.

b. $3^5 \cdot 3^5 = (3 \cdot 3 \cdot 3 \cdot 3 \cdot 3)(3 \cdot 3 \cdot 3 \cdot 3 \cdot 3)$

$= 3^{10}$

11. $n^5 \cdot n^7 = (n \cdot n \cdot n \cdot n \cdot n)(n \cdot n \cdot n \cdot n \cdot n \cdot n \cdot n)$

$= n^{12}$

Try These p. 129

12. **a.** $a \cdot a \cdot a \cdot a \cdot a = a^5$

base: a; exponent: 5

b. $2^5 = 2 \cdot 2 \cdot 2 \cdot 2 \cdot 2 = 32$

13. $(-3)^2 = 9$

14. $6^0 = 1$

15. $-8^2 = -64$

16. $1^{15} = 1$

17. $7^3 = 343$

18. $4^4 \cdot 4^2 = 4^{4+2} = 4^6$

19. $a^3 \cdot a^5 = a^{3+5} = a^8$

20. $1^2 \cdot 1^7 = 1^{2+7} = 1^9$

21. $(-5)^2 \cdot (-5)^7 = (-5)^{2+7} = (-5)^9$

22. $(3 \cdot 2)^2 + 5 = 6^2 + 5$

$= 36 + 5$

$= 41$

23. $3^2 \cdot 2 + 5 = 9 \cdot 2 + 5$

$= 18 + 5$

$= 23$

24. $-4^2 + 6 \cdot 3^2 = -16 + 6 \cdot 9$

$= -16 + 54$

$= 38$

On Your Own pp. 129–130

25. $7 \cdot 7 \cdot 7 \cdot 7 = 7^4$

26. $(-5)(-5)(-5) = (-5)^3$

27. $(-x)(-x)(-x)(-x) = (-x)^4$

28. 3 $\boxed{y^x}$ 4 $\boxed{=}$ **81** $3^4 = 81$

4 $\boxed{y^x}$ 3 $\boxed{=}$ **64** $4^3 = 64$

3^4 is larger.

29. $-4^3 = -(4)(4)(4) = -64$

30. $1^8 = 1$

31. $9^0 = 1$

32. $(-5)^2 = (-5)(-5) = 25$

33. $5^3 = (5)(5)(5) = 125$

34. I. $2^4 \cdot 2^3 = 2^7 \neq 2^{12}$

II. $2^3 \cdot 3^2 = 8 \cdot 9 = 72$

$6^6 = 46{,}656$

$2^3 \cdot 3^2 \neq 6^6$

III. $2^7 \cdot 2^0 = 2^{7+0} = 2^7$; *true*

IV. $2^4 \cdot 3^3 = 16 \cdot 27 = 432$

$6^7 = 279{,}936$

$2^4 \cdot 3^3 \neq 6^7$

Answer: A. III only is true.

35. $4 + (8 - 6)^2$

$= 4 + 2^2$

$= 4 + 4$

$= 8$

36. $4 + 8 - 6^2$

$= 4 + 8 - 36$

$= 12 - 36$

$= -24$

37. $(-3)^2 + 4^3 - 4$
$= 9 + 64 - 4$
$= 73 - 4$
$= 69$

38. $-3^2 + 4^3 - 4$
$= -9 + 64 - 4$
$= -13 + 64$
$= 51$

39. Answers may vary. Sample:
about 6; $2 < 2.3 < 3$
$2^2 < (2.3)^2 < 3^2$
$4 < (2.3)^2 < 9$
The value is between 2^2 and 3^2.
2.3 $\boxed{x^2}$ 5.29 $2.3^2 = 5.29$

40. $(b + 5)^2$ $b = 3$
$(3 + 5)^2 = 8^2 = 64$

41. $b^2 + 5^2$ $b = 3$
$3^2 + 5^2 = 9 + 25 = 34$

42. $b^2 + 5b + 5^2$ $b = 3$
$3^2 + 5(3) + 5^2 = 9 + 15 + 25 = 49$

Mixed Review p. 128

1. 100,   50,   25,   12.5, . . .

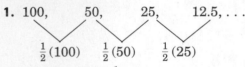

pattern: times $\frac{1}{2}$

2. 1,   11,   21,   31, . . .

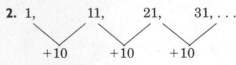

pattern: add 10

3. $C = 2\pi r$ $r = 19$ ft, $\pi \approx 3.14$
$C \approx 2\pi(3.14)(19)$
$C \approx 119.3$ ft
or $C = 2$ $\boxed{\times}$ $\boxed{\pi}$ $\boxed{\times}$ 19$=$ **119.38052**
$C \approx 119.4$ ft

4. $C = 2\pi r$ $r = 3$ yd
$C = 2\pi(3)$
$C \approx 18.8$ yd

5. Guess and Test can be used.
Conditions: The number of small drinks plus the number of large drinks is 162.
• Each small drink is $.50.
  Each large drink is $.75.
• The number of small drinks times the cost of each small drink (.50) plus the number of large drinks times the cost of each large drink (.75) is $103.
Try: 88 large drinks sold
Then: $162 - 88 = 74$ small drinks sold
$88 + 74 = 162$
$\$.75(88) + \$.50(74) = \$66 + \$37$
$= \$103$
88 large drinks and 74 small drinks satisfy the given conditions.

Checkpoint p. 130

1. $13 \cdot (-32) = -416$

2. $-4 \div (-1) = 4$

3. $-90 \div (-3 \cdot 10) = -90 \div (-30)$
$= 3$

4. $-17 \cdot (-12) - 3 \cdot (-18)$
$= 204 + 54$
$= 258$

5. $5 \cdot 19 \cdot (-10) \cdot 7$
$= -6{,}650$

6. 5 $\boxed{y^x}$ 5 $\boxed{\times}$ 3 $\boxed{x^2}$ $\boxed{=}$ **28125**
$5^5 \cdot 3^2 = 28{,}125$

7. $(-15 \div 3)(-12) = (-5)(-12)$
$= 60$

8. $3 + (-7)^4 = 3 + 2{,}401$
$= 2{,}404$

9. $(-6 + 5)^3 = (-1)^3 = -1$

10. $8[5 + (-4)]^3 = 8[1]^3 = 8(1) = 8$

11. $(-6)^2 + (9 - 7)^3 = (-6)^2 + 2^3$
$= 36 + 8$
$= 44$

12. B; $5 \cdot 6$; 5 marbles times 6 friends

Practice

Page 131

1. $-7 < 7$

2. $3 > -8$

3. $|-9| > 3$ since $9 > 3$

4. $|-8| > |-6|$ since $8 > 6$

5. $n - 18$

6. $5x$

7. $m + 10$

8. $-7 + 4 = -3$

9. $8 + 5 = 13$

10. $-6 + (-2) = -8$

11. $41 + (-26) = 15$

12. $8 - (-1) = 8 + 1 = 9$

13. $9 - 11 = 9 + (-11) = -2$

14. $-15 - (-5) = -15 + 5 = -10$

15. $|-1| - |17| = |-1| + (-|17|)$
$$= 1 + (-17)$$
$$= -16$$

16. $x + y$
$$= 5 + (-9) \qquad x = 5, y = -9$$
$$= -4$$

17. $x - z$
$$= 5 - (-1) \qquad x = 5, z = -1$$
$$= 5 + 1$$
$$= 6$$

18. $z - (-y)$
$$= (-1) - [-(-9)] \quad y = -9, z = -1$$
$$= -1 - 9$$
$$= -10$$

19. $|y| - |x|$
$$= |-9| - |5| \qquad x = 5, y = -9$$
$$= 9 - 5$$
$$= 4$$

20. $-8(-7) = 56$

21. $36 \div (-9) = -4$

22. $(-3 \cdot 8) \div (-4)$
$$= -24 \div (-4)$$
$$= 6$$

23. $6 \div (-2) \cdot (-2)$
$$= -3 \cdot (-2)$$
$$= 6$$

24. $5 + (-2) + 5 + (-8)$ Comm. and Assoc. properties
$$= (5 + 5) + [(-2) + (-8)]$$
$$= 10 + (-10)$$
$$= 0$$

25. $(-2) \cdot 43 \cdot (-5)$ Additive Inverse Comm. and Assoc. properties
$$= [(-2) \cdot (-5)] \cdot 43$$
$$= 10 \cdot 43$$
$$= 430$$

26. $50(-97)$
$$= 50(-100 + 3)$$
$$= -5000 + 150$$
$$= -4{,}850$$

27. $17(-3)$
$$= (20 - 3)(-3)$$
$$= -60 + 9$$
$$= -51$$

28. $6 \cdot \$2.99$
$$= 6(\$3 - \$.01)$$
$$= \$18 - \$.06$$
$$= \$17.94$$

29. $98 \cdot \$20$
$$= (100 - 2)(\$20)$$
$$= \$2000 - \$40$$
$$= \$1{,}960$$

30. $(-1)(-1)(-1) = (-1)^3$

31. $5 \cdot 5 \cdot 5 \cdot 5 = 5^4$

32. $(-y)(-y) = (-y)^2$

33. $-(4 \cdot 4 \cdot 4) = -4^3$

34. $(-2)^3 = (-2)(-2)(-2) = -8$

35. $(-3)^2 + 5^2 - 5$
$$= 9 + 25 - 5$$
$$= 34 - 5$$
$$= 29$$

36. $(3^2 + (6 - 2)) \cdot 5 - 4^3 - 7$
$$= (3^2 + 4) \cdot 5 - 4^3 - 7$$
$$= (9 + 4) \cdot 5 - 64 - 7$$
$$= (13)(5) - 64 - 7$$
$$= 65 - 64 - 7$$
$$= 1 - 7$$
$$= -6$$

37. $x + 5$
$$= -8 + 5 \qquad x = -8$$
$$= -3$$

38. $5n - 11$

$\qquad = 5(-3.2) - 11 \qquad n = -3.2$

$\qquad = -16 - 11$

$\qquad = -27$

39. $a^2 + 4a - 3$

$\qquad = (0.3)^2 + 4(0.3) - 3 \qquad a = 0.3$

$\qquad = (0.09) + 1.2 - 3$

$\qquad = 1.29 - 3$

$\qquad = -1.71$

Using a calculator:

.3 $\boxed{x^2}$ $\boxed{+}$ 4 $\boxed{\times}$ .3 $\boxed{-}$ 3 $\boxed{=}$ **-1.71**

3-9 Evaluating Variable Expressions

Pages 132–135

Think and Discuss pp. 132–134

1. number of days

2. Answers may vary. Sample:

$\quad (0.0165)(90) \approx (0.0165)(100)$

$\qquad\qquad\qquad = 1.65$

Round 90 to 100, and multiply by moving the decimal point 2 places to the right.

3. Sample: yes

4. .0165 $\boxed{\times}$ 90 $\boxed{=}$ **1.485**

$\quad 0.0165n = 0.0165(90) = 1.485 \qquad n = 90$

5. Answers may vary. Sample:

The distance is almost 5 times the square of the time, so it increases much more quickly than the time.

6. $-14m + 110n$

$\qquad = -14(45) + 110(2.5) \qquad m = 45, \ n = 2\frac{1}{2} = 2.5$

14 $\boxed{+/-}$ $\boxed{\times}$ 45 $\boxed{+}$ 110 $\boxed{\times}$ 2.5 $\boxed{=}$ -355

Net amount of calories is -355.

Work Together p. 134

7. a.

	A	B
1	A	$A*A-4*A$
2	-5	45
3	-4	32
4	-3	21
5	-2	12
6	-1	5
7	0	0
8	1	-3
9	2	-4
10	3	-3
11	4	0
12	5	5

b. Sample: It decreases to a low of -4, then it increases again.

c. Sample: They would be the same; all that changed was the variable name.

Try These pp. 134–135

8. $b + 5$

$\qquad = -5 + 5 \qquad b = -5$

$\qquad = 0$

9. $b - 5$

$\qquad = -5 - 5 \qquad b = -5$

$\qquad = -10$

10. $5 - b$

$\qquad = 5 - (-5) \qquad b = -5$

$\qquad = 5 + 5$

$\qquad = 10$

11. $5a - 5$

$\qquad = 5(2.45) - 5 \qquad a = 2.45$

$\qquad = 12.25 - 5$

$\qquad = 7.25$

12. $20ab$

$\qquad = 20(2.45)(-5) \qquad a = 2.45, b = -5$

$\qquad = [20 \cdot (-5)] \, (2.45)$

$\qquad = (-100) \, (2.45)$

$\qquad = -245$

13. abc

$\qquad = (2.45) \, (-5) \, (5) \qquad a = 2.45, b = -5, c = 5$

$\qquad = -61.25$

2.45 $\boxed{\times}$ 5 $\boxed{+/-}$ $\boxed{\times}$ 5 $\boxed{=}$ **-61.25**

14. $(b \div c)^3$

$= [(-5) \div 5]^3$ $\qquad b = -5, c = 5$

$= (-1)^3$

$= -1$

15. $b^2 + b + 5$

$= (-5)^2 + (-5) + 5$ $\qquad b = -5$

$= 25 - 5 + 5$

$= 25$

16. Answers may vary.

Exercises 8–10, 12, 14, 15; solved by substituting values into the expressions

17.

x	$10 - x$
-1	$10 - (-1) = 11$
0	$10 - 0 = 10$
1	$10 - 1 = 9$
2	$10 - 2 = 8$
3	$10 - 3 = 7$

  a. decreases

  b. increases

  c. yes; when $x < -10$

18. a. $t - 1$

  b. $0.65(t - 1)$

  c. $1.50 + 0.65(t - 1)$

  d. $t = 10$

$1.50 + 0.65(10 - 1)$

$= 1.50 + 0.65(9)$

$= 1.50 + 5.85$

$= 7.35$

A 10-minute call costs $7.35.

  e. $t = 11$

$1.50 + 0.65(11 - 1)$

$= 1.50 + 0.65(11 - 1)$

$= 1.50 + 0.65(10)$

$= 1.50 + 6.50$

$= 8$

An 11-minute call costs $8.00.

$t = 60$

$1.50 + 0.65(60 - 1)$

$= 1.50 + 0.65(59)$

$= 1.50 + 38.35$

$= 39.85$

An hour-length call costs $39.85.

On Your Own p. 135

19. $3n + 5$

$= 3(-2) + 5$ $\qquad n = -2$

$= -6 + 5$

$= -1$

20. $x - 8$

$= -4 - 8$ $\qquad x = -4$

$= -12$

21. $-10c$

$= -10(6)$ $\qquad c = 6$

$= -60$

22. $-3t$

$= -3(-7)$ $\qquad t = -7$

$= 21$

23. $-2xy$

$= -2(5)(11)$ $\qquad x = 5, y = 11$

$= -10(11)$

$= -110$

24. $7a + b$

$= 7(-3) + 2.5$ $\qquad a = -3, b = 2.5$

$= -21 + 2.5$

$= -18.5$

25. $p + q + r + 3$

$= -5 + (-4) + 6 + 3$ $\qquad p = -5, q = -4, r = 6$

$= -9 + 9$

$= 0$

26–29. Accept reasonable estimates. Samples given.

26. $3 + 2p; p = 4.3$

Estimate: $4.3 \approx 4$

$3 + 2(4) = 3 + 8 = 11$

Exact:

$3 + 2(4.3) = 3 + 8.6 = 11.6$

27. $m^2 + 3; m = 1.7$

Estimate: $1.7 \approx 2$

$2^2 + 3 = 4 + 3 = 7$

Exact:

$(1.7)^2 + 3 = 2.89 + 3 = 5.89$

28. $5r - 4r; r = 0.874$

Estimate: $0.874 \approx 1$

$5(1) - 4(1) = 5 - 4 = 1$

Exact:

$5(0.874) - 4(0.874) = 0.874$

29. $z^2 - 4z + 3$; $z = 5.1$

Estimate: $5.1 \approx 5$

$5^2 - 4(5) + 3 = 25 - 20 + 3 = 8$

Exact:

$(5.1)^2 - 4(5.1) + 3 = 26.01 - 20.4 + 3 = 8.61$

30. a. $8.95n + 2.95$

b. $n = 5$

$8.95(5) + 2.95 = 47.7$

$8.95 \boxed{\times} 5 \boxed{+} 2.95 \boxed{=} \mathbf{47.7}$

c. The cost of 5 cassettes is $47.70.

Mixed Review p. 135

1. $65° + 90° = 155°$

$180° - 155° = 25°$

2. $22° + 68° = 90°$

$180° - 90° = 90°$

3. $-5^2 = -25$

4. $8^4 = 8 \cdot 8 \cdot 8 \cdot 8 = 4{,}096$

5. $1,710 for 2.5-oz

$1{,}710 \div 2.5 = 684$

The price is $684/oz.

Wrap Up

Pages 136–137

1. $-8 < -1$

2. $-7 < 2$

3. $|-3| > 1$ since $3 > 1$

4. $|-4| = |4|$ since $4 = 4$

5. $(-9) + (-3) = -12$

6. $8 + (-3) = 5$

7. $(-11) - (-5) = (-11) + 5$

$\qquad = -6$

8. $(-9) - 2 = -11$

9. $-3 \cdot 18 = -54$

10. $(-34) \div (-2) = 17$

11. $-1{,}260 \div 45 = -28$

$1260 \boxed{+/-} \boxed{\div} 45 \boxed{=} \mathbf{-28}$

12. $-15 \cdot (-4) \div (-12)$

$\qquad = 60 \div (-12)$

$\qquad = -5$

13. $-8(99) + (-7) + (-93)$

$= -8(99) + [(-7) + (-93)]$ Assoc. property

$= -8(99) + (-100)$

$= -8(100 - 1) + (-100)$ $99 = 100 - 1$

$= -800 + 8 + (-100)$ Distrib. property

$= -800 + (-100) + 8$ Comm. property

$= [-800 + (-100)] + 8$ Assoc. property

$= -900 + 8$

$= -892$

14. C; A. $-15 \div (-3) - 6 = 5 - 6 = -1$

B. $2 - 3(4 - 5) = 2 - 3(-1) = 2 + 3 = 5$

C. $-2 + (-1)(-3) = -2 + 3 = 1$

D. $-4 + 3(-5 + 4) = -4 + 3(-1)$

$\qquad = -4 - 3 = -7$

15. width: w

length: $w + 6$

area: 55

Guess: width, 5

length, $5 + 6$ or 11

area, $5(11) = 55$

5 m by 11 m satisfy the given conditions.

16. total number of triangles and squares: 30

each triangle: 3 sides

each square: 4 sides

total number of sides: 103

• number of triangles times 3 sides for each + number of squares times 4 sides for each is 103

Try: 17 triangles

$30 - 17$ or 13 squares

$17 + 13 = 30$ models

$3(17) + 4(13) = 51 + 52 = 103$ sides

17 triangles and 13 squares satisfy the given conditions.

17. $3^4 + (-11)^0$

$= 81 + 1$

$= 82$

18. $2^3 \cdot 2^2$

$= 2^5$

$= 32$

19. $(6 - 8)^4$

$= (-2)^4$

$= 16$

20. $-4^2 + 1^3$

$\qquad = -16 + 1$

$\qquad = -15$

21. $b + 7$

22. $w - 8$

23. $2y + 3$

24. $\frac{x}{5}$

25. $6 \cdot (x - 1)^2$ for $x = -2.5$

$\qquad = 6 \cdot (-2.5 - 1)^2$

$\qquad = 6 \cdot (-3.5)^2$

$\qquad = 73.5$

$6 \boxed{\times} 3.5 \boxed{+/-} \boxed{x^2} \boxed{=} \mathbf{73.5}$

26. $40 \div x + 7.5$ for $x = -2.5$

$\qquad = 40 \div (-2.5) + 7.5$

$\qquad = -8.5$

$40 \boxed{\div} 2.5 \boxed{+/-} \boxed{+} 7.5 \boxed{=} \mathbf{-8.5}$

27. $40 \div (x + 7.5)$ for $x = -2.5$

$\qquad = 40 \div (-2.5 + 7.5)$

$\qquad = 40 \div (5)$

$\qquad = 8$

28. $x^2 - 7x$ for $x = -2.5$

$\qquad = (-2.5)^2 - 7(-2.5)$

$\qquad = 23.75$

$2.5 \boxed{+/-} \boxed{x^2} \boxed{-} 7 \boxed{\times} 2.5 \boxed{+/-} \boxed{=} \mathbf{23.75}$

Getting Ready for Chapter 4 p. 137

1. $a + 7 = 12$

$a + 7 - 7 = 12 - 7$

$a = 5$

2. $5b = 35$

$\frac{5b}{5} = \frac{35}{5}$

$b = 7$

3. $\frac{c}{9} = 7$

$9 \cdot \frac{c}{9} = 9 \cdot 7$

$c = 63$

4. $17 - d = 5$

$17 - d - 17 = 5 - 17$

$-d = -12$

$-1 \cdot (-d) = -1 \cdot (-12)$

$d = 12$

5. $x > -4$

$\qquad -x < -1 \cdot (-4)$

$\qquad -x < 4$

Assessment

Page 140

1. a. $-12 < 12$

$\quad$ **b.** $|-4| > -4$ since $4 > -4$

$\quad$ **c.** $0 > -1$

$\quad$ **d.** $-(-2) = |-2|$ since $2 = 2$

2. a. $-15 + (-11) = -26$

$\quad$ **b.** $26 - (-14) = 26 + 14 = 40$

$\quad$ **c.** $-9 (-6) = 54$

$\quad$ **d.** $|-21| \div (-3) = 21 \div (-3) = -7$

3. The *absolute value* of a number is its distance from zero on the number line. The *opposite* of a number is the number the same distance from zero on the number line, but on the opposite side of zero.

4. a. $y + 15$

$\quad$ **b.** $\frac{6}{c}$

$\quad$ **c.** $2n - 7$

$\quad$ **d.** $-13x$

5. a. $-8(15) + 12 \div (-4)$

$\qquad = -120 + (-3)$

$\qquad = -123$

$\quad$ **b.** $(-14) \div 2 - (-5) \cdot (-10)$

$\qquad = -7 - (50)$

$\qquad = -57$

$\quad$ **c.** $3^2 + 6 \div (-2)$

$\qquad = 9 + (-3)$

$\qquad = 6$

$\quad$ **d.** $(-24) \cdot 2 - (-13) \cdot 2$

$\qquad = -48 - (-26)$

$\qquad = -48 + 26$

$\qquad = -22$

6. a. $28 \cdot (-6) = (30 + (-2))(-6)$

$\qquad = 30(-6) + (-2)(-6)$

$\qquad = -180 + 12$

$\qquad = -168$

$\quad$ **b.** $15 \cdot 1.97 = 15(2 - 0.03)$

$\qquad = 15(2) - 15(0.03)$

$\qquad = 30 - 0.45$

$\qquad = 29.55$

7. a. $(-7)(-7)(x)(x)(x) = (-7)^2 x^3$

  b. $8 \cdot 8 \cdot 8 \cdot 8 \cdot y \cdot y = 8^4 y^2$

  c. $(a)(a)(a)(a)(-2)(-2)(-2) = a^4 (-2)^3$

8. a. $t^2 \cdot t^3 \cdot t = t^{2+3+1}$
$$= t^6$$

  b. $2^5 \cdot 2^6 \cdot 2^4 = 2^{5+6+4}$
$$= 2^{15}$$

9. C; I. $8^5 \cdot 8^4 = 8^{5+4} = 8^9 \neq 8^{20}$

  II. $(-1)^3 \cdot 1^2 = (-1) \cdot (1) = -1 \neq 1$

  III. $(-5)^2 - |-5| = 25 - 5 = 20$
$$10^2 \div 5 = 100 \div 5 = 20$$
$$(-5)^2 - |-5| = 10^2 \div 5 \qquad true$$

  IV. $3^4 \cdot 3^5 = 3^{4+5} = 3^9 \qquad true$

  Answer: C. III and IV

10. a. $-19b$ for $b = -3$
$$-19(-3) = 57$$

  b. x^3 for $x = 10$
$$10^3 = 1,000$$

  c. $|-5 - t|$ for $t = -6$
$$|-5 - (-6)| = |-5 + 6| = |1| = 1$$

  d. $-b^2 - 4b$ for $b = -3$
$$-(-3)^2 - 4(-3)$$
$$= -9 - (-12)$$
$$= -9 + 12$$
$$= 3$$

  e. $-8abc$ for $a = -5, b = 7, c = -4$
$$-8(-5)(7)(-4) = -1,120$$

  8 ⌷+/−⌷ ⌷×⌷ 5 ⌷+/−⌷ ⌷×⌷ 7 ⌷×⌷ 4 ⌷+/−⌷

  ⌷=⌷ **−1120**

11. Let b represent the number of bikes,
  c represent the number of CDs,
  p represent the number of backpacks.
  12 items were sold: $b + c + p = 12$
  Cost of bikes sold at \$120 each: $120b$
  Cost of CDs sold at \$10 each: $10c$
  Cost of backpacks sold at \$12 each: $12p$
  total cost of 12 items was \$680:
$$120b + 10c + 12p = 680$$
  Guess and Test can be used to solve the equations.
  Try: 5 bikes, 2 CDs, and 5 backpacks
  • $b + c + p = 12$
    $5 + 2 + 5 = 12 \qquad b = 5, c = 2, p = 5$
    $12 = 12$
  • $120b + 10c + 12p = 680$
    $120(5) + 10(2) + 12(5) = 680$
    $600 + 20 + 60 = 680$
    $680 = 680$

  5 bikes, 2 CDs, and 5 backpacks satisfy the conditions.

12. Answers may vary.
  Sample: Count the number of negative factors. If odd, the product is negative. If even, the product is positive.

Cumulative Review
  Page 141

1. D; $8 - 11 = 8 + (-11)$

2. C; Put the compass tip at P and draw arcs intersecting $\overleftrightarrow{XY}$ in two points.

3. D; the outliers

4. D; trapezoid

5. A; A. $5(2.99) \neq 5(3) - 0.01$
  B. $5(2.99) = 5(3 - 0.01)$
$$= 5(3) - 5(0.01) \qquad true$$
  C. $5(2.99) = 5(2 + 0.99)$
$$= 5(2) + 5(0.99) \qquad true$$
  D. $5(2.99) = \frac{10}{2}(2.99)$
$$= \frac{10(2.99)}{2} \qquad true$$

6. B; $|-2| = 2, |-1| = 1, |0| = 0, |1| = 1, |2| = 2$

7. B; $12k$; the cost (in cents) of k photocopies if each photocopy costs 12¢

8. B; the 2nd year

9. A; A. $9^2 + 12^2 \overset{?}{=} 15^2$

$81 + 144 \overset{?}{=} 225$

$225 = 225$, a right triangle

B. $(\sqrt{15})^2 + 9^2 \overset{?}{=} 10^2$

$15 + 81 \overset{?}{=} 100$

$96 \neq 100$, not a right triangle

C. $8^2 + 14^2 \overset{?}{=} 22^2$

$64 + 196 \overset{?}{=} 484$

$260 \neq 484$, not a right triangle

D. $6^2 + 28^2 \overset{?}{=} 30^2$

$36 + 784 \overset{?}{=} 900$

$820 \neq 900$, not a right triangle

10. C; Let x = side of square.

$x^2 + x^2 = 2^2$

$2x^2 = 4$

$x^2 = 2$

$x = \sqrt{2}$

area of shaded region

= area of circle − area of square

$= \pi(1)^2 - (\sqrt{2})(\sqrt{2})$ since radius of circle = 1

$= \pi - (\sqrt{2})^2$ and side of square = $\sqrt{2}$

Chapter 4 Algebraic Equations and Inequalities

4-1 Simplifying Variable Expressions
Pages 145–148

Think and Discuss pp. 145–146

1. buses: $3 + 2 = 5$
   bicycled: $6 + 7 = 13$

2. $5x$; x represents the number of students in one bus

3. $5x + 13$

4. $$\square\ \text{\tiny■■} + \square\ \text{\tiny■■} = \square\ \square\ \text{\tiny■■}\ \text{\tiny■■}$$
   $(x + 3) + (x + 3) = (x + x) + (3 + 3)$
   $\qquad 2x + 6 = 2x + 6$

Try These p. 147

5. $x + 4x = 5x$
   $$\square + \square\square\square\square = \square\square\square\square\square$$

6. $3y + 5 + 2y - 3 = 5y + 2$
   $$\square\square\square\ \text{\tiny■■■} + \square\square\ \text{\tiny■■} = \square\square\square\square\square\ \text{\tiny■}$$

7. $-5s + 2s$
   $= (-5 + 2)s$
   $= -3s$

8. $7q - 6q$
   $= (7 - 6)q$
   $= 1q$
   $= q$

9. $8n - n$
   $= (8 - 1)n$
   $= 7n$

10. $-2j - 7j$
    $= (-2 - 7)j$
    $= -9j$

11. $5(h + 12) = \boxed{5} \cdot h + 5 \cdot \boxed{12} = 5h + \boxed{60}$

12. $\left(\boxed{z} - 3\right)\boxed{6} = \boxed{z} \cdot 6 - \boxed{3} \cdot 6 = 6z - \boxed{18}$

13. $12(d - 6)$
    $= 12(d) - 12(6)$
    $= 12d - 72$

14. $3 + 5(a - 4)$
    $= 3 + 5(a) - 5(4)$
    $= 3 + 5a - 20$
    $= 5a + 3 - 20$
    $= 5a - 17$

15. $(2x + 1) + 3x$
    $= 2x + 1 + 3x$
    $= 2x + 3x + 1$
    $= (2 + 3)x + 1$
    $= 5x + 1$

16. $4 + 3p - 9q + q - 2p$
    $= 4 + 3p - 2p - 9q + q$
    $= 4 + (3 - 2)p + (-9 + 1)q$
    $= 4 + p - 8q$

17. a. Check students' work.

   b. $3(2x + 5) = 3(2x) + 3(5)$
      $\qquad\qquad = 6x + 15$
      $3(2x + 5)$ and $6x + 15$

On Your Own pp. 147–148

18. $3a + 2 + a$
    $= (3a + a) + 2$
    $= (3 + 1)a + 2$
    $= 4a + 2$

19. $9(m - 7)$
    $= 9(m) - 9(7)$
    $= 9m - 63$

20. $n + 4n - 3n$
    $= (1 + 4 - 3)n$
    $= 2n$

21. $(q + 1)5$
$\quad = (q)5 + (1)5$
$\quad = 5q + 5$

22. $4(z - 3) - 8$
$\quad = 4(z) - 4(3) - 8$
$\quad = 4z - 12 - 8$
$\quad = 4z - 20$

23. $-6 + 5(1 + r)$
$\quad = -6 + 5(1) + 5(r)$
$\quad = -6 + 5 + 5r$
$\quad = -1 + 5r$

24. $5n - 6 + 4n + 3 - 2n$
$\quad = (5n + 4n - 2n) + (-6 + 3)$
$\quad = (5 + 4 - 2)n + (-3)$
$\quad = 7n - 3$

25. $3(g + 5) + 2 + 3g$
$\quad = 3(g) + 3(5) + 2 + 3g$
$\quad = 3g + 15 + 2 + 3g$
$\quad = (3g + 3g) + (15 + 2)$
$\quad = (3 + 3)g + 17$
$\quad = 6g + 17$

26. $3x + x + 3x + x$
$\quad = (3 + 1 + 3 + 1)x$
$\quad = 8x$

27. Answers may vary. Sample:
The distributive property is when you multiply a sum or difference by another number. To evaluate, you multiply each part of the sum or difference by the number outside the parentheses and add or subtract the resulting products. So if you had $2(100 - 2)$, that would be the same as $200 - 4$, or 196. When multiplying a number by a sum, you multiply each addend by the number, then add them.

28. $3x + 2y + 189$

29. $1.07(y - 4.2)$
$\quad = 1.07(y) - 1.07(4.2)$
$\quad = 1.07y - 4.494$

30. $34 + 14p - 18 + 47p$
$\quad = (14p + 47p) + (34 - 18)$
$\quad = (14 + 47)p + 16$
$\quad = 61p + 16$

31. $9.2b + 5c + 1.2b + 1.8c$
$\quad = (9.2b + 1.2b) + (5c + 1.8c)$
$\quad = (9.2 + 1.2)b + (5 + 1.8)c$
$\quad = 10.4b + 6.8c$

32. $19k + 24(5 + k)$
$\quad = 19k + 24(5) + 24(k)$
$\quad = (19k + 24k) + 24(5)$
$\quad = (19 + 24)k + 120$
$\quad = 43k + 120$

33. $-5u + 6 + u + 4u$
$\quad = (-5u + u + 4u) + 6$
$\quad = (-5 + 1 + 4)u + 6$
$\quad = 0u + 6$
$\quad = 6$

34. $(5.1r + 2.4) - 1.009r$
$\quad = (5.1r - 1.009r) + 2.4$
$\quad = (5.1 - 1.009)r + 2.4$
$\quad = 4.091r + 2.4$

35. a. Answers may vary.
Sample: Subtract 9 from the result and move the decimal point one place to the left to get the original number.

b.

Step	Expression
1	n
2	$2n$
3	$2n + 3$
4	$10n + 15$
5	$10n + 9$

c. Begin with the last expression: $10n + 9$.
Subtract 9: $10n + 9 - 9 = 10n$.
Move one decimal place to the left (or divide by 10): $\frac{10n}{10} = n$.
n is the original number.

36. Answers may vary. Sample:
$2m + m + 8;$
$m + m + m + 8$

37.
$$x + 3 = 5$$
$$x + 3 - 3 = 5 - 3$$
$$x = 2$$

Mixed Review p. 148

1. $121 < 133 < 144$

$\sqrt{121} < \sqrt{133} < \sqrt{144}$

$11 < \sqrt{133} < 12$

$\sqrt{133} \approx 11.5$

2. $225 < 226 < 256$

$\sqrt{225} < \sqrt{226} < \sqrt{256}$

$15 < \sqrt{226} < 16$

$\sqrt{226} \approx 15$

3. $(6h + 50) \div 8 \quad$ for $h = 17$
$[6(17) + 50] \div 8$
$\quad = (102 + 50) \div 8$
$\quad = 152 \div 8$
$\quad = 19$

4. $h^2(371 - 6h) \quad$ for $h = 17$
$17^2[371 - 6(17)]$
$\quad = 17^2(371 - 102)$
$\quad = (289)(269)$
$\quad = 77,741$

5. $542.8 + 53.7 = 596.5$

6. $8,092.43 - 413.85 = 7,678.58$

7. $\frac{10}{14} = \frac{x}{8.5}$

$x = \frac{10}{14}(8.5)$

$\quad \approx \$6.07$

4-2 Addition and Subtraction Equations
Pages 149–152

Think and Discuss pp. 149–150

1.

2. $x = 3$

3.

$x = 2$

Work Together pp. 150–151

4. $x + 4 = 7$

$x + 4 - 4 = 7 - 4 \qquad$ Add -4 to each side.

$x = 3$

5. $x - 4 = -7$

$x - 4 + 4 = -7 + 4 \qquad$ Add 4 to each side.

$x = -3$

6. $x + 7 = 4$

$x + 7 - 7 = 4 - 7 \qquad$ Add -7 to each side.

$x = -3$

7. $x + 7 = -4$

$x + 7 - 7 = -4 - 7 \qquad$ Add -7 to each side.

$x = -11$

Try These p. 151

8. They are equivalent because they have the same solution.

9. Subtracting a number is the same as adding its opposite.

10.
$$y + 7 = 12$$
$$y + 7 - 7 = 12 - 7 \quad \text{Subtract 7 from each side.}$$
$$y = 5$$
Check: $y + 7 = 12$
$$5 + 7 = 12 \qquad \text{Replace } y \text{ with 5.}$$
$$12 = 12 \quad \checkmark$$

11.
$$n - 8 = -2$$
$$n - 8 + 8 = -2 + 8 \quad \text{Add 8 to each side.}$$
$$n = 6$$
Check: $n - 8 = -2$
$$6 - 8 = -2 \qquad \text{Replace } n \text{ with 6.}$$
$$-2 = -2 \quad \checkmark$$

12.
$$20 = -7 + k$$
$$20 + 7 = -7 + 7 + k$$
$$27 = k$$
Check: $20 = -7 + k$
$$20 = -7 + 27$$
$$20 = 20 \quad \checkmark$$

13.
$$7 = d - 1.4$$
$$7 + 1.4 = d - 1.4 + 1.4$$
$$8.4 = d$$
Check: $7 = d - 1.4$
$$7 = 8.4 - 1.4$$
$$7 = 7 \quad \checkmark$$

14.
$$g - \frac{1}{2} = \frac{1}{4}$$
$$g - \frac{1}{2} + \frac{1}{2} = \frac{1}{4} + \frac{1}{2}$$
$$g = \frac{3}{4}$$
Check: $g - \frac{1}{2} = \frac{1}{4}$
$$\frac{3}{4} - \frac{1}{2} = \frac{1}{4}$$
$$\frac{1}{4} = \frac{1}{4} \quad \checkmark$$

15.
$$6 + q = -8$$
$$6 - 6 + q = -8 - 6$$
$$q = -14$$
Check: $6 + q = -8$
$$6 + (-14) = -8$$
$$-8 = -8 \quad \checkmark$$

16.
$$a - 15 = -9$$
$$a - 15 + 15 = -9 + 15$$
$$a = 6$$
Check: $a - 15 = -9$
$$6 - 15 = -9$$
$$-9 = -9 \quad \checkmark$$

17.
$$64 = n + 34$$
$$64 - 34 = n + 34 - 34$$
$$30 = n$$
Check: $64 = n + 34$
$$64 = 30 + 34$$
$$64 = 64 \quad \checkmark$$

18.
$$x - 3.66 = -4.1$$
$$x - 3.66 + 3.66 = -4.1 + 3.66$$
$$x = -0.44$$
Check: $x - 3.66 = -4.1$
$$-0.44 - 3.66 = -4.1$$
$$-4.1 = -4.1 \quad \checkmark$$

19. Answers may vary. Sample: when the computation is too difficult to do mentally, or to check answers

20. D; A. $a + 3.75 = 9.30$ true
     B. $a + 3.75 - a = 9.30 - a$
$$3.75 = 9.30 - a$$
$$9.30 - a = 3.75 \quad \text{true}$$
     C. $a + 3.75 = 9.30$
$$9.30 = a + 3.75 \quad \text{true}$$
     D. $a - 3.75 \neq 9.30$ cannot be used

Mixed Review p. 151

1. $-8 \boxed{<} -6$

2. $|15| \boxed{=} |-15|$, since $15 = 15$

3. $8 + 6r + 47 - 4r$
$$= (6r - 4r) + (8 + 47)$$
$$= (6 - 4)r + 55$$
$$= 2r + 55$$

4. $3.4(s + t) + 12s - t$
$$= 3.4(s) + 3.4(t) + 12s - t$$
$$= (3.4s + 12s) + (3.4t - t)$$
$$= (3.4 + 12)s + (3.4 - 1)t$$
$$= 15.4s + 2.4t$$

5. $1.7(z + 15)$
$= 1.7(z) + 1.7(15)$
$= 1.7z + 25.5$

6. $(164 + b)22 - 6b$
$= (164)(22) + (b)22 - 6b$
$= 3{,}608 + (22b - 6b)$
$= 3{,}608 + (22 - 6)b$
$= 3{,}608 + 16b$

7. Let m represent the total amount of money.

oldest: $\frac{2}{5}m$

middle: $\frac{1}{3}m$

The youngest receives the remainder: $24,000.

$m - \frac{2}{5}m - \frac{1}{3}m = 24{,}000$

$\left(1 - \frac{2}{5} - \frac{1}{3}\right)m = 24{,}000$

$\left(\frac{15}{15} - \frac{6}{15} - \frac{5}{15}\right)m = 24{,}000$

$\frac{4}{15}m = 24{,}000$

$m = \frac{15 \cdot 24{,}000}{4}$

$m = 90{,}000$

On Your Own p. 152

21. $z - 4 = -11$
$z - 4 + 4 = -11 + 4$
$z = -7$

22. $-15 = 6 + m$
$-15 - 6 = 6 + m - 6$
$-21 = m$

23. $3.15 + w = 12.09$
$3.15 + w - 3.15 = 12.09 - 3.15$
$w = 8.94$

24. $f + \frac{1}{2} = \frac{3}{5}$
$f + \frac{1}{2} - \frac{1}{2} = \frac{3}{5} - \frac{1}{2}$
$f = \frac{6}{10} - \frac{5}{10}$
$f = \frac{1}{10}$

25. $7 + b = -13$
$7 + b - 7 = -13 - 7$
$b = -20$

26. $x - 1.75 = 19$
$x - 1.75 + 1.75 = 19 + 1.75$
$x = 20.75$

27. Let i represent the number of invitations.
$i + 8 = 52$
$i + 8 - 8 = 52 - 8$
$i = 44$
Jena mailed 44 invitations yesterday.

28. Let m represent the money Darnel had before buying the tape.
$m - 8.13 = 6.87$
$m - 8.13 + 8.13 = 6.87 + 8.13$
$m = 15$
Darnel had $15.

29. Let t represent the temperature at 6:00 A.M.
$t = 12 - 15$
$t = -3$
The temperature was $-3°F$ at 6:00 A.M.

30. $19,452; $38{,}620 - 19{,}168 = 19{,}452$

31–34. Accept reasonable estimates.

31. $r + 8.019 = -11.57$
$8.019 \approx 8, \quad -11.57 \approx -12$
$r + 8 \approx -12$
$r + 8 - 8 \approx -12 - 8$
$r \approx -20$

32. $-3.9004 = y - 61.41$
$-3.9004 \approx -4, \quad 61.41 \approx 61$
$-4 \approx y - 61$
$-4 + 61 \approx y$
$57 \approx y$

33. $j - 0.0155 = 3.029$
$0.0155 \approx 0, \quad 3.029 \approx 3$
$j - 0 \approx 3$
$j \approx 3$

34. $-14.8 + p = 2.03$

$-14.8 \approx -15, \quad 2.03 \approx 2$

$-15 + p \approx 2$

$-15 + p + 15 \approx 2 + 15$

$p \approx 17$

35–40. x indicates "is not a solution."

value of $\rightarrow$ n equation $\downarrow$	−3	−2	−1
35. $n = 3$	x	x	x
36. $\lvert n \rvert = 3$	$\lvert -3 \rvert = 3$ $n = -3$	x	x
37. $\lvert n \rvert = -3$	x	x	x
38. $\lvert n \rvert = 0$	x	x	x
39. $\lvert n \rvert + 1 = 2$ $\lvert n \rvert + 1 - 1$ $= 2 - 1$ $\lvert n \rvert = 1$	x	x	$\lvert -1 \rvert + 1 = 2$ $2 = 2$ $n = -1$
40. $\lvert n + 1 \rvert = 2$	$\lvert -3 + 1 \rvert = 2$ $\lvert -2 \rvert = 2$ $n = -3$	x	x

0	1	2	3	All Solutions
x	x	x	$3 = 3$ $n = 3$	$n = 3$
x	x	x	$\lvert 3 \rvert = 3$ $n = 3$	$n = -3$ or 3
x	x	x	x	none
$\lvert 0 \rvert = 0$ $n = 0$	x	x	x	$n = 0$
x	$\lvert 1 \rvert + 1 = 2$ $\lvert 2 \rvert = 2$ $n = 1$	x	x	$n = 1$ or −1
x	$\lvert 1 + 1 \rvert = 2$ $\lvert 2 \rvert = 2$ $n = 1$	x	x	$n = -3$ or 1

41. $a + 8.40 = 11.55$

Answers may vary. Sample:

Mr. Mann bought two packages of meat. One package weighed 8.40 lb. The total weight of the two packages was 11.55 lb. How much did the second package weigh?

42. $2x = 5$

Problem Solving Practice

Page 153

1. No; the number is not divisible by four. 24 four-digit numbers are possible.

1479	4791	<u>7914</u>	9147
1497	4719	7941	<u>9174</u>
1749	4971	<u>7194</u>	9417
<u>1794</u>	4917	7149	9471
1947	4179	7419	<u>9714</u>
<u>1974</u>	4197	7491	9741

A number divisible by 4 must be an even number since $4 = 2 \cdot 2$, so all numbers ending in 1, 7, or 9 are not divisible by 4.

Look more closely at the six remaining numbers.

$1794 = 2 \cdot 897$

$1974 = 2 \cdot 987$

$7914 = 2 \cdot 3957$

$7194 = 2 \cdot 3597$

$9174 = 2 \cdot 4587$

$9714 = 2 \cdot 4857$

When 2 is factored out of each number, the remaining factor is an odd number. To be divisible by 4, the number must be divisible by 2 twice. Thus, no possible combination is divisible by 4.

2. Let n represent the number.

$\frac{1}{3}n + 10 = n - 20$

$\frac{1}{3}n - \frac{1}{3}n + 10 = n - \frac{1}{3}n - 20$ Subtract $\frac{1}{3}n$ from each side.

$10 = \left(1 - \frac{1}{3}\right)n - 20$

$10 = \frac{2}{3}n - 20$

$10 + 20 = \frac{2}{3}n - 20 + 20$ Add 20 to both sides.

$30 = \frac{2}{3}n$

$\frac{3}{2} \cdot 30 = n$

$\frac{90}{2} = n$

$45 = n$

The number is 45.

3. Let p represent the cost of the pants. Then $p + 15$ represents the cost of the sweater.

$$p + (p + 15) = 75$$
$$(p + p) + 15 = 75$$
$$(1 + 1)p + 15 = 75$$
$$2p + 15 = 75$$
$$2p + 15 - 15 = 75 - 15$$
$$2p = 60$$
$$p = \frac{60}{2}$$
$$p = 30$$

The pants cost $30.

4. Let x represent the smallest integer. Then $x + 1$ represents the next integer and $x + 2$ represents the largest integer. The sum of the smallest and largest integers is 36.

$$x + (x + 2) = 36$$
$$(x + x) + 2 = 36$$
$$(1 + 1)x + 2 = 36$$
$$2x + 2 = 36$$
$$2x + 2 - 2 = 36 - 2$$
$$2x = 34$$
$$\frac{2x}{2} = \frac{34}{2}$$
$$x = 17$$

The smallest integer is 17.

$$x + 1 = 18$$
$$x + 2 = 19$$

The integers are 17, 18, and 19.

5. Let t represent the total hours Nathan works. For the first 15 h, he earns $4 per hour or 15($4). After 15 h, he earns $6 per hour or $(t - 15)$6. If he earns $100, then

$$15(4) + (t - 15)6 = 100$$
$$60 + 6(t) - 15(6) = 100$$
$$(60 - 90) + 6t = 100$$
$$-30 + 6t = 100$$
$$-30 + 30 + 6t = 100 + 30$$
$$6t = 130$$
$$\frac{6t}{6} = \frac{130}{6} \quad \text{Divide both sides by 6.}$$
$$t = 21\frac{2}{3}$$

Nathan must work $21\frac{2}{3}$ h to earn at least $100 in that week.

6. Let p represent the population.

$$3\% \text{ of } p = 0.03p$$

Then $p + 0.03p = (1 + 0.03)p = 1.03p$ represents an increase of 3% in population each year.
Make a table.

year	1.03p
1	$1.03(10,000) = 10,300$
2	$1.03(10,300) = 10,609$
3	$1.03(10,609) \approx 10,927$
4	$1.03(10,927) \approx 11,255$
5	$1.03(11,255) \approx 11,593$
6	$1.03(11,593) \approx 11,941$
7	$1.03(11,941) \approx 12,299$

The population will be greater than 12,000 between 6 and 7 years.
Note: Look at the pattern developed. The same result could have been obtained by multiplying repeatedly by 1.03.

year	1.03p
1	$(1.03)(10,000) = 10,300$
2	$(1.03)(1.03)(10,000) = 10,609$
3	$(1.03)(1.03)(1.03)(10,000) \approx 10,927$
4	$(1.03)(1.03)(1.03)(1.03)(10,000) \approx 11,255$
5	$(1.03)(1.03)(1.03)(1.03)(1.03)(10,000) \approx 11,593$
6	$(1.03)(1.03)(1.03)(1.03)(1.03)(1.03)(10,000) \approx 11,941$
7	$(1.03)(1.03)(1.03)(1.03)(1.03)(1.03)(1.03)(10,000) \approx 12,299$

7.

The small cubes with only 2 faces exposed will have exactly two faces painted red. There are 4 in each of 3 directions around the cube (length, width, and height).

$$4 + 4 + 4 = 12$$

12 small cubes have exactly two faces painted red.

8.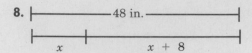

Let x represent the smaller piece.
Then $x + 8$ represents the larger piece.

$$x + (x + 8) = 48$$
$$(x + x) + 8 = 48$$
$$2x + 8 = 48$$
$$2x + 8 - 8 = 48 - 8$$
$$2x = 40$$
$$\frac{2x}{2} = \frac{40}{2}$$
$$x = 20$$
$$x + 8 = 20 + 8 = 28$$

The length of the pieces are 20 in. and 28 in.

9. The greatest product will have 4 and 5 as the leading digits, so consider only these possible numbers. The 3 as the second digit of either number will yield the greatest product.

The following are the remaining possibilities.

Numbers		Product	
532	41	21,812	
531	42	22,302	
521	43	22,403	
432	51	22,032	
431	52	22,412	← greatest product
421	53	22,313	

The two numbers are 431 and 52.

10. Let c represent the number of correct answers. Then $3c$ represents the points possible for the correct answers.
Since there are ten problems, $10 - c$ represents the number of incorrect answers. Since one point is deducted for each incorrect answer, $-1(10 - c)$ represents the points for each incorrect answer.
$3c + (-1)(10 - c)$ represents Estelle's score.

$$3c + (-1)(10 - c) = 18$$
$$3c - 1(10) - 1(-c) = 18$$
$$3c - 10 + c = 18$$
$$(3c + c) - 10 = 18$$
$$4c - 10 = 18$$
$$4c - 10 + 10 = 18 + 10$$
$$\frac{4c}{4} = \frac{28}{4}$$
$$c = 7$$

Estelle has 7 correct answers.

4-3 Multiplication and Division Equations

Pages 154–157

Think and Discuss pp. 154–155

1. Each green tile represents the amount to be saved each week.

The yellow tiles represent the total amount to be saved.

2.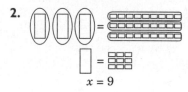
$$x = 9$$

3. $9

4. $3x = 27$
$$x = 9$$

Try These p. 155

5. $9 = 3x$

$\frac{9}{3} = \frac{3x}{3}$ Divide each side by 3.

$3 = x$

6. $2x = -10$

$\frac{2x}{2} = \frac{-10}{2}$ Divide each side by 2.

$x = -5$

7. $24 = -3s$

$\frac{24}{-3} = \frac{-3s}{-3}$ Divide each side by –3.

$-8 = s$

Check: $24 = -3s$

$24 = -3(-8)$ Replace s with –8.

$24 = 24$ √

8. $\frac{c}{-4} = -64$

$-4 \cdot \frac{c}{-4} = -4(-64)$ Multiply each side by –4.

$c = 256$

Check: $\frac{c}{-4} = -64$

$\frac{256}{-4} = -64$ Replace c with 256.

$-64 = -64$ √

9. $30 = \frac{w}{1.5}$

$(1.5)30 = (1.5)\frac{w}{1.5}$ Multiply each side by 1.5.

$45 = w$

Check: $30 = \frac{w}{1.5}$

$30 = \frac{45}{1.5}$ Replace w with 45.

$30 = 30$ √

10. $1.6a = 4.96$

$\frac{1.6a}{1.6} = \frac{4.96}{1.6}$ Divide each side by 1.6.

$a = 3.1$

Check: $1.6a = 4.96$

$1.6(3.1) = 4.96$ Replace a with 3.1.

$4.96 = 4.96$ √

11. a. Let w represent the amount Tran must save each week.

$8w = 150$

$\frac{8w}{8} = \frac{150}{8}$

$w = 18.75$

Tran must save \$18.75/wk.

b. Let w represent the number of weeks it takes to save \$150.

$7.50w = 150$

$\frac{7.50w}{7.50} = \frac{150}{7.50}$

$w = 20$

Anica will need to save \$7.50/wk for $\boxed{20}$ weeks to save \$150.

On Your Own pp. 156–157

12. $25v = -5$;   Does $v = -5$?

$25(-5) = -5$

$-125 \neq -5$ No

13. $\frac{15}{m} = -3$ Does $m = -5$?

$\frac{15}{-5} = -3$

$-3 = -3$ Yes

14. $-15 = \frac{d}{-3}$ Does $d = -5$?

$-15 = \frac{-5}{-3}$

$-15 \neq \frac{5}{3}$ No

15. $10 = -2l$ Does $t = -5$?

$10 = -2(-5)$

$10 = 10$ Yes

16. $\frac{b}{-4} = 20$ *Check*: $\frac{b}{-4} = 20$

$(-4)\frac{b}{-4} = (-4)\,20$ $\frac{-80}{-4} = 20$

$b = -80$ $20 = 20$ √

17. $35 = \frac{y}{3.5}$ *Check*: $35 = \frac{y}{3.5}$

$(3.5)\,35 = (3.5)\frac{y}{3.5}$ $35 = \frac{122.5}{3.5}$

$122.5 = y$ $35 = 35$ √

18. $270 = 1.35j$ *Check*: $270 = 1.35j$

$\frac{270}{1.35} = \frac{1.35j}{1.35}$ $270 = 1.35(200)$

$200 = j$ $270 = 270$ √

19. $-352 = -32h$ *Check*: $-352 = -32h$

$\frac{-352}{-32} = \frac{-32h}{-32}$ $-352 = -32(11)$

$11 = h$ $-352 = -352$ √

20. $0 = \frac{n}{24}$ *Check*: $0 = \frac{n}{24}$

$(24)0 = (24)\frac{n}{24}$ $0 = \frac{0}{24}$

$0 = n$ $0 = 0$ √

21. $0.3z = -1.86$

$$\frac{0.3z}{0.3} = \frac{-1.86}{0.3}$$

$$z = -6.2$$

$Check$: $0.3z = -1.86$

$$0.3(-6.2) = -1.86$$

$$-1.86 = -1.86 \checkmark$$

22. Let p represent the price of one pen.

$$8p = 9.84$$

$$\frac{8p}{8} = \frac{9.84}{8}$$

$$p = 1.23$$

The price of one pen is $1.23.

23. Let h represent the time when the temperature reached $-14°$F.

$$-2h = -14$$

$$\frac{-2h}{-2} = \frac{-14}{-2}$$

$$h = 7$$

The temperature will reach $-14°$F at 7 P.M.

24. $2|n| = 4$

$$\frac{2|n|}{2} = \frac{4}{2}$$

$$|n| = 2$$

$n = 2 \qquad |2| = 2 \ \checkmark$

$n = -2 \quad |-2| = 2 \ \checkmark$

The solutions are 2 and -2.

25. $-2|n| = -4$

$$\frac{-2|n|}{-2} = \frac{-4}{-2}$$

$$|n| = 2$$

$n = 2 \qquad |2| = 2 \ \checkmark$

$n = -2 \quad |-2| = 2 \ \checkmark$

The solutions are 2 and -2.

26. $|2n| = 4$

$n = 2 \qquad\qquad |2(2)| = 4$

$\qquad\qquad\qquad\qquad 4 = 4 \ \checkmark$

$n = -2 \qquad\qquad |2(-2)| = 4$

$\qquad\qquad\qquad\qquad |-4| = 4 \ \checkmark$

The solutions are 2 and -2.

27. $\frac{|n|}{2} = 4$

$$2 \cdot \frac{|n|}{2} = 2 \cdot 4$$

$$|n| = 8$$

$n = 8 \qquad |8| = 8 \ \checkmark$

$n = -8 \quad |-8| = 8 \ \checkmark$

The solutions are 8 and -8.

28. $\frac{|n|}{2} = -4$

$$2 \cdot \frac{|n|}{2} = 2\,(-4)$$

$$|n| = -8$$

none; No value of n will give a negative absolute value. The absolute value of a number is always nonnegative.

29. $\left|\frac{n}{2}\right| = 4$

$n = 8 \qquad\qquad \left|\frac{8}{2}\right| = 4$

$\qquad\qquad\qquad\qquad |4| = 4 \ \checkmark$

$n = -8 \qquad\qquad \left|\frac{-8}{2}\right| = 4$

$\qquad\qquad\qquad\qquad |-4| = 4 \ \checkmark$

The solutions are 8 and -8.

30. When solving $6a = -42$ and $a + 6 = -42$, you have to undo an operation involving 6. In one case you have to divide by 6, and in the other you have to subtract 6.

31. Multiply both sides by r.

32–33. Answers may vary for the estimate. Accept reasonable estimates.

32. Let x represent the number of hours Lisa worked.

$$3.75x = 69.38$$

Estimate:

$3.75 \approx 4, \qquad 69.38 \approx 68$

$$4x \approx 68$$

$$\frac{4x}{4} \approx \frac{68}{4}$$

$$x \approx 17 \text{ h}$$

Exact:

$$3.75x = 69.38$$

$$\frac{3.75x}{3.75} = \frac{69.38}{3.75}$$

$$x \approx 18.5 \text{ h}$$

33. Let x represent how much you will pay.

$$46.99 = 3x$$

Estimate: $46.99 \approx 45$

$$45 \approx 3x$$

$$\frac{45}{3} \approx \frac{3x}{3}$$

$$15 \approx x \text{ or } \$15$$

Exact: $46.99 = 3x$

$$\frac{46.99}{3} = \frac{3x}{3}$$

$$15.66 \approx x \text{ or } \$15.66$$

Mixed Review p. 157

1. 23 $\boxed{\times}$ 15 $\boxed{+/-}$ $\boxed{=}$ **−345**

$$23 \cdot (-15) = -345$$

2. 213 $\boxed{\times}$ 12 $\boxed{=}$ **2556**

$$213 \cdot 12 = 2,556$$

3. 192 $\boxed{\div}$ 12 $\boxed{+/-}$ $\boxed{=}$ **−16**

$$192 \div (-12) = -16$$

4. 5684 $\boxed{\div}$ 98 $\boxed{=}$ **58**

$$5684 \div 98 = 58$$

5.
$$22 = f - 17.6$$
$$22 + 17.6 = f - 17.6 + 17.6$$
$$39.6 = f$$

6.
$$k + 76 = 283$$
$$k + 76 - 76 = 283 - 76$$
$$k = 207$$

7. $10,000(0.1 \text{ mm})$
$$= 1,000 \text{ mm or } 1 \text{ m}$$

4-4 Solving Two-Step Equations
Pages 158–160

Think and Discuss pp. 158–159

1. $2x - 3 = 7$

2. $2x - 3 + 3 = 7 + 3$

$$2x = 10$$

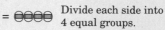

3.

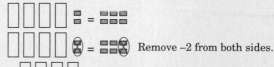

4. $x = 5$

Work Together p. 159

To solve $ax + b = c$, first subtract b from both sides, then divide both sides by a ($a \neq 0$).

$$ax + b = c$$
$$ax + b - b = c - b$$
$$\frac{ax}{a} = \frac{c - b}{a}$$
$$x = \frac{c - b}{a}$$

5.
$$2x + 8 = -6$$
$$2x + 8 - 8 = -6 - 8 \qquad \text{Subtract 8 from each side.}$$
$$2x = -14$$
$$\frac{2x}{2} = \frac{-14}{2} \qquad \text{Divide each side by 2.}$$
$$x = -7$$

6.
$$3x - 8 = 10$$
$$3x - 8 + 8 = 10 + 8 \qquad \text{Add 8 to each side.}$$
$$3x = 18$$
$$\frac{3x}{3} = \frac{18}{3} \qquad \text{Divide each side by 3.}$$
$$x = 6$$

7.
$$9 = 4x + 17$$
$$9 - 17 = 4x + 17 - 17 \qquad \text{Subtract 17 from each side.}$$
$$-8 = 4x$$
$$\frac{-8}{2} = \frac{4x}{4} \qquad \text{Divide each side by 4.}$$
$$-2 = x$$

Try These p. 159

8. $4x - 2 = -6$

Remove −2 from both sides.

Divide each side into 4 equal groups.

$$x = -1$$

9. $5 = 3x + 8$

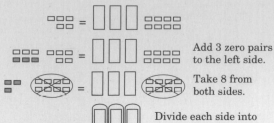

Add 3 zero pairs to the left side.

Take 8 from both sides.

Divide each side into 3 equal groups.

$x = -1$

10.
$$3s - 4 = 8$$
$$3s - 4 + 4 = 8 + 4 \qquad \text{Add 4 to each side.}$$
$$3s = 12$$
$$\frac{3s}{3} = \frac{12}{3} \qquad \text{Divide each side by 3.}$$
$$s = 4$$

Check: $3s - 4 = 8$
$$3(4) - 4 = 8 \qquad \text{Replace } s \text{ with 4.}$$
$$12 - 4 = 8$$
$$8 = 8 \;\checkmark$$

11.
$$\frac{k}{5} + 1.5 = 6.5$$
$$\frac{k}{5} + 1.5 - 1.5 = 6.5 - 1.5 \qquad \text{Subtract 1.5 from each side.}$$
$$\frac{k}{5} = 5$$
$$5 \cdot \frac{k}{5} = 5 \cdot 5 \qquad \text{Multiply each side by 5.}$$
$$k = 25$$

Check: $\frac{k}{5} + 1.5 = 6.5$
$$\frac{25}{5} + 1.5 = 6.5 \qquad \text{Replace } k \text{ with 25.}$$
$$5 + 1.5 = 6.5$$
$$6.5 = 6.5 \;\checkmark$$

12.
$$-7 = 9 + 2g$$
$$-7 - 9 = 9 + 2g - 9 \qquad \text{Subtract 9 from each side.}$$
$$-16 = 2g$$
$$\frac{-16}{2} = \frac{2g}{2} \qquad \text{Divide each side by 2.}$$
$$-8 = g$$

Check: $-7 = 9 + 2g$
$$-7 = 9 + 2(-8) \qquad \text{Replace } g \text{ with } -8.$$
$$-7 = 9 - 16$$
$$-7 = -7 \;\checkmark$$

13. Let t represent the cost of one tape.
$$4t + 5 = 33$$
$$4t + 5 - 5 = 33 - 5$$
$$4t = 28$$
$$\frac{4t}{4} = \frac{28}{4}$$
$$t = 7$$

The cost is $7 per tape.

On Your Own p. 160

14.
$$2j - 7 = 11$$
$$2j - 7 + 7 = 11 + 7$$
$$2j = 18$$
$$\frac{2j}{2} = \frac{18}{2}$$
$$j = 9$$

15.
$$\frac{x}{2} - 3 = 9$$
$$\frac{x}{2} - 3 + 3 = 9 + 3$$
$$\frac{x}{2} = 12$$
$$(2)\frac{x}{2} = (2)(12)$$
$$x = 24$$

16.
$$15 = -2x - 5$$
$$15 + 5 = -2x - 5 + 5$$
$$20 = -2x$$
$$\frac{20}{-2} = \frac{-2x}{-2}$$
$$-10 = x$$

17.
$$4m + 8 = 4$$
$$4m + 8 - 8 = 4 - 8$$
$$4m = -4$$
$$\frac{4m}{4} = \frac{-4}{4}$$
$$m = -1$$

18.
$$-11 = 1 + 3n$$
$$-11 - 1 = 1 + 3n - 1$$
$$-12 = 3n$$
$$\frac{-12}{3} = \frac{3n}{3}$$
$$-4 = n$$

19.
$$3 + \frac{m}{-10} = 6$$
$$3 + \frac{m}{-10} - 3 = 6 - 3$$
$$\frac{m}{-10} = 3$$
$$(-10)\left(\frac{m}{-10}\right) = (-10)(3)$$
$$m = -30$$

20. $5 + \frac{k}{9} = -31$

$5 + \frac{k}{9} - 5 = -31 - 5$

$\frac{k}{9} = -36$

$9 \cdot \frac{k}{9} = 9(-36)$

$k = -324$

Check: $5 + \frac{k}{9} = -31$

$5 + \frac{-324}{9} = -31$

$5 - 36 = -31$

$-31 = -31$ $\checkmark$

21. $30 = 18 + 2b$

$30 - 18 = 18 + 2b - 18$

$12 = 2b$

$\frac{12}{2} = \frac{2b}{2}$

$6 = b$

Check: $30 = 18 + 2b$

$30 = 18 + 2(6)$

$30 = 18 + 12$

$30 = 30$ $\checkmark$

22. $1.2z - 0.6 = 32.4$

$1.2z - 0.6 + 0.6 = 32.4 + 0.6$

$1.2z = 33$

$\frac{1.2z}{1.2} = \frac{33}{1.2}$

$33 \boxed{\div} 1.2 \boxed{=} \mathbf{27.5}$

$z = 27.5$

Check: $1.2z - 0.6 = 32.4$

$1.2(27.5) - 0.6 = 32.4$

$33 - 0.6 = 32.4$

$32.4 = 32.4$ $\checkmark$

23. $\frac{x}{-8} - 7 = -9$

$\frac{x}{-8} - 7 + 7 = -9 + 7$

$\frac{x}{-8} = -2$

$(-8)\left(\frac{x}{-8}\right) = (-8)(-2)$

$x = 16$

Check: $-\frac{x}{8} - 7 = -9$

$\frac{16}{-8} - 7 = -9$

$-2 - 7 = -9$

$-9 = -9$ $\checkmark$

24. $1.2 = 3s - 1.8$

$1.2 + 1.8 = 3s - 1.8 + 1.8$

$3 = 3s$

$\frac{3}{3} = \frac{3s}{3}$

$1 = s$

Check: $1.2 = 3s - 1.8$

$1.2 = 3(1) - 1.8$

$1.2 = 3 - 1.8$

$1.2 = 1.2$ $\checkmark$

25. $\frac{y}{4.5} - 9 = 3.5$

$\frac{y}{4.5} - 9 + 9 = 3.5 + 9$

$\frac{y}{4.5} = 12.5$

$4.5\left(\frac{y}{4.5}\right) = 4.5(12.5)$

$4.5 \boxed{\times} 12.5 \boxed{=} \mathbf{56.25}$

$y = 56.25$

Check: $\frac{y}{4.5} - 9 = 3.5$

$\frac{56.25}{4.5} - 9 = 3.5$

$12.5 - 9 = 3.5$

$3.5 = 3.5$ $\checkmark$

26. Answers may vary. Sample: The first is a two-step equation, and the second is a one-step equation. You must add 9 to both sides and then divide both sides by 3 to solve $3v - 9 = 12$. To solve $3v = 12$, you only divide by 3.

Real-life situations:

$3v - 9 = 12 \rightarrow$ Sample: Mrs. Woods placed a $9 deposit on three tickets for the school musical. If she owes $12, how much is each ticket?

$3v = 12 \rightarrow$ Sample: Mrs. Woods bought 3 tickets for $12. How much was each ticket?

27. $\qquad 428 = 408p + 408$

$428 - 408 = 408p + 408 - 408$

$\qquad 20 = 408p$

$\qquad \frac{20}{408} = \frac{408p}{408}$

$20 \boxed{\div} 408 \boxed{=} \textbf{0.0490196}$

$\qquad 0.05 \approx p$

$\qquad 0.05 = 0.05(100)\%$ or 5%

The percent of increase is about 5%.

28. weight × distance on one side =
weight × distance on the other side

2 oz × 6 in. = cat's weight × 4

$2 \times 6 = c \times 4$

$\qquad 12 = 4c$

$\qquad \frac{12}{4} = \frac{4c}{4}$

$\qquad 3 = c$

The cat should weigh 3 oz.

Mixed Review p. 160

1. $20 \cdot 9 \cdot 5$

$= (20 \cdot 5) \cdot 9$

$= 100 \cdot 9$

$= 900$

2. $15 + 42 + 35$

$= (15 + 35) + 42$

$= 50 + 42$

$= 92$

3. $18m = 162$

$\qquad \frac{18m}{18} = \frac{162}{18}$

$\qquad m = 9$

4. $\qquad 27 = \frac{x}{5.6}$

$27(5.6) = (5.6)\left(\frac{x}{5.6}\right)$

$27 \boxed{\times} 5.6 \boxed{=} \textbf{151.2}$

$\qquad 151.2 = x$

5. $-241.93 = -13z$

$\qquad \frac{-241.93}{-13} = \frac{-13z}{-13}$

$241.93 \boxed{+/-} \boxed{\div} 13 \boxed{+/-} \boxed{=} \textbf{18.61}$

$\qquad 18.61 = z$

6. $\qquad \frac{173.7}{c} = 19.3$

$c\left(\frac{173.7}{c}\right) = c(19.3)$

$\qquad 173.7 = 19.3c$

$\qquad \frac{173.7}{19.3} = \frac{19.3c}{19.3}$

$173.7 \boxed{\div} 19.3 \boxed{=} \textbf{9}$

$\qquad 9 = c$

7. Let m represent the amount of money Jodie had to start with.

Amount spent at amusement park: $\frac{1}{3}m$

Remainder: $\frac{2}{3}m$

Amount spent on a new shirt:

$\frac{1}{2}$ of remainder: $\frac{1}{2}\left(\frac{2}{3}m\right) = \frac{1}{3}m$

Jodie has $m - \frac{1}{3}m - \frac{1}{3}m$ or $\frac{1}{3}m$ left over.

$\qquad \frac{1}{3}m = 15$

$\qquad \frac{m}{3} = 15$

$\qquad 3\left(\frac{m}{3}\right) = 3(15)$

$\qquad m = 45$

Jodie started out with $45.

4-5 Write an Equation

Pages 161–163

1. a. $269.95

b. Paying $100 at the start.

c. He will pay the remaining $269.95 − $100 or $169.95 in five equal payments over the next five months.

The payment will be $\frac{\$169.95}{5}$ or $33.99 each month for five months.

   d. Leroy will buy a camera that costs $269.95 by making a down payment of $100 and making five monthly payments of $33.99 each.

2. subtraction and division

3.
$$100 + 5p = 269.95$$
$$100 + 5p - 100 = 269.95 - 100$$
$$5p = 169.95$$
$$\frac{5p}{5} = \frac{169.95}{5}$$
$$p = 33.99$$

4. $33.99

5.
$$100 + 5p = 269.95$$
$$100 + 5(33.99) = 269.95 \qquad \text{Replace } p \text{ with } \$33.99.$$
$$100 + 169.95 = 269.95$$
$$269.95 = 269.95 \quad \checkmark$$

6.
$$33.99 \approx 34, \quad 269.95 \approx 270$$
$$100 + 5p \approx 270$$
$$100 + 5(34) \approx 270$$
$$100 + 170 = 270$$
$$270 = 270 \quad \checkmark$$

Try These p. 162

7. a.
$$100 + 3p = 269.95$$
$$100 + 3p - 100 = 269.95 - 100$$
$$3p = 169.95$$
$$\frac{3p}{3} = \frac{169.95}{3}$$
$$p = 56.65$$

The amount of each payment would be $56.65.

   b.
$$125 + 5p = 269.95$$
$$125 + 5p - 125 = 269.95 - 125$$
$$5p = 144.95$$
$$\frac{5p}{5} = \frac{144.95}{5}$$
$$p = 28.99$$

The amount of each payment would be $28.99.

   c. Let m represent the number of months it takes to pay for the camera.
$$100 + 20m = 269.95$$
$$100 + 20m - 100 = 269.95 - 100$$
$$20m = 169.95$$
$$\frac{20m}{20} = \frac{169.95}{20}$$
$$m = 8.4975 \approx 9$$

Leroy would need 9 mo to pay for the camera.

8. C: $185 - 15n = 110$

9. Let n represent the total amount the friends earned shoveling snow. Then $\frac{n}{3}$ represents the amount each friend earned. Asheesh spent $11 on a CD and deposited $15 in a savings account.
$$\frac{n}{3} = 11 + 15$$
$$\frac{n}{3} = 26$$
$$3\left(\frac{n}{3}\right) = 26(3)$$
$$n = 78$$

The friends earned $78.

10. Let m represent the total length of a call.
$$0.35 + 0.14\,(m - 1) = 2.59$$
$$\text{or } 35 + 14\,(m - 1) = 259$$
$$35 + 14m - 14 = 259$$
$$14m + 21 = 259$$
$$14m + 21 - 21 = 259 - 21$$
$$14m = 238$$
$$\frac{14m}{14} = \frac{238}{14}$$
$$m = 17$$

The total length of the call was 17 min.

On Your Own pp. 162–163

11. Let p represent the first page number. Then $p + 1$ represents the next page number.
$$p(p + 1) = 4{,}160$$
Guess and test can be used.
$$p(p + 1) \approx p^2$$
$$p^2 \approx 4{,}160$$
$$p \approx \sqrt{4{,}160} \approx 64$$
Try: $p = 64$
$$p + 1 = 65$$
$$64(65) = 4{,}160$$

The page numbers 64 and 65 satisfy the conditions given.

12. 67 yd = 67(3) ft = 201 ft

$$x + x + 72 = 201$$
$$2x + 72 = 201$$
$$2x + 72 - 72 = 201 - 72$$
$$2x = 129$$
$$\frac{2x}{2} = \frac{129}{2}$$
$$x = 64.5$$

The unknown lengths are 64.5 ft and 64.5 ft.

13. Let n represent the total number of gallons the tank can hold.

$$\frac{3}{4}n = 18$$
$$(4)\left(\frac{3}{4}n\right) = (18)(4)$$
$$3n = 72$$
$$\frac{3n}{3} = \frac{72}{3}$$
$$n = 24$$

The tank can hold 24 gallons.

14. Let n represent the number.

$$\frac{1}{2}n + 2.36 = 9.5$$
$$\frac{1}{2}n + 2.36 - 2.36 = 9.5 - 2.36$$
$$\frac{1}{2}n = 7.14$$
$$2\left(\frac{1}{2}n\right) = 2\,(7.14)$$
$$n = 14.28$$

The number is 14.28.

15.

Item	Initial Amount	Increase/ Decrease	Revised Amount
Music	$500	+$225	$500 + $225 = $725
Refreshments	$750	$-\frac{1}{3}$($225) = $-$75	$750 - $75 = $675
Decorations	$325	$-\frac{1}{3}$($225) = $-$75	$325 - $75 = $250
Supplies	$120	$-\frac{1}{3}$($225) = $-$75	$120 - $75 = $45

The music increased by $225, and the refreshments, decorations, and supplies each decreased by the same amount, $\frac{1}{3}$($225) or $75.

16. Let p represent the number of people between 5 and 24 years old in Pennsylvania in 1991.

$$p = 27\% \text{ of } (11{,}961{,}000)$$
$$p = 0.27(11{,}961{,}000) \quad 27\% = 0.27$$

0.27 ☒ 11961000 ☐ **3229470**

3,229,470 people.

17. A Venn diagram can be used to solve this problem.

Comments	No. of Students	Music		
Students who like		Rock	Jazz	Rap
all three types	④	(4)	(4)	(4)
rock and jazz	④	(4)	(4)	
rock and rap	⑤	(5)		(5)
jazz and rap			(0)	(0)
rock only		②		
rock total	15	4 + 4 + 5 + 1 = 15		
jazz only			①	
jazz total	9		4 + 4 + 0 + 1 = 9	
rap only				③
rap total	12			4 + 5 + 0 + 3 = 12

The number of students who like rock, jazz and/or rap is the sum of the individual amounts circled in the table.

$$4 + 4 + 5 + 2 + 1 + 3 = 19$$

The total number of students polled is 25. So the number of students who didn't like any of these types is $25 - 19$ or 6.

Checkpoint p. 163

1. $9\,(4 + d)$
   $= 9(4) + 9(d)$
   $= 36 + 9d$

2. $-3m + 4 - 5m$
   $= (-3m - 5m) + 4$
   $= (-3 - 5)m + 4$
   $= -8m + 4$

3. $2h + 4(h - 5)$
$$= (2h + 4h) - 4(5)$$
$$= (2 + 4)h - 20$$
$$= 6h - 20$$

4.
$$-7 + q = 4 \qquad Check: -7 + q = 4$$
$$-7 + 7 + q = 4 + 7 \qquad\qquad -7 + 11 = 4$$
$$q = 11 \qquad\qquad\qquad 4 = 4 \;\checkmark$$

5. $16 = -2v \qquad Check:\; 16 = -2v$
$$\frac{16}{-2} = \frac{-2v}{-2} \qquad\qquad 16 = -2(-8)$$
$$-8 = v \qquad\qquad\qquad 16 = 16 \;\checkmark$$

6. $\qquad x - 7.8 = 13.75$
$$x - 7.8 + 7.8 = 13.75 + 7.8$$
$$x = 21.55$$
$$Check:\; x - 7.8 = 13.75$$
$$21.55 - 7.8 = 13.75$$
$$13.75 = 13.75 \;\checkmark$$

7. $\quad 2s + 5 = 12 \qquad Check:\; 2s + 5 = 12$
$$2s + 5 - 5 = 12 - 5 \qquad 2(3.5) + 5 = 12$$
$$2s = 7 \qquad\qquad\quad 7 + 5 = 12$$
$$\frac{2s}{2} = \frac{7}{2} \qquad\qquad\qquad 12 = 12 \;\checkmark$$
$$s = 3.5$$

8. $\quad \frac{b}{-12} = -3 \qquad Check:\; \frac{b}{-12} = -3$
$$-12\left(\frac{b}{-12}\right) = -12\,(-3) \qquad \frac{36}{-12} = -3$$
$$b = 36 \qquad\qquad\qquad -3 = -3 \;\checkmark$$

9. $\qquad 49 = 3.7z - 25$
$$49 + 25 = 3.7z - 25 + 25$$
$$74 = 3.7z$$
$$\frac{74}{3.7} = \frac{3.7z}{3.7}$$
$$20 = z$$
$$Check:\; 49 = 3.7z - 25$$
$$49 = 3.7(20) - 25$$
$$49 = 74 - 25$$
$$49 = 49 \;\checkmark$$

10. Let p represent the number of pencils.
$$0.39p + 1.19 = 3.92$$
$$0.39p + 1.19 - 1.19 = 3.92 - 1.19$$
$$0.39p = 2.73$$
$$\frac{0.39p}{0.39} = \frac{2.73}{0.39}$$
$$p = 7$$
Julia bought 7 pencils.

11. Answers may vary.
Sample: $x + 2 = 0$; $4x + 12 = 4$
Sample situations:
$x + 2 = 0$
At 11 A.M. the temperature hit 0°C. This was 2° warmer than at 7 A.M. What was the temperature at 7 A.M.?
$4x + 12 = 4$
Jon's fruit juice stand lost money for 4 days. On the fifth day it made \$12. If Jon's profit at the end of the fifth day was \$4, how much money did his fruit juice stand lose each of the four previous days?

Mixed Review p. 163

1–3.
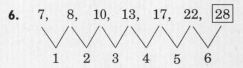

4. $\qquad 80 - \frac{b}{5} = 20$
$$80 - \frac{b}{5} - 80 = 20 - 80$$
$$\frac{-b}{5} = -60$$
$$(-5)\frac{-b}{5} = -5\,(-60)$$
$$b = 300$$

5. $\qquad 158 = 86 + 12a$
$$158 - 86 = 86 + 12a - 86$$
$$72 = 12a$$
$$\frac{72}{12} = \frac{12a}{12}$$
$$6 = a$$

6. $\quad 7, \quad 8, \quad 10, \quad 13, \quad 17, \quad 22, \quad \boxed{28}$

$\qquad 1 \qquad 2 \qquad 3 \qquad 4 \qquad 5 \qquad 6$

4-6 Simplifying and Solving Equations
Pages 164–167

Think and Discuss pp. 164–165

1. There are two groups with variables in them on the left side of the equal sign.

2. $5x + 3 = 18$

3. $5x + 3 - 3 = 18 - 3$
$$5x = 15$$
$$\frac{15x}{5} = \frac{15}{5}$$
$$x = 3$$

4. a.

Add zero pairs.

Remove −9 from each side.

Divide each side into 3 equal groups.

$x = 7$

b. $x - 9 + 2x = 12$

$$3x - 9 = 12$$
$$3x - 9 + 9 = 12 + 9$$
$$3x = 21$$
$$\frac{3x}{3} = \frac{21}{3}$$
$$x = 7$$

5.

$$-7 = (r + 1) + (r + 1) + 3$$
$$-7 = 2(r + 1) + 3$$

Work Together pp. 165–166

Let x represent any integer. $x + 1, x + 2$ represent the next two consecutive integers.

The sum of three consecutive integers is some number n.

$$x + (x + 1) + (x + 2) = n$$
$$x + x + x + 1 + 2 = n$$
$$3x + 3 = n$$

6. $n = 27$

$$3x + 3 = 27$$
$$3x + 3 - 3 = 27 - 3$$
$$3x = 24$$
$$\frac{3x}{3} = \frac{24}{3}$$
$$x = 8$$
$$x + 1 = 9$$
$$x + 2 = 10$$

integers: 8, 9, 10

7. $\quad 3x + 3 = -48$

$$3x + 3 - 3 = -48 - 3$$
$$3x = -51$$
$$\frac{3x}{3} = \frac{-51}{3}$$
$$x = -17$$
$$x + 1 = -16$$
$$x + 2 = -15$$

integers: −17, −16, −15

8. $\quad 3x + 3 = 0$

$$3x + 3 - 3 = 0 - 3$$
$$3x = -3$$
$$\frac{3x}{3} = \frac{-3}{3}$$
$$x = -1$$
$$x + 1 = 0$$
$$x + 2 = 1$$

integers: −1, 0, 1

9. $\quad 3x + 3 = 123$

$$3x + 3 - 3 = 123 - 3$$
$$3x = 120$$
$$\frac{3x}{3} = \frac{120}{3}$$
$$x = 40$$
$$x + 1 = 41$$
$$x + 2 = 42$$

integers: 40, 41, 42

Try These p. 166

10. a.

$$4x + (-8) = x + 7$$

b.

Add 8 to each side.

Remove zero pairs.

Remove an x tile from each side.

Divide each side into 3 equal groups.

$$x = 5$$

11. $-8 = z + 3z$

$-8 = 4z$

$\frac{-8}{4} = \frac{4z}{4}$ Divide each side by 4.

$-2 = z$

Check: $-8 = z + 3z$

$-8 = -2 + 3(-2)$ Replace z with -2.

$-8 = -2 - 6$

$-8 = -8$ ✓

12. $-5y = 12 - 9y$

$-5y + 9y = 12 - 9y + 9y$ Add $9y$ to each side.

$4y = 12$

$\frac{4y}{4} = \frac{12}{4}$ Divide each side by 4.

$y = 3$

Check: $-5y = 12 - 9y$

$-5(3) = 12 - 9(3)$ Replace y with 3.

$-15 = 12 - 27$

$-15 = -15$ ✓

13. $2(z - 1) = 16$

$\frac{2(z-1)}{2} = \frac{16}{2}$ Divide each side by 2.

$z - 1 = 8$

$z - 1 + 1 = 8 + 1$ Add 1 to each side.

$z = 9$

Check: $2(z - 1) = 16$

$2(9 - 1) = 16$ Replace z with 9.

$2(8) = 16$

$16 = 16$ ✓

14. $6d + 1 = 15 - d$

$6d + 1 + d = 15 - d + d$ Add d to each side.

$7d + 1 = 15$ Combine like terms.

$7d + 1 - 1 = 15 - 1$ Subtract 1 from each side.

$7d = 14$

$\frac{7d}{7} = \frac{14}{7}$ Divide each side by 7.

$d = 2$

Check: $6d + 1 = 15 - d$

$6(2) + 1 = 15 - 2$ Replace d with 2.

$12 + 1 = 13$

$13 = 13$ ✓

15. $8 - 3(p - 4) = 2p$

$8 - 3p + 12 = 2p$ Use the distributive property.

$-3p + 20 = 2p$ Combine like terms.

$3p - 3p + 20 = 3p + 2p$ Add $3p$ to each side.

$20 = 5p$

$\frac{20}{5} = \frac{5p}{5}$ Divide each side by 5.

$4 = p$

Check: $8 - 3(p - 4) = 2p$

$8 - 3(4 - 4) = 2(4)$ Replace p with 4.

$8 - 3(0) = 8$

$8 - 0 = 8$

$8 = 8$ ✓

16. $19 = 4(k + 1) - k$

$19 = 4k + 4 - k$ Use the distributive property.

$19 = 3k + 4$ Combine like terms.

$19 - 4 = 3k + 4 - 4$ Subtract 4 from each side.

$15 = 3k$

$\frac{15}{3} = \frac{3k}{3}$ Divide each side by 3.

$5 = k$

Check: $19 = 4(k + 1) - k$

$19 = 4(5 + 1) - 5$ Replace k with 5.

$19 = 4(6) - 5$

$19 = 24 - 5$

$19 = 19$ ✓

17. Let w represent the width.

$w + 7$ represents the length.

The perimeter is 38 cm.

$$(w) + (w + 7) + (w) + (w + 7) = 38$$
$$4w + 14 = 38$$
$$4w + 14 - 14 = 38 - 14$$
$$4w = 24$$
$$\frac{4w}{4} = \frac{24}{4}$$
$$w = 6$$

length: 13 cm; width: 6 cm

Mixed Review p. 166

1. $13x + 4x + 7x = 24x$

2. $18(3h + 11h) = 18(14h)$
$$= 252h$$

3. $6(n + 6) + 4n = 6n + 36 + 4n$
$$= 10n + 36$$

4. $12(-8u) + 13 - 7 = -96u + 6$

5. 4 oz fertilizes 400 ft^2

<u>1 box of fertilizer</u>

    32 oz fertilizes 3,200ft^2

<u>2 boxes of fertilizer</u>

    64 oz fertilizes 6,400 ft^2

You must buy 2 boxes to fertilize 6,000 ft^2.

On Your Own pp. 166–167

18. a.
$$2(x + 4) = 12$$
$$(x + 4) + (x + 4) = 12$$

$$2x + 4 = 12$$

$2(x + 4) = 12$ has 4 more unit blocks than $2x + 4 = 12$. The solutions are different. The solution to the first is 2, whereas the solution to the second is 4.

b.

$$2(x + 4) = 12 \qquad\qquad 2x + 4 = 12 - 4$$
$$2x + 8 = 12 \qquad\qquad 2x + 4 - 4 = 12 - 4$$
$$2x + 8 - 8 = 12 - 8 \qquad\qquad 2x = 8$$
$$2x = 4 \qquad\qquad \frac{2x}{2} = \frac{8}{2}$$
$$\frac{2x}{2} = \frac{4}{2} \qquad\qquad x = 4$$
$$x = 2$$

19.
$$2(1.5a + 4) - 6a = -7$$
$$2(1.5a) + 2(4) - 6a = -7$$
$$3a + 8 - 6a = -7$$
$$-3a + 8 - 8 = -7 - 8$$
$$-3a = -15$$
$$\frac{-3a}{-3} = \frac{-15}{-3}$$
$$a = 5$$

Check: $2(1.5a + 4) - 6a = -7$
$$2[1.5(5) + 4] - 6(5) = -7$$
$$2(7.5 + 4) - 30 = -7$$
$$2(11.5) - 30 = -7$$
$$23 - 30 = -7$$
$$-7 = -7 \quad \checkmark$$

20.
$$5y = y - 40$$
$$5y - y = y - 40 - y$$
$$4y = -40$$
$$\frac{4y}{4} = \frac{-40}{4}$$
$$y = -10$$

Check: $5y = y - 40$
$$5(-10) = (-10) - 40$$
$$-50 = -50 \quad \checkmark$$

21.
$$5(r + 3) = 2r + 6$$
$$5r + 15 = 2r + 6$$
$$5r + 15 - 2r = 2r + 6 - 2r$$
$$3r + 15 = 6$$
$$3r + 15 - 15 = 6 - 15$$
$$3r = -9$$
$$\frac{3r}{3} = \frac{-9}{3}$$
$$r = -3$$

Check: $5(r + 3) = 2r + 6$
$$5(-3 + 3) = 2(-3) + 6$$
$$5(0) = -6 + 6$$
$$0 = 0 \quad \checkmark$$

22. $0.5x + 4 + 2x = 14$

$2.5x + 4 = 14$

$2.5x + 4 - 4 = 14 - 4$

$2.5x = 10$

$\frac{2.5x}{2.5} = \frac{10}{2.5}$

$x = 4$

Check: $0.5x + 4 + 2x = 14$

$0.5(4) + 4 + 2(4) = 14$

$2 + 4 + 8 = 14$

$14 = 14$ √

23. $15 = -3(c - 1) + 9$

$15 = -3c + 3 + 9$

$15 = -3c + 12$

$15 - 12 = -3c + 12 - 12$

$3 = -3c$

$\frac{3}{-3} = \frac{-3c}{-3}$

$-1 = c$

Check: $15 = -3(c - 1) + 9$

$15 = -3(-1 - 1) + 9$

$15 = -3(-2) + 9$

$15 = 6 + 9$

$15 = 15$ √

24. $7m = 9(m + 4)$

$7m = 9m + 36$

$7m - 9m = 9m + 36 - 9m$

$-2m = 36$

$\frac{-2m}{-2} = \frac{36}{-2}$

$m = -18$

Check: $7m = 9(m + 4)$

$7(-18) = 9(-18 + 4)$

$-126 = 9(-14)$

$-126 = -126$ √

25. $0.3t + 1.4 = 4.2 - 0.1t$

$0.3t + 1.4 + 0.1t = 4.2 - 0.1t + 0.1t$

$0.4t + 1.4 = 4.2$

$0.4t + 1.4 - 1.4 = 4.2 - 1.4$

$0.4t = 2.8$

$\frac{0.4t}{0.4} = \frac{2.8}{0.4}$

$t = 7$

Check: $0.3t + 1.4 = 4.2 - 0.1t$

$0.3(7) + 1.4 = 4.2 - 0.1(7)$

$2.1 + 1.4 = 4.2 - 0.7$

$3.5 = 3.5$ √

26. $5s - 2 + 3(s - 11) = 5$

$5s - 2 + 3s - 33 = 5$

$8s - 35 = 5$

$8s - 35 + 35 = 5 + 35$

$8s = 40$

$\frac{8s}{8} = \frac{40}{8}$

$s = 5$

Check: $5s - 2 + 3(s - 11) = 5$

$5(5) - 2 + 3(5 - 11) = 5$

$25 - 2 - 18 = 5$

$5 = 5$ √

27. Let x represent the number of black and white monitors. $3x$ represents the number of color monitors.

$3x + x = 36$

$4x = 36$

$\frac{4x}{4} = \frac{36}{4}$

$x = 9$

$3x = 27$

27 color and 9 black-and-white monitors

28. Let x represent the number.

$2x - 8 = 3x - 16$

$2x - 8 - 3x = 3x - 16 - 3x$

$-x - 8 + 8 = -16 + 8$

$-x = -8$

$(-1)(-x) = (-1)(-8)$

$x = 8$

The number is 8.

29. $m + m + m + m + 5 = 21$

$4m + 5 = 21$

$4m + 5 - 5 = 21 - 5$

$4m = 16$

$\frac{4m}{4} = \frac{16}{4}$

$m = 4$

The unknown lengths are each 4 units.

30. $y + 2y + 5.05 = 10$

$3y + 5.05 = 10$

$3y + 5.05 - 5.05 = 10 - 5.05$

$3y = 4.95$

$\frac{3y}{3} = \frac{4.95}{3}$

$y = 1.65$

$2y = 3.3$

The unknown lengths are 1.65 units and 3.3 units.

31. Answers may vary. Check students' work. Sample:

1. Guess and test can be used to solve an equation. In $x + 7 = 13$, substitute values for x until you arrive at a true statement.

2. Use the properties of equality to add, subtract, multiply, or divide both sides of the equation.

3. Use the associative, commutative, and distributive properties to simplify each side of the equation and then use properties of equality to find the solution.

32. a–b.

	A	B	C
1	x	$3(4x - 55)$	$9(2x + 15)$
2	−5	−225	45
3	−4	−213	63
4	−3	−201	81
5	−2	−189	99
6	−1	−177	117
7	0	−165	135
8	1	−153	153
9	2	−141	171
10	3	−129	189
11	4	−117	207
12	5	−105	225

c. Both B and C increase, but C increases more quickly.

d. Enter additional values of x until $x = -50$. When $x = -50$

$$
\begin{aligned}
\text{B.} \quad 3(4x - 55) &= 3[4(-50) - 55] \\
&= 3(-200 - 55) \\
&= 3(-255) \\
&= -765
\end{aligned}
$$

$$
\begin{aligned}
\text{C.} \quad 9(2x + 15) &= 9[2(-50) + 15] \\
&= 9(-100 + 15) \\
&= 9(-85) \\
&= -765
\end{aligned}
$$

e. $3(4x - 55) = 9(2x + 15)$

f.

	A	B	C
1	x	$2(4x - 5) - 2$	$3(2x + 14)$
2	20	148	162
3	21	156	168
4	22	164	174
5	23	172	180
6	24	180	186
7	25	188	192
8	26	196	198
9	27	204	204
10	28	212	210

$\boxed{x = 27}$

$$
\begin{aligned}
2(4x - 5) - 2 &= 3(2x + 14) \\
8x - 10 - 2 &= 6x + 42 \\
8x - 12 &= 6x + 42 \\
8x - 12 - 6x &= 6x + 42 - 6x \\
2x - 12 &= 42 \\
2x - 12 + 12 &= 42 + 12 \\
2x &= 54 \\
\frac{2x}{2} &= \frac{54}{2} \\
x &= 27
\end{aligned}
$$

4-7 Formulas

Pages 168–170

Think and Discuss pp. 168–169

1. $i = 12f$

2. Sample: feet and yards

$f = 3y$

Try These p. 169

3. Use the area formula for a parallelogram:
$A = bh$ $b = 14$ in., $h = 8$ in.
$A = (14)(8)$
$A = 112$
The area is 112 in.^{2}.

4. Use the area formula for a triangle:

$A = \frac{1}{2}bh$ $b = 12$ cm, $h = 5$ cm

$A = \frac{1}{2}(12)(5)$

$A = 30$
The area is 30 cm^2.

5. Use the area formula for a square:
$A = s^2$ $s = 1.2$ m
$A = (1.2)^2$
$A = 1.44$
The area is 1.44 m^2.

6. a. area for a trapezoid:

$A = \frac{1}{2}h(b_1 + b_2)$

A, b_1, and b_2 are known.
Find h.

$2A = 2\left[\frac{1}{2}h(b_1 + b_2)\right]$ Multiply each side by 2.

$2A = h\,(b_1 + b_2)$

$\frac{2A}{b_1 + b_2} = h\,\frac{(b_1 + b_2)}{b_1 + b_2}$ Divide each side by $(b_1 + b_2)$.

$\frac{2A}{b_1 + b_2} = h$

b. $h = \frac{2A}{b_1 + b_2}$ $A = 133$ ft^2, $b_1 = 11$ ft, $b_2 = 17$ ft

$h = \frac{2(133)}{11 + 17}$ Replace A with 133, b_1 with 11, and b_2 with 17.

$h = \frac{266}{28}$

$h = 9.5$
The height is 9.5 ft.

7. Use the formula for distance.
$d = rt$ $r = 475$ mi/h, $t = 90$ min $= 1.5$ h
      Since the units for rate are expressed in mi/h, the time must also be expressed in hours. 90 min $= 1.5$ h.
$d = 475\,(1.5)$ Replace r with 475 and t with 1.5.
$d = 712.5$ mi

On Your Own p. 170

8. Use the perimeter and area formulas for a rectangle.
$P = 2l + 2w$ $A = lw$
$P = 2(9.8) + 2(4)$ $A = 9.8(4)$
$P = 19.6 + 8$ $A = 39.2$
$P = 27.6$
Perimeter: 27.6 cm; Area: 39.2 cm^2

9. Use the area formula for a trapezoid.
$A = \frac{1}{2}h(b_1 + b_2)$

$b_1 = 28$ in., $b_2 = 16$ in., $h = 9$ in.

$P = 28 + 16 + 9 + 15$ $A = \frac{1}{2}9(28 + 16)$

$P = 68$ $A = \frac{1}{2}9(44)$

                        $A = 198$
Perimeter: 68 in., Area: 198 in.^{2}

10. Perimeter of a rectangle: $P = 2l + 2w$
     $P = 48$ in., $w = 10$ in.
     $48 = 2l + 2(10)$
     $48 = 2l + 20$
  $48 - 20 = 2l + 20 - 20$
     $28 = 2l$
     $\frac{28}{2} = \frac{2l}{2}$
     $14 = l$
length: 14 in.

11. Area of square: $A = s^2$
     $A = 0.64$ m^2
  $0.64 = s^2$
  $\sqrt{0.64} = s$
   $0.8 = s$
length of one side of square: 0.8 m

12. a. Use the formula for distance:
     $d = rt$
     $d = 240$ mi
     7 A.M. to noon: 5 h, $t = 5$ h
     $240 = r(5)$
     $\frac{240}{5} = \frac{5r}{5}$
     $48 = r$
Their average speed is 48 mi/h.

b. $d = rt$

$d = 240$ mi, $r = 40$ mi/h

$240 = 40t$

$\frac{240}{40} = \frac{40t}{40}$

$6 = t$

The time to return home will be a 6 h drive plus a 30-min rest stop for a total time of 6 h 30 min. If they leave at 4 P.M., they will arrive home at 10:30 P.M.

13.

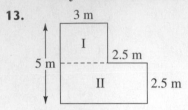

Area of figure = Area I + Area II

I. $l = 3$ m, $w = 5$ m $- 2.5$ m $= 2.5$ m

$A = lw$

$A = 3(2.5)$

$A = 7.5$

II. $l = 3$ m $+ 2.5$ m $= 5.5$ m, $w = 2.5$ m

$A = 5.5(2.5)$

$A = 13.75$

Area of figure = Area I + Area II

$= 7.5 + 13.75$

$= 21.25$

Total area: 21.25 m²

14.

Area of figure = Area I + II

I. $A = \frac{1}{2}bh$,

$b = 24$ ft, $h = 29$ ft $- 16$ ft $= 13$ ft

$A = \frac{1}{2}(24)(13)$

$A = 156$ ft²

II. $A = bh$, $b = 24$ ft, $h = 16$ ft

$A = 24(16)$

$A = 384$ ft²

Area of figure = Area I + Area II

$= 156 + 384$

$= 540$

Total area: 540 ft²

15. $F = \frac{9}{5}C + 32$

a. $F - 32 = \frac{9}{5}C + 32 - 32$

$F - 32 = \frac{9}{5}C$

$\frac{5}{9}(F - 32) = \frac{5}{9}\left(\frac{9}{5}C\right)$

$\frac{5}{9}(F - 32) = C$

$C = \frac{5}{9}(F - 32)$

b. $F = 68$

$C = \frac{5}{9}(F - 32)$

$C = \frac{5}{9}(68 - 32)$

$C = \frac{5}{9}(36)$

$C = 20$

The temperature is 20°C.

16. Make a table of the possible values for a perimeter of 24 ft.

w	l	Area
1	11	11
2	10	20
3	9	27
4	8	32
5	7	35
6	6	36

The greatest possible area for the garden is 36 ft^2.

17. Count the number of completely filled squares. Count the number of half-filled squares; divide this amount by 2. Add the number of filled and half-filled squares (divided by 2).

Completely filled squares: 66

Half-filled squares: 16

2 half-filled squares are equivalent to one completely filled square:

16 halves $=$ 8 whole squares

Total filled squares: $66 + 8 = 74$

Each filled square is 1 cm^2.

74 filled squares $= 74 \text{ cm}^2$

Mixed Review p. 170

1. $C = \pi d \quad d = 7.5$ in.
$C = \pi(7.5)$
$C \approx 23.56$ in.
$A = \pi r^2 \quad r = \frac{d}{2} = 3.75$ in.
$A = \pi(3.75)^2$
$A \approx 44.18 \text{ in.}^2$

2. $C = 2\pi r \quad r = 12$ cm
$C = 2\pi(12)$
$C = 24\pi$
$C \approx 75.40$ cm
$A = \pi r^2 \quad r = 12$ cm
$A = \pi(12)^2$
$A = 144\pi$
$A \approx 452.39 \text{ cm}^2$

3. $3x + 15 - x + 5 = 4$
$2x + 20 = 4$
$2x + 20 - 20 = 4 - 20$
$2x = -16$
$\frac{2x}{2} = \frac{-16}{2}$
$x = -8$

4. $\quad (7 + t)\,6 = 3t + 6$
$42 + 6t = 3t + 6$
$42 + 6t - 3t = 3t + 6 - 3t$
$42 + 3t = 6$
$42 + 3t - 42 = 6 - 42$
$3t = -36$
$\frac{3t}{3} = \frac{-36}{3}$
$t = -12$

5. "Emilia has the same number of sisters as brothers," which means the number of girls in the family is one more than the number of boys.

Let b represent the number of boys;
$b + 1$ represents the number of girls.
"Oscar has twice as many sisters as brothers."
The number of boys Oscar speaks of is $b - 1$.
So, sisters $= 2 \times$ brothers (minus Oscar)

$b + 1 = 2(b - 1)$
$b + 1 = 2b - 2$
$b + 1 - b = 2b - 2 - b$
$1 = b - 2$
$1 + 2 = b - 2 + 2$
$3 = b$
$b = 3$
$b + 1 = 4$

The number of boys is 3, and the number of girls is 4, for a total of 7 children in the family.

Practice

Page 171

1. $-3(x + 5) = -3x - 15$

2. $4n - 5 - 12n = -8n - 5$

3. $3h + 2(h + 1) = 3h + 2h + 2$
$\quad\quad\quad\quad\quad\quad = 5h + 2$

4. $(3s + 2) + s = 4s + 2$

5. $4j - 5j + 2j = 6j - 5j = j$

6. $9q - 2 + 4p - q + 7p = 9q - q + 4p + 7p - 2$
$$= 8q + 11p - 2$$

7. $r - 4.5 = 12$
$$r - 4.5 + 4.5 = 12 + 4.5$$
$$r = 16.5$$

Check: $r - 4.5 = 12$
$$16.5 - 4.5 = 12$$
$$12 = 12 \ \checkmark$$

8. $\frac{x}{4.5} = 12$
$$4.5\left(\frac{x}{4.5}\right) = 4.5\,(12)$$
$$x = 54$$

Check: $\frac{x}{4.5} = 12$
$$\frac{54}{4.5} = 12$$
$$12 = 12 \ \checkmark$$

9. $4m + 3m = 49$
$$7m = 49$$
$$\frac{7m}{7} = \frac{49}{7}$$
$$m = 7$$

Check: $4m + 3m = 49$
$$4(7) + 3(7) = 49$$
$$28 + 21 = 49$$
$$49 = 49 \ \checkmark$$

10. $3c + 5 = 2c - 1$
$$3c + 5 - 2c = 2c - 1 - 2c$$
$$c + 5 = -1$$
$$c + 5 - 5 = -1 - 5$$
$$c = -6$$

Check: $3c + 5 = 2c - 1$
$$3(-6) + 5 = 2(-6) - 1$$
$$-18 + 5 = -12 - 1$$
$$-13 = -13 \ \checkmark$$

11. $8 - 2(p + 3) = 4$
$$8 - 2p - 6 = 4$$
$$2 - 2p = 4$$
$$2 - 2p - 2 = 4 - 2$$
$$-2p = 2$$
$$\frac{-2p}{-2} = \frac{2}{-2}$$
$$p = -1$$

Check: $8 - 2(p + 3) = 4$
$$8 - 2(-1 + 3) = 4$$
$$8 - 2(2) = 4$$
$$8 - 4 = 4$$
$$4 = 4 \ \checkmark$$

12. $-3 = 5a - 22$
$$-3 + 22 = 5a - 22 + 22$$
$$19 = 5a$$
$$\frac{19}{5} = \frac{5a}{5}$$
$$3.8 = a$$

Check: $-3 = 5a - 22$
$$-3 = 5(3.8) - 22$$
$$-3 = 19 - 22$$
$$-3 = -3 \ \checkmark$$

13. $\frac{t}{3} - 15.7 = 12.2$
$$\frac{t}{3} - 15.7 + 15.7 = 12.2 + 15.7$$
$$\frac{t}{3} = 27.9$$
$$3\left(\frac{t}{3}\right) = 3\,(27.9)$$
$$t = 83.7$$

Check: $\frac{t}{3} - 15.7 = 12.2$
$$\frac{83.7}{3} - 15.7 = 12.2$$
$$27.9 - 15.7 = 12.2$$
$$12.2 = 12.2 \ \checkmark$$

14. $2(v - 6) = 18$

$$\frac{2(v - 6)}{2} = \frac{18}{2}$$

$$v - 6 = 9$$

$$v - 6 + 6 = 9 + 6$$

$$v = 15$$

Check: $2(v - 6) = 18$

$$2(15 - 6) = 18$$

$$2(9) = 18$$

$$18 = 18 \quad \checkmark$$

15.
$$15 = (x - 2) - 5$$

$$15 = x - 7$$

$$15 + 7 = x - 7 + 7$$

$$22 = x$$

Check: $15 = (x - 2) - 5$

$$15 = (22 - 2) - 5$$

$$15 = 20 - 5$$

$$15 = 15 \quad \checkmark$$

16.
$$2g + 7 = 8g$$

$$2g + 7 - 2g = 8g - 2g$$

$$7 = 6g$$

$$\frac{7}{6} = \frac{6g}{6}$$

$$g = \frac{7}{6} \text{ or } 1.1\overline{6}$$

Check: $2g + 7 = 8g$

$$2\left(\frac{7}{6}\right) + 7 = 8\left(\frac{7}{6}\right)$$

$$\frac{7}{3} + \frac{21}{3} = \frac{28}{3}$$

$$\frac{28}{3} = \frac{28}{3} \quad \checkmark$$

17.
$$b - \frac{1}{2} = \frac{3}{4}$$

$$b - \frac{1}{2} + \frac{1}{2} = \frac{3}{4} + \frac{1}{2}$$

$$b = \frac{3}{4} + \frac{2}{4}$$

$$b = \frac{5}{4} \text{ or } 1.25$$

Check: $b - \frac{1}{2} = \frac{3}{4}$

$$\frac{5}{4} - \frac{1}{2} = \frac{3}{4}$$

$$\frac{5}{4} - \frac{2}{4} = \frac{3}{4}$$

$$\frac{3}{4} = \frac{3}{4} \quad \checkmark$$

18. $4.5w = 9$

$$\frac{4.5w}{4.5} = \frac{9}{4.5}$$

$$w = 2$$

Check: $4.5w = 9$

$$4.5(2) = 9$$

$$9 = 9 \quad \checkmark$$

19. Area of figure = Area I + Area II

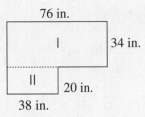

76 in.

34 in.

20 in.

38 in.

I. $A = lw, l = 76, w = 34$

$$A = 76 \cdot 34$$

$$= 2,584$$

II. $A = lw, l = 38, w = 20$

$$A = 38 \cdot 20$$

$$= 760$$

Area of figure = Area I + Area II

$$= 2,584 + 760$$

$$= 3,344$$

Area: 3,344 in.^{2}

20. Area of trapezoid: $A = \frac{1}{2}h(b_1 + b_2)$

$$h = 4.32 \text{ cm}, b_1 = 6.08 \text{ cm}, b_2 = 3.52 \text{ cm}$$

$$A = \frac{1}{2}(4.32)(6.08 + 3.52) = 0.5(4.32)(6.08 + 3.52)$$

$$0.5 \boxed{\times} 4.32 \boxed{\times} \boxed{(} 6.08 \boxed{+} 3.52 \boxed{)} \boxed{=} \mathbf{20.736}$$

Area: 20.736 cm^2

21. Area of parallelogram: $A = bh$

$$b = 27 \text{ yd}, h = 12 \text{ yd}$$

$$A = 27(12)$$

$$A = 324$$

Area: 324 yd^2

22. Let w represent the width.
Use the formula for perimeter of rectangle:
$P = 2l + 2w \qquad l = 12$ ft, $P = 64$ ft
$64 = 2(12) + 2w$
$64 = 24 + 2w$
$40 = 2w$
$\frac{40}{2} = \frac{2w}{2}$
$20 = w$
width: 20 ft

23. Let w represent the number of weeks it will take to complete the purchase.
$$150 + 50w = 995$$
$$150 + 50w - 150 = 995 - 150$$
$$50w = 845$$
$$\frac{50w}{50} = \frac{845}{50}$$
$$w = 16.9 \approx 17$$

It will take Linda 17 weeks to complete the purchase.

24. $\qquad F = \frac{n}{4} + 37 \qquad\qquad$ Find n.

$$F - 37 = \frac{n}{4} + 37 - 37$$

$$F - 37 = \frac{n}{4}$$

$$4(F - 37) = 4\left(\frac{n}{4}\right)$$

$$4(F - 37) = n$$

4-8 Formulas in Spreadsheets
Pages 172–174

Think and Discuss pp. 172–173

1.

h	$8\sqrt{h}$
25	$8\sqrt{25} = 8(5) = 40$
64	$8\sqrt{64} = 8(8) = 64$
96	$8\sqrt{96} \approx 78.4$
150	$8\sqrt{150} \approx 98.0$

2. a–c.

	A Height (h)	B Bottom Speed (v)
1		
2	5	17.89
3	10	25.30
4	15	30.98
5	20	35.78
6	25	40
7	30	43.82
8	35	47.33
9	40	50.60
10	45	53.67
11	50	56.57
12	55	59.33
13	60	61.97
14	65	64.50
15	70	66.93
16	75	69.28
17	80	71.55
18	85	73.76
19	90	75.89
20	95	77.97
21	100	80

d. Answers may vary. Sample:
As h increases, v increases, but more slowly.

e. no

3. a–d.

	A Height (h)	B Radius (r)	C Top Speed (s)
1			
2	80	40	0
3	85	40	17.89
4	90	40	25.30
5	95	40	30.98
6	100	40	35.78
7	105	40	40
8	110	40	43.82
9	115	40	47.33
10	120	40	50.60
11	125	40	53.67
12	130	40	56.57
13	135	40	59.33
14	140	40	61.97
15	145	40	64.50
16	150	40	66.93
17	155	40	69.28
18	160	40	71.55

e. Answers may vary. Sample:
As h increases, s increases, although s increases more slowly.

4. a–d.

	A	B	C
1	Height (h)	Radius (r)	Top Speed (s)
2	160	20	87.64
3	160	25	83.90
4	160	30	80
5	160	35	75.89
6	160	40	71.55
7	160	45	66.93
8	160	50	61.97
9	160	55	56.57
10	160	60	50.60

e. Answers may vary. Sample:
As r increases, s decreases.

Work Together p. 173

Answers may vary. Sample: area of a rectangle

	A	B	C
1	Length (l)	Width (w)	Area (A)
2	2	1	2
3	2	2	4
4	2	3	6
5	2	4	8
6	2	5	10

	A	B	C
1	Length (l)	Width (w)	Area (A)
2	1	3	3
3	2	3	6
4	3	3	9
5	4	3	12
6	5	3	15

As one dimension stays the same and the other increases, the area increases by a factor of the dimension that stays the same.

On Your Own p. 174

5. a–c.

	A	B
1	Height (h)	Distance (d)
2	100	12.25
3	200	17.32
4	300	21.21
5	400	24.49
6	500	27.39
7	600	30
8	700	32.40
9	800	34.64
10	900	36.74
11	1000	38.73

d. Answers may vary. Sample:
As h increases, d increases, although more slowly.

6. a–c.

	A	B
1	Speed (r)	Distance (d)
2	0	0
3	5	6.875
4	10	16.5
5	15	28.875
6	20	44
7	25	61.875
8	30	82.5
9	35	105.875
10	40	132
11	45	160.875
12	50	192.5
13	55	226.875
14	60	264
15	65	303.875

d. Answers may vary. Sample:
The braking distance at 60 mi/h is more than three times the braking distance at 30 mi/h.

7. a–d.

	A	B	C	D
1	Deposit (d)	Rate (r)	Time (t)	Amount
2	1,000	0.05	1	1,050
3	1,000	0.05	2	1,100
4	1,000	0.05	3	1,150
5	1,000	0.05	4	1,200
6	1,000	0.05	5	1,250
7	1,000	0.05	6	1,300
8	1,000	0.05	7	1,350
9	1,000	0.05	8	1,400
10	1,000	0.05	9	1,450
11	1,000	0.05	10	1,500

e. Answers may vary. Sample:
As t increases by 1, the amount increases by $50.

8. a. Answers will vary. Sample:

	A	B
1	Time (t)	Height (h)
2	0	0
3	0.5	25.335
4	1	42.67
5	1.5	52.005
6	2	53.34
7	2.5	46.675
8	3	32.01

b. 53.78 ft

9. Answers will vary. Sample:
With a spreadsheet it is easy to hold some variable constant to see what each variable does. A large number of cases can be evaluated quickly. Many values are displayed together to give an overall picture of the formula.

Mixed Review p. 174

1. Let t represent Tim's age.
$3t + 5$

2. $3x + 4y$

3. $P = 2l + 2w$ $l = 5.3$ cm, $w = 3$ cm
$P = 2(5.3) + 2(3)$
$P = 10.6 + 6$
$P = 16.6$ Perimeter: 16.6 cm
$A = lw$
$A = (5.3)(3)$
$A = 15.9$ Area: 15.9 cm^2

4. $P = 4s$ $s = 4.7$ in.
$P = 4(4.7)$
$P = 18.8$ Perimeter: 18.8 in.
$A = s^2$
$A = (4.7)^2$
$A = 22.09$ Area: 22.09 in.^{2}

5. $P = 3s$ $s = 6$ in.
$P = 3(6)$
$P = 18$ Perimeter: 18 in.
$A = \frac{1}{2}bh$ $b = 6$ in., $h = 5.2$ in.
$A = \frac{1}{2}(6)(5.2)$
$A = 15.6$ Area: 15.6 in.^{2}

6. Let n represent the number of nickels, or dimes, or quarters. (The same number for each.)
$0.05n + 0.10n + 0.25n = 10.00$
$0.4n = 10$
$\frac{0.4n}{0.4} = \frac{10}{0.4}$
$n = 25$

    25 nickels: $1.25
    25 dimes: $2.50
    25 quarters: $6.25
       total: $10.00
25 nickels, 25 dimes, 25 quarters

4-9 Inequalities
Pages 175–177

Think and Discuss pp. 175–176

1. a. $-6 < -4$; true

  b. $9 > -2$; true

  c. $5 \leq 5$; true

  d. $-5 \geq -3$; false

2. $y \geq -3$

  a. $-4 \geq -3$; no

  b. $-1 \geq -3$; yes

  c. $-3 \geq -3$; yes

  d. $0 \geq -3$; yes

  e. $\frac{1}{2} \geq -3$; yes

  f. $4.2 \geq -3$; yes

3. infinite

4. a.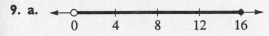

    b. $t > -4$

    c. yes; $-3.5 > -4$

    d. Sample: -4 would be included in the graph, and the inequality would be $t \geq -4$.

5. a. $t < -1$

    b. Sample: the temperature will be below $-1°$; the temperature will be colder than $-1°$.

    c. yes; because $-3.5 < -1$

6. $-4 < m$
Sample: $-3, -2, -1, 0, 1, 2$

7.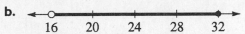

8. B. $m > -4$

Work Together p. 176

9. a.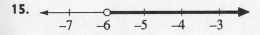

Answers may vary. Sample: The graph doesn't include negative numbers or zero because weight is always positive.

    b.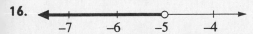

    c. for (a), $0 < w \leq 16$
       for (b), $16 < w \leq 32$

On Your Own pp. 176–177

10. $n > -1$

11. $n \leq 0$

12. $n \geq -2$

13. $n < 2$

14.

15.

16.

17.

18.

19.

20. $k \leq 0$

21. $w \geq 8.75$

22. $b \boxed{<} a$

23. $x \boxed{>} z$

24. a. $d \geq 3$

    b. $l \leq 84$

25. Answers may vary. Sample: Solutions of equalities and inequalities are solutions because they express a relationship between a variable and a number. They are different because solutions of an equation are usually finite, whereas there are infinite solutions to an inequality.

26. $h < 65$

27. $t \geq 90$

Mixed Review p. 177

1. $5(2)^3 \boxed{\phantom{<}} (5 \cdot 2)^3$

    $5(8) \boxed{\phantom{<}} (10)^3$

    $40 \boxed{<} 1{,}000$

2. $(-6)^5 \boxed{} -6^5$

    $-6^5 \boxed{=} -6^5$

3. Answers may vary.
$-40°F = -40°C$
Sample:

	Celsius (C)	Fahrenheit (F)
1		
2	15	59
3	10	50
4	5	41
5	0	32
6	−5	23
7	−10	14
8	−15	5
9	−20	−4
10	−25	−13
11	−30	−22
12	−35	−31
13	−40	−40

4.

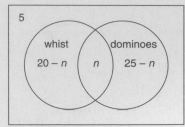

whist: 20 total

    $20 - n$ play whist only

dominoes: 25 total

    $25 - n$ play dominoes only

do not play either game: 5

total people: 30

$$(20 - n) + n + (25 - n) + 5 = 30$$
$$-n + 50 = 30$$
$$-n + 50 - 50 = 30 - 50$$
$$-n = -20$$
$$-1(-n) = -1(-20)$$
$$n = 20$$

20 people know how to play both games.

4-10 Solving One-Step Inequalities

Pages 178–181

Think and Discuss pp. 178–180

1. a. $10 > 8$; true

  b. $10 + 2 > 8 + 2$

     $12 > 10$; true

  c. $10 - 9 > 8 - 9$

     $1 > -1$; true

  d. $10(3) > 8(3)$

     $30 > 24$; true

  e. $10(-3) > 8(-3)$

     $-30 > -24$; false

  f. $10 \div 2 > 8 \div 2$

     $5 > 4$; true

  g. $10 \div (-2) > 8 \div (-2)$

     $-5 > -4$; false

2. a. $-9 < -6$; true

  b. $-9 + 4 < -6 + 4$

     $-5 < -2$; true

  c. $-9 - 1 < -6 - 1$

     $-10 < -7$; true

  d. $-9(2) < -6 \,(2)$

     $-18 < -12$; true

  e. $-9(-2) < -6(-2)$

     $18 < 12$; false

  f. $-9 \div 3 < -6 \div 3$

     $-3 < -2$; true

  g. $-9 \div (-3) < -6 \div (-3)$

     $3 < 2$; false

3. When the same number is added or subtracted from each side of an inequality, the inequality symbol remains the same. When a number greater than or equal to zero multiplies or divides each side of an inequality, the inequality symbol remains the same. When a number less than zero multiplies or divides each side of an inequality, the inequality symbol is reversed.

Mixed Review p. 179

1. $1914 \div 33 = 58$

2. $55 \times 171 = 9{,}405$

3. $18 \le -18$; false

4. $14 > 12$; true

5. $6 \ge m$

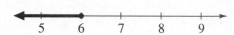

6. $k < 5$

7. Area not covered = Area of sheet of notebook paper – Area of largest circle (with diameter)

$d = 8\frac{1}{2}$ in., $r = \dfrac{8\frac{1}{2}\text{ in.}}{2} = 4.25$ in.

Area not covered $= 8.5(11) - \pi(4.25)^2$

$8.5\ \boxed{\times}\ 11\ \boxed{-}\ \boxed{\pi}\ \boxed{\times}\ 4.25\ \boxed{x^2}\ \boxed{=}\ \mathbf{36.754983}$

Area not covered ≈ 36.75 in.^{2}

Try These p. 180

4. $p + 2 > -1$ $p = -3$
$-3 + 2 > -1$
$-1 > -1$; no

5. $18 > 6j$ $j = -3$
$18 > 6(-3)$
$18 > -18$; yes

6. $-2x \le -14$ $x = -3$
$-2(-3) \le -14$
$6 \le -14$; no

7. $z - 4 > -5$ $z = -3$
$-3 - 4 > -5$
$-7 > -5$; no

8. $-1 \le \frac{r}{-3}$ $r = -3$
$-1 \le \frac{-3}{-3}$
$-1 \le 1$; yes

9. $5c < -10$ $c = -3$
$5(-3) < -10$
$-15 < -10$; yes

10. $m - 4 < -2$
$m - 4 + 4 < -2 + 4$
$m < 2$

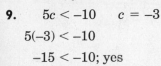

11. $3q > -15$
$\frac{3q}{3} > \frac{-15}{3}$
$q > -5$

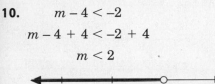

12. $\frac{y}{-4} \ge -2$
$-4\left(\frac{y}{-4}\right) \le -4(-2)$ Reverse the direction
of the inequality.
$y \le 8$

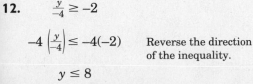

13. $9 > d + 4$
$9 - 4 > d + 4 - 4$
$5 > d$
$d < 5$

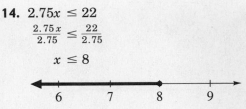

14. $2.75x \le 22$
$\frac{2.75x}{2.75} \le \frac{22}{2.75}$
$x \le 8$

15. $x - 3.4 \ge 2.6$
$x - 3.4 + 3.4 \ge 2.6 + 3.4$
$x \ge 6$

16. Let t represent their total earnings.
a. $t \le 3(60)$
$t \le 180$
b. yes; $140 \le 180$

On Your Own pp. 180–181

17. $5 - x \ge 3$ $x = 2$
$5 - 2 \ge 3$
$3 \ge 3$; yes

18. $5 - x \ge 3$ $x = 3$
$5 - 3 \ge 3$
$2 \ge 3$; no

19. $5 - x \ge 3$ $x = 1$
$5 - 1 \ge 3$
$4 \ge 3$; yes

20. $5 - x \ge 3$ $x = -5$
$5 - (-5) \ge 3$
$10 \ge 3$; yes

21. $5 - x \ge 3$ $x = -2$
$5 - (-2) \ge 3$
$7 \ge 3$; yes

22. $-4t > 20$
$\frac{-4t}{-4} < \frac{20}{-4}$
$t < -5$

23. $-1 < \frac{y}{3}$

$3(-1) < 3\left(\frac{y}{3}\right)$

$-3 < y$

$y > -3$

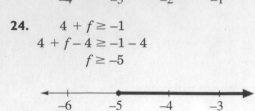

24. $4 + f \geq -1$
$4 + f - 4 \geq -1 - 4$
$f \geq -5$

25. $r - 5 < -5$
$r - 5 + 5 < -5 + 5$
$r < 0$

26. $3 \leq 0.5c$

$\frac{3}{0.5} \leq \frac{0.5c}{0.5}$

$6 \leq c$

$c \geq 6$

27. $w + 1.5 \leq 2.5$
$w + 1.5 - 1.5 \leq 2.5 - 1.5$
$w \leq 1$

28. The properties of inequalities and the properties of equality are nearly identical. Addition, subtraction, multiplication, and division by positive numbers can simplify equations and inequalities. Multiplication and division by negative numbers can simplify equations and inequalities as well, but the inequality symbol has to reverse direction.

29. Let t represent the temperature at 8:00 A.M.
$t + 17 > 65$
$t + 17 - 17 > 65 - 17$
$t > 48$
The temperature was greater than 48°F.

30. Let n represent the number.

$\frac{n}{-3} \leq 15$

$-3\left(\frac{n}{-3}\right) \geq -3(15)$ Reverse the direction of the inequality.

$n \geq -45$

The number is at least -45.

31. Let n represent the score on the fifth test.
$9 + 8 + 10 + 9 + n \geq 45$
$36 + n \geq 45$
$36 + n - 36 \geq 45 - 36$
$n \geq 9$
Amy's fifth test score must be at least 9 points.

32. $a > b$ I. $b < a$ or $a > b$ true
II. $a > b$
$a + c > b + c$ true
III. $ac > bc$ only true if $c \geq 0$
B. I and II only

33. Let n represent the number of tapes.
Estimates may vary. Sample:
$4.95 \approx 5, 37.85 \approx 35$
$5n \leq 35$

$\frac{5n}{5} \leq \frac{35}{5}$

$n \leq 7$

Estimate of the greatest number of tapes that you can buy: 7 tapes.

Checkpoint p. 181

1. $-5(w + 7) = -5w - 35$

2. $6y + 4z - y = 5y + 4z$

3. $r + 4(2 + r) = r + 8 + 4r = 5r + 8$

4. $-1 = 4 + x$
$-1 - 4 = 4 + x - 4$
$-5 = x$

Check: $-1 = 4 + x$
$-1 = 4 - 5$
$-1 = -1$ ✓

5. $-8a = 2a - 30$
$-8a - 2a = 2a - 30 - 2a$
$-10a = -30$

$\frac{-10a}{-10} = \frac{-30}{-10}$

$a = 3$

Check: $-8a = 2a - 30$
$-8(3) = 2(3) - 30$
$-24 = 6 - 30$
$-24 = -24$ ✓

6. $-16 = 5(g - 2) + 1$
$-16 = 5g - 10 + 1$
$-16 = 5g - 9$
$-16 + 9 = 5g - 9 + 9$
$-7 = 5g$
$\frac{-7}{5} = \frac{5g}{5}$
$g = -\frac{7}{5}$ or -1.4

Check: $-16 = 5(g - 2) + 1$
$-16 = 5(-1.4 - 2) + 1$
$-16 = 5(-3.4) + 1$
$-16 = -17 + 1$
$-16 = -16$ √

7. $n - 8 < -3$
$n - 8 + 8 < -3 + 8$
$n < 5$

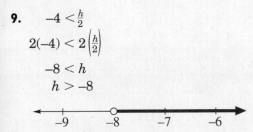

8. $-6d \geq 18$
$\frac{-6d}{-6} \geq \frac{18}{-6}$
$d \leq -3$

9. $-4 < \frac{h}{2}$
$2(-4) < 2\left(\frac{h}{2}\right)$
$-8 < h$
$h > -8$

10. Let m represent the number of miles he drove.

$27.95 + 0.14m = 45.73$
$27.95 + 0.14m - 27.95 = 45.73 - 27.95$
$0.14m = 17.78$
$\frac{0.14m}{0.14} = \frac{17.78}{0.14}$
$m = 127$

Dan drove 127 mi.

11. $370 + s > 425$

4-11 Solving Two-Step Inequalities
Pages 182–185

Think and Discuss pp. 182–183

1. a. $-2n = 14$
$\frac{-2n}{-2} = \frac{14}{-2}$
$n = -7$

b. $-2n - 5 = 9$
$-2n - 5 + 5 = 9 + 5$
$-2n = 14$
$n = -7$

c. Part (a) is a one-step equation. To solve it, divide each side by -2.
$-2n = 14$
$\frac{-2n}{-2} = \frac{14}{-2}$
$n = -7$

Part (b) is a two-step equation. To solve it, first add 5 to each side, then divide each side by -2.
$-2n - 5 = 9$
$-2n - 5 + 5 = 9 + 5$
$\frac{-2n}{-2} = \frac{14}{-2}$
$n = -7$

d. Perform addition and subtraction first. If you divide first, you could end up working with fractions.
Sample: $2x + 1 = 3$
$\frac{2x}{2} + \frac{1}{2} = \frac{3}{2}$
$x + \frac{1}{2} - \frac{1}{2} = \frac{3}{2} - \frac{1}{2}$
$x = 1$

2. $2n - 5 < 9$
$2n - 5 + 5 < 9 + 5$
$2n < 14$
$\frac{2n}{2} < \frac{14}{2}$
$n < 7$

3. Answers may vary. Sample: To solve, you need to find v, not the opposite of v.

4. a. $s \leq 4$
$s = -2, -2 \leq 4$, yes
$s = 1.5, 1.5 \leq 4$, yes

b. Answers may vary. Sample: because you cannot buy negative or fractional T-shirts.

Work Together p. 183

5. $-3n + 2 > -10$

$-3n + 2 - 2 > -10 - 2$

$-3n > -12$

$\frac{-3n}{-3} < \frac{-12}{-3}$

$n < 4$

a. where n is any number

$n < 4$

b. where n is a positive number

$0 < n < 4$

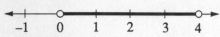

c. where n is a positive integer

$n = 1, 2, 3, 4$

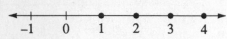

d. where n is a negative integer

$n = -1, -2, -3, -4, -5, \ldots$

Mixed Review p. 183

1. $65 + 17 + 35 + 3$

$= (65 + 35) + (17 + 3)$

$= 100 + 20$

$= 120$

2. $5(220)$

$= 5(200 + 20)$

$= 1000 + 100$

$= 1,100$

3. $n + 9 > -3$

$n + 9 - 9 > -3 - 9$

$n > -12$

Check: $n = 0$

$n + 9 > -3$

$0 + 9 > -3$

$9 > -3$ true

4. $48 = 14(s + 3) - 36$

$48 = 14s + 42 - 36$

$48 = 14s + 6$

$48 - 6 = 14s + 6 - 6$

$\frac{42}{14} = \frac{14s}{14}$

$3 = s$

Check: $48 = 14(s + 3) - 36$

$48 = 14(3 + 3) - 36$

$48 = 14(6) - 36$

$48 = 84 - 36$

$48 = 48$ $\checkmark$

5. $\frac{55}{968} = \frac{35}{x}$

$55x = 35 \cdot 968$

$x = \frac{35 \cdot 968}{55}$

$x = 616$

A car going 35 mi/h travels 616 in./s.

Try These p. 184

6. $-4d + 8 \le 15$ $d = -1$

$-4(-1) + 8 \le 15$

$4 + 8 \le 15$

$12 \le 15$; yes

7. $3z - 6 > -9$ $z = -1$

$3(-1) - 6 > -9$

$-3 - 6 > -9$

$-9 > -9$; no

8. $3 - k < 5$ $k = -1$

$3 - (-1) < 5$

$3 + 1 < 5$

$4 < 5$; yes

9. $8 - 2p \ge 10$ $p = -1$

$8 - 2(-1) \ge 10$

$8 + 2 \ge 10$

$10 \ge 10$; yes

10. $5t - 3 \le -2$

Add 3.

$5t - 3 + 3 \le -2 + 3$

$5t \le 1$

11. $-b > 1$

Multiply or divide by -1.

$-1(-b) < -1(1)$

$b < -1$

12. $16 \geq -8z - 8$

Add 8.

$16 + 8 \geq -8z - 8 + 8$

$24 \geq -8z$

13. $4 + \frac{m}{4} < 16$

Subtract 4.

$4 + \frac{m}{4} - 4 < 16 - 4$

$\frac{m}{4} < 12$

14. a. $n + 1$

b. $n + n + 1$

c. $n + n + 1 > 55$

d. $2n + 1 > 55$

$2n + 1 - 1 > 55 - 1$

$2n > 54$

$\frac{2n}{2} > \frac{54}{2}$

$n > 27$

e. 28; 29

15. $-3q + 4 < -2$

$-3q + 4 - 4 < -2 - 4$

$-3q < -6$

$\frac{-3q}{-3} > \frac{-6}{-3}$

$q > 2$

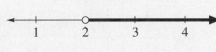

16. $9 - 2x > 15$

$9 - 2x - 9 > 15 - 9$

$-2x > 6$

$\frac{-2x}{-2} < \frac{6}{-2}$

$x < -3$

17. $\frac{a}{-4} - 3 > 0$

$\frac{a}{-4} - 3 + 3 > 0 + 3$

$\frac{a}{-4} > 3$

$-4\left(\frac{a}{-4}\right) < -4\,(3)$

$a < -12$

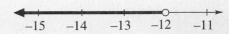

18. $-0.5 \leq \frac{w}{5} + 0.5$

$-0.5 - 0.5 \leq \frac{w}{5} + 0.5 - 0.5$

$-1.0 \leq \frac{w}{5}$

$5(-1) \leq 5\left(\frac{w}{5}\right)$

$-5 \leq w$

$w \geq -5$

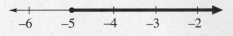

19. Let s represent the amount each student earned.

$3s + 24 > 180$

$3s + 24 - 24 > 180 - 24$

$3s > 156$

$\frac{3s}{3} > \frac{156}{3}$

$s > 52$

On Your Own pp. 184–185

20. $6 - 4r \leq -2$

$6 - 4r - 6 \leq -2 - 6$

$-4r \leq -8$

$\frac{-4r}{-4} \geq \frac{-8}{-4}$

$r \geq 2$

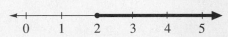

21. $\frac{y}{5} - 1 \geq -1$

$\frac{y}{5} - 1 + 1 \geq -1 + 1$

$\frac{y}{5} \geq 0$

$5(\frac{y}{5}) \geq 5(0)$

$y \geq 0$

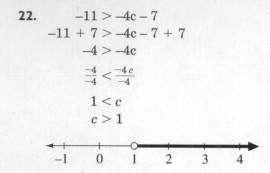

22. $-11 > -4c - 7$

$-11 + 7 > -4c - 7 + 7$

$-4 > -4c$

$\frac{-4}{-4} < \frac{-4c}{-4}$

$1 < c$

$c > 1$

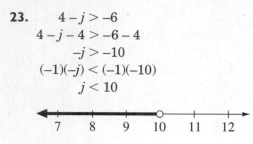

23. $4 - j > -6$

$4 - j - 4 > -6 - 4$

$-j > -10$

$(-1)(-j) < (-1)(-10)$

$j < 10$

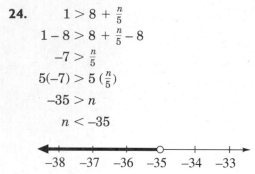

24. $1 > 8 + \frac{n}{5}$

$1 - 8 > 8 + \frac{n}{5} - 8$

$-7 > \frac{n}{5}$

$5(-7) > 5 \left(\frac{n}{5}\right)$

$-35 > n$

$n < -35$

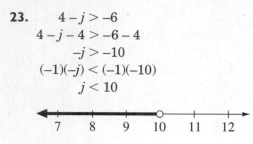

25. $1.5p - 9 \leq -3$

$1.5p - 9 + 9 \leq -3 + 9$

$1.5p \leq 6$

$\frac{1.5p}{1.5} \leq \frac{6}{1.5}$

$p \leq 4$

26. Let n represent the number.

$-2n - 4 \geq 10$

$-2n - 4 + 4 \geq 10 + 4$

$-2n \geq 14$

$\frac{-2n}{-2} \leq \frac{14}{-2}$

$n \leq -7$

27. Let h represent the number of full hours he must baby-sit to earn enough money.

$40 + 4.25h \geq 150$

$40 + 4.25h - 40 \geq 150 - 40$

$4.25h \geq 110$

$\frac{4.25h}{4.25} \geq \frac{110}{4.25}$

$h \geq 25.88 \approx 26$

Ken must baby-sit at least 26 hours.

28. Let s represent the amount of her sales.

$0.02s + 1{,}050 \geq 1{,}800$

$0.02s + 1050 - 1050 \geq 1800 - 1050$

$0.02s \geq 750$

$\frac{0.02s}{0.02} \geq \frac{750}{0.02}$

$s \geq 37{,}500$

Her sales must be at least \$37,500.

29. Let n represent the first odd integer and $n + 2$ represent the next odd integer.

$n + (n + 2) < -11$

$2n + 2 < -11$

$2n + 2 - 2 < -11 - 2$

$2n < -13$

$\frac{2n}{2} < \frac{-13}{2}$

$n < -6.5 \approx -7$

$n + 2 < -5$

The two greatest consecutive odd integers are –7 and –5.

30. Performing the addition and subtraction before the multiplication and division reduces the equation to a one-step equation and simplifies the solution.

31. B; $3y + 5 > y - 7$

$3y - y + 5 > y - 7 - y$

$2y + 5 > -7$

$2y + 5 - 5 > -7 - 5$

$2y > -12$

$\frac{2y}{2} > \frac{-12}{2}$

$y > -6$

A. I is only greater than II when $y > -6$.

B. true

C. $3y + 5 = y - 7$

$y = -6$

I equals II only when $y = -6$.

D. not true

32. a, b, d.

	A	B	C
1	x	$3.1x + 8.4$	$5.3x - 9.2$
2	-5	-7.1	-35.7
3	-4	-4	-30.4
4	-3	-0.9	-25.1
5	-2	2.2	-19.8
6	-1	5.3	-14.5
7	0	8.4	-9.2
8	1	11.5	-3.9
9	2	14.6	1.4
10	3	17.7	6.7
11	4	20.8	12.0
12	5	23.9	17.3
13	6	27.0	22.6
14	7	30.1	27.9
15	8	33.2	33.2

c. Answers may vary. Sample: the numbers in column C are less than the numbers in column B.

d. At $x = 8$, the values in columns B and C are equal. For $x < 8$, the values in column B are greater than the values in column C. For $x > 8$, the order changes, and the values in column C become greater than the values in column B.

e.

$3.1x + 8.4 \leq 5.3x - 9.2$

$3.1x + 8.4 - 3.1x \leq 5.3x - 9.2 - 3.1x$

$8.4 \leq 2.2x - 9.2$

$8.4 + 9.2 \leq 2.2x - 9.2 + 9.2$

$17.6 \leq 2.2x$

$\frac{17.6}{2.2} \leq \frac{2.2x}{2.2}$

$8 \leq x$

$x \geq 8$

f.

	A	B	C
1	x	$4(1.8x - 9)$	$6(1.7x + 4)$
2	0	-36	24
3	-5	-72	-27
4	-10	-108	-78
5	-15	-144	-129
6	-20	-180	-180
7	-25	-216	-321

$4(1.8x - 9) > 6(1.7x + 4)$

$7.2x - 36 > 10.2x + 24$

$7.2x - 36 - 7.2x > 10.2x + 24 - 7.2x$

$-36 > 3x + 24$

$-36 - 24 > 3x + 24 - 24$

$-60 > 3x$

$\frac{-60}{3} > \frac{3x}{3}$

$-20 > x$

$x < -20$

Wrap Up

Pages 186–187

1. $8x + 3(x - 4)$

$= 8x + 3x - 12$

$= 11x - 12$

2. $3(a + 2) + 5(a - 1)$

$= 3a + 6 + 5a - 5$

$= 8a + 1$

3. $4(x - 3) - 3(x - 1)$

$= 4x - 12 - 3x + 3$

$= x - 9$

4. $-2(3x - 1) + 5(x - 2)$

$= -6x + 2 + 5x - 10$

$= -x - 8$

5. Let b represent the number of bagels Randall bought.
$$0.55b + 1.60 = 6$$
$$0.55b + 1.60 - 1.60 = 6 - 1.60$$
$$0.55b = 4.40$$
$$\frac{0.55b}{0.55} = \frac{4.40}{0.55}$$
$$b = 8$$
Randall bought 8 bagels.

6. Let h represent the cost of one haircut.
$$\frac{52}{4} \cdot h = 156$$
$$13h = 156$$
$$\frac{13h}{13} = \frac{156}{13}$$
$$h = 12$$
The cost of one haircut is $12.

7.
$$x - 7 = 23$$
$$x - 7 + 7 = 23 + 7$$
$$x = 30$$

8.
$$x + 3.1 = 4.6$$
$$x + 3.1 - 3.1 = 4.6 - 3.1$$
$$x = 1.5$$

9.
$$x + 8.4 = -1.2$$
$$x + 8.4 - 8.4 = -1.2 - 8.4$$
$$x = -9.6$$

10.
$$-14 + x = -5$$
$$-14 + x + 14 = -5 + 14$$
$$x = 9$$

11. $-1.7y = -34$
$$\frac{-1.7y}{-1.7} = \frac{-34}{1.7}$$
$$y = 20$$

12. $\frac{z}{4} = -2.1$
$$4\left(\frac{z}{4}\right) = 4(-2.1)$$
$$z = -8.4$$

13. $2.5x = -8$
$$\frac{2.5x}{2.5} = \frac{-8}{2.5}$$
$$x = -3.2$$

14. $\frac{w}{3.7} = 20$
$$3.7\left(\frac{w}{3.7}\right) = 3.7(20)$$
$$w = 74$$

15.
$$2x - 5 = 19$$
$$2x - 5 + 5 = 19 + 5$$
$$2x = 24$$
$$\frac{2x}{2} = \frac{24}{2}$$
$$x = 12$$

16.
$$4 + 3q = -6.8$$
$$4 + 3q - 4 = -6.8 - 4$$
$$3q = -10.8$$
$$\frac{3q}{3} = \frac{-10.8}{3}$$
$$q = -3.6$$

17.
$$-1 = \frac{a}{5} + 2$$
$$-1 - 2 = \frac{a}{5} + 2 - 2$$
$$-3 = \frac{a}{5}$$
$$-3(5) = \frac{a}{5}(5)$$
$$-15 = a$$

18.
$$\frac{c}{-3} - 1.6 = 2$$
$$\frac{c}{-3} - 1.6 + 1.6 = 2 + 1.6$$
$$\frac{c}{-3} = 3.6$$
$$-3\left(\frac{c}{-3}\right) = -3(3.6)$$
$$c = -10.8$$

19. Answers may vary. Sample: Use the distributive property to remove the parentheses and combine like terms. Subtract $2x$ from each side to get the variable on one side of the equation. Then subtract 9 from each side. (The final step would be to divide each side by 4.)

20. Use the formula for area of a trapezoid.
$$A = \tfrac{1}{2}h(b_1 + b_2) \quad h = 5 \text{ ft}, b_1 = 3 \text{ ft}, b_2 = 11 \text{ ft}$$
$$A = \tfrac{1}{2}(5)(3 + 11)$$
$$A = \tfrac{1}{2}(5)(14)$$
$$A = 35$$
Area: 35 ft²

21. Use the formula for distance.
$$d = rt \qquad d = 270 \text{ mi}, t = 6 \text{ h}$$
$$270 = r(6)$$
$$\frac{270}{6} = \frac{6r}{6}$$
$$45 = r$$
average rate of travel: 45 mi/h

22. A; Solve each equation for A.

23.
$$5t - 1 \geq 3(t + 7)$$
$$5t - 1 \geq 3t + 21$$
$$5t - 1 + 1 \geq 3t + 21 + 1$$
$$5t \geq 3t + 22$$
$$5t - 3t \geq 3t + 22 - 3t$$
$$2t \geq 22$$
$$\frac{2t}{2} \geq \frac{22}{2}$$
$$t \geq 11$$

24.
$$-3(2b - 5) \geq 4(b - 1) + 2$$
$$-6b + 15 \geq 4b - 4 + 2$$
$$-6b + 15 \geq 4b - 2$$
$$-6b + 15 + 2 \geq 4b - 2 + 2$$
$$-6b + 17 \geq 4b$$
$$-6b + 17 + 6b \geq 4b + 6b$$
$$17 \geq 10b$$
$$\frac{17}{10} \geq \frac{10b}{10}$$
$$1.7 \geq b$$
$$b \leq 1.7$$

Getting Ready for Chapter 5 p. 187

1. $2 - (5) = 2 - 5$
$= -3$

2. $-3 - (8) = -3 - 8$
$= -11$

3. $6 - (-2) = 6 + 2$
$= 8$

4. $-5 - (-4) - -5 + 4$
$= -1$

5. $\frac{3 - 7}{5 - 2} = \frac{-4}{3}$; $\frac{7 - 3}{2 - 5} = \frac{4}{-3}$

Answers may vary. Sample: The second fraction is the first fraction multiplied by $\frac{-1}{-1}$.

Assessment

Page 190

1. a. $9 + 4r - 7 = 4r + 2$

b. $5 + (-12t) + 8t = 5 - 4t$

c. $2(3m - 5) + 6 = 6m - 10 + 6 = 6m - 4$

d. $-4(7f + 2g) - 5 = -28f - 8g - 5$

2. Answers may vary. Samples given. Advantages include that values are calculated quickly, and, since values are given in table form, comparisons can be made easily. Disadvantages include that a computer is not always available, and it may be difficult to choose appropriate beginning values.

3. Answers may vary. Sample: Three soccer players join together to buy a new soccer ball. They each contributed the same amount of money, and they bought a $12 ball. If they got $4 change in all, how much money did each contribute?

4. a.
$$4m - 9 = 27$$
$$4m - 9 + 9 = 27 + 9$$
$$4m = 36$$
$$\frac{4m}{4} = \frac{36}{4}$$
$$m = 9$$

b.
$$-3(h + 7) = -18$$
$$-3h - 21 = -18$$
$$-3h - 21 + 21 = -18 + 21$$
$$-3h = 3$$
$$\frac{-3h}{-3} = \frac{3}{-3}$$
$$h = -1$$

c.
$$\frac{r}{-5} - 3 = 14$$
$$\frac{r}{-5} - 3 + 3 = 14 + 3$$
$$\frac{r}{-5} = 17$$
$$(-5)\left(\frac{r}{-5}\right) = (-5)(17)$$
$$r = -85$$

d.
$$6 + 2d = 3d - 4$$
$$6 + 2d + 4 = 3d - 4 + 4$$
$$2d + 10 = 3d$$
$$2d + 10 - 2d = 3d - 2d$$
$$10 = d$$

5. D; $13s - 3 = 4s + 15$

$$13s - 3 + 3 = 4s + 15 + 3$$
$$13s = 4s + 18$$
$$13s - 4s = 4s + 18 - 4s$$
$$9s = 18$$
$$\frac{9s}{9} = \frac{18}{9}$$
$$s = 2$$

I. $3y = 6$
$$y = 2$$

II. $p - 2 = 0$
$$p = 2$$

III. $17k = 18$
$$k = \frac{18}{17}$$

I and II have solutions of 2.

6. Harvey can walk 1 mi every 14 min and 3.5 mi every 3.5(14) min.

$$t \geq 3.5(14)$$
$$t \geq 49$$

7. A;

A. $25 > -5w$
$$\frac{25}{-5} < \frac{-5w}{-5}$$
$$-5 < w$$
$$w > -5 \qquad \text{true}$$

B. $3x \geq -15$
$$x \geq -5 \qquad \text{not true}$$

C. $-4y > -20$
$$\frac{-4y}{-4} < \frac{-20}{-4}$$
$$y < 5 \qquad \text{not true}$$

D. $2z < -10$
$$\frac{2z}{2} < \frac{-10}{2}$$
$$z < -5 \qquad \text{not true}$$

8. a. $3x + 5 = x + 7$
$$3x + 5 - 5 = x + 7 - 5$$
$$3x = x + 2$$
$$3x - x = x + 2 - x$$
$$2x = 2$$
$$\frac{2x}{2} = \frac{2}{2}$$
$$x = 1$$

b. Let a represent the cost of one apple.
$$15a + 2.75 = 6.20$$
$$15a + 2.75 - 2.75 = 6.20 - 2.75$$
$$15a = 3.45$$
$$\frac{15a}{15} = \frac{3.45}{15}$$
$$a = 0.23$$
Each apple costs \$.23.

c. $4.5 + (3 + d) + (3 + d) = 15$
$$4.5 + 2(3 + d) = 15$$
$$4.5 + 6 + 2d = 15$$
$$10.5 + 2d = 15$$
$$10.5 + 2d - 10.5 = 15 - 10.5$$
$$2d = 4.5$$
$$\frac{2d}{2} = \frac{4.5}{2}$$
$$d = 2.25$$

9. a. $18 > \frac{w}{-9} + 3$
$$18 - 3 > \frac{w}{-9} + 3 - 3$$
$$15 > \frac{w}{-9}$$
$$(-9)(15) < \frac{w}{-9}(-9)$$
$$-135 < w$$
$$w > -135$$

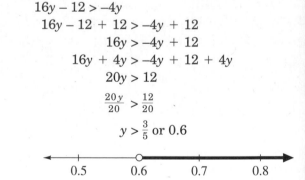

b.
$$16y - 12 > -4y$$
$$16y - 12 + 12 > -4y + 12$$
$$16y > -4y + 12$$
$$16y + 4y > -4y + 12 + 4y$$
$$20y > 12$$
$$\frac{20y}{20} > \frac{12}{20}$$
$$y > \frac{3}{5} \text{ or } 0.6$$

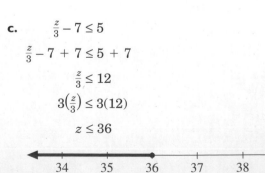

c. $\frac{z}{3} - 7 \leq 5$
$$\frac{z}{3} - 7 + 7 \leq 5 + 7$$
$$\frac{z}{3} \leq 12$$
$$3\left(\frac{z}{3}\right) \leq 3(12)$$
$$z \leq 36$$

d. $\qquad -3 + 4s \geq 4$

$-3 + 4s + 3 \geq 4 + 3$

$\qquad 4s \geq 7$

$\qquad \dfrac{4s}{4} \geq \dfrac{7}{4}$

$\qquad s \geq \dfrac{7}{4} \text{ or } 1.75$

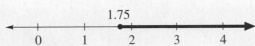

10. $A + 2B = C$

11. Samples: 3, 4, 11; 16, 12, 40

12. $d = rt \qquad\qquad d = 30 \text{ mi}, r = 12 \text{ mi/h}$

$\qquad 30 = 12t$

$\qquad \dfrac{30}{12} = \dfrac{12t}{12}$

$\qquad 2\dfrac{1}{2} = t$

time: $2\dfrac{1}{2}$ h

13. Answers may vary. Sample: Chemists use formulas for different compounds.

Cumulative Review

Page 191

1. C; $2(y + 3) = 2y + 6$

    A. $2(y) + 2(3) = 2y + 6$ equivalent

    B. $(y + 3) + (y + 3) = 2y + 6$ equivalent

    C. $2y + 3 \neq 2y + 6$ not equivalent

    D. $2(3 + y) = 6 + 2y = 2y + 6$ equivalent

2. D; 2 octagons + 1 square:

$\qquad 2(135°) + 90° = 270° + 90°$

$\qquad\qquad\qquad\quad = 360°$

3. C; $3 + 2b^2 \qquad\quad b = -3$

$\qquad = 3 + 2(-3)^2$

$\qquad = 3 + 2(9)$

$\qquad = 3 + 18$

$\qquad = 21$

4. A; $30 + 4m = 60$

5. D; A. $9 = -6w \qquad\quad w = -1.5$

    B. $-10w = 15 \qquad\; w = -1.5$

    C. $4 - 3w = 8.5 \quad -3w = 4.5, w = -1.5$

    D. $-1 - 2w = -4 \quad -2w = -3,$

$\qquad\qquad\qquad\qquad w = 1.5 \neq -1.5$

6. B; A. $-15 + 7 = -8$

    B. $22 + (-19) = 3$

    C. $-8 + (-16) = -24$

    D. $|-11| + (-12) = 11 - 12 = -1$

7. B; A. $\dfrac{1}{2}(60°) = 30°$

    B. $\dfrac{1}{2}(120°) = 60°$

    C. $\dfrac{1}{2}(60°) = 30°$

    D. $\dfrac{1}{2}(60°) = 30°$

8. D; $3(1) + 2(2)$

$\qquad = 3 + 4$

$\qquad = 7 \text{ or } \$7.00$

9. B; $x > y \quad\; y > z$

Then $x > z$ or $z < x$

10. C; Draw a line through X that intersects $\overleftrightarrow{PQ}$.

Chapter 5 Graphing in the Coordinate Plane

5-1 Graphing Points in All Four Quadrants

Pages 195–197

Think and Discuss pp. 195–196

1. red; purple
2. (4, 8); (6, 8); (9, 8); (13, 8); (17, 8); (20, 8); (22, 8); second coordinate
3. (24, 8)
4. (36, 12)
5. Start at the origin. Move 3 spaces to the left and 2 spaces up. The point is J.
6. N; L
7. $(-3, -2)$; (4, 0); (0, 0)
8. a. III
   b. IV
   c. y-axis
   d. x-axis

Work Together p. 196

9. Sample: Go to $(-1, 5)$ and lower blade. Cut to $(-5, 1)$ and raise blade. Go to $(-3, 3)$ and lower blade. Cut to $(4, -4)$ and raise blade. Go to $(6, -2)$ and lower blade. Cut to $(2, -6)$ and raise blade.
10. Yes; answers may vary. Sample: The instructions may begin and end at different points.

On Your Own p. 197

11. E
12. F
13. D
14. I
15. (0, -5)
16. (-3, 3)
17. (-5, 0)
18. (5, -3)
19. I
20. III
21. x-axis
22. IV
23. II

24. a. the letter H

b. Sample: Go to $(1, -1)$ and lower blade. Cut to $(1, -7)$ and raise blade. Go to $(4, -1)$ and lower blade. Cut to $(4, -7)$ and raise blade. Go to $(1, -4)$ and lower blade. Cut to $(4, -4)$. Raise blade.

25. C
26. Estimates may vary. Sample: St. Paul: 93°, 45°. Lincoln: 97°, 41°
27. Sample: (5, 0), (-5, 0), (0, 5), (0, -5). Yes, a circle with radius 5.
28. Check students' drawings.

Mixed Review p. 197

1. $6s = P$
   $6(7) = 42$
   42 in.

2. $3x + 4 \geq 10$
   $3x \geq 6$
   $x \geq 2$

3. $-x - 5 \leq -5$
   $-x \leq 0$
   $x \geq 0$

4. $6x + 3y = 9$
   $3y = 9 - 6x$
   $y = 3 - 2x$

5. $5y - 2x = 10$
   $5y = 2x + 10$
   $y = \frac{2}{5}x + 2$

6. Let w be width. Then length is $2w$.

$P = 2l + 2w$

$84 = 2(2w) + 2w$ Substitute and solve for w.

$84 = 6w$

$14 = w$

The width is 14 cm, and the length $2w$ is 28 cm.

5-2 Equations in Two Variables

Pages 198–201

Think and Discuss pp. 198–200

1. 2 h: Plan A $6, Plan B $7

   5 h: Plan A $15, Plan B $13

2. Answers may vary.

3. a. 3 h worked

  b. $9 earned

4. No; because $2(8) + 3 = 19$.

5. $2(4) + 3 = 11$; $11

6. Yes; for any value of x, one may find a value of y for which (x, y) is a solution.

7. a. No, you cannot work a negative number of hours or earn a negative number of dollars.

  b. $(1, 5)$ and $(2, 7)$, because 1 and 2 are positive numbers.

8. The points appear to lie on a line.

9. Check that the graph of its solutions consists of points that lie on a line.

10. Infinite; there are an infinite number of points on a line.

11. Rewrite each equation so that y is alone on one side of equation.

12. The computation is easier if you choose even numbers for x, since x is being multiplied by $-\frac{1}{2}$.

Try These pp. 200–201

13. $y = 3x + 12$; x must be an integer ≥ 0.

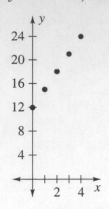

14. no; $3(4) + 9 \neq -21$

15. Table values may vary. Sample:

x	$\frac{3}{4}x - 1$	y	(x, y)
-8	$\frac{3}{4}(-8) - 1$	-7	$(-8, -7)$
-4	$\frac{3}{4}(-4) - 1$	-4	$(-4, -4)$
0	$\frac{3}{4}(0) - 1$	-1	$(0, -1)$
4	$\frac{3}{4}(4) - 1$	2	$(4, 2)$
8	$\frac{3}{4}(8) - 1$	5	$(8, 5)$

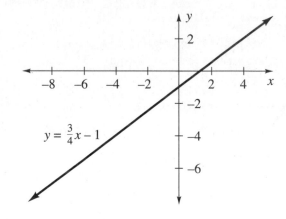

$y = \frac{3}{4}x - 1$

16. $12x + 3y = 3$

         $3y = -12x + 3$

          $y = -4x + 1$

17. a. $0x + y = 3$

$y = -0x + 3;$

$x + 0y = 3$

$x = -0y + 3$

Table values may vary. Sample:

x	$-0x + 3$	y	(x, y)
-2	$-0(-2) + 3$	3	$(-2, 3)$
-1	$-0(-1) + 3$	3	$(-1, 3)$
0	$-0(0) + 3$	3	$(0, 3)$
1	$-0(1) + 3$	3	$(1, 3)$
2	$-0(2) + 3$	3	$(2, 3)$

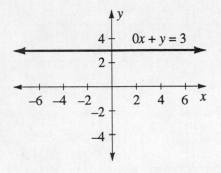

y	$-0y + 3$	x	(x, y)
-2	$-0(-2) + 3$	3	$(3, -2)$
-1	$-0(-1) + 3$	3	$(3, -1)$
0	$-0(0) + 3$	3	$(3, 0)$
1	$-0(1) + 3$	3	$(3, 1)$
2	$-0(2) + 3$	3	$(3, 2)$

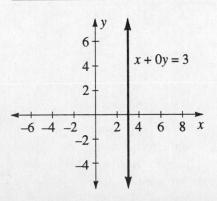

b. a horizontal line; a vertical line

On Your Own p. 201

18. yes; $31 \stackrel{?}{=} -7(-3) + 10$

$31 = 31$

19. no; $59 \stackrel{?}{=} -7(7) + 10$

$59 \neq -39$

20. yes; $10 \stackrel{?}{=} -7(0) + 10$

$10 = 10$

21. no; $46 \stackrel{?}{=} -7(8) + 10$

$46 \neq -46$

22. $3x + y = -5$

$y = -3x - 5$

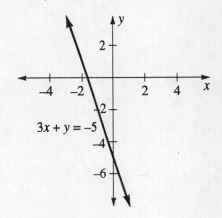

23. $-6x + 2y = -8$

$2y = 6x - 8$

$y = 3x - 4$

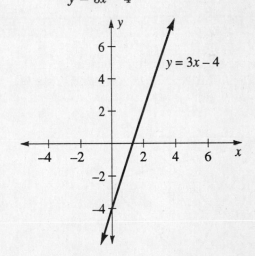

24. $-3x + 2y = 10$

$$2y = 3x + 10$$

$$y = \frac{3}{2}x + 5$$

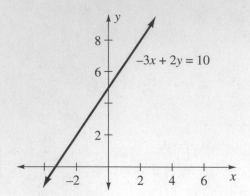

25. $-20x + 5y = 30$

$$5y = 20x + 30$$

$$y = 4x + 6$$

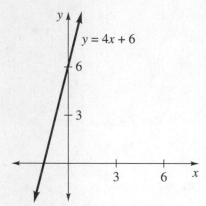

26. Trapezoid; the four lines form a quadrilateral, and $y = x + 3$ and $y = x - 2$ are parallel.

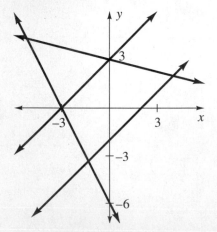

27. A is not, because it does not lie on a line with the others.

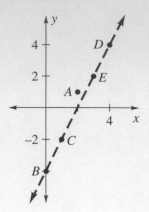

28. a.

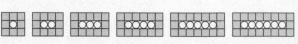

Number of circles (x)	Number of squares (y)	(x, y)
1	8	(1, 8)
2	10	(2, 10)
3	12	(3, 12)
4	14	(4, 14)
5	16	(5, 16)
6	18	(6, 18)

b.

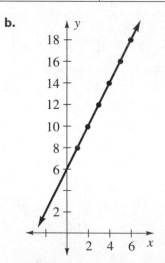

c. 36; For one circle 8 squares are needed. For each circle that is added, 2 more squares are needed. It follows that for 15 circles, we need 8 + 14(2), or 36 squares.

29. Answers may vary. Sample: (0, 150), (200, 168)

Mixed Review p. 201

1. -27; $(-3)^3 = -27$

2. -11; $-2(7) - (-3) = -14 + 3 = -11$

3. y-axis

4. IV

5. 5 packages; $50 \div 12 = 4.1\overline{6}$

5-3 The Graph of $y = mx + b$
Pages 202–205

Think and Discuss pp. 202–204

1. a. Sample: The scores rise by 1 for each basket in the first table, by 2 for each basket in the second table, and by 3 in the third table.

   b. multiply by 1; multiply by 2; multiply by 3

   c. (5, 5); (5, 10); (5, 15)

2. $y = x$: foul shots; $y = 2x$: 2-point shots; $y = 3x$: 3-point shots

3. x = number of baskets; y = number of points

4. Answers may vary. Sample: As the number of baskets increases, the number of points increases. The greater the number of baskets, the greater the number of points.

5. a. d: $y = 3x$; e: $y = 2x$; f: $y = x$

   b. Samples: As the number of baskets increases, the number of points increases. The greater the number of points per basket, the steeper the line.

6. 2

7. 3

8. 1

9. The line becomes less steep.

10. Answers may vary.

11. a. $0 < m < 1$

   b. $m < -1$

   c. $-1 < m < 0$

12. a. The line rotates clockwise around the origin until it is horizontal.

   b. The line rotates clockwise around the origin from the x-axis toward the y-axis.

13. a. M: nothing; T–Th: add 1; F–S: add 2

   b. M: (4, 4); T–Th: (4, 5); F–S: (4, 6)

14. a. x = number of rides; y = cost

   b. M: $y = x$; F–S: $y = x + 2$

   c. M: 0; T–Th: 1; F–S: 2

15. s: $y = x$; r: $y = x + 1$; q: $y = x + 2$

16. Make $b > 2$; make $b < 0$

17. The graph slides up or down the y-axis, intersecting the y-axis at b.

Work Together p. 204

18. a. $m = 2$; $b = 1$

   b. The graph rotates around $(0, b)$ as m changes and the graph slides up or down the y-axis as b changes.

On Your Own pp. 204–205

19. Bianca's plan: $y = 3x + 1$

Trevor's plan: $y = x + 3$

The graph of Bianca's plan is steeper and passes through (0, 1), while Trevor's is less steep and passes through (0, 3). Thus Bianca: k; Trevor: j.

20. a. 4; q

   b. -2; p

   c. $\frac{1}{2}$; r

21. a. -3; f

   b. 4; d

   c. $-\frac{1}{2}$; e

22. a. 2; 3; t

   b. 2; -3; v

   c. -2; 3; s

23. a. I and III

   b. II and IV

   c. I, III, and IV

   d. I, II, and IV

24. Sample: Changing b moves the graph up and down the y-axis without changing the slope of the line. Changing m rotates the line around the point $(0, b)$ on the y-axis. Increasing m rotates the graph counterclockwise, and decreasing m rotates the graph clockwise.

25. 2000

26. Answers may vary. Sample given.

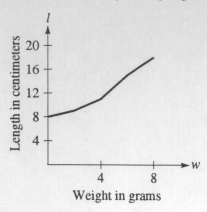
Weight in grams

Mixed Review p. 205

1. ≈ 9.75

2. ≈ 5.29

3. $y = -4x - 3$

Tables may vary. Sample given.

x	$-4x - 3$	y	(x, y)
-2	$-4(-2) - 3$	5	$(-2, 5)$
-1	$-4(-1) - 3$	1	$(-1, 1)$
0	$-4(0) - 3$	-3	$(0, -3)$
1	$-4(1) - 3$	-7	$(1, -7)$
2	$-4(2) - 3$	-11	$(2, -11)$

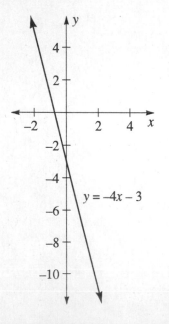
$y = -4x - 3$

4. $-3x + 2y = 18$

$$2y = 3x + 18$$

$$y = \frac{3}{2}x + 9$$

Tables may vary. Sample given.

x	$\frac{3}{2}x + 9$	y	(x, y)
-6	$\frac{3}{2}(-6) + 9$	0	$(-6, 0)$
-4	$\frac{3}{2}(-4) + 9$	3	$(-4, 3)$
-2	$\frac{3}{2}(-2) + 9$	6	$(-2, 6)$
0	$\frac{3}{2}(0) + 9$	9	$(0, 9)$

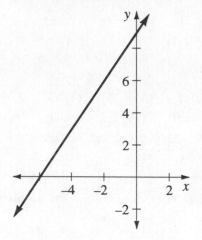

5. Let x be the number of pennies. x is then the number of dimes, of nickels, and of quarters. Thus $1x + 5x + 10x + 25x = 615$

$$41x = 615$$

$$x = \frac{615}{41}$$

$$x = 15$$

Kelly has 15 of each type of coin.

5-4 Understanding Slope

Pages 206–209

Work Together p. 206

1. **a, b, c, d, e, f.** Check students' drawings.

2. Check students' drawings.

3. **a.** b; b and c are both the steepest, but b's stairs are higher.

   b. As the ratio of rise to run increases, the steepness increases.

   c. The ratio of rise to run is the same.

Think and Discuss pp. 206–208

4. $\dfrac{\text{rise}}{\text{run}} = \dfrac{20}{24} = \dfrac{5}{6}$

5. Increase it.

6. Decrease it.

7. Sample: Decrease the rise and keep the run the same.

8. $\dfrac{\text{rise}}{\text{run}} = \dfrac{2}{3}$

9. $\dfrac{\text{rise}}{\text{run}} = \dfrac{4}{6} = \dfrac{2}{3}$; yes.

10. You can choose any 2 points on the line. Try different sets of points.

11. $\dfrac{\text{rise}}{\text{run}} = \dfrac{-3}{4} = -\dfrac{3}{4}$

12. No. The horizontal change would equal positive 5, and the slope would equal $\dfrac{9}{5}$. The value of the slope will be correct if you reverse the subtraction of the y-coordinate also.

13. It's a horizontal line. The rise is always 0, since $\dfrac{\text{rise}}{\text{run}} = 0$, and a fraction is 0 only when its numerator is 0.

Try These p. 208

14. **a.** $\dfrac{\text{rise}}{\text{run}} = \dfrac{4 - (-3)}{3 - 3} = \dfrac{7}{0}$; not defined

    b. a vertical line intersecting the x-axis at (3, 0)

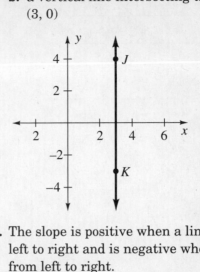

15. The slope is positive when a line rises from left to right and is negative when a line falls from left to right.

16. m must be the slope since it tells us the steepness of the line.

17. $\dfrac{5 - 1}{8 - 0} = \dfrac{4}{8} = \dfrac{1}{2}$

18. $\dfrac{5 - (-4)}{-1 - (-4)} = \dfrac{9}{3} = \dfrac{3}{1} = 3$

On Your Own pp. 208–209

19. C

20. $\dfrac{\text{rise}}{\text{run}} = \dfrac{1 - 0}{2 - 0} = \dfrac{1}{2}$

21. $\dfrac{\text{rise}}{\text{run}} = \dfrac{0}{1} = 0$

22. $\dfrac{\text{rise}}{\text{run}} = \dfrac{2 - 0}{0 - 1} = -2$

23. $\dfrac{\text{rise}}{\text{run}} = \dfrac{1}{0}$; undefined

24. $m = \dfrac{5}{3}$ for the first roof, and $m = \dfrac{8}{5}$ for the second roof. $\dfrac{8}{5} < \dfrac{5}{3}$, so the second roof is safer.

25. $\dfrac{\text{rise}}{\text{run}} = \dfrac{-4 - 0}{10 - 2} = \dfrac{-4}{8} = -\dfrac{1}{2}$

26. $\dfrac{5 - (-5)}{6 - 6} = \dfrac{10}{0}$; undefined

27. $\dfrac{6 - 1}{-3 - (-6)} = \dfrac{5}{3}$

28. $\dfrac{-7 - (-7)}{3 - 2} = \dfrac{0}{1} = 0$

29. **a.** yes; $\dfrac{1}{14} < \dfrac{1}{12}$

    b. $\dfrac{\text{rise}}{\text{run}} = \dfrac{2}{x} = \dfrac{1}{14}$; $x = 28$ ft, since $\dfrac{2}{28} = \dfrac{1}{14}$.

30. Check students' work.

Checkpoint p. 209

1. Tables may vary.

x	$2x - 6$	y	(x, y)
−2	2(−2) − 6	−10	(−2, −10)
−1	2(−1) − 6	−8	(−1, −8)
0	2(0) − 6	−6	(0, −6)
1	2(1) − 6	−4	(1, −4)
2	2(2) − 6	−2	(2, −2)

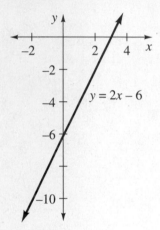

$y = 2x - 6$

2. Tables may vary.

x	$-3x + 2$	y	(x, y)
−2	−3(−2) + 2	8	(−2, 8)
−1	−3(−1) + 2	5	(−1, 5)
0	−3(0) + 2	2	(0, 2)
1	−3(1) + 2	−1	(1, −1)
2	−3(2) + 2	−4	(2, −4)

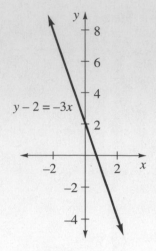

$y - 2 = -3x$

3. $m = -2, b = 4$

Mixed Review p. 209

1. 5

2. no mode

3. (0, −5); when $x = 0, y = -5$

4. (0, 8); when $x = 0, y = 8$

5. $3x + y = \frac{1}{3}$; $y = \frac{1}{3} - 3x$ or $y = -3x + \frac{1}{3}$

6. $4 + y = 3x$; $y = 3x - 4$

7. 1,800 words; $\frac{3}{4}$ h $= \frac{3}{4}$, (60) = 45; 45 min; 40(45) = 1,800; 1,800 words

Practice

Page 210

1. *I*

2. *K*

3. *J*

4. *D*

5. *A*

6. *G*

7. (−5, 1)

8. (−3, −2)

9. (0, 4)

10. (4, −1)

11. (−3, 2)

12. (−5, 5)

13. no; $3 \neq 2(2) + 1$

14. yes; $\frac{1}{2}(-6) + 2(2) = 1$

15. no; $-4 \neq -2 - 6$

16. Tables may vary.

x	$3x - 2$	y	(x, y)
−2	$3(−2) − 2$	−8	$(−2, −8)$
−1	$3(−1) − 2$	−5	$(−1, −5)$
0	$3(0) − 2$	−2	$(0, −2)$
1	$3(1) − 2$	1	$(1, 1)$
2	$3(2) − 2$	4	$(2, 4)$

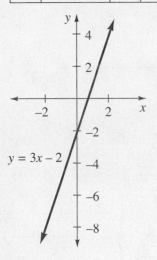

$y = 3x - 2$

17. Tables may vary.

x	$\frac{1}{4}x + 4$	y	(x, y)
−8	$\frac{1}{4}(−8) + 4$	2	$(−8, 2)$
−4	$\frac{1}{4}(−4) + 4$	3	$(−4, 3)$
0	$\frac{1}{4}(0) + 4$	4	$(0, 4)$
4	$\frac{1}{4}(4) + 4$	5	$(4, 5)$
8	$\frac{1}{4}(8) + 4$	6	$(8, 6)$

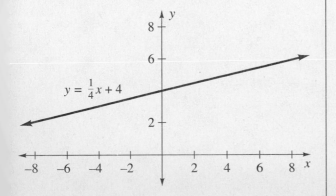

$y = \frac{1}{4}x + 4$

18. Tables may vary.

x	$−2x + 5$	y	(x, y)
−2	$−2(−2) + 5$	9	$(−2, 9)$
−1	$−2(−1) + 5$	7	$(−1, 7)$
0	$−2(0) + 5$	5	$(0, 5)$
1	$−2(1) + 5$	3	$(1, 3)$
2	$−2(2) + 5$	1	$(2, 1)$

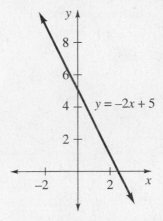

$y = -2x + 5$

19. Tables may vary.

x	$−2x$	y	(x, y)
−2	$−2(−2)$	4	$(−2, 4)$
−1	$−2(−1)$	2	$(−1, 2)$
0	$−2(0)$	0	$(0, 0)$
1	$−2(1)$	−2	$(1, −2)$
2	$−2(2)$	−4	$(2, −4)$

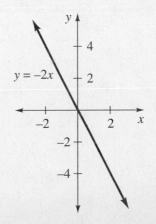

$y = -2x$

20. $m = 1; b = 9$

21. $m = -2; b = 5$

22. $m = 3; b = 0$, since the equation can be rewritten as $y = 3x + 0$

23. $2x + 4y = 12$

$$4y = -2x + 12$$

$$y = \frac{-2x + 12}{4}$$

$$y = -\frac{1}{2}x + 3$$

$$m = -\frac{1}{2}; b = 3$$

24. $m = 0$, since the equation can be rewritten as $y = 0x + 7; b = 7$

25. $m = -\frac{5}{6}; b = -9$

26. $3y = 9 - 3x$

$$3y = -3x + 9$$

$$y = -x + 3$$

$$m = -1; b = 3$$

27. $\frac{1}{2}y + 6 = 2x$

$$\frac{1}{2}y = 2x - 6$$

$$y = 2(2x - 6)$$

$$y = 4x - 12$$

$$m = 4; b = -12$$

28. b

29. a

30. c

31. e

32. d

33. $\frac{4 - 1}{3 - 2} = \frac{3}{1} = 3$

34. $\frac{-2 - 2}{3 - (-5)} = \frac{-4}{8} = -\frac{1}{2}$

35. $\frac{3 - 2}{0 - 0} = \frac{1}{0}$; undefined

36. $\frac{6 - (-3)}{-3 - 6} = \frac{9}{-9} = -1$

37. $\frac{4 - 4}{4 - (-3)} = \frac{0}{7} = 0$

38. $\frac{3 - 2}{-2 - 8} = \frac{1}{-10} = -\frac{1}{10}$

39. $\frac{6 - 3}{5 - (-10)} = \frac{3}{15} = \frac{1}{5}$

40. $\frac{-1 - (-2)}{0 - (-2)} = \frac{1}{2}$

5-5 Using Slopes and Intercepts

Pages 211–213

Think and Discuss pp. 211–212

1. Sample: A member of the opposing team catches the ball.

2. It is cut off.

3. Sample: A line intercepts an axis.

4. The slope is $\frac{3}{2}$, which is the opposite of the y-intercept divided by the x-intercept.

5. Sample:

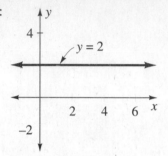

The line is horizontal; 0.

6. Sample:

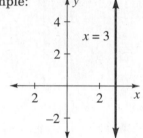

It's a vertical line; its slope is undefined.

7. $-\frac{1}{2}; 6$

8. 1; the coefficient of x is 1. -1; the coefficient of $-x$ is -1.

9. 0; because $b = 0$. 0; because $b = 0$.

Try These pp. 212–213

10. $5x + 6(0) = 30$ $5(0) + 6y = 30$

       $5x = 30$ $6y = 30$

        $x = 6$ $y = 5$

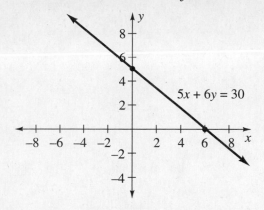

$5x + 6y = 30$

11. $4x - 6(0) = 12$ $4(0) - 6y = 12$

       $4x = 12$ $-6y = 12$

        $x = 3$ $y = -2$

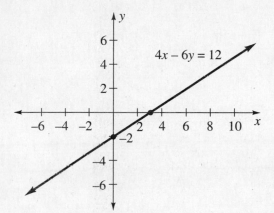

$4x - 6y = 12$

12. $6x + 2(0) = 8$ $6(0) + 2y = 8$

        $6x = 8$ $2y = 8$

       $x = \dfrac{8}{6}$ or $\dfrac{4}{3}$ $y = 4$

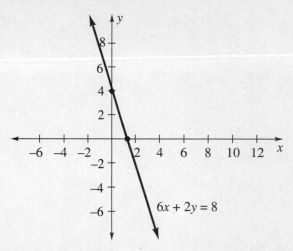

$6x + 2y = 8$

13. $1; -2$

14. $1.3; 5$

15. $0; -8;$ since the equation can be written $y = 0x - 8$.

16.

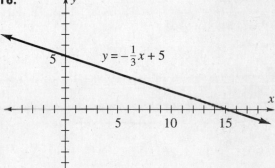

$y = -\dfrac{1}{3}x + 5$

17.

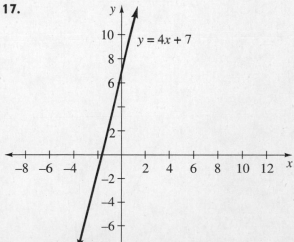

$y = 4x + 7$

18.

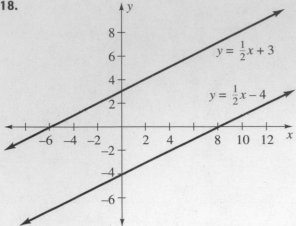

The values of *m* are the same. The lines appear to be parallel.

19. Sample:

1. Make a table of solutions and graph the ordered pairs.

2. Find *x*- and *y*-intercepts and graph them.

3. Find *y*-intercept, graph it, and use slope to find other points. Connect the points to draw a line.

On Your Own p. 213

20. −7; 4

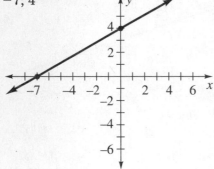

21. −3; −6

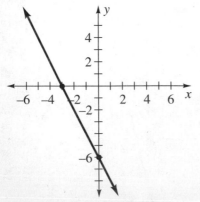

22. 8; 8

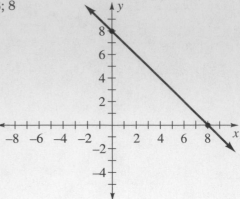

23. $\frac{1}{2}$; $\frac{3}{2}$

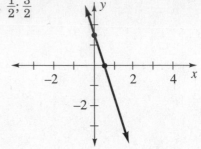

24. The same *y*-intercept: −6.

25.

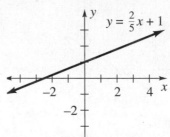

26.

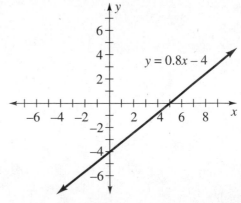

27.

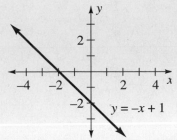

$y = -x + 1$

28. a. $\frac{9}{5}$; 32

b.

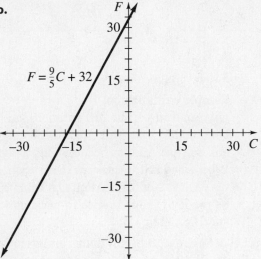

$F = \frac{9}{5}C + 32$

29. C

30. The lines are parallel.

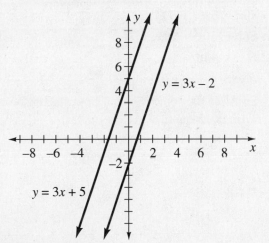

$y = 3x - 2$

$y = 3x + 5$

31. parallel lines

32. intersecting lines

Mixed Review p. 213

1. $3x - 5 = 7$

$3x = 12$

$x = 4$

2. $-2x < 6$

$x > \frac{6}{-2}$

$x > -3$

3. $\frac{-5 - 0}{0 - 5} = 1$

4. $\frac{3 - 7}{4 - 9} = \frac{-4}{-5} = \frac{4}{5}$

5. Sample:

x	$y = -5x + 8$	(x, y)
-2	$18 = -5(-2) + 8$	$(-2, 18)$
-1	$13 = -5(-1) + 8$	$(-1, 13)$
0	$8 = -5(0) + 8$	$(0, 8)$
1	$3 = -5(1) + 8$	$(1, 3)$
2	$-2 = -5(2) + 8$	$(2, -2)$

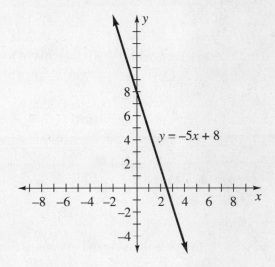

$y = -5x + 8$

6. Sample:

x	$y = 3x$	(x, y)
-2	$-6 = 3(-2)$	$(-2, -6)$
-1	$-3 = 3(-1)$	$(-1, -3)$
0	$0 = 3(0)$	$(0, 0)$
1	$3 = 3(1)$	$(1, 3)$
2	$6 = 3(2)$	$(2, 6)$

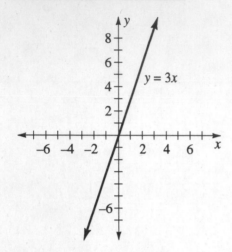

7. Yes. The score may be 9 or 10 to achieve a median of 8.5. Current: 5, 7, 7, 8, 9, 10, 10; Future: 5, 7, 7, 8, 9, 9, 10, 10; median $= \frac{8 + 9}{2} = 8.5$ or Future: 5, 7, 7, 8, 9, 10, 10, 10; median $= \frac{8 + 9}{2} = 8.5$

5-6 Draw a Diagram
Pages 214–216

1. a. 200 ft

   b. 100 ft; the pole is halfway between them

   c. Yes; if the boys walk at different speeds, their distances may vary.

   d. Sample: Two boys are 200 ft apart and walk at the same speed toward each other. After walking 50 ft the second boy turns around and walks back to his starting point. He turns around and starts to walk toward the first boy again. Where do the boys meet?

2. 50 ft

3. They would be 100 ft from the flagpole when they meet.

Try These pp. 215–216

4. a. A: 12 gal; B: 8 gal

   b.

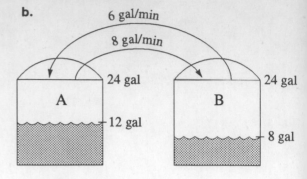

   c. A; B

   d. $8 - 6 = 2$ gal/min

   e. Sample explanation: B is gaining 2 gal/min and will be full when 16 gal have been added to it. But A contains only 12 gal, so that A must become empty before B becomes full. Answers to strategies may vary. Another sample: A table could be made of the amounts in each tank at specific times.

5. Let x be the number of hours elapsed since 7 A.M. So after x hours, Jane has traveled x hours and $40x$ miles, but Alice has traveled $x - 1$ hours and $50(x - 1)$ miles. When Alice passes Jane, their miles are the same: $40x = 50(x - 1)$.

Solve: $40x = 50x - 50$

$$50 = 10x$$
$$5 = x$$

So Alice passes Jane at 5 hours after 7 A.M. This is 12 noon.

6.

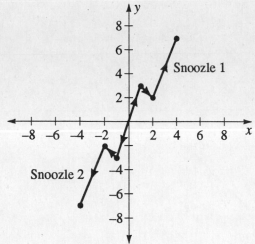

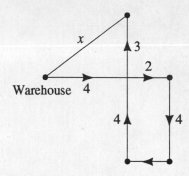

On Your Own p. 216

7. 1st bounce: $\frac{64}{2} = 32$ ft

2nd bounce: $\frac{32}{2} = 16$ ft

3rd: $\frac{16}{2} = 8$ ft

4th: 4 ft

5th: 2 ft

6th: 1 ft

7th: $\frac{1}{2}$ ft = 6 in.

after 7 bounces

8. a. Use the strategy Work Backward. Since the same number of trucks are made each day, the number of trucks must be a multiple of 30, 12, and 20. Try 60. If 60 trucks are made, 2 people are sanding, 5 are attaching wheels, and 3 are painting. Since this is a total of 10 people, it is the solution.

b. 60 trucks

c. no, since the sanders must sand before wheels are attached or painting is done.

9. $3^2 + 4^2 = x^2$

$9 + 16 = x^2$

$25 = x^2$

$5 = x$

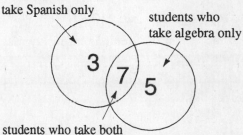

10. Use Guess and Test.

Guess: 7 more quizzes

$\frac{7(10) + 1}{8} = 8.875$

This guess is too low.

Guess: 8 more quizzes

$\frac{8(10) + 1}{9} = 9$

8 is the solution.

11. $x = 8$

students who take Spanish only

students who take algebra only

3   7   5

students who take both

The diagram demonstrates that the number taking Spanish or algebra is 15. Since this is half the class, the class must number 30 altogether.

12. $3 \times 3 \times 4 + 7 \times 2 \times 2 = 36 + 28 = 64$ and $64 = 4^3$. Thus the blocks can be stacked into a cube with 4 blocks along each edge.

Mixed Review p. 216

1. $3; -7$

2. $-\frac{5}{9}; 0$

3.

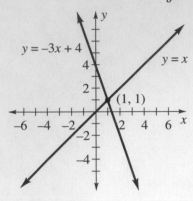

4. $x^2 = 8^2 + 15^2$

   $x^2 = 64 + 225 = 289$

   $x = 17$

5. 364, 1093, 3280. Since the number added to the first number is 3; to the 2nd number is 3^2, etc., the number added to the 5th number is 3^5, giving $121 + 243 = 364$, etc.

5-7 Systems of Linear Equations
   Pages 217–220

Think and Discuss pp. 217–218

1. infinite, since the line has infinitely many points on it.

2. infinite, since the line has infinitely many points on it

3. one

4. No; two lines either intersect at one point, do not intersect, or are the same line.

Work Together pp. 218–219

5. a.

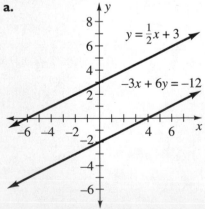

b.

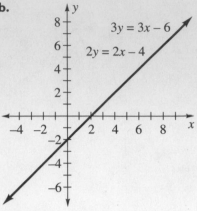

6. none

7. infinite

8. a. Answers may vary. Sample: In the first system, the slopes are the same and the intercepts are different. In the second system, both slope and intercept are the same.

   b. Sample: If the slopes are different, the system has one solution. If the slopes are the same, the system has no solutions or it has infinitely many solutions.

Try These p. 219

9. $(1, 2)$

10. Sample: $(4, 5)$

11. Sample: $(0, 3)$; $0 + 3 = 3$ but $3 \neq 0 + 1$.

12. Yes; $-3 + 1 = -2$ and $3 + 3(1) = 6$.

13. a. $y = x + 3$; $y = \frac{1}{2}x + 5$

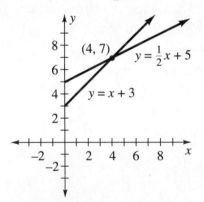

They lift the same amount at 4 mos.

   b. No, there is only one point where the lines intersect.

On Your Own pp. 219–220

14. yes: $-3 = -2(3) + 3$ and $3 - (-3) = 6$.

15. no: $-3(1) + (-5) \neq -2$ and $1 - (-5) \neq 4$.

16. yes: $16 + 2(-6) = 4$ and $16 = -3(-6) - 2$.

17. no solution

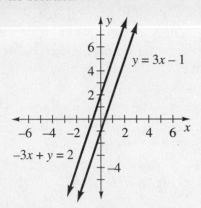

18. $(0, 4)$

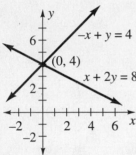

19. all points on the line

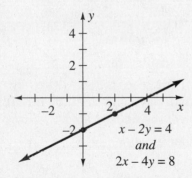

20. There is no point in common to all three lines.

21. at 6 wk; 8 km

Solution: Jan: $d = w + 2$

Ali: $d = 0.5w + 5$

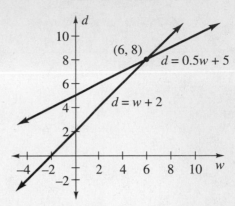

22. $3.8(18.5) = 70.3$

$70.30

23. Sample: Find two numbers whose sum is 6 and whose difference is 4.

Solution: $x + y = 6$

$x - y = 4$

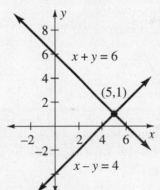

The lines intersect at $(5, 1)$. The numbers are 5 and 1.

24. Answers may vary.

Checkpoint p. 220

1. C

2.

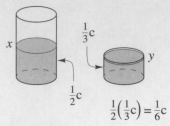

$$\frac{1}{2}\left(\frac{1}{3}c\right) = \frac{1}{6}c$$

Let c be capacity of x. Then capacity of y is $\frac{1}{3}c$. So when we add $\frac{1}{2}$ of y's capacity to x, we get

$$\frac{1}{2}c + \frac{1}{2}\left(\frac{1}{3}c\right) = \left(\frac{3}{6} + \frac{1}{6}\right)c = \frac{2}{3}c.$$

Jar x will be $\frac{2}{3}$ full.

Mixed Review p. 220

1. $s = 5h + 4$

2. $c = 0.50b + 10$

3. parallel or the same line

4. They intersect.

5. Let h be the number of hours spent swimming. Then $9 = 2h + 4h$.

Solve: $9 = 6h$

$1\frac{1}{2} = h$

When they have been swimming for $1\frac{1}{2}$ h, the time is 2:30.

5-8 Using Graphs of Equations
Pages 221–224

Work Together p. 221

Answers may vary.

Think and Discuss pp. 221–222

1. c; y interc. = 20

2. b; y interc. = 0

3. $y = x + 20$

$y = 10 + 20$

$y = 30$

$30

4. $y = 2x$

$y = 2(10)$

$y = 20$

$20

5. Expenses: $y = x + 20 = 30 + 20 = 50$; $50

Income: $y = 2x = 2(30) = 60$; $60

The income is greater.

6. **a.** (20, 40)

b. When 20 cakes are sold, the expenses and income are both $40.

c. If more than 20 cakes are sold, the income is greater than expenses, but if fewer than 20 are sold, then income is less than expenses.

7. Sample: Increase the price of each cake.

8. Sample: It might not, because fewer cakes would be sold.

9. Sample: Yes, if they believe they can sell more than 20 cakes.

On Your Own p. 223

10. A loss; expenses > income.

11. (20, 60)

12. 20

13. Extend graph to show 40 key chains. Then for 40 key chains: income − expenses = 120 − 70 = 50; $50.

14. Sample: There will be a profit when the income line is above the expense line. On the key chain graph, this occurs when the number of key chains is greater than 20.

Decision Making pp. 222–223

1. **a–d.** Check students' work.

e. Sample: You want to know whether people will pay more than the initial expense of the undecorated T-shirt.

2, 3, 4. See students' work.

5. Sample: $7, because the breakeven point for $7 is at 50 T-shirts, and we think we can sell 50 T-shirts.

6. Sample: We will manufacture 70 shirts, because we will make a profit from 70, but we are not sure we can sell more than that.

7. See students' work.

Mixed Review p. 223

1. $8x + 2y = 10$, $2y = 10 - 8x$, $y = \frac{10 - 8x}{2}$,

$y = -4x + 5$

2.

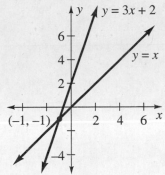

$(-1, -1)$

3.

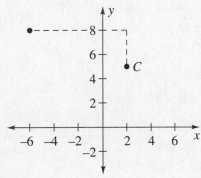

$(-6, 8)$

4. $lw = A$, $(2l)(2w) = 4A$; the area is multiplied by 4.

Problem Solving Practice

Page 224

1. a. Floor: 12 ft by 12 ft = 144 ft² = 144×144 in.² = 20,736 in.²

Each tile: 9 in. by 9 in. = 81 in.²

number of tiles: $20{,}736 \div 81 = 256$ tiles

b. number of tiles of each color:
$256 \div 2 = 128$ tiles

number of boxes of each color =
$128 \div 12 = 10\frac{2}{3}$ boxes. So 11 boxes of each color must be bought.

c. 22 boxes altogether: $22 \times 17.95 = \$394.90$

2. Sample: 3, 7, 11. Range: $11 - 3 = 8$.

Mean: $21 \div 3 = 7$.

3. Let s be the length of the shortcut. Then $2s$ is the length of the long way.

So $s + 2s = 183$

$ 3s = 183$

$ s = 61$

The shortcut is 61 mi long.

4. Let x be measure of the smallest angle. Then the measure of the other two angles are $3x$ and $5x$. Thus $x + 3x + 5x = 180$.

Solve: $9x = 180$

$ x = 20$: smallest angle

$ 3x = 60$: middle angle

$ 5x = 100$: largest angle

$20°$, $60°$, $100°$

5. Let y be the number of the year when the diary is written.

Age (400 years from then) = $145 + 400 = 545$

So in that year: Age + year = 3000

Thus

$545 + (y + 400) = 3000$

$ y + 945 = 3000$

$ y = 2055$ year when diary was written

6. First of all, change all units to inches. Then the piece of wood is 48 in. by 96 in. Thus we can cut the long edge into $96 \div 8 = 12$ 8-in. pieces, and we can cut the short edge into $48 \div 8$ in. = 6 pieces. This makes $12 \times 6 = 72$ 8-in. by 8-in. pieces.

$72 \div 6 = 12$

Then 12 birdhouses can be built, since each one takes 6 pieces.

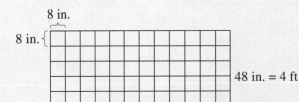

8 in.

8 in.

48 in. = 4 ft

96 in. = 8 ft

7. square

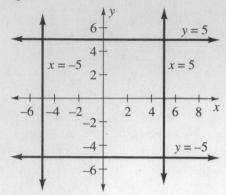

5-9 Translations
Pages 225–228

Think and Discuss pp. 225–226

1. **a.** Sample: A slide moves a figure in a plane without changing its orientation. A flip reflects an object across a line. A turn rotates an object about a point.

   b. Sample: footprints, mirror reflection, seat of a ferris wheel

2. Answers may vary.

3. **a.** B'

   b. $(3, 6)$

4. $(-1, 2)$

5. down 4 and right 4. This represents the change in the coordinates of the vertices of the figure.

6. $D'(0, -1)$; $E'(2, 1)$; $F'(5, -1)$

7. $\triangle DEF \rightarrow \triangle D'E'F'$

8. y coord.; y coord. gives the vertical distance from the x-axis.

9. x coord.; x coord. gives the horizontal distance from the y-axis.

10. Subtract 1 from the x-coord. and subtract 3 from the y-coord.

11. $(x, y) \rightarrow (x + 4, y + 5)$

12. 2 right and 11 down

13. **a.** 6

    b. 2; the lines are parallel and so have the same slope.

    c. $y = 2x + 6$

    d. same slope but different y-intercept

Work Together pp. 226–227

14. hexagon

15. Polygon A is translated up a distance x.

16. congruent

17. **a.** Check students' work.

    b. unchanged or congruent

    c. congruent

    d. congruent

    e. Answers may vary.

On Your Own pp. 227–228

18. 6 units right

19. 5 units left

20. 4 right and 3 up

21. $S'(-5, -2)$; $T'(1, -2)$; $U'(2, -5)$; $V'(-4, -5)$

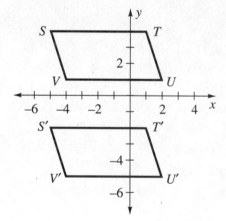

22. $S'(-8, 8); T'(-2, 8); U'(-1, 5); V'(-7, 5)$

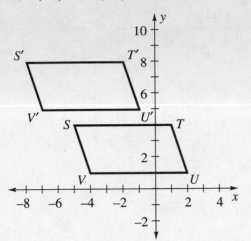

23. Add 5 to the x-coord., and subtract 2 from the y-coord.

24. 7 units right and 11 units up

25. $(1, 5)$

26. a.

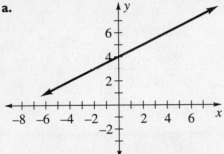

   b. $y - \frac{1}{2}x + 4$

   c. Sample: translate up 4 units

27. a.

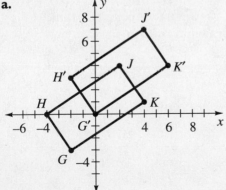

   b. right 2, up 3

   c. $G'(0, 0); H'(-2, 3); J'(4, 7); K'(6, 4)$

28. a. square

   b. See students' work.

29. Check students' work.

30. $3 + 7 - 4 = 6$ right; $5 + 11 - 2 = 14$ up

31. Sample: Translations right and left change x coordinates. Translations up and down change y coords. The size is unchanged.

Mixed Review p. 228

1. Sample:

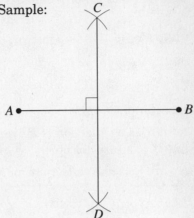

2. Sample:

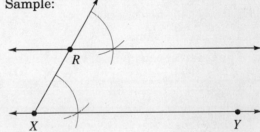

3. $(-9, 4)$

4. Let x be the side of the 1st square. Then $4x$ is the side of the 2nd square. Then
$$x^2 + (4x)^2 = 272$$

Solve:
$$x^2 + 16x^2 = 272$$
$$17x^2 = 272$$
$$x^2 = 16$$
$$x = 4$$

$x = 4$ ft: side of 1st square

$4x = 16$ ft: side of 2nd square

4 ft by 4 ft; 16 ft by 16 ft

5-10 Reflections and Symmetry
Pages 229–232

Work Together p. 229

1. **a.** See students' work.

   b. See students' work.

2. **a.** Distances are equal.

   b. Sample: Each segment is cut into 2 equal parts by the fold and is perpendicular to the fold.

   c. flip; it is like a reflection in a mirror.

Think and Discuss pp. 229–231

3. 3 units

4. y-axis is $\perp$ bisector of $\overline{CC'}$.

5. Sample: a point P' is a reflection of P over a line, if the line is a $\perp$ bisector of $\overline{PP'}$.

6. Sample: They are just like reflections in a mirror.

7. M, E; x-axis is $\perp$ bisector of $\overline{ME}$.

8. The y-axis is not $\perp$ to $\overline{MN}$.

9. The x-axis does not bisect $\overline{JK}$.

10. **a.** They are the same.

    b. The mean of each pair of y-coordinates is -1.

11. **a.** equal

    b. equal

    c. Sample: The size and shape remain the same.

12. K; J; M; L

13. Sample: They are the same, but their vertices are named by different letters.

14. Sample: $\triangle KJM$ coincides with $\triangle KLM$.

15. $\overline{JL}$ and the $\perp$ bisector of $\overline{JM}$

Try These p. 231

16. $H'(-3, -4)$

17. $G'(-2, 7)$

18. $O'(0, 8)$

19. **a.** sign of x-coord. changes

    b. sign of y-coord. changes

20. **a.** Find the $\perp$ bisector of $\overline{T'T}$.

    b. $y = x$

21. **a, b.**

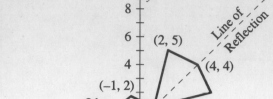
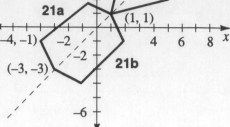

Mixed Review p. 232

1. $6^6 = 46,656$

2. m^6; $m \cdot m^2 \cdot m^3 = m^{1+2+3}$

3. $(7, -5)$

4. $(-6, 6)$; $4 + 2 = 6$ and $-3 - 3 = -6$

5. 1st week: $\frac{1}{2}(480) = \$240$

   2nd week: $\frac{1}{2}(240) = \frac{1}{2} \cdot \frac{1}{2}(480) = \$120$

   3rd week: $\frac{1}{2}(120) = \frac{1}{2} \cdot \frac{1}{2} \cdot \frac{1}{2}(480) = \$60$

   nth week: $\left(\frac{1}{2}\right)^n (480)$

   So in which week does this equal 15?

   Solve: $\left(\frac{1}{2}\right)^n (480) = 15$

   $$\left(\frac{1}{2}\right)^n = \frac{15}{480}$$

   $$\left(\frac{1}{2}\right)^n = \frac{1}{32}$$

   Thus $n = 5$, and we conclude that \$15 is withdrawn in the 5th week.

On Your Own p. 232

22. (3, 0)

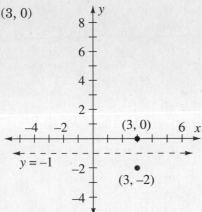

23. (0, 10)

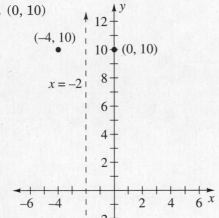

24.

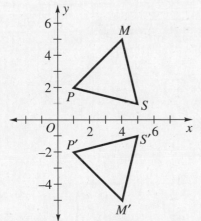

25.

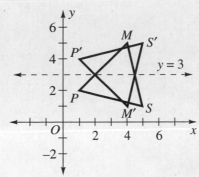

26.

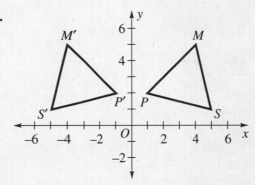

27.

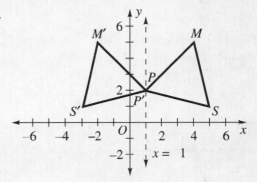

28. a, b.

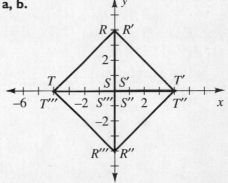

c. It's a square.

29. If you ignore the pole, the vertical line through the center of the flag is the line of symmetry.

30. Lines of symmetry are the two diagonals and the vertical and horizontal line through the center.

31. Sample:

32. Sample:

33. Sample:

34. Sample:

35. infinite; All lines passing through the center of the circle will be lines of symmetry.

36. Sample: A vertical line down the center of the tiger's face will be a line of symmetry.

5-11 Exploring Rotations

Pages 233–237

Think and Discuss pp. 233–234

1. $\frac{1}{4}$ turn; $\frac{1}{2}$ turn; $\frac{3}{4}$ turn

2. 90° counterclockwise or 270° clockwise; 180° counterclockwise or clockwise; 270° counterclockwise or 90° clockwise

3. They coincide.

4. 90°, 180°, and 270° rotational symmetry

5. a. The *x*-coord. of the pt. is same as the *y*-coord. of its image; the *y*-coord. of the pt. is the opposite of the *x*-coord. of its image.

b. Apply pattern for 90° rotation twice; apply pattern 3 times.

6. a. $(a, b) \rightarrow (-a, -b)$

b. $(a, b) \rightarrow (b, -a)$

Work Together p. 235

7.

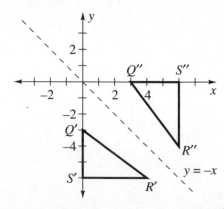

a. Sample: Step 1: Translate 5 right and 1 down.

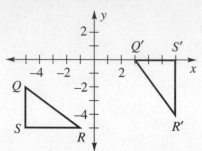

Step 2: Reflect over $y = -x$.

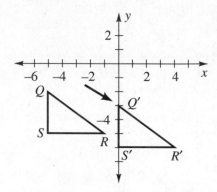

b. See students' answers.

Try These p. 235

  8. 270°

  9. 90°

10. 180°

11.

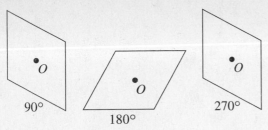

180° rotational symmetry

12.

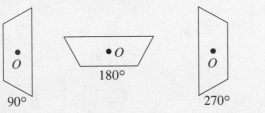

13.

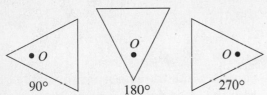

14. H, I, N, O, S, X, Z

On Your Own pp. 235–237

15. $(-3, 3)$

16. $(-2, 4)$

17. $(-3, 5)$

18. A, D

19. 180° rotation   90° rotation

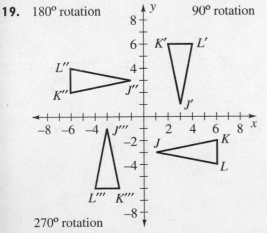

270° rotation

20.

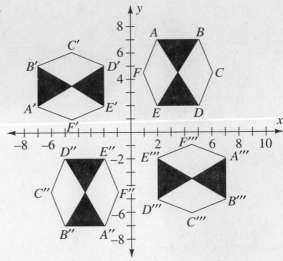

21. Sample: 45°

22. Sample: 225°

23. Sample: 135°

24. Sample: Since triangle I is isosceles and the x-axis is a line of symmetry, you can reflect it over the y-axis or you can rotate it 180° about the origin.

25. reflection about $x = \frac{3}{2}$

26. translation 3 up and 1 left

27. rotation 180°

28. translation 2 right

29. $R(4, 5)$, $S(7, 2)$, $T(5, 0)$, and $V(2, 3)$

30. Answers may vary.

Checkpoint p. 237

  1. a. income

   b. expense

2.

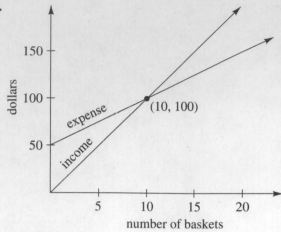

3. (10, 100); after selling 10 baskets, the income = expenses = \$100

4. B (5, −2); since −1 + 6 = 5 and 1 − 3 = −2

5. No; the resulting figure does not coincide with the original.

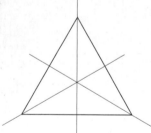

Mixed Review p. 237

1. $9x + 2$

2. $8(z + 7) + 3z = 8z + 56 + 3z = 11z + 56$

3. Sample:

4. Sample:

5. Tina: 1 quarter, 1 dime, 1 nickel, 9 pennies; Tim: 1 dime, 7 nickels, 4 pennies

Chapter 5 Wrap Up
Pages 238–239

1. A

2. F

3. G

4. B

5. $(-3, -2)$

6. $(-2, 3)$

7. $(1, -2)$

8. $(-2, -3)$

9. IV

10. $y = -2x + 3$

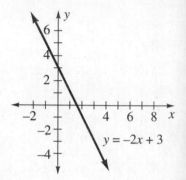

11. Sample: Since the slopes are equal, the line with the greater y-int. is above the other. Thus, $y = -7x + 1$ is above $y = -7x - 3$.

12. $\dfrac{5 - 2}{3 - 4} = \dfrac{3}{-1} = -3$

13. Slope: $\dfrac{3}{4}$; y-int.: 6

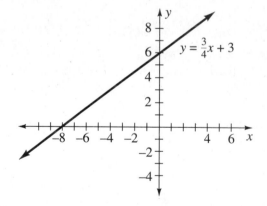

14. Slope: 0; y-int.: −5

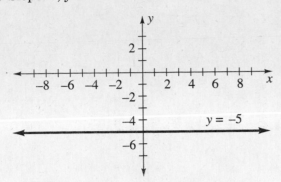

15. C, since the equation, when rewritten as $y = 2x + 1$, shows a positive slope. The other equations show a negative slope.

16. a.

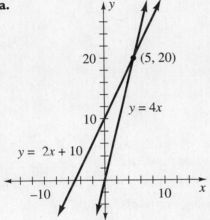

b. (5, 20), which means that after 5 barrettes are sold, both income and expenses equal $20.

17. 90° rotation about origin

18. translation right 1, down 2

19. reflection over x-axis

20. reflection over $y = 1$

21. Sample: an isosceles △

22. 180°

23. 3 pens: 1 yd by 5 yd, 2 yd by 4 yd, 3 yd by 3 yd

Getting Ready for Chapter 6 p. 239

1.

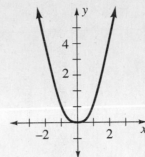

2.

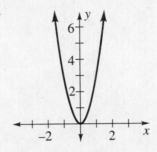

3.

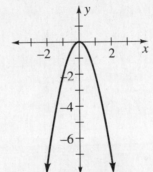

4.

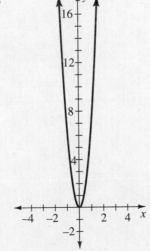

5.

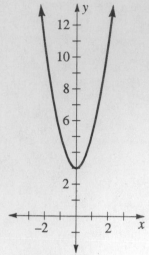

Chapter 5 Assessment

Page 242

1. a. $3; -5$

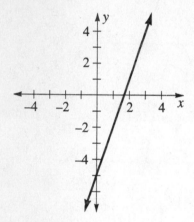

b. $2x - 4y = 12$

$$-4y = -2x + 12$$

$$y = \frac{1}{2}x - 3$$

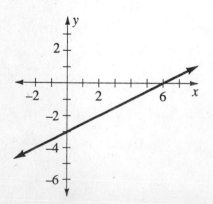

2. D, since the point must be in quad. IV

3. $\frac{-1-5}{8-(-4)} = \frac{-6}{12} = -\frac{1}{2}$

4. v

5. t

6. s

7. r

8. no; $-5 + 8 = 3$, but $2(-5) - 10 \neq -2(8)$

9.

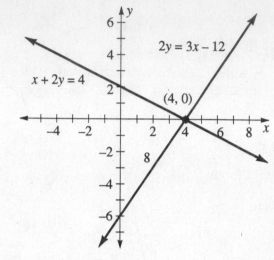

The solution is $(4, 0)$.

10. Sample: $y = x$ and $y = x + 1$. Parallel lines.

11. Sample: an equilateral triangle

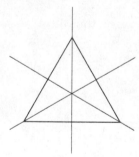

12. 2 cuts + 3 · 2 cuts = 8 cuts

13. Sample: A line with undefined slope is a vertical line, and a line with a slope of zero is a horizontal line.

14. (20, 200), which means that when 20 caps are sold, the income and expenses are equal to $200.

15.

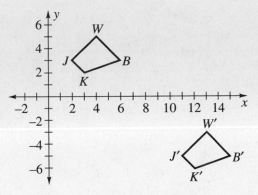

16.

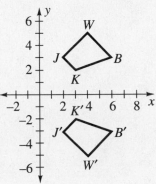

17.

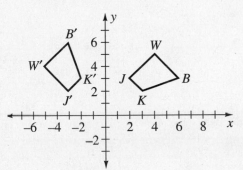

18.

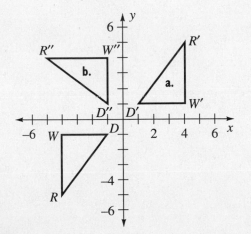

19. Sample: a fee schedule for a taxi service with a flat rate of $.50 plus $1.25 per mi.

Cumulative Review

Page 242

1. A; $2(-2) - 3 < -1$
$\quad\quad 2(-1) - 3 < -1$
$\quad$ and $2(0) - 3 < -1$

2. D; $2^3 \neq 6$

3. B; the formula for perimeter is $P = 2l + 2w$

4. B; since $2x - 3y = -6$ can be rewritten as $y = \frac{2}{3}x + 2$, the slope is $\frac{2}{3}$.

5. B; x and y are 90°, since one is the supplement of 90°, and the other is an angle inscribed in a semi-circle.

6. C; since changes over the months for one year are being compared with those from the previous year.

7. D; the reflection is over the line $x = 1$.

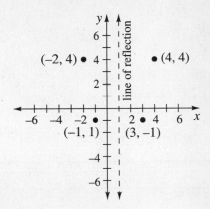

8. C

There are $(5 - 2)180°$, or 540°, in a pentagon. One angle of a regular pentagon measures $\frac{540°}{5}$, or 108°. Since 360 is not divisible by 108, a regular pentagon cannot tessellate the plane by itself.

9. C; A, B, and D will not even raise the median. With C, the median becomes 10 instead of 9, and the mean becomes $10\frac{5}{7}$ instead of 10.

Chapter 6 Functions

6-1 Sequences
Pages 247–249

Work Together p. 247

1. 4,080; 4,095; 4,000

2. Sample: Option B, because you receive the most cards

Think and Discuss pp. 247–248

3. a. Option A; 20

   b. Option B; 2

   c. Sample: Option C; you get all the cards at once, not in a sequence.

4. a. 51 in. or 4 ft 3 in.

   b. 12 days

   c. arithmetic

   d. Sample: His height could be halved every day.

5. 83; sample: If $a = 7$, $d = 4$, and $n = 3$, then $k = a + d(n-1)$ gives $k = 7 + 4(3 - 1) = 7 + 4(2) = 7 + 8 = 15$.

6. C

On Your Own pp. 248–249

7. a. 3.2, 3.5, 3.8; arithmetic; 0.3

   b. 26, 37, 50; neither

   c. −3, −9, −15; arithmetic; −6

   d. 162; −486; 1,458; geometric; −3

   e. 1.00001, 1.000001, 1.0000001; neither

   f. 8, −16, 32; geometric; −2

8. a. 10, 12.4, 14.8, 17.2, 19.6

   b. 2, 6, 18, 54, 162

   c. 23, 18, 13, 8, 3

   d. −4, 12, −36, 108, −324

9. Answers may vary. Sample: A bank account is opened with $1,000. The amount of money in the account increases by 5% each year: $1,000, $1,050, $1102.50, $1,157.63, etc. The first term is 1,000; the common ratio is 1.05.

10. a. arithmetic

    b. geometric

    c. neither

    d. arithmetic

11. a. 145

    b. neither

12. 180 min

13. 75.5

14. a. 5, 8, 11, . . .

    b. 32; 42; Sample: For the pentagons, use $p = 5 + 3(n-1)$ and for the hexagons use $p = 6 + 4(n-1)$, where p is the perimeter and n is the number of regular polygons joined to form the figure.

    c. $p = s + (s - 2)(n - 1)$, where p is perimeter, s is the number of sides of the basic regular polygon, and n is the number of polygons joined to form the figure;

    Answers may vary. Sample: The perimeter of the basic polygon is s, and each new polygon increases the perimeter by $s - 2$ units.

Mixed Review p. 249

1. $(-3, -5)$

2. $(-6, -7)$

3. 135°

4. 144°

5. 42

6. −53

6-2 Function Rules
Pages 250–253

Think and Discuss pp. 250–251

1. a. the number of containers

   b. $.30, $.60, $1.20

2. a. yes

   b. no

   c. no

3. Tables will vary. Function rules and sample tables for the given situations are shown.

$f(n) = 5.5n$		$f(n) = 1.8n + 32$		$f(n) = 3n$	
n	$f(n)$	n	$f(n)$	n	$f(n)$
1	5.5	10	50	0.5	1.5
2	11.0	20	68	1	3.0
3	16.5	30	86	1.5	4.5
4	22.0	40	104	2	6.0

Work Together p. 251

Multiply by 4; double and then add 1; $f(n) = 4n$, $f(n) = 2n + 1$; function rules that students make up will vary.

LOOK BACK: $x = 0$ makes sense in the equation and in the situation, since a person who rents a video for one night but no more will pay the base fee of $3.50.

Try These p. 252

4. yes; the larger the area of the floor, the more tiles you need to cover it.

5. no; the cost of filling the tank depends on the amount of gasoline you put in the tank, but this amount will cost the same regardless of the time of day.

6. -7

7. 5

8. 5

9. 293

10. 83.75

11. 19, 20; $f(n) = n + 4$

12. 1, 7, 17; $f(n) = n - 3$

13. 7, 25, 3.5; $f(n) = 2n + 7$

Mixed Review p. 252

1. $25, -\frac{25}{2}, \frac{25}{4}$

2. 37, 44, 51

3. $(-2, -6)$

4. $(-5, -7)$

5. -12.5

6. -4.6

On Your Own pp. 252–253

14. yes; the faster you type, the less time it takes to complete the paper.

15. no; the value of the coupon usually depends on the kind of item and the quantity purchased but not on the time of day when the purchase is made.

16–18. Answers may vary. Samples are given.

16. 8.3, 4; $f(n) = 2n + 2.3$

17. 31, 12; $f(n) = 6n - 5$

18. 20, 5; $f(n) = 6n - 4$

19. 5

20. -1

21. 3

22. -15

23. -25

24. **a.** $f(n) = n^2 - 1$

   b. Sample: Each figure is a square with one dot removed.

25. **a.** $f(n) = 2.25n$

   b. $6.75

   c. $f(n) = 2.9n$

26. **a.**

Input n (days)	Output $f(n)$ (kilowatts)
1	0.92
2	1.84

   b. $f(n) = 0.92n$

   c. 27.6 kW

27. Temperature is related to altitude and a variety of other variables. Temperature decreases in a more or less regular way the higher up you go. Research data will vary, depending on the cities selected.

28. Check students' work.

29. Answers may vary. Sample: Use equally spaced values for the input variable. Study the output values to see if they increase or decrease in a regular way as the input values change. Describe the pattern observed with a function rule. Test the rule on other input and output values.

6-3 Function Graphs

Pages 254–257

Work Together p. 254

1. $14.00

2. $f(x) = 3x + 5$

3.

x	$f(x)$
0	5
1	8
2	11
3	14
4	17
5	20

4. ordered pairs: (0, 5), (1, 8), (2, 11), (3, 14), (4, 17), (5, 20)

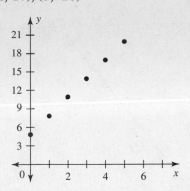

Think and Discuss pp. 254–255

5. **a** Carlos can be paid for part of an hour.

   b. No, because the points would have negative first coordinates, and Carlos cannot work a negative number of hours.

   c. lowest: yes, highest: no

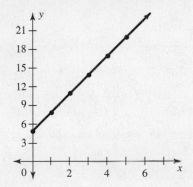

6. Answers may vary. Sample: 2.5 tickets for $64; you cannot buy half of a ticket.

7. All the *x* and *y* values must be positive in this situation.

8. yes, 28; yes, the cost of ordering all the tickets available for sale

Try These p. 256

9.

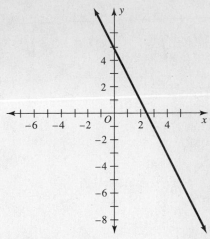

10.

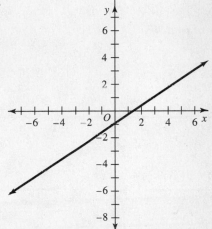

11.

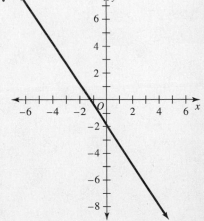

12.

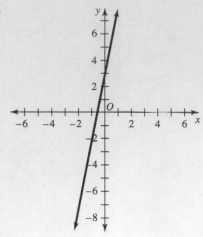

13. $f(x) = -\frac{1}{2}x - 1$

14. $f(x) = 3x + 2$

Mixed Review p. 256

1. -10

2. 14

3. $y < 4$

4. $t \geq 5$

5. 11

6. $-\frac{1}{2}$

7. $-15, 27$ or $15, -27$

On Your Own **pp. 256–257**

15. $f(x) = 50x$

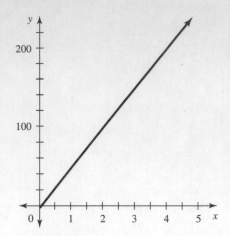

16. a.

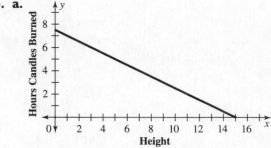

b. 15 cm; When $f(x)$ is 0 the candles have not started to burn and the height is 15.

c. 7.5 h; The height, x, is zero when $f(x)$, the hours the candle burns, is 7.5. This is the greatest value for $f(x)$.

17. $f(x) = 198 - 32x$

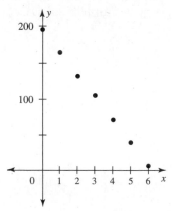

18.

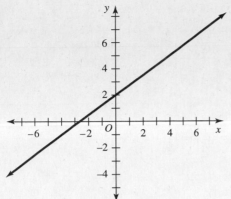

19.

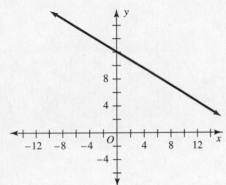

20. Answers may vary. Sample: Lucas expects to earn a 20% tip from each customer he serves over the holidays. If the customer's restaurant bill is x dollars, then the tip, $f(x)$, that Lucas expects is $f(x) = 0.2x$.

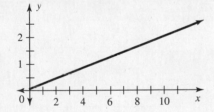

21.

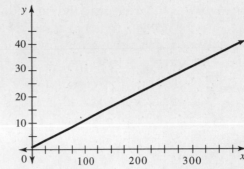

22. $-\frac{3}{2}, 2; f(x) = -\frac{3}{2}x + 2$

23. $\frac{1}{3}, 0; f(x) = \frac{1}{3}x$

Checkpoint p. 257

1. 25, 36, 49; neither
2. 0.75, 0.375, 0.1875; geometric
3. $\frac{1}{5}, -\frac{1}{25}, \frac{1}{125}$; geometric
4. 20.2, 19.9, 19.6; arithmetic
5. $0, -\frac{1}{6}, -\frac{1}{3}$; arithmetic
6. 56, 67, 78; arithmetic
7. 1
8. -17
9. -2
10. $-\frac{1}{2}$

6-4 Problem Solving: Solve a Simpler Problem

Pages 258–260

1. squares on a checkerboard
2. the total number of squares of different sizes
3. $1 \times 1, 2 \times 2, 3 \times 3, 4 \times 4, 5 \times 5, 6 \times 6,$ $7 \times 7,$ and 8×8
4. 2×2; 5 squares
5. 3×3; 14 squares
6. 4×4: $1^2 + 2^2 + 3^2 + 4^2 = 30$
   5×5: $1^2 + 2^2 + 3^2 + 4^2 + 5^2 = 55$
7. $1^2 + 2^2 + 3^2 + \cdots + 8^2 = 204$ squares
8. Answers may vary. Sample: draw a diagram

9. The number of squares equals the sum of the squares of the integers from 1 to n; yes; there is exactly one number that can result when you add the squares of the integers from 1 to n.

Try These p. 259

10. a. 13 triangles

   b. 49 triangles

   c. 19 triangles

   d. 100 triangles

   e. n^2 triangles

   f. yes; $f(n) = n^2$

11. 45 games

On Your Own pp. 259–260

12. a. 131 times

   b. 11 illustrations

13. 16 years

14. $10

15. 18 points

16. 16 arrangements

17. 7.65 mi

18. $17 - x$

19. 25 subscriptions

20. 6 packages of 15 plates, 4 packages of 20 plates

21. $-2, -14$

22. 2 tsp

23. 6 boxes

24. Check students' work.

Mixed Review p. 260

1–2. Sample tables are shown.

1.

x	$f(x)$
-2	3
0	-1
1	-3
3	-7

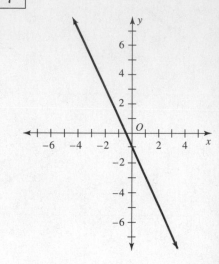

2.

x	$f(x)$
-2	-6
-1	-1
0	4
0.5	6.5

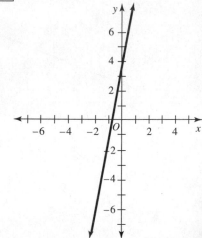

3. $a > -1$

4. $t \geq -6\frac{1}{5}$

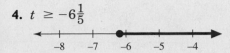

5. 10.6

6. 16.4

6-5 Interpreting Graphs
Pages 261–263

Think and Discuss *pp. 261–262*

1. 1 h

2. 4 stops

3. 50 mi/h

4. 7:35 and 7:40; 50 mi/h

5. Answers may vary. Samples: The time he left home, the traffic, the number of stops

6. yes, Graph II; Graph II shows the dots connected in order, from left to right.

7. Answers may vary. Sample: the height above the ground of a ball thrown from a height of 5 feet

8. Explanations may vary. Samples given.

   a. III; The Ferris Wheel car begins at ground level and rises to the top of the wheel before returning to ground level (peak 1). Three revolutions of the wheel yield a graph with three high points and four low points.

   b. IV; Air temperature gradually declines at night, gradually rises to a maximum during the day, and declines again in the evening.

   c. II; An athlete's pulse rate increases steadily during a warm-up period, then levels off as the exercise continues at a steady rate, and finally drops during the cool-down period.

   d. I; A parking fee increases in steps, depending on how long the car has been parked.

9. Sample: A library charges $.10 for each day a person is late in returning a book.

   a. The horizontal axis represents time and the vertical axis represents the late charge.

   b.

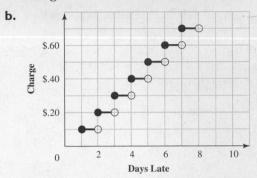

   c. Check students' answers.

Work Together *p. 263*

Sample table and graph given.

Time (seconds)	Steps (A)	Steps (B)
15	43	31
30	79	62
45	113	77
60	150	101
75	198	131
90	233	157
105	256	183
120	293	203

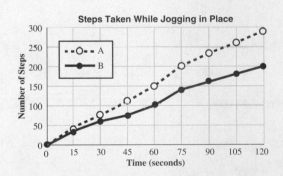

10. Answers may vary. Samples given based on the table and graph above.

   a. Each partner sped up slightly during the activity, although each person jogged at a fairly constant pace.

b. Partner A took the most steps between 60 and 75 seconds, and Partner B took the most steps between 0 and 15 seconds and between 45 and 60 seconds.

c. Yes, because you are jogging continuously.

11. Answers may vary. Sample given based on the graph above. A comparison of the progress of two boats through a channel would yield a graph similar to the graph for jogging in place.

Mixed Review p. 263

1. $y = \frac{1}{3}x - 2; \frac{1}{3}, -2$

2. $y = 5x + 10; 5, 10$

3. $\angle A \cong \angle \boxed{B}$

4. $BT = \boxed{AL}$ **5.** 420

On Your Own pp. 263–264

12.

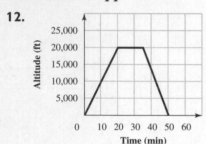

13. C

14. a. The water rises from a low-tide level of 0 ft at $h = 0$ to a high-tide level of 40 ft at $h = 6$. It then returns to low-tide level at $h = 12$.

b. about 7:30 P.M.

15. a. 11 week   **b.** 10 weeks

c. weeks 4 and 5; 15 km   **d.** 10 km

16. a. $900; $1,020

b.

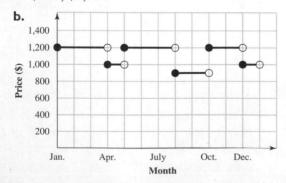

Practice
Page 265

1. 25, 28, 31; arithmetic

2. 24, 35, 48; neither

3. $-30, -15, -\frac{15}{2}$; geometric

4. 8, 13, 18; arithmetic

5. 216, 343, 512; neither

6. 1, 4, 16; geometric

7. 128

8. $f(x) = x + 5$

9. $f(x) = 3x + 3$

10. $f(x) = x^2$

11.

x	$f(x)$
-2	-2
-1	-3
0	-4
1	-5
2	-6

12.

x	$f(x)$
-2	13
-1	4
0	1
1	4
2	13

13.

x	$f(x)$
-2	-1
-1	$-1\frac{1}{2}$
0	-2
1	$-2\frac{1}{2}$
2	-3

14. $1, -3, 5, -1\frac{3}{8}$

15. $f(x) = \frac{72}{x}$; 12

16. B

6-6 Quadratic Functions
Pages 266–268

Think and Discuss pp. 266–267

1. a. 18 ft

    b. 18 ft^2

2. 32 ft²; 42 ft²

3. a. The length could be a value that is not a whole number.

    b. 5

Work Together p. 267

4. a. Sample: A curve; the rocket slows down as it rises, reaches a high point, then gains speed as it falls.

    b. $x \geq 0$; you are only interested in the height of the rocket from launch time.

    c. Quadrant I; assuming the rocket is launched at level ground, the least value of $f(x)$ is 0, and $x \geq 0$.

5. Sample:

x	$f(x)$
0	0
0.5	28
1	48
1.5	60
2	64
2.5	60
3	48
3.5	28
4	0

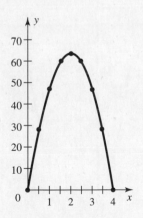

6. Check students' work.

Try These p. 268

7.

x	$x^2 - 2$	$(x, f(x))$
-3	7	$(-3, 7)$
-2	2	$(-2, 2)$
-1	-1	$(-1, -1)$
0	-2	$(0, -2)$
1	-1	$(1, -1)$
2	2	$(2, 2)$
3	7	$(3, 7)$

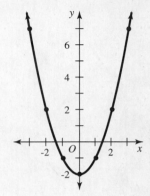

8.

x	$9 - x^2$	$(x, f(x))$
-1	8	$(-1, 8)$
0	9	$(0, 9)$
1	8	$(1, 8)$
2	5	$(2, 5)$
3	0	$(3, 0)$
4	-7	$(4, -7)$
5	-16	$(5, -16)$

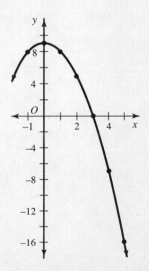

Mixed Review p. 268

1. $0; $50

2. Plumber A

3.

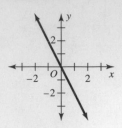

4.

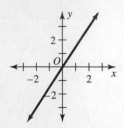

On Your Own p. 268

9. B

10–15. Table values may vary. Samples given.

10.

x	f(x)
-3	9
-2	4
-1	1
0	0
1	1
2	4
3	9

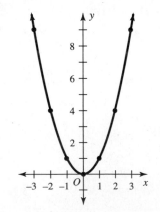

11.

x	f(x)
-3	-18
-2	-8
-1	-2
0	0
1	-2
2	-8
3	-18

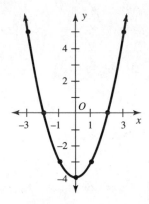

12.

x	f(x)
-3	5
-2	0
-1	-3
0	-4
1	-3
2	0
3	5

13.

x	f(x)
-3	-4
-2	1
-1	4
0	5
1	4
2	1
3	-4

15.

x	f(x)
-3	-6
-2	-2
-1	0
-0.5	0.25
0	0
1	-2
2	-6

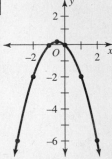

16. a. 7, 12, 15, 16, 15, 12

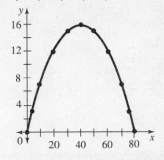

14.

x	f(x)
-2	8
-1	3
0	0
1	-1
2	0
3	3
4	8

b. Answers may vary. Sample: As the number of trees planted increases, the number of walnuts produced increases until production peaks at 16 bushels (40 trees per acre). Then walnut production decreases until no bushels are produced when 80 trees per acre are planted. This shows that when fewer than 40 trees per acre are planted, the space isn't used efficiently. For more than 40 trees per acre, the trees are too close together to produce an optimum number of walnuts. Planting 40 trees per acre produces the best crop.

Course 3 Chapter 6

17. $f(d) = \frac{\pi}{4} d^2$;

Sample (values of $f(d)$ are rounded to the nearest hundredth):

d	$f(d)$
6	28.27
10	78.54
12	113.10
16	201.06
18	254.47

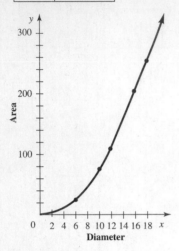

2. a–b.

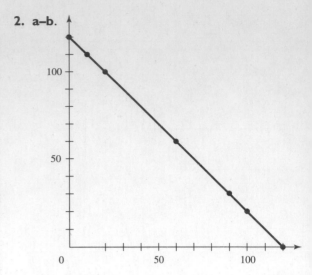

b. yes; the points of the graph are on a line that has slope -1 and y-intercept 120.

c. only the part in the first quadrant and the points (0, 120) and (120, 0)

3. a. 12 min; to find the average time, divide the total time by the number of songs.

b.

Input, x (number of songs)	Output, $f(x)$ (avg. length, min)
10	12
12	10
24	5
20	6
30	4
6	20
1	120

c. $f(x) = \frac{120}{x}$

6-7 Families of Graphs

Pages 269–272

Think and Discuss pp. 269–271

1. a. 110 min; subtract 10 from 120.

b.

Input, x (min)	Output, $f(x)$ (min left)
0	120
10	110
20	100
60	60
90	30
100	20
120	0

There are 120 min in 2 h.

c. $f(x) = 120 - x$

4. a. Answers may vary. Sample: The points will lie along a curve.

b–c.

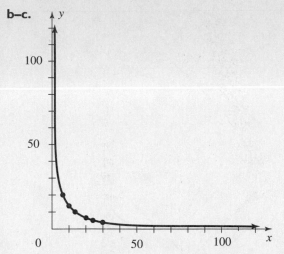

c. Answers may vary. Sample: The graph is a curve that stays in the first quadrant, getting close to the axes but never crossing them.

5. a. Answers may vary. Sample: The graph for Exercise 2 is a segment. It joins (0, 120) and (120, 0) and except for these points lies in Quadrant I. The graph for Exercise 4 is a curve in Quadrant I. It does not intersect the axes.

b. Answers may vary. Sample: The coordinates of points on the graph for Exercise 2 have a constant sum; the equation for that graph is linear. For Exercise 4, the coordinates have a constant product; the equation is not linear. Division by x results in a curve.

6. a. 1

b. 1

c. 2

d. 4

7. a.

Input, x	Output $\lvert x - 2 \rvert$
−5	7
−4	6
−3	5
−2	4
−1	3
0	2
1	1
2	0
3	1
4	2
5	3

b.

c. Answers may vary. Sample: The graph is V-shaped. It is not part of a single straight line, nor is it a smooth, rounded curve.

d. yes; check students' work.

8. a. Sample: Linear equations (ii, iii, iv), quadratic equations (v, vii), absolute value equations (vi, viii), equations with x in the denominator (i, ix)

b. yes; each family has a unique characteristic: all the linear equations will have graphs that are lines, all the quadratic equations will have U-shapes (parabolas), all absolute value equations will have V-shapes, and all the equations with x in the denominator will have two curves.

c. Straight line: equations ii, iii, iv;

U-shaped: equations v, vii;

V-shaped: equations vi, viii;

2 curves: equations i, ix

9. Graphs for Family i

$y = \dfrac{1}{x}$

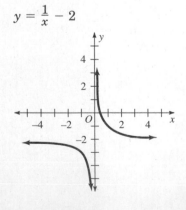

$y = \dfrac{1}{x} + 3$

$y = \dfrac{1}{x} - 2$

Graphs for Family ii

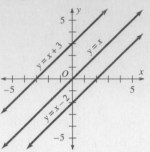

Graphs for Family iii

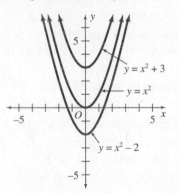

Graphs for Family iv

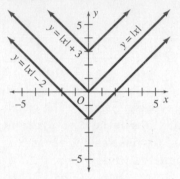

a. Answers may vary. Sample: The graph of each equation in Family i has two curves. Each graph for Family ii is a line with slope 1. Each graph for Family iii has a V-shape. Each graph for Family iv has a U-shape. The shape of the graph is related to the power of x used in the equation and to whether the variable is between absolute value bars.

b. Answers may vary. Sample: The graphs within a family differ in how high or how low they are positioned on the coordinate plane. Their shapes are exactly the same.

10.

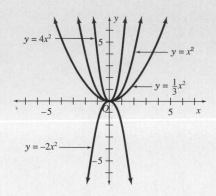

a. The graphs differ in how wide or narrow they are. The graph of $y = -2x^2$ lies below the x-axis, whereas the graphs of the other equations are above the x-axis. All the graphs are U-shaped and all touch the x-axis at $(0, 0)$.

b. The graph of $y = 5x^2$ will be narrower and steeper than the graph of $y = x^2$.

c. Sample: All the graphs are U-shaped and this seems related to the fact that they all contain x^2. The coefficient of x^2 determines how wide or narrow the graph is. The greater the absolute value of the coefficient, the narrower the graph. If the coefficient of x^2 is positive, the graph points above the x-axis; if the coefficient is negative, the graph points below the x-axis.

d. Sample: Except for the fact that the graphs are V-shaped and contain $|x|$ instead of x^2, the general relationships from part (c) apply here as they did to the quadratic equations.

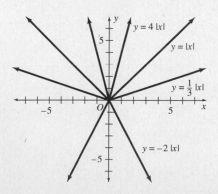

On Your Own p. 272

11. a. Answers may vary. Sample: 15 mm and 4 mm, 20 mm and 3 mm, 25 mm and 2.4 mm

b. Answers may vary. Sample: A curve that is in Quadrant I and that comes close to the x- and y-axes without ever intersecting them

c. Answers may vary. Sample: -15 and -4, -20 and -3, -25 and -2.4

d.

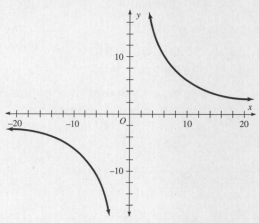

The graph is the one described in part b. Allowing negative values for x and y adds another curve in Quadrant III that is like the curve in Quadrant I.

e. The curve in Quadrant III does not have meaning for the insert, because the dimensions of a rectangle must be positive numbers.

Mixed Review p. 272

1. Graphs may vary. Sample:

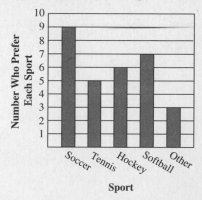

2–3.

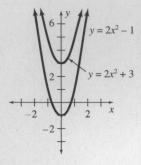

4. 12, 16; 13, 15; 14, 14

Checkpoint p. 272

1. 1981 –1990; 1931 – 1940

2. 1931 – 1940; 1941–1950

3. No; The graph gives percent of population growth, not number of immigrants.

4. D

5.

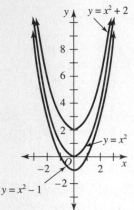

6.

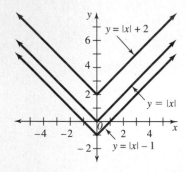

7.

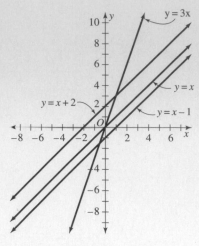

Problem Solving Practice
Page 273

1. 6 ways

2. 24 ways

3. 11 quarters

4. 160 mi

5. 2 cakes

6. $\frac{1}{4}$ in.

7. 3

8. 37

9. a. 3 P.M.

  b. 9 mi

10. 12-in. tiles; $68.40

6-8   Direct and Inverse Variation
Pages 274–277

Think and Discuss pp. 274–275

1. increases; decreases

2.

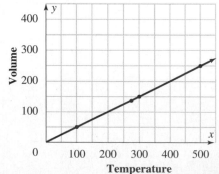

The graph is a line that passes through the origin and has slope $\frac{1}{2}$.

3.

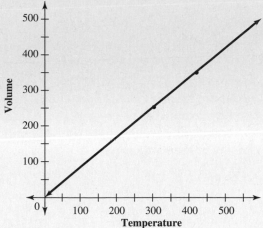

Try These p. 276

4. directly; $y = 2.5x$

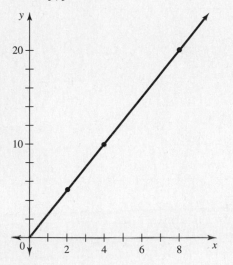

5. inversely; $xy = 12$

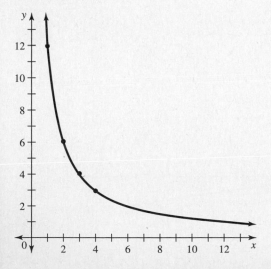

6. inversely; $xy = 18$

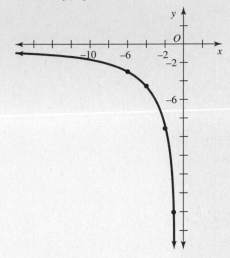

7. 200 mL	**8.** 3.6 h
9. π	**10.** $320

Decision Making pp. 276–277

1. Answers may vary. Sample: air freshener, hairspray, paint, deodorant, fixative; Products in pressurized cans give a finer spray than those in nonpressurized containers. Air does not enter the container.

2. Answers may vary. Check students' work. Sample: Do not expose the containers to high temperatures.

3. Answers may vary. Sample: It might explode.

4. Sample: If the contents are a gas, the volume will decrease (assuming that the temperature is held constant).

5. The air pressure in the plane is generally lower than that on the ground and this difference could cause the pressurized container to leak or explode.

6. Sample: yes

7. Answers may vary. Sample: Chlorofluorocarbons destroy ozone in the atmosphere.

8. Answers may vary. Sample: Containers with hand-operated "pump" dispensers

9. Answers may vary. Sample: Let manufacturers be aware of consumers' environmental concerns.

On Your Own p. 277

11. direct; 4

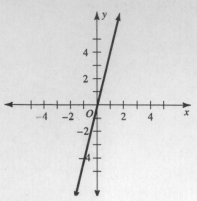

12. neither

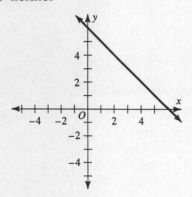

13. inverse; 6

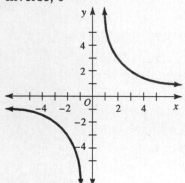

14. direct; $\frac{1}{2}$

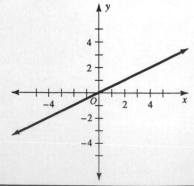

15. 5 h

16. 520 cycles/s

17. Sample: Direct variation: How is the total cost of erasers related to the number that you buy if you only buy $.20 erasers? Inverse variation: How is the number of erasers you can buy related to the price of the erasers if you spend all of your money and buy only erasers of the same price?

Mixed Review p. 277

1.

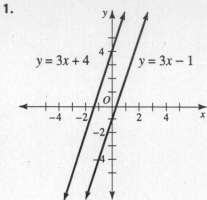

2.

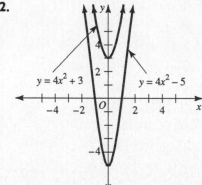

3. solution: $(2, -2)$

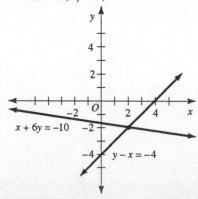

4. solution: (9, 1)

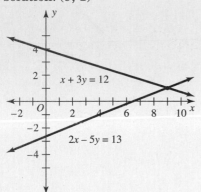

5. 1.8 h

6. 175 mi

Wrap Up

Pages 278–279

1. geometric; $\frac{25}{4}$, $\frac{25}{16}$, $\frac{25}{64}$, $\frac{25}{256}$

2. arithmetic; 42, 49, 56, 63

3. neither; −30, −25, −19, −12

4. −37

5. −1

6. −101

7. −5

8. 28

9. Answers may vary. Sample: A ski lift comes down to the bottom of a trail, stops to reload, then goes back up.

10. Answers may vary. Sample: The cost of mailing a package.

11–14. Tables may vary. Samples are shown.

11.

x	f(x)
−1	−6
0	−4
1	−2
2	0
3	2

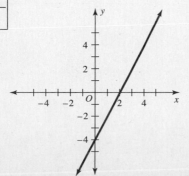

12.

x	f(x)
−4	3
−2	2
0	1
2	0
4	−1

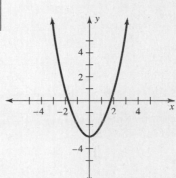

13.

x	f(x)
−2	1
−1	−2
0	−3
1	−2
2	1

14.

x	f(x)
−2	−2
−1	1
0	2
1	1
2	−2

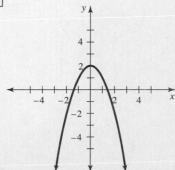

15.

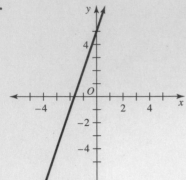

16.

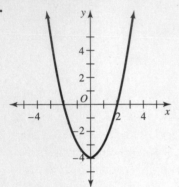

17.

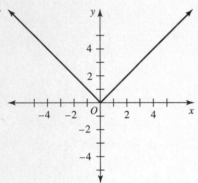

18.

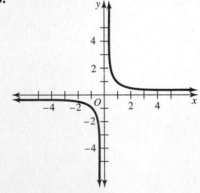

19.

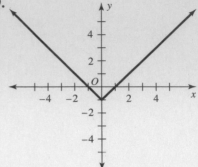

20.

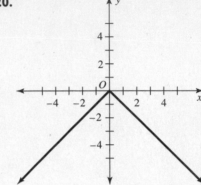

21.

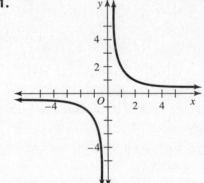

22.

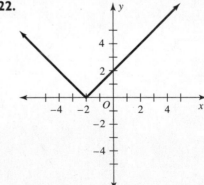

23. B

24. 64

Getting Ready for Chapter 7 p. 279

1. 540
2. 588,000
3. 7,200,000
4. $\frac{1}{4}$, 0.25, 25%

Assessment

Page 282

1. a. arithmetic; -0.15 of the original price
   b. arithmetic; -30
   c. geometric; 3
2. 100, 80, 64, 51.2
3. $12, 9\frac{1}{2}, 7, 4\frac{1}{2}, 2$
4. a. -18
   b. -22.75
   c. $1\frac{5}{9}$
5. Tables may vary. Sample:

x	$f(x)$
0.5	4.20
1.0	5.40
1.5	6.60
2.0	7.80
2.5	9.00
3.0	10.20

6. a. inverse; 26
   b. direct
   c. direct
   d. inverse; 6

7. a.

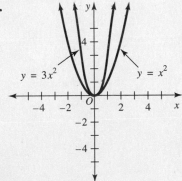

b.

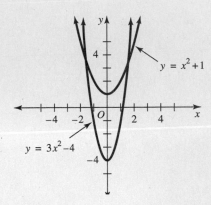

8. 190 segments
9. a. IV
   b. III
   c. II
   d. I
10. C
11. Answers may vary. Check students' work. Sample given. Joe the bus driver maneuvers his bus out of the bus yard and makes his way to the first series of stops on the way to Hollow Dale Middle School. After he picks up kids at Allen Road, Beals Terrace, and Chance Lane, he heads over to the second series of stops. He picks up kids at Rosa Avenue, Steven Court, Tracy Street, and Uma Drive. After all seven stops, Joe heads over to the school, only to encounter a traffic jam at Four Corners, causing him to drive slightly slower than he would like. Finally traffic clears, and he makes his way unimpeded to the school, where he lets off his 27 passengers.
12. 75 volts
13. Answers may vary. Sample: Lines, such as the graph of $y = x$; V-shaped graphs, such as the graph of $y = |x|$; U-shaped, parabolic graphs, such as the graph of $y = x^2$; 2-curve graphs, such as the graph of $y = \frac{1}{x}$

Cumulative Review

Page 283

1. C	2. D	3. B
4. D	5. A	6. A
7. C	8. D	9. B
10. A		

Chapter 7 Rational Numbers

7-1 Prime Factorization
Pages 287–290

Think and Discuss pp. 287–288

1. **a.** Check students' diagrams. They should show the following five kinds of rectangles: 1 by 36, 2 by 18, 3 by 12, 4 by 9, and 6 by 6.

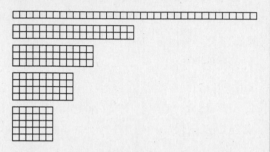

   b. 1, 2, 3, 4, 6, 9, 12, 18, 36

   c. Yes; No; When you divide 36 by 4, you get a zero remainder, but when you divide 36 by 5, you get a quotient of 7 with a remainder of 1.

2. 4 columns

3. Answers may vary. Samples: You can use factors to decide whether a group of people can be split/divided into discussion groups with the same number of people in each group. You can decide how many ways you can get a certain amount of money in traveler's checks if you want all the checks to be of the same denomination.

4. If a composite number n is a factor of the whole number m, then every prime factor of n is also a prime factor of m. To keep the number of whole numbers you must check to a minimum, it is therefore enough to check only the *prime* numbers that might be factors of m.

5. **a.**
   $$179 \div 2 = 89 \text{ R } 1$$
   $$179 \div 3 = 59 \text{ R } 2$$
   $$179 \div 5 = 35 \text{ R } 4$$
   $$179 \div 7 = 25 \text{ R } 4$$
   $$179 \div 11 = 16 \text{ R } 3$$
   $$179 \div 13 = 13 \text{ R } 10$$

Because 179 divided by 13 is about equal to 13, there are no factors of 179 other than 1 and 179, so 179 must be prime.

   b. 13; In part (a), as the divisors that are tested increase, the quotients decrease. A prime number greater than 13 that is a factor of 179 will give a division equation in which the quotient is less than 13. This quotient cannot be prime or composite, since those numbers have already been eliminated as factors of 179. The quotient will have to be 1, meaning that the prime divisor is 179.

6. **a.**

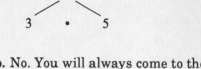

   b. No. You will always come to the same prime factors, though you may arrive at them in different ways.

Try These p. 289

7. 1, 2, 3, 5, 6, 10, 15, 30

8. 1, 31

9. 1, 5, 11, 55

10. 1, 2, 4, 8, 16, 32, 64

11. 1

12. 100 c, 101 p, 102 c, 103 p, 104 c, 105 c, 106 c, 107 p, 108 c, 109 p, 110 c

13. **a.** $54 = 2 \cdot 3^3$, $90 = 2 \cdot 3^2 \cdot 5$, $108 = 2^2 \cdot 3^3$

   b. GCF(54, 90, 108) $= 2 \cdot 3^2 = 18$

14. 21 ft

15. 1

On Your Own pp. 289–290

16. yes   17. no

18. yes   19. yes

20. Samples: 4, 36 (Any perfect square greater than 1 will do.)

21. any three of 1, 2, 3, 6, 8

22. a.

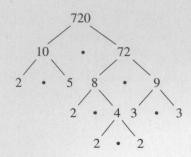

b. $2^4 \cdot 3^2 \cdot 5$

23. composite

24. prime

25. composite

26. composite

27. composite

28. Answers may vary. Sample: The definition of "prime" says the number must have exactly two factors: itself and 1. Since every number is a factor of 0 ($0 \times n = 0$), not only 0 and 1, 0 cannot be prime. And since only 1 is a factor of 1, 1 cannot be prime. The definition of "composite" says that composite numbers have more than two factors. Since 1 has only one factor, 1 cannot be composite. The definition of "composite" also says that every composite number can be written as the product of primes. Since any factorization of 0 must include 0, and 0 is not prime, 0 cannot be composite.

29. Answers may vary. Sample: Yes, the statement seems to be true, but just knowing that it is true for several numbers does not prove that it is always true.

   a. $3 + 3$

   b. $13 + 3$

   c. $19 + 5$

   d. $29 + 3$

   e. $53 + 7$

30. $2^4 \cdot 3$

31. $2 \cdot 3 \cdot 5^2$

32. $3^2 \cdot 5^2$

33. $2 \cdot 3 \cdot 31$

34. $3^3 \cdot 23$

35. Sample: 77

36. 38 students

37. 5

38. 4

39. 14

40. 1

41. B

42. a. 6 classes

   b. 20 paint brushes, 13 boxes of markers, 4 packs of paper, 9 sets of watercolors

Mixed Review p. 290

1. $42

2. 1,900

3. direct; 22

4. inverse; 63

5. $95

7-2 Rational Numbers
Pages 291–294

Think and Discuss pp. 291–292

1. a. Answers may vary. Sample: $-2.1 = \frac{-21}{10}$

   b. Answers may vary. Sample: $\frac{-21}{10}$, $-\frac{42}{20}$, $\frac{-63}{30}$, $\frac{-84}{40}$, $\frac{-105}{50}$

2. Division by zero is undefined.

3. Check students' work. $1\frac{1}{2}$ should be halfway between 1 and 2, and -1.25 should be one fourth of a unit to the left of -1.

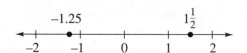

4. $2\frac{3}{4}$, $-2\frac{3}{4}$

5. a. GCF(27, 45) = 9

   b. $-\frac{3}{5}$

Try These p. 293

6. $\frac{2}{5}$

7. -20.5

8. -12

9. $2\frac{3}{4}$

10. $2\frac{1}{2}$, $2\frac{1}{2}$

11. 6.2, −6.2

12. $\frac{1}{6}$, $-\frac{1}{6}$

13. $\frac{4}{5}$, $\frac{4}{5}$

14. 0, 0

15. $-\frac{5}{6}$

16. $\frac{31}{4}$

17. $-\frac{3}{20}$

18. $\frac{1}{-3}$

19. $\frac{2}{3}$

20.

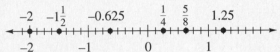

On Your Own pp. 293–294

21–24. Samples are given.

21. $\frac{8}{-1}$

22. $\frac{93}{100}$

23. $\frac{-27}{10}$

24. $\frac{19}{3}$

25. $\frac{0}{6}$

26–30. Samples are given.

26. $\frac{7}{2}$, $\frac{14}{4}$, $\frac{21}{6}$

27. $-\frac{3}{4}$, $-\frac{6}{8}$, $-\frac{9}{12}$

28. $-\frac{50}{4}$, $-\frac{75}{6}$, $-\frac{100}{8}$

29. $\frac{11}{10}$, $\frac{22}{20}$, $\frac{33}{30}$

30. $\frac{0}{1}$, $\frac{0}{2}$, $\frac{0}{3}$

31. Accept reasonable estimates. Samples are given.

$A: -1\frac{7}{10}$; $B: -\frac{3}{4}$; $C: -\frac{1}{10}$; $D: \frac{9}{10}$; $E: 1\frac{2}{5}$

32. $\frac{2}{3}$, $\frac{2}{3}$

33. $1\frac{2}{3}$, $-1\frac{2}{3}$

34. $\frac{54}{7}$, $\frac{54}{7}$

35. 5.07, 5.07

36. $\frac{9}{10}$, $-\frac{9}{10}$

37. a. Sample: true when $\frac{a}{b} = \frac{2}{5}$, false when $\frac{a}{b} = -\frac{2}{5}$

b. Sample: true when $\frac{a}{b} = -\frac{3}{5}$, false when $\frac{a}{b} = \frac{3}{5}$

38. They are equal when the number is less than or equal to 0. They are not equal when the number is greater than 0.

39. $\frac{5}{8}$

40. $-\frac{3}{4}$

41. $-\frac{9}{2}$

42. $\frac{1}{7}$

43. $\frac{2}{-5}$

44. C

45. a., b.

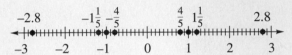

46. integer, rational

47. rational

48. rational

49. whole number, integer, rational

50. rational

51. All

52. Some

53. Some

54. No

Mixed Review p. 294

1. −9

2. −6

3. $2^5 \cdot 3$

4. $2 \cdot 5 \cdot 13$

5. $2^6 \cdot 3^2$

6. $2^4 \cdot 3^2 \cdot 7$

7.

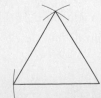

7-3 Fractions and Decimals

Pages 295–298

Think and Discuss pp. 295–296

1. a. 0.25

   b. −0.3125

   c. 3.5

2. Some calculators round.

3. a. $0.\overline{06}$

   b. $-0.08\overline{3}$

   c. $5.\overline{6}$

4. Use the same power as the number of places to the right of the decimal point.

5. a. $-\dfrac{17}{250}$

   b. $7\dfrac{2}{5}$

6. to get a number that has the same values to the right of the decimal point as n does

7. a. 10; Multiplying by 10 will give a number that has all 7s to the right of the decimal point.

   b. $\dfrac{7}{9}$

Work Together p. 297

8. a. from left to right: $0.\overline{1}, 0.\overline{2}, 0.\overline{3}, 0.\overline{4}, 0.\overline{5}$; Sample: Each numerator is a natural number less than 9. The digit indicated by the numerator repeats endlessly to the right of the decimal point in the decimal for the fraction.

   b. $0.\overline{8}$

9. a. from left to right: $0.\overline{09}, 0.\overline{18}, 0.\overline{27}, 0.\overline{36}, 0.\overline{45}$; Sample: Each numerator is a natural number less than 11. The digits that repeat endlessly in the decimal for $\frac{1}{11}$ are 0 and 9. After that, the two-digit number that you get by multiplying the numerator of the fraction by 9 tells what group of digits repeats to the right of the decimal point in the decimal for the fraction.

   b. $0.\overline{72}$

Yes, there are other such patterns.

Sample: $\dfrac{1}{33} = 0.\overline{03}, \dfrac{2}{33} = 0.\overline{06}, \dfrac{3}{33} = 0.\overline{09},$ $\dfrac{4}{33} = 0.\overline{12}$, and so on.

Try These p. 297

10. $0.\overline{71}$

11. $0.31\overline{4}$

12. $0.5\overline{28}$

13. −0.3

14. $-0.\overline{3}$

15. $2.8\overline{3}$

16. 0.5625

17. −1.875

18. $\dfrac{1}{200}$

19. $-5\dfrac{2}{9}$

20. $-\dfrac{14}{25}$

21. $\dfrac{16}{33}$

22. $6\dfrac{9}{100}$

23. 142857; Sample explanation: The calculator display indicates that the decimal has not terminated by the seventh place decimal, and you can see that the block of digits 142857 is beginning to repeat.

24. a. left to right: 0.125, $0.1\overline{6}$, 0.2, 0.25, $0.\overline{3}$, 0.375, 0.4, 0.5, 0.6, 0.625, $0.\overline{6}$, 0.75, 0.8, $0.8\overline{3}$, 0.875

   b. Sample: Reorganize by grouping repeating decimals together and terminating decimals together.

On Your Own p. 298

25. $0.58\overline{3}$

26. −4.15

27. $0.\overline{6}$

28. $1.\overline{27}$

29. −0.8

30. a. $\dfrac{14}{168} = \dfrac{1}{12}$; $0.08\overline{3}$

   b. $\dfrac{10}{370} = \dfrac{1}{37}$; $0.\overline{027}$

31. $-\dfrac{7}{25}$

32. $1\dfrac{5}{8}$

33. $\dfrac{4}{9}$

34. $12\frac{3}{250}$　　　**35.** $7\frac{16}{33}$

36. Sample: 2, 4, 5

37. Answers may vary. Sample: You might use fractions if you are giving someone a recipe or if you are making measurements for a set of bookshelves that you want to build. You might use decimals if you are buying food at the grocery store and are estimating the cost of your purchases; you would probably use decimals if you were taking your temperature to see whether you had a fever.

38. $\frac{21}{50}$

39. $\frac{23}{100}$

40. $\frac{7}{20}$

Checkpoint p. 298

1. $2^2 \cdot 3 \cdot 7 \cdot 23$

2. 52

3. $-1\frac{2}{7}; 1\frac{2}{7}, 1\frac{2}{7}$

4. 1.0625

5. $\frac{2}{5}$　　　**6.** $0.0\overline{5}$

7. $\frac{4}{25}$　　　**8.** $\frac{6}{11}$

Mixed Review p. 298

1. $t > -\frac{1}{2}$;

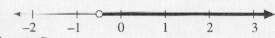

2. $x \le -5$;

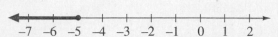

3. -10

4. -86

5. $20 for each of the three who worked all day and $10 for the one who worked half the day

7-4 Comparing Rational Numbers
Pages 299–302

Think and Discuss pp. 299–300

1. a. multiples of 8: 8, 16, 24, 32, 40, 48, . . .;
multiples of 10: 10, 20, 30, 40, 50, 60, . . .

　b. 40

2. 504; 168; 252

3. a. The numbers are the opposites of those in Example 2, so $\frac{5}{12} < \frac{4}{9}$.

　b–c. There is no need to rename the fractions. A negative number is always less than a positive number, so $-\frac{5}{12} < \frac{4}{9}$ and $\frac{5}{12} > -\frac{4}{9}$.

4. Rewrite the fractions using the LCD, which is 36: $-\frac{5}{12} = -\frac{15}{36}$, $-\frac{4}{9} = -\frac{16}{36}$, $-\frac{7}{18} = -\frac{14}{36}$. Then compare numerators. Since $-16 < -15 < -14$, the correct order of the given numbers, from least to greatest, is $-\frac{4}{9}, -\frac{5}{12}, -\frac{7}{18}$.

5. $-1\frac{5}{12} = -\frac{17}{12}$ and $-1\frac{4}{9} = -\frac{13}{9}$; $-1\frac{5}{12} > -1\frac{4}{9}$

6. Answers may vary. Write 0.32 as $\frac{32}{100}$ and put $\frac{32}{100}$ into simplest form, $\frac{8}{25}$. Next write $\frac{8}{25}$ and $\frac{5}{16}$ so that they have a common denominator: $\frac{8}{25} = \frac{128}{400}, \frac{5}{16} = \frac{125}{400}$. Since $\frac{128}{400} > \frac{125}{400}$, you know that $0.32 > \frac{5}{16}$. The method that involves changing $\frac{5}{16}$ to a decimal is better, because you can use the calculator and there are fewer steps.

Work Together p. 301

For the first two parts, check students' work.
DISCUSSION Yes; There are infinitely many points between any two points, although the number line may have to be extended or redrawn for more space.

Try These p. 301

7. a. multiples of 9: 9, 18, 27, 36, 45, 54, 63, 72, 81, 90
multiples of 15: 15, 30, 45, 60, 75, 90, 105, 120, 135, 150
two common multiples: 45, 90; LCM: 45

　b. $9 = 3^2$ and $15 = 3 \cdot 5$, so LCM(9, 15) $= 3^2 \cdot 5$ or 45

8. $>$

9. $=$

10. $>$

11. $>$

12. a. No; You need to find LCM(8, 12) to compare the negative numbers, but you do not need to change $\frac{9}{14}$, since it is positive and therefore the greatest number of the three.

   b. $-\frac{5}{8}, -\frac{7}{12}, \frac{9}{14}$

13. Karen exercises on days 3, 6, 9, 12, 15, . . . and Mai exercises on days 5, 10, 15, 20,. . . . They will meet on June 16, or 15 days after June 1.

On Your Own pp. 301–302

14. 30

15. 90

16. 45

17. 350

18. Answers may vary. Multiply all of the prime numbers in the set. Sample: LCM(5, 7, 13) = 5 • 7 • 13 or 455

19. a. 180 hot dogs and buns

   b. 5 packs of hot dogs, 9 packs of buns

20. Answers may vary. Sample: To find the GCF and the LCM, start by finding the prime factorization of each number. For the GCF, underline common prime factors, then multiply the least powers of the underlined primes. For the LCM, multiply the greatest powers of all the primes that occur in the prime factorizations.

21–24. Sample explanations are given.

21. Since 11 > 9, you know that $\frac{1}{11} < \frac{1}{9}$. When you compare the opposites of the fractions, the inequality is reversed, so $-\frac{1}{11} > -\frac{1}{9}$.

22. The numerators of the fractions are the same, so the fraction with the smaller denominator is the greater fraction; $\frac{5}{7} > \frac{5}{8}$.

23. $\frac{1}{4}$ = 0.25, so compare 0.25 and 0.3. Since 0.25 < 0.3, you know that $\frac{1}{4}$ < 0.3.

24. 0.6 is equal to $\frac{3}{5}$. The numerators of $\frac{3}{5}$ and $\frac{3}{7}$ are the same, so look at the denominators to compare the fractions. You find that $\frac{3}{5} > \frac{3}{7}$. In the original problem, you have the opposites of 0.6 and $\frac{3}{7}$, so $-0.6 < -\frac{3}{7}$.

25. Jake; Sample: Jake scored $\frac{9}{12}$ or $\frac{3}{4}$ of his field goals and Reggie scored $\frac{3}{5}$ of his. The numerators of $\frac{3}{4}$ and $\frac{3}{5}$ are the same. This means that $\frac{3}{4} > \frac{3}{5}$, since $\frac{3}{4}$ has a smaller denominator than $\frac{3}{5}$. Therefore, Jake had the better average.

26. <　　　　　　　**27.** >

28. <　　　　　　　**29.** <

30. >　　　　　　　**31.** >

32. C

33. I - B, II - D, III - E, IV - C, V - A

34. 4 turns of gear A, 3 turns of gear B

Mixed Review p. 302

1. $a \le 1$

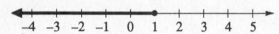

2. $y < -2$

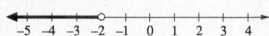

3. 8.15

4. $-0.\overline{45}$

5. about 9,350 ft

Problem Solving Practice

   Page 303

1. $\frac{3}{8}$ lb

2. Yes; The square has sides that are 1 in. long. A circle with a diameter of 1 in. would have a circumference of π in. or about 3.14 in. This circle has a circumference of only 3 in., so its diameter must be less than 1 in.

3. 6 students

4. 1.5 h

5. 1,225

6. a. 37, 50

   b. 4, 2

7. 1:24 P.M.

8. 1977

9.

7-5 Addition and Subtraction
Pages 304–307

Work Together p. 304
Check students' work.

Think and Discuss pp. 304–305

1. $17\frac{1}{6}$

2. Answers may vary.

Sample: Since $-4\frac{2}{3} = -4 + (-\frac{2}{3})$ and $6\frac{1}{2} = 6 + \frac{1}{2}$, you can find $-4 + 6$ and $-\frac{2}{3} + \frac{1}{2}$ and then add the results.

Try These p. 306

3. a. $\boxed{\frac{7}{10}} - \boxed{\frac{1}{2}} = \frac{1}{5}$

b. $\boxed{\frac{7}{10}} + \frac{-1}{2} = \frac{1}{5}$

4. a. $\boxed{\frac{11}{12}} - \frac{3}{4} = \frac{1}{6}$

b. $\boxed{\frac{11}{12}} + \frac{-3}{4} = \frac{1}{6}$

5. $\frac{7}{12}$

6. $-1\frac{1}{4}$

7. $-3\frac{1}{14}$

8. $2\frac{2}{3}$

9. a. $19\frac{5}{8}$ in.

   b. $4\frac{3}{8}$ in.

10. $\frac{1}{10}$; 0.1

11. $-\frac{1}{8}$; −0.125

12. −1

13. $1\frac{1}{2}$; 1.5

On Your Own pp. 306–307

14.

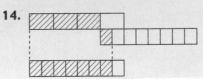

$\frac{3}{4} + \frac{1}{8} = \frac{7}{8}$

15.

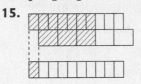

$\frac{7}{10} - \frac{3}{5} = \frac{1}{10}$

16.

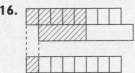

$\frac{5}{8} + (-\frac{1}{2}) = \frac{1}{8}$

17.

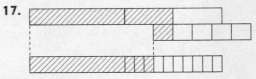

$1\frac{1}{2} - \frac{1}{5} = 1\frac{3}{10}$

18. $-1\frac{11}{12}$

19. $-10\frac{3}{20}$

20. $3\frac{1}{6}$

21. $-3\frac{8}{15}$

22. $1\frac{5}{24}$

23. $3\frac{19}{24}$

24. $-1\frac{1}{2}$

25. $-\frac{7}{8}$

26. $\frac{8}{21}$

27. $-3\frac{21}{40}$

28. a. less by $4\frac{1}{8}$ in.

$38\frac{3}{4} - 34\frac{5}{8} = \frac{155}{4} - \frac{277}{8}$

$\frac{310}{8} - \frac{277}{8} = \frac{33}{8} = 4\frac{1}{8}$

b. under by $\frac{1}{4}$ in.

$65 - 64\frac{3}{4} = \frac{1}{4}$

c. yes; wheelbase must be lengthened by at least $\frac{1}{4}$ in.

29. Sample: After the fractions have been written to have a common denominator, the addition or subtraction is performed by adding or subtracting the numerators, which are integers; the common denominator stays the same. For example, to add $-\frac{3}{8}$ and $\frac{7}{8}$, add the integers -3 and 7. The result is 4. Use the common denominator, 8, as the denominator for the sum. The final answer is $\frac{4}{8}$ or $\frac{1}{2}$.

30–33. Accept reasonable estimates. Samples are given.

30. 12

31. $-8\frac{1}{2}$

32. 0

33. -3

34. Sample: No; He used $\frac{3}{4}$ c for 4 bowls, so he needs 3 c for 16 bowls.

35. Yes; no; Subtraction of integers is neither commutative nor associative.

36. $-\frac{7}{9}$; $-0.\overline{7}$

37. $-\frac{3}{4}$; -0.75

38. 0

39. $-\frac{5}{6}$ $-0.8\overline{3}$

40. Check students' work.

Mixed Review p. 307

1. 23

2. 2.5

3. 0.9

4. 1.4

5. <

6. <

7. 97,531

7-6 Multiplication and Division
Pages 308–311

Think and Discuss pp. 308–309

1. Sample: divide numerator and denominator by 5.

2. **a.** 7

   b. $-\frac{4}{11}$

   c. 1

   d. -1

3. **a.** Sample: -4

   b. $-1\frac{3}{4}$; $-\frac{4}{7}$

   c. $-4\frac{1}{2}$

Try These p. 310

4. $\frac{5}{12} \cdot \frac{3}{4} = \frac{15}{48}$ or $\frac{5}{16}$

5. $-6\frac{2}{5} \div (-1\frac{3}{5}) = 4$

6. $\frac{12}{35}$

7. -12

8. $5\frac{1}{3}$

9. $-2\frac{14}{15}$

10. **a.** $\frac{1}{6}$

    b. $-\frac{5}{6}$

    c. $8\frac{1}{3}$

11. 9

12. -24

13. $\frac{9}{14}$

14. $-\frac{5}{4}$ or $-1\frac{1}{4}$

15. 11 banners

Mixed Review p. 310

1. $x + 2$

2. $25n + 10(n - 3)$ cents
   or $0.25n + 0.1(n - 3)$ dollars

3. $\frac{7}{36}$

4. $-\frac{1}{12}$

5. 17, 29

On Your Own pp. 310–311

16.

$\frac{1}{3} \cdot \frac{1}{4} = \frac{1}{12}$

17.

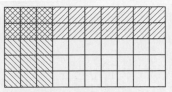

$\frac{3}{10} \cdot \frac{2}{5} = \frac{6}{50} = \frac{3}{25}$

18.

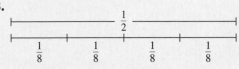

$\frac{1}{2} \div 4 = \frac{1}{8}$

19.

$-1\frac{1}{2} \div 6 = -\frac{1}{4}$

20. C

21. Answers may vary. Sample: The product of any number and zero is zero.

22. a. 120 quarters

   b. 150 half-dollars

23. $-10\frac{7}{8}$

24. $-\frac{2}{3}$

25. $6\frac{4}{5}$

26. -89

27. -40

28. $2\frac{1}{2}$

29. $1\frac{17}{64}$ in.^{2}

30. No; $\frac{1}{\frac{1}{2}} = 1 \div \frac{1}{2} = 1 \cdot 2 = 2$ and $\frac{\frac{1}{2}}{2} = \frac{1}{2}$

31. $-\frac{1}{2}$; -0.5

32. $8\frac{3}{5}$; 8.6

33. $1\frac{1}{5}$; 1.2

34. 192 muffins

35. Yes; You only need 6 cups and you have $10\frac{2}{3}$ c.

36. a. $1\frac{7}{8}$ c milk

   $3\frac{3}{4}$ c wheat bran cereal

   3 eggs (but use only $2\frac{1}{2}$ eggs)

   $1\frac{1}{4}$ c vegetable oil

   $\frac{5}{6}$ c molasses

   $3\frac{1}{8}$ c whole wheat flour

   $7\frac{1}{2}$ tsp baking powder

   $2\frac{1}{2}$ tsp salt

   b. $3.30

7-7 Work Backward

Pages 312–314

1. a. $7,500

   b. Paris, Cairo, Tokyo

   c. Paris: $\frac{2}{3}$ of the original amount; Cairo: $5,000; Tokyo: $\frac{1}{2}$ of what was left

   d. Sample: Determine how much money they had at the start of the mission.

2. a. $15,000

   b. $20,000

   c. $60,000

3. They started with $60,000.

4. a. $60,000

   b. $20,000

   c. $15,000

   d. Yes

Try These p. 313

5. a. $66,000

   b. $30,000

6. a. 108

   b. multiplication, subtraction, division, addition; They are the inverse operations.

7. 8:45 A.M.

Mixed Review p. 313

1. 4 left, 4 down

2. 5 left, 8 down

3. $8\frac{4}{7}$

4. $\frac{5}{27}$

5. 22 push ups

On Your Own pp. 313–314

8. 3 packs of 25, 5 packs of 75

9. $1, \frac{1}{2}, 2$

10. 20 bu

11. a. 14 combinations

  b. 1 quarter, 3 dimes, 2 nickels

12. 220 pens

13. white house, yellow door

14. 8:45 A.M.

15. Answers may vary. Sample: The cryptographer might use information about most frequently used letters to make some initial conjectures about what letters some of the code letters represent. For example, since "e" is the most commonly used letter in the English language, the cryptographer might be able to determine the coded word for "the." Knowing those letters could help determine other words and thus other letters.

Checkpoint p. 314

1. 168

2. $-1\frac{2}{3}, -\frac{5}{8}, -0.58, 0.72, \frac{3}{4}$

3. $\frac{7}{12}$

4. $\frac{7}{20}$

5. $-\frac{27}{32}$

6. $-6\frac{1}{12}$

7. $17.80

7-8 Rational Numbers with Exponents

  Pages 315–317

Think and Discuss pp. 315–316

1. a. $3^4 = 81$ **b.** $4^2 = 16$

  c. $2^1 = 2$ **d.** $5^3 = 125$

2. a. $2^5 = 32$

  b. $11^1 = 11$

  c. $6^3 = 216$

  d. r^3

3. 1

4. 1

5. $\frac{1}{3}$

6. $\frac{1}{8}$

7. $-\frac{1}{8}$

8. a. $\frac{1}{7^2}; 7^{-2}$ **b.** $\frac{1}{3}; 3^{-1}$

  c. $\frac{1}{2^7}; 2^{-7}$ **d.** $\frac{1}{w^4}; w^{-4}$

Work Together p. 316

9. a. $\frac{1}{2}, \frac{1}{4}, \frac{1}{8}$

  b. $2^{-1}, 2^{-2}, 2^{-3}$

10. $5^5, 5^3, 5^1, 5^{-1}, 5^{-3}, 5^{-5},$

  $3125, 125, 5, \boxed{0.2}, \boxed{0.08}, \boxed{0.00032}$

11. Sample: $81, 27, 9, 3, 1, \frac{1}{3}, \frac{1}{9}, \ldots$

On Your Own pp. 316–317

12. $\frac{1}{81}$

13. 1

14. $\frac{1}{4}$

15. $-\frac{1}{125}$

16. 1

17. $\frac{1}{81}$

18. 6^{-5}

19. $(-4)^{-8}$

20. c^{-7}

21. 9^{-1}

22. $(-8)^{-1}$

23. 100^{-1}

24. a. 2 $\boxed{y^x}$ 5 $\boxed{+/-}$ $\boxed{=}$ **0.03125**

  b. 3 $\boxed{y^x}$ 3 $\boxed{+/-}$ $\boxed{=}$ **0.0$\overline{37}$**

  c. 6 $\boxed{+/-}$ $\boxed{y^x}$ 2 $\boxed{+/-}$ $\boxed{=}$ **0.02$\overline{7}$**

  d. 4 $\boxed{+/-}$ $\boxed{y^x}$ 2 $\boxed{+/-}$ $\boxed{=}$ **0.0625**

  e. 4 $\boxed{y^x}$ 3 $\boxed{+/-}$ $\boxed{=}$ **0.015625**

25. c^2

26. $\frac{1}{s^4}$

27. 1

28. $\frac{1}{m^7}$

29. Answers may vary. The rules for multiplication involve addition, and the rules for division involve subtraction. (Numbers with base 0 are excluded from the rules for division.) The base of the answer is the same as the base of the factors, and the exponent is the sum or difference of the exponents of the factors. Also, since division is the same as multiplication by a reciprocal, the following is true.

$$\frac{a^m}{a^n} = a^m \cdot \frac{1}{a^n} = a^m \cdot a^{-n} = a^{m+(-n)} = a^{m-n}$$

30. when $a < 0$; when $a > 0$; never

31. 125

32. $\frac{1}{81}$

33. $-\frac{1}{64}$

34. 343

35. 1

36. $\frac{1}{1,296}$

37. -27

38. $\frac{1}{10,000}$

39. false; $1 \neq 4$

40. true; $1 = 1$

41. false; $1 \neq -1$

42. false; $4 \neq 1$

43. 10^{-3}

44. 10^{-1}

45. 10^{-4}

46. 10^{-6}

47. 10^1

48. C

49. 4^4; 256; $\frac{1}{4^{-4}}$

Mixed Review p. 317

1. 1,260°

2. 120°

3. 243

4. $\frac{1}{125}$

5. -9

6. 16

7-9 Scientific Notation
Pages 318–321

Work Together p. 318

1. a. $6.71 \times 10^3 = 6.71 \times 1,000 = \boxed{6,710}$

$6.71 \times 10^2 = 6.71 \times \boxed{100} = \boxed{671}$

$6.71 \times 10^1 = 6.71 \times \boxed{10} = \boxed{67.1}$

$6.71 \times 10^0 = 6.71 \times \boxed{1} = \boxed{6.71}$

$6.71 \times 10^{-1} = 6.71 \times \frac{1}{10}$

$= 6.71 \times 0.1$

$= \boxed{0.671}$

$6.71 \times 10^{-2} = 6.71 \times \frac{1}{100}$

$= 6.71 \times 0.01$

$= \boxed{0.0671}$

$6.71 \times 10^{-3} = 6.71 \times \frac{1}{1,000}$

$= 6.71 \times 0.001$

$= \boxed{0.00671}$

b. Answers may vary. Sample: As you go down the list, you can find the product in the next line by dividing by 10. If you increase the exponent of 10 by 1, the decimal point moves one place to the right. If you decrease the exponent of 10 by 1, the decimal point moves one place to the left.

Think and Discuss pp. 318–319

2. 2.59×10^{11} mi^3

3. a. Yes

   b. The first factor, 25.9, is not less than 10.

Mixed Review p. 319

1. $y = -\frac{1}{5}x - 3$; $-\frac{1}{5}$, -3

2. $y = \frac{3}{2}x - 2$; $\frac{3}{2}$, -2

3. 2,030,000

4. 0.0000429

5. $-8, -13, -19$

Try These p. 320

4. a. 72 is not less than 10.

b. $7.2 \times 10^5 = 720{,}000$

c. 0.00001 is not in exponential form.

5. 4.56×10^4 **6.** 1.3×10^{-8}

7. 8×10^7 **8.** 2×10^{-1}

9. 0.000000007 **10.** 136,200,000

11. 0.0000402 **12.** 4,000

13. 4.2×10^{-8}, 2.15×10^{-7}, 3.1×10^{-5}, 5.678×10^{-5}

14. 1.6×10^7

15. 1×10^{-5}

On Your Own p. 321

16. $7.892 \times 10^{-10} = 0.0000000007892$

17. $6 \times 10^{13} = 60{,}000{,}000{,}000{,}000$

18. $4.9 \times 10^{-12} = 0.0000000000049$

19. aluminum, glass, water, cork, air

20. 7,010,000,000,000

21. 0.000000003904

22. 1×10^{-8}

23. 4,000,000

24. 9×10^{11}

25. 3.008×10^{-8}

26. In the scientific notation for the number, the first factor is greater than or equal to 1 and less than 10. If this factor is less than 5, then the exponent of 10 remains the same when the number is doubled. But if the factor is 5 or greater, the exponent of 10 will increase by 1.

27. 5×10^{12} red blood cells

7-10 Rational Number Equations
Pages 322–325

Think and Discuss pp. 322–323

1. B; Sample: The diagram shows that the piece labeled x, when joined to the shaded strip to its right, gives a piece that is the same length as the strip of shaded pieces at the bottom.

The shaded strip at the top represents $\frac{5}{6}$, and the shaded strip at the bottom represents $\frac{11}{12}$.

2. $\frac{1}{12}$; Sample: The left and right sides of the piece labeled x line up vertically with the left and right sides of the first shaded piece at the bottom, and that piece represents $\frac{1}{12}$.

3. Sample: so that m will be alone on one side

Try These p. 323

4. $x + \frac{3}{5} = \frac{7}{10}$; $x = \frac{1}{10}$

5. $x - \frac{1}{2} = \frac{1}{12}$; $x = \frac{7}{12}$

6. $-1\frac{1}{2}$

7. $-4\frac{13}{18}$

8. $3\frac{1}{2}$ or 3.5

9. a. $60 + 1\frac{2}{3}d = 108$

b. $d = 28\frac{4}{5}$; 29 days

c. 33 days

d. 39 days

10. $-\frac{3}{4}$

11. $-\frac{1}{3}$

12. -3.6

Mixed Review p. 324

1. acute

2. obtuse

3. acute

4. $\frac{3}{5}$

5. $\frac{27}{5}$ or $5\frac{2}{5}$

6. $600

On Your Own pp. 324–325

13–14. Check students' work. Sample:

13.

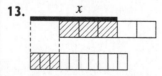

$x - \frac{3}{5} = \frac{3}{10}$

$x = \frac{3}{10} + \frac{6}{10}$

$x = \frac{9}{10}$

14.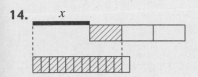

$$x + \frac{1}{3} = \frac{11}{12}$$
$$x = \frac{11}{12} - \frac{4}{12}$$
$$x = \frac{7}{12}$$

15. $-\frac{5}{12}$

16. -12

17. $\frac{19}{24}$

18. 20

19. 2.9

20. -2

21. $x + x + 9\frac{1}{8} = 25\frac{3}{4}$
$$2x + 9\frac{1}{8} = 25\frac{3}{4}$$
$$2x = 25\frac{3}{4} - 9\frac{1}{8}$$
$$2x = 16\frac{5}{8}$$
$$x = 8\frac{5}{16}$$

The unknown sides are $8\frac{5}{16}$ in. long.

22. $l \cdot 3\frac{1}{3} = 15$
$$l = 15 \div 3\frac{1}{3}$$
$$l = 15 \div \frac{10}{3}$$
$$l = \frac{15}{1} \times \frac{3}{10}$$
$$l = \frac{45}{10}$$
$$l = \frac{9}{2} = 4\frac{1}{2}$$

The rug is $4\frac{1}{2}$ yd long.

23. $\frac{3}{4}s = 9$
$$s = \frac{9}{1} \times \frac{4}{3}$$
$$s = \frac{36}{3}$$
$$s = 12$$

There are 12 sheets of plywood in the stack.

24. $2 + 0.1d = 15$
$$0.1d = 15 - 2$$
$$d = \frac{13}{0.1}$$
$$d = 130$$

The plant will be 15 in. tall in 130 days.

25. $\frac{1}{2}, -\frac{1}{2}$

26. no solution

27. $1\frac{1}{2}, -1\frac{1}{2}$

28. $1\frac{1}{2}$

29. $\frac{1}{2}, -\frac{1}{2}$

30. $\frac{1}{2}, 1\frac{1}{2}$

31. Sample: In both cases you can add, subtract, multiply or divide using the same number on each side to help solve the equation. The arithmetic involves fractions.

32. $x + 4\frac{1}{4} + x + x + 2\frac{1}{2} = 12$
$$3x + 6\frac{3}{4} = 12$$
$$3x = 12 - 6\frac{3}{4}$$
$$3x = 5\frac{1}{4} = \frac{21}{4}$$
$$x = \frac{21}{4} \times \frac{1}{3}$$
$$x = \frac{7}{4} = 1\frac{3}{4}$$

33. $4 + n + n + 10 = 24\frac{1}{2}$
$$2n + 14 = 24\frac{1}{2}$$
$$2n = 10\frac{1}{2}$$
$$n = 5\frac{1}{4}$$

34. B

35. $\sum \text{ß ß } \delta \triangle \triangle$

36. a. DeQ: $22\frac{1}{2} + x = 26\frac{1}{8}$
$$x = 3\frac{5}{8}$$

The price increased by $3\frac{5}{8}$ points.

HPG: $33\frac{3}{4} + x = 29\frac{5}{8}$
$$x = -4\frac{1}{8}$$

The price decreased by $4\frac{1}{8}$ points.

MJC: $25\frac{1}{4} + x = 19$
$$x = -6\frac{1}{4}$$

The price decreased by $6\frac{1}{4}$ points.

ZaC: $47\frac{3}{4} + x = 54\frac{3}{4}$
$$x = 7$$

The price increased by 7 points.

b. $x + 4\frac{4}{8} = 29\frac{5}{8}$
$$x = 25\frac{1}{8}$$

Checkpoint p. 325

1. $\frac{1}{27}$ 2. $\frac{1}{25}$

3. 1   4. r^8

5. $\frac{1}{d^5}$ 6. 0.00466

7. 2.23×10^8 8. 799,000

9. 4.9×10^{-4} 10. $-1\frac{1}{15}$

11. $-\frac{29}{30}$ 12. $1\frac{4}{9}$

Practice

Page 326

1. $2^3 \cdot 3^2 \cdot 5$ 2. $3^4 \cdot 5^2$

3. $2^3 \cdot 3^2 \cdot 7$ 4. $2^4 \cdot 3 \cdot 5^2$

5. $3^2 \cdot 5^3$ 6. 4; 144

7. 3; 60   8. 2; 24

9. 3; 90   10. $0.\overline{8}$

11. $1.\overline{6}$ 12. 2.75

13. 0.625   14. $18\frac{2}{5}$

15. $\frac{83}{99}$ 16. $6\frac{1}{8}$

17. $24\frac{9}{25}$ 18. >

19. =   20. <

21. >   22. $\frac{1}{24}$

23. $3\frac{1}{6}$ 24. $\frac{1}{2}$

25. $-\frac{1}{12}$ 26. 5^{-3}

27. $(-2)^{-4}$ 28. y^{-5}

29. $(-27)^{-1}$ or $(-3)^{-3}$ 30. 8^{-2}

31. 6.59×10^{-4} 32. 80,600

33. 1.75×10^7 34. 0.00004

35. −40   36. $-\frac{7}{6}$ or $-1\frac{1}{6}$

37. $\frac{44}{3}$ or $14\frac{2}{3}$ 38. $-\frac{1}{3}$

39. −96   40. 4:35 P.M.

7-11 Exploring Irrational Numbers

Pages 327–329

Think and Discuss p. 327

1. a. 0.1   b. $0.\overline{1}$

   c. 0.4375   d. $0.\overline{21}$

2. a. $\frac{3}{10}$ b. $\frac{1}{3}$

   c. $\frac{3}{25}$ d. $\frac{4}{33}$

3. a. Sample: After the decimal come one 0, one 2, one 0, two 2's, one 0, three 2's, and so on.

   b. Sample: 0.595995999. . .

   c. Answers may vary. Sample: 0.012001122000111222. . .

4. a. rational; All terminating decimals can be expressed as fractions with integers as the numerators and nonzero integers as the denominators.

   b. irrational; The digit 8 occurs repeatedly, but between one 8 and the next, the number of 1s increases by one as you go from left to right.

   c. rational; $0.\overline{81} = \frac{81}{99} = \frac{9}{11}$

   d. rational; By definition, a fraction with an integer as the numerator and a nonzero integer as the denominator represents a rational number.

Work Together p. 328

5. a. Numbers in the x^2 column are calculator-rounded values.

x	x^2
2.2	4.8
2.23	4.9729
2.236	4.999696
2.2360	4.999696
2.23606	4.999964324
2.236067	4.999995628
2.2360679	4.999999653
2.23606797	4.999999966
2.236067977	4.999999998

   b. They are getting closer to 5.

c. 2.236067978; The values in the *x* column approach $\sqrt{5}$ as you read down the column.

d. No; Answers may vary. Sample: It was stated on page 327 that $\sqrt{2}$ is irrational. There seems to be no pattern in the digits after the decimal point as you read down the *x* column. It seems possible that $\sqrt{5}$, like $\sqrt{2}$, is a nonterminating and nonrepeating decimal. $2 < \sqrt{5} < 3$.

6. a. irrational

   b. rational

   c. rational

   d. irrational

   e. irrational

7. a. No

   b. Yes

8. Answers may vary. Samples given.

   a. Sample: $\sqrt{2}$, $\sqrt{3}$

   b. Sample: $\frac{2}{3}, -\frac{2}{5}$

   c. Sample: $-2, -3$

On Your Own p. 329

9. real, rational

10. real, rational

11. real, irrational

12. real, rational

13. real, rational, integer, whole

14. real, irrational

15. real, rational, integer

16. real, irrational

17. irrational; By the Pythagorean Theorem, $AB = \sqrt{13}$. Since 13 is not a perfect square, AB must be irrational.

18. Answers may vary. Sample: I would place the set of natural numbers in their own circle or square within the rectangle for the set of whole numbers.

19. true

20. false

21. true

22. false

23. a. 0.11111111111111 . . .

   b. rational; The sum equals $0.\overline{1}$, which is a repeating decimal and therefore a rational number.

24. a. i. $2\,\boxed{\sqrt{}} \times 5\,\boxed{\sqrt{}} \boxed{=}$ **3.16227766**

    ii. $3\,\boxed{\sqrt{}} \times 6\,\boxed{\sqrt{}} \boxed{=}$ **4.242640687**

    iii. $2\,\boxed{\sqrt{}} \times 8\,\boxed{\sqrt{}} \boxed{=}$ **4**

    iv. $3\,\boxed{\sqrt{}} \times 12\,\boxed{\sqrt{}} \boxed{=}$ **6**

    v. $5\,\boxed{\sqrt{}} \times 15\,\boxed{\sqrt{}} \boxed{=}$ **8.660254038**

    vi. $5\,\boxed{\sqrt{}} \times 20\,\boxed{\sqrt{}} \boxed{=}$ **10**

   b. the products for **iii**, **iv**, and **vi**

   c. Sample: $\sqrt{2}$, $\sqrt{32}$

Mixed Review p. 329

1. 28

2. 2

3. $-\frac{1}{9}$

4. 16

5. irrational

6. rational

7. 9

Chapter 7 Wrap Up

Pages 330–331

1. $2^3 \cdot 3^2 \cdot 5$

2. $2^2 \cdot 5^2 \cdot 7$

3. $2^5 \cdot 3^2 \cdot 5$

4. $2 \cdot 3^3 \cdot 7$

5. $2^2 \cdot 3^3 \cdot 5 \cdot 13$

6. rational   **7.** rational

8. rational   **9.** rational

10. irrational   **11.** <

12. =   **13.** >

14. <   **15.** $\frac{13}{8}$ or $1\frac{5}{8}$

16. $5\frac{2}{3}$ **17.** $-1\frac{1}{2}$

18. $\frac{1}{9}$ **19.** $\frac{1}{2}$

20. $-2\frac{1}{10}$ **21.** $\frac{1}{16}$

22. $\frac{13}{4}$ or $3\frac{1}{4}$ **23.** $\frac{1}{36}$

24. 1

25. $\frac{1}{t^2}$

26. 64

27. $\frac{1}{4}$

28. 2.956×10^2

29. 8.3×10^{-3}

30. 9.056×10^4

31. 3×10^{-2}

32. 5.987×10^{-1}

33. $\frac{15}{2}$ or $7\frac{1}{2}$

34. $-\frac{19}{18}$ or $-1\frac{1}{18}$

35. $\frac{1}{3}$

36. $-1\frac{1}{3}$

37. 7:15 A.M.

Getting Ready for Chapter 8 p. 331

Answers may vary. Samples given.

1. Sample: $\frac{6}{8}, \frac{9}{12}, \frac{30}{40}$

2. Sample: $\frac{4}{6}, \frac{6}{9}, \frac{20}{30}$

3. Sample: $\frac{8}{10}, \frac{12}{15}, \frac{40}{50}$

4. Sample: $\frac{2}{12}, \frac{3}{18}, \frac{10}{60}$

5. Sample: $\frac{14}{20}, \frac{21}{30}, \frac{70}{100}$

Chapter 7 Assessment
Page 334

1. a. $-1\frac{1}{5}$

   b. $\frac{3}{5}$

   c. $-\frac{1}{5}$

   d. $1\frac{1}{5}$

2. a. 0

   b. $\frac{1}{2}$

   c. 1

   d. $\frac{1}{2}$

3. a. <

   b. <

   c. =

   d. =

4. a. 4; 48   **b.** 1; 150

   c. 3; 72   **d.** 4; 480

5. a. $\frac{7}{12}$

   b. $\frac{1}{6}$

   c. -6

   d. -9

6. a. $-\frac{4}{3}$ or $-1\frac{1}{3}$

   b. $\frac{35}{18}$ or $1\frac{17}{18}$

   c. $-\frac{11}{3}$ or $-3\frac{2}{3}$

   d. $\frac{1}{8}$

7. D

8. Sample: A rational number can be represented as a fraction $\frac{a}{b}$, where a is an integer and b is a nonzero integer. The decimal for a rational number will be terminating or repeating. Neither of these things is true for irrational numbers.

9. a. -125

   b. 64

   c. $\frac{1}{6}$

   d. 0

10. a. 4.59×10^{-3}

   b. 1.8×10^7

   c. 7.59×10^3

   d. 3×10^{-2}

11. a. 9,350

   b. 0.000153

   c. 0.6125

   d. 918

12. 27 in.

13. $-\frac{2}{3}$

14. Sample problem: Maria paid half the bill for the dinner that she and Lucas had at their favorite restaurant. Since the waiter gave special service, she left a $5 tip. In all, she left $15. What was the amount of their bill?

$$\frac{1}{2}t + 5 = 15$$
$$\frac{1}{2}t = 10$$
$$t = \frac{10}{1} \times \frac{2}{1}$$
$$t = 20$$

Chapter 7 Cumulative Review

Page 335

1. C

2. D

3. D

4. A

5. B

6. C

7. D

8. A

9. C

10. B

11. C

Chapter 8 Applications of Proportions

8-1 Exploring Ratios and Rates
Pages 339–342

Think and Discuss pp. 339–340

1. Sample: ratio of number of girls in class to number of boys; ratio of the number of students to number of teachers

2. Sample: $\frac{\text{yellow}}{\text{blue}} = \frac{9}{7}$; $\frac{\text{total}}{\text{blue}} = \frac{16}{7}$; $\frac{\text{yellow}}{\text{total}} = \frac{9}{16}$

3. Sample: $\frac{\text{wins}}{\text{losses}} = \frac{11}{7}$; $\frac{\text{losses}}{\text{wins}} = \frac{7}{11}$; $\frac{\text{total}}{\text{wins}} = \frac{22}{11}$

4. $\frac{\$8}{5 \text{ lines}} = \$1.60$ per line

Work Together p. 340

5. Bran Crisps Regular – $\frac{\$2.49}{14 \text{ oz}} = \$.18/\text{oz}$;

   Bran Crisps Giant – $\frac{\$6.39}{39 \text{ oz}} = \$.16/\text{oz}$;

   Crunchy-O's – $\frac{\$4.29}{24 \text{ oz}} = \$.18/\text{oz}$;

   The Original Toasty Flakes – $\frac{\$3.49}{18.5 \text{ oz}} = \$.19/\text{oz}$;
   So Bran Crisps Giant has the lowest unit price.

6. Sample: No; the lowest unit price may be for a larger quantity than you need.

Try These p. 341

7. Samples: $\frac{13}{24}$; $\frac{11}{24}$; $\frac{11}{13}$

8. Samples: $\frac{5}{6}$; $\frac{1}{6}$; $\frac{5}{1}$

9. $\frac{4}{9}$; $\frac{5}{9}$; $\frac{4}{5}$

10. Sample: 2 : 3; 12 : 18; 18 : 27; 1 : 1.5

11. $\frac{4}{28} = \frac{1}{7}$ or 1 : 7

12. $\frac{27}{9} = \frac{3}{1}$

13. $\frac{10}{16} = \frac{5}{8}$ or 5 out of 8

14. $\frac{30}{45} = \frac{2}{3}$

15. $\frac{12}{8} = \frac{3}{2}$ or 3 to 2

16. a. 2 : 8 = 1 : 4
    b. $5x + 1x + 2x = 24$; $8x = 24$; $x = 3$. So $5x = 15$, $x = 3$, $2x = 6$.
    So the ratio is 15 : 3 : 6 or 5 : 1 : 2.

17. $\frac{20 \text{ gal}}{4 \text{ min}} = 5$ gal/min

18. $\frac{21}{12 \text{ roses}} = \$1.75$ /rose

19. $\frac{200 \text{ m}}{22 \text{ s}} = 9.\overline{09}$ m/s

20. a. $\frac{16}{12} = \frac{4}{3}$ or 4 to 3

    b. No, in two years Gretchen will be 18 and Josh will be 14. Then the ratio will be $\frac{18}{14}$ or $\frac{9}{7}$.

    c. Ratio becomes closer to 1 : 1.

On Your Own pp. 341–342

21. a. Sample:

    b. 5 : 8; 3 : 5; 8 : 3

22. $\frac{33}{27} = \frac{11}{9}$; 1.22

23. $\frac{27}{33} = \frac{9}{11}$; 0.82

24. $\frac{33}{60} = \frac{11}{20}$; 0.55

25. $\frac{27}{60} = \frac{9}{20}$; 0.45

26. a. Let $m\angle A = 2x$, $m\angle B = x$, $m\angle C = x$.
    Then $2x + x + x = 180$; $4x = 180$; $x = 45$;
    So $m\angle A = 90°$, $m\angle B = 45°$, $m\angle C = 45°$.

    b. right isosceles triangle

27. $\frac{\$3.99}{12 \text{ cans}} = \$.3325/\text{can}$; $\frac{\$2.79}{6 \text{ cans}} = \$.465/\text{can}$;
    $0.465 - 0.3325 = 0.1325$
    about $.13/can

28. $\frac{676 \text{ mi}}{13 \text{ h}} = 52$ mi/h

29. $\frac{412 \text{ words}}{10 \text{ min}} = 41.2$ words/min

30. $\frac{\$66}{8 \text{ h}} = \$8.25/\text{h}$

31. A ratio compares two numbers or two quantities that are expressed in the same unit. A rate compares two different types of quantities that are expressed in different units.

32. midsize = $\frac{200 \text{ mi}}{7 \text{ gal}} = 28.6$ mi/gal;

    minivan = $\frac{350 \text{ mi}}{12 \text{ gal}} = 29.2$ mi/gal

    The minivan has the greater efficiency at about 29 mi/gal.

33. Let $7x$ = red marbles and $5x$ = black marbles. Then $7x + 5x = 60$, $12x = 60$, $x = 5$. So $7x = 35$ and $5x = 25$. Then 35 red marbles and 25 black marbles should be added.

34. 1,000 trees

35. $\frac{7000 \text{ gal}}{1000 \text{ trees}} = \frac{7 \text{ gal}}{1 \text{ tree}}$; 7 gal

36. $\frac{7000 \text{ gal}}{200 \text{ gal}} = \frac{35}{1}$ or 35 : 1

Mixed Review p. 342

1. rational

2. rational

3. irrational

4. rational

5. $f(-3) = 4(-3) - 3 = -12 - 3 = -15$;
$f(2.5) = 4(2.5) - 3 = 10 - 3 = 7$

6. $f(0) = 4(0) - 3 = -3$; $f(2) = 4(2) - 3 = 5$;
$f(4) = 4(4) - 3 = 13$; $f(6) = 4(6) - 3 = 21$;
$f(8) = 4(8) - 3 = 29$

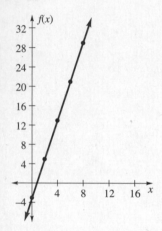

7. Use the strategy of working backward. Start with the final result of 10. Then use inverse operations to undo each operation. $10 + 5 = 15$; $15 \div 10 = 1.5$, $1.5 - 2 = -0.5$; $-0.5 \times (-6) = 3$

8-2 Using Dimensional Analysis
Pages 343–345

Think and Discuss p. 343

1. Sample: Multiply by $\frac{1 \text{ lb}}{16 \text{ oz}}$ so that the oz-units will divide out and the only unit left is the lb-unit.

2. a. $\frac{75 \text{ min}}{1} \cdot \frac{60 \text{ s}}{1 \text{ min}} = 4,500 \text{ s}$

b. $\frac{75 \text{ s}}{1} \cdot \frac{1 \text{ min}}{60 \text{ s}} = 1.25 \text{ min}$

3. $\frac{5.5 \text{ qt}}{1} \cdot \frac{2 \text{ pt}}{1 \text{ qt}} \cdot \frac{2 \text{ c}}{1 \text{ pt}} \cdot \frac{8 \text{ fl oz}}{1 \text{ c}} = 176 \text{ fl oz}$

4. Accept reasonable estimates. Sample: 6 cups

5. a. $\frac{92.4 \text{ ft}}{1 \text{ s}} \cdot \frac{1 \text{ mi}}{5280 \text{ ft}} \cdot \frac{60 \text{ s}}{1 \text{ min}} \cdot \frac{60 \text{ min}}{1 \text{ h}} = 63 \text{ mi/h}$

b. Sample: no; it is unlikely that a cheetah can maintain its top speed of 63 mi/h for 1 h.

On Your Own pp. 344–345

6. $\frac{32 \text{ in.}}{1} \cdot \frac{1 \text{ ft}}{12 \text{ in.}} = 2.67 \text{ ft}$

7. $\frac{325 \text{ da}}{1} \cdot \frac{24 \text{ h}}{1 \text{ da}} = 7,800 \text{ h}$

8. $\frac{9 \text{ gal}}{1} \cdot \frac{4 \text{ qt}}{1 \text{ gal}} \cdot \frac{2 \text{ pt}}{1 \text{ qt}} \cdot \frac{2 \text{ c}}{1 \text{ pt}} = 144 \text{ c}$

9. Check students' work.

10. $\frac{90 \text{ in.}}{1 \text{ min}} \cdot \frac{1 \text{ ft}}{12 \text{ in.}} = 7.5 \text{ ft/min}$

11. $\frac{\$27}{1 \text{ h}} \cdot \frac{1 \text{ h}}{60 \text{ min}} = \$.45/\text{min}$

12. $\frac{14 \text{ cm}}{1 \text{ s}} \cdot \frac{1 \text{ m}}{100 \text{ cm}} \cdot \frac{60 \text{ s}}{1 \text{ min}} \cdot \frac{60 \text{ min}}{1 \text{ h}} = 504 \text{ m/h}$

13. $\frac{64 \text{ yd}}{1 \text{ h}} \cdot \frac{36 \text{ in.}}{1 \text{ yd}} \cdot \frac{1 \text{ h}}{60 \text{ min}} \cdot \frac{1 \text{ min}}{60 \text{ s}} = 0.64 \text{ in./s}$

14. $\frac{95 \text{ mi}}{1 \text{ h}} \cdot \frac{5280 \text{ ft}}{1 \text{ mi}} \cdot \frac{1 \text{ h}}{60 \text{ min}} \cdot \frac{1 \text{ min}}{60 \text{ s}} = 139.3 \text{ ft/s}$

15. For the centipede: $\frac{30 \text{ m}}{1 \text{ min}} \cdot \frac{100 \text{ cm}}{1 \text{ m}} \cdot \frac{1 \text{ min}}{60 \text{ s}} =$ 50 cm/s.
Since 50 cm/s > 29 cm/s, the centipede is faster than the cockroach.

16. Sample: $\frac{65 \text{ beats}}{1 \text{ min}} \cdot \frac{60 \text{ min}}{1 \text{ h}} \cdot \frac{24 \text{ h}}{1 \text{ da}} \cdot \frac{365 \text{ da}}{1 \text{ y}} =$ 34,164,000 beats/y

17–18. Accept reasonable estimates.

17. $3.04 \approx 3$ and $\frac{3 \text{ mi}}{1} \cdot \frac{5280 \text{ ft}}{1 \text{ mi}} \rightarrow$ about 15,840 ft

18. $354 \text{ s} \approx 360$ and $\frac{360 \text{ s}}{1} \cdot \frac{1 \text{ min}}{60 \text{ s}} \rightarrow$ about 6 min

19. $\frac{141,542,000 \text{ births}}{1 \text{ y}} \cdot \frac{1 \text{ y}}{365 \text{ da}} \approx 387,786$ births/da;

$\frac{387,786 \text{ births}}{1 \text{ da}} \cdot \frac{1 \text{ da}}{24 \text{ h}} \approx 16,158$ births/h;

$\frac{16,158 \text{ births}}{1 \text{ h}} \cdot \frac{1 \text{ h}}{60 \text{ min}} \approx 269$ births/min;

$\frac{269 \text{ births}}{1 \text{ min}} \cdot \frac{1 \text{ min}}{60 \text{ s}} \approx 4.5$ births/s

Mixed Review p. 345

1. $\frac{\$16.80}{14 \text{ gal}} = \$1.20/\text{gal}$

2. $\frac{\$17.45}{5 \text{ lb}} = \$3.49/\text{lb}$

3. $\frac{292.5 \text{ mi}}{6.5 \text{ h}} = 45 \text{ mi/h}$

4. $\frac{607{,}000 \text{ people}}{61.4 \text{ mi}^2} \approx 9{,}886$ people/mi²

5.

8	3 7
9	0 4 5 7 8 9
10	0 5
11	2
12	5 7
13	4 9

6. 90–99

7. $139 - 83 = 56$

8-3 Solving Proportions

Pages 346–348

Think and Discuss pp. 346–347

1. $1.3 \cdot 18 = 23.4$; $6 \cdot 3.6 = 21.6$; No

2. Sample: $\frac{4}{15} \approx \frac{1}{4}$; $\frac{1}{4} = \frac{3}{c}$; $c \approx 12$; $\frac{4}{15} = \frac{3}{c}$; $4c = 45$; $c = 11.25$

LOOK BACK: Yes; Each U.S. dollar equals approx. 1.31 Canadian dollars.

Try These p. 347

3. $2a = 90$, $a = 45$

4. $12k = 84$, $k = 7$

5. $45 = 15y$, $y = 3$

6. $72 = 8t$, $t = 9$

7. $\frac{12 \text{ oranges}}{\$2.99} = \frac{30 \text{ oranges}}{x}$; $12x = 2.99 \cdot 30$;

$12x - 89.7$, $\frac{12x}{12} = \frac{89.7}{12}$; $x \approx 7.48$

$\$7.48$

8. $\frac{12 \text{ yd}}{2\frac{1}{2} \text{ s}} = \frac{100 \text{ yd}}{x}$; $12x = 2\frac{1}{2} \cdot 100$; $12x = 250$,

$\frac{12x}{12} = \frac{250}{12}$; $x \approx 20.83$

20.83 s

9. For C, the solution is approx. 6.03. All others have a solution of approx. 4.15.

10. a. $\frac{400 \text{ dollars}}{x \text{ pesetas}} = \frac{0.007890 \text{ dollars}}{1 \text{ peseta}}$;

$0.007890x = 400$; $\frac{0.007890\,x}{0.007890} = \frac{400}{0.007890}$;

$x \approx 50{,}697$

about 50,697 pesetas

b. $\frac{400}{x \text{ dollars}} = \frac{1 \text{ peseta}}{0.007890 \text{ dollars}}$;

$x = 400 \cdot 0.007890$; $x = 3.16$

$\$3.16$

On Your Own p. 348

11. a. Sample: $\frac{15}{20} = \frac{9}{12}$, $\frac{9}{12} = \frac{3}{4}$, $\frac{15}{20} = \frac{3}{4}$

b.

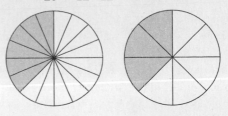

12–15. Accept reasonable estimates. Samples given.

12. $\frac{12}{47} \approx \frac{1}{4}$; $\frac{1}{4} = \frac{k}{20}$, $4k = 20$; $k \approx 5$

13. $31 \approx 30$, $\frac{5}{2} = \frac{30}{b}$; $5b = 60$, $b \approx 12$

14. $\frac{18}{5.9} \approx \frac{3}{1}$, $\frac{3}{1} = \frac{w}{7}$, $w \approx 21$

15. $\frac{2.5}{4.97} \approx \frac{1}{2}$; $\frac{1.5}{r} = \frac{1}{2}$, $r \approx 3$

16. $\frac{0.4}{1.2} = \frac{1.6}{4.8}$, $\frac{0.4}{1.6} = \frac{1.2}{4.8}$, $\frac{1.2}{0.4} = \frac{4.8}{1.6}$

17. $\frac{6}{n} = \frac{n}{1.5}$, $n^2 = 9$, $n = 3$ or -3

18–23. Methods will vary. Use cross multiplication to obtain the given equations. Then solve each equation.

18. $90 = 5m$, $m = 18$

19. $1056 = 64k$, $k = 16.5$

20. $8.1 = 3y$, $2.7 = y$

21. $18s = 544.5$, $s = 30.25$

22. $3d = 42$, $d = 14$

23. $3g = 400$, $g = 133.\overline{3}$

24. Sample: the left side is a ratio of h to mi and the right side is mi to h.

25. $\frac{1.08}{18} = \frac{x}{40}$; $18x = 1.08 \cdot 40$; $18x = 43.2$,

$\frac{18x}{18} = \frac{43.2}{18}$; $x = 2.40$; $\$2.40$

26. $\frac{50}{4} = \frac{x}{14}$; $4x = 50 \cdot 14$; $4x = 700$;

$\frac{4x}{4} = \frac{700}{4}$; $x = 175$; 175 cal

27. $\frac{241}{1{,}000} = \frac{x}{123{,}778{,}000}$;

$1{,}000x = 241(123{,}778{,}000)$; $x = 29{,}830{,}498$;

29,830,498 autos

28. $\frac{50}{x} = \frac{30}{29}$; $30x = 50 \cdot 29$; $30x = 1450$; $\frac{30x}{30} = \frac{1450}{30}$;

$x \approx 48\frac{1}{3}$; $48\frac{1}{3}$ in.

Problem Solving Practice

Page 349

1. Draw a diagram. Let a circle represent the whole amount you had to start with. Divide the circle into halves. Half represents the part given to Nadine. The other half is split among Catherine, Jerry, and yourself. One third goes to Catherine, with the rest split equally between Jerry and yourself. Since your part is $5.00, Jerry's part is also $5.00, meaning that Catherine's part is also $5.00. Thus one half the whole amount is $15.00. So you had $30.00 to start with.

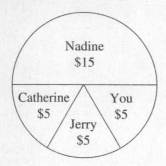

2. The first clue eliminates 0, 2, 3, 5, and 7 as possible digits. This leaves 1, 4, 6, 8, and 9 as possible digits. The third clue tells you that 1, 4, and 9 are possible digits for *B, C,* and *D.* Since $A + D = B$ and *B* and *D* are square numbers, this means $8 + 1 = 9$. So $A = 8, B = 9$, and $D = 1$. This leaves 4 and 6 as choices for *C* and *E.* But *C* has to be a square number. So $C = 4$ and $E = 6$. The number is 89,416.

3. Let x = cans of tennis balls and y = cans of racquetballs. Then $x + y = 100$ and $3x + 2y = 255$. Make a table and use Guess and Test to find the correct values for x and y.

x	y	$3x$	$2y$	$3x + 2y$
55	45	165	90	255

So 55 cans of tennis balls and 45 cans of racquetballs is the correct answer.

4. There are 100 whole numbers from 1 through 100. The numbers containing at least one 5 are 5, 15, 25, 35, 45, 50, 51, 52, 53, 54, 55, 56, 57, 58, 59, 65, 75, 85, and 95. So there are 19 out of 100 or 19% that contain at least one 5.

5. Not enough information; need to know total number of students

6. Let x = number lost. Then $x + 8$ = number won. $(x + 8) + x = 18; 2x + 8 = 18, 2x = 10, x = 5$. So there were 13 games won and 5 games lost. The ratio of games won to games lost is 13 to 5.

8-4 Similar Figures

Pages 350–353

Think and Discuss pp. 350–351

1. Sample: model airplane and actual airplane

2. **a.** $\angle R \cong \angle F; \angle S \cong \angle G; \angle T \cong \angle H; \angle U \cong \angle J$
   b. $\dfrac{RS}{FG} = \dfrac{ST}{GH} = \dfrac{TU}{HJ} = \dfrac{RU}{FJ}$

3. $\dfrac{24}{16} = \dfrac{15}{YZ}$; $24\ YZ = 16 \cdot 15$; $24\ YZ = 240$; $\dfrac{24\ YZ}{24} = \dfrac{240}{24}$; $YZ = 10$

4. $\dfrac{16}{24} = \dfrac{2}{3}$

5. $\dfrac{KH}{KL} = \dfrac{KG}{KJ}$; $\dfrac{KH}{15} = \dfrac{6}{10}$; $10\ KH = 15 \cdot 6$; $10\ KH = 90$; $\dfrac{10\ KH}{10} = \dfrac{90}{10}$; $KH = 9$
   $KL = KH + HL$; $15 = 9 + HL$; $HL = 6$

6. **a.** $\dfrac{JK}{GK} = \dfrac{10}{6} = \dfrac{5}{3}$
   b. $\dfrac{GK}{JK} = \dfrac{6}{10} = \dfrac{3}{5}$
   c. They are reciprocals.

Work Together p. 352

7. Check students' work.

8. **a.** Enlargement; reduction; A scale factor greater than 1 is an enlargement. A scale factor less than 1 is a reduction.
   b. Sample: The figures would be congruent and similar.

Try These p. 352

9. No; $\dfrac{10}{12} \neq \dfrac{6}{8}$

10. Yes, $\triangle YZX \sim \triangle YVW$; $\dfrac{2}{3}$

11. $\frac{35}{21} = \frac{x}{48}$; $21x = 35 \cdot 48$; $21x = 1680$;

$\frac{21x}{21} = \frac{1680}{21}$; $x = 80$

$\frac{35}{21} = \frac{35 + y}{48}$; $21 \cdot (35 + y) = 35 \cdot 48$;

$735 + 21y = 1680$;

$735 + 21y - 735 = 1680 - 735$; $21y = 945$;

$\frac{21y}{21} = \frac{945}{21}$; $y = 45$

12. $\frac{4.5}{6} = \frac{a}{15}$; $6a = 4.5 \cdot 15$; $6a = 67.5$; $\frac{6a}{6} = \frac{67.5}{6}$;

$a = 11.25$

$\frac{4.5}{6} = \frac{b}{10}$; $6b = 4.5 \cdot 10$; $6b = 45$; $\frac{6b}{6} = \frac{45}{6}$; $b = 7.5$

$\frac{4.5}{6} = \frac{c}{7.5}$; $6c = 4.5 \cdot 7.5$; $6c = 33.75$; $\frac{6c}{6} = \frac{33.75}{6}$;

$c = 5.625$

Mixed Review p. 352

1. $8d = 15$, $\frac{8d}{8} = \frac{15}{8}$; $d = 1.875$

2. $9y = 150$, $\frac{9y}{9} = \frac{150}{9}$; $y = 16\frac{2}{3}$

3. $\frac{3}{4}(4)^3 + \frac{4}{8} = \frac{3}{4}(64) + \frac{1}{2} = 48 + \frac{1}{2} = 48\frac{1}{2}$

4. 42; $15 - 81 \cdot 4 \div (-12)$; $15 - 324 \div (-12)$;
$15 + 27$

5. -745; $(7 + (-2) \cdot 8)^3 - 16$; $(7 + (-16))^3 - 16$;
$(-9)^3 - 16$; $-729 - 16$; -745

6. Check students' work.

On Your Own pp. 352–353

13. C is false.

14. $\frac{8}{h} = \frac{5}{3}$; $5h = 24$; $h = 4.8$

$\frac{5}{3} = \frac{8}{f}$; $5f = 24$; $f = 4.8$

$\frac{5}{3} = \frac{5}{g}$; $15 = 5g$; $g = 3$

15. $\frac{1.6}{m} = \frac{3.4}{10.2}$; $3.4m = 1.6 \cdot 10.2$;

$3.4m = 16.32$; $\frac{3.4m}{3.4} = \frac{16.32}{3.4}$; $m = 4.8$

$\frac{1.6}{4.8} = \frac{3}{3 + n}$; $1.6 \cdot (3 + n) = 4.8 \cdot 3$;

$1.6 \cdot 3 + 1.6n = 14.4$; $4.8 + 1.6n = 14.4$;

$-4.8 + 4.8 + 1.6n = -4.8 + 14.4$;

$1.6n = 9.6$; $\frac{1.6n}{1.6} = \frac{9.6}{1.6}$; $n = 6$

16. a. Sample: They are the same shape and the ratio of any two corr. sides is 1.

b. Sample: Similar figures are only congruent if the ratio of corr. sides is 1.

17.

	A	B	C
1	s	4 * s	s * s
2	1	4	1
3	2	8	4
4	3	12	9
5	4	16	16
6	5	20	25
7	6	24	36
8	7	28	49
9	8	32	64
10	9	36	81
11	10	40	100
12	11	44	121
13	12	48	144
14	13	52	169
15	14	56	196
16	15	60	225
17	16	64	256
18	17	68	289
19	18	72	324
20	19	76	361
21	20	80	400
22	21	84	441
23	22	88	484
24	23	92	529
25	24	96	576

a. doubled; quadrupled

b. tripled; multiplied by 9

c. multiplied by n, by n^2

d. Sample:

Length	Width	Perimeter	Area
L	W	2L + 2W	L * W
1	2	6	2
1	3	8	3
1	4	10	4
1	5	12	5
1	6	14	6
1	7	16	7
2	4	12	8
2	6	16	12
2	8	20	16
2	10	24	20
2	12	28	24
2	14	32	28
3	6	18	18
3	9	24	27
3	12	30	36
3	15	36	45
3	18	42	54
3	21	48	63
4	8	24	32
4	12	32	48
4	16	40	64
4	20	48	80
4	24	56	96
4	28	64	112

When the lengths of all sides of a rectangle double, the perimeter doubles and the area is multiplied by 4. When the lengths of all sides of a rectangle triple, the perimeter triples and the area is multiplied by 9. When the lengths of all sides of a rectangle are multiplied by n, the perimeter is multiplied by n and the area is multiplied by n^2.

Checkpoint p. 353

1. $\frac{12}{30} = \frac{2}{5}$

2. $\frac{\$58}{8} = 7.25$; \$7.25/page

3. $\frac{455 \text{ mi}}{1 \text{ h}} \cdot \frac{5280 \text{ ft}}{1 \text{ mi}} \cdot \frac{1 \text{ h}}{60 \text{ min}} = 40{,}040$ ft/min

4. $2 \cdot 15 = 5n$; $30 = 5n$; $\frac{30}{5} = \frac{5n}{5}$; $n = 6$

5. $\frac{3}{20} = \frac{t}{10}$; $30 = 20t$; $\frac{30}{20} = \frac{20t}{20}$; $t = 1.5$

6. $16m = 60$; $\frac{16m}{16} = \frac{60}{16}$; $m = 3.75$

7. $7k = 19.6$; $k = 2.8$

8. **a.** *RST*

   b. $\frac{3.9}{n} = \frac{1.5}{1}$; $1.5n = 3.9$; $\frac{1.5n}{1.5} = \frac{3.9}{1.5}$; $n = 2.6$

   $\frac{m}{3.6} = \frac{1}{1.5}$; $1.5m = 3.6$; $\frac{1.5m}{1.5} = \frac{3.6}{1.5}$; $m = 2.4$

8-5 Use a Proportion

Pages 354–356

1–5. Samples given.

1. A scale model is a version of an object.

2. the scale of the model

3. Find the model height if each inch of the model represents $2\frac{1}{2}$ ft in the actual silo.

4. Verify that 30 to 75 equals 1 to $2\frac{1}{2}$.

5. Yes; example: $\frac{75}{h} = \frac{2.5}{1}$

Try These p. 355

6. **a.** $\frac{1}{2\frac{1}{2}} = \frac{d}{15}$; $2\frac{1}{2}d = 15$; $\frac{2\frac{1}{2}d}{2\frac{1}{2}} = \frac{15}{2\frac{1}{2}}$; $d = 6$

   6 in.

   b. $\frac{1}{6} = \frac{h}{75}$; $6h = 75$; $\frac{6h}{6} = \frac{75}{6}$; $h = 12.5$

   12.5 in.

   $\frac{1}{6} = \frac{d}{15}$; $6d = 15$; $\frac{6d}{6} = \frac{15}{6}$; $d = 2.5$; 2.5 in.

   c. $\frac{20 \text{ in.}}{75 \text{ ft}} = \frac{1 \text{ in.}}{3.75 \text{ ft}}$; So scale is 1 in. : 3.75 ft

7. **a.** 3.2 cm

   b. $\frac{1}{160} = \frac{3.2}{d}$; $d = 160 \cdot 3.2$; d = 512; 512 km

8. $\frac{8}{6} = \frac{x}{90}$; $6x = 720$; $\frac{6x}{6} = \frac{720}{6}$; $x = 120$

   120 times

9. $\frac{1\frac{1}{2} \text{ lb}}{1} \cdot \frac{16 \text{ oz}}{1 \text{ lb}} = 24 \text{ oz}$; $\frac{6}{1.85} = \frac{24}{x}$; $6x = 1.85 \cdot 24$;

   $6x = 44.4$; $\frac{6x}{6} = \frac{44.4}{6}$; $x = 7.4$

   \$7.40

On Your Own pp. 355–356

10. total number of points divided by mean = total number of scores; $2145 \div 82.5 = 26$; $26 - 14 = 12$; 12 boys

11. The only square number between 1900 and 2000 is 1936 ($44^2 = 1936$). If Pierre were 44 years old in 1936, he would have been born in 1892. That doesn't meet the conditions. The next square number after 1936 is 2025 ($45^2 = 2025$). If Pierre is 45 in 2025, this means he was born in 1980.

12. $\frac{1}{4}{6} = \frac{1\frac{5}{8}}{l}$; $\frac{1}{4}l = 6 \cdot 1\frac{5}{8}$; $4 \cdot \frac{1}{4}l = 4 \cdot 6 \cdot 1\frac{5}{8}$; $l = 39$

   $\frac{1}{4}{6} = \frac{3}{4}{w}$; $\frac{1}{4}w = 6 \cdot \frac{3}{4}$; $4 \cdot \frac{1}{4}w = 4 \cdot 6 \cdot \frac{3}{4}$; $w = 18$

   39 ft; 18 ft

13. The length plus the width is half of 36 or 18. Make a table of possible values and find the values that give the largest area.

Length	Width	Area
1	17	17
2	16	32
3	15	45
4	14	56
5	13	65
6	12	72
7	11	77
8	10	80
9	9	81

After this point, values for the length and width switch position, but yield no value larger than 81. So the 9 m by 9 m rectangle yields the largest area.

14. Since the ginger ale and fruit juice are in the ratio 2 to 3, let $2x$ = ginger ale and $3x$ = fruit juice. Then $2x + 3x = 60$; $5x = 60$; $x = 12$. Then $2x = 24$ and $3x = 36$. So 24 cups of ginger ale are needed.
$$\frac{24\ c}{1} \cdot \frac{1\ pt}{2\ c} \cdot \frac{1\ qt}{2\ pt} = 6\ qt$$

15. The last number in each row is determined by the expression $\frac{n(n+1)}{2}$ where n is the row number. Using this formula and the guess-and-test strategy, you find that the last number in row 13 is 91 and the last number in row 14 is 105. Since seat 100 is between seats 91 and 105, it is in row 14.

16. 1 square yard = 9 square feet

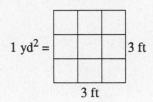

1 yd² =   3 ft

3 ft

$$\frac{\$192.24}{1\ ft^2} \cdot \frac{9\ ft^2}{1\ yd^2} = \$1,730.16/yd^2$$

17. $\frac{5\ ft}{4\ in.} = \frac{60\ in.}{4\ in.} = \frac{15}{1}$

So the scale factor is 15. The dimensions of the box must be multiplied by 15.

Length: $9\frac{1}{2}$ in. $\cdot$ 15 = 142.5 in. $\approx$ 11.9 ft

Width: $4\frac{3}{4}$ in. $\cdot$ 15 = 71.25 in. $\approx$ 5.9 ft

Height: 4 in. $\cdot$ 15 = 60 in. = 5 ft

18. Sample: Find similar figures and write a proportion involving corresponding sides.

Mixed Review p. 356

1. $\frac{MY}{KT} = \frac{BY}{GT}$; $\frac{12}{KT} = \frac{9}{10}$; $9KT = 120$; $KT = 13\frac{1}{3}$ cm

2. Since $\triangle KGT \sim \triangle MBY$, $\angle Y$ and $\angle T$ correspond and $m\angle T = 70°$. Then $m\angle K + m\angle G + m\angle T = 180°$. So $m\angle K + 55° + 70° = 180°$. Then $m\angle K + 125° = 180°$ or $m\angle K = 55°$.

3. $9a - \frac{2}{3} = \frac{5}{6}$; $9a - \frac{2}{3} + \frac{2}{3} = \frac{5}{6} + \frac{2}{3}$; $9a = \frac{3}{2}$; $\frac{1}{9} \cdot 9a = \frac{1}{9} \cdot \frac{3}{2}$; $a = \frac{1}{6}$

4. $\frac{1}{4} - 2k = \frac{1}{2}$; $\frac{1}{4} - 2k + 2k = \frac{1}{2} + 2k$; $\frac{1}{4} = \frac{1}{2} + 2k$; $\frac{1}{4} - \frac{1}{2} = \frac{1}{2} + 2k - \frac{1}{2}$; $-\frac{1}{4} = 2k$; $-\frac{1}{4} \cdot \frac{1}{2} = 2k \cdot \frac{1}{2}$; $-\frac{1}{8} = k$

5. $7z = 24$; $z = \frac{24}{7}$

6. $\frac{(n-2)180}{n} = \frac{(9-2)180}{9} = \frac{7(180)}{9} = 140$; 140°

7. $\frac{(n-2)180}{n} = \frac{(7-2)180}{7} = \frac{900}{7} = 128\frac{4}{7}$; $128\frac{4}{7}°$

8-6 Indirect Measurement

Pages 357–359

Think and Discuss pp. 357–358

1. Sample: $\frac{h}{6} = \frac{102}{17}$

2. $\frac{h}{102} = \frac{5.75}{17}$

Try These p. 358

3.

45 ft

15 ft

10 ft

30 ft

4. a. Sample: We want to find the distance d across Silver Lake using similar triangles.

b. $\frac{PQ}{ST} = \frac{QR}{TR}$

c. $\frac{d}{1.08} = \frac{1.16}{0.87}$; $1.08 \cdot 1.16 = 0.87d$; $1.2528 = 0.87d$; $\frac{1.2528d}{0.87} = \frac{0.87d}{0.87}$; $d = 1.44$ 1.44 km

5. $\frac{5}{7.5} = \frac{x}{18}$; $7.5x = 90$; $\frac{7.5x}{7.5} = \frac{90}{7.5}$; $x = 12$; 12 ft

On Your Own pp. 358–359

6. $\frac{h}{15} = \frac{16}{30}$; $15 \cdot 16 = 30h$; $240 = 30h$; $\frac{240}{30} = \frac{30h}{30}$; $h = 8$; 8 m

7. $\frac{5\frac{1}{3}}{8} = \frac{h}{20}$; $8h = 5\frac{1}{3} \cdot 20$; $8h = 106\frac{2}{3}$; $h = 13\frac{1}{3}$; 13 ft 4 in.

8. $\frac{221}{189} = \frac{h}{29}$; $189h = 221 \cdot 29$; $189h = 6,409$; $\frac{189h}{189} = \frac{6,409}{189}$; $h \approx 34$; 34 feet

9. $\frac{x}{376} = \frac{6}{8}$; $8x = 376 \cdot 6$; $8x = 2256$; $\frac{8x}{8} = \frac{2,256}{8}$; $x = 282$; 282 ft

10. $\frac{725}{482.5} = \frac{d}{780}$; $725 \cdot 780 = 482.5d$; $565,500 = 482.5d$; $\frac{565500}{482.5} = \frac{482.5d}{482.5}$; $d \approx 1172$; 1172 m

11. $\frac{60}{d} = \frac{d}{25}$; $d \cdot d = 60 \cdot 25$; $d^2 = 1500$; $d \approx 38.7$ 38.7 m

12. Sample: measure your height, your shadow, the house's shadow to form similar triangles.

13. $\frac{154}{462} = \frac{550}{550 + x}$; $154(550 + x) = 550 \cdot 462$;
$84,700 + 154x = 254,100$;
$-84,700 + 84,700 + 154x = -84,700 + 254,100$;
$154x = 169,400$; $\frac{154x}{154} = \frac{169,400}{154}$; $x = 1,100$; 1,100 ft

$550^2 = 154^2 + y^2$; $302,500 = 23,716 + y^2$;
$278,784 = y^2$; $528 = y$; 528 ft
$\frac{154}{462} = \frac{528}{z}$; $154z = 462 \cdot 528$;
$154z = 243,936$; $\frac{154z}{154} = \frac{243,936}{154}$; $z = 1,584$;
1,584 ft

14. a. Sample: Place the mirror so that the person can see the top of the basketball hoop in the mirror.

b. $\triangle XYZ \sim \triangle WVZ$

c. $\frac{XY}{WV} = \frac{XZ}{WZ}$

d. Sample: Find cross products and solve for VW.

15. Sample: Write a proportion involving corresponding sides of similar triangles. Solve the proportion for the distance you estimated.

Mixed Review p. 359

1. $\frac{2}{25} = \frac{16}{x}$; $2x = 25 \cdot 16$; $2x = 400$; $\frac{2x}{2} = \frac{400}{2}$; $x = 200$; 200 km

2. $y = -3x + 2$

3. $y = \frac{2}{5}x - 2$

4. $y = 5$

5. The smallest number is the least common multiple of 3, 5, 6, and 8. LCM(3,5,6,8) = 120.

8-7 The Tangent Ratio

Pages 360–363

Work Together p. 360

1. a. Students' values for *BC*, *AB*, *DF*, *AD*, *GH*, and *AG* will vary according to the size of the figure drawn. But the ratios in the last column will equal 0.7002.

b. Sample: Ratios in last column are equal.

2. Students' values for lengths will vary according to the size of the figure drawn, but the ratios in the last column will equal 1.8807.

3. Sample: All ratios in the third column are equal to 1.

Think and Discuss pp. 360–361

4. $\frac{3}{4}$; 0.75

5. a. $90° - 59° = 31°$

b. 0.6009

6. $\tan 37° = \frac{x}{200}$; $0.7536 \approx \frac{x}{200}$; $200 \cdot 0.7536 \approx 200 \cdot \frac{x}{200}$; $150.72 \approx x$; 150.72 ft

7. $\tan 50° = \frac{400}{x}$; $1.1918 \approx \frac{400}{x}$; $1.1918x \approx 400$; $\frac{1.1918x}{1.1918} \approx \frac{400}{1.1918}$; $x \approx 335.63$; 335.63 ft

Try These p. 362

8. a. $\overline{YZ}$; $\overline{XY}$

b. $\overline{XY}$; $\overline{YZ}$

c. $\tan X = \frac{15}{8}$; 1.875; $\tan Z = \frac{8}{15}$; $0.5\overline{3}$

d. They are reciprocals.

9. 0.2309   **10.** 11.4301

11. 0.4040   **12.** 1

13. a. $\tan 63° = \frac{m}{3.5}$; $1.9626 \approx \frac{m}{3.5}$; $3.5 \cdot 1.9626 \approx m$; $6.9 \approx m$

b. $\tan 27° = \frac{3.5}{m}$; $0.5095 \approx \frac{3.5}{m}$; $0.5095m \approx 3.5$; $\frac{0.5095m}{0.5095} \approx \frac{3.5}{0.5095}$; $m \approx 6.9$

c. $\tan 63°$ is the reciprocal of $\tan 27°$.

14. $\tan 70° = \frac{100}{x}$; $2.7475 \approx \frac{100}{x}$; $27475x \approx 100$; $\frac{2.7475x}{2.7475} \approx \frac{100}{2.7475}$; $x \approx 36$; 36 ft

On Your Own pp. 362–363

15. 0.5095; 1.9626

16. 0.5774; 1.7321

17. 1, 1

18. $\tan Q = \frac{60}{25} = \frac{12}{5}$; 2.4

19. $\tan 40° = \frac{n}{4}$; $0.8391 \approx \frac{n}{4}$; $4 \cdot 0.8391 \approx 4 \cdot \frac{n}{4}$;

$3.4 \approx n$

20. $90° - 38° = 52°$; $\tan 52° = \frac{n}{43.2}$; $1.2799 \approx \frac{n}{43.2}$;

$43.2 \cdot 1.2799 \approx 43.2 \cdot \frac{n}{43.2}$; $55.3 \approx n$

21. $90° - 59° = 31°$; $\tan 31° = \frac{n}{272}$; $0.6009 \approx \frac{n}{272}$;

$0.6009 \cdot 272 \approx \frac{n}{272} \cdot 272$; $163.4 \approx n$

22. a. 45°

b. Greater; the length of the side opposite the angle is greater than the length of the side adjacent to the angle.

c. $m\angle A < 45°$

23.

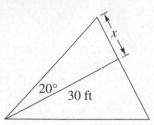

$\tan 20° = \frac{x}{30}$; $0.3640 \approx \frac{x}{30}$;

$30 \cdot 0.3640 \approx 30 \cdot \frac{x}{30}$;

$10.9 \approx x$

$10.9 \cdot 2 = 21.8$; 21.8 ft

24. Answers will vary, but the problem should involve a right triangle where one leg is known and the other is unknown and one of the acute angles is known.

25. $\tan 50° = \frac{x}{100}$; $1.1918 \approx \frac{x}{100}$; $100 \cdot 1.1918 \approx$

$100 \cdot \frac{x}{100}$; $119.2 \approx x$; 119.2 m

26. a. $\frac{1{,}248 \text{ paces}}{1} \cdot \frac{3\frac{2}{3} \text{ ft}}{1 \text{ pace}} = 4{,}576 \text{ ft}$

$\tan 20° = \frac{x}{4{,}576}$; $0.3640 \approx \frac{x}{4{,}576}$;

$4{,}576 \cdot 0.3640 \approx 4{,}576 \cdot \frac{x}{4{,}576}$; $1{,}666 \approx x$;

1,666 ft

b. $\frac{1{,}666 \text{ ft}}{1} \cdot \frac{1 \text{ mi}}{5{,}280 \text{ ft}} \approx 0.32 \text{ mi}$;

$0.32 \text{ mi} - 0.01 \text{ mi} = 0.31 \text{ mi}$

27. Check students' work.

Mixed Review p. 362

1. $\frac{x}{6} = \frac{24}{40}$; $40x = 144$; $\frac{40x}{40} = \frac{144}{40}$; $x = 3.6$; 3.6 m

2.

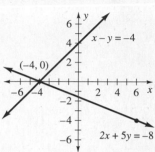

Solution: (–4, 0)

3.

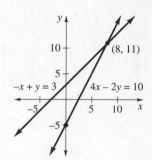

Solution: (8, 11)

4. $320 = 2 \cdot 160 = 2 \cdot 2 \cdot 80 = 2 \cdot 2 \cdot 2 \cdot 40 =$
$2 \cdot 2 \cdot 2 \cdot 2 \cdot 20 = 2 \cdot 2 \cdot 2 \cdot 2 \cdot 2 \cdot 10 =$
$2 \cdot 2 \cdot 2 \cdot 2 \cdot 2 \cdot 2 \cdot 5 = 2^6 \cdot 5$

5. $288 = 2 \cdot 144 = 2 \cdot 2 \cdot 72 = 2 \cdot 2 \cdot 2 \cdot 36 =$
$2 \cdot 2 \cdot 2 \cdot 2 \cdot 18 = 2 \cdot 2 \cdot 2 \cdot 2 \cdot 2 \cdot 9 =$
$2 \cdot 2 \cdot 2 \cdot 2 \cdot 2 \cdot 3 \cdot 3 = 2^5 \cdot 3^2$

8-8 The Sine and Cosine Ratios

Pages 364–367

Work Together p. 364

1. a. The lengths of sides will vary according to the drawing, but the ratios in the fourth column will all equal 0.8910 and the ratios in the fifth column will equal 0.4540.

b. Ratios in column 4 are the same and the ratios in column 5 are the same.

2. Ratios in column 4 will be 0.3907 and ratios in column 5 will be 0.9205.

3. 45°

Think and Discuss pp. 364–365

4. $\sin H = \frac{20}{52} = \frac{5}{13}$; $\cos H = \frac{48}{52} = \frac{12}{13}$

5. $m\angle Q = 90° - 41° = 49°$; 0.7547; 0.6561

6. $\sin 53° = \frac{200}{x}$; $0.7986 \approx \frac{200}{x}$;

$0.7986 \cdot x \approx \frac{200}{x} \cdot x$; $0.7986x \approx 200$;

$\frac{0.7986x}{0.7986} \approx \frac{200}{0.7986}$;

$x \approx 250.43$

Try These p. 366

7. $\sin J = \frac{18}{30} = \frac{3}{5}$

8. $\cos J = \frac{24}{30} = \frac{4}{5}$

9. $\sin L = \frac{24}{30} = \frac{4}{5}$

10. $\cos L = \frac{18}{30} = \frac{3}{5}$

11. $\tan J = \frac{18}{24} = \frac{3}{4}$

12. $\tan L = \frac{24}{18} = \frac{4}{3}$

13. 0.9848

14. 0.9976

15. 0.9455

16. 0.9455

17. a. $\sin 53° = \frac{x}{7.4}$; $0.7986 \approx \frac{x}{7.4}$;

$7.4 \cdot 0.7986 \approx 7.4 \cdot \frac{x}{7.4}$; $5.9 \approx x$

b. $m\angle B = 90° - m\angle A$; $m\angle B = 90° - 53° = 37°$

$\cos 37° = \frac{x}{7.4}$; $0.7986 \approx \frac{x}{7.4}$;

$7.4 \cdot 0.7986 \approx 7.4 \cdot \frac{x}{7.4}$; $5.9 \approx x$

18. a. $\sin 75° = \frac{x}{16}$; $0.9659 \approx \frac{x}{16}$; $16 \cdot 0.9659 \approx$

$16 \cdot \frac{x}{16}$; $15.5 \approx x$; 15.5 ft

b. $90° - 75° = 15°$; $\sin 15° = \frac{y}{16}$; $0.2588 \approx \frac{y}{16}$;

$16 \cdot 0.2588 \approx 16 \cdot \frac{y}{16}$; 4.1
$\approx y$; 4.1 ft

On Your Own pp. 366–367

19. $8^2 + 6^2 = n^2$; $64 + 36 = n^2$; $100 = n^2$; $n = 10$
$\sin X = \frac{6}{10} = \frac{3}{5}$; $\cos X = \frac{8}{10} = \frac{4}{5}$; $\tan X = \frac{6}{8} = \frac{3}{4}$

20. $n^2 + 8^2 = 17^2$; $n^2 + 64 = 289$;
$n^2 + 64 - 64 = 289 - 64$; $n^2 = 225$; $n = 15$
$\sin X = \frac{8}{17}$; $\cos X = \frac{15}{17}$; $\tan X = \frac{8}{15}$

21. $39^2 = 15^2 + n^2$; $1{,}521 = 225 + n^2$;

$1{,}521 - 225 = 225 + n^2 - 225$; $1{,}296 = n^2$;

$n = 36$; $\sin X = \frac{36}{39} = \frac{12}{13}$; $\cos X = \frac{15}{39} = \frac{5}{13}$;

$\tan X = \frac{36}{15} = \frac{12}{5}$

22. A

23. $\sin 36° = \frac{6}{t}$; $0.5878 \approx \frac{6}{t}$; $0.5878 \cdot t \approx \frac{6}{t} \cdot t$;

$0.5878t \approx 6$; $\frac{0.5878t}{0.5878} \approx \frac{6}{0.5878}$; $t \approx 10.2$

24. $\cos 56° = \frac{t}{3.5}$; $0.5592 \approx \frac{t}{3.5}$;

$3.5 \cdot 0.5592 \approx 3.5 \cdot \frac{t}{3.5}$; $2.0 \approx t$

25. $\sin 43° = \frac{87}{t}$; $0.6820 \approx \frac{87}{t}$; $0.6820 \cdot t \approx \frac{87}{t} \cdot t$;

$0.6820t \approx 87$; $\frac{0.6820t}{0.6820} = \frac{87t}{0.6820}$; $t \approx 127.6$

26. Check students' work.

27. a.

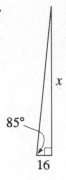

b. $\tan 85° = \frac{x}{16}$; $11.4301 \approx \frac{x}{16}$;

$x \approx 11.4301 \cdot 16$; $x \approx 183$

183 ft

28. $\sin 30° = \frac{20}{x}$; $0.5 = \frac{20}{x}$; $0.5 \cdot x = \frac{20}{x} \cdot x$; $0.5x = 20$;

$\frac{0.5x}{0.5} = \frac{20}{0.5}$; $x = 40$; 40 ft

29. Check students' work.

Checkpoint p. 367

1. $\frac{1}{3\frac{1}{2}} = \frac{x}{35}$; $1 \cdot 35 = 3\frac{1}{2} \cdot x$; $35 = 3\frac{1}{2}x$; $\frac{35}{3\frac{1}{2}} = \frac{3\frac{1}{2}x}{3\frac{1}{2}}$

$10 = x$; 10 in.

2. a. Sample: A 16-ft pole casts a 28-ft shadow.
At the same time, a tower casts a 112-ft
shadow. How tall is the tower?

b. $\frac{16}{28} = \frac{x}{112}$; $16 \cdot 112 = 28 \cdot x$; $1792 = 28x$;

$\frac{1{,}792}{28} = \frac{28x}{28}$; $64 = x$; 64 ft

3. $\sin S = \frac{28}{100} = \frac{7}{25} = 0.28$

   $\cos S = \frac{96}{100} = \frac{24}{25} = 0.96$

   $\tan S = \frac{28}{96} = \frac{7}{24} \approx 0.2917$

4. $\cos 26° = \frac{m}{16}$; $08988 \approx \frac{m}{16}$; $16 \cdot 0.8988 \approx 16 \cdot \frac{m}{16}$;

   $14.4 \approx m$

   $\sin 26° = \frac{n}{16}$; $0.4384 \approx \frac{n}{16}$; $16 \cdot 0.4384 \approx 16 \cdot \frac{n}{16}$;

   $7.0 \approx n$

Mixed Review p. 367

1. $\frac{10}{24}$

2. $\frac{24}{10}$

3. $10^2 + 24^2 = n^2$; $100 + 576 = n^2$; $676 = n^2$;
   $26 = n$

4. $90°$ (since $\angle D$ is an angle inscribed in semicircle)

5. $180° - 30° - 90° = 60°$

Practice

Page 368

1. $\frac{13}{52} = \frac{1}{4}$

2. $\frac{28}{84} = \frac{1}{3}$

3. $\frac{45 \text{ min}}{1 \text{ h}} = \frac{45 \text{ min}}{60 \text{ min}} = \frac{3}{4}$

4. $\frac{130}{5} = \frac{26}{1}$

5. $\frac{8}{20} = \frac{2}{5}$

6. $\frac{2 \text{ ft}}{8 \text{ yd}} = \frac{2 \text{ ft}}{24 \text{ ft}} = \frac{1}{12}$

7. $12 \cdot 9 = 108$ and $15 \cdot 4 = 60$. So $12 \cdot 9 \neq 15 \cdot 4$ and $\frac{12}{15} \neq \frac{4}{9}$.

8. $19 \cdot 80 = 1,520$ and $20 \cdot 76 = 1,520$.
   So $\frac{19}{20} = \frac{76}{80}$.

9. $18 \cdot 30 = 540$ and $5 \cdot 108 = 540$. So $\frac{18}{5} = \frac{108}{30}$.

0. $\frac{18 \text{ laps}}{12 \text{ min}} = 1.5$ laps/min

1. $\frac{\$3.78}{\frac{7}{8} \text{ lb}} = \frac{\$3.78}{0.875 \text{ lb}} = \$4.32/\text{lb}$

2. $\frac{195 \text{ km}}{1.3 \text{ h}} = 150$ km/h

3. $\frac{240 \text{ cal}}{8 \text{ oz}} = 30$ cal/oz

14. $\frac{10,000 \text{ ft}^2}{40 \text{ lb}} = 250$ ft^2/lb

15. $\frac{25,000 \text{ people}}{1,000 \text{ mi}^2} = 25$ people/mi^2

16. $\frac{84 \text{ m}}{1 \text{ min}} \cdot \frac{1 \text{ min}}{60 \text{ s}} = 1.4$ m/s

17. $\frac{0.075 \text{ km}}{1 \text{ s}} \cdot \frac{60 \text{ s}}{1 \text{ min}} \cdot \frac{1,000 \text{ m}}{1 \text{ km}} = 4,500$ m/min

18. $\frac{27}{n} = \frac{6}{7}$; $27 \cdot 7 = 6n$; $189 = 6n$; $\frac{189}{6} = \frac{6n}{6}$; $31.5 = n$

19. $\frac{n}{8} = \frac{9.5}{10}$; $10n = 8 \cdot 9.5$; $10n = 76$; $\frac{10n}{10} = \frac{76}{n}$;
    $n = 7.6$

20. $\frac{6}{25} = \frac{4.5}{n}$; $6n = 25 \cdot 4.5$; $6n = 112.5$; $n \approx 18.8$

21. $\frac{2.5}{x} = \frac{3}{1.6}$; $3x = 2.5 \cdot 1.6$; $3x = 4$; $\frac{3x}{3} = \frac{4}{3}$;
    $x \approx 1.3$; 1.3 cm

    $\frac{1.7}{y} = \frac{3}{1.6}$; $3y = 1.7 \cdot 1.6$; $3y = 2.72$; $\frac{3y}{3} = \frac{2.72}{3}$;

    $y \approx 0.9$; 0.9 cm

22. $\frac{4}{3.6} = \frac{z}{2.8}$; $3.6z = 4 \cdot 2.8$; $3.6z = 11.2$;
    $\frac{3.6z}{3.6} = \frac{11.2}{3.6}$; $z \approx 3.1$; 3.1 cm

23. $\frac{2}{150} = \frac{7\frac{1}{2}}{x}$; $2x = 150 \cdot 7\frac{1}{2}$; $2x = 1125$; $\frac{2x}{2} = \frac{1125}{2}$;
    $x = 562.5$; 562.5 mi

24. $\frac{116,601,000}{55,598} = \frac{x}{5}$; $55,598x = 5 \cdot 116,601,000$;
    $55,598x = 583,005,000$; $\frac{55,598x}{55,598} = \frac{583,005,000}{55,598}$
    $x = 10,486$ people

8-9 Exploring Self-Similarity and Fractals

Pages 369–371

Think and Discuss p. 369

1. a. 1, 3, 9, 27, 81

   b. powers of 3

   c. 3^6 or 729

   d. 3^n

On Your Own pp. 370–371

2. a. 1, 8, 64

   b. 512

   c. 8^n

3. a. 2^9 or 512

   b. 2^n

4. Divide each edge into three equal segments. On each middle segment draw an equilateral triangle whose base has the same length as this middle segment.

5. a.

Stage	0	1	2	3	4
Length of one side of each shaded triangle	1	$\frac{1}{2}$	$\frac{1}{4}$	$\frac{1}{8}$	$\frac{1}{16}$
Perimeter of shaded triangle	3	$\frac{3}{2}$	$\frac{3}{4}$	$\frac{3}{8}$	$\frac{3}{16}$
Total perimeter	3	$\frac{9}{2}$	$\frac{27}{4}$	$\frac{81}{8}$	$\frac{243}{16}$

b. Each new length in row 1 and each perimeter in row 2 is obtained by multiplying by $\frac{1}{2}$.

c. Each new total perimeter in row 3 is obtained by multiplying by $\frac{3}{2}$.

6. a. $\frac{3}{4}$ square unit

b. The total area becomes smaller and smaller and approaches 0.

7.

8.

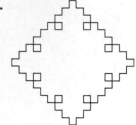

9.

The text shows Stage 3.

10.

The text shows Stage 5.

11. Check students' drawings.

Mixed Review p. 370

1. $16^2 + 30^2 = KM^2$; $256 + 900 = KM^2$; $1156 = KM^2$; $34 = KM$

2. $\sin K = \frac{16}{34}$

3. $\cos M = \frac{16}{34}$

4.

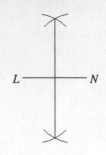

5. $n - 5 > -9$; $n - 5 + 5 > -9 + 5$; $n > -4$

6. $2 + 2n < 14$; $2 + 2n - 2 < 14 - 2$; $2n < 12$; $n < 6$

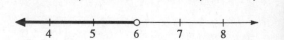

Wrap Up

Pages 372–373

1. $\frac{16}{48} = \frac{1}{3}$ or $1 : 3$

2. $\frac{32}{8} = \frac{4}{1}$

3. $\frac{12}{45} = \frac{4}{15}$ or 4 out of 15

4. $\frac{15}{9} = \frac{5}{3}$ or 5 to 3

5. $\frac{\$42}{1.5\,h} = \$28/h$

6. $\frac{826\,mi}{14\,h} \approx 59$ mi/h

7. $\frac{150\,km}{24\,L} = 6.25$ km/L

8. $\frac{\$1.98}{3\,cans} \approx \$.66$/can

9. $\frac{75\,min}{1} \cdot \frac{1\,h}{60\,min} = 1\frac{1}{4}$ h

10. $\frac{36.8\,ft}{1\,s} \cdot \frac{60\,s}{1\,min} = 2{,}208$ ft/min

11. $\frac{7900\,km}{1\,h} \cdot \frac{1\,h}{60\,min} \cdot \frac{1\,min}{60\,s} \cdot \frac{1000\,m}{1\,km} \approx 2{,}194.4$ m

12. $4 \cdot 3.9 = 5y$; $15.6 = 5y$; $\frac{15.6}{5} = \frac{5y}{5}$; $3.12 = y$

13. $10x = 8 \cdot 3$; $10x = 24$; $\frac{10x}{10} = \frac{24}{10}$; $x = 2.4$

14. $9w = 20 \cdot 2$; $9w = 40$; $\frac{9w}{9} = \frac{40}{9}$; $w = 4.\overline{4}$

15. $8 \cdot 9 = 5z$; $72 = 5z$; $\frac{72}{5} = \frac{5z}{5}$; $14.4 = z$

16. $\frac{325}{\$19.50} = \frac{400}{x}$; $19.50 \cdot 400 = 325x$; $7{,}800 = 325x$; $\frac{7{,}800}{325} = \frac{325x}{325}$; $24 = x$; \$24

17. Let $AE = x$, $\frac{x}{4} = \frac{5}{2}$; $2x = 5 \cdot 4$; $2x = 20$; $\frac{2x}{2} = \frac{20}{2}$; $x = 10$; 10 cm

18. Let $CE = y$; $\frac{y}{3} = \frac{10}{4}$; $4y = 3 \cdot 10$; $4y = 30$; $\frac{4y}{4} = \frac{30}{4}$; $y = 7.5$; 7.5 cm

19. $7.5 - 3 = 4.5$; 4.5 cm

20. $\frac{5.5}{21} = \frac{y}{45}$; $21x = 5.5 \cdot 45$; $21x = 247.5$; $\frac{21x}{21} = \frac{247.5}{21}$; $x \approx 11.8$; 11.8 ft

21. Sample: It is the ratio of a pair of corresponding sides of two similar figures. It is used to make maps or models.

22. A

23.

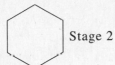

Stage 2

Getting Ready for Chapter 9 p. 373

1. Let A, B, and C represent the three friends. The possible arrangements are ABC, ACB, BAC, BCA, CAB, and CBA. There are 6 possible arrangements.

2. $2 \cdot 3 \cdot 4 = 24$ outfits

Assessment
Page 376

1. a. $\frac{6}{36} = \frac{1}{6}$ or $1 : 6$

  b. $\frac{54}{6} = \frac{9}{1}$

  c. $\frac{24}{18} = \frac{4}{3}$

  d. $\frac{23}{92} = \frac{1}{4}$ or 1 out of 4

2. a. $\frac{4\,h}{1} \cdot \frac{60\,min}{1\,h} \cdot \frac{60\,s}{1\,min} = 14{,}400$ s

  b. $\frac{448\,in.}{1} \cdot \frac{1\,ft}{12\,in.} = 37\frac{1}{3}$ ft

  c. $\frac{23\,qt}{1} \cdot \frac{1\,gal}{4\,qt} = 5.75$ gal

  d. $\frac{22\,wk}{1} \cdot \frac{7\,days}{1\,wk} \cdot \frac{24\,h}{1\,day} = 3{,}696$ h

3. a. $\frac{\$33}{1\,h} \cdot \frac{1\,h}{60\,min} = \$.55/min$

  b. $\frac{186\,ft}{1\,sec} \cdot \frac{60\,sec}{1\,min} = 11{,}160$ ft/min

4. Sample: $343 \div 3.5 \approx 300 \div 3$; $300 \div 3 = 100$

5. B (since $2 \cdot 36 = 8 \cdot 9$)

6. $\frac{160}{584} = \frac{270}{x}$; $160x = 584 \cdot 270$; $160x = 157{,}680$; $\frac{160x}{160} = \frac{157{,}680}{160}$; $x = 985.50$; \$985.50

7. $\sin 40° = \frac{x}{20}$; $0.6428 \approx \frac{x}{20}$; $20 \cdot 0.6428 \approx 20 \cdot \frac{x}{20}$; $12.9 \approx x$; 12.9 ft

8. $\frac{90}{72} = \frac{x}{4}$; $72x = 90 \cdot 40$; $72x = 3{,}600$; $\frac{72x}{72} = \frac{3{,}600}{72}$; $x = 50$; 50 m

9. $\frac{0.75}{3} = \frac{4.75}{x}$; $0.75x = 3 \cdot 4.75$; $0.75x = 14.25$; $\frac{0.75x}{0.75} = \frac{14.25}{0.75}$; $x = 19$; 19 ft

10. $\frac{AB}{EC} = \frac{AD}{ED} = \frac{BD}{CD}$

11. a. $\frac{3}{4}$; 0.75

  b. $\frac{3}{5}$; 0.6

  c. $\frac{4}{5}$; 0.8

12. $n^2 = 12^2 + 5^2$; $n^2 = 144 + 25$; $n^2 = 169$; $n = 13$

  a. $\frac{12}{13}$

  b. $\frac{5}{13}$

  c. $\frac{12}{5}$

13. $\frac{5.25}{16} = \frac{x}{90}$; $5.25 \cdot 90 = 16x$; $472.5 = 16x$; $\frac{472.5}{16} = \frac{16x}{16}$; $29.5 \approx x$; about 29.5 ft

14. Sample: any part of a figure looks like a whole; Example: snowflake

Cumulative Review

Page 377

1. C

2. D, since $\frac{12}{8} = \frac{3}{2}$

3. A

4. B, since the product of p and q is -24 in each case

5. C, since the LCD of the $\frac{13}{21}$, $\frac{25}{12}$, and $\frac{40}{49}$ is 588

6. A, since $-3 + (-8) - (-4) = -11 + 4 = -7$

7. B, since each term is obtained by dividing by -3

8. B

9. D, since $3 \cdot 4^{-2} = 3 \cdot \frac{1}{4^2} = 3 \cdot \frac{1}{16} = \frac{3}{16}$

10. A

Chapter 9 Probability

9-1 Counting and Displaying Outcomes

Pages 381–383

Work Together p. 381

1–3. Check students' work.

Think and Discuss pp. 381–382

4. 26

5. 10

6. 5 letters, since $26^5 = 11,881,376$ and $10^7 = 10,000,000$.

7. a. $5 \cdot 3 \cdot 2 = 30$

   b. All outcomes have been displayed, since at each branch every possibility is displayed.

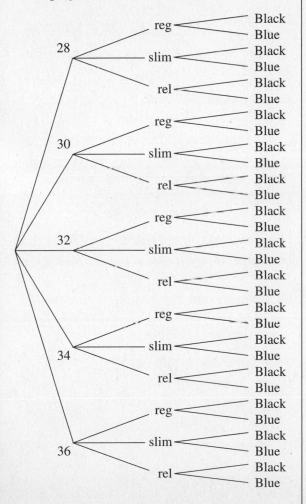

8. $26 \cdot 9 = 234$

9. Answers may vary. Sample: The counting principle is better when there is a large number of possibilities. The tree diagram gives a better picture of the possibilities, if there are not too many, especially to display non-numerical possibilities, like color. You might use both if there were not too many possibilities, in order to give both a good picture and a precise and easily read number. A tree diagram might be better to display choices in color and style for tents, for example. The counting principle would be better for counting all the possible combinations of four letters, since there are so many.

On Your Own pp. 382–383

10. Texas: $26 \cdot 26 \cdot 26 \cdot 10 \cdot 10 \cdot 26 = 45,697,600$; Massachusetts: $10 \cdot 10 \cdot 10 \cdot 26 \cdot 26 \cdot 26 = 17,576,000$

11. $(26 + 10)^6 = 36^6 = 2,176,782,336$

12. Answers will vary.

13. $3 \cdot 2 \cdot 8 = 48$

14. a. 3

   b. 18 different kinds of film

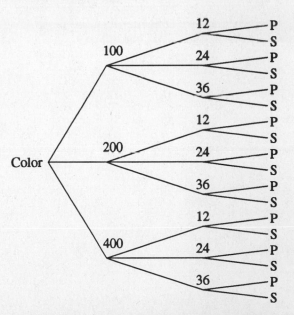

   c. 3; 12-exposure slide film comes in three different speeds.

15. a. $10^5 = 100,000$

   b. $\frac{1}{2} \cdot (100,000) = 50,000$

   c. $10^9 - 10^5 = 1,000,000,000 - 100,000 = 999,900,000$

16. $3 \cdot 5 \cdot 6 = 90$ combinations

17. a. $2 \cdot 8 \cdot 5 \cdot 2 = 160$ specials

   b. $8 \cdot 5 = 40$ choices

18. a. $2 \cdot 26 \cdot 26 = 1,352$

   b. $2 \cdot 26 \cdot 26 \cdot 26 - 1,352 = 33,800$

19. No. Sample explanation: Suppose there are 5 choices at a certain stage of a tree diagram. Even if you place these 5 choices at a different stage of the diagram, they will still result in a factor of 5 in the total number of outcomes.

Mixed Review p. 382

1. $\cos 60° = \frac{7}{x}$; $0.5 = \frac{7}{x}$; $0.5x = 7$; $\frac{0.5x}{0.5} = \frac{7}{0.5}$;

   $x = 14$; 14 cm

2. Sample: snowflake, flower blossom, tree

3. $m\angle C = 75°$, since the two $\triangle$s are congruent, and $m\angle M + m\angle C + m\angle T = 180°$. Thus $m\angle M + 75° + 35° = 180°$, which means that $m\angle M = 180° - 110° = 70°$.

4. $RZ = MC = 58$ cm and $ZY = CT = 40$ cm, since they are congruent, so the perimeter of $\triangle RZY = 42 + 40 + 58 = 140$ cm.

5. $6\left(\frac{2n}{3} + \frac{1}{2}\right) = (-8)6$

     $4n + 3 = -48$

        $4n = -51$

          $n = -12\frac{3}{4}$

6. $10\left(\frac{3}{5}\right) = \left(2\frac{7}{10}y - 48\right)10$

     $6 = 27y - 480$

   $486 = 27y$

    $18 = y$

9-2 Permutations
Pages 384–386

Think and Discuss pp. 384–385

1–3. Answers may vary. The answers given assume a class of 26 students.

1. Sample: 26

2. Sample: $26 - 1 = 25$

3. Sample: $26 \cdot 25 = 650$

4. (Matt, Raquel) represents Matt as contestant and Raquel as alternate. This is different from (Raquel, Matt), which represents Raquel as contestant and Matt as alternate.

5. MRJ, MJR, RMJ, RJM, JRM, JMR

6. $3 \cdot (3 - 1) \cdot (3 - 2) = 3 \cdot 2 \cdot 1 = 6$

7. a. $9!$

   b. $362,880$

8. $_{20}P_5 = 20 \cdot 19 \cdot 18 \cdot 17 \cdot 16 = 1,860,480$

9. (144 choices for P) $\cdot$ (143 choices for VP) $\cdot$ (142 choices for T) $= {}_{144}P_3$

Try These pp. 385–386

10. Sample for 5 letters $= 5! = 120$ ways (This assumes that all the letters are different.)

11. Sample: If two letters are repeated, some of the arrangements will look the same.

12. Agree;
$1 \cdot 2 \cdot 3 \cdot 4 \cdot 5 \cdot 6 = 6 \cdot 5 \cdot 4 \cdot 3 \cdot 2 \cdot 1 = 6!$

13. Disagree; order of letters is different.

14. Agree; $6! =$ number of permutations $= 6 \cdot 5 \cdot 4 \cdot 3 \cdot 2 \cdot 1 = {}_6P_6$

15. Answers may vary. Sample: Disagree;
$_4P_3 = 4 \cdot 3 \cdot 2 = 24$, and $_4P_4 = 4 \cdot 3 \cdot 2 \cdot 1 = 24$, so they are the same.

On Your Own p. 386

16. $10! = 3,628,800$

17. $_7P_5 = 7 \cdot 6 \cdot 5 \cdot 4 \cdot 3 = 2,520$

18. $_{14}P_3 = 14 \cdot 13 \cdot 12 = 2,184$

19. $\frac{5!}{3!} = \frac{120}{6} = 20$

20. Sample: You can multiply $8 \cdot 7 \cdot 6 \cdot ...$, etc., or you can use the ! key to get $8!$ in one step.

21. $_{50}P_6 = 50 \cdot 49 \cdot 48 \cdot 47 \cdot 46 \cdot 45 = $ 11,441,304,000

22. $7! = 5,040$

23. 1234 1243 2134 2143 3124 3142 4123 4132
1342 1324 2314 2341 3214 3241 4213 4231
1423 1432 2413 2431 3412 3421 4312 4321

24. 13 31 51 71 91
15 35 53 73 93
17 37 57 75 95
19 39 59 79 97

25. Rectangular table: $6! = 720$

Circular table: Since there is no "beginning" or "end" at a circular table, every permutation looks exactly like 5 other permutations when they are seated at a round table. For example, 123456 looks exactly like 234561, 345612, 456123, 561234, and 612345. These identities break up the entire set of permutations into distinct sets of 6 permutations each. Thus there must be $720 \div 6 = 120$ such sets, which from the point of view of the round table, are 120 distinct permutations.

26. F; $1! + 2! + 3! = 1 + 2 + 6 = 9$, but $6! = 720$.

27. T; $6! \div 4! = \dfrac{6 \cdot 5 \cdot 4 \cdot 3 \cdot 2 \cdot 1}{4 \cdot 3 \cdot 2 \cdot 1} = 6 \cdot 5$

28. F; $3! \cdot 3! = 6 \cdot 6 = 36$, but $9! = 362,880$

29. F; $7! - 3! = 5,040 - 6 = 5,034$, but $7 \cdot 6 \cdot 5 \cdot 4 = 840$.

30. T; $_{19}P_{19} = 19 \cdot 18 \cdot 17 \cdot \ldots \cdot 2 \cdot 1$, and $19! = 19 \cdot 18 \cdot 17 \cdot \ldots \cdot 2 \cdot 1$, also.

31. F; $_5P_2 = 5 \cdot 4$

Mixed Review p. 386

1. $\dfrac{1}{8}$

2. $\dfrac{81}{100}$

3. $\dfrac{1}{100}$

4. $\dfrac{1}{1,000}$

5.

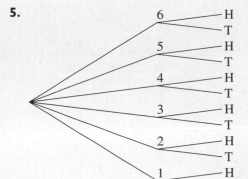

6.

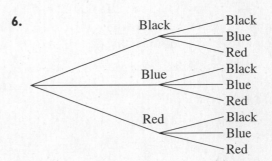

7. 12

A number of coins = 35
Let n = number of nickels
$n + 4$ = number of dimes
$(n + 4) + 3$ = number of quarters
$n + n + 4 + n + 7 = 35$
$3n + 11 = 35$
$3n = 24$
$n = 8$

8 = nickels ($.40), 12 = dimes ($1.20), 15 = quarters ($3.75), $0.40 + 1.20 + 3.75 = $5.35, $9.35 - 5.35 = 4.00$, 4 bills

9-3 Combinations

Pages 387–390

Think and Discuss pp. 387–388

1. For any two specified people, there will always be two of each pair.

2. Sample for class of 26: $26 \cdot \dfrac{25}{2} = 325$.

3. yes; order is not important

4. (Amber, Dimitri), (Amber, Carlos), (Carlos, Dimitri). There are three.

5. (A, D) and (D, A), (A, C) and (C, A), (C, D) and (D, C). Each pair occurs twice, so that we could divide the number of permutations by 2 to get the number of combinations.

6. Permutations, since there are a number of permutations of any given combination.

7. $\frac{_6P_3}{3!} = \frac{6 \cdot 5 \cdot 4}{3 \cdot 2 \cdot 1} = 20$

8. $20; \frac{_6P_3}{3!} = \frac{6 \cdot 5 \cdot 4}{3 \cdot 2 \cdot 1} = 20$

9. Sample: Since the order does not matter in a combination, we divide by the number of permutations of 5 lures, which is 5!, to get the number of combinations.

10. No; $\frac{_{12}P_7}{7!} = \frac{3,991,680}{5,040} = 792$

Work Together p. 388

11. Permutation: $4 \cdot 3 \cdot 2 \cdot 1 = 24$

12. Combination: $\frac{_{10}P_3}{3!} = \frac{10 \cdot 9 \cdot 8}{3 \cdot 2 \cdot 1} = 120$

13. Comb.: $_{15}C_5 = \frac{_{15}P_5}{5!} = 3,003$

14. Comb.: $_{52}C_6 = \frac{_{52}P_6}{6!} =$

$\frac{52 \cdot 51 \cdot 50 \cdot 49 \cdot 48 \cdot 47}{6 \cdot 5 \cdot 4 \cdot 3 \cdot 2 \cdot 1} = 20,358,520$

15. Perm.: $10! = 3,628,800$

16. Sample: If order matters, then the situation describes a permutation.

Mixed Review p. 389

1. $5 \cdot 4 \cdot 3 \cdot 2 \cdot 1 = 120$

2. $_3P_2 = 3 \cdot 2 = 6$

3. $9 \cdot 8 \cdot 7 \cdot 6 \cdot 5 \cdot 4 \cdot 3 \cdot 2 \cdot 1 = 362,880$

4. $\frac{100!}{99!} = \frac{100 \cdot 99 \cdot 98 \cdot ... \cdot 2 \cdot 1}{99 \cdot 98 \cdot ... \cdot 2 \cdot 1} = 100$

5. add 7

6. subtract 1

7.

x	$f(x)$	$x, f(x)$
−3	33	(−3, 33)
−2	13	(−2, 13)
−1	1	(−1, 1)
0	−3	(0, −3)
1	1	(1, 1)
2	13	(2, 13)
3	33	(3, 33)

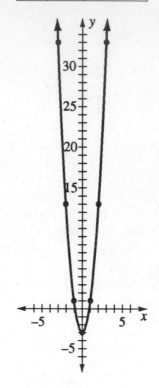

Try These p. 389

17. $_{14}C_2 = \frac{_{14}P_2}{2!} = 91$

18. $_7C_3 = \frac{_7P_3}{3!} = \frac{210}{6} = 35$

19. $_8C_5 = \frac{_8P_5}{5!} = 56$

20. $_6C_2 = \frac{_6P_2}{2!} = \frac{6 \cdot 5}{2} = 15$

21. (Juan, Ester), (Juan, Ken), (Juan, Corey), (Ester, Ken), (Ester, Corey), (Ken, Corey)

22. $_4C_2 = \frac{_4P_2}{2!} = \frac{_4P_2}{2}$, so there are twice as many permutations as combinations.

23. $_{52}P_2 = 52 \cdot 51 = 2,652$

On Your Own pp. 389–390

24. $_7C_4 = \frac{_7P_4}{4!} = \frac{7 \cdot 6 \cdot 5 \cdot 4}{4 \cdot 3 \cdot 2 \cdot 1} = 35$

25. $_3C_1 = \frac{_3P_1}{1!} = \frac{3}{1} = 3$

26. $_9C_6 = \frac{_9P_6}{6!} = 84$

27. Groups of 2: $_6C_2 = \frac{_6P_2}{2!} = \frac{30}{2} = 15$. For every group of two let on the plane, there is exactly one group of four left behind. Thus there must be 15 groups of four.

28. a. No, since $_4C_4 \neq 4!$.

    b. Yes, since $_4P_4 = 4!$.

    c. No, since $_8C_4 \neq {}_8P_4$, but $_4P_4 = 4!$.

    d. No, the 4! does not belong in the numerator.

29. $_{10}P_5 = 10 \cdot 9 \cdot 8 \cdot 7 \cdot 6 = 30,240$

30. 16 songs requested, 10 played, 6 not played.

    $_{16}C_6 = \frac{_{16}P_6}{6!} = 8,008$

31. $_{20}C_2 = \frac{_{20}P_2}{2!} = 190$

32. $_{12}C_4 = \frac{_{12}P_4}{4!} = 495$

33. $_{18}P_2 = 18 \cdot 17 = 306$

34. Sample: If you elect 2 senators from a state, that is a combination, but if you elect one governor and one lieutenant governor, that is a permutation.

35. B

36. Check students' work.

Checkpoint p. 390

1. $_{12}P_5 = 12 \cdot 11 \cdot 10 \cdot 9 \cdot 8 = 95,040$

2. $_{12}C_5 = \frac{_{12}P_5}{5!} = \frac{95,040}{120} = 792$

3. $5! = 5 \cdot 4 \cdot 3 \cdot 2 \cdot 1 = 120$

4. C

5. a. 4,845

    number of strings = $(240 \div 3) \div 4 = 20$, so number of string quartets = $_{20}C_4 =$ $\frac{_{20}P_4}{4!} = \frac{20 \cdot 19 \cdot 18 \cdot 17}{4 \cdot 3 \cdot 2 \cdot 1} = 4,845$

b. number of choices for drummer = 20, and number of choices for 2 horn players = $_{20}C_2 = \frac{20 \cdot 19}{2!} = 190$; number of choices for new players = $20 \cdot 190 = 3,800$

Problem Solving Practice

Page 391

1. Let x be Sam's number of votes. Then Sandra's number of votes is $x + 46$.

    So $x + (x + 46) = 308$

$$2x + 46 = 308$$
$$2x = 262$$
$$x = 131 \text{ votes for Sam}$$
$$x + 46 = 177 \text{ votes for Sandra}$$

2. Total number in hive is 40,251.

    $\frac{\text{workers}}{\text{total}} = \frac{40,000}{40,251}$

    $= 0.99376; 99.38\%$

    $\frac{\text{drones}}{\text{total}} = \frac{250}{40,251}$

    $= 0.00621; 0.621\%$

    $\frac{\text{queens}}{\text{total}} = \frac{1}{40,251}$

    $= 0.0000248; 0.002\%$

3. $5! = 120$ ways

4. Yellow: $\frac{1}{3}$, thus $\frac{1}{3}$ is painted, $\frac{2}{3}$ not painted.

    Blue: $\frac{1}{2}\left(\frac{2}{3}\right) = \frac{1}{3}$, thus $\frac{1}{3} + \frac{1}{3} = \frac{2}{3}$ is painted, $\frac{1}{3}$ is not.

    Green: $\frac{1}{4}\left(\frac{1}{3}\right) = \frac{1}{12}$, thus $\frac{2}{3} + \frac{1}{12} = \frac{3}{4}$ is painted, $\frac{1}{4}$ is not.

    Red: $\frac{2}{3}\left(\frac{1}{4}\right) = \frac{1}{6}$, thus $\frac{3}{4} + \frac{1}{6} = \frac{11}{12}$ is painted, $\frac{1}{12}$ is not.

    Last 9 in. is $\frac{1}{12}$ of pole, so the pole is $9 \cdot 12 = 108$ in.

5. $6 \cdot 3 \cdot 32 = 576$. There are 6 possibilities for meat, 3 possibilities for cheese, and 32 total possibilities for extras. No extras: 1 choice. 1 extra: 5 choices. 2 extras: $_5C_2 = 10$ choices. 3 extras: $_5C_3 = 10$ choices. 4 extras: $_5C_4 = 5$ choices. 5 extras: 1 choice.

6. Distance $= 1 \cdot 2 + 2 \cdot 2 + 3 \cdot 2 + \ldots + 20 \cdot 2$

$\qquad\qquad = 2(1 + 2 + \ldots + 20)$

$\qquad\qquad = 2(210)$

$\qquad\qquad = 420$ ft

A diagram:

7. $18\frac{1}{3}$ yr

Beginning Amount	1000
End of Year 1	1060
End of Year 2	1123.6
End of Year 3	1191.016
End of Year 4	1262.47696
End of Year 5	1338.22558
End of Year 6	1418.51911
End of Year 7	1503.63026
End of Year 8	1593.84807
End of Year 9	1689.47896
End of Year 10	1790.8477
End of Year 11	1898.29856
End of Year 12	2012.19647
End of Year 13	2132.92826
End of Year 14	2260.90396
End of Year 15	2396.55819
End of Year 16	2540.35168
End of Year 17	2692.77279
End of Year 18	2854.33915
End of Year 19	3025.5995
End of Year 20	3207.13547
End of Year 21	3399.5636
End of Year 22	3603.53742

The balance will be more than $3000 at the end of Year 19.

The money will triple in $110 \div x$, in this case, $110 \div 6 = 18.\overline{3}$ years.

9-4 Probability and Odds

Pages 392–395

Think and Discuss pp. 392–394

1. Samples: the sun will rise; rolling a 7 on a number cube

2. $\frac{4}{6} = \frac{2}{3}; \frac{2}{6} = \frac{1}{3}$

3. Sample: a baby is a girl; a baby is a boy

4. If odds in favor of event $= \frac{Y}{N}$, then $P(\text{event}) = \frac{Y}{(Y + N)}$.

5. Sample: $P(\text{green}) \approx \frac{2000}{8000} = \frac{1}{4}$.

$\qquad P(\text{yellow}) \approx \frac{6000}{8000} = \frac{3}{4}$

Mixed Review p. 393

1. $_6C_5 = \frac{_6P_5}{5!} = \frac{6 \cdot 5 \cdot 4 \cdot 3 \cdot 2}{5 \cdot 4 \cdot 3 \cdot 2 \cdot 1} = 6$

2. $_4C_2 = \frac{_4P_2}{2!} = \frac{4 \cdot 3}{2} = 6$

3. $_7P_3 = 7 \cdot 6 \cdot 5 = 210$

4. $\frac{12!}{3!} = 79{,}833{,}600$

5. $\frac{36}{100} = \frac{72}{x}$

$\quad 36x = 7200$

$\quad x = 200$

$\quad 72$ is 36% of 200

6. $\frac{105}{30} = \frac{x}{100}$

$\quad 10{,}500 = 30x$

$\quad 350 = x$

$\quad 105$ is 350% of 30

7. $\frac{x}{48} = \frac{66\frac{2}{3}}{100}$

$\quad 100x = \left(66\frac{2}{3}\right)(48)$

$\quad 100x = 3200$

$\qquad x = 32$

The price of the jacket is $32.

Work Together p. 394

6. No;
Divide board into quarters and then into sixteenths. Then $P(A) = \frac{(3+2)}{16} = \frac{5}{16}$, $P(B) = \frac{(4+2)}{16} = \frac{6}{16}$, and $P(C) = \frac{(3+2)}{16} = \frac{5}{16}$.

7. Check students work. Sample: $\frac{7}{12}$ of the board represents winning, and $\frac{5}{12}$ of the board represents losing.

Try These p. 394

8. Answers will vary.

9. 1

10. **a.** $P(\text{win}) = \frac{1}{(1+3)} = \frac{1}{4}$

   b. $P(\text{not win}) = \frac{3}{(1+3)} = \frac{3}{4}$

11. Sample:

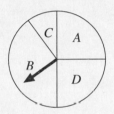

12. 1; 1 is the probability attached to absolute certainty. No probability can be higher than that.

On Your Own p. 395

13. $\frac{50}{50 + 80 + 100 + 20} = \frac{50}{250} = \frac{1}{5}$

14. $P(A) = \frac{(12 + 6 + 4)}{64} = \frac{11}{32}$, $P(B) = \frac{(8 + 4 + 16)}{64} = \frac{14}{32}$, and $P(C) = \frac{(8 + 6)}{64} = \frac{7}{32}$.

15. **a.** $P(\text{win}) = \frac{\text{favorable outcomes}}{\text{possible outcomes}} = \frac{1}{500}$,

   $\text{Odds(win)} = \frac{\text{favorable outcomes}}{\text{unfavorable outcomes}} = \frac{1}{499}$.

   b. $P(\text{win}) = \frac{2}{500} = \frac{1}{250}$.

   $\text{Odds(win)} = \frac{2}{498} = \frac{1}{249}$.

16. $P(m \text{ or } n) = \frac{11}{12}$, since there are 11 elements ending in m or n, and a total of 12 elements.

17. Sample: 25%; experimental

18. Sample: 96%; the probability of picking (blindfolded) a red apple from a bag of 24 red apples and 1 yellow one.

19. Sample: $\frac{1}{3}$; probability of randomly selecting the red jacket from a rack that holds a red jacket, a blue one, and a green one.

20. Sample: $\frac{1}{2}$, the probability of randomly selecting a green marble from a sack that has 8 green marbles and 8 white ones.

21. $P(\text{green}) + P(\text{black}) = 1$, so $P(\text{black}) = 1 - P(\text{green}) = 1 - 0.4 = 0.6$
Not enough information to find out how many olives.

22. **a.** Check students' work.

   b. Yes, but students' trials may not bear this out.

   c. Sample: There are too few trials.

23. Sample:

9-5 Independent and Dependent Events

Pages 396–399

Work Together p. 396

1. The probability is $\frac{2}{3}$.

2. yes

Think and Discuss pp. 396–398

3. **a.** independent

   b. dependent

   c. dependent

   d. independent

   e. dependent

4. **a.** $\frac{4}{10} \cdot \frac{4}{10} = \frac{16}{100} = 16\%$

   b. $P(2 \text{ blue}) + P(2 \text{ red}) = 52\%$, so $P(2 \text{ different}) = 100\% - 52\% = 48\%$

5. a. $P(GB) = \frac{2}{5} \cdot \frac{3}{4} = \frac{3}{10}$

b. $P(BG) = \frac{3}{5} \cdot \frac{2}{4} = \frac{3}{10}$

c. $P(BB) = \frac{3}{5} \cdot \frac{2}{4} = \frac{3}{10}$

6. Sample: The mouse's second choice of path depends on whether his first choice was the upper or lower path.

Mixed Review p. 397

1. $\frac{1}{999 + 1} = \frac{1}{1000}$

2.

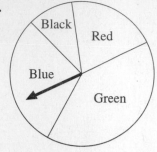

3. $\frac{3}{8} = 0.375 = 37.5\%$

4. $6\frac{3}{4} = 6.75 = 675\%$

5.

$x^2 + 40^2 = 50^2$

$x^2 = 2500 - 1600$

$x^2 = 900$

$x = 30$ ft

Try These pp. 398–399

7. $P(GG) = \frac{4}{16} \cdot \frac{3}{15} = \frac{1}{20}$, since there are 4 grape drinks out of 16 when first person chooses, but only 3 out of the 15 left are grape if the first person chooses grape.

8. a.

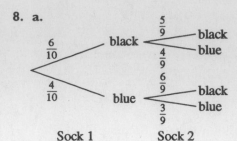

Sock 1   Sock 2

b. $P(\text{two blue}) = \frac{4}{10} \cdot \frac{3}{9} = \frac{12}{90} = \frac{2}{15}$

9. $P(\text{tail}) = \frac{1}{2}$, since these are independent events.

On Your Own p. 399

10. a. $P(I, \text{ then a vowel}) = \frac{1}{26} \cdot \frac{4}{25} = \frac{2}{325}$

b. $P(z, \text{ then a consonant}) = \frac{1}{26} \cdot \frac{20}{25} = \frac{2}{65}$

11.

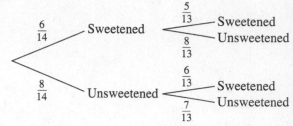

12. $P(\text{colorblind/male}) = \frac{40}{500} = 8\%$

$P(\text{colorblind/female}) = \frac{2}{500} = 0.4\%$

13. Dependent; you are more likely to be colorblind if you are male.

14. $P(\text{colorblind}) = \frac{42}{1000} \approx \frac{4}{100}$. So about 4 people out of 100 are colorblind.

15.

	Cheese
Cheese	

$P(\text{cheese}) = \frac{1}{6} + \frac{1}{3} = \frac{1}{2}$

16. a. $P(\text{4 corners}) = \frac{4}{200} \cdot \frac{3}{199} \cdot \frac{2}{198} \cdot \frac{1}{197}$

0.000000015

b. $\frac{4}{100}$; 100 pieces are left, and 4 are corners.

17. B. Sample explanation: When you go back to the box there will be a greater ratio of corners and edges to other pieces, and therefore a greater probability of picking one.

18. Sample: One event is independent of another if they have no effect on each other, like throwing dice two different times. One event is dependent on another, if the probability of one event is affected by the other event. An example is that the probability of gathering corn from a corn stalk is dependent on whether there is a cold spell in June.

9-6 Pascal's Triangle

Pages 400–403

Think and Discuss p. 400

1. Answers may vary.

2. a. The sum of the top 2 numbers is the bottom number.

b. Sample: Add the pairs to get all of the next row except for the end numbers which are just 1's.

c. row 7: 1, 7, 21, 35, 35, 21, 7, 1

row 8: 1, 8, 28, 56, 70, 56, 28, 8, 1

3. a–b. row 0: $1 = 2^0$

row 1: $2 = 2^1$

row 2: $4 = 2^2$

row 3: $8 = 2^3$

row 4: $16 = 2^4$

row 5: $32 = 2^5$

row 6: $64 = 2^6$

c. The sum of the nth row is 2^n.

Work Together pp. 401–402

4. $\frac{1}{2}$

5. Sample: If the lights work independently, the probability of three green lights in a row may be less than the probability of three green lights in a row when the lights are timed to operate in sequence.

6. There are 8 outcomes; 8 = sum of 3rd row of Pascal's triangle.

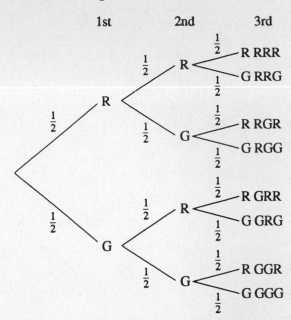

7. The numbers under the outcomes are the same as row 3 of Pascal's triangle.

8. a. $\frac{1}{8}$, since RRR is 1 out of 8 outcomes.

b. $\frac{3}{8}$

c. $\frac{3}{8}$

d. $\frac{1}{8}$

9. To find the probability of *three* green lights use Pascal's triangle by first selecting the *third* row. The first value, 1, represents the numerator for the probability and the sum of the values in that row, 8, is the denominator.

10. P(no green) = $\dfrac{1}{\text{sum of 6th row}} = \dfrac{1}{64}$

P(1 green) $= \dfrac{6}{\text{sum of 6th row}} = \dfrac{6}{64}$

P(2 green) $= \dfrac{15}{64}$

P(3 green) $= \dfrac{20}{64} = \dfrac{5}{16}$

P(4 green) $= \dfrac{15}{64}$

P(5 green) $= \dfrac{6}{64} = \dfrac{3}{32}$

P(6 green) $= \dfrac{1}{64}$

11. a. row 4: P(2H, 2T) $= \frac{6}{16} = \frac{3}{8}$

  b. P(1H, 3T) $= \frac{4}{16} = \frac{1}{4}$

12. $_5C_0$ means the number of combinations of 0 things chosen from 5 things. $_5C_0 = 1$. $_5C_5$ means the number of combinations of 5 things chosen from 5. $_5C_5 = 1$.

13. $_7C_3 = 35$, which is the 4th number in the 7th row. $_7C_3 = \frac{(7 \cdot 6 \cdot 5)}{(3 \cdot 2)} = 35$

Mixed Review p. 401

1. P(red, then red) $= \frac{7}{10} \cdot \frac{6}{9} = \frac{7}{15}$

2. P(green, then green) $= \frac{3}{10} \cdot \frac{2}{9} = \frac{1}{15}$

3. P(different colors) = P(red, then green) + P(green, then red) $= \frac{7}{10} \cdot \frac{3}{9} + \frac{3}{10} \cdot \frac{7}{9} = \frac{42}{90} = \frac{7}{15}$

4.

5.

On Your Own pp. 402–403

14. row 4, $\frac{\text{2nd number}}{\text{total of row}} = \frac{4}{16} = \frac{1}{4}$

15. row 6, 4th number = 20

16. row 6, $\frac{\text{4th number}}{\text{total of row}} = \frac{20}{64} = \frac{5}{16}$

17. P(1 girl, 1 boy) $= \frac{\text{2nd number 2nd row}}{\text{total of row}} = \frac{2}{4} = \frac{1}{2}$. P(1 boy, then girl) $= \frac{1}{2} \cdot \frac{1}{2} = \frac{1}{4}$

18. P(ninth child is a girl) $= \frac{1}{2}$ (independent events); P(nine girls in a row), for any family with nine children $= \left(\frac{1}{2}\right)^9 = \frac{1}{512}$. Sample explanation: The reason for the difference is that the family mentioned already has 8 girls, but we make no such assumption about "any family with nine children."

19. Choosing one item out of 3 is the same as choosing 2 of the opposite type item out of 3. All rows are symmetric but in a slightly different way. Even-numbered rows have an odd number of terms symmetric about a middle term. For example, 1 4 6 4 1, in row 4.

Odd-numbered rows have an even number of terms with all numbers listed twice. For example, in row 5, 1 5 10 10 5 1.

20. Sample: There are two equally likely outcomes. Probability of either event $= \frac{1}{2}$.

21. $2^{10} = 1{,}024$ possible outcomes, 1 "all correct" outcome, so odds = 1 to 1,023.

22. a. 1; 3; 3; 1

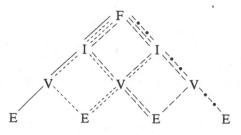

  b. They are the numbers in row 3.

23. Let U = up and R = right
Paths: <u>1</u>: R, R, R, U, U
<u>2</u>: R, R, U, R, U <u>3</u>: R, R, U, U, R
<u>4</u>: R, U, R, U, R <u>5</u>: R, U, U, R, R
<u>6</u>: R, U, R, R, U <u>7</u>: U, R, R, R, U
<u>8</u>: U, U, R, R, R <u>9</u>: U, R, U, R, R
<u>10</u>: U, R, R, U, R

There are 10 paths. This is the third entry in the fifth row of Pascal's triangle. In each case, you have a choice of U or R, so $_5C_2 = 10$ is the number of ways of choosing two U's.

  The number of routes to A, B, C, and D are 1, 3, 3, and 1. These are the numbers in the third row of Pascal's triangle. They represent $_3C_0$ (no R's), $_3C_1$ (1 R), $_3C_2$ (2 R's), and $_3C_3$ (3 R's).

24. Combination formula, since writing 24 rows of Pascal's triangle would take too long.

25. Sample: 7 out of 28 have 4-letter names. $\frac{7}{28} = 25\%$. If the school has 500 students, then 25% of 500, or 125 have 4-letter names.

Checkpoint p. 403

1. **a.** $\left(\frac{1}{2}\right)^3 = \frac{1}{8}$

   b. E and E′ are complementary events, so
   $P(E') = 1 - P(E) = 0.25$.

2. Sample: $P(0) = \frac{1}{16}$

   $P(1) = \frac{4}{16} = \frac{1}{4}$

   $P(2) = \frac{6}{16} = \frac{3}{8}$

   $P(3) = \frac{4}{16} = \frac{1}{4}$

   $P(4) = \frac{1}{16}$

   So spinner looks like this:

   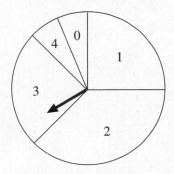

3. $P(A) = \frac{1}{2} \cdot \frac{1}{3} + \frac{2}{3} \cdot \frac{1}{3} + \frac{1}{3} = \frac{13}{18}$, so

   $P(B) = 1 - \frac{13}{18} = \frac{5}{18}$.

4. C; A and B are probabilities which can be found using Pascal's triangle, and D is a combination, which can be found using Pascal's triangle.

9-7 Simulate the Problem
Pages 404–406

1. yes; yes

2. yes; yes. Sample explanation: since he wants to lift only a cup that does not have the ball.

3. Answers may vary. Sample: It does not matter. There are equal probabilities for each.

4. Sample: The clown must lift a cup that does not contain the ball. Player must stay or switch.

5. See students' work. Sample:

Trial	Strategy	Win or Lose

6. More trials will give more accurate probabilities.

7. See students' work.
   Sample:

Strategy: Stay

Trial	Win or Lose
1	L
2	W
3	L
4	L
5	L
6	W
7	L
8	L
9	L
10	L
11	L
12	W
13	L
14	L
15	L
16	W
17	L
18	L
19	L
20	L

W = 4, L = 16

Strategy: Switch

Trial	Win or Lose
1	W
2	L
3	W
4	W
5	L
6	W
7	W
8	W
9	W
10	L
11	W
12	L
13	W
14	W
15	L
16	L
17	L
18	W
19	L
20	W

W = 12, L = 8

8. Sample: 4 out of 20

9. Sample: 12 out of 20

10. Switch; the probability of winning is higher.

11. Sample: yes; no; no

12. Sample: My reasoning was that there were equal probabilities for either cup, but this must not be true!

13. The problem can be solved by making a table.

Using the "Stay" Strategy

Ball	No Ball	No Ball	Win or Lose
√			W
	√		L
		√	L

√ represents your initial choice.

The probability of winning with the "stay" strategy is $\frac{1}{3}$.

Using the "Switch" Strategy

Ball	No Ball	No Ball	Win or Lose
√			L
	√		W
		√	W

√ represents your initial choice.

The probability of winning with the "switch" strategy is $\frac{2}{3}$.

Try These pp. 405–406

14. P(you win) = P(H, H) = $\frac{1}{2} \cdot \frac{1}{2} = \frac{1}{4}$, so

P(partner wins) = $1 - \frac{1}{4} = \frac{3}{4}$

15. P(3 sunny days) = 0.75 • 0.75 • 0.75 = 0.421875 ≈ 42%

Spinner:

A, B, C are sunny, D is not sunny. Perform 20 trials consisting of 3 spins each. Record how many times 3 "sunny's" appeared on the 20 trials.

Trial	Spins	
1	ACC	√
2	AD	
3	AD	
4	D	
5	BBD	
6	D	
7	BD	
8	CD	
9	BBD	
10	CCB	√
11	D	
12	ABA	√
13	CD	
14	CBB	√
15	CBB	√
16	CAB	√
17	BAB	√
18	CAA	√
19	BCC	√
20	BCD	

$\frac{9}{20}$ or 45% resulted in 3 sunny days. Theoretically, the probability of 3 sunny days in a row is $\left(\frac{3}{4}\right)^3 = \frac{27}{64} \approx 42\%$.

On Your Own p. 406

16. weight gain = 31(1.5) = 46.5 lb

weight = 10 + 46.5 = 56.5 lb

% gain = $\frac{46.5}{10}$ = 465%

17. Sample:

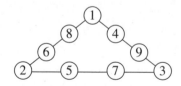

18. We can write $42 = 2x + 3(15 - x)$, where x is the number of bikes and $15 - x$ is the number of trikes.

Solve $2x + 45 - 3x = 42$

$$45 - x = 42$$

$x = 3$: number of bikes

$15 - x = 12$: number of trikes

19. $\left(\frac{1}{4}\right)^6 = \frac{1}{4,096}$

20. Switch; this is just like the red ball in the cup game.

21. Sample: To simulate a problem you perform trials of a problem with similar characteristics.

Mixed Review p. 406

1. $_6C_2 = $ 3rd number, row 6 = 15

2. $_9C_7 = $ 8th number, row 9 = 36

3. $6 \cdot 1.98 = 11.88$ and $4 \cdot 2.98 = 11.92$, so that $\frac{\$1.98}{4} < \frac{\$2.98}{6}$ and thus A is better buy.

4. B; A: $3.29 \div 6 \approx 0.548$; B: $6.49 \div 12 \approx 0.5408$

5.

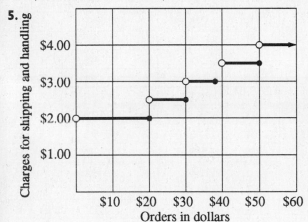

Practice

Page 407

1. $3! = 3 \cdot 2 \cdot 1 = 6$

2. $7! = 7 \cdot 6 \cdot 5 \cdot 4 \cdot 3 \cdot 2 \cdot 1 = 5,040$

3. $\frac{9!}{8!} = \frac{9 \cdot 8 \cdot 7 \cdot \ldots \cdot 1}{8 \cdot 7 \cdot \ldots \cdot 1} = 9$

4. $\frac{4!}{5!} = \frac{4 \cdot 3 \cdot 2 \cdot 1}{5 \cdot 4 \cdot 3 \cdot 2 \cdot 1} = \frac{1}{5}$

5. $\frac{8!7!}{10!} = \frac{(8 \cdot 7 \cdot 6 \cdot \ldots \cdot 1)(7 \cdot 6 \cdot 5 \cdot \ldots \cdot 1)}{10 \cdot 9 \cdot 8 \cdot 7 \cdot \ldots \cdot 1} = \frac{7!}{10 \cdot 9} = 56$

6. $\frac{75!}{73!} = 75 \cdot 74 = 5,550$

7. $\frac{8}{16} = \frac{1}{2}$

8. $\frac{4}{16} = \frac{1}{4}$

9. 0, since 20 is not on the spinner.

10. The squares are 1, 4, 9, and 16, so prob. is $\frac{4}{16} = \frac{1}{4}$.

11. $\frac{9}{16}$

12. $\frac{2}{16} = \frac{1}{8}$

13. $_{11}C_9 = \frac{11 \cdot 10 \cdot 9 \cdot 8 \cdot \ldots \cdot 3}{9 \cdot 8 \cdot \ldots \cdot 3 \cdot 2 \cdot 1} = \frac{110}{2} = 55$

14. $_5P_2 = 5 \cdot 4 = 20$

15. $_6C_6 = 1$

16. $_8P_8 = 8! = 40,320$

17. $_5C_3 = $ 4th number, row 5 = 10

18. $_7C_4 = $ 5th number, row 7 = 35

19. $_4C_3 = $ 4th number, row 4 = 4

20. $_7C_3 = $ 4th number, row 7 = 35

21. P(red, 4) $= \frac{1}{4} \cdot \frac{1}{6} = \frac{1}{24}$

22. P(not red, prime) $= \frac{3}{4} \cdot \frac{3}{6} = \frac{3}{8}$

23. P(not blue, odd) $= \frac{1}{2} \cdot \frac{3}{6} = \frac{1}{4}$

24. $\frac{4}{11}$

25. $\frac{1}{11}$

26. 0

27. P(both odd or both even) = P(both even) + P(both odd) $= \frac{1}{4} + \frac{1}{4} = \frac{1}{2}$. P(even and odd) = P(even, then odd) + P(odd, then even) $= \frac{1}{4} + \frac{1}{4} = \frac{1}{2}$. The game is fair.

28. $\frac{(3 \text{ blue socks})}{(7 \text{ socks left})} = \frac{3}{7}$, so P(no match) $= \frac{4}{7}$, so odds against match = 4 : 3.

29. $\frac{3}{5} \cdot 28,500 = 17,100$ people voted "yes."

30. 37 : 63

9-8 Fair Games and Random Digits

Pages 408–409

Work Together p. 408

1. Sample: Unfair; it's more likely not to get 1 pair of doubles.

2. Sample: no; the probabilities are unequal.

3. Check students' work.

Think and Discuss p. 408

4. Sample: 1–6; 7, 8, 9, 0

5. 4

6. A

   If students eliminate 0, 7, 8, 9 and go across from left to right, the following will result. Otherwise, answers may vary.

Round	Digits	Winner	Round	Digits	Winner
1	2341	B	16	3666	A
2	4125	B	17	4522	A
3	3554	A	18	1552	A
4	6562	A	19	2422	A
5	2231	A	20	4543	A
6	3114	A	21	3566	A
7	6441	A	22	4451	A
8	2614	B	23	3641	B
9	3344	B	24	4315	B
10	1343	A	25	6564	A
11	1451	A	26	4551	A
12	5414	A	27	4424	A
13	3312	A	28	2213	A
14	2112	B	29	3164	B
15	5411	A	30	4615	B

   Player A: 21 points
   Player B: 9 points
   Player A won.

7. Sample: A

8. Sample: Unfair, but not in the way we thought at first.

On Your Own p. 409

9. *Rolling Thunder*: unfair; A; *Three's a Crowd*: fair, since P(three heads) + P(three tails) = $\frac{4}{16} + \frac{4}{16} = \frac{1}{2}$

10. Disregard digits 7, 8, 9, 0 and use digits 1–6 to stand for the sides of the dice. Then divide these digits into groups of four digits to represent the results of throwing 2 dice by each player.

11. Sample: even digits are heads, odds are tails

12. Sample: Use 1 for heads and 0 for tails.

13. a. Sample: unfair; fair

   A random number generator was used to determine the winner of *Rolling Thunder* (RT) and *Three's a Crowd* (TC).

   Evens represent heads and odds represent tails.

Round	Digits	Sum[B]	Product[A]	Winner RT	Winner TC
1	2662	16	144	A	B
2	3516	15	90	A	A
3	3511	10	15	A	B
4	2162	11	24	A	A
5	4364	17	288	A	A
6	5445	18	400	B	B
7	1335	12	45	A	B
8	1535	14	75	A	B
9	3133	10	27	A	B
10	4232	11	48	A	A
11	5321	11	30	A	A
12	4651	16	120	A	B
13	1554	15	100	A	A
14	3523	13	90	A	A
15	2422	10	32	A	B
16	1166	14	36	A	B
17	1141	7	4	B	A
18	1216	10	12	A	B
19	5366	20	540	A	B
20	2356	16	180	A	B
21	1365	15	90	A	A
22	4552	16	200	A	B
23	2412	9	16	A	A
24	3651	15	90	A	A
25	5225	14	100	A	B
26	2425	13	80	A	A
27	2512	10	20	A	B
28	2515	13	50	A	A
29	5661	18	180	A	B
30	1165	13	30	A	A

RT	TC
Player A: 29	Player A: 14
Player B: 1	Player B: 16

Rolling Thunder is unfair. *Three's a Crowd* is fair.

b. Sample: In *Rolling Thunder*, let each player find the sum of the numbers on the dice he or she rolled.

14. Sample: P(A wins) = P(B wins)

15. Sample: Sam; he had more trials.

Mixed Review p. 409

1. Simulate this by red light-green light model. This situation is the same as the probability of 9 lights out of 15 being green.

2. Simulate this by red light-green light model. This is the same as the probability of 10 lights in a row being green.

3. $m\angle BRC = 140°; m\angle ARC = 180, 180 - 40 = 140$

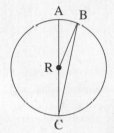

4. $m\angle ACB = 20°$; the measure of an inscribed angle is $\frac{1}{2}$ the measure of the central angle.

5. $(-4)^2 - 7 \cdot 2^3 = 16 - 7 \cdot 8 = 16 - 56 = -40$

6. $15 \div (-3) + 6^2 - 1 = -5 + 36 - 1 = 30$

9-9 Using Samples for Quality Control
Pages 410–413

Think and Discuss pp. 410–411

1. $\frac{10}{500} = \frac{1}{50}$

2. Yes; the prob. of a defect improves to $\frac{2}{800} = \frac{1}{400}$, which is less than $\frac{1}{50}$.

3. $\left(\frac{1}{400}\right) 10,000 = 25$ defective disks

4. Sample: number of cans of mushrooms; temperature of oven; how much tomato sauce; weight of pizza

5. Sample: during the process

6. 500; just above mean

7. 460 g, 540 g, 80 g; the mass must be within 40 g of 500 g.

8.

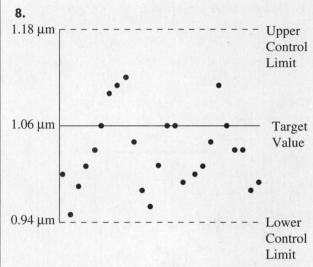

9. yes; at 0.92

10.

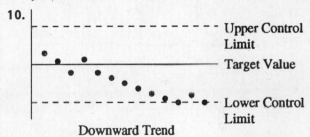

Downward Trend

Work Together p. 411

Check students' work.

On Your Own pp. 412–413

11. 2.5% of 120 = 3 air conditioners

12. Sample: Check at random times of day on random days.

13. Check students' work.

14. a. the point at which it is clear there is an upward trend

b. the point at which the point goes out of limits

15. 99.9% of 3.5 = 3.4965 to 100.1% of 3.5 = 3.5035

16. $\frac{4}{50} = \frac{20}{t}$

$4t = 1000$

$t = 250$ trout

Mixed Review p. 413

1. No; A has a greater chance of winning, since sums less than 8 are obtained from 21 out of 36 possible combinations of two number cubes, but sums greater than or equal to 8 are obtained from only 15 out of 36 possible combinations of the cubes.

2. $3n - 5 > -8$

$3n > -3$

$n > -1$

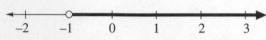

3. $\frac{1}{2} \le -6n + \frac{3}{4}$

$\frac{-3}{4} + \frac{1}{2} \le -6n + \frac{3}{4} + \frac{-3}{4}$

$\frac{-1}{4} \le -6n$

$\frac{1}{24} \ge n$

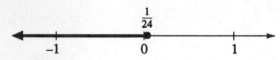

4. $m = \frac{11 - 7}{3 - (-4)} = \frac{4}{7}$

5. $m = \frac{6 - (-6)}{1 - 10} = \frac{12}{-9} = -\frac{4}{3}$

Wrap Up

Pages 414–415

1. 24

2. 5,040

3. 20

4. $\frac{12!}{9!} = \frac{12 \cdot 11 \cdot 10 \cdot 9!}{9!} = 12 \cdot 11 \cdot 10 = 1,320$

5. $3 \cdot 4 \cdot 2 \cdot 5 = 120$ outfits

6. A: $_6P_6 = 6! = 720$, $_5P_3 = 60$, $_7C_2 = 21$, $_{10}C_9 = 10$

7. $_5P_3 = 60$

8. $_{10}C_2 = \frac{10 \cdot 9}{2} = 45$

9. $_{12}C_2 = \frac{12 \cdot 11}{2} = 66$

10. $_{25}C_6 = 177,100$

11. 5th number, row 6 = 15

12. 10th number, row 9 = 1

13. 3rd number, row 5 = 10

14. 6th number, row 8 = 56

15. $\frac{1}{2}$; 1 : 1

16. $\frac{1}{2} \cdot \frac{1}{2} = \frac{1}{4}$; 1 : 3

17. Sum of 9 can be achieved by 4 different combinations out of 36, so probability = $\frac{4}{36} = \frac{1}{9}$; 1 : 8

18. Sample: An example of two independent events is that of a number cube being rolled and a card being drawn from a deck of cards. If a card is drawn from a deck and then another is drawn from the same deck without replacing the first, then the events are dependent.

19. This is simulated by the probability of 3 green lights out of 5 stoplights.

20. $\frac{7}{10} = \frac{t}{250}$

$10t = 1,750$

$t = 175$

175 toys out of 250 will not be defective.

21. When all the 8 possible outcomes are listed, it becomes clear that these outcomes will yield 6 pts for B, but 12 pts for A. The game does not appear to be fair.

Getting Ready for Chapter 10 p. 415

1. $\frac{75}{100} = 0.75$

2. $\frac{8}{10} = 0.8$

3. $\frac{5}{10} = 0.5$

4. $\frac{375}{1,000} = 0.375$

5. $\frac{4}{10} = 0.4$

6. $\frac{875}{1,000} = 0.875$

Assessment

Page 418

1. 36; 2 styles • 3 paper colors • 3 envelope colors • 2 styles = $2 \cdot 3 \cdot 3 \cdot 2 = 36$

2. 2 digits and 3 letters: $10^2 \cdot 26^3 = 1,757,600$

   7 digits: $10^7 = 10,000,000$.

   7-digit license plate has more outcomes.

3. B: There are 3 people chosen out of 20.

4. a. 40,320

   b. $4 \cdot 3 \cdot 2 = 24$

   c. $\frac{18 \cdot 17}{2} = 153$

   d. $6 \cdot 5 \cdot 4 \cdot 3 = 360$

   e. $1 - P(E) = 1 - 0.53 = 0.47$

5. $_{12}C_3 = \frac{12 \cdot 11 \cdot 10}{3!} = 220$

   a. Yes: $_{12}C_9 = \frac{12 \cdot 11 \cdot 10 \cdot 9 \cdot \ldots \cdot 4}{} = 220$

   b. No: $\frac{12!}{9!} = 12 \cdot 11 \cdot 10 = 1,320$

   c. Yes

   d. No: $_{12}P_4 = 12 \cdot 11 \cdot 10 \cdot 9 = 11,880$

6. a. $\frac{1}{400}$; $1 : 399$

   b. $\frac{5}{400} = \frac{1}{80}$; $1 : 79$

7. a. $\frac{1}{2}$

   b. 16 multiples of 3, so P(multiple of 3) = $\frac{16}{50} = \frac{8}{25}$

   c. $P(57) = 0$

8. use row 4, $\frac{\text{third number}}{\text{total of row}} = \frac{6}{16} = \frac{3}{8}$

9. All green lights out of 5 stoplights in a row: $\frac{1}{\text{total of row 5}} = \frac{1}{32}$

10. Sample: She might conclude that the game is unfair, but there are so few trials it is hard to tell.

11. a. The process would not be stopped.

    b. the point where it is clear there is a downward trend

12. $\frac{7}{126} = \frac{c}{198}$

    $126c = 1386$

    $c = 11$

    11 cracks out of 198 fenders

Cumulative Review

Page 419

1. C; II is not true if c is 0 or negative.

2. D

3. B; $\frac{6}{10} = \frac{h}{15}$, $90 = 10h$, $9 = h$

4. D

5. C

6. A; $\frac{\left(x \cdot \frac{3}{4}\right) - 3}{12} = 2$, $\frac{3}{4}x - 3 = 24$, $\frac{3}{4}x = 27$, $x = 36$

7. C

8. A; $_8P_5 = 6,720$

9. B; $\frac{16}{24} = \frac{2}{3}$

10. B; $(5 \cdot 7) + (3 \cdot 2) = 35 + 6 = 41$; 41 mm

Chapter 10 Applications of Percent

10-1 Fractions, Decimals, and Percents

Pages 423–426

Think and Discuss pp. 423–425

1. No; not every denominator is a factor of 100.

2. Sample: percents; percents can be compared more easily than fractions.

3. $41\frac{2}{3}\% = \frac{125}{3} \times \frac{1}{100} = \frac{5}{12}$

Try These p. 425

4. 36%

5. 4%

6. 0.3%

7. 520%

8. $3 \div 5 = 0.6 = 60\%$

9. $17 \div 20 = 0.85 = 85\%$

10. $1 \div 6 = 0.1\overline{6} = 16.7\%$ rounded to the nearest tenth

11. $3\frac{1}{8} = \frac{25}{8} = 25 \div 8 = 3.125 = 312.5\%$

12. $\frac{7}{10}$

13. $\frac{93}{100}$

14. $4\frac{3}{4}\% = \frac{19}{4} \times \frac{1}{100} = \frac{19}{400}$

15. $782\% = \frac{782}{100} = \frac{391}{50}$

On Your Own pp. 425–426

16. C; $52\% = 0.52 = \frac{52}{100}$

17. $60\% = \frac{60}{100} = \frac{3}{5}$

18. $5\% = \frac{5}{100} = \frac{1}{20}$

19. $120\% = \frac{120}{100} = \frac{6}{5}$

20. $2\frac{1}{5}\% = 0.022 = \frac{22}{1000} = \frac{11}{500}$

21. $\frac{7}{10} = \frac{70}{100} = 70\%$

22. $\frac{8}{5} = \frac{160}{100} = 160\%$

23. $\frac{5}{12} = 0.41\overline{6} = 41.7\%$

24. $4\frac{3}{7} = \frac{31}{7} = 4.\overline{428571} = 442.9\%$

25. $\frac{1}{7} = 0.\overline{142857} = 14.3\%$

26. Sample: $0.05 = 5\%$ not 0.05%

27. $\frac{99}{864} = 99 \div 864 = 0.114583\overline{3} = 11.5\%$

28. Hispanic, $\frac{39}{100}$; Asian, $\frac{27}{100}$; African, $\frac{3}{25}$; Caucasian, $\frac{11}{50}$

29. $835\% = 8.35$; 8.35 times

30. Sample: The incidence of rabies increased 103% this year in New Hampshire.

31. $\frac{1.5 \text{ million}}{31 \text{ million}} = \frac{1.5}{31} = 1.5 \div 31 = 0.048387096 \ldots \approx 4.8\%$

32. $0.02\% = \frac{2}{10,000} = \frac{1}{5,000}$

33. Answers will vary.

Mixed Review p. 426

1. $\frac{1}{3}$ of $30 = 10$ days

2. $\frac{3}{14}$

3. $\frac{2}{3} = 0.67$, so $0.75 \boxed{>} \frac{2}{3}$

4. $\frac{3}{8} = 0.375$, so $\frac{3}{8} \boxed{<} 0.38$

5. $5n = 32$; $n = 6.4$

6. $3n = 63$; $n = 21$

10-2 Estimating with Percents

Pages 427–429

Think and Discuss pp. 427–428

1. 25% of $64 is $16

2. **a.** $20\% = \frac{1}{5}$

   b. $65 because 65 is divisible by 5

   c. $\frac{1}{5}$ of $65 = $13

3. **a.** $37\frac{1}{2}\% = \frac{3}{8}$ and $\frac{3}{8} \times 88 = 33$

   b. $40\% = \frac{2}{5}$ and $88 \approx 90$, so $\frac{2}{5} \times 90 = 36$

   c. Sample: the estimate in 3(a) is closer to the actual answer.

4. Accept reasonable estimates.

   a. 1% of 56,246 is about 562 pilots.

   b. Since 1.8% is rounded to 2%, and 1% of 56,246 is 562, then 2% of 56,246 is 2×562 or 1,124 pilots.

5. Accept reasonable estimates.

   a. Round $29.70 to $30. 10% of $30 is $3.00, so 10% of $29.70 is about $3.00.

   b. 5% is one half of 10%, so $\frac{1}{2}$ of $3.00 is $1.50.

   c. $3.00 + $1.50 = $4.50

6. Round 590 to 600; 1% of 600 = $0.01 \times 600 = 6$; $\frac{1}{2}$ of 6 = 3

7. Answers may vary. Sample: $\frac{5}{3} \times 90 = 150$

Work Together p. 428

8. Answers may vary. An example is given.

   a. 26 students

   b. About 10 sing in the shower, about 20 prefer showers, about 4 sleep on their stomachs, about 7 squeeze toothpaste from the bottom.

9. Answers may vary.

10. Check results.

On Your Own p. 429

11–17. Accept reasonable estimates. Sample answers are given.

11. $\frac{1}{3}$ of 90 = 30

12. $\frac{2}{3}$ of 243 = 162

13. 20% of 30 = 6

14. 0.4% of 200 = $0.004 \times 200 = 0.8$

15. 40% of 75 = $0.4 \times 75 = 30$

16. 300% of 100 = $3 \times 100 = 300$

17. **a.** 50% of 68 = 34

   b. 20% of 60 = 12

   c. 25% of 64 = 16

   d. 10% of 70 = 7

18. $\frac{5}{6} = 0.8\overline{3} = 83\%$, so 85% $\boxed{>}$ $\frac{5}{6}$

19. $\frac{2}{3} = 0.6\overline{7} = 67.7\%$, so 65% $\boxed{<}$ $\frac{2}{3}$

20. $\frac{1}{8} = 0.125 = 12.5\%$, so 12.5% $\boxed{=}$ $\frac{1}{8}$

21. 10% of $35 = $3.50; 5% of $35 = $3.50 ÷ 2 = $1.75; $3.50 + $1.75 = $5.25

22. B; 20% of 300 = 60

23. A; 0.5% of 200 = 1

24. Sample: An estimate can let you know if you've entered the correct data.

25. Accept reasonable estimates.

$70\% = \frac{7}{10}$

$\frac{7}{10} \times 90 = 63$; about 63 billion cans

26. **a.** $\frac{3}{4}$ of the number of students

   b. 27 teens

Mixed Review p. 429

1. $15\% = \frac{15}{100} = 0.15$; $\frac{15}{100} = \frac{3}{20}$

2. $120\% = \frac{120}{100} = 1.2$; $\frac{120}{100} = \frac{6}{5}$

3. $0.5\% = 0.005 = \frac{5}{1000} = \frac{1}{200}$

4. $87\frac{1}{2}\% = 0.875 = \frac{875}{1000} = \frac{7}{8}$

5. 7.85×10^1

6. 4.75×10^{-2}

7. Find the perimeter: A rhombus has 4 sides that are the same length; 4×12 ft = 48 ft

10-3 Percents and Proportions

Pages 430–433

Think and Discuss pp. 430–431

1. 5% of $200 = $0.05 \times $200 = $10

2. **a.** $\frac{n}{195} = \frac{4.5}{100}$

   195 $\boxed{\times}$ 4.5 $\boxed{÷}$ 100 $\boxed{=}$ **8.775** ≈ $8.78

   b. Sample: Yes; since 4.5% and $195 are rounded up, the estimated tax is greater than the actual tax.

Work Together p. 432

3–5. Answers may vary. Examples are given for a class of 26 students.

3. **a.** about 75%;

   $\frac{19}{26} = \frac{x}{100}$, 19 $\boxed{\times}$ 100 $\boxed{÷}$ 26 $\boxed{=}$ **73.076923**, about 73%

   b. about 95%;

   $\frac{25}{26} = \frac{x}{100}$, 25 $\boxed{\times}$ 100 $\boxed{÷}$ 26 $\boxed{=}$ **96.153846**, about 96%

4. a. about 60%;

$$\frac{17}{26} = \frac{x}{100},\ 17\ \boxed{\times}\ 100\ \boxed{\div}\ 26\ \boxed{=}$$

65.384615, about 65.4%

b. about 150%;

$$\frac{38}{26} = \frac{x}{100},\ 38\ \boxed{\times}\ 100\ \boxed{\div}\ 26\ \boxed{=}$$

146.15385, about 146%

5. a. about 7;

$$\frac{x}{26} = \frac{28}{100},\ 26\ \boxed{\times}\ 28\ \boxed{\div}\ 100\ \boxed{=}\ \textbf{7.28},$$

about 7 students

b. about 34;

$$\frac{x}{26} = \frac{130}{100};\ 26\ \boxed{\times}\ 130\ \boxed{\div}\ 100\ \boxed{=}\ \textbf{33.8},$$

about 34 students

Try These p. 432

6. A; $\dfrac{\text{part}}{\text{whole}}$ $\dfrac{17}{42} = \dfrac{n}{100}$

7. B; $\dfrac{\text{part}}{\text{whole}}$ $\dfrac{n}{90} = \dfrac{35}{100}$

8. D; $\dfrac{\text{part}}{\text{whole}}$ $\dfrac{92}{n} = \dfrac{80}{100}$

9. $\dfrac{80}{100} = \dfrac{x}{72}$

$100x = 80 \times 72$

$x = \dfrac{80 \times 72}{100} = 57.6$

10. $\dfrac{33}{x} = \dfrac{15}{100}$

$15x = 33 \times 100$

$x = \dfrac{33 \times 100}{15} = 220$

11. $\dfrac{78}{50} = \dfrac{x}{100}$

$50x = 78 \times 100$

$x = \dfrac{78 \times 100}{50} = 156\%$

12. $\dfrac{70}{x} = \dfrac{20}{100}$

$20x = 70 \times 100$

$x = \dfrac{70 \times 100}{20} = 350$

13. $\dfrac{63}{x} = \dfrac{29}{100}$

$29x = 63 \times 100$

$x = \dfrac{63 \times 100}{29} \approx 217.2$

14. $\dfrac{345}{100} = \dfrac{224}{x}$

$345x = 100 \times 224$

$x = \dfrac{100 \times 224}{345} \approx 64.9$

Mixed Review p. 432

1.
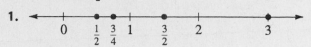

2.
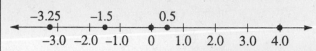

3. $0.05 \times 800 = 40$

4. $\frac{1}{3}$ of $24 = 8$

5. $2\left(\dfrac{1}{2}\right) - 3 = 1 - 3 = -2$

6. $10(0.9) + 8 = 9 + 8 = 17$

7. $0.06 \times \$45 = \$2.70;\ \$2.70 + \$45 = \$47.70$

On Your Own p. 433

15. $\dfrac{18}{30} = \dfrac{x}{100}$

$30x = 18 \times 100$

$x = \dfrac{18 \times 100}{30} = 60$

16. $\dfrac{29}{x} = \dfrac{20}{100}$

$20x = 29 \times 100$

$x = \dfrac{29 \times 100}{20} = 145$

17. $\dfrac{x}{65} = \dfrac{125}{100}$

$100x = 65 \times 125$

$x = \dfrac{65 \times 125}{100} = 81.25$

18. $\dfrac{160}{80} = \dfrac{x}{100}$

$80x = 160 \times 100$

$x = \dfrac{160 \times 100}{80} = 200\%$

19. $\dfrac{1212}{x} = \dfrac{0.03}{100}$

$0.03x = 1{,}212 \times 100$

$x = \dfrac{1212 \times 100}{0.03} = 4{,}040{,}000$

The area of the United States is 4,040,000 mi².

20. Sample: Proportions are easy to solve when one of the terms is 100.

21. $\$94.34 - \$89 = \$5.34;\ 5.34 \div 89 = 0.06 = 6\%$

22. $\dfrac{129.6}{x} = \dfrac{72}{100}$

$72x = 129.6 \times 100$

$x = \dfrac{129.6 \times 100}{72} = 180$

The teacher's budget was $180.

23. a. 23% of $500 = 0.23 \times 500 = 115$ people

b. Check students' work.

10-4 Percents and Fractions

Pages 434–437

Think and Discuss pp. 434–436

1. **a.** $3\% = 0.03$

   b. whole

   c. 3% of \$118,000 $= 0.03 \times \$118,000 =$ \$3,540

2. 12.5% of \$2,300 $= 0.125 \times \$2,300 = \$287.50$; $\$287.50 + \$115 = \$402.50$

Try These p. 436

3. $30 = P \cdot 75$

   $P = \dfrac{30}{75}$

   $P = 0.4 = 40\%$

4. $16.4 = P \cdot 5$

   $P = \dfrac{16.4}{5}$

   $P = 3.28 = 328\%$

5. $68 = 0.92 \cdot$ whole

   whole $= \dfrac{68}{0.92} \approx 73.9$

6. part $= 0.31 \cdot 82{,}150$

   part $= 25{,}466.5$

7. $300 = 0.25 \cdot$ whole

   whole $= \dfrac{300}{0.25} = 1{,}200$

8. $2 = P \cdot 360$

   $P = \dfrac{2}{360}$

   $P = 0.00\overline{5} \approx 0.6\%$

9. $935 = 0.187 \cdot$ whole

   whole $= \dfrac{935}{0.187} = 5{,}000$

   5,000 students were surveyed.

On Your Own pp. 436–437

10. $\dfrac{16}{80} = 0.2 = 20\%$

11. $\dfrac{7.3}{x} = \dfrac{2}{100}$

    $2x = 7.3 \times 100$

    $x = \dfrac{7.3 \times 100}{2} = 365$

12. 165% of 40 $= 1.65 \times 40 = 66$

13. $\dfrac{50}{42} \approx 119\%$ (rounded to the nearest whole percent)

14. $\dfrac{434{,}000}{2{,}162{,}000} \approx 20\%$

15. $438 = 0.73 \cdot$ whole

    whole $= \dfrac{438}{0.73} = 600$

    600 people were in the survey.

16. $\dfrac{1500}{800} = 1.875 = 187.5\%$

17. $\dfrac{672.30}{3735} = 0.18 = 18\%$

18. Answers may vary. Sample: Yolanda sold 32 magazine subscriptions and the fund raiser goal was 20 subscriptions. Yolanda reached 160% of the goal.

19. 39% of \$24 billion $= 0.39 \times \$24$ billion $=$ \$9.36 billion

Checkpoint p. 437

1. $0.3; \dfrac{3}{10}$

2. $12\%; \dfrac{12}{100} = \dfrac{3}{25}$

3. $2.1; \dfrac{210}{100} = \dfrac{21}{10}$

4. $5 \div 8 = 0.625 = 62.5\%$

5–7. Accept reasonable estimates. Sample answers are given.

5. 15% of 200 $= 0.15 \times 200 = 30$

6. 78% of 100 $= 0.78 \times 100 = 78$

7. $\dfrac{1}{3}$ of 150 $= 50$

8. 29% of 125 million $= 0.29 \times 125{,}000{,}000 = 36{,}250{,}000$

9. $\dfrac{63}{84} = \dfrac{x}{100}$

   $84x = 63 \times 100$

   $x = \dfrac{63 \times 100}{84} = 75\%$

10. 23% of 17 $= 0.23 \times 17 = 3.91 = 3.9$ (rounded to the nearest tenth)

Mixed Review p. 437

1. true

2. true

3. $\dfrac{80}{100} = \dfrac{24}{x}$

   $80x = 100 \times 24$

   $x = \dfrac{100 \times 24}{80} = 30$

4. $18 = P \cdot 12$

   $P = \dfrac{18}{12}$

   $P = 1.5 = 150\%$

5. $66\dfrac{2}{3}\% = 0.\overline{6} = \dfrac{2}{3}; \dfrac{2}{3}$ of 15 $= 10$

6. $\dfrac{\$64.40}{\$.35} = 184$ bags

10-5 Constructing Circle Graphs

Pages 438–440

Think and Discuss pp. 438–439

1. **a.** 21% + 47% + 32% = 100%

   b. Sample: No; a circle graph shows part of a whole, or 100%.

2. **a.** 75.6 degrees; 169.2 degrees; 115.2 degrees

   b. 75.6 + 169.2 + 115.2 = 360; Sample: The sum of the measures of the central angles of a circle equals 360°.

Work Together p. 439

Check students' work.

Try These p. 440

3. **How Rapidly Are Technological Changes Happening?**

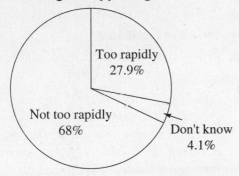

4.

Category	Amount Budgeted	Percent of Total	Degrees in Central Angle
Bus	$72	38%	136.8°
Admission	$60	32%	115.2°
Lunch	$48	25%	90°
Tolls	$10	5%	18°

Class Budget for Museum Field Trip

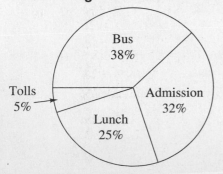

On Your Own p. 440

5. **Women's Exercise Habits**

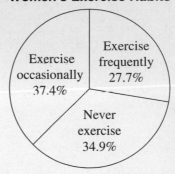

6. **Consumers' Vegetable Buying**

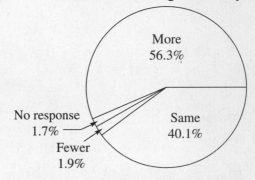

7. Answers may vary. Sample: If dollar amounts are given, you must convert each to a percentage of the entire amount and then find the number of degrees of each central angle before a circle graph can be made. If the amounts are given as percents, the process is one step shorter.

8.   Favorite School Lunches

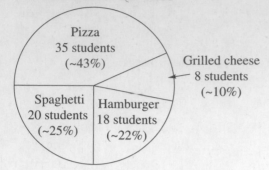

9.   Endangered Species

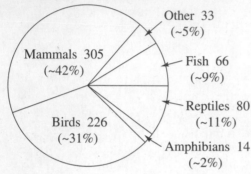

Mixed Review p. 440

1. $3(0.3) + 4(0.21) = 0.9 + 0.84 = 1.74$
2. $\frac{1}{7}(0.21) - (0.3)^3 = 0.03 - 0.027 = 0.003$
3. part = $0.075 \cdot 280$
   part = 21
4. $10 = 0.25 \cdot$ whole
   whole = $\frac{10}{0.25} = 40$
5. $25 = P \cdot 500$
   $P = \frac{25}{500} = 0.05 = 5\%$
6. Answers may vary. Sample: There are 5 red marbles and 4 green marbles in a jar. One marble is picked and not replaced. A second is picked.

Problem Solving Practice
Page 441

1. $\begin{array}{cccc} & R & Y & B \quad R \end{array}$
   Orange = ☐☐☐, ☐☐; Purple = ☐☐, ☐
   Orange is made up of 5 parts, purple of 3.
   LCM (5, 3) = 15, so you need 5 batches of purple and 3 batches of orange to have equal amounts of each.
   $$5(\text{purple}) = 10 \text{ B} + 5 \text{ R}$$
   $$3(\text{orange}) = 9 \text{ R} + 6 \text{ Y}$$
   $10 \text{ B} + 5 \text{ R} + 9 \text{ R} + 6 \text{ Y} = 10 \text{ B} + 14 \text{ R} + 6 \text{ Y}$
   14 parts out of 30 are red, or $46\frac{2}{3}\%$.

2.   the first one; 15% off $279.98 = 0.85(279.98),
   about $237.98
   20% off $299.99 = 0.80(299.99),
   about $239.99

3.   **a.** $\frac{1}{2}$; There is an equal chance that each will choose red or black.
   b. $\frac{2}{5}$; The first choice will leave 2 of one color and 3 of the second. $P = \frac{2}{5}$.
   c. 3 students; After the first student chooses, the second will either choose the same color (and be a partner) or a different color. But since there are only 2 colors, the third student will choose a color that matches one of the previous student choices.

4.   15%; 0.75(0.60) = 0.45; 60% − 45% = 15%

5.   45 games

10-6 Percent of Change
Pages 442–444

Think and Discuss pp. 442–443

1.   **a.** 167,000 − 26,000 = 141,000 decrease
   b. 167,000
   c. $P = \frac{\text{amount of change}}{\text{original amount}} = \frac{141,000}{167,000} = 0.844$
   Rounded to the nearest tenth, percent of decrease is about 84.4%.

2.   Multiply by $\frac{5}{5}$ so that the denominator is 100.
   $\frac{15}{20} = \frac{15}{20} \times \frac{5}{5} = \frac{75}{100} = 75\%$

Try These p. 443

3. Sample: The percent of change is the ratio of change to the original amount.

4. $P = \frac{5}{20} = \frac{1}{4} = 25\%$ increase

5. $P = \frac{10}{40} = \frac{1}{4} = 25\%$ decrease

6. $P = \frac{5}{50} = \frac{1}{10} = 10\%$ increase

7. $P = \frac{10}{80} = \frac{1}{8} = 12.5\%$ decrease

8. $P = \frac{22}{83} = 0.2650602$; increase of 26.5% rounded to the nearest tenth

9. $P = \frac{9.5}{21} = 0.4523809$; decrease of 45.2% rounded to the nearest tenth

10. $P = \frac{80}{15} = 5.\overline{3}$; increase of 533.3% rounded to the nearest tenth

11. $P = \frac{1.5}{7} = 0.2142857$; increase of 21.4% rounded to the nearest tenth

12. $P = \frac{138}{190} = 0.7263158$; decrease of 72.6% rounded to the nearest tenth

13. $P = \frac{3.55}{1.35} = 2.\overline{629}$; increase of 263.0% rounded to the nearest tenth

14. $P = \frac{55}{105} = 0.5238095$; decrease of 52.4% rounded to the nearest tenth

15. $P = \frac{3.5}{0.75} = 4.\overline{6}$; increase of 466.7% rounded to the nearest tenth

Mixed Review p. 443

1. total $7 + 6 + 1 + 2 + 4 = 20$; blue $\frac{7}{20} = 35\%$; black $\frac{6}{20} = 30\%$; green $\frac{1}{20} = 5\%$; red $\frac{2}{20} = 10\%$; purple $\frac{4}{20} = 20\%$

2. **Favorite Color**

Purple 20%
Blue 35%
Red 10%
Green 5%
Black 30%

3.

4. $398 - 175 = 223$, plus 1 locker at the end, $223 + 1 = 224$

On Your Own p. 444

16. $P = \frac{2.87}{0.38} = 7.5526316$; increase of 755.3% rounded to the nearest tenth

17. 18 ft $8\frac{1}{4}$ in. $= 224\frac{1}{4}$ in.

23 ft $5\frac{1}{4}$ in. $= 281\frac{1}{4}$ in.

$281\frac{1}{4} - 224\frac{1}{4} = 57$ in.

$$P = \frac{57 \text{ in.}}{224.25 \text{ in.}} = 0.2541806;$$

an increase of 25.4% rounded to the nearest tenth.

18. No; 100 increased by 20% is 120, and 120 decreased by 20% is 96.

19. 881,965; 56.1% increase is $1.561 \times 565,000 = 881,965$

20. Albuquerque: $P = \frac{2.5}{3.5} = 0.7142857$; 71.4% rounded to the nearest tenth

Boise: $P = \frac{1.5}{4} = 0.375$; 37.5%

Louisville: $P = \frac{2.5}{4} = 0.625$; 62.5%

New York: $P = \frac{2.5}{5} = 0.5$; 50%

Sioux City: $P = \frac{2.25}{3} = 0.75$; 75%

21. $P = \frac{236 \text{ million}}{1.2 \text{ billion}} = 0.19\overline{6}$; decrease of 19.7% rounded to the nearest tenth

22. Check students' work.

10-7 Markup and Discount

Pages 445–447

Think and Discuss p. 445

1. a. 65% of $.79 = 0.65 \times 0.79 = 0.5135$; $.51 rounded to the nearest cent

b. $.79 + $.51 = $1.30 selling price

c. Multiply the original cost by 1.65.

Try These p. 446

2. 60% of $89 = 0.6 \times \$89 = \$53.4$
$\$89 + \$53.40 = \$142.40$

3. 55% of $134.98 = 0.55 \times \$134.98 = \$74.24$
$\$134.98 + \$74.24 = \$209.22$

4. 40% of $180 = 0.4 \times \$180 = \$72.00$
$\$180 - \$72 = \$108.00$

5. 25% of $35.50 = 0.25 \times \$35.50 = \$8.88$
$\$35.50 - \$8.88 = \$26.62$

Mixed Review p. 446

1. $P = \frac{30}{24} = 1.25$; increase of 125%

2. $P = \frac{13.8}{41.4} = 0.\overline{3}$; increase of $33\frac{1}{3}\%$

3. $P = \frac{2.7}{3.5} = 0.7714285$; decrease of 77.1%

4. $\sin A = \dfrac{\text{opposite}}{\text{hypotenuse}} = \dfrac{6}{10} = \dfrac{3}{5} = 0.6$

5. $\cos A = \dfrac{\text{adjacent}}{\text{hypotenuse}} = \dfrac{8}{10} = \dfrac{4}{5} = 0.8$

On Your Own pp. 446–447

6. 40% of $8.99 = 0.4 \times \$8.99 = \$3.596$ or
$\$3.60; \$8.99 - \$3.60 = \$5.39; \dfrac{\$35}{\$5.39} =$
6.4935064; Thelma can buy 6 cassettes

7. 80% of $175 = \$140; \$175 + \$140 = \$315$;
No, they will be $5 short

8. $P = \frac{2.25}{3.75} = 0.6$; 60% markup

9. sale price is 80% of regular price
$\dfrac{\$335.75}{0.8} = \$419.69$

10. The store will lose money. Sample: A $10 item will be marked up to $15 and then will sell at $7.50. The result will be a loss of $2.50.

11. Yes; 40% of $40 is $16, and his sweater costs less than $40.

10-8 Simple and Compound Interest
Pages 448–451

Think and Discuss pp. 448–450

1. a. $\$100 \times 0.06 \times \$5 = \$30$

b. $\$100 + \$30 = \$130$

2. a.

	A	B	C	D	E
4	3rd	$112.36	0.06	$6.74	$119.10
5	4th	$119.10	0.06	$7.15	$126.25
6	5th	$126.25	0.06	$7.57	$133.82

b. $\$133.82 - \$130 = \$3.82$

3. Answers may vary. Sample:
$b \cdot 0.06 + b = b(0.06 + 1) = b(1.06)$,
where b is the beginning balance.

4. a. $133.82

b. Yes

c. Key strokes: 1.06 $\boxed{y^x}$ 5 $\boxed{=}$ $\boxed{\times}$ 100

5. Answers may vary. Sample: The interest is compounded quarterly, so the interest each quarter is $0.05 \div 4 = 0.0125$.

6. Need 8 rows to show 2 years. There are 2 rows there, so 6 more rows are needed.

7.

Qtr	Start of quarter	Rate	Interest	Balance
1	$200.00	0.0125	2.50	$202.50
2	$202.50	0.0125	2.53	$205.03
3	$205.03	0.0125	2.56	$207.59
4	$207.59	0.0125	2.59	$210.19
5	$210.19	0.0125	2.63	$212.82
6	$212.82	0.0125	2.66	$215.48
7	$215.48	0.0125	2.69	$218.17
8	$218.17	0.0125	2.73	$220.90

8. a. $p = 200; n = 8; r = 0.0125$

b. $A = 200(1 + 0.0125)^8 = \$220.90$ rounded to the nearest cent

c. same

Work Together p. 450

The best investment is interest compounded monthly. The final balance would be $10,831.43.

Interest Compounded	Final Balance
Annually	$10,816.00
Monthly	$10,831.43
Quarterly	$10,828.57
Semiannually	$10,824.32

Mixed Review p. 450

1. 20% of $65 = 0.2 \times \$65 = \$13$; $\$65 - \$13 = \$52$

2. 45% of $239 = 0.45 \times \$239 = \$107.55$;
$\$107.55 + \$239 = \$346.55$

3. AB

4. $\frac{6}{x} = \frac{8}{12}$; $8x = 72$; $x = 9$

5. $18 = -6 - d$; $24 = -d$; $-24 = d$

6. $12 + c = -17$; $c = -29$

On Your Own pp. 450–451

9. $900 \boxed{\times} 0.03 \boxed{\times} 2 \boxed{=} \mathbf{54}$
$900 + 54 = \$954$

10. $500 \boxed{\times} 0.05 \boxed{\times} 6 \boxed{=} \mathbf{150}$
$500 + 150 = \$650$

11. $1200 \boxed{\times} 0.075 \boxed{\times} 4 \boxed{=} \mathbf{360}$
$1200 + 360 = \$1560$

12. $1700 \boxed{\times} \boxed{(} 1 \boxed{+} 0.07 \boxed{)} \boxed{y^x} 2 \boxed{=}$
$\mathbf{1946.33}$; $\$1946.33$

13. $14000 \boxed{\times} \boxed{(} 1 \boxed{+} 0.03 \boxed{)} \boxed{y^x} 3 \boxed{=}$
$\mathbf{15298.178}$; $\$15,298.18$

14. $115 \boxed{\times} \boxed{(} 1 \boxed{+} 0.02 \boxed{)} \boxed{y^x} 4 \boxed{=}$
$\mathbf{124.4797698}$; $\$124.48$

15. $10300 \boxed{\times} \boxed{(} 1 \boxed{+} 0.02 \boxed{)} \boxed{y^x} 4 \boxed{=}$
$\mathbf{11149.051}$; $\$11,149.05$

16. $1000 \boxed{\times} \boxed{(} 1 \boxed{+} 0.005 \boxed{)} \boxed{y^x} 6 \boxed{=}$
$\mathbf{1030.3775}$; $\$1030.38$

17. **a.** $\frac{0.18}{12} = 0.015$; $\$350 - \$50 = \$300$ unpaid balance; $\$300 \times 0.015 = \$4.50$ interest charged

   b. $\$300 + \$4.50 = \$304.50$ owed

   c. Sample: The interest charged may total more than the amount saved.

8. $\frac{0.0365}{365} = 0.0001$; $\$500 \times 0.0001 \times 5 = \$0.25$; $\$500 + \$0.25 = \$500.25$

9.
Rates	Balance After 50 Years
6%	$100(1.06)^{50} = \$ \ 1,842.02$
9%	$100(1.09)^{50} = \$ \ 7,435.75$
12%	$100(1.12)^{50} = \$28,900.22$

Checkpoint p. 451

1. **Interest Rates Paid By Mortgage Holders**

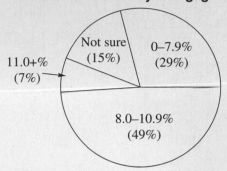

2. $P = \frac{13}{52} = 0.25 = 25\%$ increase

3. $P = \frac{2.52}{24} = 0.105 = 10.5\%$ decrease

4. $P = \frac{51,367}{30,859} = 1.6645711 \approx 166.5\%$ increase

5. A; 13

6. 20% of $36.95 = 0.2 \times \$36.95 = \$7.39$
$\$36.95 - \$7.39 = \$29.56$

7. $570 \boxed{\times} \boxed{(} 1 \boxed{+} 0.04 \boxed{)} \boxed{y^x} 4 \boxed{=}$
$\mathbf{666.81938}$; $\$666.82$

Practice

Page 452

1. $\frac{47}{100}$; 47%

2. $2\frac{6}{100} = \frac{206}{100} = \frac{103}{50}$; 206%

3. $\frac{4}{1000} = \frac{1}{250}$; 0.004

4. $\frac{872}{100} = \frac{218}{25}$; 8.72

5. $\frac{7}{9} = 0.\overline{7} = 0.78$ rounded to nearest hundredth; 77.8%

6. $\frac{5}{8} = 0.625$; 62.5%

7. $\frac{34}{10,000} = \frac{17}{5,000}$; $\frac{34}{10,000} = .0034 = .34\%$

8. $\frac{1203}{10,000}$; $\frac{1203}{10,000} = 12.03\%$

9. $3\frac{1}{2} = \frac{7}{2}$; $3\frac{1}{2} = 3.5 = 350\%$

10. $5\frac{3}{4}\% = 5.75\% = 0.0575$; $\frac{575}{10000} = \frac{23}{400}$

11–14. Accept reasonable estimates. Samples given.

11. $0.5 \times 160 = 80$

12. $0.01 \times 500 = 5$

13. $0.2 \times 40 = 8$

14. $3 \times 200 = 600$

15. $\frac{20}{100} = \frac{225}{x}$

$20x = 100 \times 225$

$x = \frac{100 \times 225}{20} = 1{,}125$

16. $\frac{61}{40} = \frac{x}{100}$

$40x = 61 \times 100$

$x = \frac{61 \times 100}{40} = 152.5$

17. $\frac{36}{x} = \frac{82}{100}$

$82x = 36 \times 100$

$x = \frac{36 \times 100}{82} \approx 43.9$

18. $\frac{2.3}{100} = \frac{x}{37}$

$100x = 2.3 \times 37$

$x = \frac{2.3 \times 37}{100} = 0.851$

19. $\frac{125}{100} = \frac{x}{6}$

$100x = 125 \times 6$

$x = \frac{125 \times 6}{100} = 7.5$

20. $\frac{35}{89} = \frac{x}{100}$

$89x = 35 \times 100$

$x = \frac{35 \times 100}{89} \approx 39.3$

21. part $= 0.2 \times 125 = 21.25$

22. $15 = P \cdot 54$

$P = \frac{15}{54} = 0.2\overline{7} \approx 27.8\%$

23. $35.7 = P \cdot 71$

$P = \frac{35.7}{71} = 0.502817 \approx 50.3\%$

24. $96 = 0.29 \cdot$ whole

whole $= \frac{96}{0.29} = 331.03448 \approx 331$

25. $30 = 0.25 \cdot$ whole

whole $= \frac{30}{0.25} = 120$

26. part $= 0.21 \cdot 627 = 131.67$

27.

How Tony Spends His Day

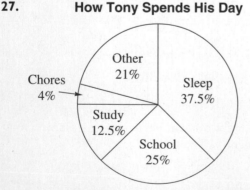

Other 21%

Chores 4%

Study 12.5%

School 25%

Sleep 37.5%

28. $P = \frac{16}{80} = 0.2$; 20% increase

29. $P = \frac{19}{32} = 0.59375 \approx 59.4\%$ decrease

30. $P = \frac{35}{63} = 0.\overline{5} \approx 55.6\%$ increase

31. $P = \frac{250}{125} = 2 = 200\%$ increase

32. $P = \frac{11.7}{15.2} = 0.7697368 \approx 77\%$ decrease

33. $P = \frac{146}{154} = 0.9480519 \approx 94.8\%$ increase

34. $P = \frac{25}{0.5} = 50 = 5{,}000\%$ increase

35. $P = \frac{3.7}{6.7} = 0.5522388 \approx 55.2\%$ decrease

36. $0.6 \times \$98 = \$58.80$; $\$58.80 + \$98 = \$156.80$

37. $0.45 \times \$143.89 = \$64.75$, rounded to the nearest cent; $\$64.75 + \$143.89 = \$208.64$

38. $0.2 \times \$267.55 = \$53.51$;
$\$53.51 + \$267.55 = \$321.06$

39. $0.15 \times \$20 = \$3$; $\$20 - \$3 = \$17$

40. $0.35 \times \$155.75 = \$54.51$, to the nearest cent; $\$155.75 - \$54.51 = \$101.24$

41. $0.3 \times \$345.50 = \$103.65$;
$\$345.50 - \$103.65 = \$241.85$

10-9 Make a Table

Pages 453–455

1. the number of questions the Madison Middle School team answered correctly

2. the number of questions asked, the number answered correctly at $50 each, the number answered incorrectly at −$25 each, and total winnings of $275

3. a.

Correct	0	1	2	3	4	5	6	7	8	9	10
Incorrect	10	9	8	7	6	5	4	3	2	1	0
Won ($)	0	0	0	0	50	125	200	275	350	425	500

b. 7

4. Sample: guess and test

5. Sample: The East School didn't win any money. How many questions did they answer correctly?

Try These p. 454

6. 10 ways; 2 quarters; 1 quarter, 2 dimes, 1 nickel; 1 quarter, 5 nickels; 1 quarter, 3 nickels, 1 dime; 10 nickels; 5 dimes; 4 dimes, 2 nickels; 3 dimes, 4 nickels; 2 dimes, 6 nickels; 1 dime, 8 nickels

7. 12 combinations

8. 19 different amounts

9. 29 palindromes; 11; 22; 33; 44; 55; 66; 77; 88; 99; 101; 111; 121; 131; 141; 151; 161; 171; 181; 191; 202; 212; 222; 232; 242; 252; 262; 272; 282; 292

10. 10 different ways

Mixed Review p. 454

1. $\$985 \times 0.075 \times 2 = \$147.75$

2. $\$1,500 \times 0.08 \times 5 = \$600$

3. $\angle A \cong \boxed{\angle D}$

4. $\overline{DJ} \cong \boxed{\overline{AY}}$

5. $x + (x + 2) + (x + 4) = 678$
$3x + 6 = 678$
$x = 224, (x + 2) = 226, (x + 4) = 228$

6. $16 = 4x - 1 + 1; x = 4; 4 + 1 + 1 = 6$
Sofia will be 6 years old next year.

On Your Own pp. 454–455

11. Not enough information; need to know the number of U.S. medals

12. 52 and 53; $52 \times 53 = 2,756$

13. Alex's ages were 1 to 6 years old; his grandfather's ages were 61 to 66 years old.

14. 11 and 27; $11 + 27 = 38$; 27 divided by 11 is 2 remainder 5.

15. a. $6 \times 485 = 2,910$ ft
b. $2,500 + 2,000 = 4,500$ years ago

16. $\frac{\$17.75}{3} = \$5.92$ rounded to the nearest cent; he paid $2 \times \$5.92$ or $\$11.84$ for one tape and one half of $\$11.84$ or $\$5.92$ for the second tape.

17. $\frac{\$95}{19}$ bundles = $5 per bundle; Michelle delivered 10 bundles at $5 each, so she should receive $50. Roscoe delivered 9 bundles at $5 each, so he should receive $45.

18. 10 holes + 20 holes + 15 holes = 45 holes

19. $\$27.50 \times 5 = \$137.50$; 600 mi − 500 mi = 100 mi above free mileage; 100 mi × $0.34 = 34.00; $\$137.50 + \$34 = \$171.50$

20. 24 cubes; cubes along edges, but not corner cubes because they will be painted on 3 sides

21. 36; multiple of 6 with a digit 6 could be 6, 36, 60, 66; 36 meets all the conditions.

Chapter 10 Wrap Up

Pages 456–457

1. $0.25 = \frac{25}{100} = \frac{1}{4}$

2. $0.062 = \frac{62}{1000} = \frac{31}{500}$

3. $0.15 = \frac{15}{100} = \frac{3}{20}$

4. $0.0003 = \frac{3}{10,000}$

5. $1.30 = 1\frac{3}{10} = \frac{13}{10}$

6. $\frac{35}{100} = \frac{7}{20}$; 35%

7. $1\frac{25}{100} = 1\frac{1}{4} = \frac{5}{4}$; 125%

8. $\frac{7}{10}$; 70%

9. $\frac{5}{100} = \frac{1}{20}$; 5%

10. $2\frac{35}{100} = 2\frac{7}{20} = \frac{47}{20}$; 235%

11–14. Accept reasonable estimates. Samples given.

11. 25% of 100 = 25

12. 7% of 60 = 4.2

13. 150% of 200 = $1.5 \times 200 = 300$

14. 70% of 80 = 56

15. $\frac{40}{50} = 80\%$

16. $\frac{30}{100} = \frac{24}{x}$
$30x = 100 \times 24$
$x = \frac{100 \times 24}{30} = 80$

17. $15 = 0.875 \cdot \text{whole}$
$\text{whole} = \frac{15}{0.875} = 17.142857 \approx 17.1$

18. $\frac{50}{35} = \frac{x}{100}$
$35x = 50 \times 100$
$x = \frac{50 \times 100}{35} = 142.85714 \approx 142.9\%$

19. **How Nell Spent Her Money**

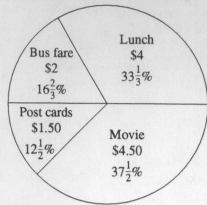

Bus fare
$2
$16\frac{2}{3}\%$

Lunch
$4
$33\frac{1}{3}\%$

Post cards
$1.50
$12\frac{1}{2}\%$

Movie
$4.50
$37\frac{1}{2}\%$

20. D; $P = \frac{3}{12} = 0.25 = 25\%$

21. $0.3 \times \$450 = \$135; \$450 - \$135 = \$315$

22. $0.75 \times \$60 = \$45; \$45 + \$60 = \$105$

23. $P = \$1{,}000 \times 0.05 \times 5 = \$250;$
$\$250 + \$1{,}000 = \$1{,}250$

24. $A = p(1 + r)^n$

$1000\ \boxed{\times}\ \boxed{(}\ 1\ \boxed{+}\ 0.07\ \boxed{)}\ \boxed{y^x}\ 3\ \boxed{=}$
1225.043; $1,225.04

25. Simple interest is money paid only on the principal, or amount deposited. Compound interest is interest paid not only on the principal but also on the accumulated interest.

26.

	1	2	3	4	5
Shirts	$18.00	$36.00	$54.00	$72.00	$90.00
Socks	$ 1.75	$ 3.50	$ 5.25	$ 7.00	$ 8.75

From the table, Uli bought 5 shirts and 4 pairs of socks for $97.

Getting Ready for Chapter 11 p. 457

1–4. Answers can be found by counting squares.

1. 12 square units

2. 8 square units

3. 14 square units

4. $8\frac{1}{2}$ square units

Chapter 10 Assessment
Page 460

1. a. $0.8\% = 0.008; 0.008 < 0.8$
   b. $\frac{5}{6} = 83\%; 83\% < 85\%$
   c. $450\% = 4.5; 450\% = 4.5$
   d. $\frac{5}{8} = 0.625$

2. a. $P = \frac{60}{180} = 0.\overline{3} = 33.3\%$ decrease
   b. $P = \frac{50}{25} = 2 = 200\%$ increase
   c. $P = \frac{25}{87.5} = 0.2857142 \approx 28.6\%$ decrease
   d. $P = \frac{33.5}{33.5} = 1 = 100\%$ increase

3. Accept reasonable estimates. Sample answers are given.
   a. $0.75 \times 48 = 36$
   b. $2.5 \times 30 = 75$
   c. $0.2 \times 36 = 7.2$
   d. $0.005 \times 500 = 2.5$

4. a. $\frac{20}{32} = \frac{x}{100}$
   $32x = 20 \times 100$
   $x = \frac{20 \times 100}{32} = 62.5\%$
   b. $\frac{18}{x} = \frac{30}{100}$
   $30x = 18 \times 100$
   $x = \frac{18 \times 100}{30} = 60$
   c. $\frac{x}{350} = \frac{95}{100}$
   $100x = 350 \times 95$
   $x = \frac{350 \times 95}{100} = 332.5$

5. a. $0.25 \times \$64 = \$16; \$64 - \$16 = \$48$
   b. $0.15 \times \$19.99 = \$3.00$ to the nearest cent
   $\$19.99 + \$3 = \$22.99$
   c. $0.1 \times \$850 = \$85.00; \$850 + \$85.00 = \$93$
   d. $0.33 \times \$90 = \$29.70; \$90 - \$29.70 =$
   $\$60.30$

6. a. $250\ \boxed{\times}\ 0.04\ \boxed{\times}\ 3\ \boxed{=}\ \mathbf{30};$
   $250 + 30 = \$280$
   b. $4500\ \boxed{\times}\ \boxed{(}\ 1\ \boxed{+}\ 0.07\ \boxed{)}\ \boxed{y^x}\ 2\ \boxed{=}$
   5152.05; $5152.05
   c. $8000\ \boxed{\times}\ \boxed{(}\ 1\ \boxed{+}\ 0.02\ \boxed{)}\ \boxed{y^x}\ 4\ \boxed{=}$
   8659.45728; $8659.46

7. D; $\frac{3}{5} = \frac{60}{100} = 0.6 = 60\%$

8. $40.80 is 85% of the regular; $\frac{\$40.80}{0.85} = \$48.00$

9. **Percent of Grade**

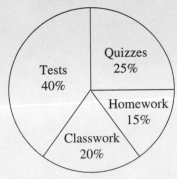

10. Sample: The markup rate is a ratio of change to the original amount, not change to new amount. Correct markup rate is 25%.

11.

Number of Boxes	Permanent Markers	Washable Markers
1	$ 15	$ 13
2	$ 30	$ 26
3	$ 45	$ 39
4	$ 60	$ 52
5	$ 75	$ 65
6	$ 90	$ 78
7	$105	$ 91
8	$120	$104
9	$135	$117
10	$150	$130
11	$165	$143
12	$180	$156
13	$195	$169
14	$210	$182

10 boxes of Permanent Markers cost $150.
14 boxes of Washable Markers cost $182.
$150 + $182 = $332

12. $P = \frac{0.5}{3} = 0.1\overline{6} \approx 16.7\%$ increase

Cumulative Review

Page 461

1. C; $3\frac{1}{2}\% = 0.035 = \frac{35}{1000} = \frac{7}{200}$

2. B; 50 ft = 50 × 12 = 600 in.
$\frac{600 \text{ in.}}{87 \text{ in.}} = 6.89655$ in.; about 7 in.

3. C

4. D; $_{10}P_5 = 10 \times 9 \times 8 \times 7 \times 6$

5. A; $\frac{1}{3}$ of $81 = $27; $81 − $27 = $54, which is about $53.

6. D; $\sin X = \frac{5}{13}$; $\cos Y = \frac{5}{13}$; $\tan X = \frac{5}{12}$; $\tan Y = \frac{12}{5}$

7. D

8. D; 60% of 80 = 48; 80% of 60 = 48;
80 − 32 = 48; 40 + 32 = 72

9. C; the first card is not replaced, so the events are not independent

10. B; $100(1 + 0.045)^1 = \$104.5$
$100(1 + 0.0225)^2 = \$104.55$
$100(1 + 0.01)^4 = \$104.06$
$100(1 + 0.00\overline{3})^{12} = \$104.07$

Chapter 11 Geometry and Measurement

11-1 Three-Dimensional Figures

Pages 465–468

Think and Discuss pp. 465–466

1. **a.** The vertical faces are rectangular.
   b. Sample: The tops and bottoms of the three prisms are different.

2. pentagonal prism

3. Sample: rectangular prism

4. **a.** Sample: All faces are congruent squares.
   b. yes; A cube has three sets of parallel and congruent polygonal faces.

5. Sample: named because of bases
   a. rectangular pyramid
   b. triangular pyramid

6. **a.** Both have bases and faces
   b. Prisms have 2 bases; pyramids have 1.

7. a triangle

8. **a.** Answers may vary. Sample: They are three-dimensional.
   b. Sample: The cylinder has 2 bases; the sphere has none; the cone has one base.

9. **a.** Answers may vary. Sample: The bases are parallel.
   b. Sample: The base of cylinder is a circle, and the base of prism is a polygon.

10. **a.** Answers may vary. Sample: Each has 1 base.
    b. Sample: Cones have circular bases, and pyramids have polygonal bases.

Work Together p. 466

Prism	Number of Faces (F)	Number of Vertices (V)	Number of Edges (E)
Triangular	5	6	9
Rectangular	6	8	12
Pentagonal	7	10	15
Hexagonal	8	12	18

11. $F + V - 2 = E$

12. yes

On Your Own pp. 467–468

13. g
14. d
15. e
16. f
17. a
18. h
19. b
20. c

21–23. Check students' drawings. Each drawing should resemble the appropriate drawing in the text.

21. cube
22. triangular prism
23. rectangular pyramid
24. Check students' drawings. Sample:

25. rectangular prism
26. sphere
27. cone or pyramid
28. pentagonal prism
29. Sample: Both are circular; a sphere is 3-dimensional and a circle is 2-dimensional.
30. Sample: edges that cannot be seen
31. Sample: The prism on the left is viewed from the top and the one on the right is viewed from below.
32. cone
33. 7
34. 18
35. triangles
36. cube
37. C; a point or a circle
38. D

Mixed Review p. 468

1. $x = 0.85 \cdot 120$ $\qquad$ $\frac{x}{120} = \frac{85}{100}$

   $x = 102$ $\qquad\qquad$ $100x = 120 \cdot 85$

   $\qquad\qquad\qquad$ $x = \frac{120 \cdot 85}{100}$

   $\qquad\qquad\qquad$ $x = 102$

2. $20 = P \cdot 60$ $\qquad$ $\frac{20}{60} = \frac{x}{100}$

   $P = \frac{20}{60}$ $\qquad\qquad$ $60x = 20 \cdot 100$

   $P = 0.\overline{3}$ $\qquad\qquad$ $x = \frac{20 \cdot 100}{60}$

   $P = 33\frac{1}{3}\%$ $\qquad\qquad$ $x = 0.\overline{3}$

   $\qquad\qquad\qquad$ $x = 33\frac{1}{3}\%$

3. $0.25x = 24$ $\qquad$ $\frac{25}{100} = \frac{24}{x}$

   $x = \frac{24}{0.25}$ $\qquad\qquad$ $25x = 2400$

   $x = 96$ $\qquad\qquad$ $x = \frac{2400}{25}$

   $\qquad\qquad\qquad$ $x = 96$

4. $65\% = 0.65 = \frac{65}{100} = \frac{13}{20}$

5. $150\% = 1.50 = \frac{150}{100} = \frac{3}{2}$

6. $37\frac{1}{2}\% = 0.375 = \frac{375}{1000} = \frac{3}{8}$

7. $83\frac{1}{3}\% = 0.8\overline{3} = \frac{83\frac{1}{3}}{100} = \frac{250}{300} = \frac{5}{6}$

8. Let q represent the number of quarters.
   Let d represent the number of dimes.
   Let n represent the number of nickels.
   Make a table of possible values. Guess and
   Test can also be used.
   Using 1, 2, 3, 4 or 5 quarters, the greatest
   amount is when the maximum number of
   dimes is used.

q	d	n	$0.25q$	$0.10d$	$0.05n$	total
1	8	1	0.25	0.80	0.05	1.10
2	7	1	0.50	0.70	0.05	1.25
3	6	1	0.75	0.60	0.05	1.40
4	5	1	1.00	0.50	0.05	1.55; not enough
5	4	1	1.25	0.40	0.05	1.70; too much
5	3	2	1.25	0.30	0.10	1.65

Cara has 5 quarters, 3 dimes and 2 nickels.

Problem Solving Practice

Page 469

1. Write an equation.
   Let b represent the number of beetles.
   Since there are 13 bugs altogether, $13 - b$
   represents the number of spiders.
   $6b$ represents the number of beetle legs.
   $8(13 - b)$ represents the number of spider legs.

   $6b + 8(13 - b) = 88$

   $6b + 104 - 8b = 88$

   $\qquad 104 - 2b = 88$

   $\qquad\qquad -2b = -16$

   $\qquad\qquad\quad b = 8$

   $\qquad 13 - b = 5$

   There are 8 beetles and 5 spiders.

2. 2 straws = 5 pencils = 16 paper clips

   1 straw = $\frac{5}{2}$ pencils = $\boxed{8 \text{ paper clips}}$

3. D;
   $\overset{+1}{\wedge}$ $\quad$ $\overset{+1}{\wedge}$ $\overset{+1}{\wedge}$ $\quad$ $\overset{+1}{\wedge}$ $\overset{+1}{\wedge}$ $\overset{+1}{\wedge}$ $\quad$ $\overset{+1}{\wedge}$

   1, 4, 5, 11, 12, 13, 22, 23, 24, 25, $\boxed{37}$ $\boxed{38}$

   $\underset{3}{\vee}$ $\quad$ $\underset{6}{\vee}$ $\qquad$ $\underset{9}{\vee}$ $\qquad$ $\underset{12}{\vee}$

4.

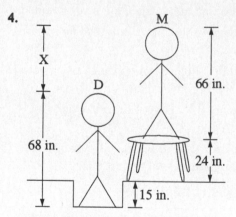

The top of Derrick's head is 68 in. − 15 in. or
53 in. above ground.
The top of Marcus's head is 66 in. + 24 in. or
90 in. above ground.
The vertical distance from the top of
Derrick's head to the top of Marcus's head is

$\qquad$ 90 in. − 53 in. = $\boxed{37 \text{ in.}}$

5. 10 angles shown;

   3 of the angles are obtuse.

6. a.

7^1	7
7^2	49
7^3	343
7^4	2,401
7^5	16,807
7^6	117,649
7^7	823,543
7^8	5,764,801

b. Look at the pattern in part (a) for the units digit:

1   2   3   4   5   6   7   8

7,   9,   3,   1,   7,   9,   3,   1, etc.

$55 \div 4 = 13$ R3

For 7^{55} the units digit will be the 3rd number in the pattern 7, 9, 3, 1, or $\boxed{3}$.

7.

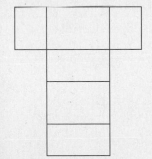

11-2 Composite Figures
Pages 470–473

Work Together p. 470

1. rectangular prism, triangular prism and cylinder

2. Check students' drawings.
Answers may vary. Sample:

Think and Discuss p. 471

3. two 4×6 rectangles,
two 3×4 rectangles, and
two 6×3 rectangles;
There are 3 pairs of congruent rectangles.

4. $2(4)(6) + 2(3)(4) + 2(6)(3)$
$= 48 + 24 + 36$
$= 108$ units^2

5. Different edges can be used as folds and cuts.

6. Sample: 3 pairs of congruent rectangles.

7. a. 5×6 rectangle,
4×6 rectangle,
3×6 rectangle,
and 2 right triangles

b. $5(6) + 4(6) + 3(6) + 2\left(\frac{1}{2}\right)(3)(4)$
$= 30 + 24 + 18 + 12$
$= 84$ units^2

c. Sample: Find the sum of the areas of each figure.

8. a. two circles with radius 2 and a $4 \times 12\frac{1}{3}$ rectangle.

b. Sample: Find the area of the circle, double it, then add the area of the rectangle.

c. $2\pi(2)^2 + 4\left(12\frac{1}{3}\right)$
$= 2\pi(4) + 4\left(\frac{37}{3}\right)$
$= 8\pi + \frac{148}{3}$
≈ 74.5 units^2

On Your Own pp. 471–473

9.

4 in.

I   4 in.

1 in.   II
6 in.

area of figure = area I + area II
area I: $A = lw$, $l = 4$ in., $w = 4$ in.
$A = 4(4) = 16$
area II: $A = \frac{1}{2}h(b_1 + b_2)$
$h = 1$ in., $b_1 = 4$ in., $b_2 = 6$ in.
$A = \frac{1}{2}(1)(4 + 6)$
$= 5$
area of figure = $(16 + 5)$
$= 21$ in.^{2}

10.

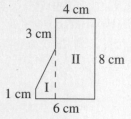

area of figure = area I + area II

area I: $A = \pi r^2$, $r = 1$ ft

$\qquad A = \pi(1)^2$

$\qquad A = \pi$

area II: $A = s^2$, $s = 2$ ft

$\qquad 2(2) = 4$

area of figure = $\pi + 4$

$\qquad \approx 7.14$ ft^2

11.

area of figure = area I + area II

area I: $h = 6$ cm $- 4$ cm $= 2$ cm

$\qquad b_1 = 8$ cm $- 3$ cm $= 5$ cm

$\qquad b_2 = 1$ cm

$\qquad A = \frac{1}{2}h(b_1 + b_2)$

$\qquad A = \frac{1}{2}(2)(5 + 1) = 6$

area II: $l = 8$ cm, $w = 4$ cm

$\qquad A = lw$

$\qquad A = 8(4) = 32$

area of figure = $6 + 32$

$\qquad = 38$ cm^2

12.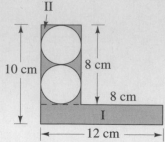

area of shaded region

$\quad$ = area of figure $-$ area of circles

area of figure = area I + area II

area I: $\; A = lw$, $l = 12$ cm

$\qquad\qquad w = 10$ cm $- 8$ cm $= 2$ cm

$\qquad A = 12 \cdot 2$

$\qquad\quad = 24$ cm^2

area II: $A = lw$, $l = 8$ cm

$\qquad\qquad w = 12$ cm $- 8$ cm $= 4$ cm

$\qquad A = 8(4)$

$\qquad\quad = 32$ cm^2

area of figure = $24 + 32$

$\qquad\qquad\quad = 56$ cm^2

area of circles: 2 circles each with radius

$\qquad\qquad r = \dfrac{12 - 8}{2}$ cm

$\qquad\qquad r = 2$ cm

$\quad A = \pi r^2$

$2A = 2\pi r^2$

$\quad\; = 2\pi(2)^2$

$\quad\; = 8\pi$ cm^2

area of shaded region

$\quad$ = area of figure $-$ area of circles

$\quad = 56 - 8\pi$

$\quad \approx 30.87$

$\quad \approx 31$ cm^2

$\boxed{(}\;12\;\boxed{\times}\;2\;\boxed{+}\;8\;\boxed{\times}\;4\;\boxed{)}\;\boxed{-}\;2\;\boxed{\times}$

$\boxed{\pi}\;\boxed{\times}\;2\;\boxed{x^2}\;\boxed{=}\;\mathbf{30.867259}$

13. Area of shaded region = $\frac{1}{2}$ area of circle =

$\frac{1}{2}\pi\left(\frac{9}{2}\right)^2 = \frac{81}{8}\pi \approx 31.8 \approx 32$ cm²

0.5 $\boxed{\times}$ $\boxed{\pi}$ $\boxed{\times}$ $\boxed{(}$ 9 $\boxed{\div}$ 2 $\boxed{)}$ $\boxed{x^2}$ $\boxed{=}$
31.808625

14. area of shaded region
= area of rectangle − 8 × area of circle
area of rectangle: $A = lw$, $l = 20$ in., $w = 10$ in.
$$A = 20(10)$$
$$A = 200 \text{ in.}^2$$
area of circle: $A = \pi r^2$ $d = \frac{20}{4} = 5$ in.
$$r = \frac{5}{2} = 2.5 \text{ in.}$$
$$A = \pi(2.5)^2 \text{ in.}^2$$

area of shaded region
= area of rectangle − 8 × area of circle
= $[200 - 8\pi(2.5)^2]$
≈ 43 in.²

200 $\boxed{-}$ 8 $\boxed{\times}$ $\boxed{\pi}$ $\boxed{\times}$ 2.5 $\boxed{x^2}$ $\boxed{=}$
42.920367

15. area of shaded region
= area of circle − area of square
area of circle: $A = \pi r^2$ $r = \frac{12}{2}$ cm = 6 cm
$$A = \pi(6)^2$$
$$A = 36\pi \text{ cm}^2$$
area of square: $A = s^2$ $s = \frac{12}{\sqrt{2}} = 6\sqrt{2}$ cm
$$A = (6\sqrt{2})^2$$
$$A = 72 \text{ cm}^2$$
area of shaded region
= area of circle − area of square
= $36\pi - 72$
≈ 41 cm²

36 $\boxed{\times}$ $\boxed{\pi}$ $\boxed{-}$ 72 $\boxed{=}$ **41.097336**

16. a.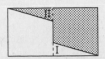

The area of I is equivalent to the area of II. Thus half the total rectangle is shaded.
Area of shaded region = $\frac{1}{2}$ area of rectangle
Area of rectangle:
$$A = lw, p = 18\frac{1}{2} = 18.5 \text{ in.}$$
$$w = 9\frac{1}{4} \text{ in.} = 9.25 \text{ in.}$$
$$A = 18.5(9.25) \text{ in.}^2$$
Area of shaded region = $\frac{1}{2}(18.5)(9.25)$
$$= 85.5625$$
$$\approx 86 \text{ in.}^2$$

b. The small triangle (area II) in the shaded region is equivalent to the small triangle (area I) in the non-shaded region. If you interchange the two areas, half of the total rectangle is shaded. Find the area of the total rectangle and multiply the result by $\frac{1}{2}$.

17. triangular prism

18. rectangular prism

19. cube

20. a. area of figure

$= 4 \times$ area of triangle + area of square

area of triangle:

$A = \frac{1}{2} \cdot b \cdot h, b = 16$ in., $h = 15$ in.

$A = \frac{1}{2}(16)(15) = 120$ in.^{2}

area of square: $A = s^2, \quad s = 16$ in.

$A = (16)^2 = 256$ in.^{2}

area of figure

$= 4 \times$ area of triangle + area of square

$= 4(120) + 256$

$= 736$ in.^{2}

b. square pyramid

21–24. Drawings may vary. Check students' work. Samples given.

21.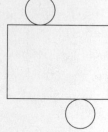

22.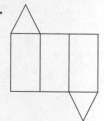

23.

24.

25. a. two rectangles, each 20 cm $\times$ 10 cm; two rectangles, each 20 cm $\times$ 12 cm; and two rectangles, each 12 cm $\times$ 10 cm

b. area $= 2(20)(10) + 2(20)(12) + 2(12)(10)$

$= 400 + 480 + 240$

$= 1{,}120$ cm^2

26–27. Accept reasonable estimates. Samples given.

Count the number of whole squares. Approximate the number of partially filled squares. Find the sum.

26. Multiply the sum by 1 cm^2 to find the answer. Sample: ≈ 91 cm^2

27. Multiply the sum by $(0.5)^2$ or 0.25 to find the answer. Sample: ≈ 23.5 cm^2

28. Check students' work.

Mixed Review p. 472

1. $\frac{7}{8} = \frac{t}{12}$

$8t = 7(12)$

$8t = 84$

$t = \frac{84}{8}$

$t = 10.5$

2. $\frac{t}{5} = \frac{2}{3}$

$3t = 10$

$t = \frac{10}{3}$ or $3\frac{1}{3}$

3.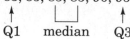

70, 79, 83, 85, 85, 85, 90, 95, 98, 100

Q1   median   Q3

mean

$= \frac{70+79+83+85+85+85+90+95+98+100}{10}$

$= 87$

mode: 85

median: 85

4. quartile 1: 83

quartile 3: 95

median: 85

lower extreme: 70

upper extreme: 100

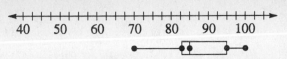

5.

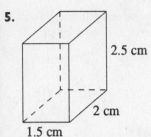

2.5 cm

2 cm

1.5 cm

6.

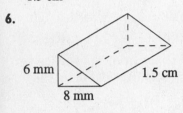

6 mm   1.5 cm

8 mm

11-3 Surface Area of Prisms

Pages 474–476

Think and Discuss p. 474

1. rectangular prism

2. Sample: two 3 in. × 1.5 in. rectangles,

two 10 in. × 1.5 in. rectangles,

two 10 in. × 3 in. rectangles,

All opposite rectangular faces are congruent.

3. surface area = [2(3)(1.5) + 2(10)(1.5) +

2(10)(3)]

= [9 + 30 + 60]

= 99

The surface area is 99 in.^{2}.

4. triangular prism

5. a. Sample: No; the triangular bases are right triangles. You can use the Pythagorean theorem to find the length of the hypotenuse.

b. 34 $\boxed{x^2}$ $\boxed{\times}$ 2 $\boxed{=}$ $\boxed{\sqrt{}}$ **48.083261**; 48 mm

c. two right triangles, two ≅ rectangles and one other rectangle

6. 15 cm = 150 mm; $A = 2(150)(34) + 2\left(\frac{1}{2}\right)(34)(34) + (48)(150) = 18{,}556$ mm^2

7. 1 mm = 0.1 cm

1 mm^2 = 0.01 cm^2

18,556 mm^2 = 18,556(0.01 cm^2)

= 185.56 cm^2

Work Together p. 475

surface area = 2(3)(10) + 2(3)h + 2(10)h,

surface area = 242 in.^{2}

242 = 60 + 6h + 20h

242 = 60 + 26h

182 = 26h

7 = h

The height of the prism is 7 in.

Mixed Review p. 475

1. $-6(m + 1) - 2m = 4$

$-6m - 6 - 2m = 4$

$-8m - 6 = 4$

$-8m = 10$

$m = \frac{-10}{8}$

$m = -\frac{5}{4}$

2. $8 - 7m = -2m + 3$

$8 - 5m = 3$

$-5m = -5$

$m = 1$

3. Estimate:

$32\% \approx \frac{1}{3}$

$32\%(18) \approx \frac{1}{3}(18) = 6$

4. Estimate:

$96\% \approx 100\% = 1.0$

$96(15) \approx 1.0(15) = 15$

5. triangular pyramid

6. triangular prism

On Your Own pp. 475–476

8. surface area = 2(3)(5) + 2(3)(20) + 2(5)(20)

= 30 + 120 + 200

= 350 in.^{2}

9. $c^2 = 3^2 + 4^2$

$c^2 = 9 + 16$

$c^2 = 25$

$c = \sqrt{25}$

$c = 5$ cm

surface area $= 2\left(\dfrac{1}{2}\right)(4)(3) + 3(15.5) +$

$\qquad\qquad 4(15.5) + 5(15.5)$

$\qquad\quad = 12 + 46.5 + 62 + 77.5$

$\qquad\quad = 198 \text{ cm}^2$

10. $c^2 = 6^2 + 8^2$

$c^2 = 36 + 64$

$c^2 = 100$

$c = \sqrt{100}$

$c = 10$ m

surface area $= 2\left(\dfrac{1}{2}\right)(6)(8) + 6(6) + 6(8)$

$\qquad\qquad + 6(10)$

$\qquad\quad = 48 + 36 + 48 + 60$

$\qquad\quad = 192 \text{ m}^2$

11. surface area $= 2(7)(6.5) + 2(7)(8.5)$

$\qquad\qquad\quad + 2(6.5)(8.5)$

$\qquad\qquad = 320.5 \text{ ft}^2$

12. surface area $= 6(4)^2$

$\qquad\qquad = 6(16)$

$\qquad\qquad = 96 \text{ cm}^2$

13. surface area $= 2(35)(7) + 2(35)(9)$

$\qquad\qquad\quad + 2(7)(9)$

$\qquad\qquad = 490 + 630 + 126$

$\qquad\qquad = 1{,}246 \text{ cm}^2$

14. surface area $= 6s^2$ $\qquad$ *s is the length*

$\qquad\quad 486 = 6s^2$ $\qquad$ *of each edge.*

$\qquad\qquad 81 = s^2$

$\qquad\qquad\ 9 = s$

The length of each edge is 9 cm.

15. D; use Guess and Test by trying some specific dimensions:

Try $l = 4, w = 2, h = 3$

Then the surface area of the prism on the left is

$\quad 2[(4 \cdot 2) + (4 \cdot 3) + (2 \cdot 3)] = 52.$

The surface area of the prism on the right is

$\quad 2[(2(4) \cdot 2) + (2(4) \cdot 3) + (2 \cdot 3)] = 92.$

The surface area of the prism on the left is *greater than half* the surface area of the prism on the right.

Try $l = 2, w = 1, h = 1.$

Then the surface area of the prism on the left is

$\quad 2[(2 \cdot 1) + (2 \cdot 1) + (1 \cdot 1)] = 10.$

The surface area of the prism on the right is

$\quad 2[(2(2) \cdot 1) + (2(2) \cdot 1) + (1 \cdot 1)] = 18.$

The surface area of the prism on the left is *greater than half* the surface area on the right.

16. surface area of first box

$\quad = 2(9)(5.5) + 2(9)(11.75) + 2(5.5)(11.75)$

$\quad = 99 + 211.5 + 129.25$

$\quad = 439.75 \text{ in.}^2$

surface area of second box

$\quad = 2(8)(6.25) + 2(8)(10.5) + 2(6.25)(10.5)$

$\quad = 399.25 \text{ in.}^2$

The first box will require more cardboard to make since the surface area is greater.

17. Answers may vary. Sample: The opposite sides of the rectangular bases are congruent, but all sides of the triangular base are only congruent if the triangle is equilateral. (One of each pair of dimensions of each rectangular non-base face is a side of the base and the other is the height of the prism.)

18. a. $17^2 \stackrel{?}{=} 8^2 + 15^2$

$289 \stackrel{?}{=} 64 + 225$

$289 = 289$ ✔

The bases are right triangles.

surface area

$= 2\left(\dfrac{1}{2}\right)(8)(15) + 8(12) + 17(12)$
$\quad + (15)(12)$

$= 120 + 96 + 204 + 180$

$= 600$ in.^{2}

b. $11^2 \stackrel{?}{=} 7^2 + 9^2$

$121 \stackrel{?}{=} 49 + 81$

$121 \neq 130$

The bases are not right triangles.

19. Check students' work.

Checkpoint p. 476

1–5. Drawings may vary. Samples given.

1.

2.

3.

4.

5.

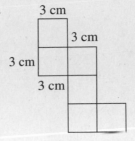

3 cm / 3 cm / 3 cm / 3 cm

6. area of shaded region

$= \pi(4)^2 - \pi(2)^2$

$= 16\pi - 4\pi$

$= 12\pi \qquad \pi \approx 3.14$

$\approx 12(3.14)$

≈ 37.68

area of shaded region ≈ 37.68 units^2

7. $d = \dfrac{18 \text{ cm}}{3} = 6$ cm $\qquad r = 3$ cm

area of shaded region

$=$ area of rectangle $- 3 \times$ area of circle

$= 6(18) - 3\pi(3)^2$

$= 108 - 27\pi \qquad \pi \approx 3.14$

$\approx (108 - 27(3.14))$

≈ 23.22 cm^2

8.

surface area $= 6(8)^2$

$= 6(64)$

$= 384$ cm^2

9.

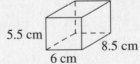

5.5 cm / 8.5 cm / 6 cm

surface area $= 2(5.5)(8.5) + 2(5.5)(6)$

$\quad + 2(8.5)(6)$

$= 261.5$ cm^2

10.

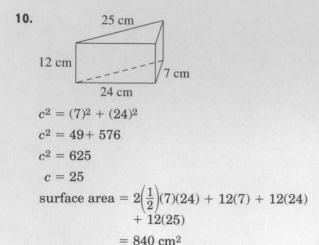

$c^2 = (7)^2 + (24)^2$

$c^2 = 49 + 576$

$c^2 = 625$

$c = 25$

surface area $= 2\left(\frac{1}{2}\right)(7)(24) + 12(7) + 12(24)$
$\qquad\qquad + 12(25)$
$\qquad = 840 \text{ cm}^2$

11-4 Surface Area of Cylinders

Pages 477–480

Work Together p. 477

diameter: $8\frac{1}{2}$ in. or 11 in.;

circumference: $\quad C = \pi d$

(1) $\quad C = 8\frac{1}{2}$ in. $= 8.5$ in.

$\qquad 2\pi r = 8.5$

$\qquad r = \frac{8.5}{2\pi}$

8.5 $\boxed{\div}$ 2 $\boxed{\div}$ $\boxed{\pi}$ $\boxed{=}$ **1.352817**

$\qquad r \approx 1.35$ in.

(2) $\quad C = 11$ in.

$\qquad 2\pi r = 11$

$\qquad r = \frac{11}{2\pi}$

11 $\boxed{\div}$ 2 $\boxed{\div}$ $\boxed{\pi}$ $\boxed{=}$ **1.7507044**

$\qquad r \approx 1.75$ in.

Check students' work.

Think and Discuss pp. 477–479

1. For $C = 8.5$ in., $r \approx \frac{8.5}{2\pi}$ in. ≈ 1.35 in., $h = 11$ in.

surface area = sum of the areas of the bases
$\qquad\qquad\qquad$ + area of the curved surface

$\qquad = 2(\pi)\left(\frac{8.5}{2\pi}\right)^2 + (8.5)(11)$

$\qquad = 2\pi\frac{(8.5)^2}{4\pi^2} + (8.5)(11)$

$\qquad = \frac{(8.5)^2}{2\pi} + (8.5)(11)$

8.5 $\boxed{x^2}$ $\boxed{\div}$ 2 $\boxed{\div}$ $\boxed{\pi}$ $\boxed{+}$ 8.5 $\boxed{\times}$ 11 $\boxed{=}$
104.99894

surface area ≈ 105.0 in.^{2}

For $C = 11$ in., $r = \frac{11}{2\pi}$ in. ≈ 1.75 in., $h = 8.5$ in.

surface area $= 2(\pi)\left(\frac{11}{2\pi}\right)^2 + (11)(8.5)$

$\qquad = \frac{2\pi(11)^2}{4\pi^2} + (11)(8.5)$

$\qquad = \frac{121}{2\pi} + (11)(8.5)$

121 $\boxed{\div}$ 2 $\boxed{\div}$ $\boxed{\pi}$ $\boxed{+}$ 11 $\boxed{\times}$ 8.5 $\boxed{=}$
112.75775

surface area ≈ 112.8 in.^{2}

2. area of one base $= \pi r^2$

area of both bases $= 2\pi r^2$

3. a. $2\pi r$ and h

b. $2\pi r h$

4. a. Sample: Area is measured in square units.

b. Sample: Area is measured in square units.

c. units^2; same as 4(a) and 4(b)

5. a. surface area $= 2\pi r^2 + 2\pi r h$; $r = 16, h = 24$
$\qquad\qquad = 4{,}021$ in.^{2}

b. 1 ft $= 12$ in.

$\qquad$ 1 ft$^2 = 144$ in.^{2}

c. $\quad 1$ in.$^2 = \frac{1}{144}$ ft^2

$\qquad 4021$ in.$^2 = \frac{4021}{144}$ ft^2

$\qquad 4021$ $\boxed{\div}$ 144 $\boxed{=}$ **27.923611**

$\qquad\qquad \approx 28$ ft^2

Try These p. 479

6. surface area $= 2\pi r^2 + 2\pi rh$

$r = 5$ cm, $h = 18.2$ cm

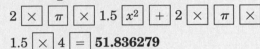

$18.2 \boxed{=} \textbf{728.8495}$

surface area ≈ 729 cm^2

7. surface area $= 2\pi r^2 + 2\pi rh$

$r = \frac{3 \text{ in.}}{2} = 1.5$ in., $h = 4$ in.

$1.5 \boxed{\times} 4 \boxed{=} \textbf{51.836279}$

surface area ≈ 52 in.^{2}

Mixed Review p. 479

1. $\quad 4b - 2 \geq 8$

$4b - 2 + 2 \geq 8 + 2$

$\qquad 4b \geq 10$

$\qquad \frac{4b}{4} \geq \frac{10}{4}$

$\qquad b \geq \frac{5}{2}$

$\qquad b \geq 2.5$

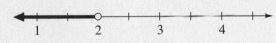

2. $\quad -3 < -2y + 1$

$-3 - 1 < -2y + 1 - 1$

$\qquad -4 < -2y$

$\qquad \frac{-4}{2} > \frac{-2y}{-2}$

$\qquad 2 > y$

$\qquad y < 2$

3. $\frac{5}{8} = 0.625$

$= 62.5\%$ or $62\frac{1}{2}\%$

4. $\frac{1}{9} = 0.\overline{11}$

$= 11.\overline{1}\%$ or $11\frac{1}{9}\%$

5.

surface area $= 6s^2$

$s = 3$ cm

surface area $= 6(3)^2$

$= 6(9)$

$= 54$ cm^2

6. surface area $= 2lw + 2lh + 2wh$

$l = 6$ cm, $w = 4$ cm, $h = 5$ cm

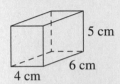

surface area $= 2(6)(4) + 2(6)(5) + 2(4)(5)$

$= 48 + 60 + 40$

$= 148$ cm^2

7.

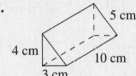

$c^2 = (3)^2 + (4)^2$

$c^2 = 9 + 16$

$c^2 = 25$

$c = 5$ cm

surface area $= 2\left(\frac{1}{2}\right)(3)(4) + (4)(10) + (3)(10)$

$+ (5)(10)$

$= 12 + 40 + 30 + 50$

$= 132$ cm^2

On Your Own pp. 479–480

8. surface area $= 2\pi r^2 + 2\pi rh$

$r = 30$ cm, $h = 45$ cm

$2 \boxed{\times} \boxed{\pi} \boxed{\times} 30 \boxed{x^2} \boxed{+} 2 \boxed{\times} \boxed{\pi} \boxed{\times}$

$30 \boxed{\times} 45 \boxed{=} \textbf{14137.167}$

surface area $\approx 14,137$ cm^2

9. surface area $= 2\pi r^2 + 2\pi rh$

$r = \dfrac{1\text{ ft}}{2} = 0.5$ ft, $h = 5$ ft

$2 \;\boxed{\times}\; \boxed{\pi} \;\boxed{\times}\; 0.5 \;\boxed{x^2} \;\boxed{+}\; 2 \;\boxed{\times}\; \boxed{\pi} \;\boxed{\times}$

$0.5 \;\boxed{\times}\; 5 \;\boxed{=}\; \mathbf{17.27876}$

surface area ≈ 17 ft^2

10.

$r = 2$ ft   These areas are equivalent.

$d = 2$ ft

8 ft

8 ft

surface area = surface area of large section
+ surface area of small section

$= 2\pi R^2 + 2\pi Rh + 2\pi rh$

    surface area   surface area of
   of large section   small section

The base of the small section is included as part of the large section since the areas are equivalent.

$R = 2$ ft, $h = 8$ ft, $r = \dfrac{2\text{ ft}}{2} = 1$ ft, $h = 8$ ft

surface area $= 2\pi(2)^2 + 2\pi(2)(8) + 2\pi(1)(8)$

$\qquad\qquad = 8\pi + 32\pi + 16\pi$

$\qquad\qquad = 56\pi$

$56 \;\boxed{\times}\; \boxed{\pi} \;\boxed{=}\; \mathbf{175.92919}$

surface area ≈ 176 ft^2

11. surface area = surface area of the cylinder side + surface area of the prism
The surface area of the exposed base is equivalent to the base that is not exposed on the prism so you can determine the surface area of the prism without any part removed.

surface area $= 2\pi rh + 2lw + 2lh + 2wh$;

$r = 1.5$ in., $h = 8$ in., $l = 10$ in., $w = 7$ in., $h = 2$ in.

surface area $= 2\pi(1.5)(8) + 2(10)(7)$

$\qquad\qquad + 2(10)(2) + 2(7)(2)$

$\qquad\quad = 24\pi + 140 + 40 + 28$

$\qquad\quad = 24\pi + 208$

$24 \;\boxed{\times}\; \boxed{\pi} \;\boxed{+}\; 208 \;\boxed{=}\; \mathbf{283.39822}$

surface area ≈ 283 in.^{2}

12. B

13. surface area $= 2\pi r^2 + 2\pi rh$

$r = \dfrac{20\text{ ft}}{2} = 10$ ft, $h = 12.5$ ft

surface area $= 2\pi(10)^2 + 2\pi(10)(12.5)$

$\qquad\qquad = 200\pi + 250\pi$

$\qquad\qquad = 450\pi$ ft^2

number of gallons of paint

$= \dfrac{\text{surface area}}{325\text{ ft}^2}$

$= \dfrac{450\pi}{325}$

$450 \;\boxed{\times}\; \boxed{\pi} \;\boxed{\div}\; 325 \;\boxed{=}\; \mathbf{4.3498975}$

surface area
$= \mathbf{1413.7167}$

More than 4 gal of paint are needed, so 5 gal of paint must be bought.

14. surface area $= 2\pi r^2 + 2\pi rh$

surface area $= 814$ in.^{2}, $r = 6\dfrac{1}{4}$ in. $= 6.25$ in.

$\qquad\qquad 814 = 2\pi(6.25)^2 + 2\pi(6.25)h$

$\quad 814 - 2\pi(6.25)^2 = 2\pi(6.25)h$

$\quad \dfrac{814 - 2\pi(6.25)^2}{2\pi(6.25)} = h$

$\boxed{(}\; 814 \;\boxed{-}\; 2 \;\boxed{\times}\; \boxed{\pi} \;\boxed{\times}\; 6.25 \;\boxed{x^2}\; \boxed{)} \;\boxed{\div}$

$\boxed{(}\; 2 \;\boxed{\times}\; \boxed{\pi} \;\boxed{\times}\; 6.25 \;\boxed{)} \;\boxed{=}\; \mathbf{14.47834}$

$h \approx 14.5$ in.

15. a. To find the area of a circle knowing its circumference, divide the circumference by 2π to find the radius; square the radius and multiply it by π.

$$C = 2\pi r \qquad A = \pi r^2$$

$r = \dfrac{C}{2\pi}$ Substitute $\dfrac{C}{2\pi}$ for r in the area formula.

$$A = \pi\left(\frac{C}{2\pi}\right)^2 = \frac{\pi C^2}{4\pi^2} = \frac{C^2}{4\pi}$$

The area of a circle is equal to the square of its circumference divided by 4π.

b. To find the circumference of a circle knowing its area, divide the area by π, then take the square root to find the radius; multiply the radius by 2π.

$$A = \pi r^2 \qquad\qquad C = 2\pi r$$

$r^2 = \dfrac{A}{\pi}$

$r = \sqrt{\dfrac{A}{\pi}}$ Substitute $\sqrt{\dfrac{A}{\pi}}$ for r in the circumference formula.

$C = 2\pi\sqrt{\dfrac{A}{\pi}} = 2\sqrt{\pi A}$

The circumference of the circle is equal to the product of 2 and the square root of πA.

16. a. surface area $= 2\pi r^2 + 2\pi rh$

    $h = r$

surface area $= 2\pi r^2 + 2\pi r(r)$ Substitute r for h.

$\qquad\qquad = 2\pi r^2 + 2\pi r^2$

$\qquad\qquad = 4\pi r^2$

b. surface area $= 1963.5$ cm^2

$1963.5 \approx 4\pi r^2$

$\dfrac{1963.5}{4\pi} \approx r^2$

$r \approx \sqrt{\dfrac{1963.5}{4\pi}}$

$1963.5 \;\boxed{\div}\; 4 \;\boxed{\div}\; \boxed{\pi} \;\boxed{=}\; \boxed{\sqrt{}}\;$ **12.500015**

$\qquad\quad r \approx 12.5$ cm

$h = r$

$h \approx 12.5$ cm

The radius and height of the cylinder are each about 12.5 cm.

c. $d = h$

$2r = h$

surface area $= 2\pi r^2 + 2\pi rh$

$\qquad\qquad = 2\pi r^2 + 2\pi r(2r)$

$\qquad\qquad = 2\pi r^2 + 4\pi r^2$

$\qquad\qquad = 6\pi r^2$

surface area ≈ 1963.5 cm^2

$1963.5 \approx 6\pi r^2$

$\dfrac{1963.5}{6\pi} \approx r^2$

$r \approx \sqrt{\dfrac{1963.5}{6\pi}}$

$1963.5 \;\boxed{\div}\; 6 \;\boxed{\div}\; \boxed{\pi} \;\boxed{=}\; \boxed{\sqrt{}}\;$ **10.206219**

$\qquad\quad r \approx 10.2$ cm

$h = d = 2r$

$h \approx 20.4$ cm

The diameter and height of the cylinder are each about 20.4 cm.

17. Estimate:

surface area $= 6s^2$

$s = 6\dfrac{3}{4}$ in. ≈ 7 in.

$s^2 \approx (7)^2$

$s^2 \approx 49 \approx 50$

surface area $\approx 6(50)$

$\qquad\qquad \approx 300$

The surface area is less than 300 in.^{2}.

18. Estimate:

surface area $= 2\pi r^2 + 2\pi rh$

$\quad r = 1$ m, $h = 2$ m

surface area $= 2\pi(1)^2 + 2\pi(1)(2)$

$\qquad\qquad = 2\pi + 4\pi$

$\qquad\qquad = 6\pi$

$\qquad\qquad \approx 6(3)$ Use $\pi \approx 3$.

$\qquad\qquad \approx 18$

The surface area is more than 18 m^2.

11-5 Volume

Pages 481–485

Think and Discuss pp. 481–482

1. Accept reasonable estimates.
   a. Sample: 24 cubes
   b. Sample: The estimated dimensions are $2 \text{ cm} \times 2 \text{ cm} \times 6 \text{ cm}$.

2. $V = Bh$

3. a. area of the base times the height
   b. $B = \frac{1}{2}(6)(8)$
   $B = 24 \text{ in.}^2$
   $h = 12 \text{ in.}$
   $V = Bh$
   $V = (24)(12)$
   $V = 288 \text{ in.}^3$
   c. No; Sample: We didn't need to use 10 in.

4. $V = lwh$ $l = 12 \text{ ft}, w = 3 \text{ ft}$
   since 12 in. = 1 ft, $h = 4 \text{ in.} = \frac{4}{12} \text{ ft} = \frac{1}{3} \text{ ft}$
   $V = (12)(3)\left(\frac{1}{3}\right)$
   $V = 12 \text{ ft}^3$

5. $V = Bh$ $B = \frac{1}{2}(6)(6) = 18 \text{ ft}^2$
                      $h = 3 \text{ in.} = \frac{3}{12} \text{ ft} = \frac{1}{4} \text{ ft}$
   $V = (18)\left(\frac{1}{4}\right)$
   $V = 4.5 \text{ ft}^3$

6. Accept reasonable estimates.
   Sample: 85 bulbs

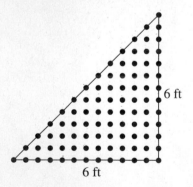

6 ft

6 ft

Each • represents a seed.

Work Together p. 482

7. area; 2-dimensional
8. volume; 3-dimensional
9. area; 2-dimensional
10. volume; 3-dimensional
11. yes; To find the volume of a 3-dimensional figure, you need to know the area of the base.

On Your Own pp. 483–485

12. $V = lwh$ $l = 10 \text{ cm}, w = 2 \text{ cm}, h = 4 \text{ cm}$
    $V = 10(2)(4)$
    $V = 80 \text{ cm}^3$

13. $V = Bh$ $B = \frac{1}{2}(8)(5) = 20 \text{ yd}^2$
                   $h = 18 \text{ yd}$
    $V = (20)(18)$
    $V = 360 \text{ yd}^3$

14. $V = Bh$ $B = \frac{1}{2}(8)(15) = 60 \text{ ft}^2$
                           $h = 22 \text{ ft}$
    $V = (60)(22)$
    $V = 1{,}320 \text{ ft}^3$

15. $V = (2.8)(3.4)(4.2) = 39.984 \approx 40 \text{ m}^3$

16. a. $V = lwh$ $l = 8 \text{ ft}, w = 4 \text{ ft}, h = 4 \text{ ft}$
       $V = 8 \cdot 4 \cdot 4 = 128 \text{ ft}^3$
    b. $V = lwh$ $l = 10 \text{ ft}, w = 8 \text{ ft}, h = 4 \text{ ft}$
       $V = (10)(8)(4) = 320 \text{ ft}^3$
       number of cords $= \frac{320}{128} = 2.5$
       $\boxed{2.5 \text{ cords}}$

17. a. $V = lwh; l = 27 \text{ ft}, w = 16 \text{ ft}, h = 6 \text{ in.} = \frac{1}{2} \text{ ft}$
       $V = (27)(16)\left(\frac{1}{2}\right)$
       $V = 216 \text{ ft}^3;$ $3 \text{ ft} = 1 \text{ yd}$
                                         $(3 \text{ ft})^3 = (1 \text{ yd})^3$
                                         $27 \text{ ft}^3 = 1 \text{ yd}^3$
                                         $1 \text{ ft}^3 = \frac{1}{27} \text{ yd}^3$
       $V = 216\left(\frac{1}{27}\right)$
       $V = 8 \text{ yd}^3$
    b. Cost = Volume $\times$ cost per yd
           $= 8(55) = \$440$

18. a. $V = lwh$

$l = 20\,\text{ft}, w = 4\,\text{ft}\ 6\,\text{in.} = 4.5\,\text{ft}, h = 4\,\text{in.} = \frac{1}{3}\,\text{ft}$

$V = 20(4.5)\left(\frac{1}{3}\right)$

$V = 30\,\text{ft}^3$

b. Cost $= 30(1.79)$

$30\ \boxed{\times}\ 1.79\ \boxed{=}\ \mathbf{53.70}$

The topsoil will cost $53.70

19. a. $V = lwh\quad l = 9\,\text{ft}\ 6\,\text{in.} = 9.5\,\text{ft}$

$\qquad\qquad w = 4\,\text{ft}$

$\qquad\qquad h = 3\,\text{in.} = \frac{1}{4}\,\text{ft}$

$V = (9.5)(4)\left(\frac{1}{4}\right)$

$V = 9.5\,\text{ft}^3$

b. You would need to buy 10 ft³. The best price would be buying two 4 ft³ and one 2 ft³.
$2(6.99) + (3.99) = \$17.97$

20. a. $V = lwh;\ l = 18\,\text{ft}, w = 6\,\text{ft}, h = 4\,\text{in.} = \frac{1}{3}\,\text{ft}$

$V = 18(6)\left(\frac{1}{3}\right)$

$V = 36\,\text{ft}^3$

b. $6.99 for 3 ft³

$2.33 for 1 ft³ $\qquad$ Divide by 3.

Cost $= 36(2.33)$

$\qquad = \$83.88$

21. No; The height of the prism is not necessarily equal to the height of the triangle base.

22. $V = lwh \qquad l = e, w = e, h = e$

$V = (e)(e)(e)$

$V = e^3$

23. a. $V = lwh\quad l = 22\,\text{in.}, w = 15\,\text{in.}, h = 14\,\text{in.}$

$V = 22(15)(14)$

$22\ \boxed{\times}\ 15\ \boxed{\times}\ 14\ \boxed{=}\ \mathbf{4620}$

$V = 4{,}620\,\text{in.}^3$

b. $\frac{4620}{231} = 20$

The aquarium filled to the top will hold 20 gallons.

24. $V = Bh \qquad\qquad V = 315\,\text{ft}^3$

$h = \frac{V}{B} \qquad\qquad B = 42\,\text{ft}^2$

$h = \frac{315}{42}$

$h = 7.5\,\text{ft}$

Mixed Review p. 484

1–4. Accept reasonable estimates.

1. $144 < 150 < 169$

$\sqrt{144} < \sqrt{150} < \sqrt{169}$

$12 < \sqrt{150} < 13$

$150 - 144 = 6$

$169 - 144 = 25$

$\frac{6}{25} = 0.2$

$\sqrt{150} \approx 12.2$

2. $64 < 75 < 81$

$\sqrt{64} < \sqrt{75} < \sqrt{81}$

$8 < \sqrt{75} < 9$

$75 - 64 = 11$

$81 - 64 = 17$

$\frac{11}{17} \approx 0.6$

$\sqrt{75} \approx 8.6$

3. $100 < 110 < 121$

$\sqrt{100} < \sqrt{110} < \sqrt{121}$

$10 < \sqrt{110} < 11$

$110 - 100 = 10$

$121 - 100 = 21$

$\frac{10}{21} \approx 0.5$

$\sqrt{110} \approx 10.5$

4. $196 < 200 < 225$

$\sqrt{196} < \sqrt{200} < \sqrt{225}$

$14 < \sqrt{200} < 15$

$200 - 196 = 4$

$225 - 196 = 29$

$\frac{4}{29} \approx 0.1$

$\sqrt{200} \approx 14.1$

5. surface area $= 2\pi r^2 + 2\pi rh$

$r = 6$ in., $h = 15$ in., $\pi \approx 3.14$

surface area $\approx 2(3.14)(6)^2 + 2(3.14)(6)(15)$

$\approx 2(3.14)(6)^2 + 2(3.14)(6)(15)$

$2 \boxed{\times} 3.14 \boxed{\times} 6 \boxed{x^2} \boxed{+} 2 \boxed{\times} 3.14 \boxed{\times}$

$6 \boxed{\times} 15 \boxed{=} \mathbf{791.28}$

surface area ≈ 791.28 in.^{2}

6. surface area $= 2\pi r^2 + 2\pi rh$

$r = 2.8$ cm, $h = 5.6$ cm, $\pi \approx 3.14$

surface area $\approx 2(3.14)(2.8)^2 + 2(3.14)(2.8)(5.6)$

$2 \boxed{\times} \boxed{\pi} \boxed{\times} 2.8 \boxed{x^2} \boxed{+} 2 \boxed{\times} \boxed{\pi} \boxed{\times}$

$2.8 \boxed{\times} 5.6 \boxed{=} \mathbf{147.7056}$

surface area ≈ 147.71 cm^2

7. surface area $= 2\pi r^2 + 2\pi rh$

$r = \dfrac{10 \text{ cm}}{2} = 5$ cm, $h = 10$ cm

surface area $= 2\pi(5)^2 + 2\pi(5)(10)$

$= 50\pi + 100\pi$

$= 150\pi$

$150 \boxed{\times} \boxed{\pi} \boxed{=} \mathbf{471.2389}$

surface area ≈ 471.24 cm^2

11-6 Changing Dimensions

Pages 486–487

Think and Discuss pp. 486–487

1. a. $V = lwh$ $l = 7$ m, $w = 3$ m, $h = 4$ m

$V = 7(3)(4)$

$V = 84$ m^3

b. $l = 14$ m, $w = 6$ m, $h = 8$ m

c. $V = 14(6)(8)$

$V = 672$ m^3

d. $\dfrac{672}{84}$

8 times greater

2. a. Answers will vary for third tank. Sample given.

Original Size		Doubled Dimensions		New Vol
Dimensions (ft)	Volume (ft^3)	Dimensions (ft)	Volume (ft^3)	÷ Old Vol
$1 \times 1 \times 1$	$1(1 \times 1)$ = 1	$2 \times 2 \times 2$	$2(2 \times 2)$ = 8	$8 \div 1$ = 8
$3 \times 3 \times 8$	$3(3 \times 8)$ = 72	$6 \times 6 \times 16$	$6(6 \times 16)$ = 576	$576 \div 72$ = 8
Sample: $2 \times 4 \times 8$	$2(4 \times 8)$ = 64	$4 \times 8 \times 16$	$4(8 \times 16)$ = 512	$512 \div 64$ = 8

b. The volume is multiplied by 8.

3. a. Answers may vary for third row. Sample given.

Original Size		Tripled Dimensions		New Vol
Dimensions (ft)	Volume (ft^3)	Dimensions (ft)	Volume (ft^3)	÷ Old Vol
$1 \times 1 \times 1$	$1(1 \times 1)$ = 1	$3 \times 3 \times 3$	$3(3 \times 3)$ = 27	$27 \div 1$ = 27
$3 \times 3 \times 8$	$3(3 \times 8)$ = 72	$9 \times 9 \times 24$	$9(9 \times 24)$ = 1,944	$1944 \div 72$ = 27
$2 \times 4 \times 8$	$2(4 \times 8)$ = 64	$6 \times 12 \times 24$	$6(12 \times 24)$ = 1,728	$1728 \div 64$ = 27

b. Answers may vary.

Sample: The volume is multiplied by 27; in 2(b), doubling the dimensions led to multiplying by 2^3 while tripling dimensions multiplies volume by 3^3.

4. a. Answers may vary for third row. Sample given.

Original Size		Quadrupled Dimensions		New Vol
Dimensions (ft)	Volume (ft^3)	Dimensions (ft)	Volume (ft^3)	÷ Old Vol
$1 \times 1 \times 1$	$1(1 \times 1)$ = 1	$4 \times 4 \times 4$	$4(4 \times 4)$ = 64	$64 \div 1$ = 64
$3 \times 3 \times 8$	$3(3 \times 8)$ = 72	$12 \times 12 \times 32$	$12(12 \times 32)$ = 4,608	$4608 \div 72$ = 64
$2 \times 4 \times 8$	$2(4 \times 8)$ = 64	$8 \times 16 \times 32$	$8(16 \times 32)$ = 4,096	$4096 \div 64$ = 64

b. The volume is multiplied by 64.

5. $V = (nl)(nw)(nh)$

$\quad = n(n)(n)lwh$

$\quad = n^3\,lwh$

The volume is multiplied by n^3.

Work Together p. 487

6. Answers may vary. Sample given for fourth prism.

Original Size		Doubled Dimensions		New S. A.
Dimensions (ft)	S. A. (ft^2)	Dimensions (ft)	S. A. (ft^2)	÷ Old S. A.
$1 \times 1 \times 1$	$6(1)(1)$ $= 6$	$2 \times 2 \times 2$	$6(2)^2$ $= 24$	$24 \div 6$ $= 4$
$3 \times 3 \times 8$	$2(3)(3)$ $+ 2(3)(8)$ $+ 2(3)(8)$ $= 114$	$6 \times 6 \times 16$	$2(6)(6)$ $+ 2(6)(16)$ $+ 2(6)(16)$ $= 456$	$456 \div 114$ $= 4$
6.5×6.5 $\times 6.5$	$6(6.5)^2$ $= 253.5$	13×13 $\times 13$	$6(13)^2$ $= 1{,}014$	$1{,}014$ $\div 253.5$ $= 4$
$2 \times 2 \times 4$	$2(2)(2)$ $+ 2(2)(4)$ $+ 2(2)(4)$ $= 40$	$4 \times 4 \times 8$	$2(4)(4)$ $+ 2(4)(8)$ $+ 2(4)(8)$ $= 160$	$160 \div 40$ $= 4$

7. The surface area is multiplied by 4.

8. When every dimension is doubled, volume is multiplied by 8, and surface area is multiplied by 4. The volume increases by a greater factor.

On Your Own pp. 488–489

9. a. surface area $= 2lw + 2lh + 2wh$

triple each dimension: $l \rightarrow 3l, w \rightarrow 3w,$ $h \rightarrow 3h$

surface area (tripled dimensions)

$\quad = 2(3l)(3w) + 2(3l)(3h) + 2(3w)(3h)$

$\quad = 9(2lw) + 9(2lh) + 9(2wh)$

$\quad = 9(2lw + 2lh + 2wh)$

$\quad = 9(\text{surface area})$

The surface area is multiplied by 9.

b. quadruple each dimension: $l \rightarrow 4l,$ $w \rightarrow 4w, h \rightarrow 4h$

surface area (quadrupled dimensions)

$\quad = 2(4l)(4w) + 2(4l)(4h) + 2(4w)(4h)$

$\quad = 16(2lw) + 16(2lh) + 16(2wh)$

$\quad = 16(2lw + 2lh + 2wh)$

$\quad = 16(\text{surface area})$

The surface area is multiplied by 16.

c. each dimension multiplied by n:

$\quad l \rightarrow nl, w \rightarrow nw, h \rightarrow nw$

surface area (multiplied by n)

$\quad = 2(nl)(nw) + 2(nl)(nh) + 2(nw)(nh)$

$\quad = n^2(2lw) + n^2(2lh) + n^2(2wh)$

$\quad = n^2(2lw + 2lh + 2wh)$

$\quad = n^2(\text{surface area})$

The surface area is multiplied by n^2.

10. a. $V = lwh$; $l = 5$ cm, $w = 8$ cm, $h = 3$ cm

$V = 5(8)(3)$

$V = 120$ cm^3

surface area $= 2(5)(8) + 2(5)(3)$

$\quad\quad\quad\quad + 2(8)(3)$

$\quad\quad\quad = 80 + 30 + 48$

$\quad\quad\quad = 158$ cm^2

b. triple dimensions: $27 \times$ volume

$\quad\quad\quad\quad\quad 9 \times$ surface area

new volume $= 27$ volume

$\quad\quad\quad\quad = 27(120)$

$\quad\quad\quad\quad = 3240$ cm^3

new surface area $= 9$ surface area

$\quad\quad\quad\quad = 9(158)$

$\quad\quad\quad\quad = 1422$ cm^2

11. a. $V = Bh = \left(\frac{1}{2} \cdot 30 \cdot 40\right)(50) = 30{,}000 \text{ cm}^3$

surface area $= (40)(50) + (30)(50)$
$$+ (50)(50) + 2\left(\frac{1}{2}\right)(30)(40)$$
$$= 7{,}200 \text{ cm}^2$$

b. double dimensions: $8 \times$ volume
$4 \times$ surface area

new volume $= 8 \times$ volume
$$= 8(30{,}000 \text{ cm}^3)$$
$$= 240{,}000 \text{ cm}^3$$

new surface area $= 4 \times$ surface area
$$= 4(7{,}200 \text{ cm}^2)$$
$$= 28{,}800 \text{ cm}^2$$

12. a. $V = lwh$ — only one dimension doubled, $l \to 2l$
$V = (2l)wh$
$V = 2(lwh)$
multiplied by 2

b. $V = lwh$ — two dimensions doubled, $l \to 2l$, $w \to 2w$
$V = 2l(2w)h$
$V = 4(lwh)$
multiplied by 4

13. D; Cube I has the same dimensions and the same volume but is only half full; Cube II has half the width but is full (volume with one dimension halved will be half); Cube III has twice the width but is only one fourth full (volume with one dimension doubled will be doubled, so one fourth the new volume will be about half the old volume).

14. 12.6 cm; Volume of cube shown is $(10)(10)(10)$, or 1000 cm³. Twice this volume is 2000 cm³. $2000 = e^3$ so use a calculator to find e.

2000 $\boxed{\sqrt[x]{y}}$ 3 $\boxed{=}$ **12.59921**

15. surface area $= 222 \text{ in.}^2$
$V = 189 \text{ in.}^3$

a. dimensions doubled: $4 \times$ surface area
$8 \times$ volume

new surface area $= 4(222 \text{ in.}^2)$
$$= 888 \text{ in.}^2$$
new volume $= 8(189 \text{ in.}^3)$
$$= 1{,}512 \text{ in.}^3$$

b. dimensions tripled: $9 \times$ surface area
$27 \times$ volume

new surface area $= 9(222 \text{ in.}^2)$
$$= 1{,}998 \text{ in.}^2$$
new volume $= 27(189 \text{ in.}^3)$
$$= 5{,}103 \text{ in.}^3$$

16. dimensions doubled: $8 \times$ volume
new weight $= 8(196 \text{ million tons})$
$$= 1{,}568 \text{ million tons}$$

17. dimensions multiplied by 5:
$5^2 \times$ surface area or $25 \times$ surface area
$5^3 \times$ volume or $125 \times$ volume
new surface area $= 25(54 \text{ m}^2)$
$$= 1{,}350 \text{ m}^2$$
new volume $= 125(40 \text{ m}^3)$
$$= 5{,}000 \text{ m}^3$$

18. dimensions halved is the same as dimensions multiplied by $\frac{1}{2}$:
$\left(\frac{1}{2}\right)^3 \times$ volume or $\frac{1}{8} \times$ volume
$\left(\frac{1}{2}\right)^2 \times$ surface area or $\frac{1}{4} \times$ surface area
volume divided by 8
surface area divided by 4

19. Answers may vary. Sample: The advertisement is misleading because the Channel 5 box doesn't seem twice as large as the Channel 4 box, even though its volume is probably twice as great. A bar graph would give a clearer picture of the comparison.

20. Volume of box shown is 14 oz.

a. volume of new box is 28 oz or $2 \times$ volume of old box

$V \to 2v$ so one dimension can be doubled
Sample: $6 \text{ in.} \times 2\left(1\frac{1}{2} \text{ in.}\right) \times 8\frac{1}{4} \text{ in.}$ double $1\frac{1}{2}$ in.

or $6 \text{ in.} \times 3 \text{ in.} \times 8\frac{1}{4} \text{ in.}$

b. Check students' work.

Mixed Review p. 489

1. probability $= \dfrac{1}{99{,}999 + 1}$

   $= \dfrac{1}{100{,}000}$

2. $\dfrac{1}{2}\left(\dfrac{1}{2}\right)\left(\dfrac{1}{2}\right) = \dfrac{1}{8}$

3. $\dfrac{4}{9} + \dfrac{1}{4} = \dfrac{16 + 9}{36}$

   $= \dfrac{25}{36}$

4. $\dfrac{2}{3} \cdot \dfrac{3}{4} = \dfrac{2 \cdot 3}{3 \cdot 4}$

   $= \dfrac{1}{2}$

5. $\dfrac{4}{5} \div \dfrac{9}{10} = \dfrac{4}{5} \cdot \dfrac{10}{9}$

   $= \dfrac{4 \cdot 10}{5 \cdot 9} = \dfrac{4 \cdot 2}{1 \cdot 9}$

   $= \dfrac{8}{9}$

6. $\dfrac{8}{9} - \dfrac{11}{12} = \dfrac{32 - 33}{36}$

   $= \dfrac{-1}{36}$

7. $V = lwh; l = 3 \text{ ft}, w = 5 \text{ in.} = \dfrac{5}{12} \text{ ft},$

   $h = 6 \text{ in.} = \dfrac{1}{2} \text{ ft}$

   4 flower pots:

   $4V = 4(3)\left(\dfrac{5}{12}\right)\left(\dfrac{1}{2}\right)$

   $= \dfrac{5}{2}$

   $= 2.5 \text{ ft}^3$

11-7 Use Multiple Strategies

Pages 490–492

1. **a.** 9 in. by 12 in.

   b. squares

   c. rectangular prism; the length of a side of one of the cut-off squares

2. **a.** $(12 - 2x)$ by $(9 - 2x)$ by x

   b. maximum value of x:

   4 since $x < 4.5$: $\quad (9 - 2x) > 0$

   $\qquad\qquad\qquad 9 - 2x > 0$

   $\qquad\qquad\qquad -2x > -9$

   $\qquad\qquad\qquad\quad x < 4.5$

   c. 0.5, 1, 1.5, 2, 2.5, 3, 3.5, 4

3.

x (in.)	length $(12 - 2x)$	width $(9 - 2x)$	height x	volume
0.5	$12 - 2(0.5)$ $= 11$	$9 - 2(0.5)$ $= 8$	0.5	44
1	$12 - 2(1)$ $= 10$	$9 - 2(1)$ $= 7$	1	70
1.5	$12 - 2(1.5)$ $= 9$	$9 - 2(1.5)$ $= 6$	1.5	**81**
2	$12 - 2(2)$ $= 8$	$9 - 2(2)$ $= 5$	2	80
2.5	$12 - 2(2.5)$ $= 7$	$9 - 2(2.5)$ $= 4$	2.5	70
3	$12 - 2(3)$ $= 6$	$9 - 2(3)$ $= 3$	3	54
3.5	$12 - 2(3.5)$ $= 5$	$9 - 2(3.5)$ $= 2$	3.5	35
4	$12 - 2(4)$ $= 4$	$9 - 2(4)$ $= 1$	4	16

4. **a.** 1.5 in.

   b. 9 in. $\times$ 6 in. $\times$ 1.5 in.

   c. 81 in.^{3}

5. Each increase of $\dfrac{1}{2}$ inch in height corresponded to a 1-inch decrease each in the length and width.

6.

x (in.)	length $(12 - 2x)$	width $(9 - 2x)$	height x	volume
1.25	$12 - 2(1.25)$ $= 9.5$	$9 - 2(1.25)$ $= 6.5$	1.25	77.1875
1.5	9	6	1.5	81
1.75	8.5	5.5	1.75	**81.8125**
2.0	8	5	2.0	80

greatest volume: 81.8125 in.^{3}

when $x = 1.75$ in.

Try These p. 491

7. Volume $= (16 - 2x)(20 - 2x)(x)$

$16 - 2x > 0$

$-2x > -16$

$x < 8$

Make a table.

x (in.)	length $(20 - 2x)$	width $(16 - 2x)$	height x	volume
0.5	19	15	0.5	142.5
1	18	14	1	252
1.5	17	13	1.5	331.5
2	16	12	2	384
2.5	15	11	2.5	412.5
3	14	10	3	**420**
3.5	13	9	3.5	409.5
4	12	8	4	384
4.5	11	7	4.5	346.5
5	10	6	5	300
5.5	9	5	5.5	247.5
6	8	4	6	192
6.5	7	3	6.5	136.5
7	6	2	7	84
7.5	5	1	7.5	37.5

The box has the greatest volume when the sides of the squares are 3 in. long.

8. We want to find the maximum area when the perimeter is 200 ft.

$2l + 2w = 200$

or $\quad l + w = 100$

Make a table.

l (ft)	w (ft)	$l + w$ (ft)	area (ft^2)
90	10	100	900
80	20	100	1600
70	30	100	2100
60	40	100	2400
50	50	100	**2500**
40	60	100	2400
30	70	100	2100
20	80	100	1600
10	90	100	900

The pen has the greatest area when the length and the width are each 50 ft.

On Your Own pp. 491–492

9. 18

10. $36 change

Make a table.

ways	bills				total ($)
	$20	$10	$5	$1	
1	1	1	1	1	36
2	1	1	0	6	36
3	1	0	2	6	36
4	1	0	3	1	36
5	0	3	1	1	36
6	0	2	3	1	36
7	0	1	5	1	36
8	0	0	7	1	36
9	0	3	0	6	36
10	0	2	2	6	36
11	0	1	4	6	36
12	0	0	6	6	36

12 ways

11. $V = lwh; l = 150$ ft, $w = 95$ ft, $h = 10$ ft

$V = (150)(95)(10)$

$\quad = 142{,}500$ ft^3

maximum number of people:

$\dfrac{142{,}500}{200} = 712.5$

Since people don't come in halves, the room holds 712 people.

12. $3(4)(2)(3)(2) = 144$ choices

13. a. $3(3)(3) = 27$

b. 8

c. 1

d. $27 + 8 + 1 = 36$

e. $64 + 27 + 8 + 1 = 100$

14. square: $A = 144$ cm^2, $s = 12$ cm

$\quad P = 4s = 48$ cm

circle: $A = \pi r^2, r = \sqrt{\dfrac{A}{\pi}} = \sqrt{\dfrac{144}{\pi}} \approx 6.8$ cm

$\quad C = 2\pi r \approx 2\pi \sqrt{\dfrac{144}{\pi}} \approx 42.5$ cm

$\quad C < P$

The circumference of the circle is less than the perimeter of the square.

15. The square root of the sum of the integers is 10, so the sum of the integers is 100.

Make a table.

odd integer n	sum of odd integers	square root of the sum
11	$1 + 3 + 5 + 7$ $+ 9 + 11 = 36$	$\sqrt{36} = 6$
13	$36 + 13 = 49$	$\sqrt{49} = 7$
15	$49 + 16 = 64$	$\sqrt{64} = 8$
17	$64 + 17 = 81$	$\sqrt{81} = 9$
19	$81 + 19 = 100$	$\sqrt{100} = 10$

The value of n is 19.

16. Six different ways. Sample:

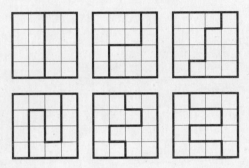

17. Distance to walk: 60 mi

Day 1 (walks 50% of the distance): 50% (60 mi)
$$= 30 \text{ mi}$$

Distance left to walk after Day 1:
$$60 \text{ mi} - 30 \text{ mi} = 30 \text{ mi}$$

Day 2 (walks 25% of remaining distance):
$$25\%(30 \text{ mi}) = 7.5 \text{ mi}$$

Distance left to the walk after Day 2:
$$30 \text{ mi} - 7.5 \text{ mi} = \boxed{22.5 \text{ mi}}$$

18. 12 different totals

1 Point	4 Points	10 Points	Total Darts	Total Score
4	0	0	4	**4**
3	1	0	4	**7**
3	0	1	4	**13**
2	2	0	4	**10**
2	0	2	4	**22**
2	1	1	4	**16**
1	3	0	4	**13**
1	0	3	4	**31**
1	2	1	4	**19**
1	1	2	4	**25**
0	4	0	4	**16**
0	0	4	4	**40**
0	3	1	4	**22**
0	2	2	4	**28**
0	1	3	4	**34**

19. 6 sides: 10 possibilities

6 all yellow:	1 way
5 yellow, 1 blue:	1 way
4 yellow, 2 blue:	2 ways; blues opposite or adjacent
3 yellow, 3 blue:	2 ways; on corner or wrapped around
2 yellow, 4 blue:	2 ways; yellows opposite or adjacent
1 yellow, 5 blue:	1 way
6 all blue:	1 way

$1 + 1 + 2 + 2 + 2 + 1 + 1$
$= 10$ ways total

Mixed Review p. 492

1. $n = 12$

$(12 - 2)(180°) = 1,800°$

2. $n = 10$

$\dfrac{(10 - 2)(180°)}{10} = 144°$

3. $(-1)^9 \div 3^2 - 5$

$= \dfrac{-1}{9} - 5$

$= -5\dfrac{1}{9}$ or $-5.\overline{1}$

4. $\sqrt{196} - (-2)^3$

$\qquad = 14 - (-8)$

$\qquad = 14 + 8$

$\qquad = 22$

5. $V = n^3$ cm^3

$\quad V$ for dimensions tripled $= (3n)^3$

$\qquad\qquad\qquad\qquad\quad = 27n^3$ cm^3

6. surface area $= 6n^2$ cm^2

$\quad$ surface area for dimensions doubled

$\qquad\qquad\quad = 6(2n)^2$

$\qquad\qquad\quad = 6(4n^2)$

$\qquad\qquad\quad = 24n^2$ cm^2

11-8 Volume of Cylinders

Pages 493–496

Think and Discuss pp. 493–494

1. Sample: Volume equals the area of the base times the height of the figure.

2. 60 m^3

3. $\boxed{\pi}$ $\boxed{\times}$ 2 $\boxed{x^2}$ $\boxed{\times}$ 5 $\boxed{=}$ **62.831853**

$\quad$ Volume ≈ 63 m^3

4. a. 1 L = 1000 mL

$\qquad$ 1000 mL occupy $\boxed{1{,}000 \text{ cm}^3}$

$\quad$ **b.** The mass of 1000 cm^3 is $\boxed{1{,}000 \text{ g}}$

Try These p. 494

5. $V = \pi r^2 h; r = \dfrac{15 \text{ cm}}{2} = 7.5$ cm, $h = 15$ cm

$\quad$ **a.** Sample:

$\qquad$ Estimate: $\pi \approx 3, r \approx 8$ cm

$\qquad V \approx 3(8)^2(15)$

$\qquad\quad \approx 3(60)(15)$

$\qquad\quad \approx 2{,}700$ cm^3

$\quad$ **b.** $V = \pi r^2 h$

$\qquad$ $\boxed{\pi}$ $\boxed{\times}$ 7.5 $\boxed{x^2}$ $\boxed{\times}$ 15 $\boxed{=}$ **2650.7188**

$\qquad V \approx 2650.7$ cm^3

$\quad$ **c.** 2650.7 cm$^3 \cdot \dfrac{1}{1000 \text{ m}^3} \approx 2.65$ L

$\quad$ **d.** $2.6057 \cdot \dfrac{1000 \text{ g}}{1 \text{ L}} = 2650.7$ g

6. 30 mL $\cdot \dfrac{1 \text{ cm}^3}{1 \text{ mL}} = 30$ cm^3

$\qquad V = \pi r^2 h; r = \dfrac{8 \text{ cm}}{2} = 4$ cm

$\qquad 30 = \pi(4)^2 h$

$\qquad 30 = \pi(16)h$

$\qquad \dfrac{30}{16\pi} = h$

$\qquad h = \dfrac{30}{16\pi}$

$\quad$ 30 $\boxed{\div}$ 16 $\boxed{\div}$ $\boxed{\pi}$ $\boxed{=}$ **0.596831**

$\qquad h \approx 0.6$ cm

On Your Own pp. 494–496

7. $V = \pi r^2 h \qquad r = 4$ in., $h = 5.5$ in.

$\quad V = \pi(4)^2(5.5)$

$\quad$ $\boxed{\pi}$ $\boxed{\times}$ 4 $\boxed{x^2}$ $\boxed{\times}$ 5.5 $\boxed{=}$ **276.46015**

$\quad V \approx 276$ in.^{3}

8. $V = \pi r^2 h \qquad r = 4$ in., $h = 11$ in.

$\quad V = \pi(4)^2(11)$

$\quad$ $\boxed{\pi}$ $\boxed{\times}$ 4 $\boxed{x^2}$ $\boxed{\times}$ 11 $\boxed{=}$ **552.92031**

$\quad V \approx 553$ in.

9. $V = \pi r^2 h; \qquad r = \dfrac{7 \text{ cm}}{2} = 3.5$ cm, $h = 42$ cm

$\quad V = \pi(3.5)^2(42)$

$\quad$ $\boxed{\pi}$ $\boxed{\times}$ 3.5 $\boxed{x^2}$ $\boxed{\times}$ 42 $\boxed{=}$ **1616.3494**

$\quad V \approx 1616$ cm^3

10. $V = \pi r^2 h; \qquad r = \dfrac{14 \text{ cm}}{2} = 7$ cm, $h = 42$ cm

$\quad V = \pi(7)^2(42)$

$\quad$ $\boxed{\pi}$ $\boxed{\times}$ 7 $\boxed{x^2}$ $\boxed{\times}$ 42 $\boxed{=}$ **6465.3977**

$\quad V \approx 6465$ cm^3

11. a. $276 : 553 \approx \boxed{1 : 2}$

$\quad$ **b.** Doubling the height doubles the volume as well.

12. a. $1616 : 5465 \approx \boxed{1 : 4}$

$\quad$ **b.** Doubling the radius increases the volume by 4.

13. C; 27 times greater

$V = \pi r^2 h$

$r \to 3r, h \to 3h$

new $V = \pi(3r)^2(3h)$

new $V = \pi(9r^2)(3h)$

new $V = 27\pi r^2 h$

new $V = 27V$

14. $V = \pi r^2 h;\qquad r = 7$ in., $h = 15$ in.

$V = \pi(7)^2(15)$

$V = \pi(49)(15)$

$\boxed{\pi}\ \boxed{\times}\ 49\ \boxed{\times}\ 15\ \boxed{=}\ \mathbf{2309.0706}$

$V \approx 2309$ in.^{3}

number of gallons: 2309 in.$^3 \cdot \dfrac{1\ \text{gal}}{231\ \text{in.}^3}$

$2309\ \boxed{\div}\ 231\ \boxed{=}\ \mathbf{9.995671}$

The tank will hold about 10 gallons.

15. a.

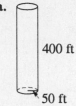

400 ft

50 ft

$V \approx 3,141,592.65$ ft^3

b.

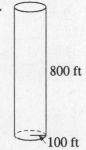

800 ft

100 ft

$V \approx 25,132,741.23$ ft^3

c. Multiply the volume in part (a) by 8.

16. a. $V = (9)(15)(15)$

$V = 2,025$ cm^3

b. $V = \pi r^2 h;\qquad r = 4$ cm, $h = 13.5$ cm

$V = \pi(4)^2(13.5)$

$V = \pi(16)(13.5)$

$\boxed{\pi}\ \boxed{\times}\ 16\ \boxed{\times}\ 13.5\ \boxed{=}\ \mathbf{678.50401}$

$V \approx 678.6$ cm^3

c. Check students' answers. Answers may vary.

d. Answers may vary. Sample: the rectangular box, because it takes less space to store.

17. a. $V = \pi r^2 h;\quad r = \dfrac{12\ \text{cm}}{2} = 6$ cm, $h = 8$ cm

$V = \pi(6)^2(8)$

$V = \pi(36)(8)$

$V \approx 904.8$ cm^3

b. $\dfrac{72.4\ \text{g}}{904.8\ \text{cm}^3} \approx 0.08$ g/cm^3

18. $V = \pi r^2 h; V = 3,534$ cm^3, $r = 7.5$ cm

3534 cm$^3 = \pi(7.5)^2 h$

$h = \dfrac{3,534}{56.25\pi}$

$3534\ \boxed{\div}\ \boxed{(}\ 56.25\ \boxed{\times}\ \boxed{\pi}\ \boxed{)}\ \boxed{=}$

$\mathbf{19.998349}$

$h \approx 20$ cm

19. $V = \pi r^2 h;\qquad V = 402$ ft^3, $h = 8$ ft

a. $\qquad 402 = \pi r^2(8)$

$\dfrac{402}{\pi(8)} = r^2$

$r^2 = \dfrac{402}{\pi(8)}$

$r = \sqrt{\dfrac{402}{8\pi}}$

$402\ \boxed{\div}\ 8\ \boxed{\div}\ \boxed{\pi}\ \boxed{=}\ \boxed{\sqrt{\ }}\ \mathbf{3.9993839}$

$r \approx 4$ ft

b. Divide 402 by 8π, then take the square root.

20. $\pi r^2 = 100,000$ mi$^2 \qquad h = 8$ mi

$r^2 = \dfrac{100,000}{\pi}$ mi^2

$r = \sqrt{\dfrac{100,000}{\pi}}$ mi

$100000\ \boxed{\div}\ \boxed{\pi}\ \boxed{=}\ \boxed{\sqrt{\ }}\ \mathbf{178.41241}$

$r \approx 178$ mi

178 mi

8 mi

Mixed Review p. 496

1. 45 to 60: $\frac{60-45}{45} = \frac{15}{45} = \frac{1}{3} = 0.\overline{3}$ or $33\frac{1}{3}\%$ increase

2. 25 to 15: $\frac{25-15}{25} = \frac{10}{25} = \frac{2}{5} = 0.4 =$ 40% decrease

3. 16 to 12: $\frac{16-12}{16} = \frac{4}{16} = \frac{1}{4} = 0.25 =$ 25% decrease

4. 10 to 50: $\frac{50-10}{10} = \frac{40}{10} = 4 = 400\%$ increase

5. $6e^2 = e^3$
   $6e^2 = e(e^2)$
   $e = 6$

   The length of the side of the cube is 6 cm.

6. The total test points for 4 tests with an average of 87 is 4(87) or 348 points. The maximum Tyra can get on a test is 100. If she does, her total points are 448 with an average of $\frac{448}{5}$ or 89.6 points.
   $\boxed{\text{No}}$; it is not possible to raise her average to 90.

Checkpoint p. 496

1. surface area = $2\pi r^2 + 2\pi rh$
   $r = 5$ cm, $h = 9$ cm, $\pi = 3.14$
   surface area = $2(3.14)(5)^2 + 2(3.14)(5)(9)$
   $\qquad = 2(3.14)(25) + 2(3.14)(45)$

   $2\;\boxed{\times}\;3.14\;\boxed{\times}\;25\;\boxed{+}\;2\;\boxed{\times}\;3.14\;\boxed{\times}\;45\;\boxed{=}$
   439.6

   surface area = 439.6 cm²

2. surface area = $2\pi r^2 + 2\pi rh$
   $r = \frac{8 \text{ cm}}{2} = 4$ cm, $h = 6$ cm, $\pi = 3.14$
   surface area = $2(3.14)(4)^2 + 2(3.14)(4)(6)$
   $\qquad = 2(3.14)(16) + 2(3.14)(24)$

   $2\;\boxed{\times}\;3.14\;\boxed{\times}\;16\;\boxed{+}\;2\;\boxed{\times}\;3.14\;\boxed{\times}\;24\;\boxed{=}$
   251.2

   surface area = 251.2 cm²

3. $V = lwh$ $l = 6.5$ cm, $w = 1.5$ cm, $h = 4$ cm
   $V = (6.5)(1.5)(4)$
   $V = 39$ cm³

4. $B = \frac{1}{2}(20)(15) = 150$ cm²
   $V = Bh;\qquad h = 12$ cm
   $\quad = (150)(12)$
   $\quad = 1800$ cm³

5. $V = \pi r^2 h$ $r = 4$ cm, $h = 12$ cm
   $V = \pi(4)^2(12)$
   $V = \pi(16)(12)$

   $\boxed{\pi}\;\boxed{\times}\;16\;\boxed{\times}\;12\;\boxed{=}\;\textbf{603.18579}$

   $V \approx 603.2$ cm³

6. D; $V = e^3$
   $e \to 2e$
   new $V = (2e)^3$
   new $V = 8e^3$
   new $V = 8V$

7. $V = lwh;$ $l = 50$ ft, $w = 35$ ft, $h = 2.5$ ft
   $V = (50)(35)(2.5)$
   $V = 4375$ ft³
   Cost = $\frac{4,375}{100} \cdot \$1.78$
   $\quad = \$77.88$

11-9 Volume of Cones and Pyramids
Pages 497–500

Think and Discuss pp. 497–499

1. $V = e^3$ $e = 6$ cm
   $V = 6^3$
   $V = 216$ cm³

2. $V = \frac{1}{6}(216)$
   $V = 36$ cm³

3. $\frac{1}{2}(6$ cm) or 3 cm

4. a. $V = lwh;$ $l = 6$ cm, $w = 6$ cm, $h = 3$ cm
      $V = (6)(6)(3)$
      $V = 108$ cm³

   b. 1 to 3

5. a. $V = \frac{1}{3}\pi r^2 h$

$V = \frac{1}{3}\pi (4.5)^2(10)$

$V \approx 212$ ft^3

b. $V = \frac{1}{3}Bh$

$V = \frac{1}{3}(9 \cdot 9)10$

$V = 270$ ft^3

c. Sample: The square base of the pyramid is larger than the circular base of the cone.

6. lower; Each factor was rounded down.

7. $V = \frac{1}{3}Bh$; $B = \frac{1}{2}(175)(90) = 7,875$ cm^2

$h = 400$ cm

a. $V = \frac{1}{3}(7875)(400)$

$\boxed{1} \boxed{\div} 3 \boxed{\times} 7875 \boxed{\times} 400 \boxed{=}$ **1050000**

$V = 1,050,000$ cm^3

b. Divide each dimension by 100, then calculate the volume, or calculate the volume and then divide by 100(100)(100) or 1,000,000.

c. $V = \frac{1}{3}(0.7875)(4) = 1.05$ m^3;

$V = 1,050,000 \div 1,000,000 = 1.05$ m^3; yes

Try These p. 499

8. Accept reasonable estimates.

$V = \frac{1}{3}Bh$; $B = 3\frac{1}{4} = 13$ in.^{2}

$h = 10\frac{1}{2}$ in.

Estimate:

$B \approx (3)(4)$

$B \approx 12$ in.^{2}, $h \approx 10$ in.

$V = \frac{1}{3}(12)(10)$

$V \approx 40$ in.^{3}

Exact:

$V = \frac{1}{3}(13)(10.5)$

$13 \boxed{\times} 10.5 \boxed{\div} 3 \boxed{=}$ **45.5**

$V \approx 46$ in.^{3}

9. Accept reasonable estimates.

$V = \frac{1}{3}\pi r^2 h$; $r = \frac{12.3 \text{ cm}}{2} = 6.15$ cm,

$h = 20.7$ cm

Estimate:

$r \approx 6$ cm, $h \approx 20$ cm, $\pi \approx 3$

$V \approx \frac{1}{3}(3)(6)^2(20)$

$V \approx 36(20)$

$V \approx 720$ cm^3

Exact:

$V = \frac{1}{3}\pi (6.15)^2(20.7)$

$\boxed{\pi} \boxed{\times} 6.15 \boxed{x^2} \boxed{\times} 20.7 \boxed{\div} 3 \boxed{=}$

819.87793

$V \approx 820$ cm^3

On Your Own pp. 499–500

10. $V = \frac{1}{3}Bh$; $B = (4 \text{ m})^2 = 16$ m^2, $h = 12$ m

$V = \frac{1}{3}(16)(12)$

$V = 64$ m^3

11. $V = \frac{1}{3}\pi r^2 h$; $r = \frac{40 \text{ in.}}{2} = 20$ in., $h = 25$ in.

$V = \frac{1}{3}\pi (20)^2(25)$

$\boxed{\pi} \boxed{\times} 20 \boxed{x^2} \boxed{\times} 25 \boxed{\div} 3 \boxed{=}$ **10471.976**

$V \approx 10,472$ in.^{3}

12. $V = \frac{1}{3}Bh$; $B = \frac{1}{2}(3 \text{ cm})(4 \text{ cm}) = 6$ cm^2

$h = 6$ cm

$V = \frac{1}{3}(6)(6)$

$V = 12$ cm^3

13. $V = \frac{1}{3}\pi r^2 h$; $r = 15$ in., $h = 35$ in.

$V = \frac{1}{3}\pi (15)^2(35)$

$\boxed{\pi} \boxed{\times} 15 \boxed{x^2} \boxed{\times} 35 \boxed{\div} 3 \boxed{=}$ **8246.6807**

$V \approx 8,247$ in.^{3}

14. Sample: $(1 \text{ m})^3 = (100 \text{ cm})^3$

100^3 is $1,000,000$.

15. rectangular pyramid:

$$V = \tfrac{1}{3}Bh; \qquad l = 6 \text{ m}, w = 3.5 \text{ m}, V = 77 \text{ m}^3$$
$$B = (6 \text{ m})(3.5 \text{ m})$$
$$77 = \tfrac{1}{3}(6)(3.5)h$$
$$77 = (2)(3.5)h$$
$$77 = 7h$$
$$\tfrac{77}{7} = h$$
$$h = 11 \text{ m}$$

16. Cone:

$$V = \tfrac{1}{3}\pi r^2 h; \; r = 7 \text{ in.}, V \approx 626 \text{ in.}^3$$
$$626 \text{ in.}^3 \approx \tfrac{1}{3}\pi(7)^2 h$$
$$\frac{3 \cdot 626}{\pi(7)^2} \approx h$$
$$h \approx \frac{3(626)}{\pi(49)}$$

$$3 \;\boxed{\times}\; 626 \;\boxed{\div}\; \boxed{\pi} \;\boxed{\div}\; 49 \;\boxed{=}\; \mathbf{12.199714}$$

$$h \approx 12.2 \text{ in.}$$

17. square pyramid:

$$V = \tfrac{1}{3}Bh; \qquad s = 9 \text{ ft}, V = 324 \text{ ft}^3$$
$$B = (9 \text{ ft})^2 = 81 \text{ ft}^2$$
$$324 = \tfrac{1}{3}(81)h$$
$$324 = (27)h$$
$$\tfrac{324}{27} = h$$
$$h = 12 \text{ ft}$$

18. square pyramid:

$$V = \tfrac{1}{3}Bh; \qquad h = 7.5 \text{ cm}, V = 40 \text{ cm}^3$$
$$B = s^2$$
$$40 = \tfrac{1}{3}s^2(7.5)$$
$$\frac{3(40)}{7.5} = s^2$$
$$s^2 = \frac{120}{7.5}$$
$$s = \sqrt{\frac{120}{7.5}}$$

$$120 \;\boxed{\div}\; 7.5 \;\boxed{=}\; \boxed{\sqrt{}}\; 4$$

$$s = 4 \text{ cm}$$

19. cone:

$$V = \tfrac{1}{3}\pi r^2 h; \qquad h = 9 \text{ in.}, V \approx 681 \text{ in.}^3$$
$$681 = \tfrac{1}{3}\pi r^2(9)$$
$$681 = 3\pi r^2$$
$$\frac{681}{3\pi} = r^2$$
$$r^2 = \frac{681}{3\pi}$$
$$r = \sqrt{\frac{681}{3\pi}}$$

$$681 \;\boxed{\div}\; 3 \;\boxed{\div}\; \boxed{\pi} \;\boxed{=}\; \boxed{\sqrt{}}\; \mathbf{8.5003732}$$

$$r \approx 8.5 \text{ in.}$$

20. Answers may vary. Accept reasonable estimates. Sample:

$$V = \tfrac{1}{3}\pi r^2 h \qquad r = 5\tfrac{1}{3} \text{ in.}, h = 18\tfrac{3}{4} \text{ in.}$$

Estimate:

$$\pi \approx 3, r \approx 5 \text{ in.}, h \approx 20 \text{ in.}$$
$$V \approx \tfrac{1}{3}(3)(5)^2(20)$$
$$V \approx 25(20)$$
$$V \approx 500 \text{ in.}^3$$

21. B; $\qquad V = \pi r^2 h \qquad r = x, h = y$

$$V = \pi x^2 y \qquad V = 600 \text{ cm}^3$$
$$600 \text{ cm}^3 = \pi x^2 y$$

I. $V = \tfrac{1}{3}\pi x^2 y \qquad\qquad \pi x^2 y = 600 \text{ cm}^3$

$$V = \tfrac{1}{3}(600)$$
$$V = 200 \text{ cm}^3; \text{ correct}$$

II. $V = \tfrac{1}{3}\pi x^2\left(\tfrac{1}{2}y\right)$

$$V = \tfrac{1}{6}\pi x^2 y \qquad\qquad \pi x^2 y = 600 \text{ cm}^3$$
$$V = \tfrac{1}{6}(600)$$
$$V = 100 \text{ cm}^3; \text{ correct}$$

III. $V = \tfrac{1}{3}\pi(2x)^2 y$

$$V = \tfrac{1}{3}\pi(4x^2)y$$
$$V = \tfrac{4}{3}\pi x^2 y \qquad\qquad \pi x^2 y = 600 \text{ cm}^3$$
$$V = \tfrac{4}{3}(600)$$
$$V = 800 \text{ cm}^3; \text{ not correct}$$

22. a. $V = e^3 = e(e)(e)$

V for one dimension doubled

new $V = 2e(e)(e)$

$= 2e^3$

$= 2V$

The volume is doubled.

V for two dimensions doubled:

new $V = 2e(2e)(e)$

$= 4e^3$

$= 4V$

The volume is multiplied by 4.

V for three dimensions doubled:

new $V = 2e(2e)(2e)$

$= 8e^3$

$= 8V$

The volume is multiplied by 8.

b. $V = \frac{1}{3}\pi r^2 h$

V for height doubled:

new $V = \frac{1}{3}\pi r^2(2h)$

$= 2\left(\frac{1}{3}\pi r^2 h\right)$

$= 2V$

The volume is doubled.

c. V for radius doubled:

new $V = \frac{1}{3}\pi(2r)^2 h$

$= 4\left(\frac{1}{3}\pi r^2 h\right)$

$= 4V$

The volume is multiplied by 4.

d. V for height and radius doubled:

new $V = \frac{1}{3}\pi(2r)^2(2h)$

$= 8\left(\frac{1}{3}\pi r^2 h\right)$

$= 8V$

The volume is multiplied by 8.

Mixed Review p. 500

1. area of shaded region

$= $ area of half circle $-$ area of triangle

$= \frac{1}{2}(3.14)(5)^2 - \frac{1}{2}(6)(8)$

$= \frac{25}{2}(3.14) - 24$

$= 12.5(3.14) - 24$

12.5 $\boxed{\times}$ 3.14 $\boxed{-}$ 24 $\boxed{=}$ **15.25**

area $= 15.25$ cm^2

2. $5^{-3} \div 5^{-9}$

$= 5^6$

$= 15,625$

3. $(-1)^{201} = -1$

4. $V = \pi r^2 h;\quad r = 2$ in., $h = 4$ in., $\pi = 3.14$

$V = 3.14(2)^2(4)$

$V = 3.14(4)(4)$

$V = 3.14(16)$

$V = 50.24$ in.^{3}

5. $V = \pi r^2 h;\quad r = \frac{6\text{ cm}}{2} = 3$ cm, $h = 10$ cm

$V = \pi(3)^2(10)$

$V = 3.14(9)(10);\qquad \pi = 3.14$

$V = 90(3.14)$ cm^3

$V = 282.6$ cm^3

Practice

Page 501

1.

2 cm

2.

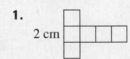

3.

4. area of shaded region

= area of rectangle − 2 • area of a circle

$\approx 12 \cdot 6 - 2 \cdot (3.14)(3)^2$

$\approx 15.48 \text{ cm}^2$

5. area of shaded region

= area of outer circle − area of middle circle

$= \pi(4)^2 - \pi(2)^2$

$= 16\pi - 4\pi$

$= 12\pi$

$\approx 12(3.14); \qquad \pi \approx 3.14$

$\approx 37.68 \text{ units}^2$

6. $V = \pi r^2 h$

$V = \pi(2)^2 7; \qquad \pi \approx 3.14$

volume $\approx 87.92 \text{ cm}^3$

$SA = \pi dh + 2\pi r^2$

$SA = \pi(4)7 + 2\pi(2)^2; \qquad \pi \approx 3.14$

surface area $\approx 113.04 \text{ cm}^2$

7. $V = Bh$

$V = \frac{1}{2}(30)(40)(65)$

volume $= 39,000 \text{ ft}^3$

$SA = (50)(65) + (40)(65) + (30)(65)$

$\qquad + \frac{1}{2}(2)(30)(40)$

surface area $= 9,000 \text{ ft}^2$

8. $V = lwh$

$V = (7.5)(4)(5)$

volume $= 150 \text{ m}^3$

$SA = 2[(7.5)(4) + (4)(5) + (7.5)(5)]$

surface area $= 175 \text{ m}^2$

9. hexagonal prism:

$V = Bh; \qquad B = 34 \text{ cm}^2, h = 3 \text{ cm}$

$V = (34)(3)$

$V = 102 \text{ cm}^3$

10. square pyramid:

$V = \frac{1}{3}Bh; \qquad\qquad s = 10 \text{ in.}, h = 7 \text{ in.}$

$\qquad\qquad\qquad\qquad B = (10 \text{ in.})^2 = 100 \text{ in.}^2$

$V = \frac{1}{3}(100)(7)$

$V = \frac{700}{3}$

$V = 233\frac{1}{3} \text{ in.}^3$

11. cone:

$V = \frac{1}{3}\pi r^2 h; \qquad r = 4 \text{ in.}, h = 8 \text{ in.}$

$V = \frac{1}{3}\pi(4)^2(8)$

$V \approx \frac{1}{3}(3.14)(16)(8); \qquad \pi \approx 3.14$

$V \approx 133.97 \text{ in.}^3$

12. cube:

V for all dimensions doubled $= 8V$;

$\quad V = 216 \text{ cm}^3$

new $V = 8(216)$

$\qquad = 1,728 \text{ cm}^3$

new $V = e^3; \qquad e = 12 \text{ cm}$

new surface area $= 6e^2$

$\qquad\qquad\qquad = 6(144)$

$\qquad\qquad\qquad = 864 \text{ cm}^2$

13. cylinder:

$V = \pi r^2 h; \qquad r = 2 \text{ in.}, h = 6 \text{ in.}$

surface area $= 2\pi r^2 + 2\pi rh$

new $V = 8\pi(2)^2(6)$

$\qquad = 8\pi(4)(6)$

$\qquad \approx 8(3.14)(4)(6); \qquad \pi \approx 3.14$

$\qquad \approx 602.88 \text{ in.}^3$

new surface area $= 4[2\pi(2)^2 + 2\pi(2)(6)]$

$\qquad\qquad\qquad = 4[2\pi(4) + 2\pi(12)]$

$\qquad\qquad\qquad = 4(8\pi + 24\pi)$

$\qquad\qquad\qquad = 4(32\pi)$

$\qquad\qquad\qquad = 128\pi; \qquad \pi \approx 3.14$

$\qquad\qquad\qquad \approx 128(3.14)$

$\qquad\qquad\qquad \approx 401.92 \text{ in.}^2$

14. 9 in. $\times$ 13 in.: area $= 9(13) = 117 \text{ in.}^2$

11 in. $\times$ 11 in.: area $= 11(11) = 121 \text{ in.}^2$

11 in. diameter: area $= \pi\left(\frac{11}{2}\right)^2 = \frac{121}{4}\pi \approx$

95.0 in.^{2}

Use the 11 in. $\times$ 11 in. square pan since the area is closest to the area of the 9 in. $\times$ 13 in. pan.

Wrap Up

Pages 502–503

1. A

2. Answers may vary. Check students' work. Sample given.
Find the area of the entire region and subtract the unshaded area.

$5^2 = 25$

$(2.5)^2\pi \approx 19.6$

Area of shaded region = $25 - 19.6 = 5.4$ cm^2

3. $2(5)(2) + 2(5)(3.5) + 2(2)(3.5) = 69$ m^2

4. $\pi dh + 2\pi r^2 = \pi(4)(10) + 2(\pi)4 = 48\pi \approx$ 150.72 cm^2

5. $\pi dh + 2\pi r^2 = \pi(12)(8) + 2\pi36 = 168\pi \approx$ 527.52 in.^{2}

6. $V = lwh;$ $l = 2\frac{3}{4}$ ft $= 24 + 9$ in. $= 33$ in.,
   $w = 6$ in., $h = 8$ in.

$V = 33(6)(8)$

$V = 1{,}584$ in.^{3}

7. rectangular prism with $V = 24$ cm^3
   and surface area $= 52$ cm^2

new volume $= 8V$

   $= 8(24)$

   $= 192$ cm^3

new surface area $= 4 \times$ surface area

   $= 4(52)$

   $= 208$ cm^2

8. cylinder with $V = 785$ in.^{3}
   and surface area $= 219.8$ in.^{2}

new volume $= 8V$

   $= 8(785)$

   $= 6{,}280$ in.^{3}

new surface area $= 4 \times$ surface area

   $= 4(219.8)$

   $= 879.2$ in.^{2}

9. Make a table.

Dimensions (cm)	Volume (cm^3)	Surface Area (cm^2)
$1 \times 1 \times 12$	12	$2(1)(1) + 2(1)(12) + 2(1)(12)$ = 50
$1 \times 2 \times 6$	12	$2(1)(2) + 2(1)(6) + 2(2)(6)$ = 40
$1 \times 3 \times 4$	12	$2(1)(3) + 2(1)(4) + 2(3)(4)$ = 38
$2 \times 2 \times 3$	12	$2(2)(2) + 2(2)(3) + 2(2)(3)$ = 32

4 ways;

largest surface area: 50 cm^2,

   dimensions: 1 cm $\times$ 1 cm $\times$ 12 cm

smallest surface area: 32 cm^2,

   dimensions: 2 cm $\times$ 2 cm $\times$ 3 cm

10. $V = \pi r^2 h$

$V = \pi(8)^2(9)$

$V = (3.14)(64)(9) = 1808.64$ m^3

11. $V = \frac{1}{3}\pi r^2 h$

$V = \frac{1}{3}\pi(6)^2(8)$

$V = \frac{1}{3}(3.14)(36)(8) = 301.44$ cm^3

12. $V = \frac{1}{3}Bh$

$V = \frac{1}{3}[(9)(9)]8$

$V = 216$ in.^{3}

13. $V = \pi r^2 h;$ $V = 376.8$ cm^3

   $r = \frac{8 \text{ cm}}{2} = 4$ cm

$376.8 = \pi(4)^2 h$

$\frac{376.8}{\pi(16)} = h$

$376.8 \boxed{\div} \boxed{\pi} \boxed{\div} 16 \boxed{=}$ **7.4961978**

   $h \approx 7.5$ cm

14. $V = \frac{1}{3}Bh;$ $V = 270$ m^3

   $s = 9$ m

   $B = (9 \text{ m})^2 = 81$ m^2

$270 = \frac{1}{3}(81)h$

$270 = 27h$

$\frac{270}{27} = h$

$h = 10$ m

15. Each can: $V = 785 \text{ cm}^3$

$$V = \pi r^2 h; \quad h = 10 \text{ cm}$$

$$785 = \pi r^2 (10)$$

$$\frac{785}{10\pi} = r^2$$

$$r = \sqrt{\frac{785}{10\pi}}$$

$$r \approx 5 \text{ cm}$$

$$d = 2r \approx 10 \text{ cm}$$

- The depth of the shelf is 22 cm, so the cans can be stacked 2 deep (2 diameter ≈ 20 cm).
- The shelf is 2 m or 200 cm long. 200 cm ÷ 10 cm = 20 cans lengthwise on the shelf.
- 2 layers of cans

Result: The shelves can be stacked with 20 × 2 × 2 or 80 cans.

Assessment

Page 506

1. Check students' work. Samples given.

a.

b.

c.

2. a.

b. 6

3. a. area of shaded region = area of square − area of circle = $100 - \pi \cdot 5^2 \approx 21.5 \text{ units}^2$

b. area of shaded region = area of circle − area of trapezoid = $25\pi - \frac{1}{2}(4)(6 + 10) \approx 46.5 \text{ units}^2$

4. a. surface area = $6e^2$; $e = 10 \text{ cm}$

$$= 6(10)^2$$

$$= 6(100)$$

$$= 600 \text{ cm}^2$$

b. surface area = $2lw + 2lh + 2wh$

$l = 6 \text{ cm}, w = 8.5 \text{ cm}, h = 9 \text{ cm}$

surface area = $2(6)(8.5) + 2(6)(9) +$
$\qquad\qquad 2(8.5)(9)$

$$= 363 \text{ cm}^2$$

c. $c^2 = (5)^2 + (12)^2$

$$c^2 = 25 + 144$$

$$c^2 = 169$$

$$c = 13 \text{ in.}$$

surface area = $2\left(\frac{1}{2}\right)(5)(12) + 5(7) +$
$\qquad\qquad 12(7) + 13(7)$

$$= 60 + 35 + 84 + 91$$

$$= 270 \text{ in.}^2$$

5. surface area = $2\pi r^2 + 2\pi rh$

$r = 5 \text{ cm}, h = 9 \text{ cm}$

surface area = $2\pi(5)^2 + 2\pi(5)(9)$

$$= 2\pi(25) + 2\pi(45)$$

$$= 50\pi + 90\pi$$

$$= 140\pi$$

$$\approx 440 \text{ cm}^2$$

6. a. prism:

$V = lwh; \quad l = 5.2 \text{ ft}, w = 3 \text{ ft}, h = 7 \text{ ft}$

$$V = (5.2)(3)(7)$$

$$V = 109.2 \text{ ft}^3$$

b. pyramid:

$V = \frac{1}{3}Bh; \quad s = 6 \text{ cm}, B = (6 \text{ cm})^2 = 36 \text{ cm}$
$\qquad\qquad h = 11 \text{ cm}$

$$V = \frac{1}{3}(36)(11)$$

$$V = 12(11)$$

$$V = 132 \text{ cm}^3$$

7. D; 3(3)(3) or $3^3 = 27$
   27 times larger

8. Answers may vary. Sample: Volume of pyramids and cones are $\frac{1}{3}$ the volume of prisms and cylinders, respectively.

9. a. cylinder:
   $V = \pi r^2 h;$ $r = 9.2$ cm, $h = 8$ cm
   $V = \pi(9.2)^2(8)$

   $\boxed{\pi}\;\boxed{\times}\;9.2\;\boxed{x^2}\;\boxed{\times}\;8\;\boxed{=}\;\mathbf{2127.2352}$

   $V \approx 2{,}127$ cm^3

   b. $V = \frac{1}{3}\pi r^2 h;$ $r = 4$ m, $h = 5.8$ m
   $V = \frac{1}{3}\pi(4)^2(5.8)$
   $V = \frac{1}{3}\pi(16)(5.8)$

   $\boxed{\pi}\;\boxed{\times}\;16\;\boxed{\times}\;5.8\;\boxed{\div}\;3\;\boxed{=}\;\mathbf{97.179933}$

   $V \approx 97$ m^3

10. surface area to be painted
   = surface area of walls
      − surface area of window
      − surface area of door
   = 2(8)(18) + 2(8)(12) − 2(3)(4) − (3)(7)
   = 16(18) + (16)(12) − 24 − 21
   = 288 + 192 − 45
   = 480 − 45
   = 435 ft^2

   At a rate of 100 ft^2 per hour, the time for Elaine to paint the wall is $\frac{435}{100} = 4.35$ h or about $\boxed{4\frac{1}{2}\text{ h}}$ to the nearest half hour.

Cumulative Review
   Page 507

1. C

2. A; $_{12}P_3 = 12 \cdot 11 \cdot 10$

3. D

4. A; area of shaded region = area of square − area of circle = 6 · 6 − $\pi(3)^2 \approx 36 - (3)(9) \approx 9$

5. D; $xy = 12$

6. C

7. C; Volume of Model 1 = $\pi(4)^2(10) \approx 480$ in.^{3}, volume of Model II = (6)(6)(11) = 396 in.^{3}, volume of Model III = (6)(8)(11) = 528 in.^{3}, volume of Model IV = (7)(7)(10) = 490 in.^{3}

8. D

9. A; $\frac{11}{50} = 22\%$, 22% of 880 = 193.6 $\approx$ 194, 194 ÷ 12 $\approx$ 16 dozen

10. B; $\frac{160}{25} = \frac{x}{40}$, 160 · 40 ÷ 25 = x, \$256 = x

Chapter 1

Page 508

1.
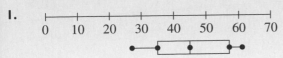

2.
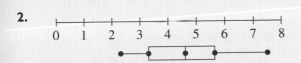

3. mean: 1+1+1+2+2+2+2+2+3+4+4+5+5+5+5=44;

$\frac{44}{15} = 2.9\overline{3}$

median = 2; mode = 2; range = 5 − 1 = 4

4. mean: $5+5+5+6+6+7+8+8+8+8+9 = 75$;

$\frac{75}{11} = 6.\overline{81}$

median = 7; mode = 8; range = 9 − 5 = 4

5. mean: $7.0 + 7.3 + 7.4 + 8.2 + 8.5 + 9.3 + 9.6 +$ $9.7 + 9.8 = 76.8$, $\frac{76.8}{9} = 8.5\overline{3}$;

median = 8.5; no mode; range = 9.8 − 7.0 = 2.8

6. can't determine mean; median = 6; can't determine mode; range = 10

7. circle graph, because it shows parts of a whole

8. line graph, because it shows changes over time

9. bar graph, because it compares amounts

10. scatterplot, because it shows relationships between sets of data

11. not enough information to solve; need to know how many students do both

12. $3 \times 4 \times 2 = 24$ lunches

13. 300

14. closed-option

15. flims

16. 10% of 300 = 0.1 × 300 = 30

Chapter 2

Page 509

1. 4 mm

2. $\frac{1}{2}$ intercepted arc; $\frac{90°}{2} = 45°$

3. isosceles right triangle

4. $c^2 = a^2 + b^2$

$c^2 = 4^2 + 4^2 = 16 + 16 = 32$

$c = \sqrt{32} \approx 5.657$

$RS \approx 5.66$ mm

5. isosceles triangle

6. $\frac{1}{2}$ intercepted arc; $m \angle TRS = \frac{135°}{2} = 67.5°$

7. A = πr^2; A = $4^2\pi = 16\pi \approx 50.265$ mm²

8. C = $\pi d = 8\pi \approx 25.12$; $\widehat{RS} = \frac{25.12}{4} = 6.28$ mm

9. rhombus

10. trapezoid

11. parallelogram

12. rectangle

13. $\triangle RST \cong \triangle NMQ$ by SAS (side/angle/side)

14. $\triangle ABC \cong \triangle FDE$ by SSS (side/side/side)

15. $\triangle JGH$ is not congruent to $\triangle MKL$.

16. $\triangle QAN \cong \triangle RDB$ by ASA (angle/side/angle)

17. No; there is space between the circles even when some points on the circles touch.

18. $\frac{360}{6} = 60$; each central angle measures 60°

19. $c^2 = a^2 + b^2$

$12^2 = 3^2 + b^2$

$144 = 9 + b^2$

$b^2 = 144 − 9 = 135$

$b = \sqrt{135} \approx 11.619$

The treehouse can be built no higher than 11.6 ft from the ground.

20. The pattern is to double the preceding number and then subtract 1.

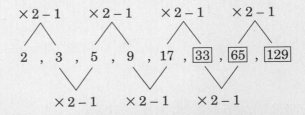

Chapter 3
Page 510

1. $-3 - 2 = -5; |5| \boxed{=} |5|$

2. $7 + (-3) = 4; 7 - (-3) = 10; 4 \boxed{<} 10$

3. $20 - (-6) = 26; 52 - 25 = 27; |26| \boxed{<} |27|$

4. -9

5. -12

6. $|-36| = 36; 36 \div 9 = 4$

7. $-45 \div 15 = -3; 5 \times (-3) = -15$

8. $-3 - 8 = -11; \frac{-11}{4} = -2.75$

9. $3(3) - 4(5) = 9 - 20 = -11$

10. $|3 - 3| + (-2) = 0 + (-2) = -2$

11. $-(5) + (-2) = -7$

12. $2(5 \times 3) = 2(15) = 30$

13. $|5| - |3| + |-2| = 5 - 3 + 2 = 4$

14. associative property of addition

15. identity property of multiplication

16. distributive property

17. identity property of addition

18. commutative property of multiplication

19. commutative property of addition

20. 3^5

21. $(-5)^{10}$

22. m^{13}

23. -4^{13}

24. $(-2)^{10} \cdot (-2)^3 = (-2)^{10+3} = (-2)^{13}$

25. $(-8) + 2 - (-3) = -3$

26. $3 + 16 - 15 = 4$

27. $1 - 1 = 0$

28. $(-9) - (-8) = -1$

29. $6(2) - 4 = 12 - 4 = 8$

30. $8 + (-5) = 3$

31. $-3(3.7) + 4(-2.8) = -11.1 + (-11.2) = -22.3$

32. $2(0.64) + 6(-0.8) + 3 = 1.28 + (-4.8) + 3 = -0.52$

33. $-1.728 + 2.88 - 1.2 + 8 = 7.952$

34. $3.7 + 13.69 = 17.39$

35. $1 + 2 + (-1) = 2$, 2 strokes above par;
$2 + 2 = 4$, 2 strokes

36. a. $\frac{316}{4} = 79$ animals

Use Guess and Test

Dromedaries	Camels	Total Animals	Total Humps	
30	49	79	128	no
35	44	79	123	no
40	39	79	118	no
37	**42**	**79**	**121**	✔

b. $37 \times \$1,200 = \$44,400; 42 \times \$1,500 = \$63,000;$
$\$44,400 + \$63,000 = \$107,400$

Chapter 4
Page 511

1. $3x + 4$

2. $2x + 2 + 6x - 12 = 8x - 10$

3. $-5 + p - 3p - 6 = -2p - 11$

4. $6b + 4d - 3d + 2 - 3b = 3b + d + 2$

5. $6n + 3 = 21$
$6n = 18$
$n = 3$

6. $10 - 7 = \frac{m}{5} + 2$
$3 = \frac{m}{5} + 2$
$\frac{m}{5} = 1$
$m = 5$

7. $-b + 2 = -\frac{1}{2}$
$-b = -2\frac{1}{2}$
$b = 2\frac{1}{2}$

8. $9g + (-4)g = 10$
$5g = 10$
$g = 2$

9. $4n - 3 > 2$
$4n > 5$
$n > \frac{5}{4}$ or $n > 1\frac{1}{4}$

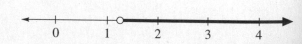

10. $\frac{-n}{3} - 4 \leq 5$

$\qquad \frac{-n}{3} \leq 9$

$\qquad -n \leq 27$

$\qquad n \geq -27$

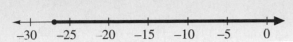

11. $4m + 3(6 - m) < -2.1$

$\qquad 4m + 18 - 3m < -2.1$

$\qquad m + 18 < -2.1$

$\qquad m < -20.1$

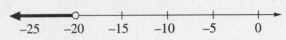

12. $6c + (-3) \geq 2c + 7$

$\qquad 6c - 3 \geq 2c + 7$

$\qquad 4c \geq 10$

$\qquad c \geq 2.5$

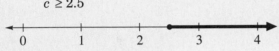

13. $A = s^2$; $3.2 \times 3.2 = 10.24$ in.^{2}

14. $A = \pi r^2$; $36\pi \approx 113.01$ mm^2

15. $A = bh$; $3 \times 4 = 12$ ft^2

16. $8 \times 7 = 56$; $56 \times 4 = 224$; $7 \times 7 = 49$;
$224 + 49 = 273$ m^2

17. $2x + 3 \geq 4 \qquad\qquad 2x + 3 > 4$

$\quad 2x \geq 1 \qquad\qquad\quad 2x > 1$

$\quad\ x \geq \frac{1}{2} \qquad\qquad\quad\ x > \frac{1}{2}$

A number that is a solution to $2x + 3 \geq 4$ that
is not a solution to $2x + 3 > 4$ is $\frac{1}{2}$.

18. $c^2 = a^2 + b^2$

$\quad c^2 = 12^2 + 9^2 = 144 + 81 = 225$

$\quad c = \sqrt{225} = 15$ m

19. $A = s^2$

$\quad 529 = s^2$

$\quad\ s = \sqrt{529} = 23$ yd

20. a. $0.0259A = I$

$\qquad\quad A = \frac{1}{0.0259} \cdot I$

$\qquad\quad A = 38.61I$

b. $A = 38.61(7)$

$\quad\ A = 270.27$ mg/dL

Chapter 5

Page 512

1. 3; $-\frac{4}{3}$; 4

2. $-\frac{2}{3}$; 3; 2

3. $-\frac{1}{4}$; 8; 2

4. -2; $-\frac{5}{2}$; -5

5. Solution: $(-2, 0)$

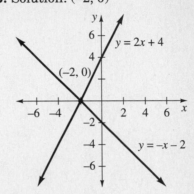

6. Solution: $(2, -3)$

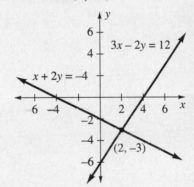

7. Solution: $\left(-\frac{17}{2}, 3\right)$

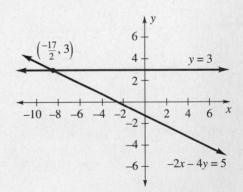

8. no solution

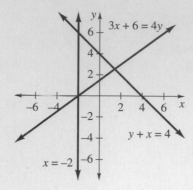

9. $\frac{y_2 - y_1}{x_2 - x_1} = \frac{1-4}{-7-2} = \frac{-3}{-9} = \frac{1}{3}$

10. $\frac{y_2 - y_1}{x_2 - x_1} = \frac{9-3}{3-5} = \frac{6}{-2} = -3$

11. $\frac{y_2 - y_1}{x_2 - x_1} = \frac{4-4}{-2-6} = \frac{0}{-8} = 0$

12. $\frac{y_2 - y_1}{x_2 - x_1} = \frac{-2-(-7)}{-3-(-3)} = \frac{5}{0}$; slope not defined

13. Quadrant IV

14. Quadrant IV

15. Quadrants I and IV

16. one

17. expenses: $y = 30 + 2x$; income: $y = 5x$

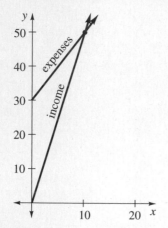

18. (10, 50)

19. more than 10

20. No; the income from 100 calendars is $500 − $230 expenses, so the net income is $270, which is less than the $300 needed.

Chapter 6
Page 513

1. 256, 1,024, 4,096; geometric; multiply by 4

2. 3, 5, 7; arithmetic; add 2

3. $\frac{1}{3}$, $\frac{1}{6}$, 0; arithmetic; subtract $\frac{1}{6}$

4. 1.5, 0.75, 0.375; geometric; multiply by $\frac{1}{2}$

5. 20, 30, 42; neither

6. 16, 32, 64; geometric; multiply by 2

7.

x	$3x - 2$	$(x, f(x))$
−2	−8	(−2, −8)
−1	−5	(−1, −5)
0	−2	(0, −2)
1	1	(1, 1)
2	4	(2, 4)

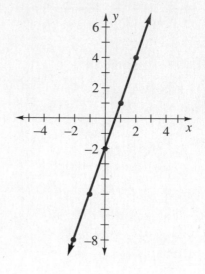

8.

x	$\frac{1}{2}x^2 + 5$	$(x, f(x))$
-2	3	$(-2, 3)$
-1	$4\frac{1}{2}$	$(-1, 4\frac{1}{2})$
0	5	$(0, 5)$
1	$4\frac{1}{2}$	$(1, 4\frac{1}{2})$
2	3	$(2, 3)$

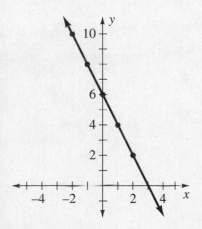

9.

x	$-2x - (-6)$	$(x, f(x))$
-2	10	$(-2, 10)$
-1	8	$(-1, 8)$
0	6	$(0, 6)$
1	4	$(1, 4)$
2	2	$(2, 2)$

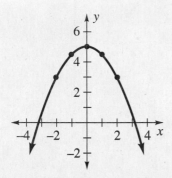

10. d

11. b

12. a

13. c

14.

x	$-x^2 + 2$	$(x, f(x))$
-2	-2	$(-2, -2)$
0	2	$(0, 2)$
2	-2	$(2, -2)$

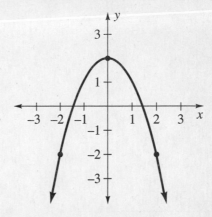

15.

x	$x^2 - 4$	$(x, f(x))$
-2	0	$(-2, 0)$
0	-4	$(0, -4)$
2	0	$(2, 0)$

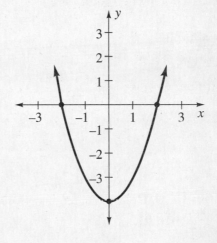

16.

x	$x^2 - 2x + 3$	$(x, f(x))$
-1	6	$(-1, 6)$
0	3	$(0, 3)$
1	2	$(1, 2)$
2	3	$(2, 3)$
3	6	$(3, 6)$

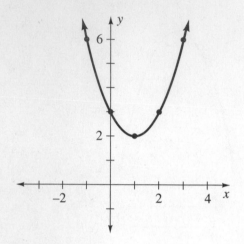

17. linear

18. quadratic

19. quadratic

20. linear

21. inverse variation; 3

22. direct variation; 7

23. direct variation; $\frac{1}{2}$

24. inverse variation; 5

25. Use $xy = k$.

$8(20) = k$

$k = 160$

$10y = 160$

$y = \frac{160}{10} = 16 \text{ ft}^3$

26. Use $y = kx$.

$175 = k(350)$

$k = \frac{175}{350} = \frac{1}{2}$

$y = \frac{1}{2}(250) = 125 \text{ mL}$

Chapter 7

Page 514

1. composite; $3^2 \times 19$

2. composite; $2^4 \times 5^3$

3. composite; $3 \times 11 \times 113$

4. composite; $2^7 \times 5$

5. prime

6. 3; 99

7. 1; 105

8. 3; 120

9. 3; 630

10. 2; 180

11. 0.1875

12. $0.9\overline{3}$

13. $\frac{177}{50} = 3\frac{27}{50}$

14. $2.\overline{3}$

15. $\frac{8}{9}$

16. $\frac{25}{36} = 0.69\overline{4}$; $\frac{25}{36}$ $\boxed{=}$ $0.69\overline{4}$

17. $\frac{10}{3} = 3.\overline{3}$; 2.7 $\boxed{<}$ $3.\overline{3}$

18. -4.3 $\boxed{<}$ -4.2

19. $-\frac{17}{3} = -5.\overline{6}$; $-5.\overline{6}$ $\boxed{>}$ -15.9

20. $\frac{15}{24} + \frac{14}{24} = \frac{29}{24} = 1\frac{5}{24}$

21. $-\frac{6}{7} \times \frac{14}{8} = -\frac{6}{4} = -1.5$

22. $6\frac{20}{15} - 6\frac{6}{15} = \frac{14}{15}$

23. $\frac{4}{9}$

24. $2^{10-7} = 2^3$

25. $\frac{1}{3}$

26. $\frac{a^6}{a^4} = a^{6-4} = a^2$

27. $\frac{8^9}{8^8} = 8^{9-8} = 8^1 = 8$

28. 0.0304

29. 1.274×10^6

30. 0.000006

31. 56,300

32. irrational

33. rational

34. rational

35. irrational

36. $x + \frac{2}{3} = \frac{5}{6}$

$x = \frac{5}{6} - \frac{2}{3}$

$x = \frac{5}{6} - \frac{4}{6}$

$x = \frac{1}{6}$

37. $d \div 5 = 7$

$d = 7 \times 5$

$d = 35$

38. $2p + \frac{4}{7} = \frac{3}{5}$

$2p = \frac{3}{5} - \frac{4}{7}$

$2p = \frac{21}{35} - \frac{20}{35} = \frac{1}{35}$

$p = \frac{1}{35} \times \frac{1}{2}$

$p = \frac{1}{70}$

39. $\frac{7}{10}s - \frac{3}{4} = 6.75$

$0.7s - 0.75 = 6.75$

$0.7s = 6.75 + 0.75 = 7.5$

$s = \frac{7.5}{0.7} = \frac{75}{7}$

40. 2 h 30 min + 10 min = 2 h 40 min;

$\frac{7}{12}$ of 60 = 35 min;

2 h 40 min + 35 min = 3 h 15 min; 2:45 P.M.

41. Work backward. $1.34 \times 5 = 6.7$

$6.7 - (-7\frac{3}{10}) = 14$

$14 \div 2 = 7$

The number is 7.

Chapter 8

Page 515

1. $\frac{4}{16} = \frac{6}{24}; \frac{7}{26}$

2. $\frac{21}{15} = \frac{7}{5}; \frac{3}{2}$

3. $\frac{1}{3} = \frac{6}{18}; \frac{4}{9}$

4. $\frac{20}{50} = \frac{8}{20}; \frac{10}{30}$

5. $7x = 84$

$x = 12$

6. $18x = 27$

$x = 1.5$

7. $80 = 15x$

$x = 5\frac{1}{3}$

8. $10 = 3x$

$x = 3\frac{1}{3}$

9. yes; $QPSR \sim XTVW$

10. yes; m $ABC \sim$ m DEF

11. not similar

12. $\frac{x}{3} = \frac{7}{2}$

$2x = 21$

$x = 10.5$

Scale factor 2 : 7

13. $\frac{3}{4} = \frac{y}{9}$

$4y = 27$

$y = 6.75$

Scale factor 3 : 4

14. $\frac{2}{1} = \frac{3}{y}$

$2y = 3$

$y = 1.5$

$\frac{z}{2} = \frac{2}{1}$

$z = 4$

Scale factor 1 : 2

15. $\tan B = \frac{6}{8} = \frac{3}{4}$

$\tan C = \frac{8}{6} = \frac{4}{3}$

16. $\cos B = \frac{8}{10} = \frac{4}{5}$

$\cos C = \frac{6}{10} = \frac{3}{5}$

17. $\sin C = \frac{8}{10} = \frac{4}{5}$

$\sin B = \frac{6}{10} = \frac{3}{5}$

18. $\sin 68° \approx 0.92718$

$\cos 34° \approx 0.82904$

$\tan 17° \approx 0.30573$

19. $\frac{6 + x}{26} = \frac{6}{8}$

$48 + 8x = 156$

$8x = 108$

$x = 13.5$

It is 13.5 ft from the sign to the top of the pole.

20. $\frac{3}{5} \overset{?}{=} \frac{4}{6}$

$\frac{3}{5} = \frac{18}{30}$

$\frac{4}{6} = \frac{20}{30}$

$\frac{18}{30} \neq \frac{20}{30}$

The photograph is not enlarged proportionally.

Chapter 9

Page 516

1. $6 \times 5 \times 4 \times 3 \times 2 \times 1 = 720$

2. $6 \times 5 \times 4 = 120$

3. $_{15}C_{12} = \dfrac{15 \cdot 14 \cdot 13 \cdot 12 \cdot 11 \cdot 10 \cdot 9 \cdot 8 \cdot 7 \cdot 6 \cdot 5 \cdot 4}{12!}$

$= \dfrac{15 \cdot 14 \cdot 13 \cdot 12 \cdot 11 \cdot 10 \cdot 9 \cdot 8 \cdot 7 \cdot 6 \cdot 5 \cdot 4}{12 \cdot 11 \cdot 10 \cdot 9 \cdot 8 \cdot 7 \cdot 6 \cdot 5 \cdot 4 \cdot 3 \cdot 2 \cdot 1}$

$= \dfrac{15 \cdot 14 \cdot 13}{3 \cdot 2 \cdot 1}$

$= \dfrac{2,730}{6}$

$= 455$

4. $7 \times 6 = 42$

5. $\dfrac{9!}{7!3!} = \dfrac{9 \cdot 8 \cdot 7 \cdot 6 \cdot 5 \cdot 4 \cdot 3 \cdot 2 \cdot 1}{7 \cdot 6 \cdot 5 \cdot 4 \cdot 3 \cdot 2 \cdot 1 \cdot 3 \cdot 2 \cdot 1}$

$= \dfrac{9 \cdot 8}{3 \cdot 2 \cdot 1}$

$= \dfrac{3 \cdot 4}{1} = 12$

6. 8

7. 126

8. 10

9. 6

10. 10

11. dependent

12. independent

13. independent

14. dependent

15. $26 \times 10 = 260$ possible outcomes

16. $\frac{1}{260}$

17. $\frac{1}{26} \times \frac{4}{10} = \frac{4}{260} = \frac{1}{65}$

18. $\frac{1}{10} \times \frac{1}{26} = \frac{1}{260}$

19. $\frac{5}{26} \times \frac{5}{10} = \frac{25}{260} = \frac{5}{52}$

20. $\frac{21}{26} \times \frac{1}{10} = \frac{21}{260}$

21. $\frac{1}{26} \times \frac{5}{10} = \frac{5}{260} = \frac{1}{52}$; 1 : 51

22. $\frac{21}{26} \times \frac{5}{10} = \frac{105}{260} = \frac{21}{52}$

23. experimental

24. theoretical

25. experimental

26. **a.** 15 g

b. 20 g and 10 g

c. 10 g

d. When the process goes above the upper control limit, it is outside the range.

Chapter 10

Page 517

1. 0.3; $33\frac{1}{3}\%$

2. 0.21; $\frac{21}{100}$

3. 347%; $\frac{347}{100}$

4. 0.042%; $\frac{42}{100,000} = \frac{21}{50,000}$

5. 0.15; 15%

6. 2.154; $2\frac{154}{1,000} = 2\frac{77}{500} = \frac{1077}{500}$

7. $x = 0.18 \cdot 36$

$x = 6.48$

8. $44 = x \cdot 32$

$x = \frac{42}{32} = 1.375 = 137.5\%$

9. $145 = 0.15 \cdot x$

$x = \frac{145}{0.15} = 966\frac{2}{3}$

10. $0.4 = x \cdot 5$

$x = 0.4 \div 5 = 0.08 = 8\%$

11. $x = 0.0009 \cdot 1024$

$x = 0.9216$

12. $x = 2.15 \cdot 20$

$x = 43$

13.

Rent	45%
Utilities	4%
Telephone	4%
Food	20%
Insurance	7%
Transportation	5%
Other	15%

14. Rent   162 degrees

     Utilities   14.4 degrees

     Telephone   14.4 degrees

     Food   72 degrees

     Insurance   25.2 degrees

     Transportation   18 degrees

     Other   54 degrees

15. rent

16. insurance

17. food

18. $20 - 16 = 4$; $\frac{4}{16} = \frac{1}{4} = 0.25 = 25\%$ increase

19. $542 - 320 = 222$

     $\frac{222}{320} = 0.69375 = 69.375\%$ increase

20. $1 - 0.4 = 0.6$; $\frac{0.6}{1} = 0.60 = 60\%$ decrease

21. $80 - 55 = 25$; $\frac{25}{80} = 0.3125 = 31.25\%$ decrease

22. $0.003 - 0.002 = 0.001$

     $\frac{0.001}{0.002} = 0.5 = 50\%$ increase

23. a. 50% of $18 = 0.5 \times 18 = 9$; $\$18 + \$9 = \$27$

     b. $\$27 - \$22.95 = \$4.05$; $\frac{\$4.05}{\$27} = 0.15 =$
        15% discount

     c. 5% of $\$22.95 = 1.1475$, rounds to $\$1.15$;
        $\$22.95 + \$1.15 = \$24.10$

     d. 8% of $\$22.95$

        $= 0.08 \times 22.95$

        $= 1.836$, rounds to $\$1.84$

     e. $\frac{94.4}{x} = \frac{8}{100}$

        $8x = 94.4 \cdot 100 = 9{,}440$

        $x = \frac{9{,}440}{8} = 1{,}180$

     The clerk sold $\$1{,}180$ worth of merchandise.

Chapter 11

Page 518

1.

2 in.   2 in.   2 in.

Area I   6 in.

Area of the shaded region =

Area I + Area I – 3(Area of one circle)

Area I = $2 \times 6 = 12$ in.²

Area of one circle = $\pi r^2 = \pi(1^2) = \pi$ in.²

12 ⊟ 3 ⊠ π ⊟ **2.5752220** ≈ 3

Area of the shaded region $\approx 12 + 3 = 15$ in.²

2.   4 m

             1 m

Area of outer ring = $\pi r^2 = \pi(2^2) = 4\pi$ m²

Area of inner ring = $\pi(1^2) = \pi$ m²

Shaded area = $4\pi - \pi = 3\pi$

3 ⊠ π ⊟ **9.424778**

Area of shaded region ≈ 9 m²

3.

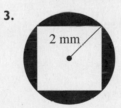

2 mm

Area of shaded region =

Area of circle – Arca of square

Area of circle = $\pi r^2 = \pi(2^2) = 4\pi$ mm²

To find area of square, first find the side length.

Use $a^2 + b^2 = c^2$

     $2^2 + 2^2 = c^2$

         $c^2 = 8$

          $c = \sqrt{8}$

Area of square = $(\sqrt{8})^2 = 8$ mm²

Area of shaded region = $4\pi - 8$

4 ⊠ π ⊟ 8 ⊟ **4.5663706**

Area of shaded region ≈ 5 mm²

4. a. $V = 1.2 \times 1.2 \times 1.2 = 1.728$ m^3

$SA = 1.2 \times 1.2 \times 6 = 8.64$ m^2

b. $V = 2.4 \times 2.4 \times 2.4 = 13.824$ m^3

$SA = 2.4 \times 2.4 \times 6 = 34.56$ m^2

5. a. $V = \pi r^2 h = \pi(1^2)8 = 8\pi$ ft^3

$8 \boxed{\times} \boxed{\pi} = \mathbf{25.132741}$

$V \approx 25.13$ ft^3

$SA = 2\pi r^2 + 2\pi r h = 2\pi(1^2) + 2\pi(1)(8)$

$= 2\pi + 16\pi = 18\pi$

$18 \boxed{\times} \boxed{\pi} = \mathbf{56.548668}$

$SA \approx 56.55$ ft^2

b. $V = \pi r^2 h = \pi(4^2)(32) = 512\pi$

$512 \boxed{\times} \boxed{\pi} = \mathbf{1608.4954}$

$V \approx 1{,}608.5$ ft^3

$SA = 2\pi r^2 + 2\pi r h = 2\pi(4^2) + 2\pi(4)(32)$

$= 32\pi + 256\pi = 288\pi$

$288 \boxed{\times} \boxed{\pi} = \mathbf{904.77868}$

$SA \approx 904.8$ ft^2

6. a. $V = 10 \times 15 \times 18 = 2{,}700$ cm^3

$SA = (2 \times 150) + (2 \times 270) + (2 \times 180) =$
$1{,}200$ cm^2

b. $V = 5 \times 7.5 \times 9 = 337.5$ cm^3

$SA = (2 \times 37.5) + (2 \times 45) + (2 \times 67.5) =$
300 cm^2

7. a. $V = \frac{1}{3}(36 \times 4) = \frac{144}{3} = 48$ in.^{3}

b. $V = \frac{1}{3}(36 \times 8) = \frac{288}{3} = 96$ in.^{3}

8. 10 faces; 16 vertices; 24 edges

9. a. $V = 4 \times 16 \times \frac{1}{4} = 16$ ft^3

b. 1 yd^3 = 27 ft^3

$\frac{16}{27} = 0.5925$, round to 1; \$50

10. $8 \times 8 \times 12 = 768$ ft^3; $\frac{768}{128} = 6$; 6 cords

11. yes; $2 \times 24 = 48$ ft^2

Working with Decimals

Pages 558

1. 9 hundred-thousandths
2. 7 tenths
3. 5 hundredths
4. 6 ten thousands
5. 4 millionths
6. 3 tens
7. 0.0041
8. 18.504
9. 0.000008
10. 7.00063
11. 0.012
12. 65.201
13. six hundredths
14. four and seven tenths
15. eleven hundred-thousandths
16. nine tenths
17. twelve thousandths
18. fifty-nine millionths
19. forty-two ten-thousandths
20. six and twenty-nine thousandths
21. five and one hundred eighty-six millionths

Comparing and Ordering Decimals

Page 559

1. 0 hundredths < 2 hundredths, so 0.003 < 0.02

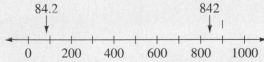

2. 0 hundreds < 8 hundreds, so 84.2 < 842

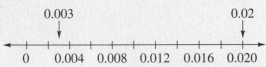

3. 6 hundredths > 0 hundredths, so 0.162 > 0.106

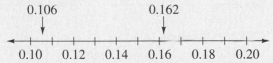

4. 0 tenths < 6 tenths, so 0.0659 < 0.6059

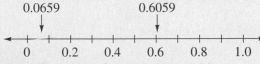

5. 1 tenth < 9 tenths, so 2.13 < 2.99

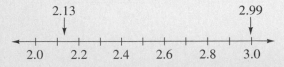

6. 3 hundredths > 2 hundredths, so 3.53 > 3.529

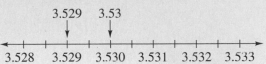

7. 6 thousandths > 5 thousandths, so 0.7562 > 0.7559

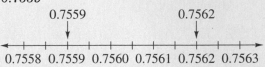

8. 0 hundredths < 7 hundredths, so 0.00072 < 0.07002

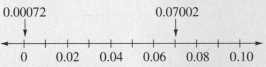

9. 0 ten-thousandths < 9 ten-thousandths, so 0.458 < 0.4589

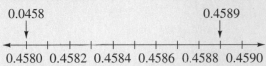

10. 2 hundredths < 4 hundredths, so 8.627 < 8.649

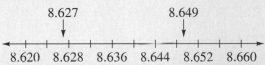

11. 1 thousandth > 0 thousandths, so 0.0019 > 0.0002

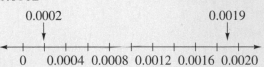

12. 3 thousandths > 2 thousandths, so 0.19321 > 0.19231

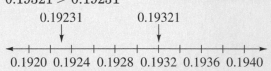

13. 23.1, 3.21, 2.31, 0.231, 0.23
14. 1.2, 1.11, 1.021, 1.02, 1.002
15. 2.22, 0.222, 0.22, 0.02, 0.002
16. 555.5, 55.555, 55.5, 5.5555
17. 0.72, 0.71, 0.7, 0.07, 0.007
18. 2.78, 2.71, 2.701, 2.7001, 2.7
19. 7.3264, 7.3246, 7.3, 7.0324, 7
20. 0.011, 0.0101, 0.0099, 0.00019

Rounding Decimals

Page 560

1. 135.91 rounds to 136.

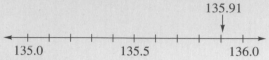

2. 3.001095 rounds to 3.

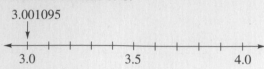

3. 96.912 rounds to 97.

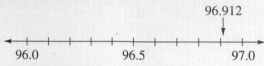

4. 101.167 rounds to 101.

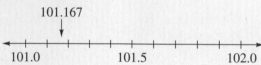

5. 299.9 rounds to 300.

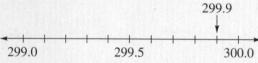

6. 823.54 rounds to 824.

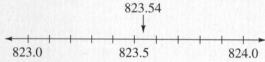

7. 10.4 rounds to 10.

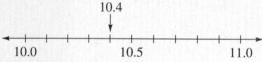

8. 79.527826 rounds to 80.

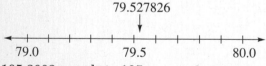

9. 105.3002 rounds to 105.

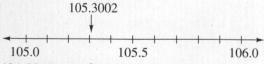

10. 431.2349 rounds to 431.

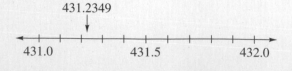

11. 82.01 rounds to 82.0.

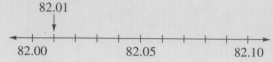

12. 4.67522 rounds to 4.7.

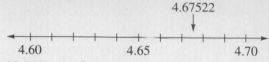

13. 20.397 rounds to 20.4.

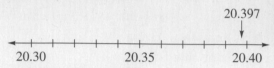

14. 399.95 rounds to 400.0.

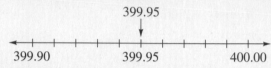

15. 129.98 rounds to 130.0.

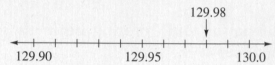

16. 9.754 rounds to 9.8.

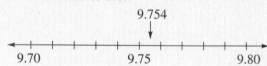

17. 3.816303 rounds to 3.8.

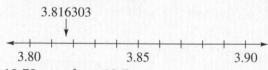

18. 19.72 rounds to 19.7.

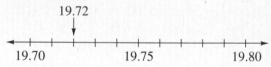

19. 401.1603 rounds to 401.2.

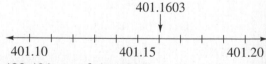

20. 499.491 rounds to 499.5.

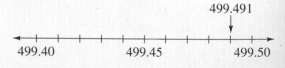

21. 13.458 rounds to 13.46.

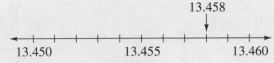

22. 96.4045 rounds to 96.40.

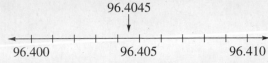

23. 0.699 rounds to 0.70.

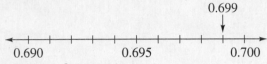

24. 4.23 rounds to 4.23.

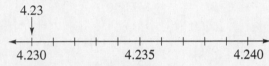

25. 12.09531 rounds to 12.10.

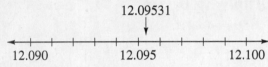

26. 8.091 rounds to 8.09.

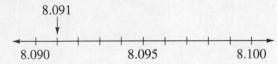

27. 14.869 rounds to 14.87.

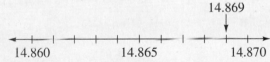

28. 1.78826 rounds to 1.79.

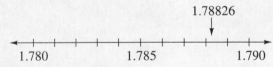

29. 0.111982 rounds to 0.11.

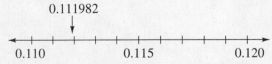

30. 736.941 rounds to 736.94.

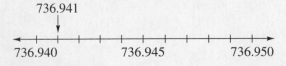

31. 7.0615 rounds to 7.062.

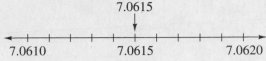

32. 5.77125 rounds to 5.771.

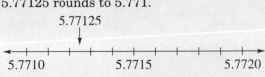

33. 125.66047 rounds to 125.660.

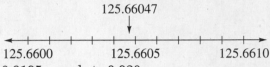

34. 0.9195 rounds to 0.920.

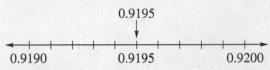

35. 4.003771 rounds to 4.004.

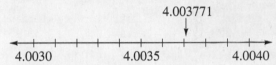

36. 6.0004 rounds to 6.000.

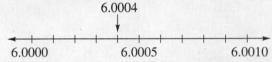

37. 0.0649 rounds to 0.065.

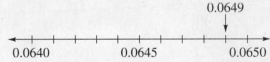

38. 3.495366 rounds to 3.495.

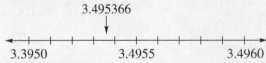

39. 8.07092 rounds to 8.071.

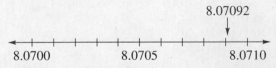

40. 0.6008 rounds to 0.601.

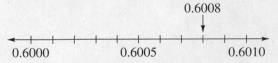

Adding and Subtracting Decimals
Page 561

1. 39.70
    −36.03
    ‾‾‾‾‾
    3.67

2. 1.08
    −0.90
    ‾‾‾‾
    0.18

3. 6.784
    +0.528
    ‾‾‾‾‾
    7.312

4. 5.01
    −0.87
    ‾‾‾‾
    4.14

5. 13.020
    +23.107
    ‾‾‾‾‾
    36.127

6. 8.634
    +1.409
    ‾‾‾‾‾
    10.043

7. 2.1
    −0.5
    ‾‾‾‾
    1.6

8. 8.23
    −3.10
    ‾‾‾‾
    5.13

9. 1.05
    +12.90
    ‾‾‾‾‾
    13.95

10. 2.600
    +0.003
    ‾‾‾‾‾
    2.603

11. 0.10
    58.21
    +1.90
    ‾‾‾‾
    60.21

12. 12.20
    3.06
    +0.50
    ‾‾‾‾
    15.76

13. 9.420
    3.600
    +21.003
    ‾‾‾‾‾
    34.023

14. 15.220
    7.400
    +8.125
    ‾‾‾‾‾
    30.745

15. 3.70
    20.06
    +16.19
    ‾‾‾‾‾
    39.95

16. 76.39
    − 8.47
    ‾‾‾‾‾
    67.92

17. 8.70
    +17.03
    ‾‾‾‾‾
    25.73

18. 32.403
    +12.060
    ‾‾‾‾‾
    44.463

19. 20.50
    −11.45
    ‾‾‾‾‾
    9.05

20. 8.90
    −4.45
    ‾‾‾‾
    4.45

21. 1.245
    +5.800
    ‾‾‾‾‾
    7.045

22. 3.90
    + 6.57
    ‾‾‾‾
    10.47

23. 14.81
    − 8.60
    ‾‾‾‾‾
    6.21

24. 11.90
    − 2.06
    ‾‾‾‾‾
    9.84

25. 3.450
    +4.061
    ‾‾‾‾‾
    7.511

26. 8.29
    + 4.30
    ‾‾‾‾
    12.59

27. 7.060
    −4.235
    ‾‾‾‾‾
    2.825

28. 6.020
    + 4.005
    ‾‾‾‾‾
    10.025

29. 7.05
    −3.50
    ‾‾‾‾
    3.55

30. 1.180
    +3.015
    ‾‾‾‾‾
    4.195

31. 2.304
    −0.870
    ‾‾‾‾‾
    1.434

32. 5.002
    −3.450
    ‾‾‾‾‾
    1.552

33. 6.80
    +3.57
    ‾‾‾‾
    10.37

34. 0.230
    +0.091
    ‾‾‾‾‾
    0.321

35. 0.50
    −0.18
    ‾‾‾‾
    0.32

36. 8.30
    2.99
    +17.52
    ‾‾‾‾‾
    28.81

37. 9.50
    12.32
    + 6.40
    ‾‾‾‾
    28.22

38. 4.521
    1.800
    +3.070
    ‾‾‾‾‾
    9.391

39. 3.602
    9.400
    +24.000
    ‾‾‾‾‾
    37.002

40. 11.60
    8.05
    + 5.13
    ‾‾‾‾
    24.78

41. 7.023
    1.480
    + 3.900
    ‾‾‾‾‾
    12.403

42. 57.0000
    0.6327
    +189.0070
    ‾‾‾‾‾‾
    246.6397

43. 741.0000
    6.0800
    + 0.0309
    ‾‾‾‾‾‾
    747.1109

44. 0.045
    16.320
    + 8.600
    ‾‾‾‾‾
    24.965

45. 4.27
    6.18
    +0.91
    ‾‾‾‾
    11.36

46. 3.856
    14.010
    + 1.720
    ‾‾‾‾‾
    19.586

47. 11.450
    3.790
    +23.861
    ‾‾‾‾‾
    39.101

Multiplying Decimals
Page 562

1. 1.48
    × 3.6
    ‾‾‾‾
    888
    +4 440
    ‾‾‾‾
    5.328

2. 191.2
    × 3.4
    ‾‾‾‾
    76 48
    +573 60
    ‾‾‾‾‾
    650.08

3. 0.05
    × 43
    ‾‾‾‾
    15
    +2 00
    ‾‾‾‾
    2.15

4. 0.27
    × 5
    ‾‾‾‾
    1.35

5. 1.36
    × 3.8
    ‾‾‾‾
    1 088
    +4 080
    ‾‾‾‾
    5.168

6. 6.23
    ×0.21
    ‾‾‾‾
    623
    +1 2460
    ‾‾‾‾‾
    1.3083

7. 0.512
    × 0.76
    ‾‾‾‾
    3072
    +35840
    ‾‾‾‾‾
    0.38912

8. 0.04
    × 7
    ‾‾‾‾
    0.28

9. 0.136
    × 8.4
    ‾‾‾‾
    544
    +1 0880
    ‾‾‾‾‾
    1.1424

10. 3
    ×0.05
    ‾‾‾‾
    0.15

11. 2.07
    ×1.004
    ‾‾‾‾‾
    828
    +2 07000
    ‾‾‾‾‾
    2.07828

12. 0.12
    × 6.1
    ‾‾‾‾
    12
    + 720
    ‾‾‾‾
    0.732

13.
$$\begin{array}{r} 3.2 \\ \times\,0.15 \\ \hline 160 \\ +\,320 \\ \hline 0.480 \\ =0.48 \end{array}$$

14.
$$\begin{array}{r} 0.74 \\ \times\,0.23 \\ \hline 222 \\ +\,1480 \\ \hline 0.1702 \end{array}$$

15.
$$\begin{array}{r} 2.6 \\ \times\,0.14 \\ \hline 104 \\ +\,260 \\ \hline 0.364 \end{array}$$

4.
$$\begin{array}{r} 7 \\ \times\,0.01 \\ \hline 0.07 \end{array}$$

5.
$$\begin{array}{r} 0.05 \\ \times\,0.05 \\ \hline 0.0025 \end{array}$$

6.
$$\begin{array}{r} 0.016 \\ \times\,0.12 \\ \hline 32 \\ +\,160 \\ \hline 0.00192 \end{array}$$

16.
$$\begin{array}{r} 0.77 \\ \times\,51 \\ \hline 77 \\ +\,38\,50 \\ \hline 39.27 \end{array}$$

17.
$$\begin{array}{r} 9.3 \\ \times\,0.706 \\ \hline 558 \\ +\,6\,5100 \\ \hline 6.5658 \end{array}$$

18.
$$\begin{array}{r} 71.13 \\ \times\,0.4 \\ \hline 28.452 \end{array}$$

7.
$$\begin{array}{r} 0.031 \\ \times\,0.08 \\ \hline 0.00248 \end{array}$$

8.
$$\begin{array}{r} 0.03 \\ \times\,0.2 \\ \hline 0.006 \end{array}$$

9.
$$\begin{array}{r} 0.27 \\ \times\,0.033 \\ \hline 81 \\ +\,810 \\ \hline 0.00891 \end{array}$$

19.
$$\begin{array}{r} 0.42 \\ \times\,98 \\ \hline 3\,36 \\ +\,37\,80 \\ \hline 41.16 \end{array}$$

20.
$$\begin{array}{r} 6.3 \\ \times\,85 \\ \hline 31\,5 \\ +\,504\,0 \\ \hline 535.5 \end{array}$$

21.
$$\begin{array}{r} 45 \\ \times\,0.028 \\ \hline 360 \\ +\,900 \\ \hline 1.26 \end{array}$$

10.
$$\begin{array}{r} 0.014 \\ \times\,0.25 \\ \hline 70 \\ +\,280 \\ \hline 0.0035 \end{array}$$

11.
$$\begin{array}{r} 0.55 \\ \times\,0.003 \\ \hline 0.00165 \end{array}$$

12.
$$\begin{array}{r} 0.74 \\ \times\,0.01 \\ \hline 0.0074 \end{array}$$

22.
$$\begin{array}{r} 76 \\ \times\,3.3 \\ \hline 22\,8 \\ +\,228\,0 \\ \hline 250.8 \end{array}$$

23.
$$\begin{array}{r} 1.35 \\ \times\,9 \\ \hline 12.15 \end{array}$$

24.
$$\begin{array}{r} 4.56 \\ \times\,7 \\ \hline 31.92 \end{array}$$

13.
$$\begin{array}{r} 0.47 \\ \times\,0.08 \\ \hline 0.0376 \end{array}$$

14.
$$\begin{array}{r} 0.76 \\ \times\,0.1 \\ \hline 0.076 \end{array}$$

15.
$$\begin{array}{r} 0.27 \\ \times\,0.3 \\ \hline 0.081 \end{array}$$

16.
$$\begin{array}{r} 0.19 \\ \times\,0.05 \\ \hline 0.0095 \end{array}$$

17.
$$\begin{array}{r} 0.018 \\ \times\,0.04 \\ \hline 0.00072 \end{array}$$

18.
$$\begin{array}{r} 0.43 \\ \times\,0.2 \\ \hline 0.086 \end{array}$$

25.
$$\begin{array}{r} 2.41 \\ \times\,5 \\ \hline 12.05 \end{array}$$

26.
$$\begin{array}{r} 704 \\ \times\,0.3 \\ \hline 211.2 \end{array}$$

27.
$$\begin{array}{r} 8.003 \\ \times\,0.6 \\ \hline 4.8018 \end{array}$$

19.
$$\begin{array}{r} 0.03 \\ \times\,0.03 \\ \hline 0.0009 \end{array}$$

20.
$$\begin{array}{r} 4.003 \\ \times\,0.02 \\ \hline 0.08006 \end{array}$$

21.
$$\begin{array}{r} 0.5 \\ \times\,0.08 \\ \hline 0.040 \\ =0.04 \end{array}$$

28.
$$\begin{array}{r} 42.2 \\ \times\,0.9 \\ \hline 37.98 \end{array}$$

29.
$$\begin{array}{r} 30.02 \\ \times\,0.6 \\ \hline 18.012 \end{array}$$

30.
$$\begin{array}{r} 11.8 \\ \times\,0.05 \\ \hline 0.59 \end{array}$$

22.
$$\begin{array}{r} 0.06 \\ \times\,0.7 \\ \hline 0.042 \end{array}$$

23.
$$\begin{array}{r} 0.047 \\ \times\,0.008 \\ \hline 0.000376 \end{array}$$

24.
$$\begin{array}{r} 0.05 \\ \times\,0.06 \\ \hline 0.0030 \\ =0.003 \end{array}$$

31.
$$\begin{array}{r} 15.1 \\ \times\,0.02 \\ \hline 0.302 \end{array}$$

32.
$$\begin{array}{r} 2.5 \\ \times\,0.04 \\ \hline 0.1 \end{array}$$

33.
$$\begin{array}{r} 6.6 \\ \times\,0.3 \\ \hline 1.98 \end{array}$$

25.
$$\begin{array}{r} 0.03 \\ \times\,0.4 \\ \hline 0.012 \end{array}$$

26.
$$\begin{array}{r} 0.036 \\ \times\,0.05 \\ \hline 0.00180 \\ =0.0018 \end{array}$$

27.
$$\begin{array}{r} 0.023 \\ \times\,0.4 \\ \hline 0.092 \end{array}$$

34.
$$\begin{array}{r} 0.901 \\ \times\,0.802 \\ \hline 1802 \\ +\,720800 \\ \hline 0.722602 \end{array}$$

28.
$$\begin{array}{r} 0.017 \\ \times\,0.3 \\ \hline 0.0051 \end{array}$$

29.
$$\begin{array}{r} 0.24 \\ \times\,0.3 \\ \hline 0.072 \end{array}$$

30.
$$\begin{array}{r} 0.67 \\ \times\,0.09 \\ \hline 0.0603 \end{array}$$

Zeros in the Product
Page 563

1.
$$\begin{array}{r} 0.03 \\ \times\,0.9 \\ \hline 0.027 \end{array}$$

2.
$$\begin{array}{r} 0.06 \\ \times\,0.5 \\ \hline 0.03 \end{array}$$

3.
$$\begin{array}{r} 2.4 \\ \times\,0.03 \\ \hline 0.072 \end{array}$$

31.
$$\begin{array}{r} 3.02 \\ \times\,0.006 \\ \hline 0.01812 \end{array}$$

32.
$$\begin{array}{r} 0.31 \\ \times\,0.08 \\ \hline 0.0248 \end{array}$$

33.
$$\begin{array}{r} 0.14 \\ \times\,0.05 \\ \hline 0.0070 \\ =0.007 \end{array}$$

34.
$$\begin{array}{r} 0.85 \\ \times\,0.07 \\ \hline 0.0595 \end{array}$$

Dividing a Decimal by a Whole Number

Page 564

1.
```
      2.56
7)17.92
    −14
      3 9
    −3 5
      42
     −42
       0
```

2.
```
      3.3
5)16.5
   −15
     1 5
    −1 5
      0
```

3.
```
      0.776
9)6.984
   −6 3
      68
     −63
      54
     −54
       0
```

4.
```
      15.24
6)91.44
   −6
    31
   −30
     1 4
    −1 2
      24
     −24
       0
```

5.
```
      8.79
4)35.16
   −32
     3 1
    −2 8
      36
     −36
       0
```

6.
```
       0.158
56)8.848
    −5 6
      3 24
     −2 80
       448
      −448
         0
```

7.
```
       0.11
22)2.42
    −2 2
      22
     −22
       0
```

8.
```
       66.3
26)1723.8
    −156
      163
     −156
        7 8
       −7 8
          0
```

9.
```
       0.184
83)15.272
    −8 3
      6 97
     −6 64
       332
      −332
         0
```

10.
```
       0.69
39)26.91
    −23 4
      3 51
     −3 51
         0
```

11.
```
      2.07
7)14.49
   −14
     49
    −49
      0
```

12.
```
      1.17
9)10.53
   −9
    1 5
    −9
     63
    −63
      0
```

13.
```
      8.76
2)17.52
   −16
     1 5
    −1 4
      12
     −12
       0
```

14.
```
      6.19
6)37.14
   −36
     1 1
    −6
     54
    −54
      0
```

15.
```
      0.0169
8)0.1352
   −8
    55
   −48
     72
    −72
      0
```

16.
```
      0.0036
9)0.0324
   −27
    54
   −54
     0
```

17.
```
      0.0147
6)0.0882
   −6
    28
   −24
     42
    −42
      0
```

18.
```
      0.1447
6)0.8682
   −6
    26
   −24
     28
    −24
     42
    −42
      0
```

19.
$$22\overline{)12.342}$$ = 0.561
$$-11\ 0$$
$$1\ 34$$
$$-1\ 32$$
$$22$$
$$-22$$
$$0$$

20.
$$32\overline{)29.792}$$ = 0.931
$$-28\ 8$$
$$99$$
$$-96$$
$$32$$
$$-32$$
$$0$$

21.
$$26\overline{)22.568}$$ = 0.868
$$-20\ 8$$
$$1\ 76$$
$$-1\ 56$$
$$208$$
$$-208$$
$$0$$

22.
$$36\overline{)11.340}$$ = 0.315
$$-10\ 8$$
$$54$$
$$-36$$
$$180$$
$$-180$$
$$0$$

23.
$$18\overline{)45.918}$$ = 2.551
$$-36$$
$$9\ 9$$
$$-9\ 0$$
$$91$$
$$-90$$
$$18$$
$$-18$$
$$0$$

24.
$$13\overline{)79.599}$$ = 6.123
$$-78$$
$$1\ 5$$
$$-1\ 3$$
$$29$$
$$-26$$
$$39$$
$$-39$$
$$0$$

25.
$$15\overline{)59.70}$$ = 3.98
$$-45$$
$$14\ 7$$
$$-13\ 5$$
$$1\ 20$$
$$-1\ 20$$
$$0$$

26.
$$12\overline{)74.664}$$ = 6.222
$$-72$$
$$2\ 6$$
$$-2\ 4$$
$$26$$
$$-24$$
$$24$$
$$-24$$
$$0$$

27.
$$84\overline{)2.100}$$ = 0.025
$$-1\ 68$$
$$420$$
$$-420$$
$$0$$

28.
$$67\overline{)89.378}$$ = 1.334
$$-67$$
$$22\ 3$$
$$-20\ 1$$
$$2\ 27$$
$$-2\ 01$$
$$268$$
$$-268$$
$$0$$

29.
$$48\overline{)0.0672}$$ = 0.0014
$$-48$$
$$192$$
$$-192$$
$$0$$

30.
$$53\overline{)171.031}$$ = 3.227
$$-159$$
$$12\ 0$$
$$-10\ 6$$
$$1\ 43$$
$$-1\ 06$$
$$371$$
$$-371$$
$$0$$

Powers of Ten

Page 565

1. $10,000 \times 0.056$

Move the decimal point 4 places to the right.

$0.056 \rightarrow 560; 10,000 \times 0.056 = 560$

2. 0.001×0.09

Move the decimal point 3 places to the left.

$0.09 \rightarrow 0.00009; 0.001 \times 0.09 = 0.00009$

3. 5.2×10

Move the decimal point 1 place to the right.

$5.2 \rightarrow 52; 5.2 \times 10 = 52$

4. $0.03 \times 1,000$

Move the decimal point 3 places to the right.

$0.03 \rightarrow 30; 0.03 \times 1,000 = 30$

5. $236.7 \div 0.1$

Move the decimal point 1 place to the right.

$236.7 \rightarrow 2,367; 236.7 \div 0.1 = 2,367$

6. $45.28 \div 10$
   Move the decimal point 1 place to the left.
   $45.28 \rightarrow 4.528$; $45.28 \div 10 = 4.528$

7. $0.9 \div 1,000$
   Move the decimal point 3 places to the left.
   $0.9 \rightarrow 0.0009$; $0.9 \div 1,000 = 0.009$

8. $1.07 \div 0.01$
   Move the decimal point 2 places to the right.
   $1.07 \rightarrow 107$; $1.07 \div 0.01 = 107$

9. 100×0.08
   Move the decimal point 2 places to the right.
   $0.08 \rightarrow 8$; $100 \times 0.8 = 8$

10. $1.03 \times 10,000$
    Move the decimal point 4 places to the right.
    $1.03 \rightarrow 10,300$; $1.03 \times 10,000 = 10,300$

11. 1.803×0.001
    Move the decimal point 3 places to the left.
    $1.803 \rightarrow 0.001803$; $1.803 \times 0.001 = 0.001803$

12. 4.1×100
    Move the decimal point 2 places to the right.
    $4.1 \rightarrow 410$; $4.1 \times 100 = 410$

13. $13.7 \div 0.001$
    Move the decimal point 3 places to the right.
    $13.7 \rightarrow 13,700$; $13.7 \div 0.001 = 13,700$

14. $203.05 \div 0.01$
    Move the decimal point 2 places to the right.
    $203.05 \rightarrow 20,305$; $203.05 \div 0.01 = 20,305$

15. $4.7 \div 10$
    Move the decimal point 1 place to the left.
    $4.7 \rightarrow 0.47$; $4.7 \div 10 = 0.47$

16. $0.05 \div 100$
    Move the decimal point 2 places to the left.
    $0.05 \rightarrow 0.0005$; $0.05 \div 100 = 0.0005$

17. 23.6×0.01
    Move the decimal point 2 places to the left.
    $23.6 \rightarrow 0.236$; $23.6 \times 0.01 = 0.236$

18. $1,000 \times 0.12$
    Move the decimal point 3 places to the right.
    $0.12 \rightarrow 120$; $1,000 \times 0.12 = 120$

19. 0.41×0.001
    Move the decimal point 3 places to the left.
    $0.41 \rightarrow 0.00041$; $0.41 \times 0.001 = 0.00041$

20. 0.01×6.2
    Move the decimal point 2 places to the left.
    $6.2 \rightarrow 0.062$; $0.01 \times 6.2 = 0.062$

21. $42.3 \div 0.1$
    Move the decimal point 1 place to the right.
    $42.3 \rightarrow 423$; $42.3 \div 0.1 = 423$

22. $0.4 \div 10,000$
    Move the decimal point 4 places to the left.
    $0.4 \rightarrow 0.00004$; $0.4 \div 10,000 = 0.00004$

23. $5.02 \div 0.01$
    Move the decimal point 2 places to the right.
    $5.02 \rightarrow 502$; $5.02 \div 0.01 = 502$

24. $16.5 \div 100$
    Move the decimal point 2 places to the left.
    $16.5 \rightarrow 0.165$; $16.5 \div 100 = 0.165$

25. $0.27 \div 0.01$
    Move the decimal point 2 places to the right.
    $0.27 \rightarrow 27$; $0.27 \div 0.01 = 27$

26. 1.05×0.001
    Move the decimal point 3 places to the left.
    $1.05 \rightarrow 0.00105$; $1.05 \times 0.001 = 0.00105$

27. 10×0.04
    Move the decimal point 1 place to the right.
    $0.04 \rightarrow 0.4$; $10 \times 0.04 = 0.4$

28. $2.09 \div 100$
    Move the decimal point 2 places to the left.
    $2.09 \rightarrow 0.0209$; $2.09 \div 100 = 0.0209$

29. 0.65×0.1
    Move the decimal point 1 place to the left.
    $0.65 \rightarrow 0.065$; $0.65 \times 0.1 = 0.065$

30. $0.03 \div 100$
    Move the decimal point 2 places to the left.
    $0.03 \rightarrow 0.0003$; $0.03 \div 100 = 0.0003$

31. $2.6 \div 0.1$
    Move the decimal point 1 place to the right.
    $2.6 \rightarrow 26$; $2.6 \div 0.1 = 26$

32. $12.6 \times 10,000$
    Move the decimal point 4 places to the right.
    $12.6 \rightarrow 126,000$; $12.6 \times 10,000 = 126,000$

33. $0.3 \div 1,000$
    Move the decimal point 3 places to the left.
    $0.3 \rightarrow 0.0003$; $0.3 \div 1,000 = 0.0003$

34. 0.01×6.7
Move the decimal point 2 places to the right.
$6.7 \to 0.067; 0.01 \times 6.7 = 0.067$

35. 100×0.158
Move the decimal point 2 places to the right.
$0.158 \to 15.8; 100 \times 0.158 = 15.8$

36. $23.1 \div 10$
Move the decimal point 1 place to the left.
$23.1 \to 2.31; 23.1 \div 10 = 2.31$

Dividing a Decimal by a Decimal
Page 566

1. Multiply by 10.
```
        84
3.2.)268.8.
   -256
     12 8
    -12 8
        0
```

2. Multiply by 10.
```
        65
1.9.)123.5.
   -114
     9 5
    -9 5
       0
```

3. Multiply by 10.
```
       452
0.3.)135.6.
   -12
     15
    -15
      6
     -6
      0
```

4. Multiply by 10.
```
        74
2.3.)170.2.
   -161
     9 2
    -9 2
       0
```

5. Multiply by 10.
```
        32
7.9.)252.8.
   -237
     15 8
    -15 8
        0
```

6. Multiply by 10.
```
       1.8
5.7.)10.2.6
   -5 7
     4 5 6
    -4 5 6
         0
```

7. Multiply by 10.
```
       31.1
2.3.)71.5.3
   -69
     2 5
    -2 3
      2 3
     -2 3
        0
```

8. Multiply by 10.
```
        5.2
3.1.)16.1.2
   -15 5
      6 2
     -6 2
        0
```

9. Multiply by 10.
```
        3.1
7.8.)24.1.8
   -23 4
      7 8
     -7 8
        0
```

10. Multiply by 10.
```
        2.3
6.3.)14.4.9
   -12 6
      1 8 9
     -1 8 9
          0
```

11. Multiply by 100.
```
         26
5.17.)134.42.
    -103 4
      31 02
     -31 02
          0
```

12. Multiply by 100.
```
        26
3.46.)89.96.
    -69 2
     20 76
    -20 76
         0
```

13. Multiply by 100.
```
         31
5.18.)160.58.
    -155 4
       5 18
      -5 18
          0
```

14. Multiply by 100.
```
         17
6.27.)106.59.
    -62 7
     43 89
    -43 89
         0
```

15. Multiply by 10.
```
       16
3.9.)62.4.
   -39
     23 4
    -23 4
        0
```

16. Multiply by 10.
```
        31
8.4.)260.4.
   -252
      8 4
     -8 4
        0
```

17. Multiply by 10.
```
        44
7.2.)316.8.
   -288
     28 8
    -28 8
        0
```

18. Multiply by 10.
```
        56
2.9.)162.4.
   -145
     17 4
    -17 4
        0
```

19. Multiply by 100.
```
         2.8
0.54.)1.51.2
    -1 08
      43 2
     -43 2
         0
```

20. Multiply by 100.
```
         7.5
0.43.)3.22.5
    -3 01
      21 5
     -21 5
         0
```

21. Multiply by 100.

$$
\begin{array}{r}
3.6 \\
0.69.\overline{)2.48.4} \\
-2\,07 \\
\hline
41\,4 \\
-41\,4 \\
\hline
0
\end{array}
$$

22. Multiply by 10.

$$
\begin{array}{r}
93 \\
5.5.\overline{)511.5.} \\
-495 \\
\hline
16\,5 \\
-16\,5 \\
\hline
0
\end{array}
$$

31. Multiply by 10.

$$
\begin{array}{r}
0.53 \\
7.4.\overline{)3.9.22} \\
-3\,7\,0 \\
\hline
2\,22 \\
-2\,22 \\
\hline
0
\end{array}
$$

32. Multiply by 100.

$$
\begin{array}{r}
24 \\
0.98.\overline{)23.52.} \\
-19\,6 \\
\hline
3\,92 \\
-3\,92 \\
\hline
0
\end{array}
$$

23. Multiply by 10.

$$
\begin{array}{r}
1.24 \\
0.8.\overline{)0.9.92} \\
-8 \\
\hline
1\,9 \\
-1\,6 \\
\hline
32 \\
-32 \\
\hline
0
\end{array}
$$

24. Multiply by 100.

$$
\begin{array}{r}
90.6 \\
0.05.\overline{)4.53.} \\
-4\,5 \\
\hline
3\,0 \\
-3\,0 \\
\hline
0
\end{array}
$$

33. Multiply by 10.

$$
\begin{array}{r}
9.5 \\
7.5.\overline{)71.2.5} \\
-67\,5 \\
\hline
3\,75 \\
-3\,75 \\
\hline
0
\end{array}
$$

34. Multiply by 10.

$$
\begin{array}{r}
31 \\
3.7.\overline{)114.7.} \\
-111 \\
\hline
3\,7 \\
-3\,7 \\
\hline
0
\end{array}
$$

35. Multiply by 100.

$$
\begin{array}{r}
1.6 \\
0.52.\overline{)0.83.2} \\
-52 \\
\hline
312 \\
-312 \\
\hline
0
\end{array}
$$

36. Multiply by 100.

$$
\begin{array}{r}
12.5 \\
0.09.\overline{)1.12.5} \\
-9 \\
\hline
22 \\
-18 \\
\hline
4\,5 \\
-4\,5 \\
\hline
0
\end{array}
$$

25. Multiply by 100.

$$
\begin{array}{r}
58.3 \\
0.06.\overline{)3.49.8} \\
-3\,0 \\
\hline
49 \\
-48 \\
\hline
1\,8 \\
-1\,8 \\
\hline
0
\end{array}
$$

26. Multiply by 10.

$$
\begin{array}{r}
74 \\
0.8.\overline{)59.2.} \\
-56 \\
\hline
3\,2 \\
-3\,2 \\
\hline
0
\end{array}
$$

37. Multiply by 10.

$$
\begin{array}{r}
3.58 \\
2.7.\overline{)9.6.66} \\
-8\,1 \\
\hline
1\,56 \\
-1\,35 \\
\hline
2\,16 \\
-2\,16 \\
\hline
0
\end{array}
$$

38. Multiply by 10.

$$
\begin{array}{r}
0.16 \\
9.1.\overline{)1.4.56} \\
-9\,1 \\
\hline
5\,46 \\
-5\,46 \\
\hline
0
\end{array}
$$

27. Multiply by 100.

$$
\begin{array}{r}
31.4 \\
0.07.\overline{)2.19.8} \\
-2\,1 \\
\hline
9 \\
-7 \\
\hline
2\,8 \\
-2\,8 \\
\hline
0
\end{array}
$$

28. Multiply by 10.

$$
\begin{array}{r}
20.4 \\
0.7.\overline{)14.2.8} \\
-14 \\
\hline
2\,8 \\
-2\,8 \\
\hline
0
\end{array}
$$

39. Multiply by 10.

$$
\begin{array}{r}
0.243 \\
1.8.\overline{)0.4.374} \\
-3\,6 \\
\hline
77 \\
-72 \\
\hline
54 \\
-54 \\
\hline
0
\end{array}
$$

40. Multiply by 100.

$$
\begin{array}{r}
5.09 \\
0.46.\overline{)2.34.14} \\
-2\,30 \\
\hline
4\,14 \\
-4\,14 \\
\hline
0
\end{array}
$$

29. Multiply by 10.

$$
\begin{array}{r}
3.96 \\
0.5.\overline{)1.9.80} \\
-1\,5 \\
\hline
4\,8 \\
-4\,5 \\
\hline
40 \\
-40 \\
\hline
0
\end{array}
$$

30. Multiply by 100.

$$
\begin{array}{r}
659 \\
0.04.\overline{)26.36.} \\
-24 \\
\hline
2\,3 \\
-2\,0 \\
\hline
36 \\
-36 \\
\hline
0
\end{array}
$$

41. Multiply by 1,000.
```
          3.44
0.021.)0.072.24
       -63
         9 2
        -8 4
          84
         -84
           0
```

42. Multiply by 100.
```
         0.77
0.18.)0.13.86
      -12 6
        1 26
       -1 26
          0
```

5. Multiply by 10.
```
        0.0095
0.2.)0.0.0190
     -18
       10
      -10
        0
```

6. Multiply by 10.
```
        1.125
0.8.)0.9.000
     -8
      10
      -8
      20
     -16
      40
     -40
       0
```

43. Multiply by 1,000.
```
          1.86
0.091.)0.169.26
       -91
        78 2
       -72 8
         5 46
        -5 46
           0
```

44. Multiply by 10.
```
        0.114
5.3.)0.6.042
     -5 3
       74
      -53
      212
     -212
        0
```

7. Multiply by 100.
```
         0.0025
0.07.)0.00.0175
      -14
        35
       -35
         0
```

8. Multiply by 100.
```
         3.55
0.04.)0.14.20
      -12
        2 2
       -2 0
         20
        -20
          0
```

45. Multiply by 100.
```
         3.77
0.62.)2.33.74
      -1 86
        47 7
       -43 4
         4 34
        -4 34
           0
```

46. Multiply by 1,000.
```
          12.9
0.078)1.006.2
      -78
       226
      -156
        70 2
       -70 2
          0
```

9. Multiply by 100.
```
         0.085
0.02.)0.00.170
      -16
        10
       -10
         0
```

10. Multiply by 10.
```
        0.005
0.6.)0.0.030
     -30
       0
```

11. Multiply by 10.
```
        0.015
0.7.)0.0.105
     -7
      35
     -35
       0
```

12. Multiply by 100.
```
         0.68
0.05.)0.03.40
      -3 0
        40
       -40
         0
```

Zeros in Decimal Division
Page 567

1. Multiply by 100.
```
         0.046
0.05.)0.00.230
      -20
        30
       -30
         0
```

2. Multiply by 100.
```
         0.0081
0.02.)0.00.0162
      -16
        2
       -2
        0
```

13. Multiply by 1,000.
```
          0.0035
0.016.)0.000.5600
       -48
         80
        -80
          0
```

14. Multiply by 10.
```
        0.0085
7.2.)0.0.6120
     -576
       360
      -360
         0
```

3. Multiply by 100.
```
         0.075
0.12.)0.00.900
      -84
        60
       -60
         0
```

4. Multiply by 10.
```
        0.0084
2.5.)0.0.2100
     -200
       100
      -100
         0
```

15. Multiply by 10.

```
        0.057
3.1.)0.1.770
    −1 55
       220
      −220
         0
```

16. Multiply by 10.

```
        0.065
0.8.)0.0.520
    −48
      40
     −40
       0
```

27. Multiply by 10.

```
        0.0330
9.3.)0.3.069
    −2 79
       279
      −279
         0
```

28. Multiply by 10.

```
         0.0015
0.3.)0.0.0045
     −3
     15
    −15
      0
```

17. Multiply by 100.

```
          0.0021
0.44.)0.00.0924
     −88
      44
     −44
       0
```

18. Multiply by 100.

```
         0.092
0.63.)0.05.796
     −5 67
       126
      −126
         0
```

29. Multiply by 10.

```
        0.073
8.9.)0.6.497
    −6 23
       267
      −267
         0
```

30. Multiply by 100.

```
          0.41
0.06.)0.00.246
     −24
       6
      −6
       0
```

19. Multiply by 10.

```
         0.00015
8.2.)0.0.01230
    −82
      410
     −410
        0
```

20. Multiply by 100.

```
         1.06
0.09.)0.09.54
     −9
      54
     −54
       0
```

31. Multiply by 10.

```
        0.0056
0.3.)0.0.0168
    −15
      18
     −18
       0
```

32. Multiply by 10.

```
        0.0024
3.4.)0.0.0816
    −68
      136
     −136
        0
```

21. Multiply by 10.

```
        0.006
1.4.)0.0.084
    −84
      0
```

22. Multiply by 10.

```
        0.074
3.5.)0.2.590
    −245
      140
     −140
        0
```

Working with Integers
Page 568

1. 6   **2.** −10   **3.** 5   **4.** −4

5. 3   **6.** −8   **7.** 12   **8.** −4

9. 0 is to the right of − 1, so 0 > − 1.

10. − 9 is to the left of 0, so − 9 < 0.

11. − 3 is to the left of 3, so − 3 < 3.

12. 7 is to the right of − 3, so 7 > − 3.

13. 0 is to the left of 1, so 0 < 1.

14. 3 is to the right of 0, so 3 > 0.

15. 1 is to the right of − 4, so 1 > − 4.

16. − 2 is to the right of − 9, so − 2 > − 9.

17. 6 is to the right of − 1, so 6 > − 1.

18. 3 is to the right of − 10, so 3 > − 10.

19. − 7 is to the left of 3, so − 7 < 3.

20. 4 is to the left of 6, so 4 < 6.

21. − 16 is to the right of − 25, so − 16 > − 25.

22. − 15 is to the left of −12, so − 15 < − 12.

23. 7 is to the right of − 8, so 7 > − 8.

24. 2 is to the left of 3, so 2 < 3.

23. Multiply by 100.

```
          0.009
0.52.)0.00.468
     −468
        0
```

24. Multiply by 100.

```
         2.08
0.05.)0.10.400
     −10
       40
      −40
        0
```

25. Multiply by 100.

```
          0.0035
0.18.)0.00.0630
     −54
       90
      −90
        0
```

26. Multiply by 100.

```
         0.044
0.25.)0.01.100
     −1 00
       100
      −100
         0
```

25. -7 is to the right of -8, so $-7 > -8$.

26. 35 is to the right of -40, so $35 > -40$.

27. -30 is to the left of -20, so $-30 < -20$.

28. 25 is to the right of -25, so $25 > -25$.

29. 9 is to the right of -9, so $9 > -9$.

30. -6 is to the left of -5, so $-6 < -5$.

31. -23 is to the left of -15, so $-23 < -15$.

32. -17 is to the right of -19, so $-17 > -19$.

33. -15 is to the right of -25, so $-15 > -25$.

Working with Fractions
Page 569

1. 12 is a common denominator. Write $\frac{1}{3}$ as $\frac{4}{12}$.

$5 > 4$, so $\frac{5}{12} > \frac{1}{3}$.

2. 24 is a common denominator. Write $\frac{5}{8}$ as $\frac{15}{24}$.

$15 < 19$, so $\frac{5}{8} < \frac{19}{24}$.

3. 12 is a common denominator.

Write $\frac{1}{6}$ as $\frac{2}{12}$ and $\frac{3}{4}$ as $\frac{9}{12}$.

$2 < 9$, so $\frac{1}{6} < \frac{3}{4}$.

4. 12 is a common denominator.

Write $\frac{2}{3}$ as $\frac{8}{12}$ and $\frac{1}{4}$ as $\frac{3}{12}$.

$8 > 3$, so $\frac{2}{3} > \frac{1}{4}$.

5. 10 is a common denominator. Write $\frac{3}{5}$ as $\frac{6}{10}$.

$9 > 6$, so $\frac{9}{10} > \frac{3}{5}$.

6. 16 is a common denominator. Write $\frac{3}{8}$ as $\frac{6}{16}$.

$6 < 9$, so $\frac{3}{8} < \frac{9}{16}$.

7. The whole numbers are the same. 6 is a common denominator.

Write $\frac{2}{3}$ as $\frac{4}{6}$.

$1 < 4$, so $5\frac{1}{6} < 5\frac{2}{3}$.

8. $4 > 1$, so $4\frac{7}{12} > 1\frac{5}{8}$.

9. The whole numbers and the denominators are the same, so compare numerators.

$5 > 2$, so $2\frac{5}{9} > 2\frac{2}{9}$.

10. $4 > 2$, so $4\frac{5}{8} > 2\frac{1}{4}$.

11. 7 is closer to 8 than to one-half of 8 or 4, so $\frac{7}{8}$ is closest to 1.

12. One-half of 9 is 4.5, so $\frac{5}{9}$ is closest to $\frac{1}{2}$.

13. 1 is closer to 0, so $\frac{1}{12}$ is closest to 0.

14. One-half of 20 is 10, so $\frac{11}{20}$ is closest to $\frac{1}{2}$.

15. One-half of 7 is 3.5, so $\frac{3}{7}$ is closest to $\frac{1}{2}$.

16. 9 is closer to 11 than to one-half of 11 or 5.5, so $\frac{9}{11}$ is closest to 1.

17. 3 is closer to 0 than to one-half of 25 or 12.5, so $\frac{3}{25}$ is closest to 0.

18. $\frac{5}{10} = \frac{1}{2}$, so by convention $2\frac{5}{10}$ rounds up to 3.

19. $\frac{5}{9} > \frac{1}{2}$, so $1\frac{5}{9}$ rounds to 2.

20. $\frac{8}{16} = \frac{1}{2}$, so by convention $7\frac{8}{16}$ rounds up to 8.

21. $\frac{3}{8} < \frac{1}{2}$, so $8\frac{3}{8}$ rounds to 8.

22. $\frac{3}{7} < \frac{1}{2}$, so $1\frac{3}{7}$ rounds to 1.

23. $\frac{3}{4} > \frac{1}{2}$, so $3\frac{3}{4}$ rounds to 4.

24. $\frac{7}{8} > \frac{1}{2}$, so $5\frac{7}{8}$ rounds to 6.

25. $\frac{7}{8} > \frac{1}{2}$, so $6\frac{7}{8}$ rounds to 7.

26. $\frac{1}{3} < \frac{1}{2}$, so $3\frac{1}{3}$ rounds to 3.

27. $\frac{1}{12} < \frac{1}{2}$, so $5\frac{1}{12}$ rounds to 5.

28. $\frac{11}{20} > \frac{1}{2}$, so $2\frac{11}{20}$ rounds to 3.

29. $\frac{5}{12} < \frac{1}{2}$, so $6\frac{5}{12}$ rounds to 6.

30. $\frac{5}{6} > \frac{1}{2}$, so $7\frac{5}{6}$ rounds to 8.

31. $\frac{9}{10} > \frac{1}{2}$, so $8\frac{9}{10}$ rounds to 9.

Adding and Subtracting Fractions with Like Denominators
Page 570

1. $\frac{4}{5} + \frac{3}{5} = \frac{4+3}{5} = \frac{7}{5} = 1\frac{2}{5}$

2. $\frac{2}{6} - \frac{1}{6} = \frac{2-1}{6} = \frac{1}{6}$

3. $\frac{2}{7} + \frac{2}{7} = \frac{2+2}{7} = \frac{4}{7}$

4. $\frac{7}{8} + \frac{2}{8} = \frac{7+2}{8} = \frac{9}{8} = 1\frac{1}{8}$

5. $1\frac{2}{5} - \frac{1}{5} = 1 + \left(\frac{2}{5} - \frac{1}{5}\right) = 1 + \frac{2-1}{5} = 1\frac{1}{5}$

6. $\frac{3}{6} - \frac{1}{6} = \frac{3-1}{6} = \frac{2}{6} = \frac{1}{3}$

7. $\frac{6}{8} - \frac{3}{8} = \frac{6-3}{8} = \frac{3}{8}$

8. $\frac{2}{9} + \frac{1}{9} = \frac{2+1}{9} = \frac{3}{9} = \frac{1}{3}$

9. $\frac{4}{5} - \frac{1}{5} = \frac{4-1}{5} = \frac{3}{5}$

10. $\frac{5}{9} + \frac{7}{9} = \frac{5+7}{9} = \frac{12}{9} = 1\frac{3}{9} = 1\frac{1}{3}$

11.
$$9\frac{1}{3}$$
$$-8\frac{1}{3}$$
$$\overline{1}$$

12.
$$8\frac{6}{7}$$
$$-4\frac{2}{7}$$
$$\overline{4\frac{4}{7}}$$

13.
$$3\frac{1}{10}$$
$$+1\frac{3}{10}$$
$$\overline{4\frac{4}{10} = 4\frac{2}{5}}$$

14.
$$2\frac{2}{9}$$
$$+3\frac{4}{9}$$
$$\overline{5\frac{6}{9} = 5\frac{2}{3}}$$

15.
$$4\frac{5}{12}$$
$$-3\frac{1}{12}$$
$$\overline{1\frac{4}{12} = 1\frac{1}{3}}$$

16.
$$9\frac{5}{9}$$
$$+6\frac{7}{9}$$
$$\overline{15\frac{12}{9} =}$$
$$16\frac{3}{9} = 16\frac{1}{3}$$

17.
$$5\frac{7}{8}$$
$$+2\frac{3}{8}$$
$$\overline{7\frac{10}{8} = 8\frac{2}{8} = 8\frac{1}{4}}$$

18.
$$4\frac{4}{7}$$
$$-2\frac{1}{7}$$
$$\overline{2\frac{3}{7}}$$

19.
$$9\frac{3}{4}$$
$$+1\frac{3}{4}$$
$$\overline{10\frac{6}{4} = 11\frac{2}{4} = 11\frac{1}{2}}$$

20.
$$8\frac{2}{3}$$
$$-4\frac{1}{3}$$
$$\overline{4\frac{1}{3}}$$

21.
$$8\frac{7}{10}$$
$$+2\frac{3}{10}$$
$$\overline{10\frac{10}{10} = 11}$$

22.
$$1\frac{4}{5}$$
$$+3\frac{3}{5}$$
$$\overline{4\frac{7}{5} = 5\frac{2}{5}}$$

23. $7\frac{1}{5} \qquad 6\frac{6}{5}$
$$-2\frac{3}{5} \rightarrow -2\frac{3}{5}$$
$$\overline{4\frac{3}{5}}$$

24. $4\frac{1}{3} \qquad 3\frac{4}{3}$
$$-1\frac{2}{3} \rightarrow -1\frac{2}{3}$$
$$\overline{2\frac{2}{3}}$$

25. $4\frac{3}{8} \qquad 3\frac{11}{8}$
$$-3\frac{5}{8} \rightarrow -3\frac{5}{8}$$
$$\overline{\frac{6}{8} = \frac{3}{4}}$$

26. $5\frac{1}{12} \qquad 4\frac{13}{12}$
$$-2\frac{7}{12} \rightarrow -2\frac{7}{12}$$
$$\overline{2\frac{6}{12} = 2\frac{1}{2}}$$

Writing Equivalent Fractions
Page 571

1. Notice that 3 has been multiplied by 2.
$$\frac{1}{3} = \frac{1 \times 2}{3 \times 2} = \frac{2}{6}$$
$$\frac{1}{3} = \frac{2}{6}$$

2. Notice that 4 has been multiplied by 4.
$$\frac{3}{4} = \frac{3 \times 4}{4 \times 4} = \frac{12}{16}$$
$$\frac{3}{4} = \frac{12}{16}$$

3. Notice that 18 has been divided by 3.
$$\frac{18}{30} = \frac{18 \div 3}{30 \div 3} = \frac{6}{10}$$
$$\frac{18}{30} = \frac{6}{10}$$

4. Notice that 3 has been multiplied by 7.
$$\frac{2}{3} = \frac{2 \times 7}{3 \times 7} = \frac{14}{21}$$
$$\frac{2}{3} = \frac{14}{21}$$

5. Notice that 3 has been multiplied by 3.
$$\frac{3}{4} = \frac{3 \times 3}{4 \times 3} = \frac{9}{12}$$
$$\frac{3}{4} = \frac{9}{12}$$

6. Notice that 3 has been multiplied by 3.
$$\frac{3}{10} = \frac{3 \times 3}{10 \times 3} = \frac{9}{30}$$
$$\frac{3}{10} = \frac{9}{30}$$

7. Notice that 5 has been multiplied by 6.
$$\frac{4}{5} = \frac{4 \times 6}{5 \times 6} = \frac{24}{30}$$
$$\frac{4}{5} = \frac{24}{30}$$

8. Notice that 2 has been multiplied by 4.
$$\frac{2}{3} = \frac{2 \times 4}{3 \times 4} = \frac{8}{12}$$
$$\frac{2}{3} = \frac{8}{12}$$

9. Notice that 55 has been divided by 11.
$$\frac{33}{55} = \frac{33 \div 11}{55 \div 11} = \frac{3}{5}$$
$$\frac{33}{55} = \frac{3}{5}$$

10. Notice that 27 has been divided by 3.
$$\frac{27}{72} = \frac{27 \div 3}{72 \div 3} = \frac{9}{24}$$
$$\frac{27}{72} = \frac{9}{24}$$

11. Notice that 3 has been multiplied by 8.

$\frac{2}{3} = \frac{2 \times 8}{3 \times 8} = \frac{16}{24}$

$\frac{2}{3} = \frac{16}{24}$

12. Notice that 11 has been multiplied by 5.

$\frac{11}{12} = \frac{11 \times 5}{12 \times 5} = \frac{55}{60}$

$\frac{11}{12} = \frac{55}{60}$

13. Notice that 3 has been multiplied by 6.

$\frac{3}{5} = \frac{3 \times 6}{5 \times 6} = \frac{18}{30}$

$\frac{3}{5} = \frac{18}{30}$

14. Notice that 60 has been divided by 6.

$\frac{60}{72} = \frac{60 \div 6}{72 \div 6} = \frac{10}{12}$

$\frac{60}{72} = \frac{10}{12}$

15. Notice that 8 has been multiplied by 3.

$\frac{7}{8} = \frac{7 \times 3}{8 \times 3} = \frac{21}{24}$

$\frac{7}{8} = \frac{21}{24}$

16. 12 is the greatest common factor.

$\frac{12}{36} = \frac{12 \div 12}{36 \div 12} = \frac{1}{3}$

The simplest form of $\frac{12}{36}$ is $\frac{1}{3}$.

17. 5 is the greatest common factor.

$\frac{25}{30} = \frac{25 \div 5}{30 \div 5} = \frac{5}{6}$

The simplest form of $\frac{25}{30}$ is $\frac{5}{6}$.

18. 2 is the greatest common factor.

$\frac{14}{16} = \frac{14 \div 2}{16 \div 2} = \frac{7}{8}$

The simplest form of $\frac{14}{16}$ is $\frac{7}{8}$.

19. 9 is the greatest common factor.

$\frac{27}{36} = \frac{27 \div 9}{36 \div 9} = \frac{3}{4}$

The simplest form of $\frac{27}{36}$ is $\frac{3}{4}$.

20. 7 is the greatest common factor.

$\frac{21}{35} = \frac{21 \div 7}{35 \div 7} = \frac{3}{5}$

The simplest form of $\frac{21}{35}$ is $\frac{3}{5}$.

21. 10 is the greatest common factor.

$\frac{40}{50} = \frac{40 \div 10}{50 \div 10} = \frac{4}{5}$

The simplest form of $\frac{40}{50}$ is $\frac{4}{5}$.

22. 8 is the greatest common factor.

$\frac{24}{40} = \frac{24 \div 8}{40 \div 8} = \frac{3}{5}$

The simplest form of $\frac{24}{40}$ is $\frac{3}{5}$.

23. 32 is the greatest common factor.

$\frac{32}{64} = \frac{32 \div 32}{64 \div 32} = \frac{1}{2}$

The simplest form of $\frac{32}{64}$ is $\frac{1}{2}$.

24. 15 is the greatest common factor.

$\frac{15}{45} = \frac{15 \div 15}{45 \div 15} = \frac{1}{3}$

The simplest form of $\frac{15}{45}$ is $\frac{1}{3}$.

25. 9 is the greatest common factor.

$\frac{27}{63} = \frac{27 \div 9}{63 \div 9} = \frac{3}{7}$

The simplest form of $\frac{27}{63}$ is $\frac{3}{7}$.

26. 11 is the greatest common factor.

$\frac{44}{77} = \frac{44 \div 11}{77 \div 11} = \frac{4}{7}$

The simplest form of $\frac{44}{77}$ is $\frac{4}{7}$.

27. 15 is the greatest common factor.

$\frac{45}{75} = \frac{45 \div 15}{75 \div 15} = \frac{3}{5}$

The simplest form of $\frac{45}{75}$ is $\frac{3}{5}$.

28. 12 is the greatest common factor.

$\frac{60}{72} = \frac{60 \div 12}{72 \div 12} = \frac{5}{6}$

The simplest form of $\frac{60}{72}$ is $\frac{5}{6}$.

29. 7 is the greatest common factor.

$\frac{77}{84} = \frac{77 \div 7}{84 \div 7} = \frac{11}{12}$

The simplest form of $\frac{77}{84}$ is $\frac{11}{12}$.

30. 12 is the greatest common factor.

$\frac{12}{24} = \frac{12 \div 12}{24 \div 12} = \frac{1}{2}$

The simplest form of $\frac{12}{24}$ is $\frac{1}{2}$.

31. 8 is the greatest common factor.

$\frac{24}{32} = \frac{24 \div 8}{32 \div 8} = \frac{3}{4}$

The simplest form of $\frac{24}{32}$ is $\frac{3}{4}$.

32. 7 is the greatest common factor.

$\frac{7}{21} = \frac{7 \div 7}{21 \div 7} = \frac{1}{3}$

The simplest form of $\frac{7}{21}$ is $\frac{1}{3}$.

33. 6 is the greatest common factor.

$$\frac{18}{42} = \frac{18 \div 6}{42 \div 6} = \frac{3}{7}$$

The simplest form of $\frac{18}{42}$ is $\frac{3}{7}$.

34. 7 is the greatest common factor.

$$\frac{35}{49} = \frac{35 \div 7}{49 \div 7} = \frac{5}{7}$$

The simplest form of $\frac{35}{49}$ is $\frac{5}{7}$.

35. 9 is the greatest common factor.

$$\frac{18}{81} = \frac{18 \div 9}{81 \div 9} = \frac{2}{9}$$

The simplest form of $\frac{18}{81}$ is $\frac{2}{9}$.

36. 6 is the greatest common factor.

$$\frac{6}{18} = \frac{6 \div 6}{18 \div 6} = \frac{1}{3}$$

The simplest form of $\frac{6}{18}$ is $\frac{1}{3}$.

37. 28 is the greatest common factor.

$$\frac{28}{56} = \frac{28 \div 28}{56 \div 28} = \frac{1}{2}$$

The simplest form of $\frac{28}{56}$ is $\frac{1}{2}$.

38. 5 is the greatest common factor.

$$\frac{10}{25} = \frac{10 \div 5}{25 \div 5} = \frac{2}{5}$$

The simplest form of $\frac{10}{25}$ is $\frac{2}{5}$.

39. 4 is the greatest common factor.

$$\frac{16}{28} = \frac{16 \div 4}{28 \div 4} = \frac{4}{7}$$

The simplest form of $\frac{16}{28}$ is $\frac{4}{7}$.

40. 6 is the greatest common factor.

$$\frac{30}{48} = \frac{30 \div 6}{48 \div 6} = \frac{5}{8}$$

The simplest form of $\frac{30}{48}$ is $\frac{5}{8}$.

41. 11 is the greatest common factor.

$$\frac{22}{55} = \frac{22 \div 11}{55 \div 11} = \frac{2}{5}$$

The simplest form of $\frac{22}{55}$ is $\frac{2}{5}$.

42. 20 is the greatest common factor.

$$\frac{80}{100} = \frac{80 \div 20}{100 \div 20} = \frac{4}{5}$$

The simplest form of $\frac{80}{100}$ is $\frac{4}{5}$.

43. 8 is the greatest common factor.

$$\frac{16}{88} = \frac{16 \div 8}{88 \div 8} = \frac{2}{11}$$

The simplest form of $\frac{16}{88}$ is $\frac{2}{11}$.

Adding and Subtracting Fractions with Unlike Denominators

Page 572

1. $\begin{array}{cc} \frac{5}{12} & \frac{5}{12} \\ -\frac{1}{3} & \rightarrow -\frac{4}{12} \\ \hline & \frac{1}{12} \end{array}$

2. $\begin{array}{cc} \frac{1}{2} & \frac{3}{6} \\ +\frac{2}{3} & \rightarrow +\frac{4}{6} \\ \hline & \frac{7}{6} = 1\frac{1}{6} \end{array}$

3. $\begin{array}{cc} \frac{2}{9} & \frac{8}{36} \\ +\frac{3}{4} & \rightarrow +\frac{27}{36} \\ \hline & \frac{35}{36} \end{array}$

4. $\begin{array}{cc} \frac{2}{3} & \frac{8}{12} \\ -\frac{1}{4} & \rightarrow -\frac{3}{12} \\ \hline & \frac{5}{12} \end{array}$

5. $\begin{array}{cc} \frac{5}{8} & \frac{15}{24} \\ +\frac{2}{3} & \rightarrow +\frac{16}{24} \\ \hline & \frac{31}{24} = 1\frac{7}{24} \end{array}$

6. $\begin{array}{cc} \frac{2}{5} & \frac{4}{10} \\ +\frac{3}{10} & \rightarrow +\frac{3}{10} \\ \hline & \frac{7}{10} \end{array}$

7. $\begin{array}{cc} \frac{19}{24} & \frac{19}{24} \\ -\frac{5}{8} & \rightarrow -\frac{15}{24} \\ \hline & \frac{4}{24} = \frac{1}{6} \end{array}$

8. $\begin{array}{cc} \frac{1}{2} & \frac{5}{10} \\ +\frac{2}{5} & \rightarrow +\frac{4}{10} \\ \hline & \frac{9}{10} \end{array}$

9.
$$\frac{1}{5} \qquad \frac{7}{35}$$
$$+\frac{3}{7} \rightarrow +\frac{15}{35}$$
$$\frac{22}{35}$$

10.
$$\frac{5}{9} \qquad \frac{20}{36}$$
$$+\frac{3}{4} \rightarrow +\frac{27}{36}$$
$$\frac{47}{36} = 1\frac{11}{36}$$

11.
$$\frac{9}{16} \qquad \frac{9}{16}$$
$$+\frac{3}{8} \rightarrow +\frac{6}{16}$$
$$\frac{15}{16}$$

12.
$$\frac{3}{10} \qquad \frac{9}{30}$$
$$+\frac{2}{15} \rightarrow +\frac{4}{30}$$
$$\frac{13}{30}$$

13.
$$\frac{3}{4} \qquad \frac{9}{12}$$
$$-\frac{1}{6} \rightarrow -\frac{2}{12}$$
$$\frac{7}{12}$$

14.
$$\frac{1}{4} \qquad \frac{5}{20}$$
$$-\frac{5}{20} \rightarrow -\frac{5}{10}$$
$$0$$

15.
$$\frac{9}{10} \qquad \frac{9}{10}$$
$$-\frac{3}{5} \rightarrow -\frac{6}{10}$$
$$\frac{3}{10}$$

16.
$$6\frac{3}{4} \qquad 6\frac{9}{12}$$
$$+1\frac{2}{3} \rightarrow +1\frac{8}{12}$$
$$7\frac{17}{12} = 8\frac{5}{12}$$

17.
$$4\frac{7}{12} \qquad 4\frac{14}{24} \qquad 3\frac{38}{24}$$
$$-1\frac{5}{8} \rightarrow -1\frac{15}{24} \rightarrow -1\frac{15}{24}$$
$$2\frac{23}{24}$$

18.
$$5\frac{4}{5} \qquad 5\frac{8}{10}$$
$$+2\frac{3}{10} \rightarrow +2\frac{3}{10}$$
$$7\frac{11}{10} = 8\frac{1}{10}$$

19.
$$5 \qquad 4\frac{4}{4}$$
$$-3\frac{3}{4} \rightarrow -3\frac{3}{4}$$
$$1\frac{1}{4}$$

20.
$$4\frac{11}{12} \qquad 4\frac{55}{60}$$
$$+3\frac{1}{5} \rightarrow +3\frac{12}{60}$$
$$7\frac{67}{60} = 8\frac{7}{60}$$

21.
$$2\frac{5}{8} \qquad 2\frac{5}{8}$$
$$-1\frac{1}{4} \rightarrow -1\frac{2}{8}$$
$$1\frac{3}{8}$$

22.
$$9\frac{5}{18} \qquad 9\frac{5}{18} \qquad 8\frac{23}{18}$$
$$-2\frac{1}{3} \rightarrow -2\frac{6}{18} \rightarrow -2\frac{6}{18}$$
$$6\frac{17}{18}$$

23.
$$7\frac{4}{9} \qquad 7\frac{8}{18}$$
$$+1\frac{5}{6} \rightarrow +1\frac{15}{18}$$
$$8\frac{23}{18} = 9\frac{5}{18}$$

24.
$$5\frac{2}{3} \qquad 5\frac{4}{6}$$
$$-2\frac{1}{6} \rightarrow -2\frac{1}{6}$$
$$3\frac{3}{6} = 3\frac{1}{2}$$

25.
$$4\frac{5}{6} \qquad 4\frac{10}{12}$$
$$+1\frac{3}{4} \rightarrow +1\frac{9}{12}$$
$$5\frac{19}{12} = 6\frac{7}{12}$$

26.
$$4\frac{5}{8} \qquad 4\frac{5}{8}$$
$$-2\frac{1}{4} \rightarrow -2\frac{2}{8}$$
$$2\frac{3}{8}$$

27.

$$7\frac{2}{3} \qquad 7\frac{10}{15}$$
$$+4\frac{4}{5} \to +4\frac{12}{15}$$
$$\overline{\qquad} \qquad \overline{11\frac{22}{15} = 12\frac{7}{15}}$$

Multiplying Fractions and Mixed Numbers

Page 573

1. $\frac{3}{4} \times \frac{3}{5} = \frac{3 \times 3}{4 \times 5} = \frac{9}{20}$

2. $\frac{2}{3} \times \frac{3}{4} = \frac{\overset{1}{\cancel{2}}}{\underset{1}{\cancel{3}}} \times \frac{\overset{1}{\cancel{3}}}{\underset{2}{\cancel{4}}} = \frac{1}{2}$

3. $6 \times \frac{2}{3} = \frac{12}{3} = 4$

4. $\frac{3}{4} \times \frac{5}{6} = \frac{3}{4} \times \frac{5}{\underset{2}{\cancel{6}}} = \frac{5}{8}$

5. $\frac{5}{8} \times \frac{2}{3} = \frac{5}{\underset{4}{\cancel{8}}} \times \frac{\overset{1}{\cancel{2}}}{3} = \frac{5}{12}$

6. $\frac{2}{5} \times \frac{3}{10} = \frac{2}{5} \times \frac{3}{\underset{5}{\cancel{10}}} = \frac{3}{25}$

7. $\frac{4}{9} \times \frac{3}{8} = \frac{\overset{1}{\cancel{4}}}{\underset{3}{\cancel{9}}} \times \frac{\overset{1}{\cancel{3}}}{\underset{2}{\cancel{8}}} = \frac{1}{6}$

8. $\frac{1}{2} \times \frac{2}{5} = \frac{1}{\cancel{2}} \times \frac{\overset{1}{\cancel{2}}}{5} = \frac{1}{5}$

9. $\frac{1}{6} \times \frac{3}{7} = \frac{1}{\underset{2}{\cancel{6}}} \times \frac{\overset{1}{\cancel{3}}}{7} = \frac{1}{14}$

10. $\frac{5}{9} \times \frac{3}{4} = \frac{5}{\underset{3}{\cancel{9}}} \times \frac{\overset{1}{\cancel{3}}}{4} = \frac{5}{12}$

11. $\frac{9}{16} \times \frac{2}{3} = \frac{\overset{3}{\cancel{9}}}{\underset{8}{\cancel{16}}} \times \frac{\overset{1}{\cancel{2}}}{\underset{1}{\cancel{3}}} = \frac{3}{8}$

12. $\frac{3}{10} \times \frac{2}{15} = \frac{\overset{1}{\cancel{3}}}{\underset{5}{\cancel{10}}} \times \frac{\overset{1}{\cancel{2}}}{\underset{5}{\cancel{15}}} = \frac{1}{25}$

13. $\frac{3}{4} \times \frac{1}{6} = \frac{3}{4} \times \frac{1}{\underset{2}{\cancel{6}}} = \frac{1}{8}$

14. $\frac{1}{4} \times \frac{5}{20} = \frac{1}{4} \times \frac{\overset{1}{\cancel{5}}}{\underset{4}{\cancel{20}}} = \frac{1}{16}$

15. $\frac{9}{10} \times \frac{1}{3} = \frac{\overset{3}{\cancel{9}}}{10} \times \frac{1}{\underset{1}{\cancel{3}}} = \frac{3}{10}$

16. $\frac{4}{9} \times \frac{3}{5} = \frac{4}{\underset{3}{\cancel{9}}} \times \frac{\overset{1}{\cancel{3}}}{5} = \frac{4}{15}$

17. $\frac{5}{9} \times \frac{2}{3} = \frac{5 \times 2}{9 \times 3} = \frac{10}{27}$

18. $\frac{3}{10} \times \frac{2}{9} = \frac{\overset{1}{\cancel{3}}}{\underset{5}{\cancel{10}}} \times \frac{\overset{1}{\cancel{2}}}{\underset{3}{\cancel{9}}} = \frac{1}{15}$

19. $\frac{4}{5} \times \frac{3}{8} = \frac{\overset{1}{\cancel{4}}}{5} \times \frac{3}{\underset{2}{\cancel{8}}} = \frac{3}{10}$

20. $\frac{5}{12} \times \frac{2}{3} = \frac{5}{\underset{6}{\cancel{12}}} \times \frac{\overset{1}{\cancel{2}}}{3} = \frac{5}{18}$

21. $1\frac{1}{3} \times 2\frac{2}{3} = \frac{4}{3} \times \frac{8}{3} = \frac{32}{9} = 3\frac{5}{9}$

22. $\frac{3}{5} \times 2\frac{3}{4} = \frac{3}{5} \times \frac{11}{4} = \frac{33}{20} = 1\frac{13}{20}$

23. $2\frac{1}{4} \times 3\frac{1}{3} = \frac{9}{4} \times \frac{10}{3} = \frac{\overset{3}{\cancel{9}}}{\underset{2}{\cancel{4}}} \times \frac{\overset{5}{\cancel{10}}}{\underset{1}{\cancel{3}}} = \frac{15}{2} = 7\frac{1}{2}$

24. $\frac{1}{4} \times 3\frac{1}{3} = \frac{1}{4} \times \frac{10}{3} = \frac{1}{\underset{2}{\cancel{4}}} \times \frac{\overset{5}{\cancel{10}}}{3} = \frac{5}{6}$

25. $6\frac{1}{4} \times 7 = \frac{25}{4} \times 7 = \frac{175}{4} = 43\frac{3}{4}$

26. $1\frac{3}{4} \times 2\frac{1}{5} = \frac{7}{4} \times \frac{11}{5} = \frac{77}{20} = 3\frac{17}{20}$

27. $2\frac{3}{4} \times \frac{1}{2} = \frac{11}{4} \times \frac{1}{2} = \frac{11}{8} = 1\frac{3}{8}$

28. $3\frac{4}{5} \times 2\frac{1}{3} = \frac{19}{5} \times \frac{7}{3} = \frac{133}{5} = 8\frac{13}{15}$

29. $2\frac{1}{2} \times 1\frac{2}{3} = \frac{5}{2} \times \frac{5}{3} = \frac{25}{6} = 4\frac{1}{6}$

30. $4 \times 2\frac{3}{11} = 4 \times \frac{25}{11} = \frac{100}{11} = 9\frac{1}{11}$

31. $5\frac{3}{4} \times 6\frac{3}{8} = \frac{23}{4} \times \frac{51}{8} = \frac{1,173}{32} = 36\frac{21}{32}$

32. $3\frac{4}{5} \times \frac{2}{3} = \frac{19}{5} \times \frac{2}{3} = \frac{38}{15} = 2\frac{8}{15}$

Dividing Fractions and Mixed Numbers

Page 574

1. $\dfrac{5}{8} \div \dfrac{5}{7} = \dfrac{5}{8} \times \dfrac{7}{5} = \dfrac{\cancel{5}^{1}}{8} \times \dfrac{7}{\cancel{5}_{1}} = \dfrac{7}{8}$

2. $\dfrac{5}{7} \div \dfrac{5}{8} = \dfrac{5}{7} \times \dfrac{8}{5} = \dfrac{\cancel{5}^{1}}{7} \times \dfrac{8}{\cancel{5}_{1}} = \dfrac{8}{7} = 1\dfrac{1}{7}$

3. $\dfrac{3}{4} \div \dfrac{6}{11} = \dfrac{3}{4} \times \dfrac{11}{6} = \dfrac{\cancel{3}^{1}}{4} \times \dfrac{11}{\cancel{6}_{2}} = \dfrac{11}{8} = 1\dfrac{3}{8}$

4. $\dfrac{1}{9} \div \dfrac{1}{9} = \dfrac{1}{9} \times 9 = 1$

5. $\dfrac{1}{9} \div 9 = \dfrac{1}{9} \times \dfrac{1}{9} = \dfrac{1}{81}$

6. $\dfrac{3}{5} \div \dfrac{3}{4} = \dfrac{3}{5} \times \dfrac{4}{3} = \dfrac{\cancel{3}^{1}}{5} \times \dfrac{4}{\cancel{3}_{1}} = \dfrac{4}{5}$

7. $\dfrac{8}{9} \div \dfrac{2}{3} = \dfrac{8}{9} \times \dfrac{3}{2} = \dfrac{\cancel{8}^{4}}{\cancel{9}_{3}} \times \dfrac{\cancel{3}^{1}}{\cancel{2}_{1}} = \dfrac{4}{3} = 1\dfrac{1}{3}$

8. $\dfrac{1}{16} \div \dfrac{1}{2} = \dfrac{1}{16} \times 2 = \dfrac{2}{16} = \dfrac{1}{8}$

9. $\dfrac{4}{5} \div \dfrac{7}{10} = \dfrac{4}{5} \times \dfrac{10}{7} = \dfrac{4}{\cancel{5}_{1}} \times \dfrac{\cancel{10}^{2}}{7} = \dfrac{8}{7} = 1\dfrac{1}{7}$

10. $\dfrac{4}{9} \div \dfrac{4}{7} = \dfrac{4}{9} \times \dfrac{7}{4} = \dfrac{\cancel{4}}{9} \times \dfrac{7}{\cancel{4}_{1}} = \dfrac{7}{9}$

11. $\dfrac{9}{10} \div \dfrac{3}{5} = \dfrac{9}{10} \times \dfrac{5}{3} = \dfrac{\cancel{9}^{3}}{\cancel{10}_{2}} \times \dfrac{\cancel{5}^{1}}{\cancel{3}_{1}} = \dfrac{3}{2} = 1\dfrac{1}{2}$

12. $\dfrac{2}{3} \div \dfrac{1}{9} = \dfrac{2}{3} \times 9 = \dfrac{18}{3} = 6$

13. $\dfrac{4}{5} \div \dfrac{5}{6} = \dfrac{4}{5} \times \dfrac{6}{5} = \dfrac{24}{25}$

14. $\dfrac{1}{5} \div \dfrac{8}{9} = \dfrac{1}{5} \times \dfrac{9}{8} = \dfrac{9}{40}$

15. $\dfrac{7}{8} \div \dfrac{1}{3} = \dfrac{7}{8} \times 3 = \dfrac{21}{8} = 2\dfrac{5}{8}$

16. $\dfrac{2}{3} \div \dfrac{3}{7} = \dfrac{2}{3} \times \dfrac{7}{3} = \dfrac{14}{9} = 1\dfrac{5}{9}$

17. $\dfrac{5}{6} \div \dfrac{3}{4} = \dfrac{5}{6} \times \dfrac{4}{3} = \dfrac{5}{\cancel{6}_{3}} \times \dfrac{\cancel{4}^{2}}{3} = \dfrac{10}{9} = 1\dfrac{1}{9}$

18. $\dfrac{2}{5} \div \dfrac{4}{5} = \dfrac{2}{5} \times \dfrac{5}{4} = \dfrac{\cancel{2}^{1}}{\cancel{5}_{1}} \times \dfrac{\cancel{5}^{1}}{\cancel{4}_{2}} = \dfrac{1}{2}$

19. $\dfrac{3}{10} \div \dfrac{3}{5} = \dfrac{3}{10} \times \dfrac{5}{3} = \dfrac{\cancel{3}^{1}}{\cancel{10}_{2}} \times \dfrac{\cancel{5}^{1}}{\cancel{3}_{1}} = \dfrac{1}{2}$

20. $4 \div \dfrac{2}{3} = 4 \times \dfrac{3}{2} = 4 \times \dfrac{3}{2} = \dfrac{12}{2} = 6$

21. $4\dfrac{1}{5} \div 2\dfrac{2}{5} = \dfrac{21}{5} \div \dfrac{12}{5} = \dfrac{21}{5} \times \dfrac{5}{12} = \dfrac{\cancel{21}^{7}}{\cancel{5}_{1}} \times \dfrac{\cancel{5}^{1}}{\cancel{12}_{4}} = \dfrac{7}{4} = 1\dfrac{3}{4}$

22. $6\dfrac{1}{4} \div 4\dfrac{3}{8} = \dfrac{25}{4} \div \dfrac{35}{8} = \dfrac{25}{4} \times \dfrac{8}{35} = \dfrac{\cancel{25}^{5}}{\cancel{4}_{1}} \times \dfrac{\cancel{8}^{2}}{\cancel{35}_{7}} = \dfrac{10}{7} = 1\dfrac{3}{7}$

23. $2\dfrac{1}{3} \div 5\dfrac{5}{6} = \dfrac{7}{3} \div \dfrac{35}{6} = \dfrac{7}{3} \times \dfrac{6}{35} = \dfrac{\cancel{7}^{1}}{\cancel{3}_{1}} \times \dfrac{\cancel{6}^{2}}{\cancel{35}_{5}} = \dfrac{2}{5}$

24. $1\dfrac{1}{2} \div 4\dfrac{1}{2} = \dfrac{3}{2} \div \dfrac{9}{2} = \dfrac{3}{2} \times \dfrac{2}{9} = \dfrac{\cancel{3}^{1}}{\cancel{2}_{1}} \times \dfrac{\cancel{2}^{1}}{\cancel{9}_{3}} = \dfrac{1}{3}$

25. $2\dfrac{1}{12} \div 4\dfrac{1}{6} = \dfrac{25}{12} \div \dfrac{25}{6} = \dfrac{25}{12} \times \dfrac{6}{25} = \dfrac{\cancel{25}^{1}}{\cancel{12}_{2}} \times \dfrac{\cancel{6}^{1}}{\cancel{25}_{1}} = \dfrac{1}{2}$

26. $4\dfrac{1}{2} \div \dfrac{3}{4} = \dfrac{9}{2} \div \dfrac{3}{4} = \dfrac{9}{2} \times \dfrac{4}{3} = \dfrac{\cancel{9}^{3}}{\cancel{2}_{1}} \times \dfrac{\cancel{4}^{2}}{\cancel{3}_{1}} = 6$

27. $3\dfrac{1}{8} \div 2\dfrac{2}{3} = \dfrac{25}{8} \div \dfrac{8}{3} = \dfrac{25}{8} \times \dfrac{3}{8} = \dfrac{75}{64} = 1\dfrac{11}{64}$

28. $14 \div 5\dfrac{1}{4} = 14 \div \dfrac{21}{4} = 14 \times \dfrac{4}{21} = \cancel{14} \times \dfrac{4}{\cancel{21}_{3}} = \dfrac{8}{3} = 2\dfrac{2}{3}$

29. $15\dfrac{2}{3} \div 1\dfrac{1}{3} = \dfrac{47}{3} \div \dfrac{4}{3} = \dfrac{47}{3} \times \dfrac{3}{4} = \dfrac{47}{\cancel{3}} \times \dfrac{\cancel{3}^{1}}{4} = \dfrac{47}{4} = 11\dfrac{3}{4}$

30. $10\dfrac{1}{3} \div 2\dfrac{1}{5} = \dfrac{31}{3} \div \dfrac{11}{5} = \dfrac{31}{3} \times \dfrac{5}{11} = \dfrac{155}{33} = 4\dfrac{23}{33}$

31. $6\dfrac{1}{4} \div 1\dfrac{3}{4} = \dfrac{25}{4} \div \dfrac{7}{4} = \dfrac{25}{4} \times \dfrac{4}{7} = \dfrac{25}{\cancel{4}} \times \dfrac{\cancel{4}^{1}}{7} = \dfrac{25}{7} = 3\dfrac{4}{7}$

32. $6\dfrac{2}{3} \div 3\dfrac{1}{8} = \dfrac{20}{3} \div \dfrac{25}{8} = \dfrac{20}{3} \times \dfrac{8}{25} = \dfrac{\cancel{20}^{4}}{3} \times \dfrac{8}{\cancel{25}_{5}} = \dfrac{32}{15} = 2\dfrac{2}{15}$

33. $15\frac{1}{2} \div 4 = \frac{31}{2} \div 4 = \frac{31}{2} \times \frac{1}{4} = \frac{31}{8} = 3\frac{7}{8}$

34. $12\frac{3}{5} \div \frac{3}{10} = \frac{63}{5} \div \frac{3}{10} = \frac{63}{5} \times \frac{10}{3} = \frac{\overset{21}{\cancel{63}}}{\underset{1}{\cancel{5}}} \times \frac{\overset{2}{\cancel{10}}}{\underset{1}{\cancel{3}}} = 42$

35. $1\frac{2}{3} \div 2\frac{1}{12} = \frac{5}{3} \div \frac{25}{12} = \frac{5}{3} \times \frac{12}{25} = \frac{\overset{1}{\cancel{5}}}{\underset{1}{\cancel{3}}} \times \frac{\overset{4}{\cancel{12}}}{\underset{5}{\cancel{25}}} = \frac{4}{5}$

36. $3\frac{1}{8} \div 1\frac{1}{4} = \frac{25}{8} \div \frac{5}{4} = \frac{25}{8} \times \frac{4}{5} = \frac{\overset{5}{\cancel{25}}}{\underset{2}{\cancel{8}}} \times \frac{\overset{1}{\cancel{4}}}{\underset{1}{\cancel{5}}} = \frac{5}{2} = 2\frac{1}{2}$

37. $5\frac{1}{4} \div 1\frac{1}{6} = \frac{21}{4} \div \frac{7}{6} = \frac{21}{4} \times \frac{6}{7} = \frac{\overset{3}{\cancel{21}}}{\underset{2}{\cancel{4}}} \times \frac{\overset{3}{\cancel{6}}}{\underset{1}{\cancel{7}}} = \frac{9}{2} = 4\frac{1}{2}$

38. $10 \div 2\frac{2}{3} = 10 \div \frac{8}{3} = 10 \times \frac{3}{8} = \overset{5}{\cancel{10}} \times \frac{3}{\underset{4}{\cancel{8}}} = \frac{15}{4} = 3\frac{3}{4}$

39. $7\frac{1}{3} \div \frac{2}{3} = \frac{22}{3} \div \frac{2}{3} = \frac{22}{3} \times \frac{3}{2} = \frac{\overset{11}{\cancel{22}}}{\underset{1}{\cancel{3}}} \times \frac{\overset{1}{\cancel{3}}}{\underset{1}{\cancel{2}}} = 11$

40. $4\frac{1}{5} \div 2\frac{1}{5} = \frac{21}{5} \div \frac{11}{5} = \frac{21}{5} \times \frac{5}{11} = \frac{21}{\cancel{5}} \times \frac{\overset{1}{\cancel{5}}}{11} = \frac{21}{11} = 1\frac{10}{11}$

Chapter 1

Page 34

1.
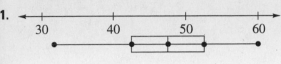

2. 48   **3.** 43   **4.** 54

5. 32   **6.** 60   **7.** $60 - 32 = 28$

Chapter 1

Page 37

1. 81%   **2.** 83%

3. Connecticut   **4.** Massachusetts and Rhode Island

5. 10–13   **6.** 18–19

7. 6,555,000   **8.** 10,976,000

Chapter 1

Page 56

Answers will vary slightly when using the calculator π key versus approximations such as $\frac{22}{7}$ or 3.14.

1. Use $C = \pi d$ and $d = 5$ cm.

3.14 ⨉ 5 = **15.7**

The circumference is about 15.7 cm.

2. Use $C = \pi d$ and $d = 6$ ft.

3.14 ⨉ 6 = **18.84**

The circumference is about 18.8 ft.

3. Use $C = \pi d$ and $d = 25$ in.

3.14 ⨉ 25 = **78.5**

The circumference is about 78.5 in.

4. Use $C = \pi d$ and $d = 3.2$ m.

3.14 ⨉ 3.2 = **10.048**

The circumference is about 10.0 m.

5. Use $C = \pi d$ and $d = 70$ mm.

3.14 ⨉ 70 = **219.8**

The circumference is about 219.8 mm.

6. Use $C = 2\pi r$ and $r = 100$ mm.

2 ⨉ 3.14 ⨉ 100 = **628**

The circumference is about 628 mm.

7. Use $C = 2\pi r$ and $r = 2.5$ mm.

2 ⨉ 3.14 ⨉ 2.5 = **15.7**

The circumference is about 15.7 mm.

8. Use $C = 2\pi r$ and $r = 14$ yd.

2 ⨉ 3.14 ⨉ 14 = **87.92**

The circumference is about 87.9 yd.

9. Use $C = 2\pi r$ and $r = 9.25$ km.

2 ⨉ 3.14 ⨉ 9.25 = **58.09**

The circumference is about 58.1 km.

10. Use $A = \pi r^2$ and $r = 4$ yd.

3.14 ⨉ 4 x^2 = **50.24**

The area is about 50.2 yd^2.

11. Use $A = \pi r^2$ and $r = 10$ ft.

3.14 ⨉ 10 x^2 = **314**

The area is about 314 ft^2.

12. Use $A = \pi r^2$ and $r = 16$ in.

3.14 ⨉ 16 x^2 = **803.84**

The area is about 803.8 in.^{2}.

13. Use $A = \pi r^2$ and $r = 0.3$ cm.

3.14 ⨉ 0.3 x^2 = **.2826**

The area is about 0.28 m^2.

14. Use $A = \pi r^2$ and $r = 2.2$ km.

3.14 ⨉ 2.2 x^2 = **15.1976**

The area is about 15.2 km^2.

15. Use $A = \pi r^2$ and $r = \frac{d}{2} = \frac{20}{2} = 10$ in.

3.14 ⨉ 10 x^2 = **314**

The area is about 314 in^2.

16. Use $A = \pi r^2$ and $r = \frac{d}{2} = \frac{1.2}{2} = 0.6$ km.

$3.14 \boxed{\times} 0.6 \boxed{x^2} \boxed{=} \mathbf{1.1304}$

The area is about 1.1 km^2.

17. Use $A = \pi r^2$ and $r = \frac{d}{2} = \frac{27}{2} = 13.5$ ft.

$3.14 \boxed{\times} 13.5 \boxed{x^2} \boxed{=} \mathbf{572.265}$

The area is about 572.3 ft^2.

18. Use $A = \pi r^2$ and $r = \frac{d}{2} = \frac{3.5}{2} = 1.75$ m.

$3.14 \boxed{\times} 1.75 \boxed{x^2} \boxed{=} \mathbf{9.61625}$

The area is about 9.6 m^2.

Chapter 2

Page 87

1. $49 \boxed{\sqrt{}} \mathbf{7}$

$\sqrt{49} = 7$

2. $900 \boxed{\sqrt{}} \mathbf{30}$

$\sqrt{900} = 30$

3. $81 \boxed{\sqrt{}} \mathbf{9}$

$\sqrt{81} = 9$

4. $256 \boxed{\sqrt{}} \mathbf{16}$

$\sqrt{256} = 16$

5. $7 \boxed{\sqrt{}} \mathbf{2.6457513}; \sqrt{7} \approx 2.6$

6. $72 \boxed{\sqrt{}} \mathbf{8.4852814}; \sqrt{72} \approx 8.5$

7. $40 \boxed{\sqrt{}} \mathbf{6.3245553}; \sqrt{40} \approx 6.3$

8. $6.4 \boxed{\sqrt{}} \mathbf{2.5298221}; \sqrt{6.4} \approx 2.5$

9. $2.89 \boxed{\sqrt{}} \mathbf{1.7}; \sqrt{2.89} = 1.7$

10. $170 \boxed{\sqrt{}} \mathbf{13.038405}; \sqrt{170} \approx 13.0$

11. $800 \boxed{\sqrt{}} \mathbf{28.284271}; \sqrt{800} \approx 28.3$

12. $3,025 \boxed{\sqrt{}} \mathbf{55}; \sqrt[3]{025} = 55$

Chapter 2

Page 92

For 1–10 let a and b be the lengths of the two legs of the right triangle and c the length of the hypotenuse. Assume b is given.

$$a^2 + b^2 = c^2$$
$$a^2 = c^2 - b^2$$
$$a = \sqrt{a^2 - b^2}$$

1. $c = 5$ cm, $b = 2$ cm

$5 \boxed{x^2} \boxed{-} 2 \boxed{x^2} \boxed{=} \boxed{\sqrt{}} \mathbf{4.5825757}$

The third side is about 4.6 cm.

2. $c = 10$ m, $b = 7$ m

$10 \boxed{x^2} \boxed{-} 7 \boxed{x^2} \boxed{=} \boxed{\sqrt{}} \mathbf{7.1414284}$

The third side is about 7.1 m.

3. $c = 20$ ft, $b = 12$ ft

$20 \boxed{x^2} \boxed{-} 12 \boxed{x^2} \boxed{=} \boxed{\sqrt{}} \mathbf{16}$

The third side is 16 ft.

4. $c = 11$ yd, $b = 4$ yd

$11 \boxed{x^2} \boxed{-} 4 \boxed{x^2} \boxed{=} \boxed{\sqrt{}} \mathbf{10.246951}$

The third side is about 10.2 yd.

5. $c = 41$ m, $b = 27$ m

$41 \boxed{x^2} \boxed{-} 27 \boxed{x^2} \boxed{=} \boxed{\sqrt{}} \mathbf{30.854497}$

The third side is about 30.9 m.

6. $c = 80$ ft, $b = 45$ ft

$80 \boxed{x^2} \boxed{-} 45 \boxed{x^2} \boxed{=} \boxed{\sqrt{}} \mathbf{66.143783}$

The third side is about 66.1 ft.

7. $c = 7.2$ cm, $b = 3.4$ cm

$7.2 \boxed{x^2} \boxed{-} 3.4 \boxed{x^2} \boxed{=} \boxed{\sqrt{}} \mathbf{6.3466527}$

The third side is about 6.3 cm.

8. $c = 26.4$ m, $b = 18.3$ m

$26.4 \boxed{x^2} \boxed{-} 18.3 \boxed{x^2} \boxed{=} \boxed{\sqrt{}} \mathbf{19.028137}$

The third side is about 19.0 m.

9. $c = 31.4$ m, $b = 10.2$ m

$31.4 \boxed{x^2} \boxed{-} 10.2 \boxed{x^2} \boxed{=} \boxed{\sqrt{}} \mathbf{29.697138}$

The third side is about 29.7 m.

10. $c = 78.6$ m, $b = 32.1$ m

$78.6 \boxed{x^2} \boxed{-} 32.1 \boxed{x^2} \boxed{=} \boxed{\sqrt{}} \mathbf{71.746428}$

The third side is about 71.7 m.

Chapter 3

Page 108

1. $7n$

2. $2n$

3. $-7n$

4. $n + 10$

5. $45n$

6. $n + (-3)$

7. $n \div (-2)$

8. $n - (-5)$

9. $14 + 3n$

Chapter 3

Page 112

1. $9 + (-4)$

$|9| - |-4| = 9 - 4 = 5$

$|9| > |-4|$, so $9 + (-4) = 5$

2. $-1 + (-6)$
$|-1| + |-6| = 1 + 6 = 7$
$-1 + (-6) = -7$

3. $2 + (-6)$
$|-6| - |2| = 6 - 2 = 4$
$|-6| > |2|$, so $2 + (-6) = -4$

4. $-14 + (-7)$
$|-14| + |-7| = 14 + 7 = 21$
$-14 + (-7) = -21$

5. $5 + (-10)$
$|-10| - |5| = 10 - 5 = 5$
$|-10| > |5|$, so $5 + (-10) = -5$

6. $-6 + 4$
$|-6| - |4| = 6 - 4 = 2$
$|-6| > |4|$, so $-6 + 4 = -2$

7. $-8 + (-5)$
$|-8| + |-5| = 8 + 5 = 13$
$-8 + (-5) = -13$

8. $-2 + 6$
$|6| - |-2| = 6 - 2 = 4$
$|6| > |-2|$, so $-2 + 6 = 4$

9. $-4 + (-5)$
$|-4| + |-5| = 4 + 5 = 9$
$-4 + (-5) = -9$

10. $15 + (-8)$
$|15| - |-8| = 15 - 8 = 7$
$|15| > |-8|$, so $15 + (-8) = 7$

11. $-9 + 0 = -9$

12. $-2 + (-2)$
$|-2| + |-2| = 2 + 2 = 4$
$-2 + (-2) = -4$

13. $6 + (-6)$
$|6| - |-6| = 6 - 6 = 0$
$6 + (-6) = 0$

14. $-7 + 11$
$|11| - |-7| = 11 - 7 = 4$
$|11| > |-7|$, so $-7 + 11 = 4$

Chapter 3
Page 114

1. $6 - 8 = 6 + (-8) = -2$

2. $2 - (-8) = 2 + 8 = 10$

3. $5 - 11 = 5 + (-11) = -6$

4. $-4 - 5 = -4 + (-5) = -9$

5. $-7 - (-5) = -7 + 5 = -2$

6. $-1 - 8 = -1 + (-8) = -9$

7. $-3 - (-8) = -3 + 8 = 5$

8. $7 - 9 = 7 + (-9) = -2$

9. $-4 - (-2) = -4 + 2 = -2$

10. $6 - (-3) = 6 + 3 = 9$

11. $4 - (-4) = 4 + 4 = 8$

12. $-2 - 6 = -2 + (-6) = -8$

13. $8 - (-17) = 8 + 17 = 25$

Chapter 3
Page 119

1. $-3 \cdot 6 = -18$

2. $-50 \div 5 = -10$

3. $-7 \cdot 10 = -70$

4. $6 \cdot (-7) = -42$

5. $-3 \cdot (-4) = 12$

6. $-12 \div (-3) = 4$

7. $-6 \cdot (-9) = 54$

8. $-32 \div 4 = -8$

9. $18 \div 6 = -3$

10. $-5 \cdot 12 = -60$

11. $-45 \div 9 = -5$

12. $3 \cdot (-15) = -45$

13. $-64 \div 8 = -8$

14. $-54 \div (-9) = 6$

15. $-2 \cdot (-8) = 16$

16. $-28 \div (-7) = 4$

Chapter 3
Page 129

1. $-4^3 = -(4)(4)(4) = -64$

2. $(-6)^2 = (-6)(-6) = 36$

3. $1.5^3 = (1.5)(1.5)(1.5) = 3.375$

4. $2^7 = 2 \cdot 2 \cdot 2 \cdot 2 \cdot 2 \cdot 2 \cdot 2 = 128$

5. $-15^1 = -15$

6. $8^0 = 1$

7. $12 + 7^2 = 12 + 49 = 61$

8. $-15 + 4^3 = -15 + 64 = 49$

9. $10^3 + 5^3 = 1,000 + 125 = 1,125$

10. $-9^2 - (-30)$
$$= -81 - (-30)$$
$$= -81 + 30$$
$$= -51$$

11. $-3^4 + 40 - 2^5$
$$= -81 + 40 - 32$$
$$= -73$$

12. $12^1 \cdot 30 - 8^2$
$$= 12 \cdot 30 - 64$$
$$= 360 - 64$$
$$= 296$$

13. $6^2 - 50 \cdot 3^3$
$$= 36 - 50 \cdot 27$$
$$= -1{,}314$$

14. $(14 + 5^2) \cdot 7^0$
$$= (14 + 25) \cdot 1$$
$$= 39 \cdot 1 = 39$$

15. $23 + (9 - 14)^2$
$$= 23 + (-5)^2$$
$$= 23 + 25 = 48$$

16. $(14 - 16)^3 + 10$
$$= (-2)^3 + 10$$
$$= -8 + 10 = 2$$

17. $-4 \cdot (2 - 8)^2$
$$= -4 \cdot (-6)^2$$
$$= -4 \cdot 36 = -144$$

18. $(-7 - 8)^2 \cdot 20$
$$= (-15)^2 \cdot 20$$
$$= 225 \times 20 = 4{,}500$$

Chapter 3

Page 135

1. $\quad -6b$
$$= -6(-2) \qquad b = -2$$
$$= 12$$

2. $\quad 12 - g$
$$= 12 - (-4) \qquad g = -4$$
$$= 16$$

3. $\quad 3c + 7$
$$= 3(-1) + 7 \qquad c = -1$$
$$= 4$$

4. $-12 - 2w$
$$= -12 - 2(3) \qquad w = 3$$
$$= -18$$

5. $\quad 7d$
$$= 7(0) \qquad d = 0$$
$$= 0$$

6. $\quad -1.5y$
$$= -1.5(6) \qquad y = 6$$
$$= -9$$

7. $\quad -2p - 6$
$$= -2(5) - 6 \qquad p = 5$$
$$= -10 - 6$$
$$= -16$$

8. $\quad 13 - z$
$$= 13 - (-11) \qquad z = -11$$
$$= 24$$

9. $\quad 4k^2$
$$= 4 \cdot 3^2 \qquad k = 3$$
$$= 4 \cdot 9$$
$$= 36$$

10. $\quad 15 - a^3$
$$= 15 - 2^3 \qquad a = 2$$
$$= 15 - 8$$
$$= 7$$

11. $-3m + 6n$
$$= -3(1) + 6(-5) \qquad m = 1,$$
$$= -3 + (-30) \qquad n = -5$$
$$= -33$$

12. $6w^3 - 2x^2$
$$= 6(-2)^3 - 2(-6)^2 \qquad w = -2,$$
$$= 6(-8) - 2(36) \qquad x = -6$$
$$= -48 - 72$$
$$= -120$$

Chapter 4

Page 148

1. $\quad -7n + 5n$
$$= n(-7 + 5)$$
$$= -2n$$

2. $-10g - g + 5g$
$$= g(-10 - 1 + 5)$$
$$= -6g$$

3. $-4(6t - 2)$
$$= -4(6t) - (-4)(2)$$
$$= -24t + 8$$

4. $(p - 1)\,12$
$$= 12(p) - 1(12)$$
$$= 12p - 12$$

5. $-2(-x + 3)$
$$= (-2)(-x) + (-2)(3)$$
$$= 2x - 6$$

6. $5c + 3(c - 6)$
$$= 5c + 3c - 3(6)$$
$$= 5c + 3c - 18$$
$$= 8c - 18$$

7. $-4(1 - m) - 5$
$$= -4(1) - (-4)(m) - 5$$
$$= -4 + 4m - 5$$
$$= 4m - 9$$

8. $-5 - 3(-z - 1)$
$$= -5 + (-3)(-z) + (-3)(-1)$$
$$= -5 + 3z + 3$$
$$= 3z - 2$$

Chapter 4
Page 150

1.
$$b + 15 = 8$$
$$b + 15 - 15 = 8 - 15$$
$$b = -7$$

2.
$$-2 = 0.5 - c$$
$$-2 + 2 + c = 0.5 - c + c + 2$$
$$c = 2.5$$

3.
$$-7 + h = 1$$
$$-7 + h + 7 = 1 + 7$$
$$h = 8$$

4.
$$p - 2 = -4$$
$$p - 2 + 2 = -4 + 2$$
$$p = -2$$

5.
$$0 = -15 + n$$
$$0 + 15 = -15 + n + 15$$
$$15 = n$$

6.
$$g - 11 = 5$$
$$g - 11 + 11 = 5 + 11$$
$$g = 16$$

7.
$$3 = t - 6$$
$$3 + 6 = t - 6 + 6$$
$$9 = t$$

8.
$$1.2 - r = 8.4$$
$$1.2 - r - 8.4 + r = 8.4 - 8.4 + r$$
$$-7.2 = r$$

9.
$$6 = e + 14$$
$$6 - 14 = e + 14 - 14$$
$$-8 = e$$

10.
$$25 + d = -10$$
$$25 + d - 25 = -10 - 25$$
$$d = -35$$

11.
$$20 - a = 32$$
$$20 - a + a - 32 = 32 + a - 32$$
$$-12 = a$$

12.
$$-5 = w + 9$$
$$-5 - 9 = w + 9 - 9$$
$$-14 = w$$

13.
$$m + 3.5 = 9$$
$$m + 3.5 - 3.5 = 9 - 3.5$$
$$m = 5.5$$

14.
$$3.5 = y - 2.5$$
$$3.5 + 2.5 = y - 2.5 + 2.5$$
$$6 = y$$

15.
$$-8 = 12 + q$$
$$-8 - 12 = 12 + q - 12$$
$$-20 = q$$

16.
$$7 = -3 - k$$
$$7 + k - 7 = -3 - k + k - 7$$
$$k = -10$$

Chapter 4
Page 155

1.
$$-4b = 76$$
$$\frac{4b}{-4} = \frac{76}{-4} \quad \text{Divide each side by } -4.$$
$$b = -19$$

2.
$$\frac{m}{-1.5} = -10$$
$$\left(\frac{m}{-1.5}\right)(-1.5) = -10(-1.5) \quad \text{Multiply each side}$$
$$m = 15 \qquad \text{by } -1.5.$$

3.
$$426 = -3d$$
$$\frac{426}{-3} = \frac{-3d}{-3} \quad \text{Divide each side by } -3.$$
$$-142 = d$$

4.
$$\frac{h}{-7} = 6$$
$$\frac{h}{-7}(-7) = 6(-7) \quad \text{Multiply each side}$$
$$h = -42 \qquad \text{by } -7.$$

5.
$$7w = 280$$
$$\frac{7w}{7} = \frac{280}{7} \quad \text{Divide each side by } 7.$$
$$w = 40$$

6.
$$5 = \frac{x}{4.2}$$
$$(5)(4.2) = \left(\frac{x}{4.2}\right)(4.2) \quad \text{Multiply each side}$$
$$21 = x \qquad \text{by } 4.2.$$

7.
$$-2 = \frac{d}{5}$$
$$-2(5) = \frac{d}{5}(5) \quad \text{Multiply each side by } 5.$$
$$-10 = d$$

8.
$$0.4 = \frac{a}{-3}$$
$$(0.4)(-3) = \frac{a}{-3}(-3) \quad \text{Multiply each side}$$
$$-1.2 = a \qquad \text{by } -3.$$

9.
$$6p = -30$$
$$\frac{6p}{6} = \frac{-30}{6} \quad \text{Divide each side by } 6.$$
$$p = -5$$

10.
$$-3.2 = -8k$$
$$\frac{-3.2}{-8} = \frac{-8k}{8}$$ Divide each side by 8.
$$0.4 = k$$

11.
$$\frac{m}{8} = -4$$
$$\frac{m}{8}(8) = -4(8)$$ Multiply each side by 8.
$$m = -32$$

12.
$$-5.6 = 0.8y$$
$$\frac{-5.6}{0.8} = \frac{0.8y}{0.8}$$ Divide each side by 0.8.
$$-7 = y$$

Chapter 4

Page 159

1.
$$-2 = 10d - 3$$
$$-2 + 3 = 10d - 3 + 3$$ Add 3 to each side.
$$1 = 10d$$
$$\frac{1}{10} = \frac{10d}{10}$$ Divide each side by 10.
$$0.1 = d$$

2.
$$\frac{h}{-3} - 6 = 8$$
$$\frac{h}{-3} - 6 + 6 = 8 + 6$$ Add 6 to each side.
$$\frac{h}{-3} = 14$$
$$\frac{h}{-3}(-3) = 14(-3)$$ Multiply each side by −3.
$$h = -42$$

3.
$$7 = -2 + 3b$$
$$7 + 2 = -2 + 3b + 2$$ Add 2 to each side.
$$9 = 3b$$
$$\frac{9}{3} = \frac{3b}{3}$$ Divide each side by 3.
$$3 = b$$

4.
$$-8 + 2g = 4$$
$$-8 + 2g + 8 = 4 + 8$$ Add 8 to each side.
$$2g = 12$$
$$\frac{2g}{2} = \frac{12}{2}$$ Divide each side by 2.
$$g = 6$$

5.
$$\frac{k}{5} + 11 = -4$$
$$\frac{k}{5} + 11 - 11 = -4 - 11$$ Subtract 11 from each side.
$$\frac{k}{5} = -15$$
$$\frac{k}{5}(5) = -15(5)$$ Multiply each side by 5.
$$k = -75$$

6.
$$-12 = \frac{m}{4} - 9$$
$$-12 + 9 = \frac{m}{4} - 9 + 9$$ Add 9 to each side.
$$-3 = \frac{m}{4}$$
$$-3(4) = \frac{m}{4}(4)$$ Multiply each side by 4.
$$-12 = m$$

7.
$$7 + \frac{c}{-6} = -3$$
$$7 + \frac{c}{-6} - 7 = -3 - 7$$ Subtract 7 from each side.
$$\frac{c}{-6} = -10$$
$$\frac{c}{-6}(-6) = (-10)(-6)$$ Multiply each side by −6.
$$c = 60$$

8.
$$-3 - 5n = -1$$
$$-3 - 5n + 3 = -1 + 3$$ Add 3 to each side.
$$-5n = 2$$
$$\frac{-5n}{-5} = \frac{2}{-5}$$ Divide each side by −5.
$$n = -0.4$$

9.
$$-1 = -4 + \frac{e}{8}$$
$$-1 + 4 = -4 + \frac{e}{8} + 4$$ Add 4 to each side.
$$3 = \frac{e}{8}$$
$$3(8) = \frac{e}{8}(8)$$ Multiply each side by 8.
$$24 = e$$

10.
$$8 + \frac{a}{-1.2} = 0.7$$
$$8 + \frac{a}{-1.2} - 8 = 0.7 - 8$$ Subtract 8 from each side.
$$\frac{a}{-1.2} = -7.3$$
$$\frac{a}{-1.2}(-1.2) = (-7.3)(-1.2)$$ Multiply each side by −1.2.
$$a = 8.76$$

11.
$$4.8 = 4p + 1.6$$
$$4.8 - 1.6 = 4p + 1.6 - 1.6$$ Subtract 1.6 from each side.
$$3.2 = 4p$$
$$\frac{3.2}{4} = \frac{4p}{4}$$ Divide each side by 4.
$$0.8 = p$$

12.
$$3.5 = -6m - 0.1$$
$$3.5 + 0.1 = -6m - 0.1 + 0.1$$ Add 0.1 to each side.
$$3.6 = -6m$$
$$\frac{3.6}{-6} = \frac{6m}{-6}$$ Divide each side by −6.
$$-0.6 = m$$

Chapter 4

Page 167

1.
$$9p - 6 = 3p$$
$$9p - 3p - 6 = 3p - 3p$$ Subtract 3p from each side.
$$6p - 6 = 0$$
$$6p - 6 + 6 = 6$$
$$6p = 6$$
$$\frac{6p}{6} = \frac{6}{6}$$ Divide each side by 6.
$$p = 1$$

2. $4m - 7 = 3m$

$4m - 7 - 3m = 3m - 3m$ Subtract $3m$ from each side.

$m - 7 = 0$

$m - 7 + 7 = 0 + 7$ Add 7 to each side.

$m = 7$

3. $5h - 2 = 28 - h$

$5h - 2 + h = 28 - h + h$ Add h to each side.

$6h - 2 = 28$

$6h - 2 + 2 = 28 + 2$ Add 2 to each side.

$6h = 30$

$\frac{6h}{6} = \frac{30}{6}$ Divide each side by 6.

$h = 5$

4. $8t - 1 = 23 - 4t$

$8t - 1 + 4t = 23 - 4t + 4t$ Add $4t$ to each side.

$12t - 1 = 23$

$12t - 1 + 1 = 23 + 1$ Add 1 to each side.

$12t = 24$

$\frac{12t}{12} = \frac{24}{12}$ Divide each side by 12.

$t = 2$

5. $5c - 2 = 6 + c$

$5c - 2 - c = 6 + c - c$ Subtract c from each side.

$4c - 2 = 6$

$4c - 2 + 2 = 6 + 2$ Add 2 to each side.

$4c = 8$

$\frac{4c}{4} = \frac{8}{4}$ Divide each side by 4.

$c = 2$

6. $2a - 1 = 4 + a$

$2a - 1 - a = 4 + a - a$ Subtract a from each side.

$a - 1 = 4$

$a - 1 + 1 = 4 + 1$ Add 1 to each side.

$a = 5$

7. $5y + 3 = 2y + 15$

$5y + 3 - 2y = 2y + 15 - 2y$ Subtract $2y$ from each side.

$3y + 3 = 15$

$3y + 3 - 3 = 15 - 3$ Subtract 3 from each side.

$3y = 12$

$\frac{3y}{3} = \frac{12}{3}$ Divide each side by 3.

$y = 4$

8. $6w + 3 = 2w + 11$

$6w + 3 - 2w = 2w + 11 - 2w$ Subtract $2w$ from each side.

$4w + 3 = 11$

$4w + 3 - 3 = 11 - 3$ Subtract 3 from each side.

$4w = 8$

$\frac{4w}{4} = \frac{8}{4}$ Divide each side by 4.

$w = 2$

9. $3(2g - 3) = 27$

$6g - 9 = 27$

$6g - 9 + 9 = 27 + 9$ Add 9 to each side.

$6g = 36$

$\frac{6g}{6} = \frac{36}{6}$ Divide each side by 6.

$g = 6$

10. $4(2m - 3) = 28$

$8m - 12 = 28$

$8m - 12 + 12 = 28 + 12$ Add 12 to each side.

$8m = 40$

$\frac{8m}{8} = \frac{40}{8}$ Divide each side by 8.

$m = 5$

11. $9 = 3(5z - 2)$

$9 = 15z - 6$

$9 + 6 = 15z - 6 + 6$ Add 6 to each side.

$15 = 15z$

$\frac{15}{15} = \frac{15z}{15}$ Divide each side by 15.

$1 = z$

12. $40 = 5(3d + 2)$

$40 = 15d + 10$

$40 - 10 = 15d + 10 - 10$ Subtract 10 from each side.

$30 = 15d$

$\frac{30}{15} = \frac{15d}{15}$ Divide each side by 15.

$2 = d$

13. $3(5 + 3q) - 8 = 88$

$15 + 9q - 8 = 88$

$9q + 7 = 88$

$9q + 7 - 7 = 88 - 7$ Subtract 7 from each side.

$9q = 81$

$\frac{9q}{9} = \frac{81}{9}$ Divide each side by 9.

$q = 9$

14. $6x - (3x + 8) = 16$

$6x - 3x - 8 = 16$

$3x - 8 = 16$

$3x - 8 + 8 = 16 + 8$ Add 8 to each side.

$3x = 24$

$\frac{3x}{3} = \frac{24}{3}$ Divide each side by 3.

$x = 8$

15. $2(3 + 4d) = 45$

$6 + 8d - 9 = 45$

$8d - 3 = 45$

$$8d - 3 + 3 = 45 + 3 \quad \text{Add 3 to each side.}$$
$$8d = 48$$
$$\frac{8d}{8} = \frac{48}{8} \quad \text{Divide each side by 8.}$$
$$d = 6$$

16. $5b - (2b + 8) = 16$
$$5b - 2b - 8 = 16$$
$$3b - 8 = 16$$
$$3b - 8 + 8 = 16 + 8 \quad \text{Add 8 to each side.}$$
$$3b = 24$$
$$\frac{3b}{3} = \frac{24}{3} \quad \text{Divide each side by 3.}$$
$$b = 8$$

17. $\qquad 3s - 3 = 3(7 - s)$
$$3s - 3 = 21 - 3s$$
$$3s - 3 + 3s = 21 - 3s + 3s \quad \text{Add } 3s \text{ to each}$$
$$6s - 3 = 21 \qquad \text{side.}$$
$$6s - 3 + 3 = 21 + 3 \quad \text{Add 3 to each side.}$$
$$6s = 24$$
$$\frac{6s}{6} = \frac{24}{6} \quad \text{Divide each side by 6.}$$
$$s = 4$$

18. $\qquad 9(n + 2) = 3(n - 2)$
$$9n + 18 = 3n - 6$$
$$9n + 18 - 3n = 3n - 6 - 3n \quad \text{Subtract } 3n$$
$$6n + 18 = -6 \qquad \text{from each side.}$$
$$6n + 18 - 18 = -6 - 18 \quad \text{Subtract 18 from}$$
$$6n = -24 \qquad \text{each side.}$$
$$\frac{6n}{6} = \frac{-24}{6} \quad \text{Divide each side by 6.}$$
$$n = -4$$

19. $\qquad 10 - 3e = 2e - 8e + 40$
$$10 - 3e = -6e + 40$$
$$10 - 3e + 6e = -6e + 40 + 6e \quad \text{Add } 6e \text{ to}$$
$$10 + 3e = 40 \qquad \text{each side.}$$
$$10 + 3e - 10 = 40 - 10 \quad \text{Subtract 10 from}$$
$$3e = 30 \qquad \text{each side.}$$
$$\frac{3e}{3} = \frac{30}{3} \quad \text{Divide each side by 3.}$$
$$e = 10$$

20. $\qquad 5 - 2k = 3k - 7k + 25$
$$5 - 2k = -4k + 25$$
$$5 - 2k + 4k = -4k + 25 + 4k \quad \text{Add } 4k \text{ to}$$
$$5 + 2k = 25 \qquad \text{each side.}$$
$$5 + 2k - 5 = 25 - 5 \quad \text{Subtract 5 from each}$$
$$2k = 20 \qquad \text{side.}$$
$$\frac{2k}{2} = \frac{20}{2} \quad \text{Divide each side by 2.}$$
$$k = 10$$

21. $\qquad 5 + 4r - 7 = 4r + 3 - r$
$$4r - 2 = 3r + 3$$
$$4r - 2 - 3r = 3r + 3 - 3r \quad \text{Subtract } 3r$$
$$r - 2 = 3 \qquad \text{from each side.}$$
$$r - 2 + 2 = 3 + 2 \quad \text{Add 2 to each side.}$$
$$r = 5$$

22. $\qquad 4 + 3a - 6 = 3a + 2 - a$
$$3a - 2 = 2a + 2$$
$$3a - 2 - 2a = 2a + 2 - 2a \quad \text{Subtract } 2a$$
$$a - 2 = 2 \qquad \text{from each side.}$$
$$a - 2 + 2 = 2 + 2 \quad \text{Add 2 to each side.}$$
$$a = 4$$

23. $\qquad 5(w + 4) = 3(w - 2)$
$$5w + 20 = 3w - 6$$
$$5w + 20 - 3w = 3w - 6 - 3w \quad \text{Subtract } 3w$$
$$2w + 20 = -6 \qquad \text{from each side.}$$
$$2w + 20 - 20 = -6 - 20 \quad \text{Subtract 20 from}$$
$$2w = -26 \qquad \text{each side.}$$
$$w = -13$$

24. $\qquad 8(3g - 2) = 4(7g - 1)$
$$24g - 16 = 28g - 4$$
$$24g - 16 - 28g = 28g - 4 - 28g \quad \begin{array}{l}\text{Subtract} \\ 28g \text{ from} \end{array}$$
$$-4g - 16 = -4 \qquad \text{each side.}$$
$$-4g - 16 + 16 = -4 + 16 \quad \text{Add 16 to each}$$
$$-4g = 12 \qquad \text{side.}$$
$$\frac{4g}{-4} = \frac{12}{-4} \quad \text{Divide each side by } -4.$$
$$g = -3$$

Chapter 4

Page 170

1. Area of rectangle: $A = lw$
$l = 8$ m, $w = 2.5$ m
$A = 8(2.5) = 20$
area: 20 m^2

2. Area of square: $A = s^2$
$s = 6.25$ cm
$A = 6.25^2 = 39.06$
area: 39.06 cm^2

3. Area of triangle: $A = \frac{1}{2}bh$
$b = 3$ ft, $h = 7$ ft
$A = \frac{1}{2}(3)(7) = 10.5$
area: 10.5 ft^2

4. Area of trapezoid: $A = \frac{1}{2}h(b_1 + b_2)$
$h = 8.5$ cm, $b_1 = 12$ cm, $b_2 = 20$ cm
$A = \frac{1}{2}(8.5)(12 + 20) = 4.25(32) = 136$
area: 136 cm^2

5. Perimeter of rectangle: $P = 2l + 2w$
$l = 1.2$ m, $w = 5$ m
$P = 2(1.2) + 2(5) = 2.4 + 10 = 12.4$
perimeter: 12.4 m

6. Perimeter of square: $P = 4s$
$s = 8.1$ cm
$P = 4(8.1) = 32.4$
perimeter: 32.4 cm

7. Perimeter of equilateral triangle: $P = 3s$
$s = 9$ in.
$P = 3(9) = 27$
perimeter: 27 in.

Chapter 4

Page 180

1.
$$4 > 7 + d$$
$$4 - 7 > 7 + d - 7$$
$$-3 > d$$
$$d < -3$$

2.
$$-5y < 35$$
$$\frac{-5y}{-5} > \frac{35}{-5}$$
$$y > -7$$

3.
$$b + 12 \leq 5$$
$$b + 12 - 12 \leq 5 - 12$$
$$b \leq -7$$

4.
$$-1.5 \geq \frac{r}{5}$$
$$-1.5(5) \geq \frac{r}{5}(5)$$
$$-7.5 \geq r$$
$$r \leq -7.5$$

5.
$$-3 < t + 7$$
$$-3 - 7 < t + 7 - 7$$
$$-10 < t$$
$$t > -10$$

6.
$$g + 9 < 2$$
$$g + 9 - 9 < 2 - 9$$
$$g < -7$$

7.
$$\frac{7}{2} < 8z$$
$$\frac{7}{2}\left(\frac{1}{8}\right) < 8z\left(\frac{1}{8}\right)$$
$$\frac{7}{16} < z$$
$$z > \frac{7}{16}$$

8.
$$-6n \leq -30$$
$$\frac{-6n}{-6} \geq \frac{-30}{-6}$$
$$n \geq 5$$

9.
$$m - 3 > -8$$
$$m - 3 + 3 > -8 + 3$$
$$m > -5$$

10.
$$\frac{e}{-4} < -3.5$$
$$\frac{e}{-4}(-4) > (-3.5)(-4)$$
$$e > 14$$

11.
$$3x \geq -42$$
$$\frac{3x}{3} \geq \frac{-42}{3}$$
$$x \geq -14$$

12.
$$18 > -2a$$
$$\frac{18}{-2} < \frac{-2a}{-2}$$
$$-9 < a$$
$$a > -9$$

13.
$$\frac{d}{8} \geq 3$$
$$\frac{d}{8}(8) \geq 3(8)$$
$$d \geq 24$$

14.
$$-6 \leq s - 13$$
$$-6 + 13 \leq s - 13 + 13$$
$$7 \leq s$$
$$s \geq 7$$

15.
$$8 < \frac{h}{-2}$$
$$8(-2) > \frac{h}{-2}(-2)$$
$$-16 > h$$
$$h < -16$$

16.
$$-6 > \frac{c}{3}$$
$$-6(3) > \frac{c}{3}(3)$$
$$-18 > c$$
$$c < -18$$

17.
$$p + 4 \leq -6$$
$$p + 4 - 4 \leq -6 - 4$$
$$p \leq -10$$

18.
$$q - 0.8 > 3.6$$
$$q - 0.8 + 0.8 > 3.6 + 0.8$$
$$q > 4.4$$

19.
$$7.2 < w + 1.6$$
$$7.2 - 1.6 < w + 1.6 - 1.6$$
$$5.6 < w$$
$$w > 5.6$$

20. $\quad -4.1 \geq k + 1.7$
$-4.1 - 1.7 \geq k + 1.7 - 1.7$
$\qquad -5.8 \geq k$
$\qquad\quad k \leq -5.8$

Chapter 4
Page 184

1. $\quad 4z + 7 > -9$
$4z + 7 - 7 > -9 - 7$
$\qquad\quad 4z > -16$
$\qquad\quad \frac{4z}{4} > \frac{-16}{4}$
$\qquad\quad z > -4$

2. $\quad 7 \geq -2 - 3h$
$7 + 2 \geq -2 - 3h + 2$
$\qquad 9 \geq -3h$
$\qquad \frac{9}{-3} \leq \frac{-3h}{-3}$
$\qquad -3 \leq h$
$\qquad\quad h \geq -3$

3. $\quad 13 < -2 + \frac{a}{-4}$
$13 + 2 < -2 + \frac{a}{-4} + 2$
$\qquad 15 < \frac{a}{-4}$
$15(-4) > \frac{a}{-4}(-4)$
$\qquad -60 > a$
$\qquad\quad a < -60$

4. $\quad \frac{m}{5} - 6 \geq 3$
$\frac{m}{5} - 6 + 6 \geq 3 + 6$
$\qquad \frac{m}{5} \geq 9$
$\qquad \frac{m}{5}(5) \geq 9(5)$
$\qquad m \geq 45$

5. $\quad -1 + 5p < 8$
$-1 + 5p + 1 < 8 + 1$
$\qquad 5p < 9$
$\qquad \frac{5p}{5} < \frac{9}{5}$
$\qquad p < 1.8$

6. $\quad 10 > \frac{w}{2} - 6$
$10 + 6 > \frac{w}{2} - 6 + 6$
$\qquad 16 > \frac{w}{2}$
$16(2) > \frac{w}{2}(2)$
$\qquad 32 > w$
$\qquad w < 32$

7. $\quad 20 < -5b - 1$
$20 + 1 < -5b - 1 + 1$
$\qquad 21 < -5b$
$\qquad \frac{21}{-5} > \frac{-5b}{-5}$
$\qquad -4.2 > b$
$\qquad b < -4.2$

8. $\quad -6 + 2y \leq 4$
$-6 + 2y + 6 \leq 4 + 6$
$\qquad 2y \leq 10$
$\qquad \frac{2y}{2} \leq \frac{10}{2}$
$\qquad y \leq 5$

9. $\quad 5 + \frac{k}{-3} < -8$
$5 + \frac{k}{-3} - 5 < -8 - 5$
$\qquad \frac{k}{-3} < -13$
$\qquad \frac{k}{-3}(-3) > (-13)(-3)$
$\qquad k > 39$

10. $\quad -3 \leq 7 - 2d$
$-3 - 7 \leq 7 - 2d - 7$
$\qquad -10 \leq -2d$
$\qquad \frac{-10}{-2} \geq \frac{-2d}{-2}(-2)$
$\qquad 5 \geq d$
$\qquad d \leq 5$

Chapter 5
Page 200

1. $\quad 2x + y = -5$
$\qquad y = -2x - 5$

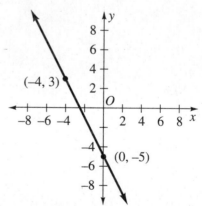

2. $-3x - 2y = 12$

$$-2y = 3x + 12$$

$$y = -\frac{3}{2}x - 6$$

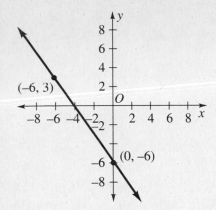

3. $6x + 2y = -16$

$$2y = -6x - 16$$

$$y = -3x - 8$$

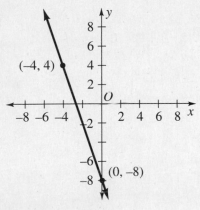

4. $-10x - 5y = 35$

$$-5y = 10x + 35$$

$$y = -2x - 7$$

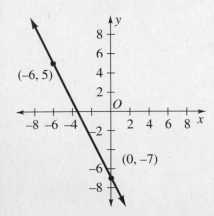

5. $6x + 3y = 18$

$$3y = -6x + 18$$

$$y = -2x + 6$$

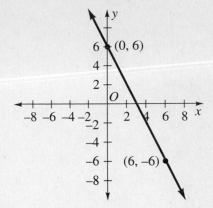

6. $x + 3y = -12$

$$3y = -x - 12$$

$$y = -\frac{1}{3}x - 4$$

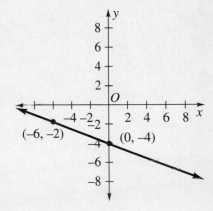

7. $24x - 4y = -16$

$$-4y = -24x - 16$$

$$y = 6x + 4$$

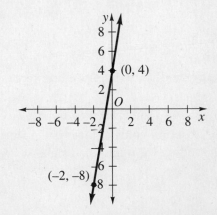

8. $-50x + 10y = -5$

$$10y = 50x - 5$$
$$y = 10x - \frac{1}{2}$$

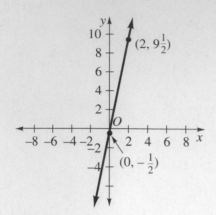

Chapter 5

Page 208

1. $\dfrac{\text{rise}}{\text{run}} = \dfrac{-1-0}{4-(-3)} = \dfrac{-1}{7} = -\dfrac{1}{7}$

2. $\dfrac{\text{rise}}{\text{run}} = \dfrac{-1-2}{-3-4} = \dfrac{-3}{-1} = 3$

3. $\dfrac{\text{rise}}{\text{run}} = \dfrac{2-2}{-5-0} = \dfrac{0}{5} = 0$

4. $\dfrac{\text{rise}}{\text{run}} = \dfrac{7-(-2)}{4-4} = \dfrac{9}{0}$ not defined

5. $\dfrac{\text{rise}}{\text{run}} = \dfrac{-1-0}{3-(-2)} = \dfrac{-1}{5} = -\dfrac{1}{5}$

6. $\dfrac{\text{rise}}{\text{run}} = \dfrac{6-(-3)}{-1-(-1)} = \dfrac{9}{0}$ not defined

7. $\dfrac{\text{rise}}{\text{run}} = \dfrac{-2-(-7)}{2-1} = \dfrac{5}{1} = 5$

8. $\dfrac{\text{rise}}{\text{run}} = \dfrac{2-(-1)}{-3-3} = \dfrac{3}{-6} = -\dfrac{1}{2}$

9. $\dfrac{\text{rise}}{\text{run}} = \dfrac{-4-(-4)}{0-2} = \dfrac{0}{-2} = 0$

10. $\dfrac{\text{rise}}{\text{run}} = \dfrac{-2-(-1)}{-6-(-2)} = \dfrac{-1}{-4} = \dfrac{1}{4}$

Chapter 6

Page 248

1. 40, 400, 4,000; multiply the preceding term by 10.

2. 27, 31, 35; add 4 to the preceding term.

3. 21, −15, 9; absolute value of term is absolute value of preceding term minus 6, signs alternate.

4. 60,006; 600,006; 6,000,006; first and last digits are 6 with number of zeros in the middle increasing by 1 each term.

5. −12, −20, −28; subtract 8 from the preceding term.

6. −2, −4, −6; subtract 2 from the preceding term.

7. 3.02222, 3.022222, 3.0222222; add a trailing digit 2 to the preceding term.

8. 3.3, 3, 2.7; subtract 0.3 from the preceding term.

9. 0.075, 0.0075, 0.00075; divide the preceding entry by 10.

10. 50, 25, 12.5; divide the preceding entry by 2.

11. −3.24, 9.72, −29.16; multiply the preceding entry by −3.

12. −16, −5, 6; add 11 to the preceding entry.

Chapter 6

Page 252

1. $f(0) = 0^2 - 2 \cdot 0 + 3 = 3$

2. $f(1) = 1^2 - 2 \cdot 1 + 3 = 2$

3. $f(-1) = (-1)^2 - 2 \cdot (-1) + 3 = 6$

4. $f(5) = 5^2 - 2 \cdot 5 + 3 = 18$

5. $f(-2) = (-2)^2 - 2 \cdot (-2) + 3 = 11$

6. $f(10) = 10^2 - 2 \cdot 10 + 3 = 83$

7. $f(1) = 3 \cdot 1^2 + 1 - 1 = 3$

8. $f(2) = 3 \cdot 2^2 + 2 - 1 = 13$

9. $f(-1) = 3 \cdot (-1)^2 + (-1) - 1 = 1$

10. $f(0) = 3 \cdot 0^2 + 0 - 1 = -1$

11. $f(6) = 3 \cdot 6^2 + 6 - 1 = 113$

12. $f(-4) = 3 \cdot (-4)^2 + (-4) - 1 = 43$

Chapter 7

Page 293

1. 0.57; 0.57

2. $\dfrac{4}{5}$; $-\dfrac{4}{5}$

3. 2.14; −2.14

4. $\dfrac{3}{4}$; GCF = 16

5. $\dfrac{-7}{10}$; GCF = 8

6. $10\dfrac{1}{3}$; $\dfrac{93}{9} = \dfrac{90}{9} + \dfrac{3}{9}$

7. $-\dfrac{10}{21}$; GCF = 12

8. $6\frac{4}{5}$; $\frac{340}{50} = \frac{300}{50} + \frac{40}{50}$

9. $-1\frac{7}{10}$; $\frac{425}{-250} = \frac{250}{-250} + \frac{175}{-250}$ and GCF $(175, 250) = 25$

Chapter 7
Page 296

For answers 1–5 use a calculator or paper and pencil to divide.

1. -0.625

2. $1.2\overline{6}$

3. $-2.58\overline{3}$

4. $0.\overline{185}$

5. $4.4\overline{5}$

6. $10n = -17.77777\ldots$

$\underline{n = -1.77777\ldots}$

$9n = -16$

$n = -\frac{16}{9} = -1\frac{7}{9}$

7. $100n = 23.33333\ldots$

$\underline{10n = 2.33333\ldots}$

$90n = 21$

$n = \frac{21}{90} = \frac{7}{30}$

8. $34{,}375 = 5^5 \cdot 11$; $100{,}000 = 10^5 = 5^5 \cdot 2^5$

GCF$(34{,}375; 100{,}000) = 5^5$, so $-0.34375 = -\frac{11}{32}$

9. $100n = 283.33333\ldots$

$\underline{10n = 28.33333\ldots}$

$90n = 255$

$n = \frac{255}{90} = 2\frac{75}{90} = 2\frac{5}{6}$

10. $100n = -305.55555\ldots$

$\underline{10n = -30.55555\ldots}$

$90n = -275$

$n = -\frac{275}{90} = -3\frac{5}{90} = -3\frac{1}{18}$

Chapter 7
Page 301

1. $\frac{7}{9} < \frac{5}{6}$, since $0.7\overline{7} < 0.8\overline{3}$.

2. $-0.35 < -\frac{4}{15}$, since $-0.35 < -0.2\overline{6}$.

3. $\frac{15}{24} = \frac{10}{16}$, since $0.625 = 0.625$.

4. $-\frac{2}{3} < -0.65$, since $-0.6\overline{6} < -0.65$.

5. $\frac{2}{5} < \frac{5}{12}$, since $0.4 < 0.41\overline{6}$.

6. $-0.375 = -\frac{3}{8}$, since $-0.375 = -0.375$.

7. $\frac{10}{27} > \frac{1}{3}$, since $0.\overline{370} > 0.33\overline{3}$.

8. $\frac{5}{9} < \frac{16}{25}$, since $0.5\overline{5} < 0.64$.

9. $-\frac{9}{11} > -0.95$ since $-0.\overline{81} > -0.95$.

10. $0.45 > \frac{3}{13}$, since $0.45 > 0.231$.

Chapter 7
Page 307

1. $\frac{2}{3} + \frac{7}{8} = \frac{16}{24} + \frac{21}{24}$

$\phantom{\frac{2}{3} + \frac{7}{8}} = \frac{37}{24} = 1\frac{13}{24}$

2. $\frac{5}{6} - \frac{3}{10} = \frac{25}{30} - \frac{9}{30}$

$\phantom{\frac{5}{6} - \frac{3}{10}} = \frac{16}{30} = \frac{8}{15}$

3. $-\frac{4}{5} + \frac{3}{8} = -\frac{32}{40} + \frac{15}{40}$

$\phantom{-\frac{4}{5} + \frac{3}{8}} = -\frac{17}{40}$

4. $\frac{5}{12} - \left(-\frac{3}{4}\right) = \frac{5}{12} + \frac{9}{12}$

$\phantom{\frac{5}{12} - \left(-\frac{3}{4}\right)} = \frac{14}{12} = 1\frac{1}{6}$

5. $\frac{1}{8} - \frac{2}{3} + \frac{5}{6} = \frac{3}{24} - \frac{16}{24} + \frac{20}{24}$

$\phantom{\frac{1}{8} - \frac{2}{3} + \frac{5}{6}} = \frac{7}{24}$

6. $\frac{2}{9} + \frac{5}{6} - \frac{1}{4} = \frac{8}{36} + \frac{30}{36} - \frac{9}{36}$

$\phantom{\frac{2}{9} + \frac{5}{6} - \frac{1}{4}} = \frac{29}{36}$

7. $5\frac{1}{6} - 1\frac{3}{4} = \frac{62}{12} - \frac{21}{12}$

$\phantom{5\frac{1}{6} - 1\frac{3}{4}} = \frac{41}{12} = 3\frac{5}{12}$

8. $1\frac{2}{3} - \left(-6\frac{4}{5}\right) = \frac{25}{15} + \frac{102}{15}$

$\phantom{1\frac{2}{3} - \left(-6\frac{4}{5}\right)} = \frac{127}{15} = 8\frac{7}{15}$

9. $-3\frac{7}{8} + 1\frac{1}{6} = -\frac{93}{24} + \frac{28}{24}$

$\phantom{-3\frac{7}{8} + 1\frac{1}{6}} = -\frac{65}{24} = -2\frac{17}{24}$

10. $-2\frac{1}{12} - 5\frac{7}{10} = -\frac{125}{60} - \frac{342}{60}$

$\phantom{-2\frac{1}{12} - 5\frac{7}{10}} = -\frac{467}{60} = -7\frac{47}{60}$

Chapter 7
Page 310

1. $-\frac{4}{5} \cdot \frac{3}{8} = -\frac{12}{40}$

$\phantom{-\frac{4}{5} \cdot \frac{3}{8}} = -\frac{3}{10}$

2. $-\frac{5}{6} \div \left(-\frac{2}{3}\right) = -\frac{5}{6} \cdot \left(-\frac{3}{2}\right)$

$\phantom{-\frac{5}{6} \div \left(-\frac{2}{3}\right)} = \frac{15}{12} = 1\frac{1}{4}$

3. $-15 \div \frac{3}{8} = -15 \cdot \frac{8}{3}$

$\phantom{-15 \div \frac{3}{8}} = -40$

4. $\frac{7}{9} \cdot 45 = 7 \cdot 5 = 35$

5. $-2\frac{3}{4} \div \frac{7}{12} = -\frac{11}{4} \cdot \frac{12}{7}$

$\qquad = -\frac{33}{7} = -4\frac{5}{7}$

6. $4\frac{1}{8} \cdot \left(-5\frac{1}{3}\right) = \frac{33}{8} \times -\frac{16}{3}$

$\qquad = -22$

Chapter 7
Page 316

1. $7^0 = 1$ by definition

2. $5^{-3} = \frac{1}{5^3} = \frac{1}{125}$

3. $\frac{6^{10}}{6^8} = 6^{10-8} = 6^2 = 36$

4. $\frac{(-1)^5}{(-1)^6} = (-1)^{5-6} = (-1)^{-1} = \frac{1}{-1} = 1$

5. $\frac{-2^9}{(-2)^5} = \frac{-2^9}{-2 \cdot -2 \cdot -2 \cdot -2 \cdot -2} = \frac{-2^9}{-2^5} = \frac{2^9}{2^5} =$
$2^4 = 16$

6. $(-1)^{-9} = \frac{1}{(-1)^9} = \frac{1}{-1} = -1$

7. $\frac{-3^5}{-3^8} = \frac{3^5}{3^8} = 3^{5-8} = 3^{-3} = \frac{1}{3^3} = \frac{1}{27}$

8. $-8^{-2} = -\frac{1}{8^2} = -\frac{1}{64}$

9. $2^{-7} = \frac{1}{2^7} = \frac{1}{128}$

10. $(-3)^{-4} = \frac{1}{(-3)^4} = \frac{1}{81}$

11. $\frac{(-4)^3}{4^6} = \frac{-4 \cdot -4 \cdot -4}{4^6} = \frac{-(4^3)}{4^6} = \frac{-1}{4^3} = \frac{-1}{64}$

12. $(-20)^{-1} = \frac{1}{-20} = -\frac{1}{20}$

Chapter 7
Page 320

1. 2.3×10^4 **2.** 1.01×10^{-2}

3. 8.1×10^3 **4.** 6.25×10^6

5. 3×10^{-3} **6.** 0.95

7. $132{,}000$ **8.** 0.0005

9. $70{,}000{,}000$ **10.** 0.0036

Chapter 7
Page 323

1. $-\frac{2}{3}g = 18$

$\qquad g = 18 \cdot \left(\frac{3}{-2}\right)$

$\qquad g = -27$

2. $0.78 - w = -3.4$

$\qquad -w = -3.4 - 0.78$

$\qquad -w = -4.18$

$\qquad w = 4.18$

3. $-0.2b + 0.8 = -0.4$

$\qquad -0.2b = -0.4 - 0.8$

$\qquad -0.2b = -1.2$

$\qquad b = \frac{-1.2}{-0.2} = 6$

4. $\frac{1}{8}m = 2\frac{3}{4}$

$\qquad m = \frac{11}{4} \cdot 8$

$\qquad m = \frac{88}{4} = 22$

5. $-\frac{5}{6} + d = 1\frac{1}{3}$

$\qquad d = \frac{4}{3} + \frac{5}{6} = \frac{8}{6} + \frac{5}{6}$

$\qquad d = \frac{13}{6} = 2\frac{1}{6}$

6. $\frac{1}{4}k - 4 = -1$

$\qquad \frac{1}{4}k = -1 + 4$

$\qquad \frac{1}{4}k = 3$

$\qquad k = \frac{4}{1} \times 3 = 12$

7. $\frac{1}{5} + \frac{3}{10}a = 2$

$\qquad \frac{3}{10}a = 2 - \frac{1}{5} = \frac{10}{5} - \frac{1}{5}$

$\qquad \frac{3}{10}a = \frac{9}{5}$

$\qquad a = \frac{9}{5} \cdot \frac{10}{3}$

$\qquad a = \frac{30}{5} = 6$

8. $1.8 - 0.2p = -0.5$

$\qquad -0.2p = -0.5 - 1.8$

$\qquad -0.2p = -2.3$

$\qquad p = \frac{-2.3}{-0.2} = 11.5$

Chapter 7
Page 328

1. irrational   **2.** irrational   **3.** rational

4. rational   **5.** irrational   **6.** 4.47

7. 5.48   **8.** 4.90   **9.** 3.74

10. 7.75

Chapter 8
Page 341

1. $\frac{24}{36} = \frac{4}{6} = \frac{2}{3}$ **2.** $\frac{40}{15} = \frac{8}{3} = 8 \text{ to } 3$

3. $\frac{18}{8} = \frac{9}{4} = 9 : 4$ **4.** $\frac{64}{36} = \frac{32}{18} = \frac{16}{9}$

5. $\frac{15}{50} = \frac{3}{10}$ **6.** $\frac{10}{55} = \frac{2}{11} = 2 \text{ out of } 11$

7. $\frac{33}{15} = \frac{11}{5}$ **8.** $\frac{4}{16} = 1 : 4$

9. $\frac{27}{12} = \frac{9}{4} = 9 : 4$ **10.** $\frac{96}{8} = \frac{12}{1} = 12 \text{ to } 1$

Chapter 8

Page 348

1. $\frac{x}{8} = \frac{3}{10}$
   $10x = 24$
   $x = 2.4$

2. $4 : 9 = 15 : n$
   $\frac{4}{9} = \frac{15}{n}$
   $4n = 135$
   $n = 33.75$

3. $5 : g = 8 : 25$
   $\frac{5}{g} = \frac{8}{25}$
   $8g = 125$
   $g = 15.625$

4. $\frac{16}{7} = \frac{4}{a}$
   $16a = 28$
   $a = 1.75$

5. $\frac{h}{12} = \frac{18}{45}$
   $45h = 216$
   $h = 4.8$

6. $6 : 25 = c : 30$
   $\frac{6}{25} = \frac{c}{30}$
   $25c = 180$
   $c = 7.2$

Chapter 8

Page 363

1. 0.36   2. 11.43   3. 3.08   4. 0.27

5. 1.96   6. 55°   7. 0.70   8. 1.43

9. $\tan B = \frac{AC}{BC}$
   $AC = BC \cdot \tan B$
   $AC = 24 \cdot \tan 55° \approx 34.3$

10. $AC = BC \cdot \tan B$
    $AC = 50 \cdot \tan 55° \approx 71.4$

11. $\tan A = \frac{BC}{AC}$
    $BC = AC \cdot \tan A$
    $BC = 8.5 \cdot \tan 35° \approx 6.0$

12. $BC = AC \cdot \tan A$
    $BC = 34.6 \cdot \tan 35° \approx 24.2$

Chapter 9

Page 385

1. 24   2. 5,040   3. 6
4. 120   5. 40,320   6. 13,800
7. 306   8. 29,760   9. 1,680
10. 159,600 11. 95,040   12. 132,600
13. 720   14. 5,040

Chapter 9

Page 389

1. $_{10}C_3 = \frac{_{10}P_3}{3!} = \frac{720}{6} = 120$

2. $_6C_2 = \frac{_6P_2}{2!} = \frac{30}{2} = 15$

3. $_{13}C_5 = \frac{_{13}P_5}{5!} = \frac{154,440}{120} = 1,287$

4. $_9C_2 = \frac{_9P_2}{2!} = \frac{72}{2} = 36$

5. $_7C_3 = \frac{_7P_3}{3!} = \frac{210}{6} = 35$

6. $_{16}C_3 = \frac{_{16}P_3}{3!} = \frac{3,360}{6} = 560$

7. $_{10}C_2 = \frac{_{10}P_2}{5!} = \frac{90}{2} = 45$

8. $_{12}C_5 = \frac{_{12}P_5}{5!} = \frac{95,040}{120} = 792$

9. $_5C_3 = \frac{_5P_3}{3!} = \frac{60}{6} = 10$

10. $_9C_4 = \frac{_9P_4}{4!} = \frac{3,024}{24} = 126$

11. $_{20}C_4 = \frac{_{20}P_4}{4!} = \frac{116,280}{24} = 4,845$

12. $_{16}C_2 = \frac{_{16}P_2}{2!} = \frac{240}{2} = 120$

Chapter 10

Page 426

1. $6\% = \frac{6}{100} = \frac{3}{50}$; 0.06

2. $37.5\% = \frac{375}{1,000} = \frac{3}{8}$; 0.375

3. $180\% = \frac{180}{100} = 1\frac{4}{5}$; 1.8

4. $43.75\% = \frac{4,375}{10,000} = \frac{7}{16}$; 0.4375

5. 3%   6. 240%   7. 7.5%
8. 80%   9. 171.4%   10. 46.7%
11. 24%   12. 15%   13. 77.8%
14. 266.7%

Chapter 10
Page 429
1–12. Answers may vary. Samples given.

1. $\frac{4}{5}$ of $30 = 24$

2. $\frac{1}{20}$ of $80 = 4$

3. $\frac{1}{2}$ of $60 = 30$

4. $\frac{1}{10}$ of $140 = 14$

5. $\frac{1}{4}$ of $40 = 10$

6. $\frac{1}{50}$ of $400 = 8$

7. $\frac{3}{5}$ of $100 = 60$

8. $\frac{1}{5}$ of $50 = 10$

9. $\frac{2}{5}$ of $200 = 80$

10. $\frac{1}{10}$ of $650 = 65$

11. $\frac{1}{4}$ of $16 = 4$

12. $\frac{1}{2}$ of $9 = 4.5$

Chapter 10
Page 433

1. $\frac{15}{100} = \frac{18}{x}$

    $15x = 100 \times 18$

    $x = \frac{100 \times 18}{15} = 120$

2. $\frac{30}{100} = \frac{x}{48}$

    $100x = 30 \times 48$

    $x = \frac{30 \times 48}{100} = 14.4$

3. $\frac{2.4}{60} = \frac{x}{100}$

    $60x = 2.4 \times 100$

    $x = \frac{2.4 \times 100}{60} = 4$

4. $\frac{55}{100} = \frac{110}{x}$

    $55x = 100 \times 110$

    $x = \frac{100 \times 110}{55} = 200$

5. $\frac{10.8}{180} = \frac{x}{100}$

    $180x = 10.8 \times 100$

    $x = \frac{10.8 \times 100}{180} = 6$

6. $\frac{2}{100} = \frac{1.4}{x}$

    $2x = 100 \times 1.4$

    $x = \frac{100 \times 1.4}{2} = 70$

7. $\frac{85}{100} = \frac{x}{400}$

    $100x = 85 \times 400$

    $x = \frac{85 \times 400}{100} = 340$

8. $\frac{13.5}{75} = \frac{x}{100}$

    $75x = 13.5 \times 100$

    $x = \frac{13.5 \times 100}{75} = 18$

9. $\frac{105}{100} = \frac{630}{x}$

    $105x = 100 \times 630$

    $x = \frac{100 \times 630}{105} = 600$

10. $\frac{x}{100} = \frac{210}{84}$

    $84x = 100 \times 210$

    $x = \frac{100 \times 210}{84} = 250$

11. $\frac{60}{100} = \frac{x}{355}$

    $100x = 60 \times 355$

    $x = \frac{60 \times 355}{100} = 213$

12. $\frac{4.5}{300} = \frac{x}{100}$

    $300x = 4.5 \times 100$

    $x = \frac{4.5 \times 100}{300} = 1.5$

Chapter 10
Page 436

1. $50 = P \cdot 118$

    $P = \frac{50}{118} \approx 0.424 = 42.4\%$

2. part $= 0.23 \cdot 67 \approx 15.4$

3. $65 = 1.12 \cdot$ whole

    whole $= \frac{65}{1.12} \approx 58.0$

4. $3.5 = 0.12 \cdot$ whole

    whole $= \frac{3.5}{0.12} \approx 29.2$

5. part $= 0.13 \cdot 250 = 32.5$

6. part $= 0.73 \cdot 28 \approx 20.4$

7. $430 = 0.95 \cdot \text{whole}$

whole $= \frac{430}{0.95} \approx 452.6$

8. $20 = P \cdot 370$

$P = \frac{20}{370} \approx 0.054 = 5.4\%$

9. $25 = 0.35 \cdot \text{whole}$

whole $= \frac{25}{0.35} \approx 71.4$

10. $120 = P \cdot 175$

$P = \frac{120}{175} \approx 0.686 = 68.6\%$

11. $10 = P \cdot 18$

$P = \frac{10}{18} \approx 0.556 = 55.6\%$

12. $0.04 = 0.023 \cdot \text{whole}$

whole $= \frac{0.04}{0.023} \approx 1.7$

Chapter 10
Page 443

1. $P = \frac{10}{25} = 40\%$ decrease

2. $P = \frac{15}{65} \approx 23.1\%$ increase

3. $P = \frac{15}{45} \approx 33.3\%$ decrease

4. $P = \frac{25}{120} \approx 20.8\%$ decrease

5. $P = \frac{35}{75} \approx 46.7\%$ increase

6. $P = \frac{3.5}{4} = 87.5\%$ increase

7. $P = \frac{4.1}{12.3} \approx 33.3\%$ decrease

8. $P = \frac{12.3}{34} \approx 36.2\%$ decrease

9. $P = \frac{7.8}{55.2} \approx 14.1\%$ increase

Chapter 10
Page 447

1. 35% of $9.50 = 0.35 \times \$9.50 = \$3.33$
$\$9.50 + \$3.33 = \$12.83$

2. 70% of $45.70 = 0.70 \times \$45.70 = \$31.99$
$\$45.70 + \$31.99 = \$77.69$

3. 45% of $176.80 = 0.45 \times \$176.80 = \$79.56$
$\$176.80 + \$79.56 = \$256.36$

4. 30% of $55.89 = 0.30 \times \$55.89 = \$16.77$
$\$55.89 - \$16.77 = \$39.12$

5. 15% of $76.29 = 0.15 \times \$76.29 = \$11.44$
$\$76.29 - \$11.44 = \$64.85$

6. 45% of $163.19 = 0.45 \times \$163.19 = \$73.44$
$\$163.19 - \$73.44 = \$89.75$

Chapter 10
Page 451

1. 600 ⊠ 0.04 ⊠ 2 ⊟ **48**
$600 + 48 = \$648$

2. 1500 ⊠ 0.08 ⊠ 4 ⊟ **480**
$1,500 + 480 = \$1,980$

3. 850 ⊠ 0.05 ⊠ 3 ⊟ **127.5**
$850 + 128 = \$978$

4. 3000 ⊠ 0.062 ⊠ 0.5 ⊟ **93**
$3,000 + 93 = \$3,093$

5. 700 ⊠ (1 ⊞ 0.04) y^x 2 ⊟ **757.12;**
$\$757$

6. 1600 ⊠ (1 ⊞ 0.07) y^x 4 ⊟
2097.2736; $2,097

7. 800 ⊠ (1 ⊞ 0.05) y^x 3 ⊟
926.1; $926

8. 2500 ⊠ (1 ⊞ 0.015) y^x 4 ⊟
2653.4089; $2,653

9. 3200 ⊠ (1 ⊞ 0.01) y^x 2 ⊟
3264.32; $3,264

Chapter 11
Page 475

1. surface area $= 2(5)(4) + 2(5)(8) + 2(4)(8)$
$= 40 + 80 + 64$
$= 184 \text{ in.}^2$

2. surface area $= 2(12)(9) + 2(12)(15) +$
$2(9)(15)$
$= 216 + 360 + 270$
$= 846 \text{ cm}^2$

3. surface area $= 2(24)(20) + 2(24)(6) +$
$2(20)(6)$
$= 960 + 288 + 240$
$= 1{,}488 \text{ ft}^2$

4. surface area $= 2(50)(45) + 2(50)(60) +$
$2(45)(60)$
$= 4{,}500 + 6{,}000 + 5{,}400$
$= 15{,}900 \text{ m}^2$

5. surface area = 2(32)(28) + 2(32)(10) + 2(28)(10)
= 1,792 + 640 + 560
= 2,992 ft^2

6. surface area = 2(70)(70) + 2(70)(85) + 2(70)(85)
= 9,800 + 11,900 + 11,900
= 33,600 in.^{2}

7. surface area = 2(8.2)(6.5) + 2(8.2)(10) + 2(6.5)(10)
= 106.6 + 164 + 130
= 400.6 m^2

8. surface area = 2(12.4)(10) + 2(12.4)(10) + 2(10)(10)
= 248 + 248 + 200
= 696 m^2

Chapter 11
Page 480

Use surface area of cylinder = $2\pi r^2 + 2\pi rh$. Answers may vary slightly when using a calculator's π key versus approximations such as $\frac{22}{7}$ or 3.14.

1. r = 12 ft, h = 15 ft
2 $\times$ π $\times$ 12 x^2 $+$ 2 $\times$ π $\times$ 12 $\times$ 15 $=$ **2035.7520**
surface area ≈ 2,036 ft^2

2. r = 6 cm, h = 10 cm
2 $\times$ π $\times$ 6 x^2 $+$ 2 $\times$ π $\times$ 6 $\times$ 10 $=$ **603.18579**
surface area ≈ 603 cm^2

3. r = 2 yd, h = 14 yd
2 $\times$ π $\times$ 2 x^2 $+$ 2 $\times$ π $\times$ 2 $\times$ 14 $=$ **201.06193**
surface area ≈ 201 yd^2

4. r = 5 mm, h = 9 mm
2 $\times$ π $\times$ 5 x^2 $+$ 2 $\times$ π $\times$ 5 $\times$ 9 $=$ **439.82297**
surface area ≈ 440 mm^2

5. r = 2.5 m, h = 6.5 m
2 $\times$ π $\times$ 2.5 x^2 $+$ 2 $\times$ π $\times$ 2.5 $\times$ 6.5 $=$ **141.37167**
surface area ≈ 141 m^2

6. d = 8 ft (r = 4 ft), h = 12 ft
2 $\times$ π $\times$ 4 x^2 $+$ 2 $\times$ π $\times$ 4 $\times$ 12 $=$ **402.12386**
surface area ≈ 402 ft^2

7. d = 20 in. (r = 10 in.), h = 15 in.
2 $\times$ π $\times$ 10 x^2 $+$ 2 $\times$ π $\times$ 10 $\times$ 15 $=$ **1570.7963**
surface area ≈ 1,571 in.^{2}

8. d = 6 ft (r = 3 ft), h = 8 ft
2 $\times$ π $\times$ 3 x^2 $+$ 2 $\times$ π $\times$ 3 $\times$ 8 $=$ **207.34512**
surface area ≈ 207 ft^2

9. d = 3 cm (r = 1.5 cm), h = 6 cm
2 $\times$ π $\times$ 1.5 x^2 $+$ 2 $\times$ π $\times$ 1.5 $\times$ 6 $=$ **70.685835**
surface area ≈ 71 cm^2

10. d = 4.2 m (r = 2.1 m), h = 5.3 m
2 $\times$ π $\times$ 2.1 x^2 $+$ 2 $\times$ π $\times$ 2.1 $\times$ 5.3 $=$ **97.640700**
surface area ≈ 98 m^2

Chapter 11
Page 483

1. $V = lwh$; l = 16 in., w = 12 in., h = 20 in.
V = (16)(12)(20) = 3,840 in.^{3}

2. $V = lwh$; l = 8 ft, w = 7 ft, h = 10 ft
V = (8)(7)(10) = 560 ft^3

3. $V = lwh$; l = 10 cm, w = 8 cm, h = 15 cm
V = (10)(8)(15) = 1,200 cm^3

4. $V = lwh$; l = 12 yd, w = 12 yd, h = 20 yd
V = (12)(12)(20) = 2,880 yd^3

5. $V = lwh$; l = 4 mm, w = 3 mm, h = 10 mm
V = (4)(3)(10) = 120 mm^3

6. $V = lwh$; l = 20 ft, w = 15 ft, h = 8 ft
V = (20)(15)(8) = 2,400 ft^3

7. $V = lwh$; l = 5 in., w = 2 in., h = 17 in.
V = (5)(2)(17) = 170 in.^{3}

8. $V = lwh$; l = 3.5 cm, w = 3 cm, h = 8 cm
V = (3.5)(3)(8) = 84 cm^3

9. $V = lwh$; l = 6.1 m, w = 5.5 m, h = 3.3 m
V = (6.1)(5.5)(3.3) ≈ 110.7 m^3

10. $V = lwh; l = 0.2$ m, $w = 0.1$ m, $h = 3.5$ m

$V = (0.2)(0.1)(3.5) = 0.07$ m^3

Chapter 11
Page 494

Use the formula volume of a cylinder $V = \pi r^2 h$.
1–10. Answers vary slightly when using a calculator π key versus approximations 3.14 or $\frac{22}{7}$.

1. $r = 3$ yd, $h = 9$ yd

   3.14 $\boxed{\times}$ 3 $\boxed{x^2}$ $\boxed{\times}$ 9 $\boxed{=}$ **254.34**

   $V \approx 254$ yd^3

2. $r = 20$ cm, $h = 10$ cm

   3.14 $\boxed{\times}$ 20 $\boxed{x^2}$ $\boxed{\times}$ 10 $\boxed{=}$ **12560**

   $V \approx 12,560$ cm^3

3. $r = 5$ ft, $h = 8$ ft

   3.14 $\boxed{\times}$ 5 $\boxed{x^2}$ $\boxed{\times}$ 8 $\boxed{=}$ **628**

   $V \approx 628$ ft^3

4. $r = 4$ in., $h = 12$ in.

   3.14 $\boxed{\times}$ 4 $\boxed{x^2}$ $\boxed{\times}$ 12 $\boxed{=}$ **602.88**

   $V \approx 603$ in.^{3}

5. $r = 10$ m, $h = 15$ m

   3.14 $\boxed{\times}$ 10 $\boxed{x^2}$ $\boxed{\times}$ 15 $\boxed{=}$ **4710**

   $V \approx 4,710$ m^3

6. $d = 16$ ft ($r = 8$ ft), $h = 6$ ft

   3.14 $\boxed{\times}$ 8 $\boxed{x^2}$ $\boxed{\times}$ 6 $\boxed{=}$ **1205.76**

   $V \approx 1,206$ ft^3

7. $d = 5$ mm ($r = 2.5$ mm), $h = 4$ mm

   3.14 $\boxed{\times}$ 2.5 $\boxed{x^2}$ $\boxed{\times}$ 4 $\boxed{=}$ **78.5**

   $V \approx 79$ mm^3

8. $d = 70$ in. ($r = 35$ in.), $h = 40$ in.

   3.14 $\boxed{\times}$ 35 $\boxed{x^2}$ $\boxed{\times}$ 40 $\boxed{=}$ **153860**

   $V = 153,860$ in.^{3}

9. $d = 9$ m ($r = 4.5$ m), $h = 8.5$ m

   3.14 $\boxed{\times}$ 4.5 $\boxed{x^2}$ $\boxed{\times}$ 8.5 $\boxed{=}$ **540.4725**

   $V \approx 540$ m^3

10. $d = 7.6$ m ($r = 3.8$ m), $h = 7.1$ m

    3.14 $\boxed{\times}$ 3.8 $\boxed{x^2}$ $\boxed{\times}$ 7.1 $\boxed{=}$ **321.92536**

    $V \approx 322$ m^3

Chapter 11
Page 499

1–7. Answers vary slightly when using a calculator π key versus approximations 3.14 or $\frac{22}{7}$. Answers are given to the nearest cubic unit.

1. $V = \frac{1}{3}Bh; B = 20$ ft^2 , $h = 12$ ft

   $V = \frac{1}{3}(20)(12) = 80$ ft^3

2. $V = \frac{1}{3}Bh; B = 9$ in.^{2} , $h = 4.5$ in.

   $V = \frac{1}{3}(9)(4.5) = 14$ in.^{3}

3. $V = \frac{1}{3}Bh; B = 16.25$ m^2 , $h = 6$ m

   $V = \frac{1}{3}(16.25)(6) \approx 33$ m^3

4. $V = \frac{1}{3}Bh; B = 50$ cm^2 , $h = 6.5$ cm

   $V = \frac{1}{3}(50)(6.5) \approx 108$ cm^3

5. $V = \frac{1}{3}\pi r^2 h; r = 3$ in., $h = 7$ in.

   $V = \frac{1}{3}\pi (3)^2 (7) \approx 66$ in.^{2}

6. $V = \frac{1}{3}\pi r^2 h; r = 5$ ft, $h = 12$ ft

   $V = \frac{1}{3}\pi (5)^2 (12) \approx 314$ ft^2

7. $V = \frac{1}{3}\pi r^2 h; r = \frac{4}{2}$ m $= 2$ m, $h - 4.5$ m

   $V = \frac{1}{3}\pi (2)^2 (4.5) \approx 19$ m^2